MW01071061

THE INDO-ARYAN CONTROVERSY

For the first time in a single volume, this book presents the various arguments in the Indo-Aryan controversy by some of the principal scholars in this field of study. Its essays provide a template for the basic issues involved in the debates by addressing four major areas. First, archaeologists consider some of the recent findings and interpretations of the archaeological record, focusing particularly on the issue of the relationship between the Indus Valley archaeological complex and the culture of the Indo-Aryans as expressed in the Vedic texts. These chapters consider whether there was more continuity between the two civilizations than has been assumed in earlier works, and evaluate whether there is enough evidence to establish a definitive scholarly consensus as to whether or not the Indus civilization was actually Indo-Aryan. Second, scholars take on some of the linguistic issues in the debate, particularly the relationship between Indo-Aryan and its parent language Indo-European, as well as the linguistic borrowings between languages and language families. The discussion here rests on whether the traditional rules of linguistic derivation for Indo-European languages allow for the possibility that the origins of the Indo-Aryan languages developed in India itself. Additionally, authors debate whether contact between Indo-Aryan and non-Indo-Aryan languages (such as Dravidian or Munda) is the result of Indo-Aryan as a language intruding into the subcontinent, or whether other types of mutual interactions between those languages can account for such contacts. Third, philological scholars sieve through the Vedic texts to find clues that might situate the Vedic Aryans in space and time by correlating them with the archaeological record. Different scholars examine references to items associated with the Indo-Aryans such as iron, the horse, and chariot, as well as astronomical data, to consider the implication such references have for the dating of the Veda, a crucial issue in this debate, and the geography of its horizons. Finally, historians contribute historiographical contexts for the debates, stressing the ways in which positions on this issue might be influenced by socio-political or ideological currents, both in the early debates in the nineteenth century as well as today.

Edwin F. Bryant received his doctorate from Columbia University in 1997, where he taught Sanskrit and Hindi. He was the Lecturer in Hinduism at Harvard University for three years, and is presently Associate Professor in Hinduism at Rutgers University, New Jersey. His publications include books on the Indo-Aryan invasion debate and on the Krishna tradition. He is presently working on a translation of the Yoga Sutras and its commentaries.

Laurie L. Patton is Professor of Early Indian Religions at Emory University and Winship Distinguished Research Professor in the Humanities. She is the author of two books and twenty-five articles on early Indian myth and poetry, as well as a book of poetry, *Fire's Goal: Poems from a Hindu Year*. She is presently completing a translation of the Bhagavad Gita. Her current book project is a collection and analysis of a series of life histories of women Sanskritists in India.

THE INDO-ARYAN CONTROVERSY

Evidence and inference in Indian history

Edited by
Edwin F. Bryant and
Laurie L. Patton

Routledge
Taylor & Francis Group
LONDON AND NEW YORK

First published 2005
by Routledge
2 Park Square, Milton Park, Abingdon, Oxon, OX14 4RN

Simultaneously published in the USA and Canada
by Routledge
270 Madison Ave, New York NY 10016

Routledge is an imprint of the Taylor & Francis Group

Transferred to Digital Printing 2008

Typeset in Times New Roman by
Newgen Imaging Systems (P) Ltd, Chennai, India

British Library Cataloguing in Publication Data
A catalogue record for this book is available from the British Library

Library of Congress Cataloging in Publication Data
A catalog record for this book has been requested

ISBN 0–700–71462–6 (hbk)
ISBN 0–700–71463–4 (pbk)

CONTENTS

CONTRIBUTORS

Edwin F. Bryant is Associate Professor of Hinduism at Rutgers University, where he teaches Hindu religion and philosophy. His publications include *The Quest for the Origins of Vedic Culture: The Indo-Aryan Migration Debate* (2001). He is translator of *Krishna: The Beautiful Legend of God, Srimad Bhagavata Purana Book Ten* (2004). He is also editor of *Sources of the Krishna Tradition* (in press) and with Maria Ekstrand, of *The Hare Krishna Movement: The Postcharismatic Fate of a Religious Transplant* (2004). Bryant is currently at work on a translation of Patanjali's Yoga Sutras and its commentaries.

Christian Carpelan is Researcher at the Department of Archaeology at the University of Helsinki. His special field is archaeology of northern and eastern Europe. He has presented papers on the early contacts between Uralic and Indo-European in a number of international settings. He is the co-editor (with Tony Hackens and Hagne Jungner) of *Time and Environment: A PACT Seminar* (1992) and *Early Contacts Between Uralic and Indo-European: Archaeological and Linguistic Considerations* (2001).

Madhav M. Deshpande received his MA (1968) at the University of Pune in India and his PhD (1972) at the University of Pennsylvania. In 1972 he joined the University of Michigan where he is currently Professor of Sanskrit and Linguistics. He has published several books and hundreds of articles on Indo-Aryan and Paninian linguistics, religion, and philosophy.

Koenraad Elst earned MA degrees in Philosophy, Chinese Studies and Indo-Iranian Studies at the Catholic University of Leuven, Belgium. His PhD dissertation on Hindu nationalism, *Decolonizing the Hindu Mind*, became a best-seller in India. Making his living mostly by journalism, he has been active as an independent scholar in the fields of comparative religion and philosophy and of the history of India. Among twenty published titles, most attention has been drawn by his *Update on the Aryan Invasion Debate; Gandhi and Godse* (a close discussion of the apology of Mahatma Gandhi's assassin Nathuram Godse); *The Saffron Swastika: The Notion of "Hindu Fascism"*; and *Ayodhya, the Case against the Temple.*

Lars Martin Fosse is an independent scholar with a doctorate in Sanskrit. He has also studied Hindi and Middle Indic languages, as well as Greek and Latin, at the Universities of Oslo, Heidelberg, and Bonn. His research interests involve stylometry (statistical analysis of the language and style of Sanskrit texts) as well as Vedic and epic studies. In addition to authoring several articles in these areas, he has taught at the University of Oslo in Sanskrit, linguistic statistics, and Hinduism.

Hans Henrich Hock is Professor of Linguistics and Sanskrit at the University of Illinois Urbana. His research interests include Sanskrit linguistics, especially with an emphasis on phonology, syntax, and sociolinguistics. He has written extensively on historical Indo-Aryan linguistics and the Indo-Iranian and comparative Indo-European backgrounds of Sanskrit. Among other works, he is the author of *Principles of Historical Linguistics* (1991), senior author (with Brian D. Joseph) of *Language History, Language Change, and Language Relationship* (1996), Editor of *Studies in Sanskrit Syntax* (1991) and of *Historical, Indo-European, and Lexicographical Studies: A Festschrift for Ladislav Zgusta on the Occasion of his 70th Birthday* (1997).

Subhash Kak is the Delaune Distinguished Professor of Electrical Engineering and Professor in the Asian Studies Program at Louisiana State University in Baton Rouge. His research interests include foundations of physics and information, cognitive science, history of science, and Vedic studies. His recent books are *The Astronomical Code of the Rgveda*, *The Wishing Tree*, *The Gods Within*, and *The Architecture of Knowledge*. He has also published several books of poems.

Jonathan Mark Kenoyer is Professor of Anthropology, and teaches archaeology and ancient technology at the University of Wisconsin, Madison. He has a BA in anthropology from the University of California at Berkeley and completed his MA and PhD (1983) in south Asian archaeology at the same university. He has conducted archaeological research and excavations at both Mohenjo-daro and Harappa, two of the most important early sites in Pakistan, and has also worked in western and central India. Since 1986 he has been the Co-director and Field Director of the Harappa Archaeological Research Project in Pakistan, a long-term study of urban development in the Indus Valley. His work is most recently featured in the July 2003 issue of *Scientific American* and on the website www.harappa.com

B. B. Lal served as the Director General of the Archaeological Survey of India from 1968 to 1972. In the latter year, he took voluntary retirement from that coveted post, better to pursue his research programs independently. Soon thereafter he joined Jiwaji University, Gwalior, as Professor and Head of the School of Studies in Ancient Indian History, Culture and Archaeology. In 1976 he moved on to the renowned Indian Institute of Advanced Study, Simla, of which he was also the Director for a number of years, finally retiring in 1986. He has held prestigious visiting lectureships at the University of Chicago and University of London, and in 1994 he was awarded an honorary degree by the Institute of Archaeology (St Petersberg), Academy of Sciences, Russia. The same year he was elected the President of World Archaeological Congress-3, held in Delhi. He has also been President and Member of several Committees of UNESCO.

Carl C. Lamberg-Karlovsky received his PhD from the University of Pennsylvania and then worked as the Director of Archaeological Survey in Syria as well as at the Director of Excavations at Tempe Yahya in southeastern Iran. There he has been engaged in collaborative excavations in the Turkmenistan, Uzbekistan, and the Altai Mountains of southern Siberia. In 1999 he launched what is anticipated as a long-term excavation of the site of Panj Piye in Balochistan, Pakistan, a major urban Bronze Age settlement. Dr Lamberg-Karlovsky's current research interests are in the cultural interaction and trade patterns that brought distant centers into contact such as Mesopotamia, the Gulf, and Central Asia. Dr Lamberg-Karlovsky is the Director of Graduate Studies for Stephen Phillips, Archaeology and Ethnology at Harvard University.

Diane A. Lichtenstein received her PhD from the University of Wisconsin, Madison, in 1977 and is Adjunct Professor of Anthropology at Baldwin-Wallace College and the Cleveland Institute of Art, Cleveland, Ohio. Her dissertation research, conducted among the Langi of northern Uganda in 1970–72, focused on village social dynamics in the context of the advent of national military rule. She has participated in archaeological fieldwork in Egypt, Pakistan, and India and has maintained a long-term research interest in South Asian prehistory. She has co-authored several articles with Jim G. Shaffer, which focus on archaeological details of the Indus Valley (Harappan) civilization.

Satya Swarup Misra was Professor of Indology and Linguistics at the Benaras Hindu University. He was the author of many books on comparative Indo-European linguistics, including *New Lights on Indo-European Comparative Grammar* (1996); *The Aryan Problem: A Linguistic Approach* (1992); *The Old Indo-Aryan: A Historical and Comparative Grammar* (1991); and *Avestan: A Historical and Comparative Grammar* (1979).

Asko Parpola PhD, is Professor of Indology at the Institute for Asian and African Studies at the University of Helsinki. He has published several books and over one hundred articles on the Indus civilization; Indus script and religion; Vedic ritual, particularly the Samaveda and the Jaiminiya Samaveda texts and rituals; the religious history and archaeology of South India; the prehistory of Indian languages, and the prehistoric archaeology of South Asia and (in a broad sense) Central Asia. His home page with a list of publications is: www.helsinki.fi/~aparpola/

Laurie L. Patton is Winship Distinguished Research Professor in the Humanities and Professor of Early Indian Religions at Emory University. Her interests are in the interpretation of early Indian ritual and narrative, comparative mythology, and literary theory in the study of religion. She is author or editor of six books and thirty articles in these fields. Most recently, she is the editor of *Jewels of Authority: Women and Text in the Hindu Tradition* (2002), and the author of a book on the use of poetry in *Vedic ritual, Bringing the Gods to Mind* (University of California Press, 2004). Her book of poetry, *Fire's Goal: Poems from a Hindu Year* (2003) will be followed by a translation of the Bhagavad Gita (forthcoming) from Penguin Press Classics.

Jim G. Shaffer received his PhD from the University of Wisconsin, Madison, in 1972 and is Associate Professor of Anthropology at Case Western Reserve University, Cleveland, Ohio. His academic career focus on South Asian prehistory began with his dissertation research of Bronze Age Afghanistan, detailed in *Prehistoric Baluchistan: A Systematic Approach*. Additionally, he has conducted extensive archaeological fieldwork at Bronze Age and Neolithic sites in Pakistan and in north and south India. He is author of numerous articles analyzing details of the Indus Valley (Harappan) civilization and other cultures of South and Southwest Asia, with a research emphasis on the origin and processes of domestication, metallurgy, urbanization and state formation, and archaeological application of the concept of paleoethnicity and paleogroup migration.

Shrikant G. Talageri was educated in Bombay where he lives and works. He has been interested in wildlife, comparative music, religion and philosophy, history and culture, and linguistics. He has made a special study of the Konkani language, his mother tongue. He has devoted several years, and much study, to the theory of an Aryan invasion of India, and interpreted the Vedas with the help of the Puranas. He is the author of *The Aryan Invasions Theory: A Reappraisal* (1993) and *The Rig Veda: A Historical Analysis* (2000).

Michael Witzel is the Wales Professor of Sanskrit at Harvard University. He received his PhD from the University of Erlangen in 1972 and has continued to work in the fields of Indology, Indo-European, Indo-Iranian philology and linguistics, and Japanology. In addition to teaching positions at the University of Tuebingen and the University of Leiden, he has taught at the Sanskrit Campus, Tribhuvan University, Kathmandu, and served as the Director of the Nepal Research Center of the German Oriental Society. He has served as the chief editor of the *Indo-Iranian Journal*, and, since 1990 he has been the editor of the *Harvard Oriental Series* as well as the founding editor of *Electronic Journal for Vedic Studies*. He is the author or editor of over 100 articles and books in early Indian history and philology.

ACKNOWLEDGMENTS

This volume has been very long in incubation. Since its inception, arguments have been refined and conducted across the ethernet in a myriad of ways. We would like to thank the participants of the original panel of the American Academy of Religion, 1998: Frederick M. Smith, Beatrice Reusch, George Thompson, as well as the two editors. Their thoughts and contributions at that panel gave us the inspiration to gather together a body of literature that is rigorous and yet accessible to Indologists and their students from a variety of subfields, and that represented a variety of scholars in their own voices. Our hope is that this volume will provide a new template for inquiry into Aryan origins, and perhaps even a new impetus for an international consensus on scholarly methods and common questions. All the colonialist and nationalist motives have already been suspected and attributed; perhaps now we can get down to work.

Editorial assistance was provided ably by Michelle Roberts and Joy Wasson in various stages of preparation of this manuscript. Special thanks go to Russell Cambron, who has spent innumerable hours standardizing references and following through on small editorial details. Jonathan Price has given us indefatigable editorial grounding and inspiration, even as Curzon passed through its own transitions into Routledge. Since the beginning of this project, Dr S. S. Misra has passed away, and we honor his work with the posthumous publication of his essay in this volume.

INTRODUCTION

Laurie L. Patton

In June of 1997, at a celebration of the twenty-first birthday of a young man in an upper middle-class neighborhood in Bombay, a high school teacher was heard to say, "The Indo-Europeans! No one believes in those anymore. They've been disproven by Indian scholars for decades now." Six months later, at an academic reception in New York City, a well-known intellectual raised his eyebrows when asked about the indigenous Aryan theory, and said: "Those theories coming out of India? Pure, unreasoned polemics...." There were more than oceans separating these views, but also on both sides a dismissive unwillingness to engage in the debate, and clear assumptions about the motivations of the other point of view.

In Indological studies, we now exist in an era where one's use of evidence is inevitably suspect of being linked to nationalist, colonialist, or cultural agendas. If one is "Western," one is suspect of neocolonialism or Orientalism. If one is "Indian," one is suspect of nationalism or Marxism. If one is the wrong color, and takes the wrong point of view, one is suspect of being co-opted by the false consciousness of the other side.

No issue is more illustrative of this impasse than the debate about Aryan origins. Until recently, publications by Indo-Europeanists and Indigenous Aryanists have continued on with very little conversation between the opponents, and great opportunity for creating straw men on both sides. The purpose of this volume is to present various sides of the arguments in their own voices, as well as provide a kind of template for the basic issues involved. Recent public debate has allowed for some direct contact between sparring partners;[1] it is the point of view of the editors of the present volume that more juxtaposition of views, more contact, and more agreement on the rules of evidence is necessary. This book is one small step in that direction.

The chapters represent a huge diversity of opinion, and by no means fully representative of all the voices in the debate. Rather, we have chosen articles that raise certain important issues that deserve further scrutiny. It is our expectation that both sides of the debate will find us overly accepting and affirming of the other side. (Given the acrimonious and over-determined nature of much of the discussion to date, we think it best to view this anticipated critique as an intellectual virtue, and proof that we have represented the state of things fairly accurately.)

There is no way out of this impasse, except by taking extraordinarily difficult and small steps. Such steps involve several elements: agreeing upon rules of evidence and abiding by those rules; allowing a hypothesis to remain exactly that, and not become an automatic claim; allowing a challenge to be answered, and not simply be taken for an automatic demolishing of a theory. Scholars might make the daring move of allowing the questions themselves to unite, rather than suspicions divide them.

The chapters

How might one make sense of the massive amount of data in this volume? Most South Asianists do not have the time to master it, and yet they feel the pressure of the controversy weighing down on them in everyday scholarly intersections with colleagues and students, such as the ones described earlier. Let me begin with a basic description of the arguments of the chapters.

Part I, "Archaeology" addresses some of the recent findings and arguments in these areas. Part II, "Archaeology and Linguistics," takes on some of the linguistic issues in the debate, particularly those of linguistic borrowing and parent languages. Part III, "Philology and Linguistics," takes up the related concerns of interpretation of texts and their historical contexts. Part IV, "Historiography," comprises articles that give both histories of the debates, as well as assessments of the state of the current arguments and their ideological roots.

Mark Kenoyer begins Part I with his chapter, "Culture Change during the Late Harappan period at Harappa: New Insights on Vedic Aryan Issues." He argues that, on the basis of new archaeological research, there is evidence for cultural change in the Late Harappan period (1900–1700 BCE). Kenoyer is clear that there is no evidence for the use of the horse by the occupants of the Late Harappan cities and towns. This would mitigate against the idea that Indus Valley and Aryan culture were one and the same. He does argue, however, that there are significant changes in burial practices and new decorative motifs of on pottery, "indicating that some of those urban communities had developed new ideologies that were inconsistent with the religious practices of early Harappan communities (pp. 43–44)." New use of material for bead technology also suggests the emergence of a new elite.

Given that there seems to be no significant change in population during this period, Kenoyer thinks that the archaeological data reflect social, economic, and ideological restructuring that involved previously marginal communities. These communities cannot be called "Aryan" or "non-Aryan," but it is also clear that these terms do not even represent a single community in the Veda. Kenoyer acknowledges that there is moreover clearly no support for the idea of invasion and destruction of cities and towns. He goes on to state that it is equally wrong to conclude that the Indus Valley inhabitants were Aryans; the total absence of writing in the Vedic system precludes this. He does suggest that the absence of writing in the Late Harappan period, combined with the change in decorative motifs and burial practices are consonant with Vedic culture. He goes on to speculate that it is not improbable that some Vedic communities were passing through Harappan towns, some of which were named in the Vedas. Kenoyer ends by arguing that more research needs to be done on human remains, as none of this evidence is conclusive. But the necessity of building a transitional chronology is crucial.

In "Aryan Invasion of India: Perpetuation of a Myth," B. B. Lal begins by tracing first the intellectual history of the idea of an Aryan invasion, beginning with William Jones and moving through Max Mueller and Mortimer Wheeler. As he argues, there is no evidence of attacks on the citadels of the Harappan cities, which would be the first structures to be destroyed in the case of an attack. Second, many of the skeletal remains are from a lower level of buildings, not what one would expect in the case of warriors fallen in a battle. His view is that Harappa gradually transformed itself into the later Rangpur culture. Still, for Lal, ideas from the Aryan invasion theory remain. For instance, arguments about the placement and dating of the drying up of the Sarasvati river, which are relevant to the debate due to its prominence both in the Ṛgveda literary record and the Harappan archaeological record, still hinge on whether one believes the Sarasvati mentioned in the texts should be placed inside or outside of India. The Gagghar–Sarasvati River complex has been studied through Landsat imagery (Yash Pal *et al.* 1984) and tentative conclusions are that it supported a lush and more fluid eco-system before drying up.

Lal goes on to say that, as early as 1951, and then more convincingly in the 1980s, studies have pointed to evidence of gradual evolution from the Seventh millennium onward in Baluchistan. This evolution moved from Neolithic to Chalcolithic culture to Bronze Age culture. This area distinguishes itself from Western Asian culture by a particular emphasis on barley (and not as much wheat) and on cattle (and not as much sheep and goats). Metal tools replaced stone, granaries emerged (4500 BCE), and the mature Harappan civilization (3000 BCE) included street designs and distinctive pottery. Seals and script emerged in 2600 BCE. By the second millennium BCE, a degeneration due to climate change, agricultural over extension, a decline in trade, and the drying of the Sarasvati began to force the civilization into decline. Moreover, Hemphill *et al.* (1991) provide biological evidence in the continuity of cranial structure of skeletons in this area, with interaction between Iran and the South Asian subcontinent. Despite the strength of the evidence, Lal argues that some historians still cling to the invasion theory, "in disguised" garb, as migration or as contacts between pastoral herders.

Yet Lal is also cautious in moving to the assumption that Aryans were the authors of Harappan civilization. He shows that none of the claims to decipher Indus Valley seals meets the criterion of a consistent reading of all the seals – whether the claim is that the seals were Dravidian or Aryan. Moreover, if the Indus Valley inhabitants were Dravidian people that moved southward, there is a lack of archaeological and place-name evidence along their hypothesized route southward to make that a convincing possibility. Finally, Lal argues that in the *Ṛgveda*, the Aryans showed evidence of being urban, not just pastoral peoples. He finishes by saying that, given the evidence of Naushuro and Lothal, the possibility of the presence of the horse cannot be ruled out. More work needs to be done in order for any of these hypotheses to be convincing.

Finally, in "South Asian Archaeology and the Myth of Indo-Aryan Invasions," Jim Shaffer and Diane Lichtenstein describe the basic ways in which archaeologists begin building their cases: basic potsherds, pots *in situ*, stone tools, flora and fauna remains, and human remains. Stratigraphic chronology is measured against carbon dating. Given the aggregate of these basic building blocks, they argue that the migration/invasion hypothesis of people needs to be assessed against newer archaeological data. Basing their analysis on recent findings over the last two decades, they argue that South Asian prehistory shows a cultural complexity and urbanization process that develops over a long chronology based on indigenous, but not isolated, cultural innovations. The excavations at Mehrgarh, for example, establish food production technologies as an indigenous Indus Valley phenomenon that requires neither migration nor invasion as an explanatory paradigm. So, too Harappan culture is a result of indigenous cultural developments but stood among several culturally similar but distinct neighbors with whom they traded both directly and indirectly. It was a cultural mosaic responding to particular ecological changes affecting the greater Indus Valley area from the third millennium BCE to the first millennium BCE. This was a combination of increasing aridity and the capture of Gagghar-Hakra (aka Sarasvati) River system by adjacent rivers, so that these waters were diverted eastward.

Shaffer and Lichtenstein go on to assess different areas in terms of their population and settlement changes in Harappan civilization. In Cholistan, there is a 48 percent decline in the Late Harappan period, and by the first millennium BCE an 83 percent decline. They conjecture that this may have been a cultural response to the crisis of the river changes and climactic changes mentioned earlier. Relatedly, in the eastern Punjab, there is a significant population influx in the area with a 304 percent increase in settlements over a similar period. In central Haryana, there is a 98 percent increase in habitation sites between the Harappan and the Late Harappan periods, and then perhaps a growing occupational stability which led to a stabler pattern. Sindh reflects a pattern similar to Cholistan, and Gujarat reflects a pattern similar to Haryana. Finally, the authors mention that one archaeological site of Bhagwanpura seems to link the Late Harappan and the subsequent Painted Gray Ware periods, associated with the traditional "Aryan" groups. However, they argue that there is much more work to be done on the precise nature of these continuities.

In sum, Shaffer and Lichtenstein argue for considerably more cultural continuity for early South Asian history, and further argue against historical linguistic scholars who try to link culture, race, and population movements in their reconstruction of a proto-Indo-European language, linking that language to a homeland, and defining population migration away from that seminal geographical base. Instead, they propose an Indo-Gangetic cultural tradition. In contrast to the idea of discontinuity based on outside influences, they think that there was significant *indigenous discontinuity*, which can be indexed to geological and environmental changes in the period. They conjecture that this may be the migration so focused on in ancient oral Vedic tradition.

Part II titled "Archaeology and Linguistics," begins with Asko Parpola and Christian Carpelan's chapter "The Cultural Counterparts to Proto-Indo-European, Proto-Yralic and Proto-Aryan." Their contribution is to sketch out a scenario in which the archaeological data matches the cultural and linguistic data in the hypotheses of Indo-European expansion. They argue first through etymological data, and then through archaeological discussion, that Indo-European and Uralic proto-languages were both spoken in the archaeological cultures of Eastern Europe. Building on the work of David Anthony (1995, 1998), they also attempt to correlate Indo-European and Uralic linguistic groups with archaeological cultures. They see the invention of the wheel as the *terminus post quem* of the earliest dispersal of the Indo-European culture, as it is shared by all Indo-European languages. The parent language that gave birth to proto-Indo-European was the Khvalynsk culture in the mid-Volga region (5000–4500 BCE). According to their scenario, the Khvalynsk culture spread east and west, intersecting with Uralic speaking peoples (8500 BCE).

In the southern Ukraine, the authors hypothesize that a proto-Indo-European culture was born from this Khvalynsk culture. They suggest that the Srednij Stog culture expanded after the wheel was invented in 3500 BCE, and expanded into the Pit Grave culture. In their view, Early Pit Grave culture gave rise to two subsequent cultures, the middle Dneiper and the Corded Ware cultural complex. The expanding Corded Ware to the northwest gave rise to Italo-Celtic, proto-Baltic, Slavic, and proto-Germanic. The Corded Ware culture also expanded into rural Russia, also creating distinct subcultures and interactions between Indo-European groups and proto-Uralic speaking groups.

This scenario is a background for Parpola's and Carpelan's new hypothesis of the split between Indo-Aryans and Indo-Iranians. According to their scenario, Eastern Pit Grave cultures (2200–1800 BCE) thrived in the southern Urals and developed horse-drawn chariots; this was called the Sintashta-Arkaim culture and was made up of two dialects: Poltavka in the west (pre-proto-Iranian) and Abashevo (pre-proto-Indo-Aryan) in the east. The split where these two dialects became more marked and distinct from each other must have occurred in 1800 BCE. At this time the Ural River became the border between them. Moving westward, the Indo-Iranian speaking groups developed their characteristic 'h' change from Indo-European 's' words. The Indo-Iranian speaking group was called the Timber Grave culture, and was able to expand into central Asia through the use of horses. The proto-Indo-Aryan speakers were the rulers of the Mitanni Kingdom – famous for its seals which name the five Indo-European deities. According to Parpola and Carpelan, they in all likelihood came to Syria from southern central Asia and northern Iran. A recent find in Tajikistan shows an aristocratic warrior with accouterments that are clearly Sintashta-Arkaim in nature (Bobomulloev 1999). Thus, this hypothesis would bring the Sintashta-Arkaim culture to the borders of South Asia in which the horse-drawn chariot played a central role in the Vedic-Aryans' movements and cultures.

C. C. Lamberg-Karlovsky's chapter, "Archaeology and Language: The Case of the Bronze Age Indo-Europeans," also addresses the theories of the last few decades about Androvono (which Parpola and Carpelan call the Sintashta-Arkaim) culture, as well as the Bactrian Margiana Archaeological Complex (BMAC). He is particularly concerned with the possibility of either culture being identified as positively Indo-Iranian speaking. Unlike Parpola and Carpelan, he is interested not in creating possible scenarios of links between archaeological and linguistic cultures, but on showing the lack of evidence for most of them.

Focusing particularly on Russian archaeologists (such as the recent works of E. E. Kuzmina), he argues that while there are many general parallels to be made between Androvono culture and Indo-Iranian ideas, such as the emphasis on the horse, the pattern of large houses, and so on, there is no specific archaeological evidence for Androvono culture reaching or influencing the cultures of Northern India or Iran in the second millennium – the date by which it should have reached these areas if the traditional Indo-Iranian scenario is played out. As he suggests, there is no archaeological evidence for the horse in Iran until the very late second millennium BCE, and in South Asia in the 1700 BCE. (We have seen some suggestions of earlier dates, but there is no scholarly consensus on this issue.) Lamberg-Karlovsky also argues that, despite the euphoria of recent discoveries such as that of Arkhaim, insufficient attention has been paid to the dramatic variations within Androvono culture, and the relative chronological dating of these variations.

The BMAC culture, excavated by the Soviets in the last two decades in Afghanistan, however, is a slightly different story. Houses and forts, temples and palaces contain parallels in Iran as well as other parts of South Asia, and BMAC seems to be basically contemporaneous with Androvono culture. Archaeologists generally agree that the question of contact between BMAC and Androvono is paramount, and many argue that such contact was possible and proveable, even if the nature of the contact (trade, domination, warfare) is impossible to determine. What is more, the use of ephedra as a kind of mild intoxicant (*homa/soma*), the presence of animal sacrifice and fire altars have inspired scholars to argue for an Indo-Iranian and proto-Zoroastrian identity of the BMAC.

And yet here is the final paradox for Lamberg-Karlovsky: the only intrusive archaeological culture that directly influences Iran and India is the BMAC, but it remains impossible to link the BMAC with the developments of the later second and first millennium archaeological cultures on the Irian Plateau. Lamberg-Karlovsky ends with a plea for restraint on simplified notions of an archaeological culture identified with an ethnic group. Most of these identifications are in his view no more than mere speculations with political agendas. Archaeological cultures tend to proceed in linear fashion, whereas many different simultaneous factors may influence linguistic change, and many different languages can co-exist in a single society with a single archaeological record.

Satya Swarup Misra's (posthumously published) article, "The Date of the Ṛgveda and the Aryan Migration: Fresh Linguistic Evidence," begins Part III, "Philology and Linguistics." He argues for an early linguistic date of 5000 BCE for the *Ṛgveda*, matching the linguistic archaism of Sanskrit. He posits that, since no other Indo-European language can be traced to such an early date, India might well be the original home of Aryans. He introduces the evidence of the Gypsy languages, which originated in India, as further evidence in this regard, arguing that the sound changes they exhibit are consistent with earlier sound changes differentiating Sanskrit (which he holds to be the Indo-European language closest to the proto-language), from the other Indo-European languages.

Building on S. R. Rao's reading of the Indus Valley seals, he takes the language of these seals to be a transitional language from Old Indo-Aryan to Middle Indo-Aryan, comparable to Buddhist Hybrid Sanskrit. (As Edwin Bryant notes [2001: 180], Rao's work is used in official government publicity, and therefore should be better addressed.) Misra also argues for a closer study of the relationship between Dravidian and Indo-Aryan words, with a view toward an affinity or common source. Following Harmatta (1981, 1992), he argues that Aryan loan words present in Uralic languages show the loans belong to an early age, which thus may not be Indo-Iranian but Indo-Aryan. Gypsy evidence shows more characteristically independent changes in different Indo-European language groups. Iranian languages are less archaic, showing continuities with Middle Indo-Aryan, and Iranian language place names tend to refer to Aryan evidence. His analysis of Anatolian evidence proceeds on similar grounds. Misra also argues for a closer study of the relationship between Dravidian and Indo-Aryan, with a view towards a possible affinity.

Koenraad Elst's chapter, "Linguistic Aspects of the Aryan Non-Invasion Theory," argues that, while the evidence is inconclusive, the Out of India Theory deserves a hearing. Like Misra, Elst's essay is based on acceptance of the linguistic paradigms of the academic guild. He argues that immigration theory must have involved some kind of military conquest, but points out that Shaffer and Litchenstein (1999) following Rao and Lal, argue that there is no archeological indication of Aryan immigration post Harappa. Even invasionists like Ratnagar admit that there is no evidence, even though she also argues that in other cultures parallels of no archeological evidence for invasion also exist. Hock (1999) also affirms that the lack of horse evidence is of significance for our understanding of Aryan culture. Elst responds that the paucity of horse evidence does not rule out the Out of India Theory, as the comparable evidence for Aryan culture is also weak. Elst goes on to argue that those critics of the Out of India theory who dismiss evidence do not accept the fact that linguistic rules are far more rigorous than ancient archeological ones, as archaeologist David Anthony (1991) also admits. Elst argues that the palatization of words, usually a one-way process, allows for the possibility that the homeland was originally in India and not outside. The discovery of groups in India with palatization suggests this possibility. He goes on to say that archaic laryngeal features of Hittite also do not prove that Hittite was older and closer to proto-Indo-European.

Elst also answers Hock's observation that the dialectological relationships and the lateral sharing of isoglosses between linguistic groups suggest an origin outside of India. Elst posits another scenario, where the same linguistic changes could have reflected successive waves of migration out of India, and the lateral changes post-migration changes, rather than signs of proto-Indo-European status. The expansion might have also included native influence of Indo-European speakers; in addition, Elst argues other examples in history show a singular direction of movement. Moreover, what Indo-Europeanists argue are foreign origins of words may well be spontaneous variations without adstratal or substratal influence. While he acknowledges the scholarly consensus that Dravidian seems to have been eliminated as a source for the Harappan language, Elst argues against too much dependence on the idea of borrowing from Munda or para-Munda languages. If we do accept borrowing, he argues, it may well be that such borrowing is not an influence of a substratum language in a superimposed foreign language. It is possible that the absorption of foreign words could have taken place after the emigration of other branches of Indo-Europeans from India.

Finally, Elst argues that linguistic paleontology – "flora and fauna" words which all Indo-Europeans share – is not necessarily proof of their Northern geographical area of origin. Northern words are shared in India, too, and many animal names are indigenous or metaphoric extensions and not necessarily proof of proto-Indo-European status. Elst finishes with studies of contact with other languages, again concluding that the evidence does not rule out the Out of India hypothesis.

Hans Hock's article, "Philology and the Historical Interpretation of the Vedic Texts," begins the related section on philology and interpretation. Hock also takes up the question of internal Vedic evidence. He examines five different cases of Vedic interpretation and a related case of Avestan interpretation concerned with the problem of Aryan origins. First he takes on the idea that Vedic references to outsiders indicate that the outsiders' speech was influenced by Dravidian. Hock argues that, if anything, such statements refer to ritually impure speech, rather than dialectical Dravidian influence. Second, the idea that *Ṛgveda* passages refer to racial differences between *ārya* and *dāsa* is also not supportable, as most of the passages may not refer to dark or light skinned people, but dark and light worlds. Other words, such as, *anas* (noseless) may well be interpreted as mouthless, or possessing bad speech, and bull-lipped (*vṛṣaśipra*) may not necessarily be a negative characteristic.

Third, the Vedic passages suggesting immigration from outside are in Hock's mind ambiguous, as neither their "directionality" nor their geographical referents, are assured. Relatedly, the Avestan arguments for migration out of India are not convincing. It is not clear whether the regions named in the Avesta as "having been abandoned" refer to the South Asian places that Out of India theorists claim, nor do they necessarily refer to an outside origin at all.

The fifth case, of astronomical evidence, evaluates the *Kauṣītaki Brāhmaṇa* passage of how the new moon of Māgha and the winter solstice could have coincided. This observation involves a large tolerance of variation in fixing the time, so much so that variations of 576 and 1950 years are possible. It is, moreover, impossible to adjudicate between various scholarly claims of its accuracy. Finally, Hock evaluates the claim that *brahman* means a solstice. He argues that it is not clear from the textual evidence that *brahman* can mean a solstice; nothing in the relevant passages actually calls for an astronomical interpretation. All of these arguments, Hock is careful to note, may be resolved by further evidence; for the present, he argues that it is more appropriate to wait for further evidence than use any of the evidence to support a particular claim. They are, at present, unresolvable.

In "Vedic astronomy and Early Indian Chronology," Subhash Kak argues that astronomical evidence (*jyotiṣa*) can be used for dating Vedic chronology, along with philological measures and standards. After establishing the presence of *jyotiṣa* in the Vedas, Kak goes on to show that altars were used as symbolic representations of knowledge. Using Frankfort's date of 1900 BCE for the drying up of the Sarasvati River, he argues that the Vedic references to this phenomenon should place the *Ṛgveda* as at least that old. Vedic ritual was based on times for the full and the new moon, the solstices and the equinoxes. The Vedic year was divided into lunar year of 358 days, or 360 and 5 days. Lists of *nakṣatra*s (lunar asterisms) were also present in the Vedic works, and served as the names of the months. According to Kak, dates can be calculated backwards on the basis of the months shifting about 2000 years per *nakṣatra*. The changes in the lists of *nakṣatra*s in Vedic texts can help us date the Veda.

Other examples of Ṛgvedic astronomical sophistication, according to Kak, are the texts' understanding of the irregular motions of the moon and the sun, the occurrences of the equinoxes, and the descriptions of solar eclipses. From his calculations of the position of the vernal equinoxes in the *nakṣatra*s, Kak argues that the Vedic people were in India during the "Rohinī" period of 4000 BCE. If one proceeds with an astronomical interpretation of the story of Prajāpati in the form of a stag (Orion) pursuing his daughter, Rohinī, then one can argue that this period represents the astronomical time when the vernal equinox was moving from Mṛga Śiras to Rohinī.

Shrikant Talageri's chapter, "The Textual Evidence: The Ṛgveda as a Source of Indo-European History," also argues for an earlier date of the *Ṛgveda*. Talageri's contribution in this volume is a summary of his book, in which he argues that the uniquely primitive and representative character of Vedic mythology is totally incompatible with a theory which treats the Ṛgveda as the end-product of long and complete events and circumstances. According to him, there could not have been a long period of separation from the original Indo-European homeland, racial transformations en route, a long stay in Punjab, and then the development of a uniquely Indian language. Based on his analysis of internal referents to ancestors and kings in the Ṛgveda, he proposes a new chronological order of the books. From earliest to latest, he proposes the order of 6, 3, 7, 4, 2, 5, 8, 9, 10, with book 1 stretching from the pre-middle to late periods. The geographical referents in each of these books, he argues, show the earliest books in

Uttar Pradesh and the later in the Punjab. The battles of "the ten kings" in the Ṛgveda refers to a battle between the Vedic Aryans, settled east of the Sarasvati, and Iranian groups (the Vedic "Anu" tribes), settled west of the Sarasvati.

In his chapter, "Indocentrism: Autochthonous Visions of Ancient India," Michael Witzel begins by examining the positive evidence for the scholarly views currently agreed upon by Indo-Europeanists. The Ṛgveda does not know of large cities but only ruins and forts; thus we can argue that the text is later than the disintegration of the cities. He further argues that the Ṛgveda is earlier than the appearance of iron in 1200–1000 BCE, as Ṛgveda does not know iron, but only copper/bronze metal. If one strictly observes Indo-European rules of linguistic change and archaeological dating, the Mittani gods represent an earlier linguistic form of around 1400 BCE. Witzel argues that the western relatives of the Indo-Aryans, the Parsumas, and the people of the Mittani culture were all intrusive cultures, and they share much with the Indo-Aryan culture. He posits a long period of initial acculturation, most likely between Old-Indo-Aryan speakers and those speakers of the local language in the Punjab.

Witzel goes on to assert that if one follows Indo-European rules of linguistic change, the substratum words of local languages could not be Indo-European, thus ruling out the possibility of Indo-Aryan indigenous origins. Scholars who claim that such words have Indo-European origins, even though they were previously thought to be substratum words, are simply not following well-accepted linguistic procedures. Moreover, Witzel argues that a truly Vedic archaeological site would have to include several factors all at once – chariots, horse furnishing, three fire places, specific settlement patterns, tools of stone and copper, gold and silver ornaments, local pottery, barley, milk, and some wild animals. The site that best fits this description is Swat, *c.*1400 BCE known in the Ṛgveda (8.19.37). Thus, pottery styles alone, he argues, cannot support the autochthonous Aryan argument.

Witzel, too, dismisses the old hordes of invaders model as an outdated, nineteenth-century view; he turns instead to Ehret's theory of culture change, in which cultural and linguistic shifts can happen with the coming of a relatively small group who make choices in new prestige equipment and vocabulary (Ehret's "prestige kit"). Pottery, even in moments of great change, does tend to be continuous; this would explain the archaeological data in which pottery styles remain continuous.

Witzel then turns to the denial of this theory by three different groups: (1) the indigenous school, who see the Indo-Aryans originating from the Punjab; (2) the Out of India school, which views Iranians emigrating from the Punjab; (3) and the *devabhāṣya* school which claims that all the Indo-European languages originated from Sanskrit. Focusing mostly on the first two, Witzel begins by saying that interaction between Aryans and indigenous groups has been assumed for decades by linguists and historians; the assertion by these theorists is nothing new. Rather, he argues that the indigenous school's use of archaeological arguments for cultural continuity is too narrow and cited out of context. Moreover he argues that the indigenous theorists also need to explain archaeological, linguistic, textual and astronomical data in a general framework in order to become credible as a general framework. He goes on to critique the linguistic methods used by these theorists, saying that such methods are not based on regularity of linguistic shifts nor on the possibility of predicting language shifts. Moreover, the indigenous theories' sources for early history are based on later texts such as the Puranas, taken as fact and read back into the Ṛgveda itself. Moreover, the evidence such as Misra's for an early date for the Ṛgveda (5000 BCE) mistakenly relies on Harmatta (1992) whose date for proto-Finno-Ugric has been challenged by scholars. Moreover, the proponents of a common South Asian proto-language of Sanskrit and Dravidian confuse the outcome of borrowings from a long stay together, and genetic descent, which involves similarities in basic grammar and vocabulary.

Turning to the Out of India Theory, Witzel argues that such a theory would need both to explain historically and to predict the linguistic changes according to known phenomena of linguistic expansion as well as linguistic origin. Moreover, Witzel goes on to say that if we accept the Out of India Theory, the dialectical differences hypothesized in proto-Indo-European, now originating in India, would have to have been reproduced exactly all over Europe and the Near East. This is a highly unlikely scenario. Finally, Witzel goes on to show there are very few typically Indian characteristics in languages occurring west of India. They do not possess Indian grammatical features, nor words for plants, animals, or technology. The Out of India Theory cannot explain why none of these features survive. This is especially the case with retroflection; there is an absence of retroflex sounds in Old Iranian, whereas it is typical for South Asia compared with its neighboring regions. In Old Iranian, there is also an absence of local Indian words and grammatical innovations, and there is no evidence of Indian skeletons, which look very different from Western ones. Finally, Witzel argues that the autochthonous theory would have the Ṛgveda anywhere from 5000 BCE or 2600 BCE; therefore the Iranians should have exported the horse-drawn chariot from South Asia at that time. However, the horse-drawn chariot is only found in 2000 BCE in Ural Russia and at Sintashta, discussed by Parpola and Carpelan. Thus, Witzel states the word and the object itself would have occurred before its invention. The same case goes for the wheel. In addition, Witzel argues that the changes of Centum languages and Satem languages follow a clear pattern in the Indo-European scenario; such changes would become nonsensical if they were reversed in the Out of India scenario. Thus the Out of India Theory requires a multiple special pleading that no other scientist would tolerate. Witzel argues that its assertions are monolateral, and not holistic.

With this rich background in place, Part IV continues with the historiography of the contemporary debates themselves. In his "Aryan Origins: Arguments from Nineteenth-century Maharashtra," Madhav Deshpande uses little known details to analyze the history of the debate about Aryan origins in nineteenth-century Maharashtra. He does so by analyzing several factors: (1) the sense of Brahmin identity as one of only two classes (Brahmin and Śūdras); (2) the emerging British attempts to promote a certain kind of Sanskrit learning; (3) the counterclaims of such Brahmins to reassert traditional learning; (4) and the education of the non-Brahmin groups. Deshpande begins with the moderate R. G. Bhandarkar who accepted much of Indo-European philology, but attempted to develop a historical idea of the development of Sanskrit into Pali, through contact with non-Aryans. Yet Bhandarkar's views raised the unsettling question of Aryan contact with non-Aryans in the process of migration, and the even more unsettling possibility of Aryan descent from peoples who would be considered non-Aryan today.

Another theorist, M. M. Kunte, was similar to some contemporary theorists. He called the British "Western Aryas" and tried to focus on the racial affinity between colonizer and colonized. For Kunte, the original Aryan settled in India, while the Western Aryan settled only when he made a fortune. Similarly, the social reformer, M. G. Ranade, identifies the social customs of the British Aryans as continuities from the pure ancestral Aryan period, unaffected by the degrading influence of non-Aryans. So, too, the dilemma of Brahmin Aryan descent from non-Brahmin non-Aryan origins, and the divide between Aryan North and Dravidian South, posed a problem for Ranade's nationalism.

In contrast, Jotirao Phule, of the *mali* or "gardeners" caste, restudied Brahmin myths and epics and exposed them for their cruelty and subjugation. His nemesis, Vishnushastri Chiplunkar, waged an intellectual war against this Śūdra perspective, as well as the British one. In the midst of all this debate, Deshpande observes that the now famous B. G. Tilak presented the least political views of his day. He based his scholarly evidence instead on the presence of constellations and their mention in various books of the Ṛgveda. Although Tilak did not discuss archeological or linguistic data, he did establish the Aryans as senior brothers to the Western Aryan British, who subjugated them.

Finally, N. B. Pavgee was one of the first to argue for the "Out of India" model, basing his evidence on a scenario where the Arctic home was a colony of the original "Aryavasta home" in India. Deshpande argues that all of these ancestors of the Hindu nationalist movement were caught up, in some way or another, with their identities, both political and caste.

Our final article before Edwin Bryant's "Concluding Remarks," is Lars Martin Fosse's "Aryan Past and Post-Colonial Present: The Polemics and Politics of Indigenous Aryanism." Fosse takes on four theorists of the Indigenous Aryan school, and, like Deshpande, examines their political perspectives. He is careful to point out that his concern is not to undermine all of the arguments challenging the present Indo-European perspective on Aryan origins, but rather to see how indigenous Aryan arguments can function as an ideology as well as a set of academic challenges. He begins by discussing Dipesh Chakrabarty's *Colonial Indology* (1997), and argues that while Chakrabarty's critique of a biased European construction of the Indian past is at times appropriate, it is not balanced by constructive alternatives and is content with sowing seeds of doubt about scholarly motives of Western Indologists. He goes on to make the point that, given the hypothetical nature of Indo-European origins and its status as "inferred history," the nature of the evidence opens up a vast argumentative space in which contradictory hypotheses are admissible. Yet such a space also lends itself to a kind of emotional and polemic debate which compensates for a lack of conclusive data.

Fosse goes on to analyze the work of K. D. Sethna, Bhagwan Singh, N. S. Rajaram, and Shrikant Talageri. Sethna responds to a paper by Asko Parpola (1988) which conjectures a set of complex migrations and interactions to account for Aryan culture. Many of their arguments are based on elements which will by now be familiar to readers – the early date of the *Ṛgveda*, new archaeological data describing the ecology of the Sarasvatī River and Northwest India, the lack of textual evidence for an invasion, astronomical evidence based on the equinoxes, etc. While each of these authors have their own set of arguments which Fosse discusses at length, he sees some moves which are common to all of the theorists: First, they tend to rely on arguments *ex silencio*, in which lack of evidence substitutes for positive evidence; thus the lack of evidence for a migration or the questionable evidence for the presence of the horse previous to 1600 BCE cannot constitute positive arguments for an indigenous civilization. Second, they do not follow the established scholarly rules of linguistic derivation and etymology; thus, their arguments about the early date of the *Ṛgveda* or the relationship between Dravidian and Aryan languages do not hold credibility.

Fosse continues his piece with a history of the various views of the Aryan/Dravidian relationship. Theorists move along a continuum between the two extremes of establishing Tamil culture as the origins of the Aryan culture to the more Indigenist view that Aryan and Dravidian were part of a single Aryan identity, with Aryan designating culture unity and Dravidian simply indicating a "place." Talageri, for instance, assumes a common parentage for the two cultures and Kak assumes interaction between the two groups in South Asia and a subsequent migration northward.

Fosse concludes with a view that the ideological aspects of indigenous Aryanism come to full force with a challenge to the cultural and political Left in India – particularly its inability to give India the proper cohesion it needs in a postcolonial environment. He views it as a complex movement, partly motivated by caste and political interests, but also by a legitimate need to resist the colonial distortions that began in the nineteenth century. He argues that many of the movement's legitimate questions and challenges to Indo-European hypotheses are undermined by its political rhetoric.

The issues

Edwin Bryant's recent volume, *The Quest for the Origins of Vedic Culture* (2001), goes a long way toward summarizing these basic issues, and it is not worth rehearsing all the issues here done so masterfully in that volume. The basic terms of the argument are organized in his chapters: Vedic philology (including dating), linguistic substrata in India texts, linguistic evidence outside of India, archaeological evidence, both within South Asia including the Indus Valley civilization, and outside subcontinent.

How do these issues fare in the present volume? The issue of Vedic philology and dating is taken on by many of our authors – Misra, Talageri, Elst, Hock, and Witzel. Misra argues for an earlier date of the Veda based on three factors: the work of S. R. Rao's interpretation of the Indus Valley seals, the possibility of a closer relationship between Dravidian and Indo-Aryan words, and Harmatta's argument that Aryan loan words in Uralic languages show that the loans belong to an early age. Witzel takes on some of these arguments, questioning the viability of a connection between Dravidian and Indo-Aryan words, as well as reminding us that Harmatta's work has been corrected to suggest a later date for Uralic borrowings. Parpola and Carpelan, moreover, account for these borrowings in Uralic and Aryan by an entirely different scenario, which locates the homeland in Khvalynsk culture. Some response by those who agree with Misra's arguments is now the next step.

Talageri argues on the basis of reference to kings and ancestors for a reordering of the books of the Veda. He is therefore working on the internal evidence alone for the basis of his theory. The next step might be: how might we assess this method for establishing chronology for the Vedic books, as opposed to the more traditional linguistic methods for establishing their chronology? Following Hock's insights on other internal Vedic arguments, are there other more traditional linguistic methods for ways to interpret the battle of the ten kings, or does Talageri's view make the most sense out of the most data?

Hock's examination of key internal evidence within the Veda is also helpful in shedding light on the issue at stake: why are we imputing meaning to distinctions in the Veda that may not be there, such as claiming the *ārya/dāsa* distinction as necessarily a racial distinction? Moreover, assertions about directionality based on internal Vedic evidence in either direction, are at best ambiguous, and the case cannot be made on internal Vedic evidence alone. Fosse's comments on some of the Indigenous Aryan school's use of Vedic evidence parallels these questions.

The same issues arise with astronomical evidence. Hock questions the purely astronomical interpretation of certain Brāhmaṇa passages, particularly whether common words such as *brahman* can be interpreted as an astronomical term. The issue of astronomical dating and accuracy seems to depend, in part, on how one chooses to interpret certain Vedic passages that could be literary or scientific statements. Yet we might also take heed of Deshpande's observation that Tilak's use of astronomical evidence was an attempt to move beyond the entrenched and overly polemicized debates of the nineteenth- and twentieth-century day, and turn to more objective method of dating. In this volume, Hock also argues that the margin of error in astronomical calculation is too wide to come to any definitive conclusions. However, Kak is right to point out the astronomical sophistication of certain Vedic texts, particularly the fact that certain understandings of the *nakṣatra*s in the Vedas seem to be astronomically accurate and important in the history of science.

The question of linguistic adstratum and substratum influence is also key in this volume. We must understand that a substratum assumes that the dominant language overtook another less powerful language and absorbed words from it; while adstratum assumes mutual contact between languages. Witzel has argued against Dravidian presence in the earliest part of the *Ṛgveda*, but he does posit a possible proto-Munda substratum. Elst argues against too much dependence of Munda substratum. Arguing that there is nothing to rule out the case of linguistic change developing spontaneously within indigenous Indo-Aryan. Other cases of spontaneous linguistic change have been shown in other languages; what is more, borrowing or absorption of foreign words could have taken place after certain branches emigrated from India. Witzel, in turn, argues that several words commonly posited as substratum words could not possibly be Indo-European in origin if one follows basic rules of linguistic change. Fosse's concern with a basic lack of a shared paradigm for linguistic analysis between Indigenous Aryanists and Indo-Europeanists mirrors these concerns.

The same kinds of issues occur in the issue of words for flora and fauna. While Witzel argues that flora and fauna words do not show a pattern of borrowing which would reflect a westward migration theory, Elst in turn argues that Indo-European words do no necessarily point to a Northern origin of Indo-European. As Talageri, Masica, and others have pointed out, because obscure etymological pedigrees would appear to be the norm for most plant and animal terms in proto-Indo European in general, etymological obscurity need not necessarily indicate a non-Indo-European source unless that source can be specifically demonstrated (quoted in Bryant 2001: 96).

Evidence of an archaeological nature within India seems to be the most intriguing for the building of a common set of questions in this debate. Shaffer and Lichtenstein paint a picture of a Harappan culture, trading with other related and nearby cultures, which underwent a massive shift eastward by the second millennium BCE due to climactic and economic reasons. They argue for an Indo-Gangetic civilization which suggests more cultural continuity between Harappan and Aryan, yet more study has to be done for this to be proved conclusively. Because of this lack of evidence, Shaffer and Lichtenstein refrain from making any more definitive cultural scenarios, yet their work is frequently cited by the Indigenist Aryan writers (certainly Kak and Talageri in this volume) in the building of a case of Aryan origins.

The question of Indo-Iranian languages and archaeology outside the subcontinent present us with the same forms of disagreement in this volume. Misra argues that Iranian language could well be less archaic, showing more continuity with middle Indo-Aryan. Witzel, on the other hand, argues that because there is an absence of local Indian words in Old Iranian, and an absence of Indian-like skeletons in the archaeological finds in Iran, it is impossible to posit an Out of India Theory in which Iranian languages developed out of an Indian proto-Indo-European.

In addition to these linguistic ideas, the actual archaeological evidence outside of India is equally controversial. Using a variation of the basic Indo-European hypothesis of expansion through the central Caucasus, Parpola and Carpelan try to correlate the archaeological data outside of India, particularly recent archaeological discoveries in Central Asia and Russia by David Anthony (1995 and 1998), and linguistic observations about Finno-Ugaritic and its relationship to proto-Indo-European. Yet Lamberg-Karlovsky is quite clear that there is great danger in trying to make these correlations, particularly with the most likely archaeological candidates to be identified as "Indo-Iranian" culture – the Androvono and the BMAC cultures. Even the most likely connecting link, the BMAC culture, could have still sponsored several different spoken languages within its impressive fortifications and temples.

More generally: for many theorists, Indo-Aryan origins is best explained by the hypothesis that accounts for the most facts, and that takes into account the most consistent patterns of linguistic and archaeological change. For others, the large lacunae still left by these theorists means that other narratives must be possible, or, a more modest claim, that another narrative cannot be ruled out. It is the burden of the alternative theory to account for the consistencies, and not just the inconsistencies, in the previous theory.

How then, might this global academy begin to tell even the rudiments of a common story? Or, to put it another way: What might a professor of Indian culture whose area of expertise is not ancient India say to the eager faces of an introductory class in light of all this complexity? One might attempt something like the following: There are significant differences as well as some continuities between Indus Valley and Aryan civilizations and ideas. Recent archaeological evidence in the north west of India suggests that Harappan culture interacted with Aryan culture, but there is still a debate as to whether this interaction came from migration or from indigenous changes from within. And, that with a scholarly lack of consensus on the meaning of the Harappan script, it is difficult to ascertain the nature of the connection between Harappan and Aryan cultures. Moreover, present debates about the linguistic evidence focus on the nature of the Sanskrit language, and whether it was a dominant language which borrowed certain elements from indigenous languages, or whether that scenario should be changed to reflect more interactive relationships or even change from within Sanskrit itself. In addition, those who argue for the origin of Aryan civilization *within* India and those who argue for an origin *outside* of India do not share the same paradigms for linguistic derivation. Archaeological discoveries in other, related areas, such as Iran and Russia, also seem to suggest a connection between these cultures. The basic challenge for all scholars remains in matching the linguistic evidence with the archaeological evidence in a way that explains most data.

We exist in a world of global conflict without global governance; and the question of Aryan origins has become a global academic conflict with a dire need for common rules of debate. Without anticipating Edwin Bryant's excellent and cohesive "Concluding Remarks," I might end by observing that, even in these articles there are, however, emerging consensuses of a certain sort: First, very few, if any, archaeologists or linguists embrace the invasion theory, and have not done so for several decades. Second, there is a general agreement that in the pre-Vedic period, prolonged contact between Aryan and other cultures led to major changes in religious, material, and linguistic life that led to what we now call the Vedic culture. Third, if the status of the Indus Valley script is ever deciphered, theories would have to change dramatically; equally importantly, if the horse is ever discovered to be contemporaneous with early Indus Valley culture, or pre-Vedic South Asian civilization, the migrationist theories would have to change dramatically. In the absence of such discoveries, definitive conclusions cannot be based on the absence of evidence.

Several opportunities for colloquies and conferences present themselves from this volume: the need for scholars to gather to evaluate Vedic astronomy, and claims about Vedic astronomy, in the larger context of the history of science. Scholars also need to gather to re-establish a set of agreed upon rules about internal Vedic evidence, and internal Vedic chronology. Finally, scholars need to confer about the possibility and rules for linguistic "flip-flopping," where, in linguistic paleontology and studies of palatization in particular, arguments have been made about the reverse directionality of linguistic change.

Barring any new discoveries, neither internal evidence from the Veda, nor archaeological evidence, nor linguistic substrata alone can make the turning point in any given hypothesis. This situation should be the most persuasive case of all for scholars to allow the questions to unite them in interdependence, rather than suspicions to divide them in monistic theory-making. It is far too early for scholars to begin taking positions and constructing scenarios as if they were truths. Rather, it is time for scholars to rewrite and then share a set of common questions, such as the ones articulated earlier. Then, a lack of conclusive evidence can be a spur for further research, rather than a political bludgeon which wastes precious intellectual resources.

Note

1 See in particular the recent exchange in "The Open Page" of *The Hindu* between Michael Witzel and David Frawley, June 18, June 25, July 9, July 16, August 6, and August 13 (2002). Also see Witzel's "Westward Ho! The Incredible Wanderlust of the Rgvedic Tribes Exposed by S. Talageri, A Review of: Shrikant G. Talageri, The Rigveda. A historical analysis." in *Electronic Journal of Vedic Studies* (EJVS) 7(2) (2001), March 31 (At http://nautilus.shore.net/~india/ejvs/ejvs0702/ejvs0702a.txt). See also responses in http://www.bharatvani.org/indology.html and http://www.tri-murti.com/ancientindia

This volume does not address the recent discovery in the Gulf of Cambay, off the coast of Gujarat, since there is as of yet no scholarly consensus about its date and significance.

References

Anthony, D., 1991. "The Archaeology of Indo-European Origins," *Journal of Indo-European Studies*, 19(3/4): 193–222.

——, 1995. "Horse, Wagon, and Chariot: Indo-European Languages and Archaeology," *Antiquity*, 69(264): 554–65.

Anthony, D., 1998. "The Opening of the Eurasian Steppe at 2000 BCE." In *The Bronze Age and Iron Age Peoples of Eastern Central Asia* (*The Journal of Indo-European Studies Monograph*, 26), edited by V. H. Maire, Vol. 1. Washington, DC: Institute for the Study of Man, pp. 94–113.

Bobomulloev, S., 1999. "Discovery of a Bronze Age Tomb on the Upper Zerafshan," *Stratum Plus* (in Russian) No. 2:307–14.

Bryant, E., 2001. *The Quest for The Origins of Vedic Culture: The Indo-Aryan Migration Debate*. New York: Oxford University Press.

Chakrabarty, D., 1997. *Colonial Indology: Sociopolitics of the Ancient Indian Past*. New Delhi: Munshiram Manoharlal Publishers Pvt, Ltd.

Harmatta, J., 1981. "Proto Iranians and Proto Indians in Central Asia in the 2nd Millennium BC (Linguistic Evidence)." In *Ethnic Problems of the History of Central Asian in the Early Period*, edited by M. S. Asmiov *et al.* Moscow: Nauka, pp. 75–82.

——, 1992. "The Emergence of the Indo-Iranians: The Indo-Iranian Languages." In *History of Civilizations of Central Asia*, edited by A. H. Dani and V. M. Masson. UNESCO, Vol. 1, pp. 357–78.

Hemphill, B. E., J. R. Lukaes, and K. A. R. Kennedy, 1991. "Biological Adaptations and Affinities of Bronze Age Harappans." In *Harappa Excavations 1986–1990*, edited by R. H. Meadow. Madison, WI: Prehistory Press, pp. 137–82.

Hock, H. H., 1999. "Through a Glass Darkly: Modern 'Racial' Interpretations vs. Textual and General Pre-historical Evidence on ārya and dāsa/dasyu in Vedic Society." In *Aryan and Non-Aryan in South Asia: Evidence, Interpretation, and Ideology*, edited by J. Bronkhorst and M. Deshpande. Harvard Oriental Series, Opera Minora, Vol. 3. Columbia, MO: South Asia Books, pp. 145–74.

Parpola, A., 1988. "The Coming of the Aryans to Iran and India and the Cultural and Ethnic Identity of the Dasas." *Studia Orientalia*, 64: 195–302.

Witzel, M., 1999a. "Aryan and Non-Aryan Names in Vedic India. Data for the Linguistic Situation, *c.*1900–500 BC." In *Aryans and Non-Aryans in South Asia*, edited by J. Bronkhorst and M. Deshpande. Harvard Oriental Series, Opera Minora. Cambridge, MA: Harvard University Press.

——, 1999b. "Substrate Languages in Old Indo-Aryan," *Electronic Journal of Electronic Studies*, September 1999.

Yash Pal, B., R. K. Snood, and D. P. Agrawal, 1984. "Remote Sensing of the 'Lost' Sarasvati River." In *Frontiers of the Indus Civilization*, edited by B. B. Lal, S. P. Gupta, and Shashi Asthana. New Delhi: Books and Books, pp. 491–7.

Part I

ARCHAEOLOGY

1

CULTURE CHANGE DURING THE LATE HARAPPAN PERIOD AT HARAPPA

New insights on Vedic Aryan issues

Jonathan Mark Kenoyer

1.1 Introduction

In the course of the early excavations at Harappa and Mohenjo-daro in the 1920s–1930s, the Indus Valley civilization came to be recognized by the world as the first urban culture of South Asia. In the beginning, scholars such as Sir John Marshall claimed that the Indus Valley civilization represented an indigenous culture that set the foundation for later Vedic, Buddhist, and Hindu civilization (Marshall 1931). Even though some scholars proposed that the "idea" of civilization had diffused from the West (Wheeler 1968), the achievements of this culture soon came to be regarded as an important validation for the antiquity of Indian civilization as a whole. In this capacity it was occasionally used by political and religious leaders of the subcontinent in their struggle for independence from British rule. Some of the artifacts used to link the Indus cities to later Indian culture were decorative motifs such as the swastika, pipal leaf, and endless knot mandala. Seals with depictions of individuals seated in yogic positions and "post cremation burial urns" served to confirm the Indianness of the Harappan culture.

After the independence of India and Pakistan in 1947, the Indus Valley civilization came to be viewed from several different perspectives. Scholars using Western historical, anthropological, or archaeological paradigms studied this civilization to determine its relationships to other known civilizations in West and East Asia. This perspective has continued to be the predominant framework for archaeological research in both India and Pakistan. However, many scholars in Pakistan have come to view the Indus cities as an example of a pre-Islamic civilization that had little relationship to the modern Islamic state. Since the major excavated Indus sites of Mohenjo-daro, Harappa, and Chanhudaro were located in what became Pakistan, archaeological research in India after 1947 focused on the discovery and excavation of new sites, such as Kalibangan and Lothal. At these sites, the discovery of comparable artifacts, such as seals, Indus script, burials, city walls, and monumental architecture were interpreted as being identical to those found at the major sites of Mohenjo-daro and Harappa. However, other features, such as hearths, that were at first interpreted as being domestic in nature, soon came to be referred to as "fire altars" and mundane artifacts such as triangular terra cotta cakes began to take on a new significance as ritual objects (Lal and Thapar 1967).

Over the past several decades there have been numerous attempts to define the relationship of the Harappan culture and the Indus Valley civilization as a whole to the Vedic literature and culture. These studies often fade into broader discussions that include later Indian religious traditions that have come to be referred to collectively as Hinduism. This chapter will focus only on three major arguments regarding the Harappans and the Vedic Aryans, all of which use the same basic archaeological and literary data, but interpreted in different ways. One view is that the Harappan culture was destroyed by invading hordes of horse- and chariot-riding Indo-Aryan warriors (Wheeler 1968). In this view, the Indus civilization did not leave a significant legacy, but was replaced by new cultural and religious traditions as well as new populations that have continued up to the present. This view has been strongly contested by archaeologists (Shaffer 1984; Shaffer and Lichtenstein 1999) and others (Singh 1995). A second view is that the Harappans were themselves the communities referred to in the Vedic texts and that they were the ones to introduce the domestic horse and iron technology in the northern subcontinent, along with Early Vedic ideology (Singh 1995; Gupta 1996). Many of the arguments used to support this view are so tenuous that few if any scholars have bothered to address the issues. A third view is that the Harappan culture was earlier and distinct from Vedic culture, but that there is an important Harappan legacy in later cultures (see Kenoyer 1998 for summary).

The archaeological identification of Vedic culture has been very difficult because the material culture associated with Vedic communities is either ephemeral and not preserved in the archaeological record or it is indistinguishable from that of other Late Chalcolithic cultures. Since the Early Vedic people did not use a system of writing, there are no written records or inscriptions. Furthermore, there are no known monuments, temples, or distinctive sculptures that can be attributed to this elusive period. Whereas scholars tend to agree that Vedic communities did leave some form of archaeological record, most claims have not withstood the scrutiny of scientific research (see Gaur 1997 for a summary). Current candidates for Early Vedic communities are the Ochre Colored Pottery Cultures of the northern subcontinent (Gaur 1997) or the grey ware using cultures of northern Pakistan (Dani 1967, 1991). Some scholars feel that later Indo-Aryan communities can be associated with the Painted Grey Ware Cultures (Lal 1981, 1998) which overlap with the Late Harappan occupation at the site of Bhagwanpura (Lal 1982, 1998; Joshi 1993). Many other variations on these three themes can be found in the literature, but it is not possible to address all of them individually.

The uncritical use of the archaeological data from excavations throughout northern India and Pakistan has led to serious misrepresentations about the nature of the Indus culture, its decline and its legitimate legacy. Much of the confusion is due to the paucity of well-documented excavations of the critical period at the end of the Indus cities, generally referred to as the Late Harappan period (1900–1300 or 1000 BC). An additional complication is that the Late Harappan period has several different regional variations that have been grouped together on the basis of the modern regions of Punjab, Sindh, and Gujarat (Shaffer 1992; Kenoyer 1995) (Figure 1.1). The period following the Late Harappan is also quite poorly represented in the critical areas of the Punjab, Sindh, and Gujarat. A review of the data from excavations in both Pakistan and India show that although there are numerous continuities with later periods, significant changes were also occurring during the latest phase of the Indus Tradition and the rise of new urban centers in the Indo-Gangetic Tradition (Kenoyer 1995).

One of the most important developments is the emergence of new peripheral centers in the Gangetic region concomitant with the eclipse of urban centers in the old core of the Indus Valley. This suggests that the Late Harappan period is not so much a time of decline in the Indus Valley, but rather of social, economic, and political reorganization on a larger scale that includes both the Indus and Gangetic regions as well as the adjacent Malwa Plateau.

In order to provide a more reliable perspective on the Late Harappan period of the Punjab region, recent excavations at Harappa have included examination of the uppermost levels of the site (Meadow 1991; Meadow *et al.* 1996; Meadow and Kenoyer 2001). The Late Harappan phenomenon at the site is generally referred to as the Cemetery H culture because it was first discovered in the course of excavations in a cemetery located in the portion of the site grid referred to as Area H (Vats 1940). This chapter presents a critical examination of the Late Harappan data from the earlier excavations at Harappa followed by the recent discoveries from new excavations conducted by the Harappa Archaeological Research Project in collaboration with the Department of Archaeology and Museums, Government of Pakistan. These new excavations indicate that the Late Harappan occupation at the site was much more widespread than originally thought (Figure 1.2). Baked brick architecture was constructed with both newly made bricks as well as reused bricks from earlier structures. During the Late Harappan period there is evidence of over-crowding and encroachment rather than abandonment and decline (Kenoyer 1991).

Furthermore, people using pottery identical to that found in Cemetery H were living together with people who were still using Harappan styles of pottery (Meadow *et al.* 1999). Instead of technological stagnation and reversals, we see evidence of more highly refined techniques of firing pottery and making faience. The earliest evidence for glass production is seen during this time along with new techniques for drilling hard stone beads (Meadow *et al.* 1996).

With all of these new developments, it is also important to note the relatively sudden disappearance of cubical stone weights, the Indus script, and Indus seals with script and animal motifs (Kenoyer 1998). The unicorn motif and other distinctive symbols of the Indus elites are no longer produced. New types of pottery

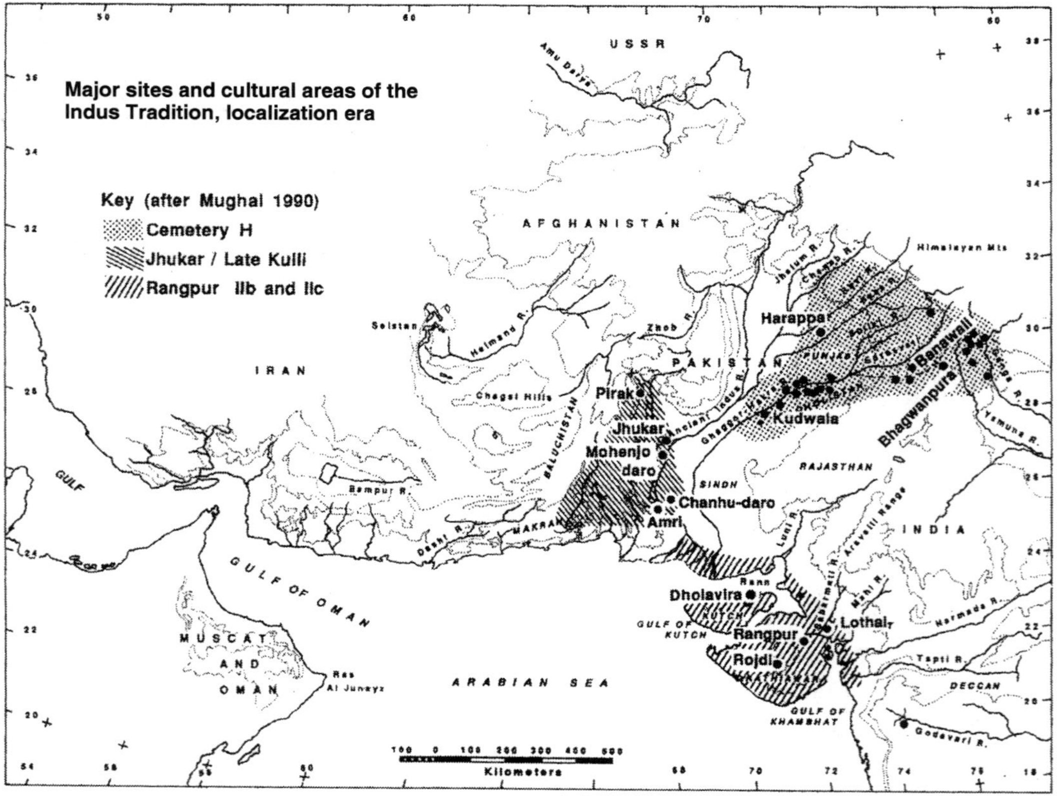

Figure 1.1 Major sites of the Late Harappan period.

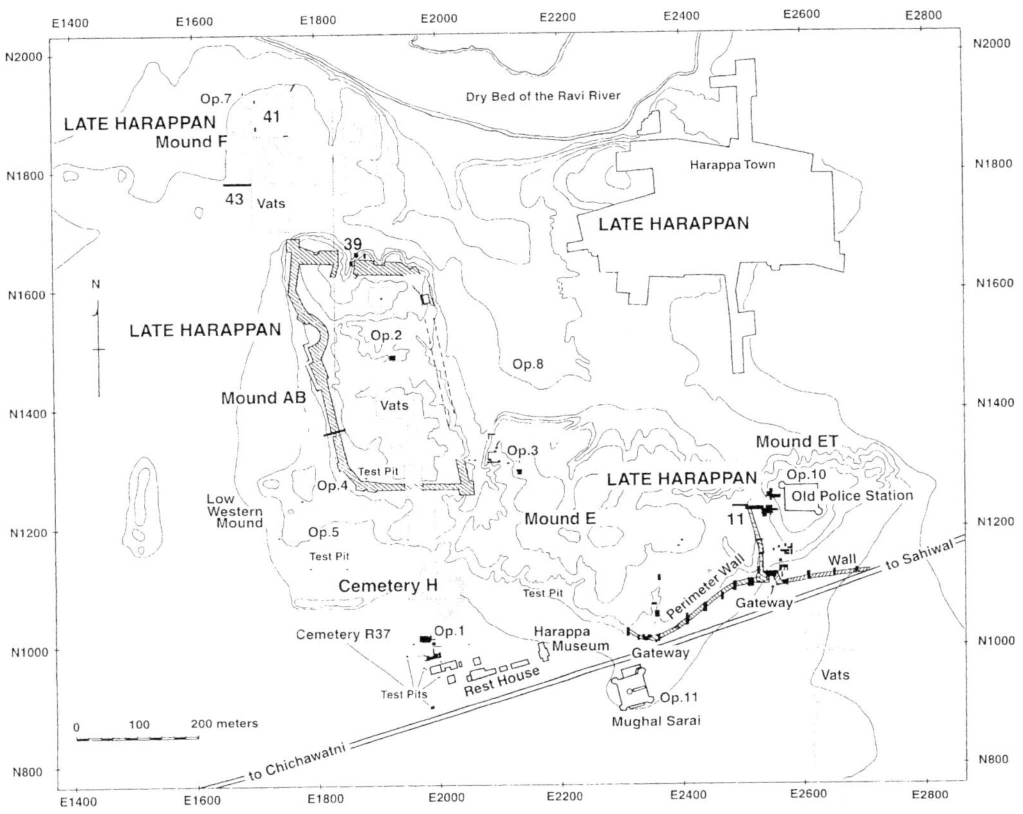

Figure 1.2 Harappa: Late Harappan occupation areas.

vessels and the disappearance of traditional Harappan forms indicate changes in food preparation. While there is no evidence for a new set of food crops, the increasing importance of rice and millets indicates a significant change or intensification of the subsistence economy (Weber 1992, 1998; Meadow 1996, 1998). The economic and ritual importance of new animals such as the horse and camel are still not fully understood (Meadow 1998), though they were present by the end of the Late Harappan period and beginning of the Painted Grey Ware Period. Finally, the changes in burial practices attest to a major shift in ideology, but it is important to note that there is no concrete evidence for the appearance of a new biological population (Hemphill *et al.* 1991; Kennedy 1992, 1995). This suggests that the changes and discontinuities reflect a transformation of the local population rather than the appearance of new people and the eradication of the Harappan inhabitants.

Given the new information it is necessary to reevaluate not only the relationship between the Harappan and the Late Harappan periods, but also the relationship of the Late Harappan to the archaeological cultures of the Early Historic period. Furthermore, archaeologists, linguists, and historians of religion who have been trying to understand the origin of Vedic Aryan communities and their relationship to the Indus civilization must also take into account this new information. It is not possible in this chapter to critically evaluate these earlier interpretations (e.g. Godbole 1961; Sharma 1978, 1999; Wheeler 1979; Erdosy 1989; Bajpai 1992; Deshpande 1995; Lal 1998; Bryant 1999; Kochhar 2000), even though some of them still have some validity. Instead, it is more constructive to begin with a fresh new perspective on the socio-economic, technological, and symbolic/ritual transformations going on at the site. When these data can be correlated to information from other sites, it will be possible to finally shed new light on the time period between the end of the Indus cities and the rise of Early Historic cities in the northern subcontinent.

1.2 Chronological framework

In the past there was considerable disagreement over the dating of the Indus Valley civilization and the period leading up to the rise of the Early Historic cities. However, the large number of radiocarbon dates from careful excavations during the past 50 years now make it possible to date the major chronological periods quite reliably (Table 1.1). The major qualification to the chronology presented is that the decline of the Indus civilization occurred at different times depending on the specific region. Some settlements, such as Harappa, may never have been totally abandoned, while other sites such as Mohenjo-daro and Jhukar were abandoned for centuries and then re-inhabited for short periods in later historical periods. In the Punjab, the dates for the Late Harappan are generally 1900–1300 BC, but in some sites the dates go as late as 1000 BC (Shaffer 1992). In the region of Sindh the Late Harappan is generally referred to as the Jhukar culture, but there are no radiocarbon dates from the late levels of sites with Jhukar pottery and artifacts. According

Table 1.1 Chronology of the Indus and Indo-Gangetic Traditions

Archaeological/historical events	*General dates*
Indus Tradition	
Early Food Producing Era	*c.*6500–5000 BC
Regionalization Era	*c.*5000–2600 BC
Harappa Period 1A/B	3300–2800 BC
Harappa Period 2	2800–2600 BC
Integration Era	2600–1900 BC
Harappa Period 3A	2600–2450 BC
Harappa Period 3B	2450–2200 BC
Harappa Period 3C	2200–1900 BC
Localization Era	1900–1300 (or 1000) BC
Late Harappan – Harappa Period 4	1900–1800 BC
Late Harappan – Harappa Period 5	1800–1700 BC
Post-Indus Painted Grey Ware	+1200–800 BC
Mahabharata Battle	*c.*836 BC
Indo-Gangetic Tradition: beginning of Regionalization Era for Indo-Gangetic Tradition	
Early Historic Period begins around	600 BC
Northern Black Polished Ware	(?700) 500–300 BC
Ramayana Episode (early NBP period)	
Panini (Sanskrit grammarian)	*c.*500–400 BC
Buddha (Siddhartha Gautama)	563–483 BC (or 440–360 BC)
Mauryan Empire (Integration Era)	
Chandragupta Maurya	?317–298 BC
Bindusara	298–274 BC
Ashoka	274–232 BC

to Mughal, " 'Jhukar' is only a pottery style emerging in association with the continuing Mature Harappan ceramic tradition without any break or sudden change in cultural continuity" (Mughal 1990: 3). Another Late or post-Harappan culture from this region is seen at the site of Pirak which can be dated from 1700–700 BC (Jarrige and Santoni 1979) or 2000–1300 BC (Shaffer 1992). In Gujarat, the Late Harappan period is characterized by a pottery referred to as Lustrous Red Ware (LRW), which is found in levels associated with the Harappan pottery and continues until around 1400 BC (Bhan 1992). The LRW pottery is also often found in association with a style of pottery referred to as Black and Red ware which has strong cultural affinities to peninsular sites. Furthermore, the discovery of LRW at the sites of Navdatoli (Phase III) and Ahar (Phase IC) provides additional support for interaction with the east rather than with the west (Bhan 1992). After 1400 BC there is a break in the archaeological record at most sites between 1400 and 600 BC when another diagnostic style of pottery appears. This is the famous Northern Black Polished Ware that is associated with the Early Historic period. At present there are no sites in the Punjab, Sindh, or Gujarat that provide a convincing link between the Late Harappan and Early Historic periods. However, it is not unlikely that they will be discovered, since all of these regions played an important role in the initial phases of the Early Historic period.

1.3 The Late Harappan period

The Late Harappan period at the site of Harappa was first identified in the excavations of Cemetery H that was discovered by K. N. Sastri in 1928 (Sastri 1965) and excavated by M. S. Vats from 1928 to 1934 (Vats 1940: 203ff.) (Figure 1.2). The collection of burial pottery from the upper levels of the cemetery, referred to as Stratum I (Figure 1.3), were stylistically different from the pottery associated with the Harappan occupation at the site (Figure 1.4). Fractional secondary burials of one or more adult individuals were found in some of the pots, and it was suggested that the bodies had been exposed for some time before the bones were collected and buried in the funerary vessels (Sastri 1965) (Figure 1.5). Some of the vessels contained the entire body of infants buried in embryonic position, presumably wrapped with cloth (Sastri 1965: 6).

In all but one example, the bones found in the pot burials appear to have been exposed without any evidence of burning. One partly eroded pot contained "ashy earth freely mixed with pieces of charcoal, some blackened potsherds, and numerous fragments of charred and un-charred bones, including one charred bone of a bird" (Vats 1940: 219). Although many scholars have used this evidence to speak of cremation being practiced by the people of the Cemetery H period (Sankalia 1979), the contents of this pot appear to conform to the type of Harappan trash matrix in which the pot burials were being buried. One other vessel was found with some charred fragmentary bone, but none of the charred bone has been identified as being human (Vats 1940: appendix I).

In addition to the burials in Cemetery H, Vats reports the discovery of post-cremation burial urns that were never found with burned human bones. Nonetheless, these urns were identified as post-cremation urns because large urns with partly burned human bones had been found at a site in Baluchistan and because similar ones from Mohenjo-daro had been identified as such by Sir John Marshall (Vats 1940: 251–3). All of the ones pictured in the Harappa report appear to be trash bins or sump pots that may have collected differing amounts of animal bone and in one case an un-burned human tibia (Vats 1940: 252). Recent excavations at Harappa using modern techniques of recording and analysis confirm that the so-called "post-cremation burial urns" are in fact secondary accumulations of bone resulting from periodic discard. It is clear from a critical reading of the excavation report and recent work at Harappa that there is no evidence for cremation during either the Harappan or the Late Harappan period at Harappa.

After removal of the upper layer of burial vessels additional graves were discovered at a lower level, designated Stratum II and commonly referred to as "earth burials" (Figure 1.6). These burials were different from the fractional pot burials and consisted of complete skeletons buried on their side with flexed or extended legs and generally oriented northeast to southwest. The orientations

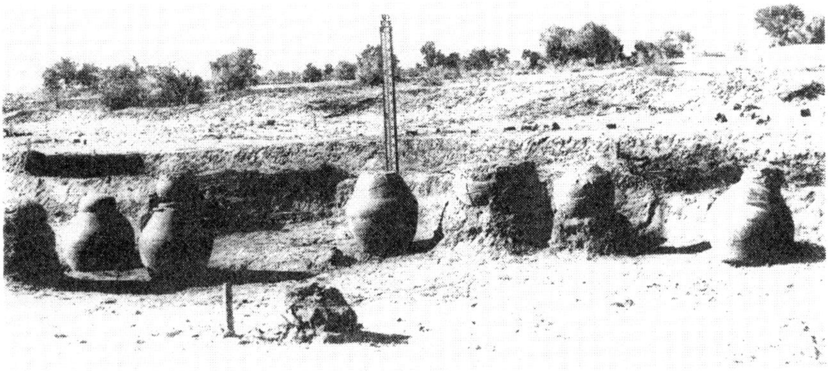

Figure 1.3 Cemetery H: Stratum I burials. Group No. H206a–k from east.

Source: Punjab Volume 44, pl. 4563, 1929–30. Photo: Courtesy of Archaeological Survey of India.

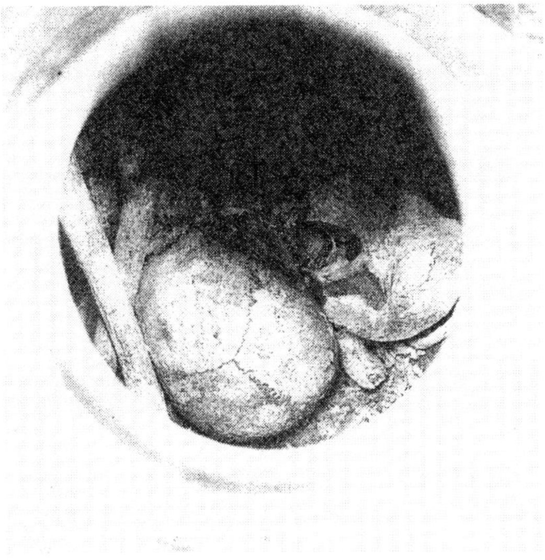

Figure 1.4 Detail of contents in burial jar H245a.

Source: Punjab Volume 44, pl. 4567, 1929–30. Photo: Courtesy of Archaeological Survey of India.

were not uniform however, and some skeletons were oriented with head to the east, and one had the head to the west. Most of these burials were accompanied by burial pottery and occasionally ornaments (Vats 1940; Sastri 1965). The burial pottery found with the Stratum II burials (Figure 1.7) is stylistically different

Figure 1.5 Cemetery H: Stratum I burial pottery.

Source: Punjab Volume 44, pl. 4573, 1929–30. Jars no. H206a,b and H245b. Photo: Courtesy of Archaeological Survey of India.

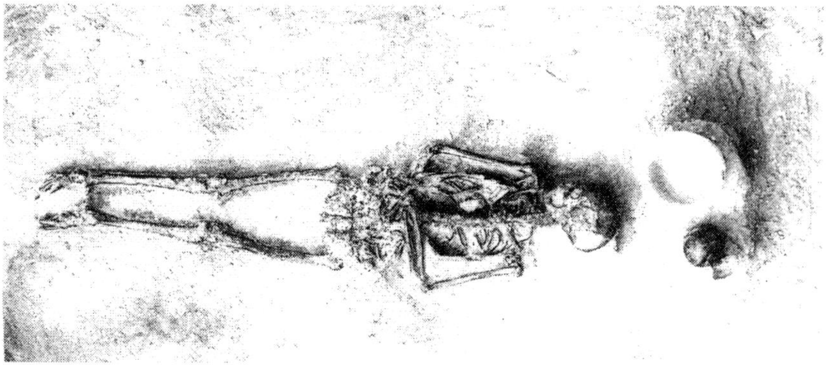

Figure 1.6 Cemetery H: Stratum II burial no. H306.

Source: Punjab Volume 44, pl. 4566, 1929–30. Photo: Courtesy of Archaeological Survey of India.

from that found with the Stratum I burials and is also distinct from the Harappan pottery found in the Harappan Cemetery R37 and in the occupation areas of the site. Some of these vessels, particularly the ones with tall everted rims (Figure 1.7) are stylistically similar to vessels from sites in Baluchistan and Afghanistan. However, the ware and manufacturing conforms to the rest of the pottery in the assemblage, and together the ceramics represent a local industry.

Although the pottery from both Stratum I and II do not reveal any direct parallels with Harappan pottery, there does appear to be a stylistic evolution beginning with the Harappan pottery and continuing through both Stratum II and Stratum I. Furthermore, the same general area of the site continued in use as a cemetery from the Harappan (2600 BC) through the Late Harappan period

Figure 1.7 Pottery from Stratum II burials.
Source: Punjab Volume 44, pl. 4671, 1929–30. Photo: Courtesy of Archaeological Survey of India.

(1700 BC or later). Almost 1,000 years of continuous use suggests that there were some important continuities in concepts of sacred burial areas and afterlife.

According to Hemphill *et al.* (1991) the main biological discontinuities are between 6000 and 4500 BC and then again around 800 BC.

> With closest biological affinities outside the Indus Valley to the inhabitants of Tepe Hissar 3 (3000–2000 BC), these biological data can be interpreted to suggest that peoples to the west interacted with those in the Indus Valley during this and the preceding proto-Elamite period and thus may have influenced the development of the Harappan civilization.
>
> The second biological discontinuity exists between the inhabitants of Harappa, Chalcolithic Mehrgarh, and post-Harappa Timarghara on one hand and the Early Iron Age inhabitants of Sarai Khola on the other.
>
> (Hemphill *et al.* 1991: 174)

They go on to state emphatically that

> The Harappan Civilization does indeed represent an indigenous development within the Indus Valley, but this does not indicate isolation extending back to Neolithic times. Rather, this development represents internal continuity for only 2000 years, combined with interactions with the West and specifically with the Iranian Plateau.
>
> (Ibid.)

It is important to note that these biological discontinuities are based on a very limited data set and do not indicate massive movements of populations. It is not certain what the cause of these changes is, but they could result from gene flow during the annual movements of traders traveling between the Iranian Plateau and the Indus settlements. Trade interactions can be documented from the earliest Neolithic period (+7000 BC) and continued through the Harappan period (2600–1900 BC). There is some question as to the degree of trade between the northern Indus sites such as Harappa and the highlands to the west during the Late Harappan period.

When looked at in the larger context of the Indus Valley, all of the burials from Indus Valley sites bear strong affinities, except for the late burials at Mohenjo-daro (Hemphill *et al.* 1991: 173). On a smaller scale, studies comparing the cranial measurements of only burials at Harappa itself indicate that the burials of the Harappan period have the closest biological affinity with those of the Late Harappan Stratum II burials. There is no close relationship between the Late Harappan Stratum II and Stratum I burials. The significance of these similarities or dissimilarities should not be taken too seriously since the biological anthropologists themselves caution that this is only a tentative suggestion due to the small sample size of the Late Harappan burials. Generally speaking, the biological evidence does not support any hypothesis involving the movements of new populations into Harappa from outside the Indus Valley during the Harappan or Late Harappan periods. While there is some suggestion that the individuals buried in the Harappan cemetery are more closely linked to those of the Late Harappan Stratum II earth burials than to the Stratum I pot burials, the sample is too small to make any conclusive statements. Therefore, it is necessary to look to the archaeological evidence from the habitation areas until a larger sample of burials can be recovered and studied. Excavations of Late Harappan houses in the various areas of the site were undertaken by the Harappa Project to look for new types of evidence to understand additional cultural features of the people who were buried in Cemetery H.

1.3.1 Cemetery H occupation extent

During the initial surface surveys of Harappa begun in 1986 and 1987, pottery of the Late Harappan (Cemetery H) occupation was recovered primarily from Mounds AB and E, with a higher proportion found on the deflated and barren surfaces of Mound AB (Figure 1.2). However, by 1999, evidence for Cemetery H occupation had been recovered from all of the major mounds. In addition, excavations by the Department of Archaeology and Museums along the western edge of Harappa town discovered the presence of Cemetery H occupation levels and substantial architectural units made with fired brick (unpublished). It is not unlikely that additional Late Harappan structures exist beneath Harappa City itself. These discoveries indicate that the Cemetery H occupation was much more widespread than previously thought. Although the total area of the Cemetery H occupation is difficult to estimate due to the massive scale of brick robbing and the lack of detailed excavations in Harappa City, the total habitation area is probably as much as 100 hectares, only slightly less than that of the Harappan period.

1.3.2 Cemetery H architecture

Excavations in various trenches between 1987 and 2000 have convincingly demonstrated that the Late Harappans were constructing their houses in much the same pattern as during the Harappan period. They made large mud brick platforms as foundations for brick buildings that were serviced by brick-lined drains. The orientation of the houses was based on the cardinal directions and, except for encroachments, the streets remained along the same plans as during the preceding Harappan period.

In 1987, excavations on the top northwestern corner of Mound E, mud brick platforms associated with Cemetery H styles of pottery were found overlying Harappan occupation deposits (Dales and Kenoyer 1991: 221). In excavations along the top edge of the mound a drain made of fired bricks was discovered associated with Late Harappan (Cemetery H) pottery (Dales and Kenoyer 1989). The brick sizes were slightly smaller than those of the Harappan period, but they had the same general proportion of 1 : 2 : 4 (i.e. thickness : width : length).

The initial investigation of Late Harappan occupation on Mound AB was undertaken in a large step trench in the center of the mound in 1988 and 1989. Structures made of mud brick were identified along the uppermost edges of the trench, but further excavations indicated that these fragmentary structures had been badly disturbed by brick robbing. Even though no complete structures were identified, it was possible to determine that the mud bricks did not conform to the standard Harappan sizes (Dales and Kenoyer 1991: 235). Further excavations in this area did not reveal any significant occupation deposits.

Continued excavations down the northwestern edge of Mound E in 1988 provided new information on the overall chronology of the settlement, beginning with the Early Harappan period through the Harappan and Late Harappan occupations (Dales and Kenoyer 1991). When combined with the results from excavations on Mound AB, it was possible to establish an internal chronology for the site (Table 1.1), beginning with Periods 1 and 2 – Early Harappan, Period 3 – Harappan, and Periods 4 and 5 – Late Harappan (Kenoyer 1991).

Period 4 was a transitional phase following the final phase of the Harappan period and was characterized by the presence of brick drains, fragmentary brick walls, and mud brick structures. Due to the lack of extensive habitation contexts it was difficult to determine the precise nature of the ceramic assemblage, but it appeared to include a mixture of Cemetery H and Harappan forms, particularly the pointed base goblet.

Period 5 was the Late Harappan occupation with pottery related to the Cemetery H, pot burials of Stratum I. Initially, no architectural features were found associated with these types of pottery, but in 1986, one area with *in situ* pottery, hearths, and some fragmentary brick architecture was discovered west of the tomb of Baba Noor Shah Wali on Mound AB (Figure 1.2). These features were found at the top of a circular plinth of the original mound, left standing in the middle of the extensive excavations made by Rai Bahadur Daya Ram Sahni between 1920 and 1925 (Vats 1940: 136). Every year the eroding vessels and hearths of this feature were carefully observed, and in 1994 samples of ash and sediment from inside the lower portion of a large storage vessel were collected for botanical analysis. Finally, in 1996, it was necessary to excavate the area because of excessive erosion and disturbance by local children looking for "treasures." Designated Trench 38, this area actually did reveal numerous treasures in the form of architecture, pottery, beads, and hearths that made it possible to obtain a good date for the elusive Late Harappan period. The initial studies of the pottery and artifacts from this and other contexts at Harappa are providing a new understanding of the material culture of the Late Harappan phase, which up to now has been known primarily from cemetery contexts and surface collections. A detailed study of this area is under preparation by Manabu Koiso who supervised the excavations, but a summary of the major points is provided next.

1.3.3 Cemetery H domestic space

Although the area of excavation in Trench 38 was very limited, only about 5 by 5 meters, it proved to be extremely rich in a wide variety of domestic artifacts and architectural features. Directly below the surface a baked brick wall [13] was encountered that was oriented east-west, with connecting walls at either end oriented north-south (Figure 1.8a). These walls were made of generally complete fired bricks that were slightly smaller than those normally used during the Harappan period, but as with the drain found on Mound E, the proportions of the bricks were 1 : 2 : 4. On the floor associated with this wall was a large oval hearth [43] that has been dated to *c.*1701–37 cal BC (Meadow *et al.* 1996). The pottery directly associated with this hearth and floor were almost exclusively attributable to the Cemetery H period, except for a few plain storage vessels that are also found in the preceding Harappan period. It is important to note that pointed base goblets were found in these latest levels along with Cemetery H pottery. Other finds include steatite beads, carnelian beads, terra cotta bangles, and some terra cotta figurine fragments.

Beneath the floor level associated with brick wall [13] were a series of habitation surfaces with *in situ* hearths and ceramic vessels characteristic of the Late Harappan phase. The hearths were basically a shallow depression on the floor, filled with charcoal and ash with underlying red burned soil. Large undecorated globular storage jars were set into the floor and eventually became filled with trash that included terra cotta nodules and terra cotta cake fragments. These large storage jars were almost identical to those used during the Harappan period. Other plain wares include shallow dishes, deep bowls, and small jars, including the pointed base goblet.

A large globular pot with a lid made from an overturned ceramic bottle was found under the corner of the later wall. This vessel may have been used for storing or heating water, but it was then reused as a refuse pit set into the floor near a cooking area. The upper fill inside this vessel was the result of later sediments washing into the empty pot, but in the bottom was an ashy layer that had a bone tool, possibly used in weaving or basketry. Several small bowls with red slip and black bands were found on or near the floor levels. In addition a small round-bottomed pot was discovered on the floor (Figure 1.8b). Careful excavation of the

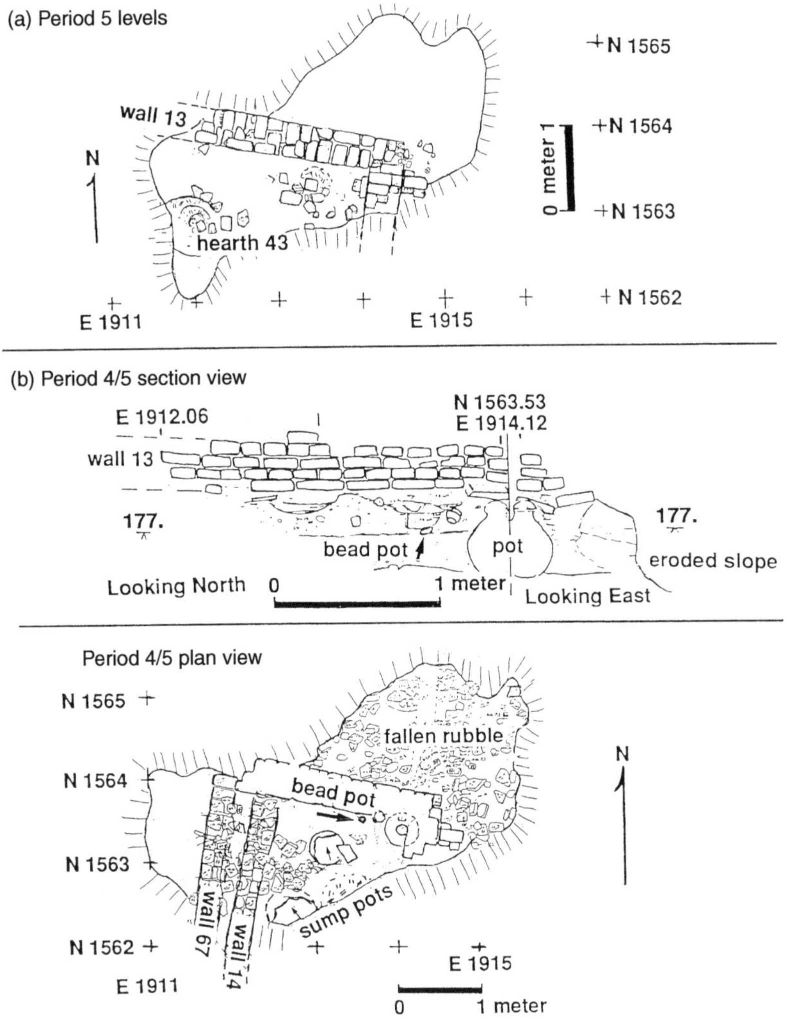

Figure 1.8 (a) Harappa 1996: Trench 38, wall 13 and hearth 43. (b) Harappa 1996: trench 38, house floor with bead pot.

fill of this vessel revealed a collection of 133 beads, amulets, and copper fragments (Figure 1.9). This assemblage includes beads that were derived from the earliest occupations at the site (Ravi Phase, 3300 BC) as well as some beads from the Harappan period (2600–1900 BC). The rest of the beads were made during the Late Harappan period (1900–1700 BC) and reflect the development of new materials and manufacturing techniques.

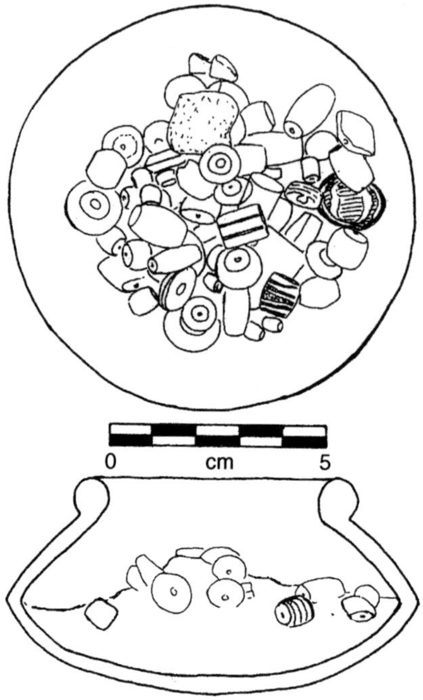

Figure 1.9 Harappa 1996: bead pot with beads.

Even today, children make similar collections of beads from the modern town of Harappa as they scamper across the mounds after a heavy rainfall. It is not unlikely that a child of the Late Harappan period collected these beads and put them in a pot, only to forget about them as the years passed. Eventually the house was remodeled and the scattered pottery was covered with fill and eventually a later building. There is no sign of any conflagration or destruction in this or any of the occupation layers of the Late Harappan period at Harappa.

Along with the *in situ* pottery, the floors contained a fragment of a wavy stone ring generally interpreted as a ritual object during the Harappan period. A typical Harappan female figurine made of terra cotta was also found on the same floor. The presence of these types of artifacts could indicate continuity in some Harappan ritual traditions or, as was the case of the bead pot, that later inhabitants occasionally collected curious objects from the earlier times.

A similar explanation can be made for the fragment of a badly eroded faience molded tablet that was found in the lowest excavated levels, which correspond to the interface between Periods 3C and 4/5. There are no inscribed seals from the Late Harappan levels (Period 5 levels) and only a few examples of pottery with possible script or graffiti (Meadow *et al.* 1996). Some scholars have argued that the Indus script did not disappear totally with the end of the Harappan period (Lal 1962, 1998; Possehl 1996), but the types of evidence presented are not very convincing. There is no clear evidence from Harappa that inscribed seals or pottery with Indus script were produced after *c.*1900 BC.

1.4 Trade and technology through bead analysis

Information derived from the beads in the bead pot found in 1996 include aspects of technological innovation, changing trade networks, and socio-economic hierarchies during the Late Harappan period. It is not possible to go into great detail in this chapter, but some of the basic findings and interpretations will be summarized next.

The Late Harappan beads include a variety of faience beads made in unique shapes and with different coloring than during the Harappan period. The azure blue faience beads were mistaken for lapis until they were carefully examined under the microscope. This suggests that they may have been intended to replicate this blue stone, possibly because it was difficult to obtain, or to create a new form of blue material that did not dull easily as happens with natural lapis. Blue green faience had been made since the Early Harappan times, but some of the blue green faience of the Late Harappan period are extremely compact and glassy, almost to the point of being primarily made up of vitreous silica. These beads may have been made to replicate turquoise, a stone that can turn a dull green if worn against sweaty skin in the hot summers of the Punjab. The glassy faience would have remained a flashy blue green and was much more durable than the natural turquoise.

One of the most important beads in this pot is a red-orange colored glass bead that was mistaken for carnelian until it was more carefully examined. Since carnelian does not discolor or become dull, it is possible that this glass replica was made to create a new form of material because the carnelian was difficult to obtain and also difficult to drill and polish.

Once glass became more common during the Early Historic period, stone beads became less common and were rapidly replaced by glass beads. Regardless of the motives behind the production of this glass bead, it is the earliest evidence for glass in the subcontinent. There is also evidence of glass bangles and beads from the site of Bhagwanpura (Sub-period 1B), which represents a period of overlap between the final phases of the Late Harappan and the Painted Grey Ware Period, dating from 1400 to 1000 BC (Joshi 1993: 219; Lal 1998: 444). The increasing evidence for the use of glass for beads and bangles during the Painted Grey Ware (Roy 1983) and later Northern Black Polished Ware (Gaur 1983; Roy 1986) periods provides an important link between the glass of the Late Harappan period and the subsequent Early Historic period. Between 1700 and 800 BC, glass production developed into a common industry and became quite widespread throughout the northern subcontinent. It is important to note that although there is no mention of glass in the Ṛg Veda, it was known to later Vedic communities and is referred to in the Satapatha Brahmana (Lal 1998: 444).

In Mesopotamia the earliest manufacture of glass beads and glassy inlays can be dated to around 2500–2200 BC, but glass was not commonly produced until around 1600 BC. In Egypt the date for intentionally produced glass ornaments is closer to 1500 BC (Moorey 1994: 190ff.). The dating of glass in the Indus Valley and northern India, between 1900 and 1700 BC suggests that this industry was becoming common in all three regions at about the same time. Whereas there is evidence for considerable interaction between Mesopotamia and Egypt during this time, there is no concrete evidence for trade between the Indus and either Mesopotamia or Egypt. No analysis of the recently discovered Late Harappan glass has been undertaken, but the styles of beads and the presence of a highly developed faience industry suggests that the Indus glass technology was an indigenous development.

The stone beads found in the pot tell a different story. During the Harappan period, stone beads were being drilled with a hard stone called Ernestite. It is important to note that none of the Late Harappan-style stone beads appear to have been drilled with this type of drill. This could mean that the source of the rare Ernestite drill material was no longer available or that new bead makers without the knowledge of this technique had taken over the bead industry at the site. The Late Harappan beads are drilled with fine abrasives and a tiny copper tube. This is a unique technique that was clearly not as effective as the stone drills, but was apparently the only technique available. One unfinished carnelian bead was found in the pot indicating that the tubular drilling was actually being done at Harappa.

Other types of stone beads were made with a new variety of banded black and white agates that was not commonly used during the Harappan period. It is not clear where this agate comes from, but beads of this material are quite abundant in Late Harappan to Early Historic sites of the Gangetic region and even in Kashmir (e.g. Burzahom late levels) (Pande 2000). This suggests that the source may be in the central Deccan Plateau or the Vindhya Mountains. If this can be determined then the presence of these beads at Harappa would indicate an expansion of trade networks to the east. This change in trade focus could also explain the lack of lapis lazuli which would have come from Baluchistan and the absence of the Ernestite drill materials, which came either from Baluchistan or Gujarat. During Harappan times, carnelian is thought to have been obtained primarily from Gujarat though some small carnelian nodules may have been obtained from Baluchistan and Afghanistan. The production of carnelian colored glass beads could indicate a shortage of this natural raw material.

Another important material that came from the coastal areas to the south and southeast was marine shell that was used to make bangles, beads, and ritual objects such as ladles and libation vessels. During the Late Harappan period in the northern regions marine shell ornaments are conspicuously absent (Kenoyer 1983). It is possible that the long-distance trade networks that brought carnelian and marine shell to Harappa from the south were disrupted because of changing river patterns and other socio-economic changes in the intervening sites. A similar breakdown in trade from the northwest may have resulted in the scarcity of lapis lazuli.

The need for new types of beads and new materials such as lapis-colored faience, carnelian-colored glass, and a wide variety of new shapes indicate that ornaments continued to be used as important symbols of status and wealth in the context of the Late Harappan period. Stone beads made from exotic colored rocks, such as variegated jaspers and banded agates, were also being produced during this period, adding to the variety of ornaments available to the diverse urban population. The lack of ornaments in the Cemetery H, Stratum I and II burials makes it difficult to assign specific types of beads to different communities or classes. However, based on general assumptions about categories of wealth (Kenoyer 2000), there is little doubt that new and rare materials would have been in demand by elite communities. In contrast, the common people may have continued to wear ornaments of terra cotta or other more easily produced materials such as steatite.

1.5 Pottery production

Pottery is one of the most important sources of information for dating an occupation level or site. During the Late Harappan period new features of decoration, form and manufacture provide strong evidence for changes in the ceramic corpus, but there are equally strong indications of continuities in the use of some earlier pottery forms and manufacturing techniques. Therefore it is necessary to develop a method for characterizing the pottery that provides a relatively objective perspective on what comprises the Late Harappan pottery assemblage. At the urban site of Harappa, this is done by careful analysis of the pottery fragments from each stratigraphic excavation unit using a comprehensive methodology that begins with the gross characterization of sherds and ends with a detailed recording of the form, surface treatment, manufacturing, and absolute measurements. It is not possible to discuss this procedure in detail here, but the initial results of the pottery analysis from Trench 38 on Mound AB reveal the gradual increase in Cemetery H pottery styles and the disappearance of specific types of Harappan pottery, spanning Periods 4 and 5.

In 1998 and 1999, excavations in Trench 43 on Mound F (Figure 1.10) revealed additional evidence for the concurrent use of both Harappan and Late Harappan pottery (i.e. Period 4), and also a kiln (Figure 1.11) in which Late Harappan pottery (Periods 4 and 5) had been fired (Meadow *et al.* 1998, 1999; Meadow and Kenoyer 2001).

Just inside the city wall of Mound F were found traces of fallen brick walls of buildings that had been abandoned at the end of Harappan Period 3C or during the Late Harappan Periods 4 and 5. The walls and floor levels had been disturbed by tunneling of brick robbers, but it was possible to confirm that these structures were oriented in the cardinal directions and many were associated with brick drains, cooking areas, and well-defined activity areas.

Initially, the presence of pointed base goblets scattered in the fallen rubble was taken as an indication that these buildings were used during the final occupation of Harappan Period 3C. A few sherds of Cemetery H pottery found

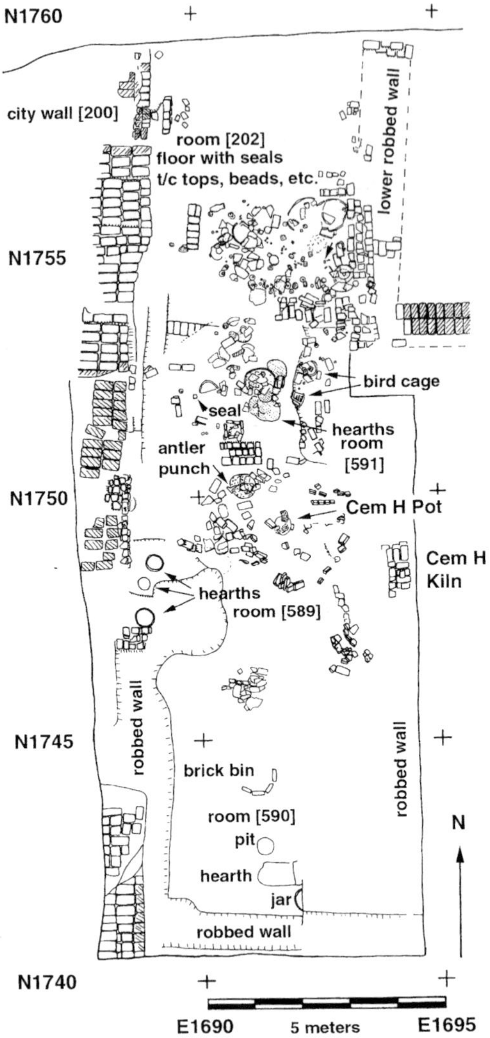

Figure 1.10 Harappa 1998–99: Trench 43, houses with fallen walls and pottery.

mixed in with the fallen rubble of the walls were thought to be the result of later mixing. However, further excavations revealed numerous complete vessels (Figure 1.12) crushed by the walls that were similar to Late Harappan Period 4 pottery from Cemetery H and Mound AB. In addition, a distinctive Cemetery H style (Period 5) globular cooking pot was found crushed by the fallen walls, and this vessel was stratigraphically associated with pointed base goblets and other Harappan-style pottery.

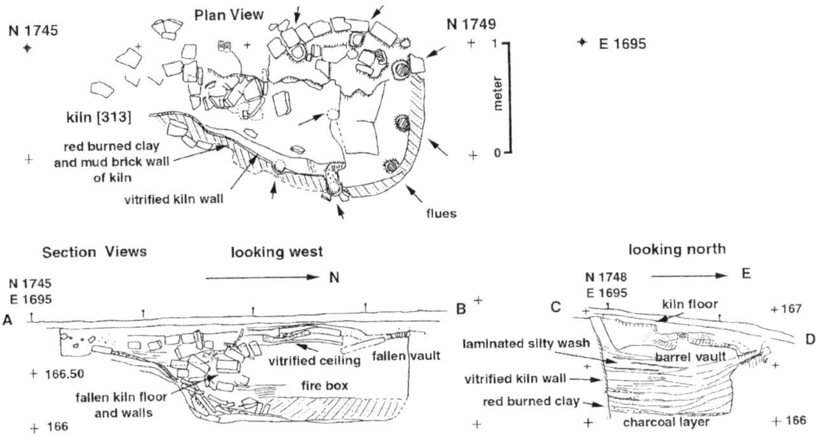

Figure 1.11 Harappa 1999: Cemetery H kiln.

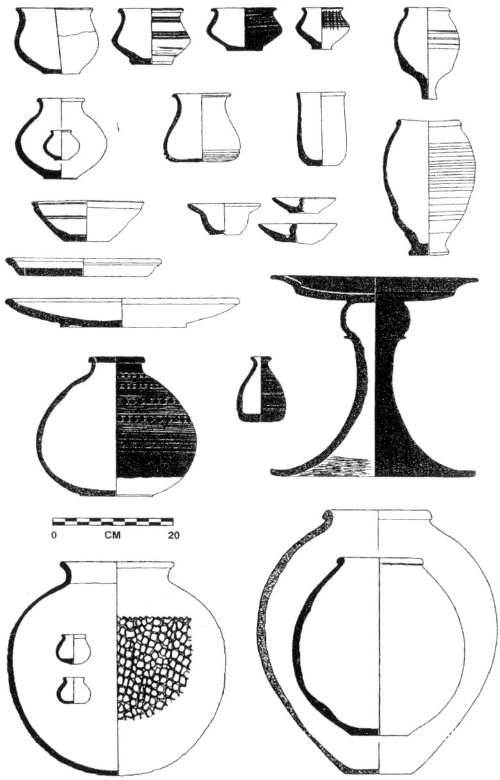

Figure 1.12 Harappa 1998–99: Period 4 pottery.

The extremely thin body wall of this globular shaped vessel was made with the paddle and anvil technique in a manner totally unlike anything the Harappan potters would have done. The exterior below the shoulder was coated with a thick layer of sandy appliqué that had been pressed with the fingertips to create a honeycomb design. After firing, this rough, sandy honeycomb surface was coated with straw tempered sandy clay slurry. The lower exterior surfaces of the vessel were blackened from cooking fires, but it is not certain what form of food or beverage was being prepared. The discovery of this new form of cooking pot indicates not only the introduction of a new manufacturing technique (paddle and anvil), but also possibly a new method of food preparation. Many other fragments of Cemetery H pottery were found in the fallen rubble associated with this cooking pot, and one fragment of this type of cooking pot was found inside a large kiln just to the east.

1.6 Late Harappan (Cemetery H) Phase kiln

Excavations by Vats in this area of Mound F in the 1920s and 1930s resulted in the discovery of many pottery-firing kilns that were found scattered between houses (Vats 1940: 472ff.). In the course of excavations in Trench 43, it was not surprising therefore to find a large kiln just below the surface of the mound (Meadow *et al.* 1998). After excavation it became clear that this was a new form of kiln and the associated pottery confirms that it belongs to the Late Harappa Phase (Period 4 or 5). Although it had the general "pear-shaped" plan of Harappan kilns, the structure shows a clear discontinuity with the traditional form of Harappan pottery kilns. In this new form, a barrel vault made from curved slabs of fired clay (Figure 1.11) supported the floor of the firing chamber, while Harappan kilns were constructed with a central column to support the floor. Eight flues perforated the floor to allow fire from the lower firebox to circulate around the pottery, and there was probably a tall chimney to help create a strong draft. Recent experimental studies suggest that this innovative construction was more fuel-efficient than Harappan kilns and may have reached higher temperatures as indicated by the semi-vitrified surface of the kiln floor. The need for more efficient kilns could indicate a decline in the availability of good fuel near the city, but a more likely explanation would be increased demand, not only from the urban population, but also from regional consumers. Although this is the first example of a barrel vaulted updraft kiln in South Asia, it is possible that other examples will be found at the Late Harappan industrial sites reported by Mughal in Cholistan (Mughal 1997). This same type of kiln continues to be used in many regions of the northwestern subcontinent even today (Rye and Evans 1976; Saraswati 1978).

Other aspects of Late Harappan technology and craft traditions remain to be investigated, but even these few examples indicate a vigorous urban economy that continued to support innovation and large-scale production.

1.7 Summary and conclusion

Although studies of the Late Harappan occupations at Harappa are not yet complete, this brief overview suggests that earlier models of the Late Harappan period need to be substantially revised. Important continuities are seen in basic features of architectural traditions as well as many other technologies, such as faience production and certain aspects of pottery making. On the other hand, discontinuities in the use of seals, weights, and writing provide evidence for significant changes in key technological and cultural features that were associated with the earlier Harappan period. The breakdown of long-distance trade networks in the northern regions are revealed by the absence or decline in shell working. The establishment of new trade networks are suggested by the appearance of new raw materials, such as banded black and white agate, for the manufacture of ornaments. The introduction of new technologies, such as paddle and anvil techniques of pottery making and new types of kilns suggest a major reorganization of crafts needed to supply the basic domestic needs of urban communities. Furthermore, innovations in faience and glass making, and new bead drilling techniques, suggest a creative environment stimulated by demand for high-status items by new groups of elites in a diverse urban population.

There are still important unanswered questions regarding Late Harappan subsistence systems (Meadow 1996; Weber 1998), but one thing for certain is that there is no evidence for the use of the horse by the occupants of either the Harappan or the Late Harappan cities and towns (Meadow and Patel 1997). The horse and camel were clearly known in the foot hills of Baluchistan since they are represented in terra cotta figurines at the site of Pirak (Jarrige and Santoni 1979) and date to *c*.1700–700 BC.

The role of rice and millets during the Harappan period is still not well understood, but it did become more common in the Late Harappan and subsequent Painted Grey Ware Period (Gaur 1983). Earlier reports have argued for the use of rice during the Harappan period (Vishnu-Mittre and Savithri 1982) and even though recent excavations at Harappa have recovered evidence for rice from the Harappan and Late Harappan levels, it was clearly not an important subsistence grain (Weber 2000, pers. comm.). Three varieties of millet have also been found from the Harappan and Late Harappan levels at Harappa, but it is still not clear if they reflect a major change in the subsistence economy or simply a change in processing or discard (Weber 2000, pers. comm.). These same varieties of millet are also found in the Late Harappan period at sites such as Rojdi in Gujarat (Weber 1992, 1998). A variety of millets and pulses are also common in the Orange Colored Pottery sites such as Atranjikhera (Gaur 1983). Although the new discoveries indicate that there are changes occurring in subsistence practices as well as in the utilization of new animals for transport or traction, these changes are not abrupt, and therefore may have affected only a small proportion of the population.

Finally, the biological evidence from Harappa does not indicate a significant change in population. However, there are significant changes in burial practices and new decorative motifs on pottery, indicating that some of these urban communities had developed new ideologies that were inconsistent with the religious practices of the earlier Harappan elites.

I would interpret the various developments summarized earlier as reflecting social, economic, and ideological restructuring that involved previously marginal or minority communities. On the basis of Late Harappan pottery associated with Harappan pottery at the site of Harappa, this process appears to have begun during the final phases of the Harappan period and continued through the Late Harappan period. The origin of these communities is unknown, but it is not unlikely that one or more of them may represent communities referred to in the early Vedic literature. Whether these communities can be considered "arya" or "non-arya" is impossible to determine because it is abundantly clear that these terms, as used in the Vedas, do not represent a single distinct community. (For the most recent discussion of this topic see Bronkhorst and Deshpande 1999.) Nevertheless, it is possible to clarify some points regarding the relationship between the Harappan and Late Harappan period to the culture and peoples reflected in the Vedic literature.

One of the most important results of the current work at Harappa is that there continues to be no support for the earlier interpretations of Vedic-Aryan invasions and the destruction of Harappan settlements. Many scholars have argued that the site of Harappa can possibly be associated with a reference in the Ṛg Veda (6.27.4–8) to a place called Hariyupia (Majumdar *et al.* 1961; Wheeler 1968; Singh 1995; Joshi 1999). In this Vedic reference, there is a description of a battle between two forces, one led by Abhyavartin, son of Chayamana (Puru clan) and the other by Turuvasa (Turuvasa clan), leader of the Vrichivat, seed of Varasika (Majumdar *et al.* 1961: 25–6; Sen 1974). The battle was fought at Hariyupia, which appears to have been situated to the east of the Yabyabati River (possibly the Ravi). Half of the attacking force was scattered in the west, presumably on the other side of the river, while the other portion was defeated by Abhyavartin, aided by Indra (Singh 1995). There is no evidence for a battle or conflagration in either the Harappan or the Late Harappan levels at the site, but given the nature of many historical conflicts it is possible that the battle may have taken place outside of the city. Since the invading forces were defeated, there is no need to find destruction levels in the city itself and the identification of the place called Hariyupia remains unresolved.

However, there is a more serious issue regarding the interpretation of this text that must be addressed. The correct translation of the text indicates that Wheeler was totally mistaken in his assumption that Hariyupia was a "non-arya" settlement and that it was being attacked by a hoard of Indo-Aryan invaders. In fact, both the winner, Abhyavartin, and the defeated leader, Turuvasa, belonged to "arya" clans (Majumdar *et al.* 1961; Sen 1974). The army led by Turuvasa is referred to as the Vrichivat, race of Varasika. Some scholars argue that the Vrichivats were a local community and presumably "non-arya" who were allied with the "arya" leader Turuvasa (Majumdar *et al.* 1961: 26), but this cannot be confirmed. Regardless of the identification of the Vrichivat, this often quoted text does not convincingly refer to the simple model of superior forces of "arya" conquering indigenous "non-arya" communities. On the contrary it reflects the complex politics of the Vedic "arya" communities and their propensity for armed conflict against each other as well as against possible "non-arya" communities.

At the opposite end of the spectrum is the misconception that the Indus people as a whole represent the communities referred to in the Vedic literature (Gupta 1996). The details of these arguments are beyond the scope of this chapter, but an example of how this view is supported is reflected in the discussion of settlement types. Although the pastoral nature of Vedic communities and their settlements is clearly the dominant theme in the Ṛg Veda, there are references to forts and towns that were inhabited by "arya" communities (Bisht 1999). In fact, the text about Hariyupia referred to earlier is used by some scholars to argue that, since the people of Hariyupia (i.e. Harappa) were "arya," therefore the entire Indus civilization can be associated with Vedic Aryans (Singh 1995).

S. P. Gupta claims that the Indus-Saraswati civilization does reflect the Vedic literature, but that "...we cannot determine the percentage at this stage of our study when the script remains undeciphered. However it may be 50 percent." (Gupta 1996). In making this statement he inadvertently highlights the one aspect of Indus technology that is clearly not mentioned in any of the Vedas, that is, the technology of writing. Although the training of the three highest castes is explicitly outlined in the later texts, there is no mention of learning the art of writing or reading itself (Dandekar 1947). Furthermore, there are no words for pens, reading, writing, inscription, or any other materials associated with writing in the Vedas (Macdonell and Keith 1967).

The presence of a well-defined system of writing during the Harappan period clearly precludes this culture from having any direct connection with Vedic culture. However, the general lack of writing during the Late Harappan could be correlated to the absence of any reference to writing in the Vedic period. The change in the Late Harappan burial practices and introduction of new symbols on Late Harappan painted pottery also may have some correlation with Vedic burial traditions and decorative arts (Sankalia 1979). The Ṛg Veda refers to several types of burial, including earth burials and cremation. It is clear from the careful reading of the excavation reports of Vats that there is no evidence for cremation at Harappa, but there are earth burials in Stratum II of Cemetery H. In later texts dating to *c.*800 BC, there are detailed instructions on how to collect bones that have been either buried or exposed for a specified length of time and place them in a pot with a lid that is then buried in a pit (Grihya-Sutra 4.4.1 and 4.5.1–6) (Oldenberg 1964). Pot burials from the later Stratum I in Cemetery H could reflect an earlier example of this type of secondary or fractional burial. However, the limited nature of the data make it impossible to make any conclusive statements about the presence or absence of Vedic communities at Harappa.

According to many scholars, the chronological framework for the final phases of the Harappan and the Late Harappan occupation at Harappa does correspond broadly with the time frame for the Ṛg Vedic period. Therefore, it is not improbable that some communities referred to in the Vedas were passing through or living in the regions controlled by Harappa during both the Harappan (Period 3C 2250–1900 BC) and the Late Harappan times (1900–1700 or 1300 BC). However, instead of trying to identify Indo-Aryans who are a modern construct, it is more important to focus future research on the more complex array of cultures that are identified in the Vedic literature. Further archaeological studies must be undertaken at sites that are more directly linked to the Vedic period in order to build a transitional chronology from the Harappan period through the Late Harappan and on into the Early Historic period. In order to complement the studies of artifacts and architecture, it is necessary to undertake new and more intensive studies of the human remains from these same periods. By increasing the sample size of human skeletons and developing more detailed studies of the artifacts associated with the burials, it will be possible to make more meaningful comparisons with reference to material culture and the many different communities identified in the Vedic literature.

Acknowledgments

I would like to express my gratitude to the Department of Archaeology, Government of Pakistan for providing the opportunity to work at Harappa. Special thanks to all of the team members who have been involved in the Harappa Archaeological Research Project, and particularly those involved in the study of the levels dating to the Late Harappan period; the late Dr George F. Dales, Dr Richard H. Meadow, Rose Drees, Carl Lipo, John Berg, Manabu Koiso, and Paul Christy Jenkins. I would also like to acknowledge the facilities provided by the Archaeological Survey of India in obtaining copies and permission to use photographs from the earlier excavations at Harappa from their archives.

References

Bajpai, K. D., 1992. "The Harappan and Vedic Civilizations: An Analysis of Legacy," *Puratattva*, 22: 115–16.

Bhan, K. K., 1992. "Late Harappan Gujarat," *Eastern Anthropologist*, 45(1–2): 173–92.

Bisht, R. S., 1999. "Harappans and the Rgveda: Points of Convergence." In *The Dawn of Indian Civilization (up to c.600 BC)*, edited by G. C. Pande. Delhi: Munshiram Manoharlal Publishers Pvt Ltd, pp. 393–442.

Bronkhorst, J. and M. M. Deshpande, eds, 1999. *Aryan and Non-Aryan in South Asia: Evidence, Interpretation and Ideology*. Harvard Oriental Series, Opera Minora. Columbia, MO: South Asia Books.

Bryant, E. F., 1999. "Linguistic Substrata and the Indigenous Aryan Debate." In *Aryan and Non-Aryan in South Asia: Evidence, Interpretation and Ideology*, edited by J. Bronkhorst and M. M. Deshpande. Columbia, MO: South Asia Books, pp. 59–84.

Dales, G. F. and J. M. Kenoyer, 1989. "Excavation at Harappa – 1988," *Pakistan Archaeology*, 24: 68–176.

——, 1991. "Summaries of Five Seasons of Research at Harappa" (District Sahiwal, Punjab, Pakistan). In *Harappa Excavations 1986–1990*, edited by R. H. Meadow. Madison, WI: Prehistory Press, pp. 185–262.

Dandekar, R. N., 1947. *The Antecedents and the Early Beginnings of the Vedic Period*. Indian History Congress, 10th session.

Dani, A. H., 1967. "Timargarha and Gandhara Grave Culture," *Ancient Pakistan*, 3.

——, 1991. *History of Northern Areas of Pakistan*. Islamabad: National Institute of Historical and Cultural Research.

Deshpande, M. M., 1995. "Vedic Aryans, Non-Vedic Aryans, and Non-Aryans: Judging the Linguistic Evidence of the Veda." In *The Indo-Aryans of Ancient South Asia: Language, Material Culture and Ethnicity*, edited by G. Erdosy. Berlin: W. DeGruyter, pp. 67–84.

Erdosy, G., 1989. "Ethnicity in the Rigveda and its Bearing on the Question of Indo-European Origins," *South Asian Studies*, 5: 35–47.

Gaur, R. C., 1983. *Excavations at Atranjikhera: Early Civilization of the Upper Ganga Basin*. Delhi: Motilal Banarsidass.

——, 1997. *Studies in Indian Archaeology and Ancient India*, Vol. 1. Jaipur: Publication Scheme.

Godbole, N. N., 1961. "Rg Vedic Saraswati," *Annals of the Bhandarkar Oriental Research Institute* (Poona), XLII(1–4): 1–40.

Gupta, S. P., 1996. *The Indus-Sarasvati Civilization. Origins, Problems and Issues*. Delhi: Pratibha Prakashan.

Hemphill, B. E., J. R. Lukacs, and K. A. R. Kennedy, 1991. "Biological Adaptations and Affinities of Bronze Age Harappans." In *Harappa Excavations 1986–1990*, edited by R. H. Meadow. Madison, WI: Prehistory Press, pp. 137–82.

Jarrige, J.-F. and M. Santoni, 1979. *Fouilles de Pirak*. Paris: Diffusion de Boccard.

Joshi, J. P., 1993. *Excavations at Bhagwanpura 1975–76*. New Delhi: Archaeological Survey of India.

——, 1999. "Religious and Burial Practices of Harappans: Indian Evidence." In *The Dawn of Indian Civilization (up to c.600 BC)*, edited by G. C. Pande. Delhi: Munshiram Manoharlal Publishers Pvt Ltd, pp. 377–91.

Kennedy, K. A. R., 1992. "Biological Anthropology of Human Skeletons from Harappa: 1928–1988," *Eastern Anthropologist*, 45(1–2): 55–86.

——, 1995. "Have the Aryans Been Identified in the Prehistoric Skeletal Record from South Asia? Biological Anthropology and Concepts of Ancient Races." In *The Indo-Aryans of Ancient South Asia: Language, Material Culture and Ethnicity*, edited by G. Erdosy. Berlin: W. DeGruyter, pp. 32–66.

Kenoyer, J. M., 1983. *Shell Working Industries of the Indus Civilization: An Archaeological and Ethnographic Perspective*. Berkeley, CA: University of California Press.

——, 1991. "Urban Process in the Indus Tradition: A Preliminary Model from Harappa." In *Harappa Excavations 1986–1990*, edited by R. H. Meadow. Madison, WI: Prehistory Press, pp. 29–60.

——, 1995. "Interaction Systems, Specialized Crafts and Culture Change: The Indus Valley Tradition and the Indo-Gangetic Tradition in South Asia." In *The Indo-Aryans of Ancient South Asia: Language, Material Culture and Ethnicity*, edited by G. Erdosy. Berlin: W. DeGruyter, pp. 213–57.

——, 1998. *Ancient Cities of the Indus Valley Civilization*. Karachi: Oxford University Press.

Kenoyer, J. M., 2000. "Wealth and Socio-Economic Hierarchies of the Indus Valley Civilization." In *Order, Legitimacy and Wealth in Early States*, edited by J. Richards and M. Van Buren. Cambridge: Cambridge University Press, pp. 90–112.

Kochhar, R., 2000. *The Vedic People: Their History and Geography*. Hyderabad: Orient Longman.

Lal, B. B., 1962. "From the Megalithic to the Harappan: Tracing Back the Graffiti on the Pottery," *Ancient India*, 16: 4–24.

——, 1981. "The Two Indian Epics vis-a-vis Archaeology," *Antiquity*, LV: 27–34.

——, 1982. "The Painted Grey Ware Culture." In *A History of the Civilizations of Central Asia*, edited by A. H. Dani and V. M. Masson. Paris: UNESCO Publishing, pp. 421–40.

——, 1998. "Rigvedic Aryans: The Debate Must Go On," *East and West*, 48(3–4): 439–48.

Lal, B. B. and B. K. Thapar, 1967. "Excavation at Kalibangan: New Light on the Indus Civilization," *Cultural Forum*, 9(4): 78–88.

Macdonell, A. A. and A. B. Keith, 1967. *Vedic Index of Names and Subjects*. New Delhi: Motilal Banarsidass.

Majumdar, R. C., H. C. Raychaudhuri, and K. Datta, 1961. *An Advanced History of India*. London: Macmillan & Co.

Marshall, S. J., 1931. *Mohenjo-daro and the Indus Civilization*. London: A. Probsthain.

Meadow, R. H., ed., 1991. *Harappa Excavations 1986–1990*. Monographs in World Archaeology. Madison, WI: Prehistory Press.

Meadow, R. H., 1996. "The Origins and Spread of Agriculture and Pastoralism in South Asia." In *The Origins and Spread of Agriculture and Pastoralism in Eurasia*, edited by D. R. Harris. Washington, DC: Smithsonian Institution Press, pp. 390–412.

——, 1998. "Pre- and Proto-Historic Agricultural and Pastoral Transformations in Northwestern South Asia," *The Review of Archaeology*, 19(2): 12–21.

Meadow, R. H. and J. M. Kenoyer, 2001. "Harappa Excavations 1998–1999: New Evidence for the Development and Manifestation of the Harappan Phenomenon." In *South Asian Archaeology 1999*, edited by K. R. van Kooij and E. M. Raven. Leiden Netherlands: International Institute of Asian Studies.

Meadow, R. H. and A. Patel, 1997. "A Comment on 'Horse Remains from Surkotada' by Sándor Bökönyi," *South Asian Studies*, 13: 308–15.

Meadow, R. H., J. M. Kenoyer, and R. P. Wright, 1996. "Harappa Archaeological Research Project: Harappa Excavations 1996." Report submitted to the Director General of Archaeology and Museums, Government of Pakistan, Karachi.

——, 1998. "Harappa Archaeological Research Project: Harappa Excavations 1998." Report submitted to the Director General of Archaeology and Museums, Government of Pakistan, Karachi.

——, 1999. "Harappa Archaeological Research Project: Harappa Excavations." Report submitted to the Director General of Archaeology and Museums, Government of Pakistan, Karachi.

Moorey, P. R. S., 1994. *Ancient Mesopotamian Materials and Industries*. Oxford: Clarendon Press.

Mughal, M. R., 1990. "The Decline of the Indus Civilization and the Late Harappan Period in the Indus Valley," *Lahore Museum Bulletin*, 3(2): 1–17.

——, 1997. *Ancient Cholistan: Archaeology and Architecture*. Lahore: Ferozsons.

Oldenberg, H. (translator), 1964. *The Grihya-Sutras: Rules of Vedic Domestic Ceremonies*. Delhi: Motilal Banarsidass.

Pande, B. M., 2000. Burzahom Beads. In *South Asian Archaeology 1997*, edited by M. Taddei. Rome: Is. A. I. O.

Possehl, G. L., 1996. *Indus Age: The Writing System*. New Delhi: Oxford and IBH Publishing Company.

Roy, T. N., 1983. *The Ganges Civilization: A Critical Archaeological Study of the Painted Grey Ware and Northern Black Polished Ware Periods of the Ganga Plains of India*. New Delhi: Ramanand Vidya Bhawan.

——, 1986. *A Study of Northern Black Polished Ware Culture: An Iron Age Culture of India*. New Delhi: Ramanand Vidya Bhawan.

Rye, O. S. and C. Evans, 1976. *Traditional Pottery Techniques of Pakistan*. Washington, DC: Smithsonian Institution.

Sankalia, H. D., 1979. "The 'Cemetery H' Culture." In *Ancient Cities of the Indus*, edited by G. L. Possehl. New Delhi: Vikas Publishing House Pvt Ltd, pp. 323–30.

Saraswati, B., 1978. *Pottery-Making Cultures and Indian Civilization*. New Delhi: Abhinav.

Sastri, K. N., 1965. *New Light on the Indus Civilization*, Vol. II. Delhi: Atma Ram and Sons.

Sen, U., 1974. *The Rig Vedic Era: India (3500–2000 B.C.)*. Calcutta: Sumitre Sen.

Shaffer, J. G., 1984. "The Indo-Aryan Invasions: Cultural Myth and Archaeological Reality." In *The People of South Asia: The Biological Anthropology of India, Pakistan, and Nepal*, edited by J. R. Lukacs. New York: Plenum Press, pp. 77–90.

——, 1992. "The Indus Valley, Baluchistan and Helmand Traditions: Neolithic Through Bronze Age." In *Chronologies in Old World Archaeology*, 3rd edition, edited by R. Ehrich. Chicago, IL: University of Chicago Press, pp. 441–64.

Shaffer, J. G. and D. A. Lichtenstein, 1999. "Migration, Philology and South Asian Archaeology." In *Aryan and Non-Aryan in South Asia: Evidence, Interpretation and Ideology*, edited by J. Bronkhorst and M. M. Deshpande. Columbia, MO: South Asia Books, pp. 239–60.

Sharma, R. S., 1978. "Archaeology and Tradition: The Later Vedic Phase and the Painted Grey Ware Culture." *Puratattva*, 8(1975–76): 63–7.

——, 1999. *Advent of the Aryans*. New Delhi: Manohar, 1999.

Singh, B., 1995. *The Vedic Harappans*. New Delhi: Aditya Prakashan.

Vats, M. S., 1940. *Excavations at Harappa*. Delhi: Government of India Press.

Vishnu-Mittre and R. Savithri, 1982. "Food Economy of the Harappans." In *Harappan Civilization*, edited by G. L. Possehl. New Delhi: Oxford and IBH Publishing Co., pp. 205–21.

Weber, S. A., 1992. "South Asian Archaeobotanical Variability." In *South Asian Archaeology 1989*, edited by C. Jarrige. Madison, WI: Prehistory Press, pp. 283–90.

——, 1998. "Out of Africa: The Initial Impact of Millets in South Asia," *Current Anthropology*, 39(2): 267–74.

Wheeler, M., 1979. "Harappan Chronology and the Rig Veda." In *Ancient Cities of the Indus*, edited by G. L. Possehl. New Delhi: Vikas Publishing House Pvt Ltd, pp. 289–92.

Wheeler, R. E. M., 1968. *The Indus Civilization*, 3rd edition. Cambridge: Cambridge University Press.

2

ARYAN INVASION OF INDIA

Perpetuation of a myth

B. B. Lal

When, as far back as 1786, a Calcutta High Court judge, Sir William Jones, made a very significant linguistic observation, little did he realize that his findings, in subsequent centuries, would involve scholars from all over the world in a furious debate over an issue termed "The Aryan invasion of India." All that Sir William had stated was:

> The Sanskrit language, whatever be its antiquity, is of wonderful structure, more perfect than the Greek, more copious than the Latin, and more exquisitely refined than either, yet bearing to both of them stronger affinity both in the roots of verbs and in the forms of grammar than could have been produced by accident, so strong indeed, that no philologer [*sic*] could examine them all three, without believing them to have sprung from some common source, which perhaps no longer exists...
>
> (Jones 1788: 422–3)

This simple observation led, in the course of time, to the propounding of a theory that there existed a "race" which was the carrier of these languages westward to Europe and eastward to India. And somewhere in Central Asia was thought to be the "original home" of these envisioned Indo-Europeans, though many scholars preferred this "home" to have been located in Russia or northern Europe. This envisaged migration from Central Asia/Europe to India via Iran and Afghanistan marked the beginning of a subsequently more aggressive invasion theory.

Nearly a century later, an eminent Sanskrit scholar, F. Max Müller, made yet another very significant pronouncement, namely, that the *Ṛigveda* was to be dated around 1200 BC. Though no doubt this dating gave to Sanskrit a respectable antiquity in world literature, Max Müller's computation, it must at once be added, was purely *ad hoc*. Accepting that the *Sūtra* literature existed at the time of the Buddha around the sixth to fifth century BC, he assigned a period of 200 years to each of the successively preceding groups of literary productions, namely, the *Āraṇyakas*, *Brāhmaṇas*, and *Vedas*. It is in this arbitrary manner that the date of

1200 BC was arrived at. When criticized by a host of his contemporaries, such as Goldstucker, Whitney and Wilson, Max Müller raised his hands up by stating in his preface to the text of the *Ṛigveda*:

> I have repeatedly dwelt on the merely hypothetical character of the dates, which I have ventured to assign to first periods of Vedic literature. All I have claimed for them has been that they are minimum dates, and that the literary productions of each period which either still exist or which formerly existed could hardly be accounted for within shorter limits of time than those suggested.
>
> (Max Müller 1890, reprint 1979)

And then came the final surrender:

> If now we ask as to how we can fix the dates of these periods, it is quite clear that we cannot hope to fix a *terminum a qua* [*sic*]. Whether the Vedic hymns were composed [in] 1000 or 2000 or 3000 years BC, no power on earth will ever determine.
>
> (Ibid.)

Unfortunately, in spite of such a clear-cut retreat by the clergy himself, his earlier fatwa still holds the ground. Many Western scholars and their Indian followers continue to swear by 1200 BC as the date of the *Ṛigveda* and do not dare cross this *Lakṣmaṇa rekhā*.

That was the scenario on the literary front toward the end of the nineteenth century. But the ground reality still was that even as late as 1920, Western scholars denied to India any iota of civilization prior to the invasion of Alexander in 326 BC.

Tables, however, turned when in 1921 Daya Ram Sahni and in 1922 R. D. Banerjee carried out trial excavations respectively at Harappa in Punjab and Mohenjo-daro in Sindh and brought to light archaeological evidence that threw back, with a single stroke, the antiquity of Indian civilization from the fourth century BC to the third millennium BC. The initial discovery was followed up by large-scale excavations, by John Marshall and E. J. H. Mackay at Mohenjo-daro, and M. S. Vats at Harappa. The emergent picture was that as far back as the third millennium BC India did have a civilization of its own, which in some ways even excelled the contemporary civilizations of Egypt and Mesopotamia. Not only did the Indian civilization cover a much vaster terrain than did either of the aforesaid Western civilizations, but it also produced ample evidence of systematic town-planning and an underground system of drainage. The use of kiln-fired bricks, unknown to the then Western world, was a common feature at the Indian sites. The people produced all kinds of objets d'art, so much so that the excellently carved steatite seals can well be the envy of any seal-cutter, past or present.

At this point begins the next phase of the "Aryan invasion" theory. Since Max Müller had given the fatwa that the Vedas were not earlier than 1200 BC and this newly discovered civilization was ascribable to the third millennium BC, it was argued that it could never have been the creation of the Vedic people, who were termed as the Aryans. (Here, perhaps it needs to be clarified that in the Vedic texts the word "*Arya*" was not used in any racial sense; it only meant the "noble one.") Further, since India has two dominant language groups, namely, the Sanskritic and the Dravidian, it was held that the Dravidian-speakers were the authors of this civilization.

Then came the master stroke of the "Aryan invasion" theory. In the year 1944, a British Brigadier, Robert Eric Mortimer Wheeler (later knighted), operating on the soil of Egypt in the Second World War, was invited by the then Viceroy of India, Lord Wavell, to take charge of the Archaeological Survey of India, as its Director General. He was attracted by the site of Harappa and in 1946 took up further excavations. And although an officer of the Survey had already noticed the remains of a mud-brick wall around one of the mounds (Mound AB), to Wheeler must go the credit of duly establishing the existence of a fortification around it. However, the manner in which he interpreted his newly found data is, to say the least, not only dramatic but also unwarranted. He averred:

> The Aryan invasion of the Land of Seven Rivers, the Punjab and its environs, constantly assumes the form of an onslaught upon the walled cities of the aborigines. For these cities the term used in the *Ṛigveda* is *pur*, meaning a "rampart," "fort" or "stronghold."... Indra, the Āryan War god, is *puraṁdara*, "fort-destroyer." He shatters "ninety forts" for his Aryan protégé Divodasa. [...]
>
> Where are – or were – these citadels? It has in the past been supposed that they were mythical, or were "merely places of refuge against attack, ramparts of hardened earth with palisades and a ditch." The recent excavation of Harappa may be thought to have changed the picture. Here we have a highly evolved civilization of essentially non-Āryan type, now known to have employed massive fortifications, and known also to have dominated the river-system of north-western India at a time not distant from the likely period of the earlier Aryan invasions of that region. What destroyed this firmly settled civilization? Climatic, economic, political deterioration may have weakened it, but its ultimate extinction is more likely to have been completed by deliberate and large-scale destruction. It may be no mere chance that at a late period of Mohenjo-daro men, women and children appear to have been massacred there. On circumstantial evidence, Indra stands accused.
>
> (Wheeler 1947: 82)

We may now examine the validity of Wheeler's assertion, and begin with the so-called massacre. Altogether thirty-seven skeletons, some full and others fragmentary, were found at Mohenjo-daro during the course of nine years of excavation at the site. All these come from the Lower Town, which was the general habitation area, but none from the Citadel, the seat of government. If there was an invasion, how come that the Citadel remained completely unaffected? Anyway, the thirty-seven skeletons turned up from different stratigraphic levels: some from the Intermediate one, some from the Late; and yet some others are reported to have been found in deposits subsequent to the abandonment of the site. If these skeletons do really represent a massacre by invaders, they should have come from the uppermost level of the site. But this was not the case at all. Second, one does expect some evidence, by way of some vestiges, left behind by the invaders. Nothing whatsoever of the kind has been found at the site. Still more, some of the skeletons bore cut-marks which had healed. Had the death occurred as a result of an invasion, it would have been immediate and there would have been no time available for the cuts to have healed. Indeed, George F. Dales (1964) very aptly decried this so-called massacre as "The Mythical Massacre at Mohenjo-daro."

In this context it needs to be added that no site of Harappan civilization, be it Kot Diji or Amri in Sindh or Harappa itself in Punjab or Kalibangan in Rajasthan or Banawali in Haryana or Lothal, Surkotada, or Dholavira in Gujarat, has yielded any evidence whatsoever of any violent destruction, much less of an invasion. On the other hand, most of these sites have given evidence of a transition from the Mature Harappan stage to that of a localized, degenerated culture-complex. Thus, for instance, Amri and Mohenjo-daro have yielded the remains of what is known as the Jhukar culture, and it has been demonstrated by Mughal (1992) that the Jhukar complex is nothing but a devolution of the Harappa culture itself. Likewise, the current excavators of Harappa, Kenoyer and Meadow, have shown that the so-called Cemetery H culture is nothing but a localized change from the Harappa culture. A similar scenario is available in Rajasthan and Haryana. Lothal and Rangpur, put together, have amply demonstrated that the Harappa culture gradually transformed itself into what has been labeled as the Rangpur culture. Thus, nowhere in the entire area occupied by the Harappan civilization do we have any evidence of wanton destruction or invasion, much less by Aryan marauders!

In spite of the foregoing evidence, the champions of the Aryan invasion theory keep harping on some old arguments. For example, it is held by them that the river Sarasvatī mentioned in the *Ṛigveda* is not the present-day Sarasvatī-Ghaggar of India, but the Helmand of Afghanistan. Thus, they argue, the Aryans must have come from outside, via Afghanistan. A noted historian, R. S. Sharma, writes:

> The fundamentalists want to establish the superiority of the Sarasvati river over the Indus because of communal considerations. In the Harappan context they think that after partition the Indus belongs to the Muslims and only the Sarasvati remains with the Hindus (S. P. Gupta in S. P. Gupta, ed. 1995: 181–3). [Dr S. P. Gupta informs me that he never made any such statement.] The Sarasvati receives much attention in the *Ṛg Veda* and several *sūktas* are devoted to it; so they want to use it for their purpose. But it seems that there are several Sarasvatīs, and the earliest Sarasvati cannot be identified with the Hakra and the Ghaggar. In the *Ṛg Veda* the Sarasvati is called the best of rivers (*nadītamā*). It seems to have been a great river with perennial water. Hakra and Ghaggar

> cannot match it. The earliest Sarasvati is considered identical with the Helmand in Afghanistan which is called Harakhwati in the *Avesta*.
> (1999: 35–6)

But, in the same breath he confesses

> But the archaeology of the Helmand valley in the second millennium BC needs adequate attention. Its two large cities Shahr-i-Sokhta and Mundigak show decay in this period. In place of wheel-turned pottery Mundigak V shows hand-turned pottery. The users of this pottery may have come from outside, but we need more information about them.
> (Ibid.)

However, in spite of his own confession, he insists:

> In any case the linguistic time–place proximity of the Avesta and the *Ṛg Veda* leaves no doubt that the early Vedic Sarasvati is the same as the Harakhwati or the Helmand. As the Ṛgvedic people expanded they took the name Sarasvati to Punjab, Haryana and Rajasthan, and also to Garhwal.
> (Ibid.)

That the equation of the Sarasvatī with the Helmand is patently wrong would be amply clear from the Vedic texts themselves. The famous *Nadī Sūkta* of the *Ṛigveda* (10.75.5) places the Sarasvatī between the Yamunā and the Sutlej, as would be seen from the following:

> *Imam me Gaṅge Yamune Sarasvati Śutudri stomam sachatā Paruṣṇyā*
>
> Since there are no rivers by the names of the Yamunā and Śutudrī in Afghanistan, it is futile to look over there for the Vedic Sarasvatī which lay between the two aforesaid rivers.

Again, as categorically mentioned in the following verse of the *Ṛigveda* (7.95.2), the Sarasvatī rose from the mountains and fell into the ocean:

> *Ekāchetat Sarasvatī nadīnām śuchiryatī giribhya āsamudrāt*
>
> The Helmand does not fall into the ocean; the ocean is just not there.

Further, the *Ṛigveda* (3.23.4) mentions the Dṛiṣadvatī and Āpayā as tributaries of the Sarasvatī:

> *Dṛiṣadvatyām manuṣa Āpayāyām Sarasvatyām revad agne didhi*
>
> These two rivers are in Haryana (India) and not in Afghanistan.

If none of the aforesaid associations of the Ṛigvedic Sarasvatī can be found out in the Afghan region, how can we transport the Ṛigvedic Sarasvatī to that region?

Mere similarity in name does not mean much. The transference of name could as well have been the other way about. It is well known that the *Avestā* is later than the *Ṛigveda*.

There is yet another point which calls for comments. According to Sharma (1999), "the earliest Sarasvati cannot be identified with the Hakra and the Ghaggar. In the *Ṛg Veda* the Sarasvati is called the best of the rivers (*nadītamā*). It seems to have been a great river with perennial water. The Hakra and the Ghaggar cannot match it." Perhaps Sharma is blissfully unaware of, or maybe he deliberately ignores, the path-breaking work that teams of geologists and other scientists have carried out during the past two decades on the various aspects of the river-system that now goes by the names of the Sarasvatī-Ghaggar in Haryana and Rajasthan in India and the Hakra and Nara in Cholistan and Sindh in Pakistan. Without going into the enormous details of the findings of these experts, it may perhaps suffice here to quote from two of their papers. Based on a critical study of Landsat imagery, Yash Pal and his colleagues observe:

> The ancient bed of the Ghaggar has a constant width of about 6 to 8 km from Shatrana in Punjab to Marot in Pakistan. The bed stands out very clearly having a dark tone in the black-and-white imagery and reddish one in false colour composites. There is a clear palaeo-channel south-east of the river Markanda which joins the bed of the Ghaggar near Shatrana. The present Sarasvatī mostly flows through this channel.
>
> (1984: 495)

> Our studies show that the Satluj was the main tributary of the Ghaggar and that subsequently the tectonic movements may have forced the Satluj westward and the Ghaggar dried.
>
> (Ibid.: 494)

> As discussed above, during the period 4–5 millennia BP northwestern Rajasthan was a much greener place with the Sarasvati flowing through it. Some of the present rivers joined to make the Sarasvati a mighty river which probably discharged into the sea (Rann of Kutch) through the Nara, without joining the Indus.
>
> (Ibid.: 497)

Another highly scientific study, made by V. M. K. Puri and B. C. Verma (1998), has established that the Sarasvatī originated from the glaciers in the Himalayas and thus had a perennial supply of water on its own. These experts observe:

> Drainage analysis, basin identification, glaciological and terrace studies suggest that the Vedic Saraswati originated from a group of glaciers in Tons fifth order basin at Naitwar in Garhwal Himalaya. In early stages,

> it occupied the present day drainage of Tons river up to Paonta Doon and took a westerly swing after receiving nourishment from Algar, Yamunā and Giri. West of Paonta, it followed a westerly and southwesterly course along Bata valley and entered plains at Adh Badri.
>
> (Puri and Verma 1998: 19)

May it be hoped that the foregoing scientific evidence dispels all doubts in the minds of Sharma and his associates about the river now going by the names of Sarasvatī-Ghaggar-Hakra-Nara as having been the Ṛigvedic Sarasvatī?

There is yet another issue which needs to be dealt with. Drawing his inspiration from Walter A. Fairservis Jr (1995), R. S. Sharma writes (1999: 77): "According to Fairservice [*sic*], the pastoralists who moved to the Indian borderland came from Bactria-Margiana Archaeological Complex or the BMAC which saw the genesis of the culture of the *Ṛg Veda.*" But Sharma completely ignores the inherent weakness of the case, even though admitted by Fairservis himself when he wrote the concluding line of his paper under reference (1995: 211): "Whatever the case, we are justified by our evidence in making these speculations, remote as they may be from the truth."

Speculations, bravo! But can someone please cite even a single site in India, east of the Indus (which was the main scene of activity of the Ṛigvedic people), where the remains of the BMAC Complex, have been found? Insofar as the present author is aware, there is no such evidence. Then, why indulge in such speculations?

Just as a drowning person tries to catch hold of every bit of straw that comes his way, so does Sharma when he cites every conceivable archaeological outfit to uphold the theory of Aryan invasion of India. He says:

> Lying in the geographical area of the *Ṛg Veda*, Cemetery-H and Pirak show traits of Aryan culture. More importantly, similar sites appear in the valleys of the *Ṛg Vedic* rivers Suvāstu (Swat), Gomatī (Gomal) and Yavyāvatī (Zhob). All these sites found in the river valleys or outside furnish adequate archaeological data to establish the arrival of the Ṛg Vedic people in the first half of second millennium BC.
>
> (Sharma 1999: 67)

While detailed comments on this equation will be offered in a subsequent publication, it would suffice here to point out that no archaeologist worth his salt would venture to argue that these various disparate culture-complexes, namely, those of the Gandhara Graves, Pirak, Cemetery H, and Zhob valley are creations of one and the same people. There may have been some minor interaction between Pirak and the Gandhara Grave sites, but there was none whatsoever between these two and the Cemetery H culture on the one hand and the Zhob culture on the other. To equate the Pirak culture with the Painted Grey Ware culture (ibid.: 73) is another example of sheer desperation.

To underpin his argument about the Zhob culture being that of the Aryans, Sharma says:

> We may note that the river Zhob is identical with Yavyāvatī of the *Ṛg Veda* and Indra with his two red steeds is said to have destroyed three thousand warriors in a tribal war on this river.
>
> (Ibid.: 63)

From Sharma's line of argument it would follow that any archaeological culture falling in the valleys of rivers mentioned in the *Ṛigveda* should be ascribed to the Aryans. If that be so, what is wrong with the Harappan civilization itself which spread in the valleys of almost all the rivers mentioned in the *Ṛigveda*? Anyway, Sharma ought to be aware of the fact that the Zhob culture has been placed by knowledgeable archaeologists in the third millennium BC. Does he mean to give up his mid-second millennium BC-"Aryan invasion" theory and take it back to the third millennium BC? The choice is his.

In order to project a clear picture of what actually transpired on the Indo-Pakistan subcontinent during the prehistoric/protohistoric times it becomes necessary to go into the whole question of the genesis, evolution, and devolution of the Harappan civilization itself. For long it had been propagated by certain scholars that it was a peripheral offshoot of the West Asian cultures. When called upon to produce concrete evidence in support of their thesis, and failing to do so, the proponents took shelter under a saying "ideas have wings." But indeed there were no ideas, much less wings.

Recent excavations on the Indo-Pakistan subcontinent have fully demonstrated that there was a gradual evolution of the Harappa culture from a Neolithic-Chalcolithic beginning in the seventh to sixth millennium BC, demonstrating that the Harappans were the "sons of the soil." And although space does not permit me to go into the details of this evolution, some basic facts substantiating it must nevertheless be stated.

As far back as 1951, Walter A. Fairservis had discovered the remains of a pre-pottery Neolithic assemblage at Kile Ghul Mohammad, 3 kilometers northeast of Quetta, in Baluchistan, and radiocarbon dates assigned the upper levels of these deposits to the fifth millennium BC. But no serious notice was taken of these findings. Maybe because the excavations were on a small scale, but more likely because at that point of time it was generally believed that such early cultures were the preserve of Western Asia.

Anyway, this erroneous impression was rectified some twenty-five years later by large-scale excavations carried out by J. F. Jarrige and his colleagues at Mehrgarh, a site on the Kachhi plains, about a hundred kilometers southeast of Kile Ghul Mohammad (Jarrige and Lechevallier 1979; Jarrige 1981, 1982, 1984). The occupational deposits, divided into seven cultural periods, yielded, from bottom upwards, the remains of a Neolithic complex, followed by a Chalcolithic complex, on to early and mature bronze ages. The Neolithic deposits, accounting for a total thickness of 10 meters and on the basis of radiometric chronology dating back to the seventh millennium BC, were divisible into two sub-periods, namely, 1A and IB, of which the former was bereft of pottery. The inhabitants used polished stone axes and microliths, hunted wild animals and only rarely domesticated them. By Sub-period IB, there was regular domestication of animals, among which the cattle predominated over sheep and goat. A handmade coarse ware with mat-impressed designs also began to be used. The cultivated cereals included barley and wheat, with much greater emphasis on the former. The subsistence pattern, it needs to be emphasized, was quite different from that of Western Asia, where wheat and not barley, and sheep and goat but not the cattle dominated the scene. It is, thus, clear that the two areas developed their own subsistence patterns, quite independent of the other. In other words, even as far back as the seventh millennium BC the Indian subcontinent had started laying the foundation of its own cultural evolution.

In the context of the subsistence pattern, it may be well worth mentioning that barley and not wheat was the mainstay of the Ṛigvedic people. Likewise, the cattle and not goat and sheep were their main animal wealth.

The Neolithic period was followed by a Chalcolithic one (Period II) wherein stone tools became less dominant and metal (copper) began to be exploited. Further, the hand-made pottery began to be discarded and a wheel-turried red ware with designs painted in black came into being. All this happened around 4500 BC. Period III produced evidence of what may be called public granaries, implying a surplus economy as well as an organizational set-up. Subsequent periods of Mehrgarh, supplemented by the evidence from a nearby site called Nausharo, carried the story right into the Harappan times and even later.

The combined evidence from sites like Kot Diji in Sindh, Harappa itself in Punjab, Kalibangan in Rajasthan and Banawali and Kunal in Haryana shows that many of the characteristic features of the Mature Harappan civilization had begun to manifest themselves by about 3000 BC. For example, the houses were oriented along the cardinal directions, with the streets naturally following suit. The typical Harappan brick-size ratio of 4 : 2 : 1 had also come into being. Some of the settlements, like Kot Diji, Kalibangan, and Banawali were also fortified. In the pottery repertoire, many of the shapes and painted designs duly anticipated the upcoming Harappan pottery. And so was the case with other household objects. The pottery bore certain graffiti marks which, for all one can guess, may have contributed in some way toward the make-up of the Harappan script. However, what were lacking were weights and measures and inscribed seals and sealings and, of course, the monumental script. It appears that *c*.2600 BC there was a big spurt in both internal as well as external trade (the latter with regions now comprising Iraq, Arabia, Iran, and Central Asia), which necessitated the creation of a system of weights and measures, of seals to mark the cargo and a script to keep accounts. This mature stage of the Harappan civilization continued till about the beginning of the second millennium BC, after which a degeneration began to set in. Many factors contributed to this economic regression, some man-made and some natural. Overexploitation of land without taking adequate steps to maintain its fertility and the cutting down of forests for firing billions of bricks may have been the human contribution.

But no less significant were the natural causes. There is ample evidence to show that the Sarasvatī, to which a reference has already been made earlier, dried up around the beginning of the second millennium BC. Originating from the glaciers in the Himalayas, in antiquity this river had ample water of its own, which was further augmented by the waters of the Sutlej. However, tectonic movements in the Himalayan region not only blocked the passage of this river through the Siwaliks but also diverted the Sutlej into the Indus system.

This is what the experts, Puri and Verma, have to say about the matter:

> The cumulative effect of the above-mentioned events, viz. reactivation of Yamunā tear, constriction of catchment area of Vedic Saraswati by 94.05%, emergence and migration of river Drishadvati towards southeast acquiring the present day Yamunā course and finally shifting of Shatudri (Satluj) forced Vedic Saraswati to change drastically from the grandeur of a mighty and a very large river to a mere seasonal stream that depended for its nourishment on monsoon precipitation only.... [Thus] Vedic Saraswati was completely disoriented and attained the present day status of oblivion.
>
> (1998: 19)

With the drying up of the Sarasvatī, the impoverished folks of the Harappan settlements in its valley were obliged to move eastwards where they could get reasonable water-supply, to sites like Hulas and Alamgirpur in the upper Gaṅgā–Yamunā Valley. Perhaps a change of climate to aridity may have also added to the troubles of the Harappans. And the final blow to the prosperity of the Harappans seems to have been delivered by the snapping of the trade with Western Asia. Thus, as already discussed, there was a gradual decline of the Harappan civilization and there is clearly no evidence whatsoever for invoking an "Aryan invasion" for its downfall.

At this point it may be worth while to draw attention to a very telling piece of biological evidence. Hemphill and his colleagues have the following to say:

> As for the question of biological continuity within the Indus Valley, two discontinuities appear to exist. The first occurs between 6000 and 4500 BC and is reflected by the strong separation in dental non-metric characters between neolithic and chalcolithic burials at Mehrgarh. The second occurs at some point after 800 BC and before 200 BC. In the intervening period, while there is dental non-metric, craniometric, and cranial non-metric evidence for a degree of internal biological continuity, statistical evaluation of cranial data reveals clear indication of an interaction with the West specifically with the Iranian Plateau.
>
> (1991: 137)

It is thus clear that even though there may have been some sporadic "interaction" between Iran and the Indo-Pakistan subcontinent between *c.*4500 BC and 800 BC, there was a basic biological continuity in the subcontinent during this period – a fact which leaves no room for any infiltration of an "alien" stock.

The biological evidence fully endorses the archaeological data adduced earlier, which too rules out any hypothesis of newcomers devastating the Harappan civilization. To summarize what has been stated previously, it is a continuous story of evolution from the Chalcolithic stage in the fifth millennium BC to the Mature Harappan in the third millennium BC. Then, at the beginning of the second millennium BC there sets in a devolution process, brought about by a variety of causes such as overexploitation of the landscape, changes in climate and river-courses and a steep fall in trade. The affluence graph, which dramatically soared up around the middle of the third millennium BC, fell sharply in the first quarter of the second millennium BC. Parodying Tennyson's *The Brook*, the impoverished Harappan villages must have whispered to one another

> C'ties may come c'ties may go
> But we go on for ever.

There is no case whatsoever for any cultural break, much less for an "Aryan invasion."

We may now have a brief look at what some scholars, Indian and Western, have to say. Writing in the *Journal of the Asiatic Society of Bombay*, a noted Indian historian, Romila Thapar, states:

> it is now generally agreed that the decline of Harappan urbanism was due to environmental changes of various kinds, to political pressures and possible break in trading activities, and not to any invasion. Nor does the archaeological evidence register the likelihood of a massive migration from Iran to northwestern India on such a scale as to overwhelm the existing cultures.
>
> If invasion is discarded then the mechanism of migration and occasional contacts come into sharper focus. The migrations appear to have been of pastoral cattle-herders who are prominent in the Avesta and Rig Veda.
> (1988–91: 259–60)

Once it is conceded that there is no evidence to support the invasion theory, where indeed is the need to flog the dead horse by formulating another theory, namely that of sporadic "migration and occasional contacts" by "pastoral cattle-herders?" What archaeological evidence is there to substantiate the theory even in its new garb?

Now let us see what some Western scholars have to say on this subject. I will take one example each from the UK and the USA, the two countries whose scholars are very much involved in this debate. Commenting on the issue, the distinguished archaeologist from the UK, Colin Renfrew wrote:

> When Wheeler speaks of "the Aryan invasion of the Land of the Seven Rivers, the Punjab," he has no warranty at all, so far as I can see. If one checks the dozen references in the Rig Veda to the seven rivers, there is nothing in any of them that to me implies an invasion.

> ...Despite Wheeler's comments, it is difficult to see what is particularly non-Aryan about the Indus Valley.
>
> (1987: 188, 190)

And here is what Jim G. Shaffer, who has done a lot of archaeological field-work in India, and Diane Lichtenstein, both from the USA, have to say:

> A few scholars have proposed that there is nothing in the "literature" firmly placing the Indo-Aryans... outside of South Asia, and now archaeological record is confirming this. ... As data accumulate to support cultural continuity in South Asian prehistoric and historic periods, a considerable restructuring of existing interpretive paradigms must take place. We reject most strongly the simplistic historical interpretations, which date back to the eighteenth century, that continue to be imposed on South Asian cultural history. These still prevailing interpretations are significantly diminished by European ethnocentrism, colonialism, racism and antisemitism.
>
> (1999: 256)

It would thus be seen that the Aryan invasion theory, which was in an embryonic stage in the eighteenth century, acquired adolescence in the nineteenth and entered its full adulthood in the first part of the twentieth century, is today clearly on its death-bed, breathing its last in spite of some attempts to revive it by using life-saving drugs like the "sporadic migration and occasional contacts" theory. One need not be surprised if with the dawn of the twenty-first century there takes place a ceremonial burial as well.

The foregoing discussion is not an end in itself. It has only established that the Aryan invasion theory is a myth. Now, if the Aryans were not the destroyers of the Harappan civilization, does it automatically follow that they themselves were its authors? The answer should be a "No," unless it is proved to be so.

Over the years claims have been raised in respect of the Dravidians as well as the Aryans to have been the authors of the Harappan civilization. No third claim has come up so far, though there could be nothing to bar it. In this context it needs to be restated that the two terms, namely, Dravidian and Aryan, were once used in a racial sense, which definition appears to have faded away. These terms are now used in a linguistic sense. So the question boils down to: Were the Harappans speakers of a Dravidian language or of a Sanskritic one? Here it must be remembered that the entire population extending over such a vast territory may not have spoken exclusively one language. While one of the aforesaid languages may have predominated the other may still have been present there, though in a smaller section of the society. In fact, one need not be surprised if a third language, of Austric affiliation, may also have been present.

Scholars like Asko Parpola (1969) and Walter A. Fairservis (1992) have claimed that the Harappans were a Dravidian-speaking people, whereas S. R. Rao (1982),

M. V. N. Krishna Rao (1982), and Richter-Ushanas (1992) hold that the language spoken by the Harappans was Sanskrit. In fact, the last-named, a German scholar, reads Vedic verses in the inscriptions on the seals. I have reviewed most of these claims and have demonstrated that not only are the readings arrived at untenable but even the methodology adopted by these scholars is questionable (Lal 1970, 1974, 1983). An amusing part of these decipherments is that no two Dravidianists among themselves see eye to eye, and so is the case with the Sanskritists. There are a few simple tests that can be applied to these decipherments. In the first place, a value assigned to a sign must remain constant throughout the readings; it should not be changed according to the whim and fancy of the decipherer. Second, the key thus used should be capable of unlocking all the inscriptions. Third, the readings arrived at should make sense in the language concerned. If these criteria are met with, one would be only too glad to accept the decipherment, but unfortunately, nobody has succeeded as yet. Nevertheless, all attempts should be directed toward an acceptable decipherment for it is indeed the script that may be said to hold the master key.

Anyway, even in the absence of a successful decipherment, the two claims about the authorship of the Harappan civilization still loom large. We would perhaps do well to examine the arguments put forward in support of both these claims and see the outcome.

To begin with the Dravidian claim. It may be recalled that toward the end of the nineteenth century Max Müller gave the fatwa that the Vedas were unlikely to have been earlier than 1200 BC. Thus, when in the early twentieth century the Harappan civilization was discovered and, on the basis of its contacts with the Mesopotamian civilization, was dated to the third millennium BC, it was but natural to assert that the Vedic people could not have been its authors. Since the other dominant group in the country was that of the Dravidian-speaking people, it was taken as a gospel truth that the Harappans must have belonged to this group.

In support of this thesis many other ingenuous arguments have been adduced. In a small pocket of Baluchistan a dialect called Brahui is spoken today. It is asserted that when the Dravidian-speaking Harappans were ousted by the invading Indo-Aryans, a small community of the Harappans managed to escape the onslaught and is now available to us in the form of the Brahui-speaking population in a tiny area of Baluchistan. There are quite a few drawbacks in such a postulation. In the first place, not all linguists agree that Brahui is indeed a Dravidian tongue. According to some, it is more similar to "modern colloquial eastern Elamite." Some others hold that the Brahui-speaking people are not the original inhabitants of the area but migrated to it during the medieval times.

Similarly baseless are other arguments in favor of the Harappan–Dravidian equation. For instance it has been suggested that the invading Aryans pushed the Dravidian-speaking Harappans all the way down to South India. This stand is prima facie wrong. Had the Harappans indeed been sent away to that region, we should have come across Harappan sites in the Dravidian-speaking areas, namely, Tamil Nadu, Andhra Pradesh, Karnataka, and Kerala. The fact, on the contrary, is that there is not even a single site of the Harappan civilization in any of these states. The only archaeological remains of a comparable antiquity in these regions are those of the southern Neolithic culture. Are we then to believe that a full-fledged Bronze Age civilization overnight degenerated into a Neolithic one, with nothing whatsoever common between the two? This is just not possible.

Let us look at the issue from another perspective. It has been observed that if in an area where the inhabitants speak a particular language, say X, there is an influx of another set of people speaking a language called Y, there will still remain remnants of the earlier language X. This is particularly reflected in the names of some of the rivers and mountains and even of some localities. Thus, for example, the names of the well-known North American rivers Missouri and Mississippi or of cities like Chicago and states like Massachusetts are carry-overs from the language of the original American inhabitants now called the American Indians. This is the case in spite of the fact that after the European migration to the USA, the European languages, in particular English, are spoken by the people. The same is the story in Europe where names of many places, rivers, and mountains of the earlier languages have continued even after the spread of the present-day European languages. On this analogy, one expects that at least some places, rivers, and mountains would have retained Dravidian names if the Harappans spoke that language, even if they had been ousted from their original habitat, which was the entire region from the Indus in the west to the Yamunā on the east. The total absence of any Dravidian names in this region clearly militates against the Harappan–Dravidian equation.

To discuss yet another argument that has been adduced in favor of the Harappan–Dravidian equation, there occur in the Vedas a few words which may have been derived from the Dravidian languages. On this basis it has been held that the invading Vedic Aryans picked up these words from the Dravidian-speaking Harappans whom they conquered. While there is no doubt that the Dravidian words could have been borrowed by the Vedic people only through some kind of contact with the Dravidian-speaking people, it has been shown earlier that there was no Aryan invasion whatsoever. Hence, the borrowing of the Dravidian words by the Vedic Aryans cannot be explained by this mechanism. Under such a situation, there is another possibility which can explain this borrowing. As a working hypothesis, let it be assumed for a while that the Harappans themselves were a Sanskrit-speaking people (more will be said about it later). In that case they could have easily borrowed some Dravidian words from the southern Neolithic people, who are the most likely candidates for having spoken that language. (Ever since the dawn of history, Dravidian is the only language known to have been spoken in that region.) We also know that the Harappans got their gold supply from the mines in South India. Because of this line of contact it would have been normal for the Harappans to have picked up some words from the South Indian Neolithic people.

We have so far established that: (i) the "Aryan-invasion" theory is nothing but a myth and (ii) the Harappans are unlikely to have been a Dravidian-speaking people. These formulations lead us to yet another enquiry, namely, were the Harappans themselves the much-debated Aryans? Against the Harappan–Aryan equation, however, several objections have been raised from time to time, and we shall now deal with them.

The first and most formidable mental barrier that had been created against a Harappan–Aryan equation is that of chronology. Since the Harappan civilization dates back to the third millennium BC and since according to the fatwa of Max Müller the Vedas are only as old as 1200 BC, it was but natural for all concerned to hold that the two cannot be equated. However, as we have already noted, Max Müller clearly distanced himself from this hard line (pp. 50–1). Yet it is a pity that even now some scholars with a particular mind-set, both in the west and east, are trying to hold on to the sinking ship.

Many distinguished astronomers have drawn our attention to the data given in the Vedic texts about the position of the *Nakṣatras*. For example, the *Aitareya Brāhmaṇa* refers to the shifting of the vernal equinox from the *Nakṣatra Mṛigaśiras* to *Rohiṇī*. According to these astronomers this event is likely to have taken place *c.*3500 BC. The implication of this would be that the *Ṛigveda* will have to be dated still earlier. Not being an astronomer myself, I am in no position to offer any comments. All that I would urge is that it would be unscientific to just pooh-pooh the idea. It is high time that experts from all over the world, having a knowledge of both Sanskrit and astronomy, sat together and thrashed out the issue.

However, let us see what archaeology has to say in the matter. We are all familiar with the Bughaz Keui inscription assignable to the fourteenth century BC. It records a treaty between the Mitanni king Matiwaza and a Hittite king Suppiluliuma. In it four deities are invoked, namely Indra, Mitra, Varuṇa, and Nāsatya. These are clearly Vedic gods. The presence of the Vedic Aryans in that region is once again attested to by a treatise which offers instructions regarding horse-training. Terms like *ekavartana*, *trivartana*, *pañchavartana*, etc. have been used, which are nothing but Sanskrit. There are many more documents from Western Asia which point to their Sanskritic origin. Analyzing the entire issue, the distinguished scholar T. Burrow (1955: 29) has very aptly remarked: "The Aryans appear in Mitanni from 1500 BC as the ruling dynasty, which means that they must first have entered the country as conquerors." Conquerors from where, one might ask. At that point of time there was no other country in the world where these gods – Indra, Mitra, Varuṇa, Nāsatya – were worshiped, except India. One cannot, therefore, escape the conclusion that the conquerors must have gone from this region. Anyway, on the basis of this evidence, the Vedas must antedate 1500 BC.

We may now move on to another very significant evidence. It comes from a combination of Vedic texts, archaeology and geomorphology. As discussed in some detail earlier, the *Ṛigveda* is full of references to the river Sarasvatī. It was a mighty flowing river during the Ṛigvedic times. The *Pañchaviṁśa Brāhmaṇa* gives two very significant pieces of evidence regarding the Sarasvatī. In the first place, it confirms the Ṛigvedic statement that the Dṛiṣadvatī was a tributary of the Sarasvatī (25.10.13–14). This further knocks the bottom out of the assumption that the Sarasvatī is to be equated with the Helmand since in Afghanistan there is no river by the name of Dṛiṣadvatī. Second, it states: "At a distance of a journey of forty days on horseback from the spot where the Sarasvatī is lost (in the sand of the desert), (is situated) Plakṣa Prasravaṇa" (Calad 1931: 636) (25.10.16). Although with the horse-back-journey distance it may not be possible to identify the exact place where the Sarasvatī disappeared, it is nevertheless clear that by the time of the *Pañchaviṁśa Brāhmaṇa* it was no longer alive. And it is here that archaeology, geomorphology, and Landsat imagery come to our help. As already stated earlier, the dry bed of the Sarasvatī has been duly identified with the help of Landsat imagery.

The excavations at Kalibangan in Rajasthan have demonstrated that the Harappan settlement at the site had to be abandoned because of the drying up of the adjacent river, now called the Ghaggar but anciently going by the name of the Sarasvatī. Another Harappan site, Banawali, which lay further upstream along this very river, had a similar fate. According to the radiocarbon dates, the end of Kalibangan and Banawali seems to have come *c*.2000–1900 BC. In other words, the Sarasvatī dried up *c*.2000 BC. This clearly establishes that the *Ṛigveda*, which speaks of the Sarasvatī as a mighty flowing river, has to be assigned to a period prior to 2000 BC. By how many centuries, it cannot be said for certain.

Those who have a mind-set that the Aryans must have come from outside put forward arguments which are sometimes quite frivolous. For example, Witzel argues:

> Indirect references to the migration of Indo-Aryan speakers include reminiscences of Iran, Afghanistan and Central Asia. Thus, the mythical Indo-Aryan river **Rasā* corresponds to the Vedic *Rasā* (RV, JB), the East Iranian *Ranhā* and the north Iranian *Rahā*, which is preserved in Greek as *Rhā*, where it designates the river Volga. This is a good example of the "migration" of river names, a topic discussed in the previous paper. In the same category might fall the rather vague identification of Ṛgvedic *rip-* with the Rhipaean mountains, the modern Urals (Bongard-Levin 1980).
> (1995: 321)

While, from the phonetic point of view, there may not be any objection to the *Rasā–Rahā* equation, why must it necessarily indicate a "migration" from west to east? It could as well have been the other way about. Let us not forget that the Rasā was one of the many tributaries of the Indus, as mentioned in the *Ṛigveda* (10.75.6)

> *Tṛiṣṭāmayā prathamam yātave sajūḥ Susartvā Rasayā Śvetyā tyā*
> *Tvam Sindho Kubhayā Gomatīm Krumum Mehantvā saratham yābhirīyase*

It would thus be clear that the Ṛigvedic Rasā cannot be placed in Iran. The identification of *rip-* with the Ural Mountains is indeed a good example of the heights to which flights of imagination can take us.

Anyway, there are yet two other major objections to an Aryan–Harappan equation. It has been argued that whereas the Harappan civilization was urban, the culture reflected in the Vedas is nomadic. So how can the two be equated? The other objection relates to the horse. The argument is that while the Vedic texts speak so often of the horse, the Harappans were unfamiliar with it. We shall now examine the validity of these two objections.

To take up the first, it is entirely wrong to say that the Vedic Aryans were nomads or, granting a concession, living in small hamlets, but had no urban component. Perhaps we may begin with references to *pur* in the *Ṛigveda*. As Macdonell and Keith (1912, reprint 1982, Vol. I: 538) rightly pointed out, this word connotes " 'rampart', 'fort' or 'stronghold'." And here we quote a few of the relevant verses, which show that there existed even varieties of forts during the Ṛigvedic times: some made of stone, while some others having a hundred (in the sense of many) arms. Thus, RV 4.30.20 states:

Śatamaśmanmayīnām puramindro vyāsyat Divodasaya daśuṣe

For Divodāsa, him who brought oblations, Indra overthrew
A hundred fortresses of stone.
(Griffith 1973, reprint: 221)

Through verse RV 10.101.8, the devotee desires that the fort ought to be very strong:

... varma sīvyadhvam bahulā pṛithūni
puraḥ Kṛiṇudhvamāyasīradhṛiṣṭā ...

... stitch ye [oh gods] the coats of armour, wide and many;
make iron forts, secure from all assailants.
(Griffith 1973, reprint: 615)

Here it needs to be clarified that the word *ayas* in the *Ṛigveda* stands for metal in general and it is only in later texts that two separate words came to be used: *kṛiṣṇā yasa*, that is, black metal, for iron; and *lohāyasa*, that is, red metal, for copper/ bronze. Anyway, what was really prayed for in the verse under consideration was that the gods may construct such a strong fort that the enemy was not able to penetrate it.

Through another hymn (RV 7.15.14), the devotee further prays that the fort ought to have a hundred arms, that is, be very large:

Adhaḥ Mahī na āyasyanādhṛiṣṭo nṛipītaye pūrbhavā śatabhujiḥ

And, irresistible, be thou a mighty iron fort to us,
With hundred walls for man's defence.
(Griffith 1973, reprint: 340)

Even though the context and meaning of the word *pur* is very clear in the above-mentioned verses, scholars who have been looking at the Ṛigvedic text with colored glasses keep on repeating the old view that the word does not connote a fort or city.

In his latest book, Sharma (1999: 39) once again holds out: "But those who have adequately examined references to *pur* in the Vedic texts, particularly in the *Ṛigveda* do not consider it a fortified town." May not one ask these "those" a simple question: When Wheeler (1947: 82) accused Indra of destroying the Harappan forts, on the basis of his epithet "*puraṁdara*" (*pura* = fort, and *dara* = destroyer), they had no hesitation in accepting that the word *pur* did mean a fort. Now, when the same word is found associated with the Aryans themselves, it loses its meaning. What kind of logic is this? Unless it be a case of: "Head I win, and tail you lose."

Looking for an escape route, Sharma goes on to say:

> In our opinion the myths and metaphors relating to the *pur* suggest that it was either a dwelling unit or a cluster of such units as appeared in the post-Harappan phase. Particularly the early Vedic stone *purs* may represent the recently discovered rock shelters in which pastoralists lived in the hilly tracts of North-West Frontier.
>
> (1999: 39)

Sharma has not given any reference to the publication detailing these "rock-shelters," but surely one is entitled to ask: What archaeological evidence has he found in these caves to associate them with the Ṛigvedic Aryans?

It is true that the *Ṛigveda* does not provide us details of the inner layout of these forts, but surely the text was not meant to be a treatise on *Vāstuśāstra*. May it be remembered that it is essentially a compilation of prayers to gods and should be looked at as such. All the evidence that it provides regarding the material culture of the then people is only incidental.

While discussing the urban–rural dichotomy between the Harappans and the Ṛigvedic people, it needs also to be emphasized that the entire Harappan population did not live in cities. There were many more Harappan villages and small towns than the metropolitan cities. Thus, if the *Ṛigveda* also speaks of rural life, besides referring to *purs*, it is perfectly in order. Whether in the past or at present, whether in India or elsewhere, rural and urban components have always been and are parts of the same cultural ethos. Hence not much should be made of this issue.

Unlike nomads (as they are dubbed), the Ṛigvedic Aryans were engaged in trade, maybe even sea-trade, and also had a very well organized civic and administrative set-up. A reference to RV 10.33.6 throws valuable light on the Ṛigvedic sea-trade:

> *rāyaḥ samudrāñśchaturo asmabhyam soma viśvataḥ ā pavasva sahasriṇaḥ*
>
> From every side, O Soma, for our profit, pour thou forth four seas filled full [*sic*] of riches thousand fold.
>
> (Griffith 1973, reprint: 483)

For carrying out the sea-trade the Ṛigvedic people used a variety of boats, some of which had as many as a hundred oars, as could be seen from the following verse (RV 1.116.5):

> *anārambhaṇe tadvīrayethāmanāsthāne agrabhaṇe samudre /*
> *yadaśvinā ūhathurbhujyumastam śatāritram nāvamātasthivānsam //*
>
> Ye wrought that hero exploit in the ocean which giveth no support, or hold or station,
> What time ye carried Bhujyu to his dwelling, borne in a ship with hundred oars, O Aśvins.
>
> (Griffith 1973, reprint: 77)

That the Ṛigvedic Aryans were socially and administratively well integrated is duly attested to by the occurrence in the text of such terms as *sabhā*, *samiti*, *samrāṭ*, *rājan*, *rājaka*, *janarāja*, etc. If the first two terms do not refer to some kind of assemblies which took collective decisions on matters of public interest, what else do they mean? Likewise, if the next four terms do not point to a hierarchy of rulers, where was the need to have these separate words? And here we shall quote from the *Ṛigveda* itself to show that these terms were indeed used to denote the difference in the status of the rulers concerned. Thus, for example, Abhyāvartin Chāyamāna, who was a very distinguished ruler, has been referred to as a *samrāṭ*. In contrast, Chitra, a ruler of lesser importance, has been called a *rājan*. Rulers of still lesser status have been called only *rājaka*. The relevant verses are as follows:

RV 6.27.8 states:

> *dvyāṁ agne rathino viṁśatim gā vadhūmato maghavā mahyam* samrāṭ /
> *Abhyāvartī Chāyamāno dadāti dūrṇāśeyam dakṣiṇā parthavānām //*
>
> Two wagon-teams, with damsels, twenty oxen, O Agni, Abhyāvartin Chāyamāna,
> The liberal Sovran, giveth me. This guerdon of Pṛithu's seed is hard to win from others.
>
> (Griffith 1973, reprint: 302)

In contrast, there is a verse RV 8.21.18:

> *Chitra id rājā rājakā idanyake yake Sarasvatīmanu /*
> *parjanya iva tadanaddhi vṛiṣṭyā sahasramayutā dadāt //*
>
> Chitra is King and only kinglings are the rest who dwell beside Sarasvatī.
> He, like Parjanya with his rain, hath spread himself with thousand, yea, with myriad gifts.
>
> (Griffith 1973, reprint: 412)

That there was definitely a difference between the status of a *samrāṭ* on the one hand and of a *rājan* on the other is clear from the explanatory note provided in the *Śatapatha Brāhmaṇa* (V.1. 1.12–13):

> *Rājā vai rājasūyeneṣṭvā bhavati, samrāḍ vājapeyena / avaram hi rājyam param sāmrājyam / kāmayeta vai rājā samrāḍ bhavitum avaram hi rājyam param sāmrājyam / na samrāṭ kamayeta rājā bhavitum avaram hi rājyam param sāmrājyam //*
>
> By offering the *rājasūya* he becomes rājā and by the *vājapeya* he becomes samrāj, and the office of *rājan* is lower and that of *samrāj*, the higher; a *rājan* might indeed wish to become *samrāj*, for the office of *rājan* is lower and that of *samrāj* the higher; but the *samrāj* would not wish to become a *rājā* for the office of *rājan* is the lower, and that of *samrāj* the higher.

What greater authority is needed to settle the issue?

Now to the horse. Dealing with the terracotta animals from his excavations at Mohenjo-daro, Mackay wrote (1938, Vol. 1: 289; Vol. 2, pl. LXXVIII, no. 11): "Perhaps the most interesting of the model animals is the one that I personally take to represent a horse." Confirming this identification, Wheeler stated:

> One terracotta, from a late level of Mohenjo-daro, seems to represent a horse, reminding us that a jaw-bone of a horse is also recorded from the same site, and that the horse was known at a considerably earlier period in Baluchistan.
>
> (1968: 92)

These pieces of evidence, however, were ignored by those who wished to portray the Harappan civilization as one without the horse, since the (alleged) absence of the horse has been made out to be a strong point against any association of the Harappan civilization with the Vedic Aryans. Another reason for doubting the presence of the horse in the Harappan civilization seems to have been the absence of this animal from the seals. But then the camel is also absent. So why should the horse be singled out on that count?

Anyway, in recent years a lot of evidence has accumulated from Harappan sites, both in India and Pakistan. For example, Phase III of Lothal in Gujarat, which is Mature Harappan in contents, has yielded a terracotta figure of the horse. It has a stumpy tail and the mane is indicated by a low ridge over the neck. And this figure is not the only evidence regarding the presence of the horse at Lothal. Reporting on the faunal remains from the site, two experts, namely, Bholanath of the Zoological Survey of India and G. V. Sreenivas Rao of the Archaeological Survey, have the following to say:

> The single tooth of the horse referred to above indicates the presence of the horse at Lothal during the Harappan period. The tooth from Lothal resembles closely with that of the modern horse and has the pli-caballian

> (a minute fold near the base of the spur or protocone) which is a well distinguishable character of the cheek teeth of the horse.
>
> (S. R. Rao 1985: 641)

From practically all the Harappan occupational sub-periods (IA, IB, and IC at Surkotada, another site in Gujarat, come a large number of bones of the horse (A. K. Sharma in Joshi 1990: 381). Since the occurrence of the horse in a Harappan context has all along been a matter of debate, opinion of an international expert was also sought that of Professor Sandor Bökönyi, a renowned archaeo-zoologist and the then Director of the Archaeological Institute, Budapest, Hungary. And here is what he had to convey, through a letter dated 13 December 1993, addressed to the then Director General of the Archaeological Survey of India:

> Through a thorough study of the equid remains of the protohistoric settlement of Surkotada, Kutch, excavated under the direction of Dr. J. P. Joshi, I can state the following: The occurrence of true horse (*Equus Caballus* L.) was evidenced by the enamel pattern of the upper and lower cheek and teeth and by the size and form of the incisors and phalanges (toe bones). Since no wild horses lived in India in post-Pleistocene times, the domestic nature of the Surkotada horse is undoubtful. This is also supported by an inter-maxilla fragment whose incisor tooth shows clear signs of crib-biting, a bad habit only existing among domestic horses which are not extensively used for war.
>
> (Bökönyi, December 13, 1993)

Giving measurements, other details and photographs of the faunal remains in a paper published subsequently, Bökönyi (1997: 300) confirmed his findings: "All in all, the evidence enumerated above undoubtedly raises the possibility of the occurrence of domesticated horses in the mature phase of the Harappa Culture, at the end of the third millennium BC."

However, those who have a mind-set to the contrary are not inclined to accept Bökönyi's well argued case. Thus, referring to a discussion that Meadow and Patel had with Bökönyi before the latter's death, they write (1997: 308): "We went through each point that we had raised and in some cases agreed to disagree. He (i.e. Bökönyi) remained firmly convinced that there are the bones of true horse (*Equus Caballus*) in the Surkotada collection, and we remain skeptical."

While Meadow and Patel have every right to "remain skeptical," it needs no emphasis that Bökönyi was an internationally recognized and respected expert on the anatomy of horses.

Anyway, Rupnagar (formerly known as Ropar) in Punjab and Kalibangan in Rajasthan have also given evidence of the presence of the horse in Harappan contexts. At the latter site have been found an upper molar, a fragment of a shaft of the distal end of a femur and the distal end of a left humerus (A. K. Sharma 1993).

Insofar as the situation in Pakistan is concerned, we have already referred to the evidence from Mohenjo-daro. Ross reported a few teeth of the horse from Rana

Ghundai, a pre-Harappan site in Pakistan, though some scholars, as usual, expressed doubt about the identification. The current excavators of Harappa, namely, Kenoyer and Meadow, have not reported so far of any remains of horse from there. But an earlier faunal collection from Harappa was examined by an expert of the Zoological Survey of India, who categorically stated that there were horse remains also in it (Bholanath 1959). However, the latest evidence regarding the association of the horse with the Harappan civilization comes from the excavations carried by J.-F. Jarrige and his colleagues at the well-known site of Nausharo (Report in press, but type-script privately circulated). Over here a few definitely identifiable terracotta figurines of the horse have been found.

From the foregoing it is clear that the Harappans did use the horse, although one would certainly welcome more evidence. As I have said elsewhere (Lal 1997: 286; 1998: 109–12), the truant horse has crossed the first hurdles!

There is yet another very important piece of evidence which needs to be brought into focus. I am currently working on the flora and fauna mentioned in the *Ṛigveda* and hope to publish a book on the subject in the near future. Meanwhile, it may be stated that almost all the plants and animals mentioned in this text relate to the region extending from Afghanistan on the west to the whole of the Indo-Pakistan subcontinent. While full details will be published in the book under preparation, some examples may nonetheless be given here.

The *aśvattha* (*Ficus religiosa*) tree, mentioned in a number of verses in the *Ṛigveda* (e.g. 1.35.8; 10.97.5) occurs in sub-Himalayan forests from Panjab eastwards, Bengal, Orissa, central India, upper Myanmar (Burma), and Sri Lanka. Likewise, *Khadira* (*Acacia catechu*), referred to in RV 3.53.19, grows only in India and Pakistan. Another noteworthy tree, *śiṁśapā* (*Dalbergia sissoo*; RV 3.53.19) is found in India, Pakistan, and Afghanistan and scantily in some adjacent parts of Iran. Incidentally, it may be mentioned that the *sissoo* is mentioned in certain Mesopotamian texts of the third millennium BC, wherein it is recorded that this valuable wood was imported from eastern regions called Magan and Meluḫḫa, the latter being generally identified as the Harappan region. All the Ṛigvedic trees show the above-mentioned kind of distribution pattern. On the other hand, the *Ṛigveda* does not refer to any tree which is typical of cold regions such as Russia or northern Europe.

Similar is the story about the Ṛigvedic fauna. For example, the elephant and peacock are typical of the Indo-Pakistan subcontinent but have nothing to do with the colder climes of Europe or Russia. (The occurrence of the elephant in Africa or of the peacock in southeast Asia has no relevance in the present context.)

Hence the combined evidence of the flora and fauna militates against the thesis of the immigration of the Ṛigvedic people from a hypothetical "cold-climate home."

Finally, we may refer to the Ṛigvedic geography itself. The *Nadī Sūkta*, already referred to earlier, enumerates the rivers with which the Ṛigvedic people were familiar. Starting from the Gaṅgā in the east, the *Sūkta* continues to mention the western rivers more or less in a serial order, subject, of course, to the constraints of poetic metrology. While dealing with the Indus, it mentions a large number of its tributaries which joined it from the west. These include, among others, the

Kubhā, Krumu, and Gomatī, which are now known respectively as the Kabul, Kurram, and Gomal. It is known that these rivers originate in Afghanistan. Thus, the Ṛigvedic Aryans inhabited not only the present-day northwestern India and Pakistan but also a good part of Afghanistan.

Further, as shown earlier (p. 65), the combined evidence of archaeology, radiocarbon-dating, hydrology and literature shows that the *Ṛigveda* is to be dated prior to 2000 BC, and, indeed, the third millennium BC. Thus, both spatial and temporal factors do point to a Vedic Harappan equation (see Figure 2.1). Can all this compelling evidence be brushed aside as mere coincidence?

Please think.

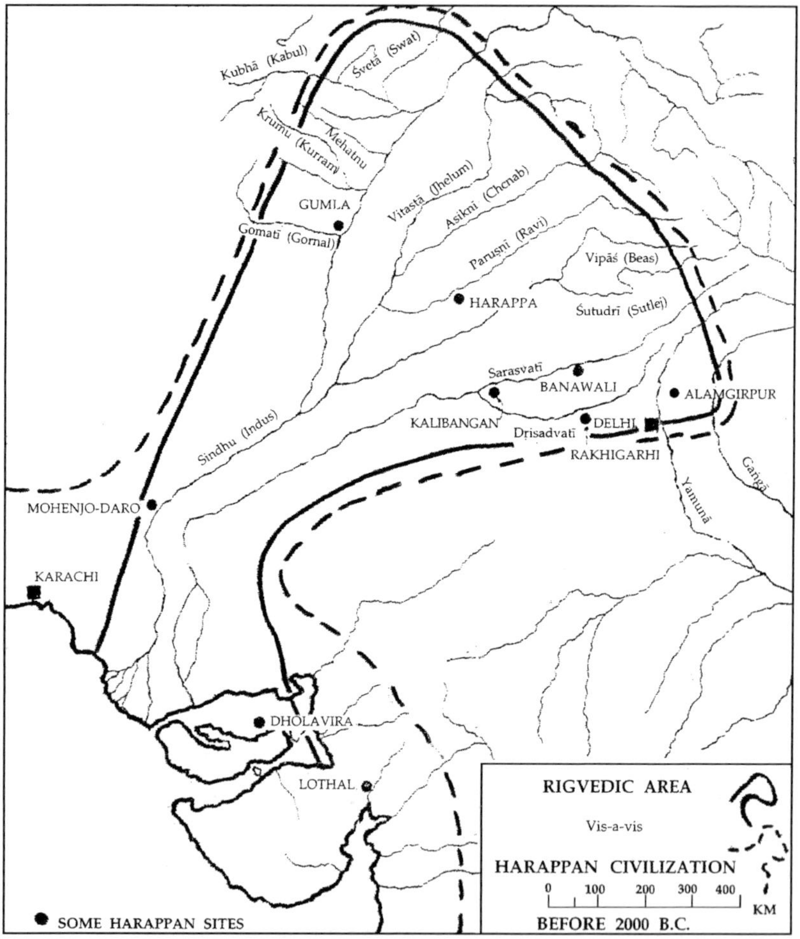

Figure 2.1 Map showing a correlation between the Ṛigvedic area and the spread of Harappan civilization, before 2000 BC.

References

Bholanath, 1959. "Remains of the horse and Indian elephant from the protohistoric site of Harappa (West Pakistan)," *Proceedings of First All-India Congress of Zoologists*, pt. 2. pp. 1–4.

Bökönyi, S., 1997. "Horse Remains from the Prehistoric Site of Surkotada, Kutch, Late 3rd Millennium BC," *South Asian Studies*, 13: 297–307.

Bongard-Levin, G. M., 1980. *The Origin of the Aryans: From Scythis to India*. Delhi: Arnold-Heineman.

Burrow, T., 1955. *The Sanskrit Language*. London: Faber and Faber.

Calad, W., 1931 [1982]. *Pañchavinmśa Brāhmaṇa*. Calcutta: Asiatic Society.

Dales, G. F., 1964. "The Mythical Massacre at Mohenjo-daro," *Expedition*, 6(3): 36–43.

Fairservis, W. A., 1992. *The Harappan Civilization and its Writing*. New Delhi: Oxford and IBH Publishing Co.

——, 1995. "Central Asia and the Rigveda: The Archaeological Evidence." In *Indo-Aryans of Ancient South Asia*, edited by George Erdosy. Berlin: Walter de Gruyter, pp. 206–11.

Griffith, R. T. H., 1973 [reprint]. *The Hymns of the Ṛigveda*. Delhi: Motilal Banarsidass.

Gupta, S. P., 1996. *The Indus-Sarasvati Civilization: Origins, Problems and Issues*. Delhi: Pratibha Prakashan.

Hemphill, B. E., J. R. Lukaes, and K. A. R. Kennedy, 1991. "Biological Adaptations and Affinities of Bronze Age Harappans." In *Harappa Excavations 1986–1990*, edited by R. H. Meadow. Madison, WI: Prehistory Press, pp. 137–82.

Jarrige, J.-F., 1981. "Economy and Society in Early Chalcolithic/Bronze Age of Baluchistan – New Perspectives from the Recent Excavations at Mehrgarh." In *South Asian Archaeology 1979*, edited by H. Haertel. Berlin: Dietrich Reimer Verlag, pp. 93–114.

——, 1982. "Excavations at Mehrgarh: Their Significance for Understanding the Background of the Harappan Civilization." In *Harappan Civilization: A contemporary Perspective*, edited by G. L. Possehl. New Delhi: Oxford and IBH Publishing Co., pp. 79–84.

——, 1984. "Towns and Villages of Hill and Plain." In *Frontiers of the Indus Civilization*, edited by B. B. Lal., S. P. Gupta, and S. Asthana. New Delhi: Books and Books, pp. 289–300.

Jarrige, J.-F. and M. Lechavallier, 1979. "Excavations at Mehrgarh, Baluchistan: Their Significance in the Prehistorical Context of the Indo-Pakistani Borderlands." In *Asian Archaeology 1977*, edited by M. Taddei. Naples: Instituto Universitario Orientale, pp. 463–535.

Jarrige, J.-F. *et al.* (in press). *Excavations at Mehrgarh-Nausharo, 16th to 20th Seasons (1990–94)*. Report submitted to the Director General of Archaeology and Museums, Government of Pakistan (unpublished but privately circulated).

Jones, William, 1788. "The Third Anniversary Discourse," *Asiatick Researches*, 1: 415–31.

Joshi, J. P., 1990. *Excavations at Surkotada 1971–72 and Explorations in Kutch*. New Delhi: Archaeological Survey of India.

Lal, B. B., 1970. "Some Observations on the Harappan Script." In *India's Contribution to World Thought and Culture*, edited by L. Chandra *et al.* Madras: Vivekanand Rock Memorial Committee, pp. 189–202.

——, 1974. *Has the Indus Script been Deciphered? An Assessment of Two Latest Claims*. Shimla: Indian Institute of Advanced Study.

——, 1983. "Reading the Indus Script," *Indian and Foreign Review*, 20(13): 33–36.

——, 1997. *The Earliest Civilization of South Asia*. New Delhi: Aryan Books International.

——, 1998. *India 1947–1997: New Light on the Indus Civilization*. New Delhi: Aryan Books International.

Macdonell, A. A. and A. B. Keith, 1912 [1982]. *Vedic Index of Names and Subjects*, 2 vols. Delhi: Motilal Banarsidass.
Mackay, E. J. H., 1938. *Further Excavations al Mohenjo-daro*, 2 vols. Delhi: Government of India.
Meadow, R. H. and Ajita Patel, 1997. "A Comment on 'Horse Remains from Surkotada' by Sandor Bokonyi," *South Asian Studies*, 13: 308–15.
Mughal, M. R., 1992. "Jhukar and the Late Harappan Cultural Mosaic of the Greater Indus Valley." In *South Asian Archaeology 1989*, edited by C. Jarrige. Madison, WI: Prehistory Press.
Müller, F. Max, 1890 [1979]. *Physical Religion*. New Delhi: Asian Educational Services.
Parpola, A., S. Koskenniemi, S. Parpola, and P. Alto, 1969. *Decipherment of the Proto-Dravidian Inscriptions of the Indus Civilization*. Copenhagen: Scandinavian Institute of Asian Studies.
Puri, V. M. K. and B. C. Verma, 1998. "Glaciological and Geological Source of Vedic Saraswati in the Himalayas," *Itihas Darpan*, IV(2): 7–36.
Rao, M. V. N. Krishna, 1982. *Indus Script Deciphered*. Delhi: Agam Kala Prakashan.
Rao, S. R., 1982. *The Decipherment of the Indus Script*. Bombay: Asia Publishing House.
——, 1985. *Lothal – A Harappan Port Town (1955–62)*, Vol. 2. New Delhi: Archaeological Survey of India.
Renfrew, C., 1987. *Archaeology and Language*. London: Jonathan Cape.
Richter-Ushanas, E., 1992. *The Fifth Veda: The Indus Seals in Comparison with the Ṛigveda*. Germany.
Shaffer, Jim G. and Diane Lichtenstein, 1999. "Migration, Philology and South Asian Archaeology." In *Aryan and Non-Aryan in South Asia: Evidence, Interpretation and Ideology*, edited by J. Bronkhorst and M. Deshpande. Cambridge, MA: Harvard University.
Sharma, A. K., 1993. "The Harappan Horse was buried under Dune of...," *Puratattva*, 23: 30–4.
Sharma, R. S., 1999. *Advent of the Aryans in India*. New Delhi: Manohar Publishers.
Singh, B., 1995. *The Vedic Harappans*. New Delhi: Aditya Prakashan.
Thapar, R., 1988–91. *Journal Asiatic Society of Bombay*, 64–66: 259–60.
Wheeler, R. E. M., 1947. "Harappa 1946: 'The Defences and Cemetery R-37'," *Ancient India*, 3: 58–130.
——, 1968. *The Indus Civilization*, 3rd edition. Cambridge: Cambridge University Press.
Witzel, M., 1995. "Rigvedic History, Poets, Chieftains and Polities." In *The Indo-Aryans of Ancient South Asia*, edited by George Erdosy. Berlin: Walter de Gruyter, pp. 307–52.
Yash Pal *et al.*, 1984. "Remote Sensing of the 'Lost' Sarasvati River." In *Frontiers of the Indus Civilization*, edited by B. B. Lal, S. P. Gupta, and Shashi Asthana. New Delhi: Books and Books, pp. 491–7.

Postscript

This paper was written in 1999. Since then a lot has been published by me on the topic under discussion. I would, therefore, like to draw the reader's attention to at least the following: *The Sarasvatī Flows On: The Continuity of Indian Culture*. New Delhi: Aryan Books International, 2002; "Should One Give up All Ethics for Promoting One's Theory?," in *East and West*, 53: 1–4; December 2003, pp. 285–8 *The Homeland of the Aryans: Evidence of Ṛigvedic Flora and Fauna*. New Delhi: Aryan Books International, 2005.

3

SOUTH ASIAN ARCHAEOLOGY AND THE MYTH OF INDO-ARYAN INVASIONS

Jim G. Shaffer and Diane A. Lichtenstein

The material, tangible, archaeological record is a most vital "hard data" record for establishing knowledge about the ways of life, and identities, of prehistoric peoples. It is a record that presents the patterns of prehistoric life in both a relative, stratigraphic, chronology, and absolute chronology, through radiometric techniques. It helps inform us of that part of human existence before written records, some 99 percent of human existence.

In our earlier discussions of the prehistory of South Asia (Shaffer and Lichtenstein 1995, 1999), we have described the "cultural tradition" and "paleoethnicity" concepts in reference to the mosaic of peoples living between the Indus and Gangetic Valleys in the mid-third millennium BC. Their patterns of cultural adaptation and cultural expression describe a more structured "Indo-Gangetic Cultural Tradition," characterized by, among other features, an economic focus on cattle together with agricultural production. In the following pages, we summarize an earlier presentation of more recently available South Asian archaeological data, placing it in the context of assessing the eighteenth- and nineteenth-century interpretative scholarly paradigms for the study of ancient India (Shaffer 1984, 1992, 1993; Shaffer and Lichtenstein 1999). These are arguments premised on a conflating of language, culture, "race," and population movements. Despite a plea by one South Asian scholar to be "... hopefully somewhat free from the ghosts of the past" (Bryant 2001: 14), the legacy of a post-Enlightenment western scholarship concerning South Asian prehistory and history has been for the arguments to be repeated so often as to become dogma.

3.1 "The Language of Paradise"

Sir William "Oriental" Jones delivered a lecture on February 2, 1786 to the Royal Asiatic Society of Bengal; it contained his now famous "philologer" paragraph in which he proposed a linguistic relationship linking, at some point in the ancient past,

Sanskrit with Latin, Greek, and other European languages (Jones 1788, as quoted in Poliakov 1974: 190 and cited in Franklin 1995: 361; see also Mukherjee 1987). European scholars earlier had considered some of this same issue (Poliakov 1974; Trautmann 1997, 1999; Bryant 2001), but Jones' status as a legal, philological, and historical scholar, as well as a Judge for the East India Company, established a gravity for this linguistic hypothesis which continues today. Perhaps no other scholarly hypothesis of the eighteenth century, outside of the natural sciences, has continued to so influence such diverse disciplines as linguistics, history, biology, ethnology, and political science. The timing of Jones' lecture is significant in a broader social context. With the American colonies lost, England was beginning a global expansion of colonization and the generally agreed upon era of the modern nation-state had begun. Fewer than one-third of the some current 200 modern nation-states are over thirty years old, a point worth noting when present day social identities are defined with descriptive terminology of the scholarly disciplines of the eighteenth and nineteenth centuries. Academic discourse in philology, ethnology, archaeology, paleontology, biology, and religion was plumbed in the eighteenth and nineteenth centuries to substantiate a sense of self and shared identity in a newly expanded view of the known geographic world and in a reassessment of a chronology of human antiquity beyond a Biblical interpretation of human origins. Archaeology's "hard evidence," discordant with Biblical interpretations of human origins, European knowledge of other cultures' self-asserted antiquity, especially that of India, and Jones' hypothesis of Indo-European language relationships combined to structure European scholarship of the eighteenth and nineteenth centuries toward a reconsideration of the characteristics which seemed to unambiguously establish a shared, common identity – language, culture, "race."[1]

Certainly by the eighteenth century, language was increasingly manipulated by European political elites as a source of social identity and power. As the fledgling European industrial revolution expanded, the need for an increasingly literate population, and availability of "cheap newsprint," invited an even more intense manipulation of language as a source of identity, along with other characteristics such as physical appearance, dress, and food (Smith 1986; van den Berge 1987; Anderson 1991). Linguistically based European nation-states in the eighteenth and nineteenth centuries emerged from the hodgepodge of languages/cultures/religions essentially by fiat. Less than 3 percent of the population spoke Italian as their "mother tongue" when Garibaldi united a group of provinces into what was to become Italy (Robbins 2002: 107).

But what of the language of paradise? How to relate the "language of Adam to the pluralism of Babel?" (Olender 1992, 1997). Language's powerful ability to establish ordered existence is reflected in the Biblical tale of a "... faceless God with an unutterable Name, creating the Universe in six days, divulging several words in a language that dissipates primeval Chaos" (Olender 1997: 51). Such an "original" language, initially considered to be Hebrew, as common source for all later languages, is established in biblical chronology. Noah's three sons were the accepted progenitors of all humanity, dispersed throughout the world and speaking a common language. In Babel, the immediacy and translucency of the Adamic language was lost. As Olender notes (1997: 55), the quest of the European nation-state to attribute its source of identity to this "original" language established the impetus of more than one nationalist ideology.

Hebrew was the "original" language of the Bible, and, at the time, it was the oldest language known until the Rosetta Stone's discovery and decipherment yielded even more ancient languages. Hebrew also was the language of the Jews. In the eighteenth and nineteenth centuries, European scholars who felt compelled to accept Biblical "history" in its Hebraic account of human origins may have been reluctant, in the light of European anti-Semitism, to accept Hebrew as the "original" language of paradise. Jones' linguistic hypothesis linking Sanskrit with Latin and Greek, and his further detailed studies of Indian chronology, provided the impetus for a disaffection with Genesis, a neat out for the troubled scholars of the day. The philological chronologies of Jones' day, and after, helped reconstruct an "original" proto-language form, presumed to have been spoken by a specific group of people living in a circumscribed area. While India was at first promoted as the Indo-European homeland, Indian civilization was later demoted to being the end result of an invading Indo-Aryan branch of the Indo-Europeans combined with indigenous non-Indo-European peoples (Shaffer and Lichtenstein 1999; Bryant 2001: *passim*).

3.2 Language, culture, "race"

A broad review of the scholarly paradigm shifts which eighteenth- and nineteenth-century European scholars experienced in dealing with human origins within the context of the natural sciences, and, later, social sciences is well beyond the scope of this discussion (Stepan 1982; Bowler 1989; Van Riper 1993; Trautmann 1997, 1999).

Epistemological linking of language, culture, "race" in the European scholarship of the eighteenth and nineteenth centuries was a continuation of earlier efforts to assess the unity of monogenic descent from Adam described in Biblical narrative *vis-à-vis* European recognition of human physical variation. It was an effort to assess a "unity of reason" underlying linguistic diversity (Olender 1997: 56–7) and it was an effort to assess a chronology recognized in population movements both in ancient times and in the period of the growth of the modern nation-state. The way in which Indo-European studies approached the issue of a linguistic dispersal of the Indo-European language group ultimately relied on the principle of the segmentary structure of a Mosaic ethnology (Trautmann 1997: 55–7), in the metaphor of an endless branching tree of patrilineal descent. The tree paradigm of European philologists in the nineteenth century also acknowledges an emphasis, not quite complementary, on the feminine, in its use of the "mother tongue" reproducing "daughter" languages. What is important about the use of the tree metaphor by linguists is that it asserts a genealogical connectedness among humans speaking a particular language and an endless branching of linguistic change establishing a chronology by which to describe the movements of specific language speakers in space. For the eighteenth- and nineteenth-century philologists, the superiority of a particular language/"race" was revealed in the verifiable accomplishments of a culture/"civilization" of great antiquity. The goal was to use the reconstructed proto-Indo-European/Aryan language to locate its speakers in a region which, ultimately, was placed outside India and assess the migration of peoples/languages away from the nodal area in both west and southeasterly directions. This linguistic paradigm is modified but remains a basic point of debate in various modern scholarship on South Asian prehistory (Renfrew 1987; Mallory 1989, but see Lamberg-Karlovsky 1988, 2002; Shaffer 1990; Yoffee 1990 for critical reviews) when chronology, area of language origin, and migrations (Allchin 1995) are considered.[2]

In the mid-nineteenth century, Max Müller wrote of the "... 'Aryan' language, spoken in Asia by a small tribe, nay, originally by a small family living under one and the same roof" (1880, cited in Leach 1990: 234), careful to separate the study of language from "ethnology," which was the discipline which could describe population movements.

Muller stresses, "There are Aryan and Semitic languages, [but] it goes against all rules of logic to speak, without an expressed or implied qualification, of an Aryan race, of Aryan blood, or Aryan skulls" (1880, cited in Leach 1990: 234). Less than a century later in Europe, courtesy of language, there were indeed just such identifying characteristics in the Nazi Reich.[3] The intellectual atmosphere in which correlations of "race" and language from the comparative linguistics side occasionally continue "to haunt" Indo-European studies has been recently reviewed (Bryant 2001: 17). It is a viewpoint that can overwhelm, at times, the discussion of the prehistoric patterns of adaptation, stability, and change revealed in the archaeological record of South Asia.[4] Few scholars have addressed these issues from a South Asian archaeological perspective based on archaeological data gathered over the past century (see Erdosy 1989, 1995a,b; Shaffer and Lichtenstein 1999). We now turn to such a consideration.

3.3 The British archaeologists

British archaeologists have been the dominant influence in South Asian archaeology from the beginning of its inception there, in 1861, through the independence period and beyond (until recently). The Archaeological Survey of India was created, organized, and staffed by British scholars since the 1860s (for extensive discussions of this history, see Chakrabarti 1982; Kennedy 2000; Possehl 1996, 1999a, 2002). However, it is important to note that the Archaeological Survey of India has attempted always to integrate indigenous scholars into its activities at all administrative and field research levels. Harappa was excavated and published on by M. S. Vats (1940); research was conducted in Sindh by N. G. Majumdar (1934). Among the most important of the British archaeologists are Sir John Marshall, Sir Ernest Mackay, Sir Mortimer Wheeler, and Stuart Piggott. Marshall (1931), Mackay (1938), and

Vats (1940) were responsible, with others, for the excavation of many, critically important, prehistoric and early historic South Asian sites including Mohenjo-daro and Harappa. Marshall and Mackay interpreted and presented to the academic world South Asia's Bronze Age Harappan (Indus) civilization as a result of their research. Their interpretation of this Bronze Age civilization was different than expected. By the 1930s, enough ancient documents had been translated to reveal an ancient Old World much like that of twentieth-century Europe, with urban elites engaged in trade and promoting warfare for their own aggrandizement and profit from earliest historic times to the present. Note that for Marshall and Mackay, their contemporary period had just witnessed the First World War, the "war to end all wars." In anticipating revelations about a prehistoric world, there was no reason to suspect that, in this case, it would be much different from the early and later historical periods known for the Old World. However, based on their research, Marshall and Mackay described a Bronze Age, South Asian culture/civilization that had urban centers, writing, public, but not monumental, architecture, with no direct evidence for warfare, an essentially homogeneous and sophisticated craft technology distributed over a vast geographic area, and one, no less, without elite status burials of the kind found in Sumeria or Egypt. The geographic area encompassed by this Harappan (Indus) culture was understood to be much larger than that of either Sumeria or Egypt. Marshall and Mackay's interpretation of the Harappan data was that it was a complex civilization of priests, literati, traders in contact with western areas, craftsmen, sailors, successful agriculturalists and pastoralists and, perhaps, philosophers – the "priest-king" figurine of Mohenjo-daro. Additionally, they maintained that the Harappan culture was too early in date to be connected to the Vedic tradition of an invasion by Aryans. In general, their interpretation of Harappan culture was similar to that of Greek scholars such as Megasthenes (Greek ambassador to India *c.*302–291 BC) who wrote *Indika*, a work that would influence Western scholarly perspectives of South Asia until about the sixteenth century AD. (Interestingly this interpretation of the Harappan culture as a peacefully integrated, sophisticated, complex culture is very similar to that proposed until recently by New World archaeologists to describe aspects of Maya civilization.)

Since India's and Pakistan's independence, South Asian archaeology was significantly influenced by Sir Mortimer Wheeler (born 1890, died 1976) and, to a lesser degree, by the late Stuart Piggott. Wheeler secured a reputation as one of the most prominent archaeologists in the English speaking world. He had served in the First World War and was on active duty in north Africa during the Second World War when he received the order to proceed to India and reorganize the Archaeological Survey of India. His responsibility was to train the next generation of Indian archaeologists who would work in the post-independence era (Wheeler 1956; Clark 1979). Wheeler did accomplish his task of reorganizing the Survey and he embarked on an ambitious program of stratigraphic excavations at various sites, with the goals of training his staff in the modern, for the day, archaeological field techniques and gaining critical new data about ancient cultures to help in building an informed chronology of prehistoric and ancient South Asia. Very quickly, he proposed a very different interpretation of what the archaeological record revealed about Harappan culture (Wheeler 1956: 192) versus the then prevailing descriptions of Marshall and Mackay (Childe 1934, 1953). Rather than mere enclosing walls for sites, Wheeler envisioned the citadels present in other Old World ancient civilizations; Harappan culture's homogenous material remains marked strong bureaucratic centralization and its widespread geographical distribution, as recorded in its many sites, was the result of a "militaristic imperialism" (Wheeler 1956: 192), establishing a pattern known for other Old World civilizations. It was a pattern of conflict for resources and hegemony comparable to that Wheeler and Piggott had each experienced in their respective war service. Theirs was a defining stamp of description widely accepted at all public levels in Europe and South Asia, via the writings of V. Gordon Childe (1953) and one which persists today (e.g. Mallory 1989; but see Shaffer and Lichtenstein 1999).

If Jones' had his "philologer paragraph," Wheeler had his "Aryan paragraphs" which directed archaeological, historical, linguistic, and biological interpretations within South Asian studies for over a half century. Wheeler (1968, 3rd edition) proposed the following:

> It is, simply, this. Sometime during the second millennium B.C. – the middle of the millennium has been suggested, without serious support – Aryan-speaking peoples invaded the Land of Seven Rivers, the Punjab and its neighboring region. It has long been accepted that the tradition of this invasion is reflected in the older hymns of the Rigveda, the composition of which is attributed to the second half of the millennium. In the Rigveda, the invasion constantly assumes the form of an onslaught upon walled cities of the aborigines. For these cities, the term used is *pur*, meaning a "rampart," "fort," "stronghold." One is called "broad" (prithvi) and "wide" (urvi). Sometimes strongholds are referred to metaphorically as "of metal" (dyasi). "Autumnal" (saradi) forts are also named: "this may refer to the forts in that season being occupied against the Aryan attacks or against inundations caused by overflowing rivers." Forts "with a hundred walls" (satabhuji) are mentioned. The citadel may be of stone (*aśmanmayi*): alternatively, the use of mud-bricks is perhaps alluded to by the epithet *ama* (raw, unbaked); Indra, the Aryan war-god is *purandara*, "fort-destroyer." He shatters "ninety forts" for his Aryan protégé, Divodasa. The same forts are doubtless referred to where in other hymns he demolishes variously ninety-nine and a hundred "ancient castles" of the aboriginal leader Sambara. In brief, he renders "forts as age consumes garment."
>
> If we reject the identification of the fortified citadels of the Harappans with those which the Aryans destroyed, we have to assume that, in the short interval which can, at the most, have intervened between the end of the Indus civilization and the first Aryan invasions, an unidentified but formidable civilization arose in the same region and presented an

> extensive fortified front to the invaders. It seems better, as the evidence stands, to accept the identification and to suppose that the Harappans of the Indus valley in their decadence, in or about the seventeenth century BC, fell before the advancing Aryans in such fashion as the Vedic hymns proclaim: Aryans who nevertheless, like other rude conquerors of a later date, were not too proud to learn a little from the conquered...
>
> (1968: 131–2)

Wheeler definitely links the "end" of Harappan culture with a human, physical, invasion correlated with linguistic change associated with Aryans in South Asia and Europe. He, and Piggott, attributed to the Harappan culture a conservative, centralized, state organization dominated by priest-kings, which had become stagnant. It was only after the "Aryan invasions" that the indigenous population was reinvigorated with Aryan warriors and Aryan intellect and a new language that was fated to decline through interaction with and contamination by the language of the indigenous population. This authoritative description has become the received wisdom guiding much of the discussion about the Pre- and Early Historic periods of South Asia until the period of the 1980s. What new data challenged this authoritative description?

3.4 Recent archaeological developments

Archaeologists and non-archaeologists (Renfrew 1987; Mallory 1989; Ratnagar 1991; Mallory and Mair 2000), linguists (Witzel 1999), historians (Robb 2002), and biologists (Cavalli-Sforza *et al.* 1994) have used those portions of the South Asian archaeological record which seemed to most support their goals of determining a well-defined nodal area of proto-Indo-European culture at a time sufficient to allow for the development of later cognate languages linked to genealogically defined human populations. It is singularly refreshing, against this dogmatic pursuit of what may be an unobtainable goal, to know there are South Asian scholars who "...do not believe that the available data are sufficient to establish anything very conclusive about an Indo-European homeland, culture, or people" (Bryant 2001: 11; see also Kennedy 2000). We do acknowledge that cognate languages exist over a vast area from India to Europe, but see little attention directed to a consideration of language convergence as well as divergence for assessing prehistoric population interaction (see Lamberg-Karlovsky 2002; Sherratt and Sherratt 1988: 585). We note too Ehret's cautionary proviso of the relative ease of language shift among "small-scale" social groups (Ehret 1988: 569).[5] The existing interpretative discussions postulating large-scale human "invasions" (Renfrew 1987; Allchin 1995) simply do not correlate with the physical, archaeological, or paleoanthropological, data (Kennedy 2000). No matter how prevalent some population intrusions have been within the South Asian context since the time of Alexander the Great, the archaeological data currently available do not support a parallel scenario being drawn for the prehistoric context.

Within the context of South Asian archaeology, the available material record is the initial avenue for reconstructing prehistoric patterns of immediate environmental adaptation and cultural organization of specific groups. That same record assists in determining the kind and degree of interactions among groups within defined geographic areas over a period of time. Potsherds are a humble beginning; pots *in situ* describe more; chipped stone tools and polished stone tools and metals reveal specific craft techniques and possible areas of resource availability; flora and fauna remains describe still more; human remains are a definite confirmation of, at least, some aspects of human physical variation; the ways in which human remains were dealt with by prehistoric populations describe something of cultural beliefs concerning cultural identity both in life and death, and a relative stratigraphic chronology of the material record is evaluated against the calendric chronology of carbon-14 dating. There are never enough prehistoric sites excavated, and excavated well, and there are never enough carbon-14 dates. Still, the efforts by archaeologists working in South Asia, especially in the last two decades, have revealed data by which earlier interpretative hypotheses of South Asian cultures can be reviewed for their strengths and weaknesses (Shaffer 1996). The migration/invasion hypothesis of people entering South Asia from the West in a prehistoric period is one to be assessed against newer archaeological data.

3.5 Mehrgarh: the origins of food production

The excavations at Mehrgarh (Jansen *et al.* 1991; Jarrige *et al.* 1995) near Sibri, Pakistan, do demonstrate an indigenous development of agricultural food production by people living there as early as the seventh millennium BC. As a cultural occupation, Mehrgarh Period IA dates to the seventh millennium BC period (Shaffer 1992); because of the essential cultural complexity in that occupation stratum, some scholars posit an even earlier period for the cultural innovation there of achieving plant and animal domesticates. Most important was the identification at Mehrgarh of *wild* representatives of domesticable plants and animals, indicating their use by groups in the area. Mehrgarh's seventh millennium BC population had a plant economy using domesticated wheats and barley, with a high percent (90 percent) of naked six-row barley, a variety which occurs only in a post-domestication context. Wild sheep, goat, cattle, water buffalo, and gazelle were hunted.

The small size of some goats, a post-domestication characteristic, and intentional use of immature goats within human burials suggests that goats were being herded. By Mehrgarh Period IB, *c.*6000–5500 BC, fully domesticated sheep, goats, and cattle were the *major* animals being exploited. In Mehrgarh Period II, 5500–4500 BC, nearly all the faunal remains indicate domestication. After Mehrgarh Period II, some 60 percent of the animals consumed were domesticated cattle. This emphasis on domesticated cattle, though variable, persisted into the second millennium BC, a rare pattern in the ancient Old World where domesticated sheep/goats become the most exploited fauna. Moreover, during the Harappan period, after 2500 BC, groups of specialized cattle pastoralists have been identified in the prehistoric record (Rissman and Chitalwala 1990). More recently, and importantly, cattle mtDNA studies (Loftus *et al.* 1994; Wuethrich 1994; Bradley *et al.* 1996) indicate that South Asia is a primary world area where at least one species of cattle, *Bos indicus*, was domesticated.

Other important aspects of the Mehrgarh occupation sequence indicate that humans were emphasizing surplus resource production, establishing a precocious and varied craft industry and making use of early "public" architectural units. The crucial point is that the site of Mehrgarh establishes food production technology as an indigenous South Asian, Indus Valley cultural phenomenon. No intruding/invasive/migrating population coming into the area can be referred to as the source of such cultural innovation, as suggested by Renfrew (1987). The current data (Shaffer 1992) delineates a South Asian prehistoric cultural complexity and urbanization process that develops over a long chronology based on indigenous, but not isolated, cultural innovations. The available archaeological record does not support the explanatory paradigm of a culturally superior, intrusive/invasive Indo-Aryan people as being responsible for the cultural accomplishments documented archaeologically for prehistoric South Asia.

Archaeology documents a great deal of cultural development in South Asia between 6000 and 1000 BC, and certain other data are noteworthy. During the early third millennium BC, a variety of similar but distinctive cultural groups coexisted in the Indus Valley, several of which continued into the second millennium BC. During the mid-third millennium BC, one, or more, of these groups developed rather quickly into the Harappan culture (Shaffer and Lichtenstein 1989, 1995, 1999; Possehl 1990), Marshall's Indus Valley civilization, one which became widespread for several reasons. Mughal (1970, 1973) has strongly argued that the Kot Dijian cultural group of this area was *the* direct predecessor to the Indus Valley civilization, based on stratigraphy and material artifact analysis. At some sites, Kot Dijian culture is chronologically earlier than the Indus Valley/Harappan culture sites; other Kot Dijian sites are contemporary with those of the Indus Valley/Harappan culture, while other Kot Dijian sites are later than those of the Indus Valley/Harappan culture (Allchin 1984; Possehl 1984; Shaffer and Lichtenstein 1989; Shaffer 1992). Lacking fullest data, there is, nonetheless, a growing consensus that Harappan culture is the result of indigenous cultural developments, with no "Mesopotamian" people or diffusions of Western inventions, by whatever means, needed to explain it.

Earlier, Harappan culture was described as *the* single, monumental social entity in the Indus Valley area. However, we now know that there were several contemporaneous cultural groups occupying the same and immediately adjacent geographic areas. These include the cultural groups of the Kot Dijian, Amrian, Hakran, and final Mehrgarh occupations, to note but a few (Shaffer and Lichtenstein 1989, 1995, 1999; Shaffer 1992). Culturally, the Harappan was certainly the most impressive of these, but it was not alone; rather, it was part of a greater cultural mosaic in this geographic area which we are just now beginning to appreciate (Shaffer and Lichtenstein 1989, 1995, 1999).

Harappan culture groups, and their culturally similar but distinct neighbors, were aware of and interacted with a range of other social groups living in a greater hinterland (Shaffer and Lichtenstein 1989, 1995; Shaffer 1993). These additional social groups were food foragers, pastoralists and agriculturalists, some of whom practiced small-scale craft industries. These diverse other groups were situated geographically from Baluchistan to the Yamuna–Ganges divide, and from Swat and Kashmir to the central Deccan Plateau. Direct and indirect trade though intermediary groups occurred. There is, for instance, an Harappan site located on the Oxus River, while Kot Dijian and Hakran sites are found in Swat and a Kot Dijian presence is recorded for Kashmir (Shaffer 1992). Harappans and their immediate neighbors had indirect and direct access to a large and ecologically varied, resource-rich, eastern hinterland, an area moreover which was underpopulated compared to the Indus Valley proper, a circumstance unusual in the Bronze–Iron Age ancient Old World.

The "identity" of the encompassing Indus Valley cultural mosaic has been much scrutinized by interested scholars (Chakrabarti 1990; Ratnagar 1991; Lal 1997; Possehl 2002), with a focus on the kinds of relationships comprising it, (the political, economic, and religious organizational relationships), as well as the nature and degree of interactions between the groups of the Indus Valley cultural mosaic and groups located elsewhere. Space precludes full discussion here of these details. More vital is the apparent cultural mosaic response to ecological changes affecting the greater Indus Valley area beginning in the mid-third millennium BC and intensifying during the second through first millennium BC.

South Asian paleoenvironmental data are minimal compared to other regions, but important details emerge. Pollen cores from Rajasthan (Singh 1971; Singh *et al.* 1974; Bryson and Swain 1981; Bhatia and Singh 1988; Singh *et al.* 1990; Deotare and Kajale 1996) seem to indicate that by the mid-third milennium BC, climatic conditions of the Indus Valley area became increasingly arid. Data from the Deccan region (Dhavalikar 1988) also suggests a similar circumstance there by the end of the second millennium BC (for alternative views about Rajasthan, see Misra 1984; Possehl 1997a,b, 1999b, 2002). Additionally, and more directly devastating for the Indus Valley region, in the early second millennium BC, there was the capture of the Ghaggar-Hakra (or Saraswati) river system (then a focal point of human occupation) by adjacent rivers, with subsequent diversion of these waters eastwards (Shaffer 1981, 1982, 1986, 1993; Mughal 1990, 1997; Shaffer and Lichtenstein 1995, 1999). At the same time, there was increasing tectonic activity in Sindh and elsewhere. Combined, these geological changes meant *major* changes in the hydrology patterns of the region (Flam 1981, 1993). These natural geologic processes had significant consequences for the food producing cultural groups throughout the greater Indus Valley area. Archaeological surveys have documented a cultural response to these environmental changes creating a "crisis" circumstance and we note them here.

3.6 Archaeological considerations

The archaeological database is never complete. Newer archaeological data with corresponding radiometric dates can corroborate earlier anthropological interpretations of a specific group's cultural patterns at any time and over time and also perhaps alter those earlier interpretations of a group's way of life. More specifically, radiometric dating techniques for the periods considered in this chapter essentially refer to carbon-14 dating, which can provide a *range* of possible dates, with varying degrees of accuracy for specific dates. With the confidence of relying on the testing of hundreds of carbon samples, it is possible to describe the mature Harappan culture as dating to between 2600 and 1900 BC. Nonetheless, it is not as easy to state, within that chronological range, precisely when, and for how long, each of the eighty-three recorded mature Harappan habitation sites in Cholistan existed (Mughal 1997). For the 2600–1900 BC period, the Cholistan archaeological survey data indicate that some human habitation sites were abandoned, others persisted and other sites were newly created throughout that region. The following evaluation of the Harappan site survey data is presented with such considerations in mind.

From a broader theoretical perspective, we note that, in describing other world regions, archaeologists generally have retreated from the use of human migration/invasion as a specified cause of cultural innovations in a different area, recognizing the difficulty in distinguishing such a causal factor from "diffusion" (Clark 1966; Adams *et al.* 1978; Trigger 1989). Successful archaeological documentation of human migration (Rouse 1986) nearly always has been correlated, to some degree, with verifiable historical population movements (e.g. Polynesians, Inuit, Japanese, Tainos, Europeans to North America). Cultural anthropology does document the ease of cultural borrowing, but it is useful to recall that humans are selective in their borrowing patterns. Objects, ideas, technologies, language can be used by a borrowing group and, in the absence of historical records, it is difficult to determine with certainty whether a changed distribution pattern of cultural traits/styles in a given area reflects physical population movement or stimulus diffusion. Where archaeology has been able to convincingly document human physical movement is with regionally based human site distribution patterns, which demonstrate the abandonment of sites and/or establishment of new sites in a given region. For the greater Indus Valley area, those habitation site survey data have been available only recently.

3.6.1 The regional data

Beginning in the late third millennium BC and continuing throughout the second millennium BC, many, *but not all*, Indus Valley settlements, including urban centers, were abandoned as a cultural response to the environmental "crisis" described earlier.

Other areas, such as Baluchistan, were also affected by the same environmental changes affecting the Indus Valley, but the relative and absolute cultural chronologies of the western fringe areas are not known well enough to incorporate that information into this discussion. Even within the Indus Valley, the cultural response of abandoning habitation sites varied. In Cholistan, along the Ghaggar-Hakra River, it was a dramatic response of abandonment. Yet all areas were affected in the Indus Valley. While the quality of the survey data is regionally variable, it is sufficient to show a gradual and significant population shift from the Indus Valley eastward into the eastern Punjab and Gujarat, beginning in the late third millennium BC and continuing throughout the second millennium BC. This is a significant human population movement which parallels that attributed to the mid-second millennium BC and described within the Vedic oral tradition.[6] The data gained by these archaeological surveys are presented next.

Cholistan

Mughal's 1974–77 (1990, 1997) archaeological surveys of this area, together with archaeological surveys in the eastern Punjab (see later), indicate considerable population settlement dynamics in this region from the third through second millennium BC. Knowledge of a diagnostic Hakra cultural pattern is limited. It is described essentially on the basis of Mughal's survey data of pottery samples and a few excavations. Mughal (1990, 1997) considers the Hakra culture to be earlier than Kot Dijian, *now designated as Early Harappan by Mughal and others*, and earlier than the Harappan. That may be correct. It is also quite likely that some Hakran settlements, like related Kot Dijian ones, persisted and were contemporary with, or even later than, the Harappan (Shaffer 1992). Only more archaeological fieldwork excavations and radiometric dates may resolve these issues. It should be noted that Mughal's culturally defined Hakra and Early Harappan groups correspond to the "Early Harappan" as applied by researchers to groups in other nearby regions. And from the survey data, only habitation sites are considered here. As we note, "*Industrial sites without associated habitation areas, camp sites and cemeteries are excluded, since they do not reflect long-term human daily activity usage (habitation) or, in the case of camp sites, only temporary use*" (Shaffer and Lichtenstein 1999); see Figure 3.1.

The published report for the site survey data of Cholistan includes site sizes, a detail of information not now available for other known sites in different regions. Hakra habitation sites, and Early Harappan habitation sites, in total area occupied, are essentially the same. Together, the Hakra and Early Harappan habitation site area occupied is similar to that of the Harappan. In striking contrast, the habitation area of Late Harappan sites in Cholistan declines by 48 percent. By the late second through early first millennium BC period (i.e. Painted Gray Ware cultural groups/early Iron Age), another habitation area decline of 83 percent occurs. By the early Iron Age, in other words, the habitation area of sites is only 8 percent of the habitation area of sites occupied during the Harappan cultural period. It is evident, based upon habitation area size changes, that a major population decline in this region was happening by the beginning of the second millennium BC.

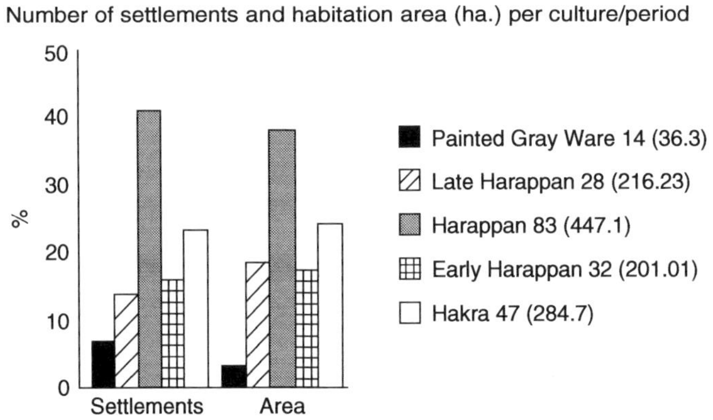

Figure 3.1 Cholistan.

This site habitation history is outlined in Figure 3.2 and supports the interpretation just stated, a significant, major, population decline was evidenced in the Cholistan region by the beginning of the second millennium BC. Together, the number of Early Harappan and Hakran sites occupied equals the number of Harappan sites occupied (Shaffer and Lichtenstein 1999). If Mughal's chronology is correct, with Hakra predating the Early Harappan, then 40 percent of known sites are described as changed in habitation status. That is, they either were abandoned or were inhabited for the first time between the Hakran and Early Harappan cultural developments. Some 57 percent of the sites changed their habitation status between the Early Harappan and Harappan. However one evaluates Mughal's description of cultural development, habitation changes occur during the Late Harappan, with the total number of settlements declining by 66 percent. Of these, 54 percent exhibit a change in their occupation status, with 96 percent of them being newly established settlements. By the first millennium BC, that is, Painted Gray Ware culture, the total number of habitation settlements declines by another 50 percent, or, in comparison with Harappan, the total number of habitation sites declines by 83 percent. Significantly, *all* these new habitation settlements were in the dry Ghaggar-Hakra River channel. Between the Harappan and Late Harappan periods, the Cholistan region was being abandoned as the cultural response to the "crisis" of the river changes described earlier.

Given the rarity of Painted Gray Ware sites in the Indus Valley proper, and their exclusive location in a dry river channel, these first millennium BC settlements may represent a very small backward population shift. Only five small Early Historic period habitation settlements were recorded and they were new settlements. This region was significantly reoccupied during the Medieval period. Thus, it is clear that this region was extensively, but not completely, abandoned during the second millennium BC.

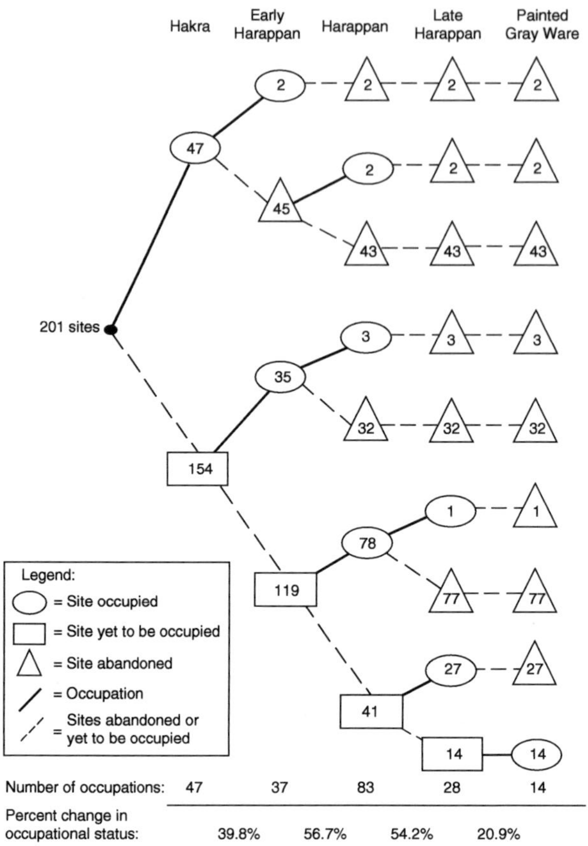

Figure 3.2 Cholistan.

Eastern Punjab

The eastern Punjab designation used here incorporates the modern Indian states of the Punjab, northern Rajasthan, Haryana, Delhi Territory, and the western districts of Uttar Pradesh. The most detailed published accounts of archaeological research (Joshi *et al.* 1984) organize the data into three cultural/chronological categories: Early Harappan, Harappan, and Late Harappan. As used to interpret the site survey data, the authors' category of Early Harappan corresponds to Mughal's Hakra and Early Harappan (previously Kot Dijian) cultures and to what has been referred to as Sothi and early Siswal in the Indian literature. Also, with regard to the designation of cultural categories, some, but not all, of the "Early Harappan" occupations of the eastern Punjab were contemporary with the Harappan and with, perhaps, even the Late Harappan occupation sites found throughout the

Harappan culture area. It is important again to note that these archaeological surveys essentially recorded only habitation sites.

The number of designated Early Harappan and Harappan occupations in the eastern Punjab are almost the same, with only 24 percent of the potentially inhabitable settlements changing their occupation status (Figure 3.3). However, the settlement dynamics of the Harappan and Late Harappan are significantly different. The number of occupied settlements increases by 304 percent, of which 82.5 percent are newly occupied settlements, whereas 80 percent of habitation settlements change their occupation status. Despite limitations of archaeological data, with the abandonment of habitation sites recorded for the Cholistan region and the magnitude of increase of new occupied settlements in the eastern Punjab, a significant population influx into the eastern Punjab occurred between the Harappan and Late Harappan cultural periods (see also Possehl 1997a,b, 2002; Shaffer and Lichtenstein 1999).

Central Haryana

The central Haryana data (Bhan 1975, and pers. comm.; Bhan and Shaffer 1978; Shaffer 1981, 1986; Shaffer and Lichtenstein 1989, 1995, 1999) are incorporated

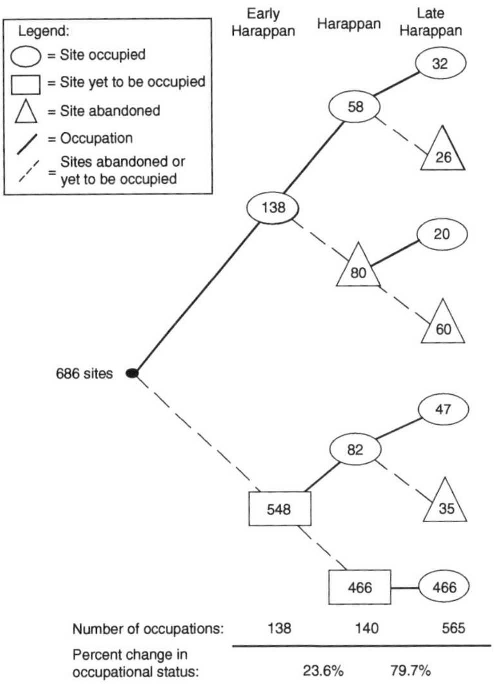

Figure 3.3 Eastern Punjab.

within those for the eastern Punjab presented earlier. However, this central Haryana data includes the Painted Gray Ware and Early Historic culture complexes (Figure 3.4). It is considered separately here now to focus on the occupation settlement changes in this area. The number of Early Harappan and Harappan habitation settlements are essentially the same, with only 1 percent of the sites changing habitation status. Between the Harappan and Late Harappan, however, there is a 98 percent increase in the number of habitation sites, with 63 percent changing their occupation status. Although there is a 15 percent decline in the number of sites between the Late Harappan and Painted Gray culture periods, there is still considerable settlement mobility, since 82 percent of sites change occupation status. The Early Historic culture period yields another 20 percent decline in the number of occupied sites, with 41 percent changing their occupation status. However, *no new settlements are established*. Although a degree of

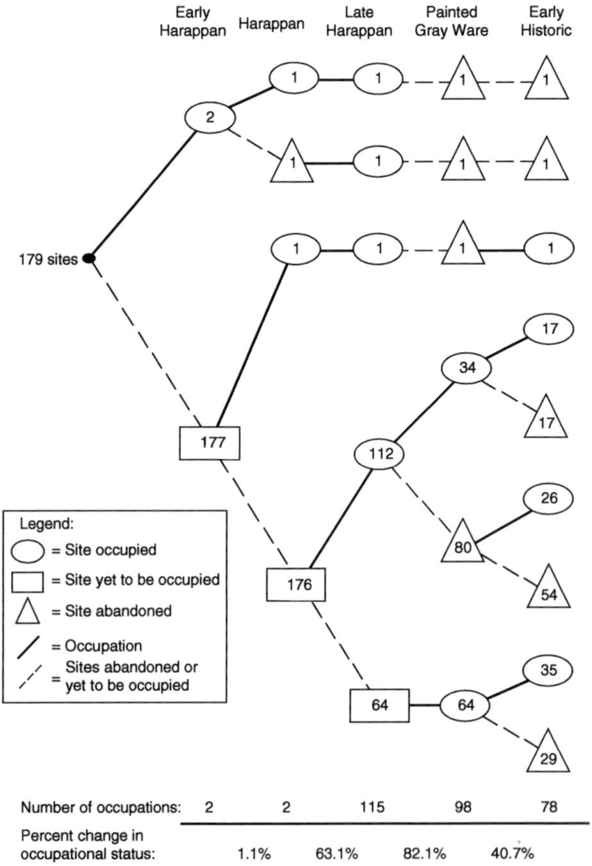

Figure 3.4 Central Haryana.

settlement mobility continues into the Early Historic context, there was more cultural occupation site stability by that time, perhaps reflecting the emergence of the first South Asian states in the Ganga Valley.

Sindh

Presently, the most comprehensive archaeological survey data have been compiled by Flam (1981, 1993, 1999; see also Possehl 1999b). However, these data focus on the Early-to-Mature Harappan cultural relationships. The Late Harappan cultural period may be underrepresented in the survey data. Nonetheless, the settlement pattern dynamics (Figure 3.5) are very similar to those in Cholistan. The number of Early Harappan and Harappan habitation sites occupied are comparable in number, with 68 percent changing occupation status. In the Late Harappan, there is an 89 percent decline in the number of habitation settlements, with 65 percent changing their occupation status and no new sites are established. Like Cholistan, the Sindh region reveals a significant population decline, probably for similar geological and ecological reasons.

Gujarat

After the publication of the archaeological survey data used here (Joshi *et al.* 1984), excavations have identified a few Early Harappan occupations. Still, with the

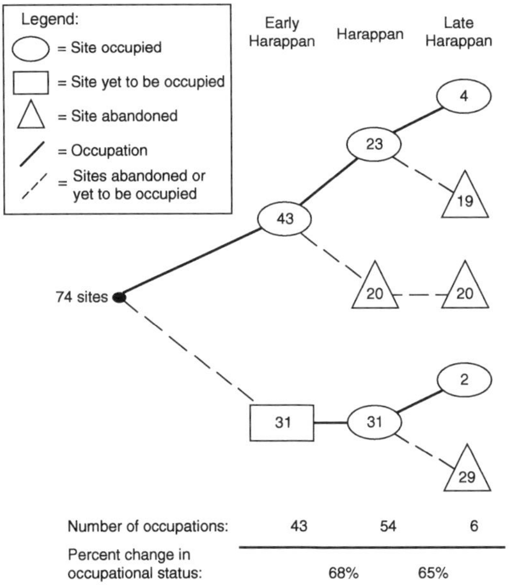

Figure 3.5 Sindh.

intensity of the surveys conducted, it is reasonable to conclude that Early Harappan settlements in this region are rare. Available survey data (Figure 3.6) indicate a significant population shift during the Harappan period, with almost 46 percent of the total inhabited settlements being established. Between the Harappan and Late Harappan culture periods, 96 percent of the settlements change occupation status, with 93 percent being new settlements. In Gujarat then, as in the eastern Punjab, there was a considerable settlement status change.

Bhagwanpura

It should be noted that archaeological excavations at Bhagwanpura (Joshi 1993), and at a few other sites, have defined a stratigraphic chronology linking the Late Harappan and Painted Gray Ware culture periods. No chronological gap separates these culture periods (Shaffer 1993; Shaffer and Lichtenstein 1995, 1999), but the precise nature of the cultural relationships indicated by the data remains to be determined in future archaeological excavations. The Painted Gray Ware complex (Tripathi 1976; Roy 1983; Gaur 1994) is an Early Iron Age culture and a direct predecessor to the historic Northern Black Polished Ware culture of the Early Historic period. Given the meticulous archaeological efforts to identify culture patterns for the geographic areas described, and with the relative and radiometric chronologies established for the archaeological record, it seems that there is no "Vedic night" (Fairservis 1975) separating the prehistoric/protohistoric from the early historic periods of South Asian culture history. Rather, these data reinforce what the site of Mehrgarh so clearly establishes, an indigenous cultural continuity in South Asia of several millennia.

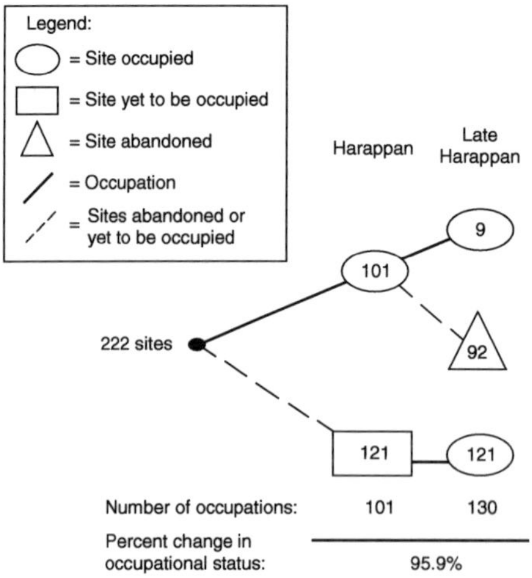

Figure 3.6 Gujarat.

3.7 Conclusions

The modern archaeological record for South Asia indicates a history of significant cultural continuity; an intrepretation at variance with earlier eighteenth through twentieth-century scholarly views of South Asian cultural discontinuity and South Asian cultural dependence on Western culture influences (but see Allchin and Allchin 1982; Allchin 1995). We have already noted that the scholarly paradigm of the eighteenth and nineteenth centuries in conflating language, culture, race, and population movements has continued, with historical linguistic scholars still assiduously attempting to reconstruct a Proto-Indo-European language and attempting to link that language to a specific "homeland," in order to define population migration away from that seminal geographic base (but see Poliakov 1974). Suggestions for such a Proto-Indo-European homeland range from Siberia to more recent efforts tracing the "homeland" to Anatolia (Renfrew 1987) and the Ukraine (Gamkrelidze and Ivanov 1985a,b; Gimbutas 1985; Mallory 1989; Allchin 1995), and these efforts now incorporate human genetic studies (Cavalli-Sforza *et al.* 1994) to verify the linguistic chronologies.[7] The current archaeological and paleoanthropological data simply do not support these centuries old interpretative paradigms suggesting Western, intrusive, cultural influence as responsible for the supposed major discontinuities in the South Asian cultural prehistoric record (Shaffer and Lichtenstein 1999; Kennedy 2000; Lamberg-Karlovsky 2002). The image of Indo-Aryans as nomadic, conquering warriors, driving chariots, may have been a vision that Europeans had, and continue to have, of their own assumed "noble" past. If Indo-Aryans ever existed, and we do dispute their existence as identified in the scholarly literature to date, they are much more likely to have been "... impoverished cowboys in ponderous ox-carts seeking richer pasture ..." (Kohl 2002: 78). It is currently possible to discern cultural continuities linking specific prehistoric social entities in South Asia into one cultural tradition (Shaffer and Lichtenstein 1989, 1995, 1999; Shaffer 1992, 1993). This is *not* to propose social isolation *nor* deny any outside cultural influence. Outside cultural influences did affect South Asian cultural development in later, especially historic, periods, but an identifiable cultural tradition has continued, an Indo-Gangetic Cultural Tradition (Shaffer 1993; Shaffer and Lichtenstein 1995, 1999) linking social entities over a time period from the development of food production in the seventh millennium BC to the present.

The archaeological record and ancient oral and literate traditions of South Asia are now converging with significant implications for South Asian cultural history. Some scholars suggest there is nothing in the "literature" firmly locating Indo-Aryans, the generally perceived founders of modern South Asian cultural tradition(s) outside of South Asia (see Erdosy 1988, 1989, 1995a,b), and the archaeological record is now confirming this (Shaffer and Lichtenstein 1999). Within the chronology of the archaeological data for South Asia describing cultural continuity (Shaffer and Lichtenstein 1989, 1995, 1999; Shaffer 1992, 1993), however, a significant *indigenous discontinuity* occurs, but it is one correlated to significant geological and environmental changes in the prehistoric period. This indigenous discontinuity was a regional population shift from the Indus Valley area to locations east, that is, Gangetic Valley, and to the southeast, that is, Gujarat and beyond. Such an indigenous population movement can be recorded in the ancient oral Vedic traditions as perhaps "the" migration so focused upon in the linguistic reconstructions of a prehistoric chronology for South Asia.[8] As archaeological data accumulate which refute earlier interpretations of South Asian cultural prehistory as due to Western influences, it is surprising to see the same scholarly paradigm used for describing another geographic area's culture history. The example in mind is of Mallory and Mair's (2000) interpretation of the Tarim mummies as an Indo-Aryan, Western, intrusion, despite the fact that the burials correspond to the pattern of Pazyryk burials to the northeast (Polosmak and Molohdin 2000 – there are other relevant articles in this journal issue). We reemphasize our earlier views, namely that scholars engaged in South Asian studies must describe emerging South Asia data objectively rather than perpetuate interpretations, now more than two centuries old, without regard to the data archaeologists have worked so hard to reveal (Shaffer and Lichtenstein 1999).[9]

Notes

1 The concept of "race" in its biological deterministic sense has been a negatively powerful, at times horrific, tool for asserting immutable identities of specific human groups. Such "race" identities, in their continued common use are measured on primarily visible human physical differences. Beyond the mere correlation of human physical, visible, variations with specific group identities, the concept of "race" implies a ranking, with perceived visible identities ranged on a gradual ascending scale. In the eighteenth and early nineteenth centuries, European ethnological discussion had not turned fully to a use of "race" in a biological deterministic sense of causality. Instead, European philological studies stressed commonality of group identity achieved through shared language, with "race" used to reinforce the notion of group identity in a way that is now done with the term ethnicity (e.g. Trautmann 1997; and see Shanklin 1994; Shipman 1994).

2 In the European scholarship of the eighteenth and nineteenth centuries, with a focus on recognizing Indo-European connections, a coupling of language and "race" asserted an inclusionary geneological kinship for diverse populations. However, against the backdrop of European world conquest and colonial rule of the day, as nineteenth-century European scholars addressed issues of species variation and natural selection, courtesy of the biological sciences, the "concept" of race did acquire more biological deterministic qualities. In his very excellent discussion of the British Sanskrit scholars, and other philological scholars of the period, Trautmann (1997, 1999) notes that the linked language/ "race" identity of inclusionary status shared by certain populations was replaced by a bolder imperative of exclusionary status, identified by visible human physical differences. Aryan by complexion, versus Aryan by language, was to suggest the true "white man's burden" of nation-building within imperial rule.

For the British Sanskritists, to handle the competing identity claims of "language," with its inclusionary notion of commonality shared by Europeans and Indians of the subcontinent, and of "complexion," with its more deterministic, exclusionary view of distinct identities for these groups, the scholarly synthesis became what Trautmann describes as the "...racial theory of Indian civilization. This is the theory that Indian civilization was formed by a big bang, caused by the conquest of light-skinned, Aryan, civilized invaders over dark-skinned savage aboriginal Indians, and the formation of the caste system which bound the two in a single society, at once mixed and segregated" (1999: 287). Trautmann notes that in the racial reading of the ancient texts, "... the image of the dark-skinned savage is only imposed on the Vedic evidence with a considerable amount of text-torturing, both 'substantive' and 'adjectival' in character" (1997: 208). His further admonition concerning the flimsy foundation of this "racial" interpretation of Indian civilization is succinct; "That the racial theory of Indian civilization has survived so long and so well is a miracle of faith. It is high time to get rid of it" (1999: 290; cf. Leach 1990: *passim*).

3 That the Nazi Reich existed only a few decades ago, about a two-generation time depth, is noted by both Olender, "We shall remember the immense importance the Nazi Reich – occupying Europe barely 50 years ago – assigned to the ideas of the purity of the Aryan language, race and nation..." (1997: 55) and Leach, when, in reference to the "myth of Aryan invasions," he describes the hold the idea has for his fellow country-men "... even today, 44 years after the death of Hitler..." (1990: 243). If, in Leach's words, it is the use of the remembered past that defines "what we are now" (1990: 227), scholarship that picks and chooses its preferred histories risks the criticism of elaborating just-so stories (cf. Anderson 1991).

Trautmann's summary remarks on aspects of eighteenth- and nineteenth-century South Asian historiography are valuable here also. Having so deftly demonstrated the contingent way in which many scholars of this period used the South Asian data to establish specific congruences of identity via language, "race," culture, nation, which are framed mostly as polar opposites, he calls for a scholarship that is far more pluralistic in its perspectives and "... one that stresses continuities with the deeper past in the formation of modernity and downplays discontinuities" (1997: 223). As he notes, "... the political consequences of the Aryan or Indo-European idea do not reside within the idea itself as a kind of hidden virus or all-determining genetic code but vary with circumstance and are the creatures of historical conjuncture and human purpose" (1997: 228).

4 Africa is another immensely important geographic area receiving the intense focus of the paleoanthropologist, archaeologist, historian, linguist, and geneticist in an effort to describe its prehistory and more recent past. It is noteworthy that group/population identities and cultural chronologies described for Africa's prehistory and for the present-day (now "ethnic" identity) via history and archaeology are almost as contentious as in the case of the South Asian data. Vansina (1995), historian, and Robertshaw (1999), archaeologist, summarize some concerns over epistemological goals, methods, and descriptive results in their respective, and each other's, disciplines. The difficulties of relying on genetic research to help inform issues of African population history and prehistory are reviewed in MacEachern (2000). We note too that the dangers of human conflict couched in the framework of present-day ethnic identities are no less substantive and horrific than earlier human conflicts defined as "racial" (see de Waal 1994 and Maybury-Lewis 1997: 99–107 for a case in point).

5 A discussion on present-day language shift in the Hatay province of Turkey offers insight into the process of human identity achieved via specific language use, politics and religion (Smith 2001: 36–9). Additional discussion of language maintenance and change and an assessment of modern linguistics' efforts at language reconstruction are found in Dixon (1997).

6 Fauna remains are a crucial archaeological data set. It would be useful to have more complete faunal data from South Asian Early Historic sites, but it is possible to note that the large number of cattle documented in the greater Indus Valley prehistoric sites of the third millennium BC possibly diminish in economic emphasis as population groups inhabit the Gangetic Plain, Gujarat, and the eastern Punjab in the first millennium BC. An increasingly agricultural and land tenure-based economy within the constraints of a new physical

environment may have meant a diminished focus on cattle's economic aspect while, nonetheless, cattle's symbolic value was maintained (see Shaffer 1993 for discussion).

7 The Gladstone bag of "race science" that meshed with nineteenth-century European philological studies to interpret human differences has become, in the twentieth and twenty-first centuries, a very large steamer trunk of modern genetic essentialism which, with impressive irony, must still resort to the older philological linguistic typologies to impose an order on newer genetic data now available (Cavalli-Sforza *et al.* 1994). Cavalli-Sforza *et al.* (1994: 80) claim that they give no "racial" meaning to the named population classifications derived from their studies using modern analytical concepts and methods of human population genetics. Their goal is impressive – a single compelling narrative detailing bio-historical origins and human relationships derived from genetic data. However, a strong claim of authority by the modern science of genetics to address fundamental issues of identity and descent, "to tell people who they really are" is noticeably similar to earlier "racial histories of man" (Marks 2001: *passim*; 2002a: *passim*). As Marks (2001: 361) notes, "... irreconcilable tensions ..." within genetic analysis itself and "... unrealistic assumption about human population histories ..." are subsumed in presentation as dichotomous (bifurcating) tree diagrams representing evolutionary genetic-cum-linguistic descent. One critic notes that, "Dichotomous tree diagrams may not be the most appropriate models for describing either the genetic or the linguistic histories of large proportions of the world's current and former populations" (Armstrong 1990: 13). The same critic suggests that "... anastomoses of linguistics stocks call into question the application of tree diagrams to linguistic diversification (The same can equally be said of genetically defined populations.)" (Armstrong 1990: 14). Focusing on human biological history, Marks (2001: 360, 2002a: *passim*) assesses the difficulties of tree construction subsuming an array of complex data. When population isolation and less genetic admixture is posited, a reticulating evolution is simplified into a bifurcating one. Cavalli-Sforza *et al.* acknowledge the implicit bias in their work:

> The presence of mixed populations in standard tree reconstruction may sometimes alter the shape of the reconstructed tree. It is therefore good practice to try reconstruction with and without populations suspected of admixture, or to avoid including them. The full analysis of reticulate evolution remains an important task for the future.
>
> (1994: 59)

The issues of how social-cultural groups are constructed and constituted through time, the role of heredity in establishing self-identity in the biological and social realms, the use of genealogies to determine "who we really are" (Marks 2001: 377), all these modern genetic studies may address. In constructing its authoritative approach, however, population genetics' value is diminished when it is presented within a framework of archaic language and loaded assumptions of human differences (Marks 2001: 370). We note too that genetic research, presently, has no claim to any precision of chronometric dating comparable to that used by archaeology. The same is true of linguistics. The controversies created by the linking of modern population genetics and linguistics, and some of the controversial uses of modern population genetics in the goal of establishing a single bio-history of humankind, are considered in Bateman *et al.* (1990), Shipman (1994), Mirza and Dungworth (1995), Pluciennik (1995), Evison (1996), Fix (1996), Clark (1998), Sims-Williams (1998), Brown and Pluciennik (2001), MacEachern (2000), and Marks (2000a,b, 2001, 2002a,b). It is notable that geneticists working on such a large-scale synthesis of human prehistory and history pay more attention to correlating their data with linguistic rather than archaeological data. While genetics may be considered by some a possible "third arbiter" to resolve issues of relationship between archaeological culture and language (Lamberg-Karlovsky 2002: 75), for the moment, we are more skeptical.

8 The linguistic designation of a category of "Indo-European/Aryan" languages is not the question here. However, the historical, and prevailing, use of the language designation is the issue. For two centuries, scholars concentrating on the South Asian data have described an Indo-European/Aryan migration/invasion into South Asia to explain the formation of Indian civilization. The conflating of language, people/culture, "race" to maintain the "myth of the Aryan invasion" continues, perhaps, as Leach (1990: 237) so cogently notes, due to the academic prestige at stake. The distinguished scholar Colin Renfrew (1987) opts to distort the archaeological record rather than to challenge it. Failing to identify archaeological evidence for such a migration in the European post-Neolithic periods, Renfrew argues instead for an Indo-European/Aryan human migration associated with the spread of food production economies from Anatolia. In doing so, he ignores critical archaeological data from Southwest Asia (Lamberg-Karlovsky 1988) and South Asia (Shaffer 1990). The South Asian archaeological data reviewed here does not support Renfrew's position nor any version of the migration/invasion hypothesis describing western population movement into South Asia. Rather, the physical distribution of prehistoric sites and artifacts, stratigraphic data, radiometric dates, and geological data describing the prehistoric/proto-historic environment perhaps can account, in some degree, for the Vedic oral tradition describing a cultural discontinuity of what was an indigenous population movement in the Indo-Gangetic region.

9 Over one hundred years ago, in a review of William Z. Ripley's publication *The Races of Europe*, Franz Boas called for the conceptual separation of biology (i.e. racial type) from culture (i.e. ethnography/history) and from language. In his words, "The misconception of what constitutes a racial type, a cultural group and a linguistic stock has caused a vast amount of futile speculation" (1899, reprinted in 1940: 159). He elaborated this viewpoint in more detail in his 1911 publication, *The Mind of Primitive Man.*

> It is obvious, therefore, that attempts to classify mankind, based on the present distribution of type, language and culture, must lead to different results, according to the point of view taken; that a classification based primarily on type alone will lead to a system which represents more or less accurately the blood-relationships of the people; but these do not need to coincide with their cultural relationships. In the same way classifications based on language and culture do not need to coincide with a biological classification.
>
> (1911, reprinted 1965: 142)

Recognizing that the characteristics commonly used to construct individual and group identity which establishes presumed type/class "...is never more than an abstraction hardly ever realized in a single individual," Boas observes that even those efforts to assign human differences to a type/class are "...often not even a result of observation, but an often heard tradition that determines our judgment" (1911, reprinted 1965: 241–2).

Eloquently, in his closing paragraph, Boas reminds us that in having no preconceived estimate of an individual's ability and character, we obtain a freedom of judgment. "Then we shall treasure and cultivate the variety of forms that human thought and activity has taken, and abhor, as leading to complete stagnation, all attempts to impress one pattern of thought upon whole nations or even upon the whole world" (1911, reprinted 1965: 242).

While Boas was thus remarking on the negative consequences of preconceived constructs of human and group identity which specify a causal relationship between thought and accomplishment, we suggest that some of his views can be extended to the epistemology and analytical methods used to construct preconceived accounts of South Asian prehistory and history. Such efforts still rely on interpretative paradigms established in western European scholarship of the eighteenth and nineteenth centuries. In the end, such preconceived accounts of South Asian prehistory and history lead to a complete stagnation of interpretation. Scholars exercising a "freedom of judgment" cannot ignore new archaeological data pertaining to South Asia's prehistory and history.

Bibliography

Adams, W. Y., D. P. Van Gerven, and R. S. Levy, 1978. "The Retreat from Migrationism," *Annual Review of Anthropology*, 7: 483–532.
Agrawal, D. P., 1982. *The Archaeology of India*. London: Curzon Press.
Allchin, B. and F. R. Allchin, 1982. *The Rise of Civilization in India and Pakistan*. London: Cambridge University Press.
Allchin, F. R., 1984. "The Northern Limits of the Harappan Culture Zone." In *Frontiers of the Indus Civilization*, edited by B. B. Lal and S. P. Gupta. New Delhi: Books and Books, pp. 51–4.
——, 1995. *The Archaeology of Early Historic South Asia: The Emergence of Cities and States*. Cambridge: Cambridge University Press.
Anderson, B., 1991. *Imagined Communities*. New York: Verso.
Armstrong, D., 1990. "Comments on Speaking of Forked Tongues: The Feasibility of Reconciling Human Phylogeny and the History of Language," *Current Anthropology*, 31(1): 13–14.
Bateman, R., I. Goddard, R. O'Grady, V. A. Funk, R. Mooi, W. J. Kress, and P. Cannell, 1990. "Speaking of Forked Tongues: The Feasibility of Reconciling Human Phylogeny and the History of Language," *Current Anthropology*, 31(1): 1–24.
Bernal, M., 1987. *Black Athena*, Vol I. New Brunswick, NJ: Rutgers University Press.
Bhan, S., 1975. *Excavations at Mitathal (1968) and Other Explorations in the Sutlej–Yamuna Divide*. Kurukshetra: Kurukshetra University Press.
Bhan, S. and Jim G. Shaffer, 1978. "New Discoveries in Northern Haryana," *Man and Environment*, 2: 59–68.
Bhatia, S. B. and N. Singh, 1988. "Middle Holocene Palaeoclimatic and Palaeo-Environmental Events in Southern Harayana." In *Palaeoclimatic and Oalaeoenvironmental Changes in Asia: During the Last 4 Million Years*, edited by D. P. Agrawal, P. Sharma, and S. K. Gupta. New Delhi: Indian National Science Academy, pp. 236–46.
Boas, F., 1899, 1940 [1966]. *Race, Language and Culture.* New York: The Free Press.
——, 1911 [1965]. *The Mind of Primitive Man*, revised edition. New York: The Free Press.
Bowler, P., 1989. *The Invention of Progress: The Victorians and the Past*. Oxford: Basil Blackwell.
Bradley, D. G., D. E. MacHugh, P. Cunningham, and R. T. Loftus, 1996. "Mitochondrial Diversity and the Origins of African European Cattle," *Proceedings of the National Academy of Science (USA)*, 93: 5131–5.
Brown, K. and M. Pluciennik, 2001. "Archaeology and Human Genetics: Lessons for Both," *Antiquity*, 75: 101–6.
Bryant, E., 2001. *The Quest for Origins of Vedic Culture: The Indo-Aryan Migration Debate*. New York: Oxford University Press.
Bryson, R. A. and A. M. Swain, 1981. "Holocene Variations of Monsoon Rainfall in Rajasthan," *Quarterly Research*, 16: 135–45.
Cavalli-Sforza, L., P. Menozzi, and A. Piazza, 1994. *The History and Geography of Human Genes*. Princeton, NJ: Princeton University Press.
Chakrabarti, D. K., 1982. "The Development of Archaeology in the Indian Subcontinent," *World Archaeology*, 13: 326–44.
——, 1990. *The External Trade of the Indus Civilization*. New Delhi: Munshiram Manoharlal Publishers.

Childe, V. G., 1934. *New Light on the Most Ancient East: The Oriental Prelude to European History*. London: Kegan Paul.

——, 1953. *New Light on the Most Ancient East*. New York: W. W. Norton.

Clark, G., 1966. "The Invasion Hypothesis in British Archaeology," *Antiquity*, 40: 172–89.

——, 1979. *Sir Mortimer and Indian Archaeology*. New Delhi: Archaeological Survey of India.

——, 1998. "Multivariate Pattern Searches, the Logic of Inference, and European Prehistory: A Comment on Cavalli-Sforza," *Journal of Anthropological Research*, 54: 406–11.

Cohn, B. S., 1996. *Colonialism and Its Forms of Knowledge: The British in India*. Princeton, NJ: Princeton University Press.

Deotare, B. C. and M. D. Kajale, 1996. "Quaternary Pollen Analysis and Palaeoenvironmental Studies of the Salt Basins at Panchpadra and Thob, Western Rajasthan, India: Preliminary Observations," *Man and Environment*, 21: 24–31.

de Waal, A., 1994. "Genocide in Rwanda," *Anthropology Today*, 10(3): 1–2.

Dhavalikar, M. K., 1988. *The First Farmers of the Deccan*. Pune: Ravish Publishers.

Dikotter, F., 1992. *The Discourse of Race in Modern China*. Stanford, CA: Stanford University Press.

Dixon, R. M. W., 1997. *The Rise and Fall of Languages*. Cambridge: Cambridge University Press.

Ehret, C., 1988. "Language Change and the Material Correlates of Language and Ethnic Shift," *Antiquity*, 62: 564–74.

Erdosy, G., 1988. *Urbanization in Early Historic India*. Bar International Series No. 430. Oxford: British Archaeological Reports.

——, 1989. "Ethnicity in the Rigveda and its bearing on the Question of Indo-European Origins," *South Asian Studies*, 5: 35–47.

——, 1995a. "Language, Material Culture and Ethnicity: Theoretical Perspectives." In *The Indo-Aryans of Ancient South Asia: Language, Material Culture and Ethnicity*, edited by G. Erdosy. Berlin: Walter de Gruyter, pp. 1–31.

——, 1995b. "The Prelude to Urbanization: Ethnicity and the Rise of Late Vedic Chiefdoms." *The Archaeology of Early South Asia*, edited by F. R. Allchin. Cambridge: Cambridge University Press, pp. 75–98.

Evison, M., 1996. "Genetics, Ethics and Archaeology," *Antiquity*, 70: 512–14.

Fairservis, W. A., 1975. *The Roots of Ancient India*, 2nd edition. Chicago, IL: University of Chicago Press.

Fix, A. G., 1996. "Gene Frequency Clines in Europe: Demic Diffusion or Natural Selection," *Journal of the Royal Anthropological Institute* (n.s.), 2: 625–43.

Flam, L., 1981. "The Palaeogeography and Prehistoric Settlement Patterns in Sind, Pakistan (*ca.*4000–2000 B.C.)," PhD dissertation, South Asia Regional Studies. University of Pennsylvania, PA.

——, 1993. "Fluvial Geomorphology of the Lower Indus Basin (Sindh, Pakistan) and the Indus Civilization." In *Himalaya to the Sea*, edited by J. F. Schroder. New York: Routledge, pp. 265–326.

——, 1999. "Ecology and Population Mobility in the Prehistoric Settlement of the Lower Indus Valley, Sindh, Pakistan." In *The Indus River: Biodiversity-Resources-Humankind*, edited by A. Meadows and P. Meadows. Oxford: Oxford University Press, pp. 313–23.

Franklin, M. J. (ed.), 1995. *Sir William Jones: Selected Poetical and Prose Works*. Cardiff: University of Wales Press.

Gamkrelidze, T. and V. V. Ivanov, 1985a. "The Ancient Near East and the Indo-European Question: Temporal and Territorial Characteristics of Proto-Indo-European Based On Linguistic and Historical-Cultural Data," *Journal of Indo-European Studies*, 13: 3–48.

——, 1985b. "The Migrations of Tribes Speaking the Indo-European Dialects from their Original Homeland in the Near East to their Historical Habitations in Eurasia," *Journal of Indo-European Studies*, 13: 49–91.

Gaur, R. C., ed., 1994. *Painted Grey Ware*. Jaipur: Publication Scheme.

Gimbutas, M., 1985. "Primary and Secondary Homeland of the Indo-Europeans," *Journal of Indo-European Studies*, 13: 185–202.

Harrell, S., 1995. *Cultural Encounters on China's Ethnic Frontiers*. Seattle, WA: University of Washington Press.

Inden, R., 1986. "Orientalist Construction of India," *Modern Asian Studies*, 20: 401–46.

——, 1990. *Imagining India*. Oxford: Basil Blackwell.

Jansen, M., L. Maire, and G. Urban, eds, 1991. *Forgotten Cities on the Indus: Early Civilization in Pakistan from the 8th to 2nd Millennium BC*. Mainz: Verlag Phillip Von Zabern.

Jarrige, C., J. F. Jarrige, R. Meadow, and G. Quivron, eds, 1995. *Mehrgarh: Field Reports 1974–1985 – From Neolithic Times to the Indus Civilization*. Karachi: Department of Culture and Tourism, Government of Sindh, Pakistan.

Jones, S., 1997. *The Archaeology of Ethnicity: Constructing Identities in the Past and Present*. London: Routledge.

Joshi, J. P., 1993. *Excavations at Bhagwanpura 1975–1976 and Other Explorations and Excavations 1975–81 in Haryana, Jammu and Kasmir, and Punjab*. Memoirs of the Archaeological Survey of India No. 89. New Delhi: Archaeological Survey of India.

Joshi, J. P., M. Bala, and J. Ram, 1984. "The Indus Civilization: Reconsidering on the Basis of Distribution Maps." In *Frontiers of the Indus Civilization*, edited by B. B. Lal and S. P. Gupta. New Delhi: Books and Books, pp. 511–31.

Kennedy, K. A. R., 2000. *God-Apes and Fossil Men: Paleoanthropology in South Asia*. Ann Arbor, MI: University of Michigan Press.

Kenoyer, J. M., 1991. "The Indus Valley Tradition of Pakistan and Western India," *Journal of World Prehistory*, 5: 1–64.

——, 1998. *Ancient Cities of the Indus Valley Civilization*. Karachi: Oxford University Press.

Kohl, P. L., 2002. " 'Comment on Archaeology and Language: The Indo-Iranians' by C.C. Lamberg-Karlovsky," *Current Anthropology*, 43: 77–8.

Lal, B. B., 1997. *The Earliest Civilization of South Asia*. New Delhi: Aryan Books International.

Lamberg-Karlovsky, C. C., 1988. "Indo-Europeans: A Near-Eastern Perspective," *Quarterly Review of Archaeology*, 9: 1, 8–10.

——, 2002. "Archaeology and Language: The Indo-Iranians," *Current Anthropology*, 43: 63–88.

Leach, E., 1990. "Aryan Invasions Over Four Millennia." In *Culture Through Time: Anthropological Approaches*, edited by E. Ohnuki-Tierney. Stanford, CA: Stanford: University Press.

Loftus, Ronan, T., David E. MacHugh, Daniel G. Bradley, and Paul M. Sharp, 1994. "Evidence for Two Independent Domestications of Cattle," *Proceedings of the National Academy of Science (USA)*, 91: 2757–61.

MacEachern, S., 2000. "Genes, Tribes, and African History," *Current Anthropology*, 41(3): 357–84.

Mackay, E. J. H., 1938. *Further Excavations at Mohenjo-daro, Being an Official Account of Archaeological Excavations Carried out by the Government of India between the Years of 1927–1931*. Vol. 1. New Delhi: Government Press.
Majumdar, N. G., 1934. "Explorations in Sind," *Memoirs of the Archaeological Survey of India*, No. 48. Delhi.
Mallory, J. P., 1989. *In Search of the Indo-Europeans: Language, Archaeology, and Myth*. London: Thames and Hudson.
Mallory, J. P. and Victor H. Mair, 2000. "The Tarim Mummies: Ancient China and the Mystery of the Earliest Peoples From the West." London: Thames and Hudson.
Marks, J., 2000a. "Heredity and Genetics After the Holocaust." In *Humanity at the Limit: The Impact of the Holocaust on Jews and Christians*, edited by M. A. Singer. Bloomington, IN: Indiana University Press, pp. 241–9.
——, 2000b. "Can a Holistic Anthropology Inform a Reductive Genetics?" Paper presented at the 99th meeting of the Annual Meeting of the American Anthropological Association, 16 November 2000, San Francisco, CA.
——, 2001. " 'We're Going to Tell These People Who They Really Are': Science and Relatedness." In *Relative Values: Reconfiguring Kinship Studies*, edited by S. Franklin and S. McKinnon. Chapel Hill, NC: Duke University Press, pp. 355–83.
——, 2002a. "Contemporary Bio-Anthropology: Where the Trailing Edge of Anthropology Meets the Leading Edge of Bioethics," *Anthropology Today*, 18(4): 3–7.
——, 2002b. "What is Molecular Anthropology? What can it be?," *Evolutionary Anthropology*, 11: 131–5.
Marshall, J., 1931. *Mohenjo-daro and the Indus Civilization, Being an Official Account of Archaeological Excavations at Mohenjo-daro Carried out by the Government of India between the Years 1922 and 1927*. 3 Vols. London: Arthur Probsthain.
Maybury-Lewis, D., 1997. *Indigenous Peoples, Ethnic Groups and the State*. Boston, MA: Allyn and Bacon.
Mirza, M. N. and D. B. Dungworth, 1995. "The Potential Misuse of Genetic Analyses and the Social Construction of 'Race' and 'Ethnicity'," *Oxford Journal of Archaeology*, 14(3): 345–54.
Misra, V. N., 1984. "Climate, a Factor in the Rise and Fall of the Indus Civilization." In *Frontiers of the Indus Civilization*, edited by B. B. Lal and S. P. Gupta. Delhi: Books and Books, pp. 461–9.
Mughal, R. M., 1970. "The Early Harappan Period in the Greater Indus Valley and Northern Baluchistan (*c*.3000–2400 B.C.)," PhD dissertation, Department of Anthropology, University of Pennsylvania, PA.
——, 1973. *Present State of Research on the Indus River Valley Civilization*. Department of Archaeology and Museums. Karachi: Government of Pakistan.
——, 1990. "Harappan Settlement Systems and Patterns in the Greater Indus Valley," *Pakistan Archaeology*, 25: 1–72.
——, 1997. *Ancient Cholistan: Archaeology and Architecture*. Karachi: Ferozsons (Pvt.) Ltd.
Mukherjee, S. N., 1987. *Sir William Jones: A Study in Eighteenth-Century British Attitudes to India*, 2nd edition. Hyderabad: Orient Longman Ltd.
Olender, M., 1992. *The Languages of Paradise: Race, Religion and Philology in the Nineteenth Century*. Cambridge, MA: Harvard University Press.
——, 1997. "From the Language of Adam to the Pluralism of Babel," *Mediterranean Historical Review*, 12(2): 51–9.

Olson, S., 2002. *Mapping Human History: Discovering the Past Through Our Genes.* Boston, MA: Houghton Mifflin Company.

Piggott, S., 1950. *Prehistoric India.* Middlesex: Penguin Books.

Pluciennik, M., 1995. "Genetics, Archaeology and the Wider World," *Antiquity*, 70: 13–14.

Poliakov, L., 1974. *The Aryan Myth: A History of Racist and Nationalist Ideas in Europe.* New York: Basic Books.

Polosmak, N. V. and V. I. Molohdin, 2000. "Grave Sites of the Pazyryk Culture on the Ukok Plateau," *Archaeology, Ethnology and Anthropology of Eurasia*, 4: 66–87.

Possehl, G. L., 1984. "A Note on Harappan Settlement Patterns in the Punjab." In *Studies in the Archaeology and Palaeoanthropology of South Asia*, edited by K. A. R. Kennedy and G. L. Possehl. New Delhi: Oxford and IBH Publishing Company, pp. 83–7.

——, 1990. "Revolution in the Urban Revolution: the Emergence of Indus Urbanization," *Annual Review of Anthropology*, 19: 261–81.

——, 1996. *Indus Age: The Writing System.* New Delhi: Oxford and IBH Publishing Company.

——, 1997a. "Climate and the Eclipse of the Ancient Cities of the Indus." In *Third Millennium BC Climatic Change and Old World Civilizations*, edited by H. N. Dalfes, G. Kukla, and H. Weiss. NATO ASI Series, Series 1: Global Environmental Changes, Vol. 49. Berlin: Springer, pp. 193–243.

——, 1997b. "The Transformation of the Indus Civilization," *Journal of World Prehistory*, 11: 425–72.

——, 1999a. *Indus Age: The Beginning.* New Delhi: Oxford and IBH Publishing Company.

——, 1999b. "Prehistoric Population and Settlement in Sindh." In *The Indus River: Biodiversity-Resources-Humankind*, edited by A. Meadows and P. Meadows. Oxford: Oxford University Press, pp. 393–405.

——, 2002. *The Indus Civilization: A Contemporary Perspective.* Walnut Creek, CA: AltaMira Press, a division of Rowman and Littlefield Publishers, Inc.

Possehl, G. L. and P. C. Rissman, 1992. "The Chronology of Prehistoric India: From Earliest Times to the Iron Age." In *Chronologies in Old World Archaeology*, edited by R. W. Ehrich. Chicago, IL: University of Chicago Press, Vol. I, pp. 465–90, Vol. II, pp. 447–74.

Ratnagar, S., 1991. *Enquiries Into the Political Organization of Harappan Society.* Pune: Ravish Publishers.

Renfrew, C., 1987. *Archaeology and Language: The Puzzle of Indo-European Origins.* New York: Cambridge University Press.

Rissman, P. C. and Y. M. Chitalwala, 1990. *Harappan Civilization and Oriyo Timbo.* New Delhi: Oxford and IBH Publishing Co.

Robb, P., 2002. *A History of India.* New York: Palgrave, St. Martin's Press.

Robbins, R. H., 2002. *Global Problems and the Culture of Capitalism.* Boston, MA: Allyn and Bacon.

Robertshaw, P., 1999. "Sibling Rivalry? The Intersection of Archaeology and History," *H-Africa, H-Net, Humanities and Social Sciences OnLine.*

Rouse, I., 1986. *Migrations in Prehistory: Inferring Population Movement from Cultural Remains.* New Haven, CT: Yale University Press.

Roy, T. N., 1983. *The Ganges Civilization.* New Delhi: Ramanand Vidya Bhawan.

Schwab, R., 1984. *The Oriental Renaissance: Europe's Rediscovery of India and the East, 1680–1880.* New York: Columbia University Press.

Shaffer, J. G., 1981. "The Protohistoric Period in the Eastern Punjab: A Preliminary Assessment." In *Indus Civilization: New Perspectives*, edited by A. H. Dani. Islamabad: Quaid-I-Azam University, pp. 65–101.

——, 1982. "Harappan Culture: a Reconsideration." In *Harappan Civilization: A Contemporary Perspective*, edited by G. L. Possehl. New Delhi: Oxford and IBH Publishing Company, pp. 41–50.

——, 1984. "The Indo-Aryan Invasions: Cultural Myth and Archaeological Reality." In *The Peoples of South Asia*, edited by J. R. Lukacs. New York: Plenum Press, pp. 74–90.

——, 1986. "Cultural Development in the Eastern Punjab." In *Studies in the Archaeology of India and Pakistan*, edited by J. Jacobson. New Delhi: Oxford and IBH Publishing Company, pp. 74–90.

——, 1990. "Review of Language and Archaeology: The Puzzle of Indo-European Origins by Colin Renfrew," *Ethnohistory*, 37: 354–6.

——, 1992. "Indus Valley, Baluchistan and the Helmand Traditions: Neolithic Through Bronze Age." In *Chronologies in Old World Archaeology*, edited by R. W. Ehrich. Chicago, IL: University of Chicago Press, Vol. I, pp. 441–64, Vol. II, pp. 425–46.

——, 1993. "Reurbanization: the Eastern Punjab and Beyond." In *Meaning in South Asia: The Shaping of Cities from Prehistoric to Precolonial Times*, edited by H. Spodek and D. M. Srinivasan. Washington, DC: National Gallery of Art, pp. 53–67.

——, 1996. "South Asian Archaeology 1995: New Data/Subdued Interpretations," *Antiquity*, 70: 995–8.

Shaffer, J. G. and D. A. Lichtenstein, 1989. "Ethnicity and Change in the Indus Valley Cultural Tradition." In *Old Problems and New Perspectives in the Archaeology of South Asia*, edited by J. M. Kenoyer. University of Wisconsin, Madison, WI: Wisconsin Archaeological Reports No. 2, pp. 117–26.

——, 1995. "The Concepts of Cultural Tradition and Paleoethnicity in South Asian Archaeology." In *The Indo-Aryans of Ancient South Asia: Language, Material Culture and Ethnicity*, edited by G. Erdosy. Berlin: Walter de Gruyter, pp. 126–54.

——, 1999. "Migration, Philology and South Asian Archaeology." In *Aryan and Non-Aryan in South Asia: Evidence, Interpretation and Ideology*, edited by J. Bronkhurst and M. M. Deshpande. Harvard Oriental Series, Opera Minora Vol. 3, Cambridge, MA: Department of Sanskrit and Indian Studies, Harvard University, pp. 239–60.

Shanklin, E., 1994. *Anthropology and Race*. Belmont, CA: Wadsworth Publishing Company.

Sherratt, A. and S. Sherratt, 1988. "The Archaeology of Indo-European: An Alternative View," *Antiquity*, 62: 584–95.

Shipman, P., 1994. *The Evolution of Racism: Human Differences and the Use and Abuse of Science*. New York: Simon and Schuster.

Sims-Williams, P., 1998. "Genetics, Linguistics, and Prehistory: Thinking Big and Thinking Straight," *Antiquity*, 72: 505–27.

Singh, G., 1971. "The Indus Valley Culture (seen in the context of post-glacial climatic and ecological studies in north-west India)," *Archaeological and Physical Anthropology in Oceania*, 6: 177–89.

Singh, G., R. D. Joshi, S. K. Chapra, and A. B. Singh, 1974. "Late Quaternary History of Vegetation and Climate of the Rajasthan Desert, India." In *Philosophical Transactions of the Royal Society of London* (Biological Sciences) 267: 467–501.

Singh, G. R., R. J. Wasson, and D. P. Agrawal, 1990. "Vegetational and Seasonal Climatic Changes Since the Last Full Glacial in the Thar Desert, Northwestern India," *Review of Paleobotany and Palynology*, 64: 351–8.

Smith, A. D., 1986. *The Ethnic Origins of Nations*. Oxford: Basil Blackwell.

Smith, J., 2001. "For Reasons Out of Our Hands: A Community Identifies the Causes of Language Shift," *Cultural Survival Quarterly*, 25(2): 36–9.
Stepan, N., 1982. *The Idea of Race in Science: Great Britain 1800–1960*. London: Macmillan.
Trautmann, T. R., 1997. *Aryans and British India*. New Delhi: Vistaar Publications.
——, 1999. "Constructing the Racial Theory of Indian Civilization." In *Aryan and Non-Aryan in South Asia: Evidence, Interpretation and Ideology*, edited by J. Bronkhurst and M. M. Deshpande, Harvard Oriental Series, Opera Minora Vol. 3, Cambridge, MA: Department of Sanskrit and Indian Studies, Harvard University, pp. 277–93.
Trigger, B. G., 1989. *A History of Archaeological Thought*. Cambridge: Cambridge University Press.
Tripathi, V., 1976. *The Painted Grey Ware: An Iron Age Culture of Northern India*. Delhi: Concept Publishing Company.
van den Berge, P. L., 1987. *The Ethnic Phenomenon*. New York: Prager.
Van Riper, A. B., 1993. *Men Among the Mammoths: Victorian Science and the Discovery of Human Prehistory*. Chicago, IL: University of Chicago Press.
Vansina, J., 1995. "Historians, are Archaeologists your Siblings?" *History in Africa*, 22: 369–408, reprinted on *H-Africa, H-Net, Humanities and Social Sciences OnLine.*
Vats, M. S., 1940. *Excavations at Harappa*. New Delhi: Government of India.
Wheeler, Sir M., 1956. *Still Digging*. New York: E. P. Dutton.
——, 1968. *The Indus Civilization*, 3rd edition. London: Cambridge University Press.
Witzel, M. 1999. "Aryan and Non-Aryan Names in Vedic India: Data for the Linguistic Situation, *c*.1900–500 BC." In *Aryan and Non-Aryan in South Asia: Evidence, Interpretation and Ideology*, edited by J. Bronkhurst and M. M. Deshpande. Harvard Oriental Series, Opera Minora Vol. 3, Cambridge, MA: Department of Sanskrit and Indian Studies, Harvard University, pp. 337–404.
Wuethrich, B., 1994. "Domesticated Cattle Show Their Breeding," *New Scientist*, 142: 16–17.
Yoffee, N., 1990. "Before Babel, a Review Article," *Proceedings of the Prehistoric Society*, 56: 299–313.

Part II

ARCHAEOLOGY AND LINGUISTICS

4

THE CULTURAL COUNTERPARTS TO PROTO-INDO-EUROPEAN, PROTO-URALIC AND PROTO-ARYAN

Matching the dispersal and contact patterns in the linguistic and archaeological record

Asko Parpola and Christian Carpelan

4.1 Introductory note

The present chapter summarizes the main results of a much longer study (Carpelan and Parpola 2001). In that study (where detailed documentation can be found; 15 out of the 37 illustrations are reproduced here), we argue that the Indo-European and Uralic proto-languages were both spoken in archaeological cultures of eastern Europe, and that even the predecessors and some of the successors of these cultures were in contact with each other. The last part of the chapter correlating Indo-European and Uralic linguistic groups with definite archaeological cultures just reproduces the summary of the above-mentioned study. It is preceded by slightly modified and rearranged excerpts from other parts of that same study, focusing on some aspects of the linguistic record, especially issues related to Proto-Aryan.

4.2 The linguistic record

A serious search for the homeland (original speaking area) of a particular linguistic group has to take as its starting point the earliest historically known distribution of the languages belonging to that group. Early distribution of the Indo-European languages (Figure 4.1) is well known, and good expositions of the earliest evidence relating to each language group are easily accessible, for instance in J. P. Mallory's book *In Search of the Indo-Europeans* (1989) which even otherwise ought to be known to the readers of the present book. The Uralic language family is much less known, even though several good and recent books dealing with it are available (see Hajdú 1975, 1987; Sinor 1988; and Abondolo 1998, each with further literature). We therefore begin with a brief survey, from

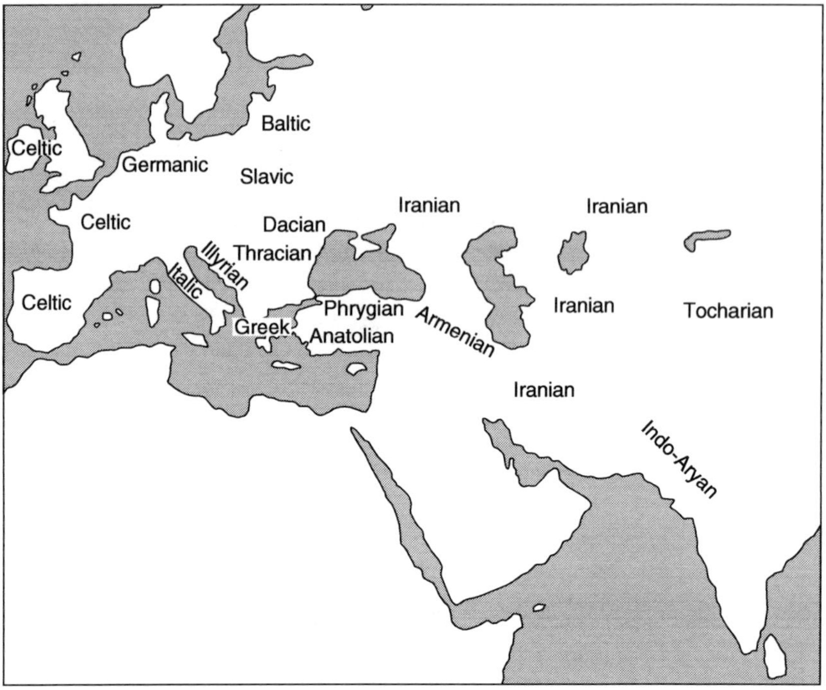

Figure 4.1 Early distribution of the principal groups of Indo-European languages.
Source: Mallory and Mair 2000: 119, fig. 50.

west to east, of the Uralic languages (Figure 4.2) and their known history and internal relations.

4.3 The Uralic language family and its main branches

The *Saami* (non-native name: *Lapp* or *Lappish*) languages are nowadays spoken in northernmost Fennoscandia, in Norway, Sweden, Finland, and the Kola Peninsula of Russia; but it is known from historical sources and place names (which attest to phonological changes typical of Saami) that Saami was spoken in various parts of Finland and Russian Karelia until medieval times.

The *Finnic* alias *Baltic Finnic* languages are nowadays spoken in Finland (*Finnish*, native name: *Suomi*), in Estonia (*Estonian*) and northern Latvia (*Livonian*), in Russian Karelia (*Karelian*), and in discontinuous areas from the southeastern shores of the Gulf of Finland to Lake Lagoda (*Inkerois* alias *Ingrian; Vote* alias *Votyan*) and further to Lake Onega (*Veps* alias *Vepsian* and *Lude* alias *Lydic*).

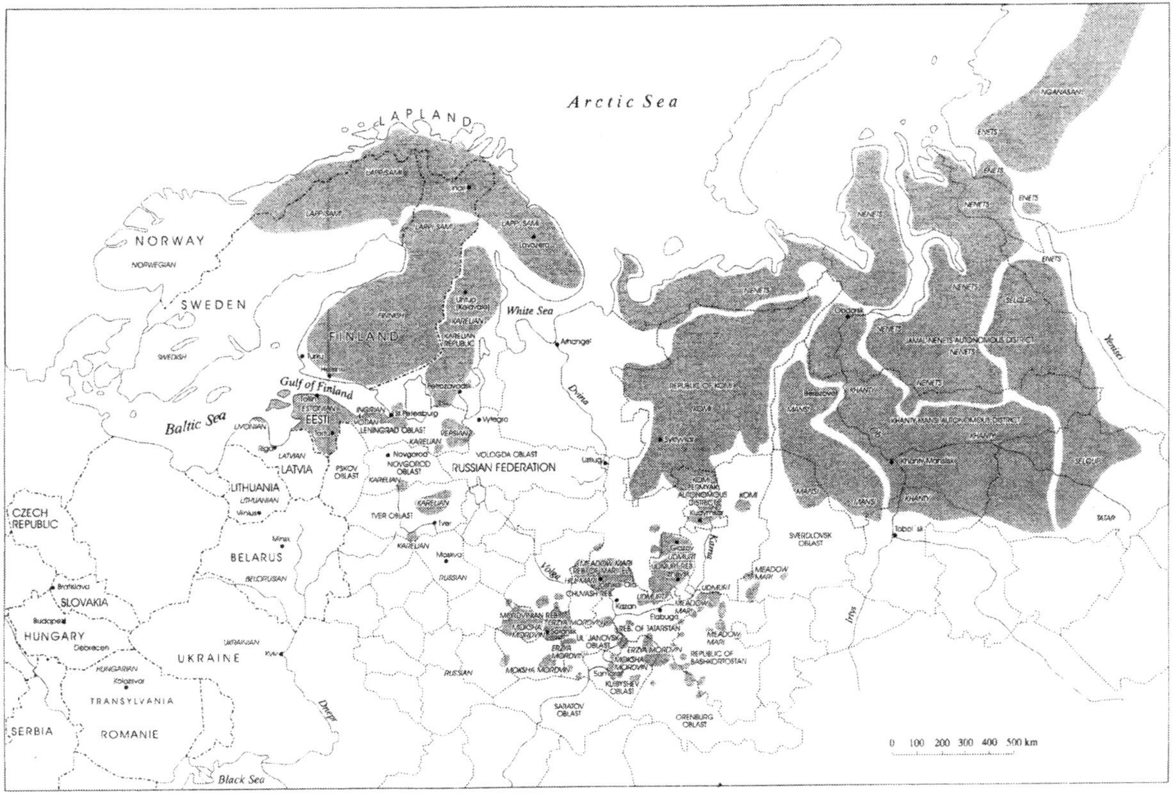

Figure 4.2 Present distribution of Uralic languages.

Source: Pirkko Numminen, Department of Geography, University of Helsinki.

Before the expansion of the Russian language from the southwest since the eighth century AD, the areas south and southwest of Vote and Veps were undoubtedly inhabited by nowadays extinct Finno-Ugric languages that would have bridged Finnic with Mordvin. Medieval Russian chronicles mention such people as the *Chud'* (different peoples between Estonia and the northern Dvina), the *Merya* (on the upper Volga and in the Volga–Oka interfluve) and the *Muroma* and the *Meshchera* (who lived on the left, i.e. northern, side of the Oka). *Mordvin* is spoken in two distinct dialects (Erzya Mordvin and Moksha Mordvin), originally on the right (southeastern) side of the Oka, while *Mari* (non-native name: *Cheremis*) is spoken on the mid-Volga (between the Oka and the Kama) and (since *c.* AD 1600) in present Bashkiristan; Mari, too, has two dialects (Meadow Mari and Mountain Mari). These *Volgaic* languages were previously thought to form a separate branch, but nowadays Mordvin and Mari are no longer thought to be particularly close to each other.

The *Udmurt* (non-native name: *Votyak*) and *Komi* (non-native name: *Zyryan* alias *Zyryene*) form the *Permic* branch of Finno-Ugric. The Udmurt have more or less remained in the old Permic homeland in the Kama–Vyatka interfluve on the European side of northern Russia. The Komi are divided in two groups, the Komi-Permyak on the upper reaches of the Kama and the Komi-Zyryan, who since *c.* AD 700 have moved northwards to their present habitats that extend up to the Pechora River.

The *Hungarian* (native name: *Magyar*) speakers arrived in Hungary by the tenth century AD. The starting point of their migration was the present Bashkiristan in the southern Urals, where Old Hungarian survived until late medieval times, when the last of its speakers adopted the Turkic Bashkir language. The nearest linguistic relatives of the Hungarians, the *Ob-Ugric* peoples of *Khanty* (non-native name: *Ostyak*) and *Mansi* (non-native name: *Vogul*), live in a wide area in northwestern Siberia between the Urals and the river Ob and its tributaries. Their former habitats included (until early 1900s) areas west of the Urals, but the arrival of Russians some 500 years ago started their move eastwards to the Irtysh and to the Ob. The homeland of the *Ugric* branch is thought to have been in the forests and forest steppe of the southern Urals.

The *Samoyed* languages form the easternmost branch of the Uralic language family. Proto-Samoyedic is thought to have disintegrated as late as only *c.*2000 years ago. On the basis of Turkic and Ketic (Yeniseic) loan words in Proto-Samoyedic, the earliest habitats of the Samoyeds were in the forest steppe zone of Siberia between the Urals and the Sayan and Altai mountains. The now extinct Samoyed languages *Kamassian* (with the related *Koibal*) and *Motor* alias *Mator* (with the related *Taigi* and *Karagas*) were spoken in the Sayan region partly until the early nineteenth century; the only surviving Samoyed language of the southern group is *Selqup* (non-native name: *Ostyak Samoyed*) spoken along the upper reaches of the Ob and Yenisei rivers. The ancestors of the *Nenets* (non-native name: *Yurak*), the *Enets* (non-native name: *Yenisei Samoyed*), and the *Nganasan* (non-native name: *Tavgi*) are thought to have arrived in northern Siberia *c.* AD 500, the Nenets continuing westwards to the tundra areas of northeast Europe. The first historical source to mention the Samoyeds is the Old Russian so-called “Nestor’s Chronicle,” according to which they lived as the neighbors of the Ob-Ugrians (*Yugra*) in 1096.

Although only about 130 words of those about 700 that can be reconstructed for Proto-Samoyedic go back to the Uralic proto-language (cf. Janhunen 1977, 1981), Samoyedic in its long isolation has in many respects remained remarkably archaic, so that its comparison with the likewise archaic Finnic branch at the other end of the language family constitutes the most reliable means to reconstruct Proto-Uralic.

Traditionally the genetic classification of the Uralic languages starts with the division of the proto-language into two, Proto-Finno-Ugric and Proto-Samoyedic. While the Samoyedic languages are spoken in Siberia, practically all Finno-Ugric languages (including some extinct ones) appear to have been originally spoken in the forest area of northeastern Europe west of the Ural mountains.

4.4 Early Indo-European loanwords in Uralic languages

Uralic languages contain many loanwords from Indo-European languages. A brief “list of Indo-European loan-words” was included by Björn Collinder in his *Fenno-Ugric Vocabulary: An Etymological Dictionary of the Uralic Languages* (Collinder 1955: 128–41). The early contacts between Indo-European and Uralic languages were discussed in detail by Aulis J. Joki in his monograph on this subject from 1973 (with 222 etyma), and Károly Rédei’s *Uralisches etymologisches Wörterbuch* (Rédei 1988–91) as well as the two etymological dictionaries of the Finnish language (SKES 1955–78 and SSA 1992–2000) naturally also take a stand in the matter. Jorma Koivulehto with his rare double competence in Indo-European as well as Uralic linguistics has been able to increase the number of such etymologies considerably, and to refine earlier proposed etymologies. Koivulehto’s recent summary article (2001) provides the most up-to-date survey of the topic; it analyzes a large number of words and the linguistic criteria that enable them to be assigned to a specific source and temporal horizon.

It is fairly generally accepted that the reconstructed protoforms of a considerable number of these loanwords often constitute the earliest existing external evidence of the languages involved. This is true not only of the Indo-European proto-language itself, but also of its Aryan, Baltic, and Germanic branches. In such cases the Uralic loanword represents an earlier stage of development than the respective proto-language has in the reconstruction based on its surviving descendents. A case in point is Proto-Volga-Finnic **kešträ* ‘spindle’ < pre-Proto-Aryan **ket*^{s}*tro-* ‘spindle’ (whence Old Indo-Aryan *cattra-, cāttra-* and Old Iranian **častra-* > Pashto *čāṣ̌ai*), from Proto-Indo-European **kert*^{s}*tro-* < **kert-tro-* < **kert-* ‘to spin’ (whence Sanskrit *kart-* ‘to spin’) (cf. Koivulehto 1979). In this example, the shape of the Finno-Ugric words for ‘spindle’ suggests that the borrowing took place before Proto-Aryan (the only branch of Indo-European to have comparable nominal derivatives) had reached the stage reconstructed on the basis of the Aryan languages descended from it.

In the following we focus on some words that are of particular importance for the question as to where the Uralic and Aryan homelands were situated.

4.5 The Proto-Indo-European or Proto-Aryan loanwords for 'honey' and 'bee'

It is generally accepted that Proto-Finno-Ugric **mete* 'honey' (distributed in Finnic, Saami, Mordvin, Udmurt, Komi, and Hungarian) is borrowed from Proto-Indo-European = pre-Proto-Aryan **medhu-* (which became **madhu-* in Proto-Aryan) (cf. Joki 1973: 283–5; Rédei 1988: I, 655f.; Mayrhofer 1996: II, 302f.). The same pre-Proto-Aryan vowel **e* is found in Proto-Finno-Ugric **mekše* 'bee' (distributed in Finnic, Mordvin, Mari, Udmurt, Komi, and Hungarian) which on the Indo-European side has a reasonable counterpart only in the Aryan branch (cf. Joki 1973: 281f.; Rédei 1988: I, 655; Mayrhofer 1996: II, 287). Fëdor Keppen (1886: 84–6, 107–13) alias Theodor Köppen (1890) and other scholars including Péter Hajdú have rightly stressed that the Indo-European loanwords for 'honey' and 'bee' are key terms for locating the oldest habitats of the Finno-Ugric speakers. The honeybee

> was unknown in Asia, until relatively recent times, with the exception of Asia Minor, Syria, Persia, Afghanistan, Tibet and China, none of which can be taken into account for our purposes. The bee was not found in Siberia, Turkestan, Central Asia and Mongolia; indeed, it was introduced to Siberia only at the end of the eighteenth century. On the other hand, the bee is found west of the Urals in eastern Europe, mainly from the northern limit of the oak (. . .), or from Latitude 57°–58° southwards. Moreover, the middle Volga region was known of old as a bee-keeping area.
>
> (Hajdú 1975: 33)

Hajdú's statements conform to the latest state of research summarized in Eva Crane's extensive book, *The World History of Beekeeping and Honey Hunting* (1999). *Apis mellifera* is native to the region comprising Africa, Arabia and the Near East up to Iran, and Europe up to the Urals in the east and to southern Sweden and Estonia in the north; its spread further north was limited by arctic cold, while its spread to the east was limited by mountains, deserts, and other barriers. Another important limiting factor was that the cool temperate deciduous forests of Europe extend only as far east as the Urals and do not grow in Siberia (see later). The distribution of *Apis mellifera* was confined to this area until *c.* AD 1600, when it started being transported to other regions (Crane 1999: 11–14). Thus hive bee-keeping was extended to Siberia from the 1770s, when upright log hives were taken from the Ukraine and European Russia to Ust'-Kamenogorsk and Tomsk, from where it started spreading (Keppen 1886: 109–11; Crane 1999: 232, 366f.).

Another species of cavity-nesting honeybee, *Apis cerana*, is native to Asia east and south of Pakistan, Afghanistan, China, Korea, and Japan (cf. Crane 1999: 13–14).

Tree bee-keeping is one of the oldest methods of exploiting *Apis mellifera*. Tree bee-keeping is supposed to have developed early in the area of the Oka, mid-Volga, and lower Kama – areas long inhabited by Finno-Ugric speaking peoples. This zone has had rich deciduous forests with broad-leaved trees which shed their leaves before winter; the leaves foster the growth of herbs and shrubs, which together with the flowers of the trees provide forage for honey bees. This region has been particularly rich in limes, the flowers of which were the principal source of honey here; it remained the most important area of tree bee-keeping until the early 1900s, when the bee forests largely disappeared. Besides the limes and other flowering trees, the cool temperate deciduous forests of Europe had big oaks that develop large and long-lasting cavities for the bees to nest in (the bees prefer cavities having a volume of around 50 liters). Large pines and spruces enabled tree bee-keeping also in such coniferous forests of northern Europe that were not too cold in the winter and had enough forage for the bees, especially in northern Russia, in the Baltic region and in Poland and east Germany (Crane 1999: 62, 127).

The natural habitat of the oak (*Quercus robur*) and the lime (*Tilia cordata*), which have been the most important trees for tree bee-keeping in central Russia, grow in Europe as far east as the southern Urals (60° E). Today, *Quercus robur* is not found in Siberia at all (cf. Hultén and Fries 1986: I, 315, map 630; III, 1031), but there are scattered occurrences of *Tilia cordata* in western Siberia (cf. Hultén and Fries 1986: II, 651, map 1301). According to palynological investigations the lime spread to central Russia from the (south)west in the early Boreal period (*c*.8150–6900 cal BC). In the favorable Atlantic conditions (*c*.6900–3800 cal BC), the spread of *Tilia cordata* continued to western Siberia, but in the unfavorable conditions of the Subboreal period (*c*.3800–600 cal BC) a considerable reduction of elements of broad-leaved forests is seen east of the Urals leaving isolated occurrences at some favorable spots. The disjunct distribution of another species, *Tilia sibirica*, is found between the upper Syr Darya and the upper Yenisei (cf. Hultén and Fries 1986: II, 651, map 1301). In any case, the scattered isolated occurrences of the lime in western Siberia cannot be compared with the dense lime forests that have long existed in central Russia, and the Siberian limes can hardly have provided a basis for prehistoric bee-keeping.

'Bee' or 'honey' are not among the meanings of those around 700 words that are found in at least one language of both the northern and the southern group of the Samoyedic languages and can thus be reconstructed for Proto-Samoyedic (cf. Janhunen 1977). It is possible that pre-Proto-Samoyedic did inherit these words from Proto-Finno-Ugric (from which they seem to have departed), but lost them in Siberia, because bee and honey did not exist there. There are indeed no old words for 'bee' in Samoyedic languages: Kamassian *pinekü*ʙ 'bee' literally means 'searching wasp'. In Nenets there are four words for 'honey', but one is a native neologism literally meaning 'good-tasting water' and three are relatively recent loans: *ma* < Komi *ma*; *m'āb* < Khanty *mav*; *m'ōd/m'ot* < Russian *mëd* (cf. Joki 1973: 284f.).

Tree bee-keeping is to be distinguished from honey hunting, in which honey is simply stolen and bees may be killed, and from the later hive bee-keeping, which started in forest areas in the twelfth century when trees were cut down on land taken for agriculture. Climbing the tree unaided or with the help of rope, footholds, or ladder, the beekeeper on his frequent rounds tended the bee nests located either in natural tree cavities or in holes that he himself had made with axe and chisel. In either case, an upright rectangular opening to the cavity was made and furnished with a removable two-part door having small flight entrances for the bees. The entrances and the inner surfaces were kept clean, and the nest was protected against bears, woodpeckers, and thieves. During winter, all openings but one were closed and straw was tied around the trunk to insulate it. The honeycombs were harvested in spring (which is the main flowering season) and at the end of summer; with the help of smoke put into the nest, the bees were kept in the upper part, while the honeycombs were taken with a wooden ladle from the lower part; something was left for the bees. The Mari traditionally did this at full moon, with prayers said at each stage of the operation and addressed to the Great God, God of Heaven, God of Bees, Mother of Plenty, and so on (Crane 1999: 127–35).

Old Russian historical records tell that by AD 1000 or earlier, the aristocracy and monasteries owned many and often large bee woods (with 100–500 tree cavities, but only some 10–20 occupied at a time). These were looked after by a special class of peasants called bortnik, who could also own bee trees (usually between 100 and 200), but had to pay the landlord a rent. Cut ownership marks were put on the trees, sometimes on the back wall of the cavity. Large amounts of honey and beeswax were produced in Russia, and the honey was both eaten and used for making mead. The aristocracy needed mead for its parties in large quantities. At a seven-day feast held in AD 996 to celebrate the Russian victory over the Turks, 300 large wooden tubs or about 5000 liters of mead was drunk. Bee-keeping declined in the late seventeenth century as Tsar Peter the Great imposed a tax on bee-keeping income and founded a sugar industry. This reduced the demand for honey, and vodka and wine were produced instead of mead, which until then had been the usual alcoholic drink in Russia. Conditions improved again when Catherine the Great abolished all taxes on bee-keeping: in 1800, there were 50 million beehives in the Russian Empire (Crane 1999: 63, 129–35, 232f., 515).

For the Proto-Indo-Europeans, too, honey (**medhu*) was important as the source of mead, which was also called **medhu*: this original meaning is preserved in the Celtic, Germanic, and Baltic cognates, while the Greek cognate *méthu* has come to denote another alcoholic drink, wine, and Sanskrit *mádhu* in Vedic texts usually denotes the honey-sweetened variety of the sacred Soma drink, and in later Indian texts often wine (grown in, and imported from, Afghanistan). The ancient Aryans, however, also drank some kind of mead, for according to the Vedic manuals, an honored guest had to be received by offering him a drink mixed with honey (*madhu-parka* or *madhu-mantha*, cf. e.g. *Kauśikasūtra* 90). Moreover, the Greek lexicographer Hesychios mentions *melítion* (from Greek *méli* gen. *mélitos* 'honey') as 'a Scythian drink'. The Ossetes of the Caucasus, descended from the Scythians, are said to have worshipped a bee goddess (Crane 1999: 602); Ossetic *mid/mud* has preserved the meaning 'honey', while Avestan *maδu*, Sogdian *mδw*, and Modern Persian *mai* mean 'wine'.

In the Vedic religion, *madhu* as a cultic drink was connected with the *Aśvins*, the divine twins 'possessing horses', who function as cosmic charioteers and saviours from mortal danger (cf. e.g. *Atharva-Veda* 9.1). The *Śatapatha-Brāhmaṇa* (14.1.1) relates a myth in which the *Aśvins* learn the secret 'knowledge of the *madhu*' which enables its possessor to revive a dead person. They learn it from the demon *Dadhyañc*, whom the god Indra had forbidden to reveal the secret to anyone, threatening to cut off the head of the offender. The *Aśvins*, however, promised to revive *Dadhyañc* after he had taught them the secret, and replaced the head of their teacher with the head of a horse. After Indra in punishment had cut off *Dadhyañc*'s horse head, the *Aśvins* replaced it with the original one and revived him. This myth seems to be connected with an earlier form of the Vedic horse sacrifice, in which a young warrior and a horse were beheaded, and their heads swapped in a ritual of "revival" (cf. Parpola 1983: 62–3).

The Vedic tradition seems to have a predecessor in the mid-Volga region in the beginning of the second millennium BC: a grave belonging to the Potapovka culture (Figure 4.10), which succeeded the Abashevo culture (Figure 4.9) and possessed the horse-drawn chariot, was found to contain a skeleton which was otherwise human except for the skull which belonged to a horse (cf. Vasil'ev *et al.* 1994: 115, Fig. 11; cf. Anthony and Vinogradov 1995). Sulimirski (1970: 295) quotes some evidence for human sacrifice accompanied by beheaded calves and burnt cows from an Abashevo culture site in the southern Urals. There may be a reminiscence of this ancient Aryan tradition in the Finnish folk poetry incorporated in the Kalevala, where the mother of the slain hero Lemminkäinen with the help of the bee and honey revives the body of her son, who has been cut into pieces (cf. Parpola 1999: 201).

Proto-Finno-Ugric **mete* 'honey' is formed like Uralic **wete* 'water', which (along with the similar Uralic word **nime* 'name' and Proto-Finno-Ugric **sixne* 'sinew') has always been considered to be among the oldest Indo-European loanwords (cf. e.g. Hajdú 1987: 300; Koivulehto 1999: 209–10). Perhaps they were borrowed together with the earliest Uralic word for 'pot', **pata*, when the ancestors of the later Proto-Uralic speakers learnt the technique of pottery making and the process of making mead or honey-beer from their southern neighbors, ancestors of the later Proto-Indo-Europeans. This would have taken place with the appearance of the earliest ceramics in the forest region of eastern Europe, *c.*6000 BC. Unless the reward was something very desirable, like storing honey that constituted a very valuable food resource or social celebrations with an alcoholic drink made of honey, it is difficult to understand what could have induced hunter-gatherers – not practising agriculture – to make enormous pots that were difficult to move. It could also explain why such a basic word as 'water' would have been borrowed. However, with the arrival of the Aryan speakers of the Abashevo culture, honey-keeping apparently became more effectively organized. The bronze axes and adzes of the Abashevo culture were undoubtedly used in tree bee-keeping, to prepare new nests for captured bee-swarms and to maintain and protect them.

4.6 A new Proto-Indo-Aryan etymology for a Volga-Permic word for 'beeswax'

Beeswax, which keeps indefinitely, is easily transported, and has various technical uses, especially in metallurgy, was the second most important export article after fur in ancient and medieval Russia. Before the coming of Christianity in the tenth century AD, Russia exported much of its beeswax to Byzantium and beyond, for churches and monasteries that needed wax for candles. But as early as the fifth century BC, Scythia was one of the main exporters of beeswax. The Scythians also used wax for coating the body of their king when he died, so that it could be put on a wagon and carried around all the subject nations before the burial (Herodotus 4.71). According to Herodotus (1.140.2), the Persians, too, coated the dead body with wax before burying it in the ground (Crane 1999: 538).

Besides mead, beeswax in the form of a sacred candle occupied a central position in the religion of the Finno-Ugric peoples of the Oka, mid-Volga and Kama region, who had beekeeping as one of their main occupations. The mead and wax-candle accompanied practically all of their ceremonies. Thus a candle was lighted in front of the honey vat after the honey harvest had been taken home, with prayers addressed to the God of the Bees, and to the Bee-Mother, and so on. Each clan further had its own clan candle lighted once a year, during Easter, when the dead ancestors were remembered (Hämäläinen 1937).

Beeswax produced in great quantities in the forest region of the mid-Volga was certainly a major incentive for the metallurgists of the early Aryan speakers to get this region under their control. The smiths needed beeswax to make molds for casting metal. There was some metallurgy in the mid-Volga region as early as the Volosovo culture (Figure 4.7: H), but it reached another level in the succeeding Balanovo (Figure 4.6: B) and Abashevo (Figure 4.9) cultures.

Estonian and Finnish *vaha* < **vakša* 'beeswax' is derived from Proto-Baltic **vaška-* (Lithuanian *vãškas*, Latvian *vasks* 'wax'), which like Old Slavonic *vosku* and Russian *vosk* comes from Proto-Indo-European **wosko-*; Proto-Germanic **waχsa* comes from the variant **wokso-*. Another word for 'beeswax' in Finno-Ugric languages, Estonian *kärg*, Mordvin *k'eras*, Mari *käräš*, *karaš*, *karas*, and Udmurt *karas*, is likewise of Baltic origin, cf. Lithuanian *korỹs* 'honey-comb', Latvian *kāre(s)* 'honey-comb': the vowel of the first syllable can only come from Baltic **ā*, not from **ē* in Greek *kērós* 'wax', *kēríon* 'honey-comb', and Latin *cera* 'wax' (which is a loanword from Greek), whence Irish *cēir* 'wax' and Welsh *cwyr* 'wax'; the Turkic languages of the Volga region have borrowed the word from Finno-Ugric: Kazan *käräz, käräs*, Bashkir *kärä-*, Chuvas *karas* 'honey-comb'.

In the Volga-Permic languages there is yet another appellation for 'beeswax' that has been thought to be the old native Finno-Ugric word, apparently because no external etymology has been proposed for it so far: Mordvin (Moksha dialect) *šta*, (Erzya dialect) *kšta, šta*, Mari *šište*, Udmurt *śuś* < **śuśt*, Komi *śiś* (*śiśt-, śiśk-, śiś-*), *ma-siś*; all these words denote 'beeswax', but in Komi the usual meaning is 'wax candle, light' (the word *ma* in the compound *ma-siś* means 'honey'). Heikki Paasonen (1903: 112) reconstructed the protoform as **śikšta* or **šiks[']ta*. Károly Rédei in his *Uralisches etymologisches Wörterbuch* (1988: II, 785f.), summarizing twelve scholars' studies of these words gives us the reconstruction **šikśt3*; he notes, however, that while it is possible to derive the forms of all the languages from this reconstruction, its *k* is based on the Mordvin dialectal variant only, and this *k* may be just an epenthetic glide that has come into being inside the word; moreover, the *ś* in the middle of the word has caused an assimilation **š* > *ś* at the beginning of the word in Permic languages, while in the Komi compound *ma-siś*, a dissimilation **ś* > *s* has taken place; and the change **i* > *u* in Udmurt is irregular. But the assimilation **š* > *ś* in Permic may have taken place in the middle of the word as well as at the beginning, because in Mari **ś* always became *š* at the beginning of a word and inside the word, *š* in front of voiceless stops, while original **š* was preserved in these positions (cf. Bereczki 1988: 335). In the Mordvin words the vowel has first been reduced in the unstressed first syllable and then dropped, cf. E *kšna*, E M *šna* < **šĕkšna* < **šukšna* 'strap' (cf. Bereczki 1988: 321). In this Baltic loanword the *k* is etymological (cf. Lithuanian *šikšnà*, Latvian *siksna* 'strap'), but in the 'wax' word it may be due to the analogy of this "very similar" word (cf. Jacobsohn 1922: 166). Thus it seems that the reconstruction of the word for 'wax' could equally well be **śikšta* (as proposed by Paasonen) or **śišta*.

In Indian sources, a formally and semantically perfect match can be found for Proto-Volga-Permic **śišta* 'beeswax', namely Sanskrit *śiṣṭá-* < Proto-Indo-Aryan **śištá-*, preterite participle regularly formed with the suffix *-tá-* from the verbal root *śiṣ-*'to leave (over)'. In *Rāmāyaṇa* 5.60.10. 'beeswax' is called *madhu-śiṣṭa-*, literally 'what is left over of honey' and in some other texts synonymous terms *madhūcchiṣṭa-* and *madhu-śeṣa-*. *Śiṣṭa-* is used as a neuter noun meaning 'remainder, remnant' in Vedic texts (cf. *Śatapatha-Brāhmaṇa* 11.5.4.18: interestingly, this passage speaks of eating honey). Sanskrit *śiṣṭa-* has become *siṭṭha-* 'left over, remainder' in Middle Indo-Aryan; its cognates in Modern Indo-Aryan languages usually mean 'dregs', but in Singhalese 'wax' (cf. Turner 1966: nos 12478 and 12480).

There is an exact correspondence even between the Sanskrit compound *madhu-śiṣṭa-* 'beeswax' and the Komi compound *ma-siś* 'beeswax', for Komi *ma* corresponding to Udmurt *mu* goes back to Proto-Permic **mo* and this to Proto-Finno-Ugric **mete* 'honey', just as Komi *va* corresponding to Udmurt *vu* goes back to Proto-Permic **wo* and Proto-Uralic **wete* 'water' (cf. Itkonen 1953–54: 319f.).

Besides, there is the following undoubtedly related etymon in Indo-Aryan: Sanskrit *śiktha-, siktha-, sikthaka-* n., Middle Indo-Aryan *sittha-, sitthaka-, sitthaya-* n., Kashmiri *syothu* m. and Lahnda and Punjabi *sitthā* m., all meaning 'beeswax' (cf. Turner 1966: no. 13390). This variant suggests contamination by Sanskrit *siktá-* (Middle Indo-Aryan *sitta-*, whence Khowar *sit* 'silt, dregs', cf. Turner 1966: no. 13388): the latter is the past participle of the verb *sic-* 'to pour (out) (something liquid)', which is used also of 'casting liquid metal' (cf. *Atharva-Veda* 11.10.12–13; *Taittirīya-Samhitā* 2.4.12.5; 2.5.2.2; *Aitareya-Brāhmaṇa* 4.1; all these texts speak of casting the demon-destroying thunderbolt-weapon). Beeswax plays a central role in the lost-wax method of metal casting, which was used in Abashevo metallurgy. If the contamination of **śišta-* and **sikta-* took place in the (pre-)Proto-Indo-Aryan language of the Abashevo culture, it offers yet another possibility to explain the 'epenthetic' *k* in the Erzya Mordvin variant *kšta* 'beeswax'.

The formal and semantic match between these Volga-Permic and Indo-Aryan words for 'beeswax' is so close that there can hardly be doubt about this etymology. It is particularly significant, because these words, like the very root *śiṣ* – < **ćiš-* 'to leave (over)' (possibly from Proto-Indo-European **k'(e)i-s-* 'to leave lying') with all its verbal and nominal derivatives, are missing in the entire Iranian branch. Thus the Volga-Permic word can hardly be from an early Iranian language, and strongly suggests that the Abashevo culture (Figure 4.9) was dominated by Aryans belonging to the "Indo-Aryan" branch. Several Finno-Ugric loanwords have previously been suspected to be of specifically Proto-Indo-Aryan origin (cf. Koivulehto 1999: 227), but the new etymology narrows the Proto-Indo-Aryan affinity down to the Abashevo culture. Among the other early Proto-Indo-Aryan loanwords in Finno-Ugric is **ora* 'awl' < Proto-Aryan **ārā* = Sanskrit *ārā-* 'awl' (cf. Koivulehto 1987: 206f.), which is likewise not found in the Iranian branch at all. Also Proto-Finno-Ugric **vaśara* 'hammer, axe' (cf. Joki 1973: 339) on account of its palatalized sibilant is from Proto-Aryan or Proto-Indo-Aryan rather than Proto-Iranian, where depalatalization took place (cf. Mayrhofer 1989: 4, 6), cf. Sanskrit *vajra-* 'thunder-bolt, weapon of *Indra* the god of thunder and war' versus Avestan *vazra-* 'mace, the weapon of the god *Mithra*', possibly from the Proto-Indo-European **weg'-* 'to be(come) powerful'.

In Proto-Volga-Permic **śišta* 'beeswax', the Proto-Finno-Ugric palatal sibilant **ś* corresponds to the Proto(-Indo)-Aryan palatal affricate **ć* or palatal sibilant **ś*. Jorma Koivulehto (pers. comm.) has pointed out that this does not necessarily imply that the satemization had already taken place in the donor language, because Proto-Finno-Ugric (Proto-Uralic) **ś* already substitutes the palatalized velar stop **k'* of the Indo-European proto-language: with one uncertain exception, there are no examples of the PIE palatalized velar stops being substituted with Proto-Uralic/Proto-Finno-Ugric **k*. This makes us wonder whether the satemization of the Baltic and Aryan branches was triggered by the substratum of the Finno-Ugric majority language in the area of the Fat'yanovo/Balanovo (Figure 4.6: F, B) and Abashevo (Figure 4.9) cultures respectively, and spread from them to the other cultures speaking Proto-Baltic and Proto-Aryan languages (cf. also Kallio 2001).

On the other hand, the second affrication of velars before a front vowel has not yet taken place in the Aryan donor language of Saami *geavri* < **kekrä* 'circular thing' (actual meanings in Saami: 'ring, circular stopper of the ski stick, shaman's circular drum') and Finnish *kekri* < **kekrä-j* 'ancient pagan new year feast', which go back to early Proto-Aryan **kekro-*, whence, through the intermediate form **cekro-*, Proto-Aryan (and Sanskrit) *cakrá-* 'wheel, circle, cycle of years or seasons' (other branches of Indo-European do not have the development **r* < **l* from Proto-Indo-European **k^{w}ek^{w}lo-* 'wheel, cycle') (cf. Koivulehto 2001: no. 42; Pokorny 1959: 640). These words have probably come to Saami and Finnish through the Netted Ware culture (Figure 4.8) and the Sejma-Turbino Intercultural Phenomenon (Figure 4.11), the ruling elite of which seems to have come both from the Abashevo culture (Figure 4.9, assumed to have spoken early 'Proto-Indo-Aryan') and from the Pozdnyakovo culture (assumed to have spoken early 'Proto-Iranian').

What the Volga-Permic reconstruction **śišta* 'beeswax' does suggest is that the RUKI rule was already functioning when the word was borrowed: Proto-Indo-European **s* became **š* after **i* (and after **r, *u* and **k*) in Proto-Aryan (and in varying measure in Proto-Balto-Slavic, cf. Porzig 1954: 164f.).

4.7 Aryan ethnonyms of Finno-Ugric peoples

The former presence of an Aryan-speaking elite layer among the Finno-Ugric speaking peoples of the Oka–Volga–Kama region (Figure 4.2) is clearly visible in the ethnonyms of these peoples. The name *Mari* goes back to Proto-Aryan **márya-* 'man', literally 'mortal, one who has to die'. It is quite possible that this ethnic name is of Bronze Age origin, for *marya-* is used in Mitanni Aryan of Syria (*c.*500–1300 BC) for the nobility with horse chariots. The name *Mordvin* seems to go back to early Proto-Aryan *mórto-* 'mortal, man'. The same word was separately borrowed into Finnic after the change *o* > *a* had taken place in Proto-Aryan, so as to yield *márta-* 'mortal, man' preserved in Old Indo-Aryan: Finnish *marras*, stem *marta-* 'dying, dead; manly, male'. The corresponding appellative reconstructed for Volga-Permic, **mertä* 'man, human being' is likewise a loanword from Proto-Aryan: *er* substitutes vocalic *r̥* in Proto-Aryan and Old Indo-Aryan *mr̥tá-* 'mortal, man'. This same Proto-Aryan word occurs as the second element of the ethnonym *Udmurt* as well. The ethnonym *Arya/Ārya* appears as a loanword in Finnish and Saami, the reconstructed original shape being **orya*, written *orja* in modern Finnish, where it denotes 'slave'; this meaning can be explained as coming from 'Aryan taken as a war-captive or prisoner', as English *slave* comes from 'captive Slav'. Besides **orya*, there are several other early Aryan loanwords where the labial vowel *o* (or *ō*) of Proto-Finno-Ugric corresponds to Proto-Aryan *a/ā*, reflecting a somewhat labialized realization on the Aryan side, apparently in early Proto-Indo-Aryan.

The Ugric languages share several very early Aryan loanwords (e.g. Hungarian *méh* 'bee'). The ethnic name *Yugra* is used of the Ob-Ugrians in the Old Russian "Nestor's Chronicle." As shown by Tuomo Pekkanen (1973), this ethnic name was used of the Hungarians as well and has an Aryan etymology. Proto-Aryan **ugrá-* 'mighty, strong, formidable, noble' occurs in Old Indo-Aryan and Old Iranian not only as an adjective but also as a tribal name and as a proper name. The Greek historian Strabo (64 BC–AD 19) in his *Geography* (7.3.17) says that the Scythian tribe of 'Royal Sarmatians' were also called *Oûrgoi*. This is a metathesis form of the word *ugra*, attested also in Scythian proper names such as *Aspourgos* (= Old Iranian *aspa-* 'horse' + *ugra-*). These Oûrgoi were settled between the Dniester and the Dnieper; according to Strabo, they "in general are nomads, though a few are interested also in farming; these peoples, it is said, dwell also along the Ister (i.e. the Danube), often on both sides." The Oûrgoi seem to have included also Hungarians, since a third- or fourth-century Latin inscription (CIL III, 5234) from the borders of Hungary mentions raiders called *Mattzari*, which agrees with the later Byzantine transcriptions of *Magyar*, the self-appellation of the Hungarians, called *Majqhari* in the tenth-century Muslim sources.

4.8 The archaeological record

In order to function, a human community needs both means of making a living (reflected by the material cultures of archaeology) and means of communication (in the form of languages); and the shared material culture and the shared language are both among the strongest sources of ethnic identity. If various peoples lived in isolation, their material cultures and their languages could be expected to change only little over time (cf. the case of Icelandic), and essentially there would be continuity in both spheres. But very few people have lived in isolation. Contact with other communities has normally led to changes, the extent and pace of which depend on the intensity of the contact. Trade contacts may result in the introduction of new kinds of artifacts and loanwords denoting new ideas and objects. Conquests or immigrations usually lead to radical changes: a community may abandon its previous way of life or language, and adopt a new one. Language shift is realized through bilingualism, when parts of the population become able to speak two (or more) languages.

Continuities as well as cultural contacts and their intensity can usually be seen both from the archaeological record and from a language (inherited vocabulary versus loanwords, structural changes) when analyzed with the comparative method. Archaeology and linguistics both have developed their own special methods and techniques to do this, and they must be respected in a serious attempt to correlate the results of the two disciplines. Unlike reconstructed protoforms of languages, prehistoric archaeological cultures can usually be placed on the map and dated; but since they by definition have not left any readable written remains, their correlation with definite languages or language groups poses a number of problems. Correlations proposed without acceptable methodology are worthless. Concerning the methodology to be followed in an attempt to correlate linguistic and archaeological evidence we are in full agreement with J. P. Mallory and refer the reader to his excellent systematic exposition (Mallory 2001). A few points may be emphasized, however.

Adequate dating and chronology are crucial for the correlation. In archaeology, dating and chronology has traditionally been based on the classical typological method. We believe, however, that the radiocarbon method offers the only feasible basis for building a realistic prehistoric archaeological chronology in eastern Europe and western Siberia as well as elsewhere. The survey and use of a continuously growing corpus of radiocarbon dates from eastern Europe and western Siberia has recently been made easier with the publication of date lists, in addition to scattered articles with notes on new dates. In total there are several hundred dates available today. The radiocarbon ages are calibrated by Carpelan according to the 'Original Groningen Method' based on the median of the cumulative probability of a date and the INTCAL98 calibration curve (cf. Plicht 1993). Calibrated calendar dates are marked cal BC.

Isolated correlations of one language with one archaeological culture may look plausible in some respects, but they do not allow the results to be checked. A holistic solution that covers the entire spectrum of relevant cultures and languages does make some control possible. An archaeological culture has not only its geographical and temporal extent and a specific content (e.g. the use of certain tools, plants, and animals) but also specific relationships to other archaeological cultures diachronically and synchronically. Each language, too, has similar, though often less exact parameters, particularly its genetic and areal relationships to other languages. This means that the correlation of an archaeological culture with a specific language or language group can be tested by checking how well the implied external archaeological and linguistic relationships match, and whether these matches will stand if the whole web of these relationships is worked out systematically.

The earliest historical seats of the various Indo-European languages are widely separated from each other (Figure 4.1), but these languages all go back to a single proto-language. Is there any one archaeological culture, from which one could derive cultures that are intrusive in all (or all but one) of these widely dispersed areas? A crucial temporal clue is given by the fact that all Indo-European languages possess inherited vocabulary related to wheeled transport (Figure 4.3). The Indo-European proto-language had these terms before its disintegration, and the daughter languages have not borrowed them from one another after the dispersal. Therefore, the speakers of the Indo-European proto-language knew and used wheeled vehicles, and the wheeled vehicles were first invented around the middle of the fourth millennium BC (cf. Anthony 1995). The earliest evidence of

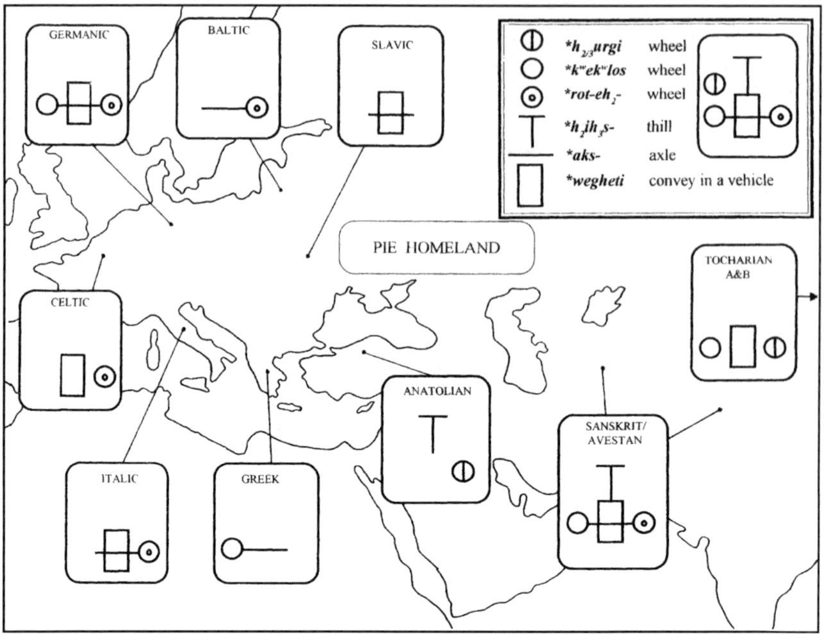

Figure 4.3 Distribution of inherited terminology related to wheeled transport in Indo-European languages.

Source: Anthony 1995: 557, fig. 1, Meid 1994.

wheeled vehicles comes from Bronocice in Poland (Figure 4.4). It is a drawing of a wagon on a clay vessel belonging to occupational Phase III which is dated to *c.*3470–3210 cal BC (cf. Piggott 1983). The dispersal of Late Proto-Indo-European, then, cannot have taken place much earlier than 3500 cal BC. Just about this time, when the ox-drawn cart or wagon with two or four solid wheels became locally available, the pastoral Pit Grave (alias Yamna or Yamnaya) culture (Figures 4.5, 4.6: Y), according to a number of radiocarbon dates, emerged in the Pontic steppe and began to expand.

This is the starting point for the following scenario, which is put forward as a set of theses for further substantiation or falsification. Undoubtedly, many details need adjustment and are subject to correction. However, this is a holistic attempt to fit together several interacting factors, and it seems difficult to find any other archaeological model which in general could equally well explain the areal and temporal distribution of the Indo-European and Uralic languages and the internal contacts between them at different times and in different places. This applies especially if the invention of wheeled transport is taken as the *terminus post quem* for the dispersal of Late Proto-Indo-European.

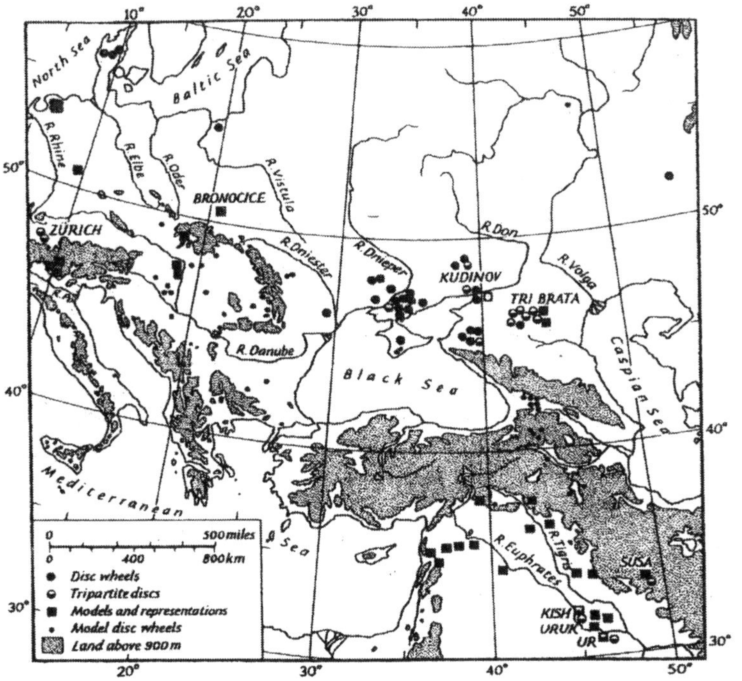

Figure 4.4 Distribution of the earliest finds of wheeled vehicles, 3500–2000 cal BC.
Source: Piggott 1983: 59, fig. 27.

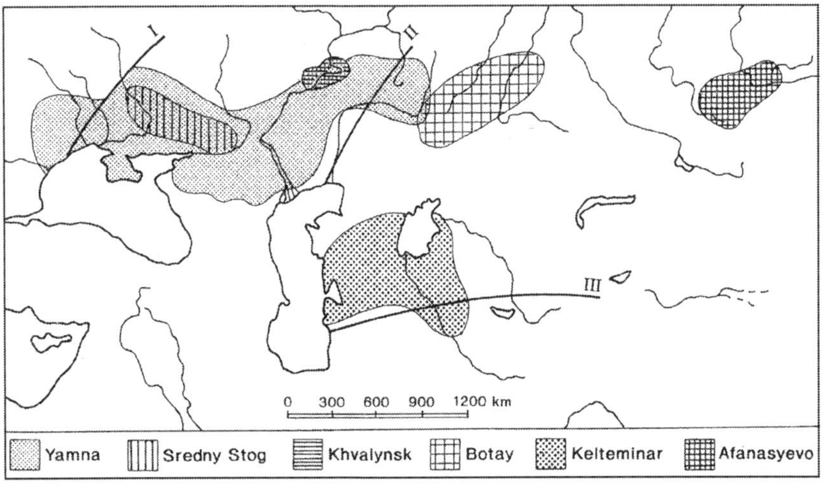

Figure 4.5 The Eurasian steppe region in the fifth–third millennium BC.
Source: Mallory 1994–95: 254, fig. 3.

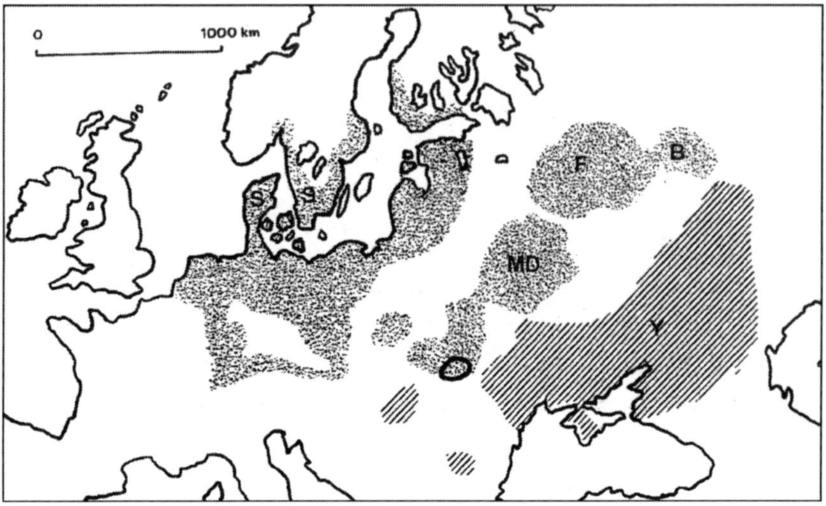

Figure 4.6 The distribution of the Pit Grave (Yamnaya) culture (Y and diagonal lines) and the Corded Ware cultural entity (stippled).

Source: Carpelan and Parpola 2001, fig. 6, adapted from Rowlett 1987: 194, map 1.

Notes
Within the Corded Ware area, the circle indicates the Sub-Carpathian group, MD = the Middle Dnieper culture, F = the Fat'yanovo culture, B = the Balanovo culture and S = the Scandinavian Corded Ware culture. The Pit Grave culture formed *c.*3500 cal BC and began to give way to the Catacomb Grave and Poltavka cultures *c.*2700 cal BC. The Middle Dnieper culture and the Sub-Carpathian group formed by 3300 cal BC, whereafter the Corded Ware culture expanded rapidly to the eastern Baltic and Finland on the one hand, and central Europe and the North European plain on the other, but did not enter Scandinavia until *c.*2800 cal BC. At the same time, the Middle Dnieper culture on the one hand, and the Baltic–Belorussian Corded Ware culture on the other, expanded toward the Volga–Oka interfluve forming the Fat'yanovo culture. Probably *c.*2200 cal BC the Balanovo culture formed on the mid-Volga as a result of movement and adaption of Fat'yanovo communities. It is necessary to remember that the Volosovo culture formed in the region as early as 3650 cal BC and existed there together with Fat'yanovo and Balanovo until assimilation led to the formation of the Netted Ware culture along the upper, and the Chirkovo culture along the mid-Volga, in the beginning of the second millennium BC.

4.9 A systematic correlation of the Indo-European and Uralic linguistic groups with specific archaeological cultures

The parent language that immediately preceded and gave birth to Proto-Indo-European was spoken in the Eneolithic Khvalynsk culture (5000–4500 cal BC) of the mid-Volga forest steppe (Figure 4.5), descended from the Samara culture (6000–5000 cal BC) of the same area. Like its predecessors, the Khvalynsk culture interacted with the Sub-Neolithic hunter-gatherers occupying the forests of the upper Volga region. Here the Lyalovo culture (5000–3650 cal BC) spoke an early variety of Proto-Uralic, which with the Pitted Ware typical of Lyalovo culture soon spread to Russian Karelia in the north, to the forest steppe between the Dnieper and the Don in the southwest and almost to the Kama basin in the east. A later variety of Proto-Uralic spread rapidly with new immigrants arriving around 3900 cal BC (with Combed Ware Style 2 and semisubterranean houses) from the Lyalovo culture of the upper Volga to Finland and Russian Karelia up to the Arctic Circle as well as to Estonia and Latvia; the entire area up to the Urals was united by an efficient exchange network.

The Khvalynsk culture expanded both east and west along the border of the steppe and forest-steppe. In the east, Khvalynsk immigrants, after a long trek, eventually reached southern Siberia and founded the Afanas'evo culture (3600–2500 cal BC) (Figure 4.5). In the west, the expansion of the Khvalynsk culture created the Mariupol' and Chapli type burials (5000–4500 cal BC) in the Pontic steppe part of the Dnieper–Donets culture, in the area next occupied by the Srednij Stog culture (4500–3350 cal BC) (Figure 4.5).

The Khvalynsk influence reached even further west, being represented by the Decea Muresului cemetery of Romania (4500 cal BC). The Suvorovo culture (4500–4100 cal BC) of Moldavia and Bulgaria probably belongs to the same wave of immigration, for it has been considered as resulting from an early Srednij Stog expansion to the west. Thus both the Afanas'evo culture of central Siberia, which is considered to be related to the Quäwrighul culture (2000–1550 cal BC) of Sinkiang, the region where Tocharian was later spoken, and the Suvorovo culture of Bulgaria would both have preserved the pre-Proto-Indo-European language of the Khvalynsk culture. This more archaic language would have largely prevailed in the subsequent fusions with later Proto-Indo-European speaking immigrants, who arrived at both areas with wheeled vehicles after the Srednij Stog culture was transformed into the Pit Grave culture (Figures 4.5, 4.6: Y) *c.*3500–3350 cal BC. The Ezero culture (3300–2700 cal BC) of Bulgaria, which resulted from the fusion with the early Pit Grave immigrants, took this pre-Proto-Indo-European language in a somewhat changed form into Anatolia 2700 cal BC, where it became Hittite, Luwian, etc.

The Indo-European proto-language was spoken in the Srednij Stog culture (4500–3350 cal BC) of southern Ukraine, an offshoot of the Khvalynsk culture with a Dnieper-Donets culture substratum. It developed in interaction with the non-Indo-European speaking prosperous Tripol'e culture (5500–3000 cal BC) (cf. Figure 4.7: F), but had contact also with the early Proto-Uralic speaking Lyalovo culture (5000–3650 cal BC) which extended to the forest-steppe between the Dnieper and the Don. After acquiring wheeled transport *c.*3500 cal BC, the Srednij Stog culture started expanding and disintegrating. It was first transformed into the Pit Grave (Yamnaya) culture (3500–2200 cal BC) distinguished by kurgan burials. Expanding northward to the forest-steppe zone, early Pit Grave culture participated in the formation of the Middle Dnieper culture (Figures 4.6: MD; 4.7: I) by 3300 cal BC and thus contributed to the formation of the new Corded Ware cultural complex (Figures 4.6, 4.7), which quickly spread over wide areas of central and northern Europe, appearing in the Baltic countries and southwestern Finland 3200–3100 cal BC and a little later in the Netherlands. The language of the Corded Ware culture,

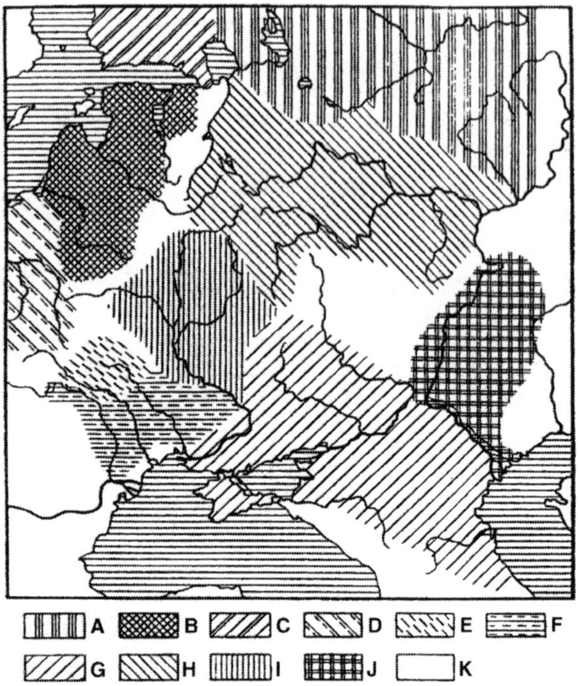

Figure 4.7 Middle Bronze Age cultures in eastern Europe *c*.2500 cal BC.

Source: Bader *et al.* 1987: 61, map 6.

Notes

A: Subneolithic/Eneolithic cultures of northern Russia. B: The Corded Ware culture of the eastern Baltic. C: The Corded Ware culture of Finland. [The distribution shown in the map is too extensive: it is limited to the coastal zone, while the Subneolithic/Eneolithic zone of A extended to eastern Finland.] D: The Globular Amphora culture. E: The Early Corded Ware culture. F: The Late Tripol'e culture. G: The Catacomb Grave culture. H: The Fat'yanovo culture. [The Volosovo culture existed simultaneously in the same area.] I: The Middle Dnieper culture. J: The Poltavka culture. K: Areas not studied. The white spot in the middle of the Catacomb Grave, Poltavka and Fat'yanovo cultures is the area where the Abashevo culture emerged.

Proto-Northwest-Indo-European, was still close to Proto-Indo-European, but started to diverge into Proto-Italo-Celtic, Proto-Germanic, and Proto-Balto-Slavic under the influence of the local substratum languages. In southwestern Finland and in Estonia (Figure 4.7: B and C), the Corded Ware superstratum was absorbed and integrated in the local population, which spoke late Proto-Uralic. This created a cultural boundary between the (southwestern) Corded Ware area and the rest of Finland and Karelia, and led to the differentiation between Finnic and Saami.

The Corded Ware culture of the southern Baltic and Belorussia, whose language had become (pre-)Proto-Baltic, expanded to central Russia *c*.2800 cal BC. Here it formed the Fat'yanovo culture (2800–1900 cal BC) in the Volga–Oka interfluve

(Figure 4.6: F; Figure 4.7: H) and the Balanovo culture (2200–1900 cal BC) in the mid-Volga region (Figure 4.6: B). These cultures lived in symbiosis with the Proto-Finno-Ugric speaking peoples of the Volosovo culture (3650–1900 cal BC) (Figure 4.7: H), which had succeeded the late Proto-Uralic speaking Lyalovo culture (5000–3650 cal BC). The Volosovo people, who continued having exchange relationships with their linguistic relatives in Finland and Russian Karelia, eventually absorbed linguistically these Proto-Baltic speakers, whose language and culture deeply influenced the Finno-Ugric languages and cultures of the northwest. A cultural border (similar to that between Finnic and Saami) formed between the Proto-Volgaic speakers in the west and the unmixed Proto-Permic speakers in the east. Possibly under the pressure of the Fat'yanovo–Balanovo culture, part of the Volosovo population moved east to the Kama Valley, participating there in the development of the Garino–Bor culture and becoming the linguistic ancestors of the Ugric branch of the Uralic family (cf. Krajnov 1987a,b, 1992).

From northern Germany the Corded Ware culture expanded also to southern Scandinavia (Figure 4.6: S) about 2800 cal BC, around which time (pre-)Proto-Germanic came into being. Proto-Germanic loanwords in Finnic languages are likely to date from 1600 cal BC onwards, when the Nordic Bronze Age culture (1700–500 cal BC) started exerting a strong influence on coastal Finland and Estonia. Proto-North-Saami speakers, expanding to northern Fennoscandia with the Lovozero Ware (1900–1000 cal BC), eventually came into direct contact with Proto-Germanic.

The main sources of the earliest Aryan loanwords in Finnic and Saami are the Abashevo and Sejma-Turbino cultures (representing the Indo-Aryan branch) and the Pozdnyakovo culture (representing the Iranian branch), all to be discussed further. In the eighteenth century BC, both the Abashevo and the Pozdnyakovo culture contributed to the development of the probably Proto-Volga-Finnic speaking Netted Ware culture of the upper Volga, which in turn exerted a strong influence on eastern Finland and Russian Karelia (Figure 4.8).

The main area of the Pit Grave culture (3500–2200 cal BC) comprised the Proto-Indo-European homeland of the preceding Srednij Stog culture, with some further penetration in the west to the Danube, and an eastern extension from the Pontic and forest-steppe to the southern Urals, which was reached by 3000 cal BC. Thus the Pit Grave culture came to occupy much the same area as the Eneolithic Khvalynsk culture that we have suggested was linguistically pre-Proto-Indo-European speaking. Hence the Late Proto-Indo-European languages of this central group are not likely to have had non-Indo-European substrata and consequently preserved their inherited structure and vocabulary much better than many other groups. The differentiation of the Pit Grave culture into several subcultures started in 2800 cal BC and was undoubtedly accompanied by linguistic differentiation, so that Proto-Graeco-Armenian developed in the Catacomb Grave culture of the Pontic steppes (Figure 4.7: G), and Proto-Aryan in the Poltavka culture of the Volga-Ural steppe (Figure 4.7: J) and the Abashevo culture of the upper Don forest steppe (Figure 4.7: K; Figure 4.9: K).

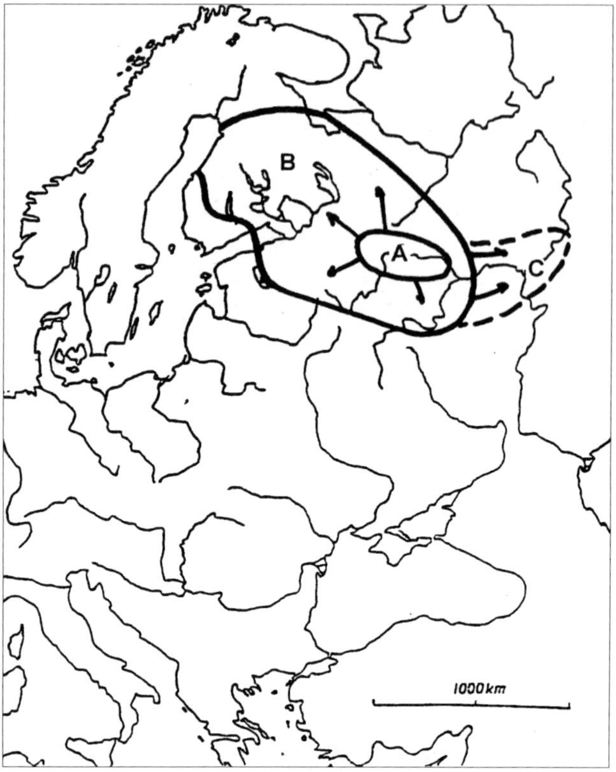

Figure 4.8 Distribution of Netted Ware.

Source: Carpelan in Carpelan and Parpola 2001, fig. 16.

Notes

A: Emergence of Netted Ware on the upper Volga *c.*1900 cal BC. B: Spread of Netted Ware by *c.*1800 cal BC. C: Early Iron Age spread of Netted Ware.

The dialectal differentiation of Proto-Aryan into its two main branches seems to have started with this early cultural divergence in the eastern Pit Grave culture, so that people of the Poltavka culture in the southern treeless steppe spoke pre-Proto-Iranian, while the language of the Abashevo culture in the northern forest-steppe was pre-Proto-Indo-Aryan. The Poltavka culture was throughout in closer contact with the Catacomb Grave culture, which probably spoke Proto-Graeco-Armenian, while the Abashevo culture, in its quest for the copper of the mid-Volga region, first established contact with the more northerly Fat'yanovo–Balanovo and Volosovo cultures of the forest zone, where (pre-)Proto-Baltic and Proto-Finno-Ugric respectively were spoken. Early Aryan loanwords in Proto-Finno-Ugric connected with honey and wax industry, which has flourished especially in the mid-Volga region, strongly suggest that the elite language

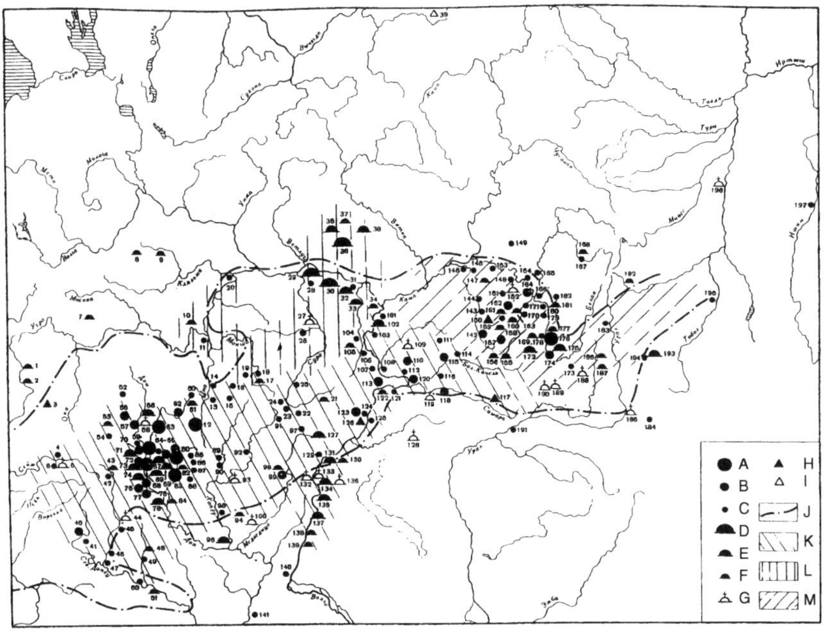

Figure 4.9 Sites and area of the Abashevo cultural-historical community.

Source: Pryakhin and Khalikov 1987: 126, map 23.

Notes

A: a cluster of six to ten habitation sites with Abashevo ceramics. B: a cluster of two to five Abashevo sites. C: a single Abashevo site. D: a cluster of six to ten cemeteries with kurgan burials. E: a cluster of two to five cemeteries with kurgan burials. F: a single cemetery with kurgan burials. G: isolated kurgan burials and cemeteries with a few kurgans or burials of the Abashevo type. H: cemetery without kurgan burials. I: an isolated non-kurgan burial. J: the present border of the forest-steppe. K: Area of the Don–Volga variant of the Abashevo culture. L: Area of the mid-Volga variant of the Abashevo culture. M: Area of the southern Urals variant of the Abashevo culture.

of the Abashevo culture was Aryan, and the here proposed new etymology for a Proto-Volga-Permic word for 'beeswax' narrows the identification to pre-Proto-Indo-Aryan.

The differences between the languages of the Poltavka and Abashevo cultures are likely to have remained on a dialectal level until 1800 cal BC. The period of the Sintashta-Arkaim cultural expression (2200–1800 cal BC) (Figure 4.10; Gening *et al.* 1992; Vasil'ev *et al.* 1994; Zdanovich 1997) seems to be the last phase of the relatively unified Proto-Aryan speech. Both Poltavka and Abashevo participated in the creation of this powerful and dynamic culture in the southern Urals which appears to have developed the horse-drawn chariot (Figures 4.11, 4.15: 4; Anthony and Vinogradov 1995; Anthony 1998). The profound influence that radiated from Sintashta-Arkaim into both Poltavka and Abashevo horizons is likely to have had

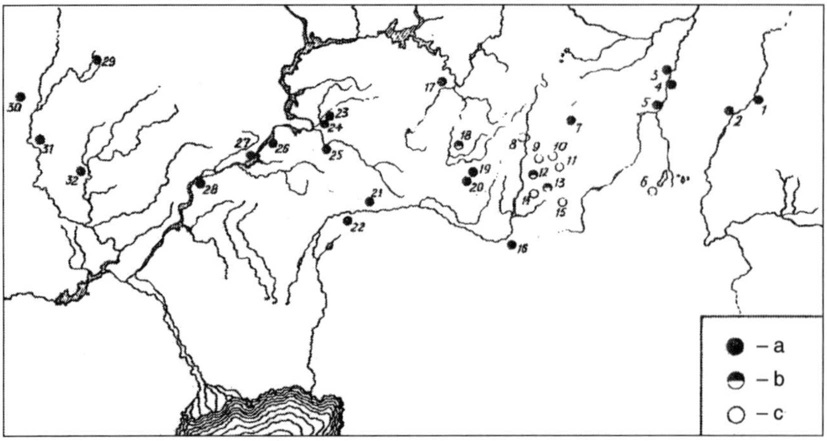

Figure 4.10 Map of important Pre-Timber Grave and Pre-Andronovo sites of the Potapovka-Sintashta-Petrovka horizon (2200–1800 cal BC).

Source: Vasil'ev *et al.* 1994: 166, fig. 62.

Notes

a = habitation site, b = habitation and cemetery, c = cemetery. 1 = Petrovka, 3 = Tsarev Kurgan, 11 = Krivoe Ozera, 12 = Arkaim, 13 = Sintashta, 16 = Novyj Kumak, 23 = Potapovka, 25 = Utevka, 28 = Pokrovsk, 32 = Vlasovka.

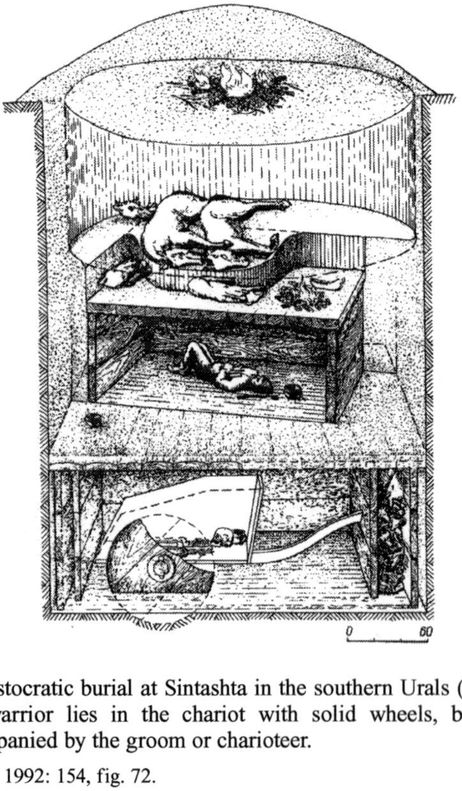

Figure 4.11 An aristocratic burial at Sintashta in the southern Urals (2200–1800 cal BC). The warrior lies in the chariot with solid wheels, beneath two horses accompanied by the groom or charioteer.

Source: Gening *et al.* 1992: 154, fig. 72.

some unifying effect. This could have included the transference of "satemization," possibly triggered by the Proto-Finno-Ugric substratum influence upon the pre-Proto-Indo-Aryan spoken in the Abashevo culture, over to the pre-Proto-Iranian spoken in the pre-Timber Grave horizon of the Late Poltavka/Potapovka and Pozdnyakovo cultures. Yet the palatal affricates or sibilants resulting from the satemization in pre-Proto-Indo-Aryan seem to have lost their palatalization in pre-Proto-Iranian which did not have a "palatalizing" language as a substratum. (For very early Finno-Ugric loanwords from pre-Proto-Iranian attesting to this depalatalization, cf. Koivulehto 1999: 224–6, 2001: 49.) Archaeologically, the pre-Timber Grave horizon in the west does not yet essentially differ from the pre-Andronovo horizon in the east, which in addition to the Sintashta-Arkaim itself (succeeded in the southern Urals by the Alakul' culture of the Andronovo complex), includes the Petrovka cultural expression in northern Kazakhstan.

Proto-Greek did not become a Satem language, while Proto-Armenian did. In our estimate, the most likely of the various alternative scenarios presented by different scholars for the coming of the Proto-Greek speakers to Greece (cf. Mallory and Adams 1997: 243–5) is the violent break in the archaeological record between Early Helladic II and III, *c.*2200 BC; tumulus burials and the domesticated horse are found in Greece in the succeeding Middle Helladic period. This suggests that Proto-Greek descends from the Proto-Graeco-Armenian language of the early Catacomb Grave culture. After the separation of Proto-Greek, the Catacomb Grave culture was transformed into the Multiple-Relief-band (Mnogovalikovaya) Ware culture (*c.*2000–1800 cal BC) (cf. Figure 4.13: 5) and its Proto-Graeco-Armenian language into (pre-) Proto-Armenian, which became a Satem language due to its contact with Proto-Iranian. The Multiple-Relief-band Ware culture extended from the Don up to Moldavia, and was eventually overlaid and assimilated by the Proto-Iranian speaking Timber Grave (Srubnaya) culture (1800–1500 cal BC) (Figure 4.12, 4.13: 6). The Armenians are assumed to have come to Anatolia from the Balkans in the twelfth century BC, being possibly the invaders called Muški in Assyrian sources (cf. Mallory 1989: 33–5; Mallory and Adams 1997: 26–30).

The final split of Proto-Aryan into its "Indo-Aryan" and "Iranian" branches appears to have taken place *c.*1800 BC, when the Ural river more or less became the border between Proto-Iranian spoken to the west of it in the Timber Grave (Srubnaya) culture (which evolved from the earlier pre-Timber Grave cultures), and Proto-Indo-Aryan spoken to the east of it in the Andronovo cultural complex (which evolved from the earlier pre-Andronovo cultures) (Figure 4.12; Avanesova 1991; Kuzmina 1994) (cf. Parpola 1998). Excepting some interference in the immediate neighborhood of the border area, the two branches stayed apart and expanded into opposite directions until the fifteenth century BC. The early Andronovo phase (1800–1500 cal BC), principally represented by the Alakul' Ware of the southern Urals and western Siberia but also by early Fedorovo Ware, which in Siberia reached as far as the upper Yenisei, was succeeded by the late Andronovo phase (1500–1200 cal BC), the Fedorovo horizon proper, which in the southeast reached as far as the Tien-shan mountains.

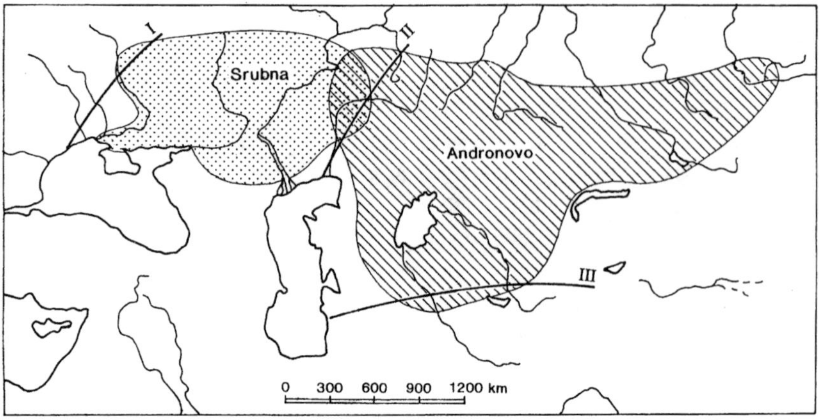

Figure 4.12 Distribution of the cultures belonging to the Timber Grave (Srubnaya) and Andronovo horizons.

Source: Mallory 1994–95: 252, fig. 1.

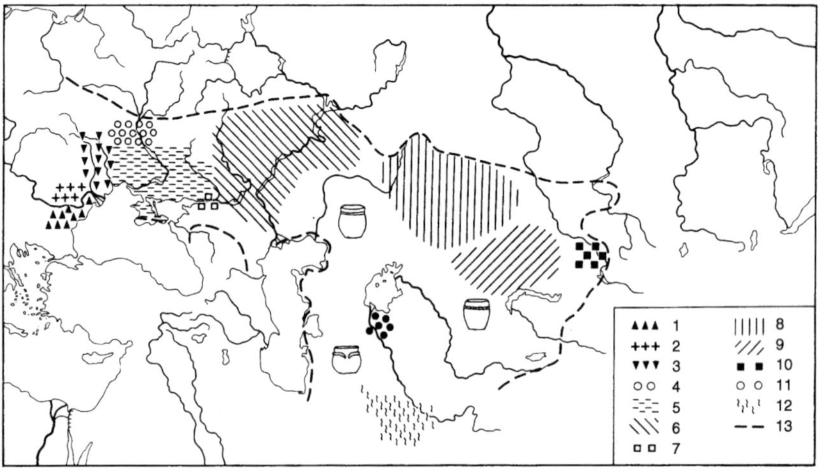

Figure 4.13 Distribution of cultures distinguished by the Single Relief-band (Valikovaya) pottery. 5 = Sabatinovka and Belozerka (occupying the area formerly occupied by the Multiple Relief-band culture), 6 = Timber Grave culture, 12 = Yaz I culture.

Source: Chernykh 1992: 236, fig. 79.

Some of the principal sound changes differentiating Proto-Iranian from Proto-Indo-Aryan (which in these respects agrees with Proto-Aryan) seem to have resulted from the substratum influence of the languages spoken in the areas into which Timber Grave culture expanded (cf. Parpola 2002a,b). It has long been observed that the change *$s > h$ in similar phonic contexts (between vowels and word-initially before a vowel, and in some other contexts, but not before and after stops) is a significant isogloss connecting Greek, Armenian, and Iranian languages; moreover, it has taken place in all these languages before their earliest historical records came into being. Yet from the point of view of Proto-Indo-European it is a relatively late change, being in Iranian posterior to the RUKI change of $s > \check{s}$ (cf. Meillet 1908: 86–8). We now know that in Greek the *$s > h$ change predates even the Mycenaean texts. It was proposed by Karl Hoffmann (1975: 14) that this Proto-Iranian sound change was still productive when the first Iranian languages arrived in the Indo-Iranian borderlands in the neighborhood of the Ṛgvedic tribes sometimes around the fifteenth century BC, changing the Vedic river name *Sindhu* into Avestan *Hindu*, Vedic *Sarasvatī* into Avestan *Haraxvaitī*, and so on. Temporally and areally this coincides with the introduction of the Yaz I culture (1400–1000 cal BC) (Figure 4.13: 12) into southern Central Asia (cf. Hintze 1998). If the Catacomb Grave culture spoke Proto-Graeco-Armenian, it is difficult to believe that its *$s > h$ change is independent from that of Proto-Iranian, for the Catacomb Grave culture was transformed into the Multiple-Relief-band Ware culture (2000–1800 cal BC); the latter probably spoke Proto-Armenian and was in 1800 cal BC overlaid and assimilated by the Timber Grave culture (Figure 4.12, 4.13: 5), the derivative of which from 1500 cal BC onward spread to southern Central Asia with the simple Relief-band (Valikovaya) Ware (Figure 4.13).

Similarly, the deaspiration of voiced aspirates is an isogloss connecting Iranian with Balto-Slavic (as well as with Albanian and Celtic, cf. Meillet 1908: 75). In Iranian it might have been triggered by the absorption of late Corded Ware cultures into the Timber Grave culture in the more northerly parts of eastern Europe.

The Sintashta-Arkaim culture appears to have mainly continued the Abashevo culture, which pushed eastward into the Siberian forest steppe in order to take possession of the important metal ores in the Altai region. As demonstrated by Carpelan with reference to the evolution of the socketed spearhead (Carpelan and Parpola 2001), this led to the formation of the Sejma–Turbino Intercultural Phenomenon (Figure 4.14), which mediated new types of high-quality metal tools and weapons along a zone connecting the Altai mountains over the Urals with northeastern Europe. (So far, the Sejma–Turbino Intercultural Phenomenon has been thought to originate in the Altai region, cf. Chernykh 1992: 215–34.) The Andronoid cultures and the Samus' cultural expression emerged in the forest zone of western Siberia under the influence of the Andronovo and Sejma–Turbino complexes. The language of the Sejma–Turbino complex and the Andronoid cultures continued the Finno-Ugric speech of that part of the bilingual Abashevo community which crossed the Urals and headed toward the Altai mountains, becoming the ancestors of the Proto-Samoyed speakers (cf. Carpelan 1999). If this is correct, the Samoyed branch

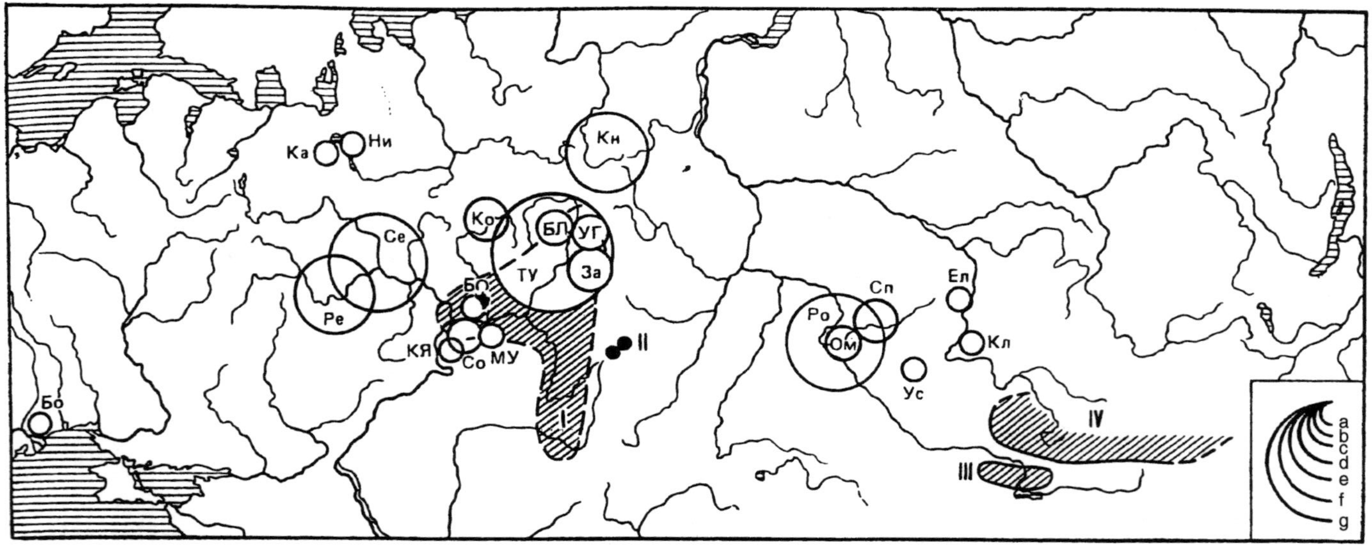

Figure 4.14 Location of copper ores (I = the Urals region, IV = Altai) and the Sejma–Turbino cemeteries (Ce = Sejma, Ty = Turbino, Po = Rostovka, Ел = Elunino, УГ = Ust' Gajva). The size of the circular markings indicates the number of finds according to the following scale: a = 1–2 , b = 2–5, c = 5–10, d = 10–20, e = 20–50, f = 50–100, g = more than 100 finds.

Source: Bader *et al*. 1987: 87, map 13.

originally belongs to the same group of Volosovo people who came to the Kama basin as the Proto-Ugric speakers, although the future Samoyed speakers did not stay on the Kama and there develop common innovations with the Ugric branch.

After the Timber Grave culture had developed horseback warfare, the Proto-Iranian speakers became very mobile and expanded from the Pontic-Caspian area also east of the Ural river into the Asiatic steppes, overlaying and assimilating there the earlier Andronovo cultures. They seem to have come to southern Central Asia with the Yaz I culture (Figure 4.13: 12) and to southern Siberia in the thirteenth century BC in the closing Fedorovo phase of the Andronovo cultural complex. Here the Andronovo culture was succeeded by the at least partly genetically related Karasuk culture (1200–1000 cal BC), which flourished around the upper Yenisei, Mongolia, and the Ordos region of China. The Karasuk culture preceded the transition from the Late Bronze Age to the Early Iron Age of the "Scythian culture," when the extensive use of the saddled horse, the composite bow and the "animal style art" had become integral parts of steppe life (cf. Askarov *et al.* 1992). Around 1000 BC, the Eurasiatic steppes from Mongolia to Hungary became more or less uniform culturally, and for the next thousand years and more Old and Middle Iranian Scythian/Saka languages were spoken there; descendants of these languages survive now only in the Ossete language of the Caucasus and the Wakhi language of the Pamirs, the latter related to the Saka once spoken in Khotan. The varieties of Old Iranian that in the late second millennium BC came from the northern steppes to southern Central Asia and Afghanistan – the regions where the Avestan language is assumed to have been spoken – seem to have given rise to most of, if not all, the other Iranian languages of today. (On the Iranian languages, see especially Schmitt 1989.) Cuyler Young (1985) derives the Late West Iranian Buff Ware, which *c.*950 BC appears in the regions where Median and Old Persian were first attested, from the Gurgan Buff Ware (*c.*1100–1000 BC) of southern Central Asia.

The fate of the Indo-Aryan branch beyond Central Asia lies outside the scope of our paper (Carpelan and Parpola 2001), but a few observations on this topic may be made in conclusion (this theme is dealt with extensively in Parpola 2002a,b). It has been noted earlier that the horse-drawn chariot was probably developed in the Sintashta-Arkaim culture (Figure 4.11, 4.15: 4). The Proto-Indo-Aryan speaking rulers of the Mitanni kingdom in 1500–1300 BC were famed for their horse-chariotry (cf. Mayrhofer 1966, 1974). The Mitanni Aryans in all likelihood came to Syria from southern Central Asia and northern Iran, where a cylinder seal with the image of a horse-drawn chariot was discovered from Tepe Hissar III B (cf. Ghirshman 1977). Tepe Hissar III B–C represents an extension of the Bactria and Margiana Archaeological Complex (BMAC) (cf. Hiebert and Lamberg-Karlovsky 1992; Hiebert 1994: 177). The rich, semiurban, agriculturally based BMAC had local roots, but its rule seems to have been taken over by Aryan speakers coming from the northern steppes (cf. Parpola 1988; Hiebert 1993, 1995). The Proto-Indo-Aryan expansion to northern Iran and Syria may have been triggered by the tin trade with Central

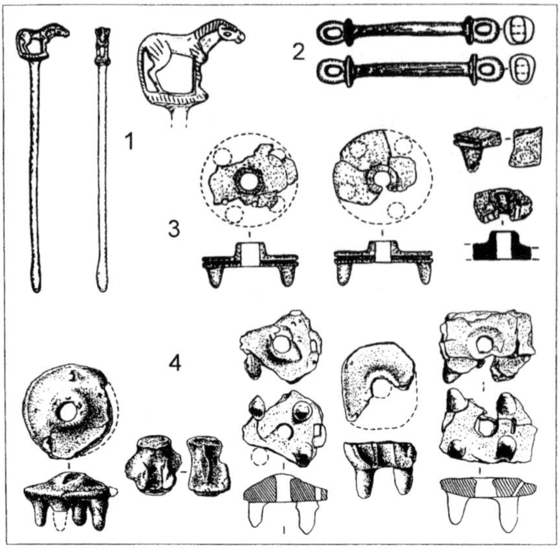

Figure 4.15 A horse-headed "sceptre" pin of bronze (1), two horse bits of bronze (2) and fragments of cheek-pieces of bone (3) from an aristocratic burial at Zardcha Khalifa in Zeravshan Valley, Tajikistan. The horse-headed "sceptre" has close parallels in the steppe, and the cheek pieces are of the same type as those found at Sintashta (4). Not to scale.

Source: Bobomulloev 1997: 126, Abb. 3: 14 [= 1] and 12–13 [= 2] and 128: Abb. 4: 1–4 [= 3]. The horse-headed "sceptre" has close parallels in the steppe (see Carpelan and Parpola 2001, fig. 27.) Gening *et al.* 1992: 133, fig. 57: 7–8, 10–12 [= 4].

Asia in which the Assyrian merchants of Cappadocia were engaged in 1920–1850 BC: the glyptic evidence suggests that the BMAC, too, was directly involved in this trade (cf. Collon 1987: 41, 142). An aristocratic grave recently discovered in the Zeravshan Valley of Tajikistan contained typical BMAC pottery (cf. Sarianidi 2001: 434), but also horse furnishings, including two bronze bits and two pairs of Sintashta-Arkaim type cheek pieces, as well as a bronze "sceptre" topped with the image of the horse (cf. Bobomulloev 1997) (Figure 4.15: 1–3). This find heralds the coming of Proto-Indo-Aryan speakers to the borders of South Asia, where the horse-drawn chariot played an important role in the culture of the Vedic Aryans (cf. Sparreboom 1983).

References

Abondolo, D., ed., 1998. *The Uralic Languages* (Routledge language family descriptions). London and New York: Routledge.

Anthony, D. W., 1995. "Horse, Wagon and Chariot: Indo-European Languages and Archaeology," *Antiquity*, 69(264): 554–65.

——, 1998. "The Opening of the Eurasian Steppe at 2000 BCE." In *The Bronze Age and Iron Age Peoples of Eastern Central Asia* (The Journal of Indo-European Studies Monograph, 26), Vol. I, edited by V. H. Mair. Washington, DC: Institute for the Study of Man, pp. 94–113.

Anthony, D. W. and N. B. Vinogradov, 1995. "Birth of the chariot," *Archaeology*, 48(2): 36–41.

Askarov, A., V. Volkov, and N. Ser-Odjav, 1992. "Pastoral and Nomadic Tribes at the Beginning of the First Millennium B.C." In *History of Civilizations of Central Asia*, Vol. I, edited by A. H. Dani and V. M. Masson. Paris: UNESCO, pp. 459–72.

Avanesova, N. A., 1991. *Kul'tura pastusheshkikh plemen èpokhi bronzy Aziatskoj chasti SSSR (po metallicheskim izdeliyam)*. Tashkent: Izdatel'stvo 'Fan' UzSSR.

Bader, O. N., D. A. Krajnov, and M. F. Kosarev, eds, 1987. *Èpokha bronzy lesnoj polosy SSSR (Arkheologiya SSSR)*. Moskva: Izdatel'stva "Nauka."

Bereczki, G., 1988. "Geschichte der wolgafinnischen Sprachen." In *The Uralic Languages: Description, History, and Foreign Influences* (Handbuch der Orientalistik, Abt. 8: 1), edited by D. Sinor. Leiden: E. J. Brill, pp. 314–50.

Bobomulloev, S., 1997. Ein bronzezeitliches Grab aus Zardča Chalifa bei Pendžikent (Zeravšan-Tal). *Archäologische Mitteilungen aus Iran und Turan*, 29: 121–34.

Carpelan, C., 1999. "Käännekohtia Suomen esihistoriassa aikavälillä 5100. . . 1000 eKr." In *Pohjan poluilla: Suomalaisten juuret nykytutkimuksen mukaan* (Bidrag till kännedom av Finlands natur och folk, 153), edited by P. Fogelberg. Helsinki: Societas Scientiarum Fennica, pp. 249–80.

Carpelan, C. and A. Parpola, 2001. "Emergence, Contacts and Dispersal of Proto-Indo-European, Proto-Uralic and Proto-Aryan in Archaeological Perspective." In *Early Contacts Between Uralic and Indo-European: Linguistic and Archaeological Considerations* (Mémoires de la Société Finno-Ougrienne, 242), edited by C. Carpelan, A. Parpola, and P. Koskikallio. Helsinki: Suomalais-Ugrilainen Seura, pp. 55–156.

Chernykh, E. N., 1992. *Ancient Metallurgy in the USSR: The Early Metal Age*. Translated by Sarah Wright. Cambridge: Cambridge University Press.

Collinder, B., 1955. *Fenno-Ugric Vocabulary: An Etymological Dictionary of the Uralic Languages*. Stockholm: Almqvist and Wiksell.

Collon, D., 1987. *First Impressions: Cylinder Seals in the Ancient Near East*. London: British Museum Publications.

Crane, E., 1999. *The World History of Beekeeping and Honey Hunting*. London: Duckworth.

Gening, V. F., G. B. Zdanovich, and V. V. Gening, 1992. *Sintashta. Arkheologicheskie pamyatniki arijskikh plemen uralo-kazakhstanskikh stepej*. Chelyabinsk: Yuzhno-Ural'skoe knizhnoe izdatel'stvo.

Ghirshman, R., 1977. *L'Iran et la migration des Indo-Aryens et des Iraniens*. Leiden: E. J. Brill.

Hajdú, P., 1975. *Finno-Ugrian Languages and Peoples*. Translated and adapted by G. F. Cushing (The language library). London: André Deutsch.

——, 1987. "Die uralischen Sprachen." In *Die uralischen Sprachen und Literaturen* (Bibliotheca Uralica, 8), edited by P. Hajdú and P. Domokos (Hrsg.). Budapest: Akadémiai Kiadó and Hamburg: Helmut Buske Verlag, pp. 21–45.

Hämäläinen, A., 1935. "Beiträge zur Geschichte der primitiven Bienenzucht bei den finnisch-ugrischen Völkern," *Journal de la Société Finno-Ougrienne*, 47(1): 1–40.

——, 1937. "Das kultische Wachsfeuer der Mordvinen und Tscheremissen. Beiträge zur Erforschung der Religion und der Glaubensvorstellungen der finnisch-ugrischen Völker in Ostrussland," *Journal de la Société Finno-Ougrienne*, 48: 1–158.

Hiebert, F. T., 1993. "Chronology of Margiana and Radiocarbon Dates," *Information Bulletin of the International Association for the Study of Cultures of Central Asia*, 19: 136–48.

——, 1994. *Origins of the Bronze Age Oasis Civilization in Central Asia* (American School of Prehistoric Research Bulletin, 42). Cambridge, MA: Peabody Museum.

——, 1995. "South Asia from a Central Asian perspective (3500–1750 B.C.)," In *The Indo-Aryans of Ancient South Asia: Language, Material Culture and Ethnicity* (Indian Philology and South Asian Studies, 1), edited by G. Erdosy. Berlin and New York: Walter de Gruyter, pp. 192–205.

Hiebert, F. T. and C. C. Lamberg-Karlovsky, 1992. "Central Asia and the Indo-Iranian Borderlands," *Iran*, 30: 1–15.

Hintze, A., 1998. "The Migrations of the Indo-Iranians and the Iranian Sound-change *s* > *h*." In *Sprache und Kultur der Indogermanen* (Innsbrucker Beiträge zur Sprachwissenschaft 93), edited by W. Meid (Hrsg.). Innsbruck: Institut für Sprachwissenschaft der Universität Innsbruck, pp. 139–53.

Hoffmann, K., 1975. *Aufsätze zur Indoiranistik*, I–II, edited by J. Narten (Hrsg.). Wiesbaden: Dr Ludwig Reichert Verlag.

Hultén, E. and M. Fries, 1986. *Atlas of North European Vascular Plants North of the Tropic of Cancer*, I–III. Königstein: Koeltz Scientific Books.

Itkonen, E., 1953–54. "Zur Geschichte des Vokalismus der ersten Silbe im Tscheremissischen und in den permischen Sprachen," *Finnisch-Ugrische Forschungen*, 31: 149–345.

Jacobsohn, H., 1922. *Arier und Ugrofinnen*. Göttingen: Vandenhoeck und Ruprecht.

Janhunen, J., 1977. *Samojedischer Wortschatz: Gemeinsamojedische Etymologien* (Castrenianumin toimitteita, 17). Helsinki: (distributor) Suomalais-Ugrilainen Seura.

——, 1981. "Uralilaisen kantakielen sanastosta," *Journal de la Société Finno-Ougrienne*, 77: 219–74.

Joki, A. J., 1973. *Uralier und Indogermanen. Die älteren Berührungen zwischen den uralischen und indogermanischen Sprachen* (Mémoires de la Société Finno-Ougrienne, 151). Helsinki: Suomalais-Ugrilainen Seura.

Kallio, P., 2001. "Uralisms in Indo-European?" In *Early Contacts Between Uralic and Indo-European: Linguistic and Archaeological Considerations* (Mémoires de la Société Finno-Ougrienne, 242), edited by C. Carpelan, A. Parpola, and P. Koskikallio. Helsinki: Suomalais-Ugrilainen Seura, pp. 221–34.

Koivulehto, J., 1979. "Phonotaktik als Wegweiser in der Lehnwortforschung: Die osfi. *-str-* Wörter," *Finnisch-Ugrische Forschungen*, 43: 67–79.

——, 1987. "Zu den frühen Kontakten zwischen Indogermanisch und Finnisch-Ugrisch." In *Parallelismus und Etymologie: Studien zu Ehren von Wolfgang Steinitz anlässlich seines 80. Geburtstags am Februar 1985*, edited by E. Lang and G. Sauer (Hrsg.) (Linguistische Studien, Reihe A, 161, II.). Berlin: Akademie der Wissenschaften der DDR, pp. 195–218.

——, 1999. "Varhaiset indoeurooppalaiskontaktit: aika ja paikka lainasanojen valossa." In *Pohjan poluilla: Suomalaisten juuret nykytutkimuksen mukaan* (Bidrag till kännedom av Finlands natur och folk, 153), edited by P. Fogelberg. Helsinki: Societas Scientiarum Fennica, pp. 207–36.

——, 2001. "The earliest contacts between Indo-European and Uralic speakers in the light of lexical loans." In *Early Contacts between Uralic and Indo-European: Linguistic and Archaeological Considerations* (Mémoires de la Société Finno-Ougrienne, 242), edited by C. Carpelan, A. Parpola, and P. Koskikallio. Helsinki: Suomalais-Ugrilainen Seura, pp. 235–63.

[Köppen, Th.] Keppen, F., 1886. *Materialy k voprosu pervonachal'noj rodině pervobytnom rodstvě indo-evropejskago i finno-ugorskago plemeni.* Sankt-Peterburg.

Köppen, Th., 1890. "Ein neuer tiergeographischer Beitrag zur Frage über die Urheimat der Indoeuropäer und Ugrofinnen." *Das Ausland*, 63(51): 1001–7.

Krajnov, D. A., 1987a. "Volosovskaya kul'tura." In *Èpokha bronzy lesnoj polosy SSSR* (Arkheologiya SSSR), edited by Bader *et al.* Moskva: Nauka, pp. 10–28.

——, 1987b. "Fat'yanovskaya kul'tura." In *Èpokha bronzy lesnoj polosy SSSR* (Arkheologiya SSSR), edited by Bader *et al.* Moskva: Nauka, pp. 58–76.

——, 1992. "On the Problem of Origin, Chronology and Periodization of the Fatyanovo-Balanovo cultural community." In *Die kontinentaleuropäischen Gruppen der Kultur mit Schnurkeramik* (Praehistorica, 19), edited by M. Buchvaldek and C. Strahm (Hrsg.). Praha: Univerzita Karlova, pp. 321–7.

Kuzmina, E. E., 1994. *Otkuda prishli indoarii? Material'naya kul'tura plemen andronovskoj obshchnosti i proiskhozhdenie indoirantsev.* Moskva: "Kalina."

Mallory, J. P., 1989. *In Search of the Indo-Europeans: Archaeology, Language and Religion.* London: Thames and Hudson.

——, 1994–95. "The Indo-European Homeland: An Asian perspective," *Bulletin of the Deccan College Post-Graduate and Research Institute*, 54–55: 237–54.

——, 1998. "A European Perspective on Indo-Europeans in Asia." In *The Bronze Age and Iron Age Peoples of Eastern Central Asia* (The Journal of Indo-European Studies Monograph, 26), Vol. I, edited by V. H. Mair. Washington, DC: Institute for the Study of Man, pp. 175–201.

——, 2001. "Uralics and Indo-Europeans: Problems of Time and Space." In *Early Contacts Between Uralic and Indo-European: Linguistic and Archaeological Considerations* (Mémoires de la Société Finno-Ougrienne, 242), edited by C. Carpelan, A. Parpola, and P. Koskikallio. Helsinki: Suomalais-Ugrilainen Seura, pp. 345–66.

Mallory, J. P. and D. Q. Adams, eds, 1997. *Encyclopedia of Indo-European Culture.* London: Fitzroy Dearborn Publishers.

Mallory, J. P. and V. H. Mair, 2000. *The Tarim Mummies: Ancient China and the Mystery of the Earliest Peoples from the West.* London: Thames and Hudson.

Mayrhofer, M., 1966. *Die Indo-Arier im alten Orient. Mit einer analytischen Bibliographie.* Wiesbaden: Otto Harrassowitz.

——, 1974. *Die Arier im Vorderen Orient – ein Mythos? Mit einem bibliographischen Supplement.* (Österreichische Akademie der Wissenschaften, Philosophisch- historische Klasse, Sitzungsberichte 294: 3.) Wien: Verlag der Österreichischen Akademie der Wissenschaften.

——, 1989. "Vorgeschichte der iranischen Sprachen; Uriranisch." In *Compendium linguarum iranicarum*, edited by R. Schmitt (Hrsg.). Wiesbaden: Dr Ludwig Reichert Verlag, pp. 4–24.

——, 1992–2001. *Etymologisches Wörterbuch des Altindoarischen*, I–III. (Indogermanische Bibliothek, Zweite Reihe.) Heidelberg: Carl Winter – Universitätsverlag.

Meid, W., 1994. "Die Terminologie von Pferd und Wagen im Indogermanischen." In *Die Indogermanen und das Pferd* (Archaeolingua, 4), edited by B. Hänsel and S. Zimmer (Hrsg.). Budapest: Archaeolingua Alapítvány, pp. 53–65.

Meillet, A., 1908. *Les dialectes indo-européens.* (Collection linguistique publiée par La Société de Linguistique de Paris, 1). Paris: Librairie ancienne Honoré Champion.

Paasonen, H., 1903. *Die finnisch-ugrischen s-Laute, I: Anlaut*. Helsingfors: Finnische Litteraturgesellschaft.

Parpola, A., 1983. "The Pre-Vedic Indian Background of the śrauta Rituals." In *Agni: The Vedic Ritual of the Fire Altar*, Vol. II, edited by F. Staal. Berkeley, CA: Asian Humanities Press, pp. 41–75.

——, 1988. "The Coming of the Aryans to Iran and India and the Cultural and Ethnic Identity of the Dāsas," *Studia Orientalia*, 64: 195–302.

——, 1995. "The Problem of the Aryans and the Soma: Textual-linguistic and archaeological evidence." In *The Indo-Aryans of Ancient South Asia: Language, Material Culture and Ethnicity* (Indian Philology and South Asian Studies, 1), edited by G. Erdosy. Berlin and New York: Walter de Gruyter, pp. 353–81.

——, 1998. "Aryan Languages, Archaeological Cultures, and Sinkiang: Where did Proto-Iranian come into Being, and How did it Spread?" In *The Bronze Age and Iron Age Peoples of Eastern Central Asia* (The Journal of Indo-European Studies Monograph, 26), Vol. I, edited by V. H. Mair. Washington, DC: Institute for the Study of Man, pp. 114–47.

——, 1999. "Varhaisten indoeurooppalaiskontaktien ajoitus ja paikannus kielellisen ja arkeologisen aineiston perusteella." In *Pohjan poluilla: Suomalaisten juuret nykytutkimuksen mukaan* (Bidrag till kännedom av Finlands natur och folk, 153), edited by P. Fogelberg. Helsinki: Societas Scientiarum Fennica, pp. 180–206.

——, 2002a. "From the dialects of Old Indo-Aryan to Proto-Indo-Aryan and Proto-Iranian." In *Indo-Iranian Languages and Peoples* (Proceedings of the British Academy, 116), edited by N. Sims-Williams. Oxford: Oxford University Press for The British Academy, pp. 43–102.

——, 2002b. "Pre-Proto-Iranians of Afghanistan as initiators of Śākta Tantrism: On the Scythian/Saka affiliation of the Dāsas, Nuristanis and Magadhans," *Iranica Antiqua*, 37: 233–324.

Pekkanen, T., 1973. "On the oldest relationship between Hungarians and Sarmatians: From Spali to Aspali," *Ural-Altaische Jahrbücher*, 45: 1–64.

Piggott, S., 1983. *The Earliest Wheeled Transport: From the Atlantic Coast to the Caspian Sea*. London: Thames & Hudson.

Plicht, J. van der, 1993. "The Groningen Radiocarbon Calibration Program," *Radiocarbon*, 35: 231–7.

Pokorny, J., 1959. *Indogermanisches etymologisches Wörterbuch*, I. Bern: Francke Verlag.

Porzig, W., 1954. *Die Gliederung des indogermanischen Sprachgebiets* (Indogermanische Bibliothek, Dritte Reihe: Untersuchungen). Heidelberg: Carl Winter – Universitätsverlag.

Pryakhin, A. D. and A. Kh. Khalikov, 1987. "Abashevskaya kul'tura." In *Èpokha bronzy lesnoj polosy SSSR* (Arkheologiya SSSR), edited by Bader *et al.* Moskva: Izdatel'stvo "Nauka," pp. 124–31.

Rédei, K., 1988–91. *Uralisches etymologisches Wörterbuch*, I–III. Wiesbaden: Otto Harrassowitz.

Rowlett, R. M., 1987. "Grave Wealth in the Horodenka Group of Sub-Carpathian Corded Ware," In *Proto-Indo-European: The Archaeology of a Linguistic Problem. Studies in Honor of Marija Gimbutas*, edited by S. N. Skomal and E. C. Polomé. Washington, DC: Institute for the Study of Man, pp. 191–202.

Sarianidi, V., 2001. "The Indo-Iranian Problem in the Light of Latest Excavations in Margiana." In *Vidyārṇavavandanam: Essays in Honour of Asko Parpola* (Studia

Orientalia, 94), edited by K. Karttunen and P. Koskikallio. Helsinki: The Finnish Oriental Society, pp. 417–41.

Schmitt, R., ed., 1989. *Compendium linguarum Iranicarum*. Wiesbaden: Dr Ludwig Reichert Verlag.

Sinor, D., ed., 1988. *The Uralic languages: Description, History, and Foreign Influences* (Handbuch der Orientalistik, Abt. 8: 1). Leiden: E. J. Brill.

SKES = Toivonen, Y. H. [I–II], Erkki Itkonen [II–VI], Aulis J. Joki [II–VI] and Reino Peltola [V–VI], 1955–78. *Suomen kielen etymologinen sanakirja*, I–VI (Lexica Societatis Fenno-Ugricae, XII: 1–6). Helsinki: Suomalais-Ugrilainen Seura.

Sparreboom, M., 1983. "Chariots in the Veda." PhD dissertation, University of Leiden, Leiden.

SSA = *Suomen sanojen alkuperä: Etymologinen sanakirja*, 1–3 (Suomalaisen Kirjallisuuden Seuran Toimituksia, 556; Kotimaisten kielten tutkimuskeskuksen julkaisuja 62), 1992–2000. Helsinki: Suomalaisen Kirjallisuuden Seura.

Sulimirski, T., 1970. *Prehistoric Russia: An Outline*. London: John Baker, and New York: Humanities Press.

Turner, R. L., 1966. *A Comparative Dictionary of the Indo-Aryan Languages*. London: Oxford University Press.

Vasil'ev, I. B., P. F. Kuznetsov, and A. P. Semënova, 1994. *Potapovskij kurgannyj mogil'nik indoiranskikh plemën na Volge*. Samara: Izdatel'stvo "Samarskij universitet."

Watkins, C., 1995. *How to Kill a Dragon: Aspects of Indo-European Poetics*. New York: Oxford University Press.

Young, T. C., Jr, 1985. "Early Iron Age Iran Revisited: Preliminary Suggestions for the Re-analysis of Old Constructs." In *De l'Indus aux Balkans. Recueil à la mémoire de Jean Deshayes*, edited by J.-L. Huot, M. Yon, and Y. Calvet. Paris: Éditions Recherche sur les Civilisations, pp. 361–77.

Zdanovich, G. B., 1997. "Arkaim: kul'turnyj kompleks èpokhi srednej bronzy yuzhnogo Zaural'ya," *Rossijskaya Arkheologiya*, 2: 47–62.

Postscript

Václav Blažek has independently (and before us) briefly suggested the derivation of "FP **śi(k)šta* 'Wachs' < IA **śi(k)šta* 'beeswax'" (p. 43, no. 15) in his paper published in 1990, "New Fenno-Ugric – Indo-Iranian lexical parallels," in *Uralo-Indogermanica: Balto-slavyanskie yazyki i problema uralo-indoevropejskikh svyazej*, Vol. II. Moskva: Akademiya Nauk SSSR, Institut slavyanovedeniya i balkanistiki, pp. 40–5.

5

ARCHAEOLOGY AND LANGUAGE

The case of the Bronze Age Indo-Iranians

Carl C. Lamberg-Karlovsky

Once upon a time, no one really knows how long ago, there lived a community that spoke a common language. For almost two centuries scholars have been trying to locate the time and the place, and to reconstruct the language of that community. The language is referred to as Proto-Indo-European (PIE) and is ancestral to the Germanic, Slavic, Romance, Iranian, Indic, Albanian, and Greek languages. Several recent works by archaeologists and linguists, involving the origins and eventual spread of PIE related languages from India to England, offer new perspectives on this centuries long debate. Among these the work of Renfrew (1987), Mallory (1989), and Gamkrelidze and Ivanov (1984, 1995) are of great interest. Renfrew, the archaeologist, contends that the PIE settlement was located in Anatolia *c.*7000–6500 BC. Its subsequent spread he attributes to a superior technology: their invention of agriculture. Gamkrelidze and Ivanov, the linguists, situate the homeland of the PIE a few millennia later in the nearby Caucasus. Mallory agrees with their fifth to fourth millennium date but places the homeland in the Pontic-Caspian steppe region.

There is an agreement that the PIE community split into two major groups from wherever its homeland was situated, and whatever the timing of its dispersal. One headed west for Europe and became speakers of Indo-European (all the languages of modern Europe save for Basque, Hungarian, and Finnish) while others headed east for Eurasia to become Indo-Iranians (see Figure 5.1). The Indo-Iranians were a community that spoke a common language prior to their branching off into the Iranian and Indo-Aryan languages. Iranian refers to the languages of Iran (Iranian), Pakistan (Baluch), Afghanistan (Pashto), and Tadjikistan (Tadjik) and Indo-Aryan, Hindi and its many related languages. In this review our concern is with the location and dating of the Indo-Iranian community. The search for the Indo-Europeans, within an archaeological context, is almost as old as archaeology. In 1903 Raphael Pumpelly's (1908) highly regarded excavations at Anau, in Turkmenistan, were motivated by a search for the Indo-Europeans. The results, as well as the motivation for these excavations, had a profound influence on V. G. Childe (1926).

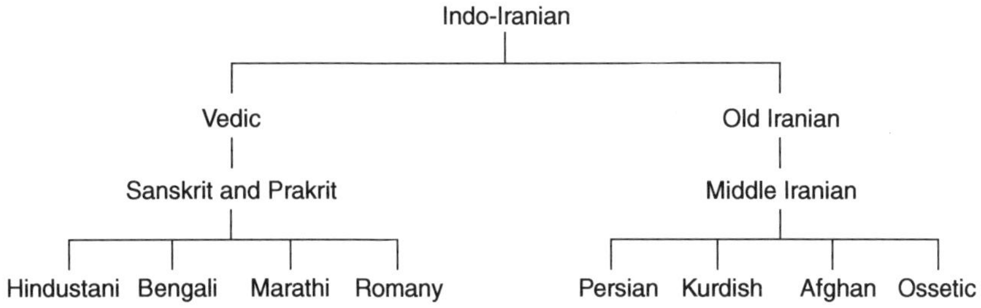

Figure 5.1 Hypothetical development of the Indo-Iranian languages.

Recently, Colin Renfrew (1999) has reviewed the status of the origins and dispersal of the Indo-European languages. In his reconstruction he finds, "The Indo-Iranian languages however represent . . . a later development [than the earlier Proto-Indo-European whose emergence he places in Anatolia ca. 7000–6500 B.C.] and their immediate ancestor may perhaps find its material counterpart in the Cucuteni-Tripolye culture of the Ukraine" (Renfrew 1999: 280). After 3000 BC he argues for an eastward dispersal of Indo-Iranian speakers. He offers no "cause" for this dispersal but believes it unrelated to horseriding which he believes to be a later second millennium adaptation. He positions the dispersal of Indo-Iranian on to the Indian sub-continent *c.*1700 BC and invokes his "elite dominance model," that is, the subordination of the local populations by an elite group of charioteers, as described in the Rigveda. This perspective, along with others, will be reviewed later.

Elena Kuzmina (1994), in search of the homeland of the Indo-Europeans, examines the regions from the Balkan-Carpathian-Danube to the Urals and the eastern steppes of Kazakhstan. She sets the period in which the PIE community existed as broadly between 4500 and 2500 BC and its subsequent spread in the range of 3200–2200 BC. She favors an Indo-European homeland in the Pontic-Caspian zone and advocates a series of eastward migrations to the Urals. The migratory movement of tribes along the Don basin in the north Caspian regions, and from the western steppes and mountainous Crimea to the eastern steppes beyond the Urals, is seen as resulting in the spread of a productive subsistence economy based on cattlebreeding and wheat and barley farming. The large-scale migrations of the PIE, she believes, were motivated by reduced food resources, resulting from deteriorating climatic conditions, as well as by a conscientious search for new productive lands and modes of subsistence economy. The reliance upon migrations as the principal agent of social change was typical of archaeological interpretations throughout the Soviet period. To the importance of migrations can be added a blurred distinction between ethnic, linguistic, racial, and cultural entities; a concern for the isolation of racial/ethnic groups by craniometric methods of physical anthropology; and the use of linguistic paleontology to reconstruct the cultural development of cultural groups.

In the fourth millennium, archaeologists identify various "tribes" of the Pit Grave culture, that is, the Mariupol culture, as inhabiting the regions between the

Dnieper and the Urals. The formation of cattle breeding and the domestication of the horse are taken to be major fifth/fourth millennium developments that took place on the Russian/Ukrainian steppes. These archaeological cultures are typically identified as Indo-European. Kuzmina believes that the horse was first intensively hunted for food, then domesticated as a food source, later used as a beast of burden for the pulling of wagons, and finally, toward the very end of the second millennium, used for riding.

Kuzmina is insistent that the Bandkeramik farmers of the Danube played a decisive role in the spread of farming to the Dneiper basin in the fourth millennium. She portrays a complex picture of a multitude of seemingly distinctive archaeological cultures, from the Danube of southeastern Europe to the southern Urals, migrating and assimilating. The resultant picture is one in which Indo-European speaking tribes spread, following the introduction of agriculture from southeastern Europe, from the Pontic-Caspian zone to the southern Urals and beyond. These migrations are believed to be evident in a bewildering number of related archaeological cultures, all said to have varying degrees of affinity. No two authors, however, seem able to agree upon the extent of the relatedness of these cultures. Perhaps this is not surprising for there is a conspicuous absence of formal descriptions, ceramic typologies, chronological sequences and/or distributional analyses of the artifact types that are said to characterize these cultures. The principal actors on the archaeological stage are the Pit Grave culture(s) in the Pontic-Caspian steppe 4000–2800 BC, which evolved into the Catacomb Grave culture(s) 2800–2000 BC, which, in turn, was succeeded by the Timber Grave (Srubnaja) culture(s) 2000–1000 BC and the related Andronovo cultures 2000–900 BC. Each of these major archaeological cultures is divisible into archaeological variants and each variant has its proponent supporting their Indo-Iranian identity.

The Andronovo culture is almost universally implicated by Russian archaeologists with the Indo-Iranians and we shall concentrate on them. On the basis of pottery type and its technology of production, the absence of pig, the presence of camel, horse, and cattle, the evolution of cheek pieces, and the presence of the chariot, Kuzmina argues for a cultural continuity of the Andronovo extending from 2000–900 BC. There is little doubt in her mind that the Andronovo culture is Indo-Iranian. She attempts to verify the southern Urals as the homeland of the Indo-Iranians by an extensive use of ethnohistoric evidence. The Iranian speaking Sakas and Sauromatians, of the first millennium, are traced back to the Andronovo tribes, while various Indo-Iranian texts, the Rigveda and the Avesta, to mention but two of the many referred to, are believed to reflect the world of the Andronovo. The ethnohistoric parallels and the textual citations are of such general nature that they do not convince. Thus, in the Rigveda there is an admonition against the use of the wheel in the production of pottery. As Andronovo pottery is handmade this is taken as evidence of their Indo-Iranian identity. Ethnic and linguistic correlations are generally not based on rigorous methodologies; they are merely asserted.

Kuzmina (1995) formulates a set of what she believes to be universal rules for "the methods of ethnic attribution." These are: (1) retrospective comparison, that is an ethnic identity is established for an archaeological culture by comparing it to a descendent culture whose ethnicity is established by written documents; (2) the linguistic method, which involves the ethnic attribution derived from the retrospective method and then comparing that with lexicostatistic data on the level and type of economy; (3) verification by establishing migration routes, the search for indicators of migrations, and plotting such indicators through time and space; (4) the employment of an anthropological method; which involves a study of craniometric analyses, believed to indicate a group's biological affinity; (5) verification by linguistic contact, which involves the study of linguistic substrates and toponymic correlations; and finally, (6) the reconstruction of culture and world view ("spiritual culture") derived from an analysis of the archaeological and linguistic data. This "methodology" is utilized by Kuzmina for establishing the "ethnic indicators" of the Andronovo culture as Indo-Iranian, and, more specifically, of the Federovo culture (a late variant of the Andronovo) as Indo-Aryan. The "ethnic indicators" are: (1) the absence of swine in the domestic diet; (2) the presence of the Bactrian camel; (3) the special significance of horsebreeding; (4) the special role of chariots; (5) a cult of the horse associated with burial contexts; (6) the technology of making vertically oriented tripartite vessels by coiling; (7) pots of unique quadrangular shape; (8) burials rites of cremation; and, (9) houses with high, gabled roofs. In an enthusiastic review of Kuzmina's volume Igor Diakonoff (1995) concludes that her methodology, which juxtaposes linguistic, archaeological, textual, and ethnological data, allows for an ethnic identification of archaeological cultures. He writes, "Hence the bearers of a certain archaeological culture can securely be identified with the bearers of a language of a certain group or with their ancestors." Such optimism remains unfounded.

Although there is a consensus among archaeologists working on the steppes that the Andronovo culture is in the right place at the right time, and thus is to be considered Indo-Iranian, there is neither textual, ethnohistoric, nor archaeological evidence, individually or in combination, that offers a clinching argument for this consensus. Kuzmina's carefully constructed methodology simply cannot be applied to the Andronovo culture. The Andronovo culture is well over a thousand years distant from any textual tradition, making any linguistic and/or ethnohistoric attribution extremely tenuous. Furthermore, ethnicity is permeable and multidimensional. It is difficult to accept the notion that for over a millennium the Andronovo culture remained an unchanging entity. Finally, the categories of "ethnic indicators" utilized by Kuzmina: horsebreeding, horse rituals, shared ceramic types, avoidance of pig, shared burial patterns, and architectural templates can be used to identify the Arab, the Turk, and the Iranian; three completely distinctive ethnic and linguistic groups. Ethnicity and language are not so easily wedded to an archaeological signature. Material residues as well as the units of analysis in archaeology are too frequently incongruent with what we wish to investigate. The Arab, Turk, and Iranian may share a laundry list of general attributes but they are neither linguistically nor culturally similar entities.

Kuzmina (1994) is not alone in believing that the domestication of the horse introduced a new stage in the evolution of civilization. On the steppes the horse allowed for the increasing role of cattlebreeding, the intensification of interethnic communication, the development of plough traction, and the use of carts and wagons. By the middle of the third millennium, from the Danube to the Urals, these new innovations were utilized by the tribes of the Pit Grave culture. The fourth millennium Pit Grave culture was characterized by large fortified settlements (Mihajlovka), four- and two-wheeled wagons pulled by bulls or horses, intensive cattlebreeding and farming, an extensive use of metal tools, and burials under mounds (kurgans) containing carts, wagons, and sacrificed horses. The migrations of the Pit Grave culture(s) are taken by some to be responsible for the emergence of stockbreeding and agriculture in distant Siberia (brought there by the related Afanasievo culture). Following the Pit Grave culture two great cultural entities flourished: the Timber Grave (Srubnaja) culture, which many archaeologists believe evolved from the Pit Grave culture, and the Andronovo culture, whose genesis, periodization, and cultural variants, are the subject of decade-long debates.

The Andronovo culture was first described by Teploukhov in 1927 and has been the focus of archaeological research on the Ural/Kazakhstan steppe and Siberia ever since (for a review of the history of research see Jettmar 1951). Kuzmina (1994) is among the majority of Russian scholars who believe that the Andronovo forms a single cultural entity. Increasingly, however, the concept of a single homogenous culture covering 3 million square kilometers, and enduring for over a millennium, has become untenable. Archaeologists working on the steppes are involved in giving new definition, that is, distinctive chronological and cultural phases, to the cultures of the steppes (Kutimov 1999, and the papers in Levine *et al.* 1999). Similarly, the nature of Andronovo interaction, its periodization, and the unstructured chronology accompanying the steppic cultural-historical community are all subjects of heated discussion. Numerous subcultures have been defined: Petrov (also called Sintashta-Arkhaim-Petrov = SAP), Alakul, Fedorov, Sargarin, Cherkaskul, Petrovalka, Abashevo, Novokumak, etc. Differences in the Andronovo subcultures are based upon variations in ceramic decoration, house forms, settlement pattern, as well as mortuary facilities and rituals. We still lack a comprehensive synthesis bringing together the vast amount of information available and much of what has been excavated is not published. Evidence for variations in material culture is poorly documented, hypothetical population movements are asserted not demonstrated, direct contradictions of interpretations between different researchers are left unresolved, and there is simply no chronological control over the cultural variations existing within the millennium long expanse of the Andronovo culture. Attempts are made to identify the physical types of the different Andronovo populations, invariably by craniometric means (Alekseev 1986, 1989). These studies are more closely related to racial typology, that is, the more recent studies that attempt to gauge degrees of biological affinity between populations residing in distinctive geographical settings (Mallaspina *et al.* 1998).

The earliest of the Andronovo cultures would seem to be the Petrov which is closely related to, if not identical with, the Sintashta-Arkhaim culture, dated to the first centuries of the second millennium. The Petrov is succeeded by the Alakul which, in turn, is followed by the Fedorov, dated to the second half of the second millennium. Among the Andronovo cultures of the southern Urals, the Alakul and the Fedorov are most frequently assigned an Indo-Iranian identity. In the minority are those that believe in the multiethnic identity of the Andronovo tribes. Thus, V. N. Chernetsov (1973) argues for an Ugric substrate among the Andronovo tribes and a specific Indo-Iranian identity for the Alakul tribe. Stokolos (1972), on the other hand, argues for an Ugric identity for the Andronovo, a local development for the Fedorov tribe, and an Indo-Iranian one for the Alakul tribe. Linguistic/ethnic identities are frequently asserted but the reasons for doing so are very rarely elucidated. Kuzmina (1994) accepts the cultural subdivisions of the Andronovo culture yet she often refers to cultural contact and migrations within the context of a singular Andronovo identity. She refers to Andronovo influence with regard to the introduction of specific axes and adzes of Andronovo type in distant Xinjiang. The relationships of the Andronovo with the cultures of Xinjiang is documented in an important paper by Jianjun and Shell (1999). P'yankova (1993, 1994, 1999) and Kuzmina (1994) are specific in connecting the second millennium agricultural communities of Central Asia, the Bactrian-Margiana Archaeological Complex (the BMAC), with the Andronovo culture. Sites of the BMAC, and the related mid-second millennium Bishkent culture, are seen by P'yankova as influenced by the Fedorovo tribes. Fedorovo ceramics, funeral rites, metal types (alloyed with tin), as well as skulls of the Andronovo anthropological type, are said to be present on a number of Central Asian sites. There is a consensus view that throughout the second millennium migratory movements of the Andronovo tribes resulted in contact with the Central Asian oases (BMAC), cultures of the Tien Shan mountains of Xinjiang, as well as with the indigenous tribes of the Altai, Tuva, and the Pamir Mountains.

The "push" motivating these migratory movements from the steppes is universally attributed to deteriorating climatic conditions. Khazanov puts it this way:

> Almost all paleoclimatologists accept that the second millennium B.C. was characterized by a dry climate which, it will appear, was at its driest at the turn of the second and first millennium B.C. . . . The fact that these dates coincide with the period of the emergence of pastoral nomadism, as has been established by archaeological data and written sources, is scarcely due to chance. It would appear that the dry climate was the first stimulus for pastoralists to abandon agriculture once and for all and become fully nomadic.
>
> (1983: 95)

Thus, the "cause" for these large-scale migratory movements as well as for the emergence of pastoral nomadism is environmental: the result of increasing aridity.

Climate is no doubt relevant but it remains unlikely that it constituted the first cause for either the migratory movements or for the emergence of pastoral nomadism. It is of interest to note that Bar-Yosef and Khazanov (1992), in a review of the evidence for pastoral nomadism in the ancient Near East, doubt that a pristine stage of socioeconomic pastoral nomadism ever existed. It is more than likely that the same conclusion, one that argues for the existence of a mixed economy wherein the percentage of dependence upon farming and pastoral nomadism varies, also holds for the cultures of the steppes. It is increasingly evident that where the fauna and flora have been collected, agriculture and pastoral nomadism characterize all of the cultures of the steppes.

Warrior attributes are frequently assigned to the Pit Grave culture and are certainly evident in the Andronovo culture. Axes, spears, bow, and arrow, a rich variety of dagger types, and chariots all speak of conflict and confrontation, as do the heavily fortified communities of "The Country of Towns" (see later). Sharp definitions of rank are attested in burial sites. Kuzmina (1994) suggests that social position was defined more by social, ideological, and ritual activities than by ranking based upon property ownership. Russian archaeologists view steppe cultures as being a "transitional type" the concept of a "military democracy," derived from the work of Lewis Henry Morgan, remains popular and is expressed by the presence of a chief, council, and a peoples' assembly. Khazanov (1979), while regarding "military democracy" as a specific form of transitional society, suitable for discussing the social forms of Central Asian pastoral nomads, has also advocated the adoption of the concept of a "chiefdom" as a transitional form preceding the origin of the state.

The Andronovo culture has also been seen as responsible for large-scale metallurgical production and as the principal agent in the exchange of metals throughout Eurasia in the second millennium. The recent discovery of stannite deposits and tin mining at Muschiston, Tadjikistan, associated with Andronovo sherds (Alimov *et al.* 1998), adds to the already considerable evidence for the mining of copper deposits by the Andronovo (Chernykh 1994a,b). Given the existence of an extensive Andronovo metallurgical inventory, their association with the mining of both copper and tin, evidence for the production of metal artifacts on numerous sites, and their presumed extensive migratory movements, the Andronovo are frequently seen as responsible for the dissemination of metallurgical technology. Some authors have even suggested that the pastoral nomads of the steppes, that is, the Andronovo and the even earlier Afanasiev cultures, were the agents responsible for the dissemination of metallurgical technology into China (Bunker 1998; Mei and Shell 1998; Peng 1998).

Commenting upon the vehicle burials of the earlier Pit and Catacomb Grave cultures, Stuart Piggott (1992: 22) took the opportunity to mention the deplorable state of archaeology in the Soviet Union. His disparaging remarks refer specifically to the use of outdated excavation techniques and publication standards. He points out that over the past forty years over a hundred kurgans with vehicles have been excavated, but fewer than half are published and then only in the briefest form. In this regard, of outstanding significance is the discovery, excavation, and publication of the site of Sintashta. Piggott's comments certainly do not pertain to the excellent Sintashta volume produced by V. F. Gening, G. B. Zdanovich, and V. V. Gening (1992). This volume was published in the same year in which Piggott made his unduly harsh criticism. The settlement and cemetery of Sintashta is located in the southern Urals along a river of the same name. Here ten-spoked chariots, horse sacrifices, and human burials are radiocarbon dated to the first century of the second millennium BC. This volume is exceptionally well illustrated and details the nature of a complex series of settlements and burials. Although Kuzmina (1994) identifies the third millennium Timber Grave culture as Indo-Iranian it is only in the following Andronovo culture, and specifically at the site of Sintashta, that she believes one can document a cluster of specific Indo-Iranian cultural traits: (1) a mixed economy of pastoralism and agriculture, (2) hand-made ceramics, (3) horse-drawn chariots, (4) the cultic significance of the horse, fire, and ancestor worship, and (5) the high status of charioteers.

Excavations at Sintashta were initiated in 1972 under the direction of V. I. Stepanov and resumed in 1983 under the direction of G. B. Zdanovich and V. F. Gening. The site of Sintashta consists of a number of different features:

1 The fortified settlement. The settlement of a sub-circular form is 140 meters in diameter. Its elaborate fortification system consists of an outer wall, a moat, and an inner wall having periodic buttresses believed to form towers. Entrance to the settlement is by way of two gates, each offering angled access and a movable bridge placed over a moat. The settlement is 62,000 square meters. Several 2–3 room houses were excavated containing hearths and constructed of timber, wattle, and daub, and unbaked brick. Evidence for the production of metal, as well as ceramics was found in some of the houses.

2 The large kurgan. Two hundred meters to the northwest of the settlement a burial complex consisting of 40 graves with 60–65 inhumations was uncovered. The burials were placed in pits in which wooden structures were constructed and roofed with wooden beams. Single and multiple burials, adults and children, were placed within these wooden structures. The burials contained a wealth of material: vessels, daggers, pins, awls, needles, axes, mortars, pestles, stone tools, bone artifacts, etc. Five graves contained cheek pieces for horses and two "battle chariots" were recovered. Twenty-five graves had evidence for the sacrifice of horses, cattle, sheep/goat, as well as dog. The animals, and at times only parts of the animal, were placed directly within the burial or in associated pits. From one to six horses were placed in individual graves. There was little doubt in the minds of the excavators that differential wealth, placed in particular tombs, indicated a rank ordering of social strata. Significantly, several burials containing considerable wealth were of females and children. In some burials the excavators record the presence of "altars" and associated "ritual" fires.

3 The barrow burial. This consisted of a circular barrow 32 meters in diameter containing three burial clusters. The first group had a great richness of grave offerings all placed within individual chambers containing numerous sacrificed horses. The second group of burials was placed within a central structure 18 meters in diameter. Within this burial a large "battle chariot" was uncovered with a very rich inventory of material remains and numerous sacrificed animals. The entire complex is interpreted as the burial of an extremely important person. A third group of burials, consisting mostly of women and children, was placed within simple shallow pits at the edge of the barrow. These burials also contained rich grave goods and sacrificial animals.

4 A small kurgan. This barrow was located 400 meters northwest of the Large Burial Complex. It is 12 meters in diameter and contained six adults and three children, all placed within a square wooden structure. Burial 7, a male, was particularly rich in material remains as was burial 10, a female. Both burials contained a rich inventory of metals. The male burial contained daggers and knives, the female bracelets and needles. Both burials contained sacrificial animals. The authors suggest that this burial complex contained a number of related kin.

5 A little barrow. This barrow was 15–16 meters in diameter and contained a single wooden chamber with five bodies. A large "battle chariot" was uncovered and near each of the deceased a rich material inventory. Four additional graves were found outside of the structure. Some Russian archaeologists believe that human sacrifice, as well as the defleshing of the dead, were components of Andronovo burial ritual. If so, perhaps these are candidates for such practice.

6 A big barrow. This barrow is 85 meters in diameter and is located almost immediately adjacent to the Large Burial Complex. Around the barrow there is evidence for a 12 meters wide moat. Within the barrow there are numerous "ritual fires" surrounding two wooden structures and a large "temple" structure of wood. Unfortunately, this impressive barrow was looted in antiquity. The principal burial was placed within a vaulted dromos. Over the looted burial chambers an impressive "temple" was constructed.

All of the principal structures described are exceedingly well illustrated both by axiometric drawings as well as detailed plans of the structures and associated features. The book (Gening *et al.* 1992) is accompanied by a wealth of photographs of which a number are in color. A second volume promises to offer a detailed typology and an analysis of the finds. The settlement and cemetery of Sintashta, whose material remains closely resemble the Petrov culture, a variant of the Andronovo, is usually mentioned together with the settlement of nearby Arkhaim as the SAP culture. In the opinion of the Zdanovichs (1995) this culture is characterized by a common cultural style represented by heavily fortified communities with moats and walls forming circular or sub-rectangular settlements. The SAP burials at Sintashta are affiliated with such settlements (Zdanovich 1997). The burial sites consist of kurgans containing several burials situated around a central grave. The burial chamber consisted of several superimposed layers. At Sintashta a chariot was buried within a wooden construction at the bottom of the tomb. On the roof of the tomb were sacrificed horses; above the horses a single male was interred with a rich variety of prestige goods: daggers, axes, and ceramics. Traces of fire were discovered around the burial. At Sintashta the excavators interpreted the entire kurgan as a "fire temple." Gennadi Zdanovich (1995, 1997) who excavated both Sintashta and Arkhaim refers to the SAP as the "Country of Towns." Nineteen settlements of the Arkhaim type are known within a region 450 by 150 square kilometers. In this "Country of Towns" fortified settlements are spaced about 20–30 kilometers from each other. The horse drawn chariot, a rich inventory of weaponry, tin-bronze alloying, and disc-like bone cheek pieces (psalia) are all believed to be innovations of the SAP culture. To some the psalia suggest the presence of horseback riding. Many specialists, including Elena Kuzmina and Marsha Levine (1999), believe that horse riding appears only toward the very end of the second millennium (for contrary opinions see later).

The search for new metal resources, the alloying of copper with tin, an intensive dependence on cattlebreeding, the construction of fortified settlements, and the development of the horse-driven chariot are all important innovations of the "Country of Towns." Less attention has been paid to the preservation and study of plant remains. At Arkhaim archaeologists recovered sowing millet (*Panicum miliaceum*) and Turkestan barley (*Hordeum turkestan*). The excavator has also argued for the presence of "irrigated farming" in "kitchen gardens," narrow parallel beds, 3–4 meters wide, divided by deep ditches (Zdanovich 2002: 380). The site of Arkhaim is the most intensively studied and occupies an area of 20,000 square meters. [A recent booklet pertaining to the publications dealing with Arkhaim and related subjects list 381 published items between 1987 and 1997 (Zdanovich 1999a).]

The site of Arkhaim was discovered by two schoolboys on June 20, 1987. Arkhaim is a circular fortified settlement approximately 150 meters in diameter. It is estimated that between 1,000 and 2,000 people inhabited the community. The settlement is surrounded by two concentric defensive walls constructed of adobe and clay placed within a log frame. Within the circle, and abutting the defensive walls, are some sixty semi-subterranean dwellings. Each house contains hearths, cellars, wells, and some have metallurgical furnaces. A drainage gutter with water-collecting pits was uncovered in the circular street that surrounds the inner portion of the settlement. In the center of the settlement was a rectangular "plaza." Entrance into the settlement was effected by four elaborately constructed angular passages, constructed over moats, and terminating in an elaborate gate. Clearly, access for the unfamiliar would have been very difficult. Today, larger fortified settlements with far more impressive stone architecture are known but remain unexcavated. Settlements in the "Country of Towns" are interpreted as military forts, proto-cities, and as ceremonial and religious centers. Russian archaeologists believe that the SAP culture consisted of three classes: military and religious leaders, nobles, and peasants. Today among Russian archaeologists there is a preference to refer to this culture as a "chiefdom" rather than as a "military democracy" (Koryakova 1996).

The discovery and "saving" of Arkhaim is of special significance. Initially, the site of Arkhaim was to be flooded by the construction of a reservoir to be built by the Ministry of Water Resources of the USSR. Construction of the reservoir was scheduled for completion in 1989 which would have completely submerged Arkhaim. In 1989, with the rapid dissolution of the USSR and the concomitant rise of regional authorities, the Ministry of Water Resources began to lose its authority. In April 1991 the Council of Ministers of the Russian Federation decided to halt the construction of the reservoir and make Arkhaim and its environs a protected site. In subsequent years a scientific campus was built, as were tourist facilities, and, in 1999 an impressive Museum of Natural History and Man was under construction. Today the site of Arkhaim has become a center for followers of the occult and super-nationalist Russians. It has become a theater of, and for, the absurd and dangerous. It is advocated by some that Arkhaim was planned to reproduce a model of the universe; it was built by the legendary King Yima, as described in the Avesta, the sacred book of the Persians and Zoroastrians (Medvedev 1999); it was a temple-observatory comparable to Stonehenge; it was the birthplace of the prophet Zoroaster who at death was buried at Sintashta; it is a model for contemporary society of harmonious relationships between culture and the natural environment; it is the homeland of the ancient Aryans; and the oldest example of a Slavic state. Arkhaim also is identified with Asgard, the secret homeland of the Germanic god Odin; it is the "city of the Aryan hierarchy and racial purity." The swastika, which appears incised on pottery from Arkhaim, is proclaimed as the symbol of Aryanism by Russian ultranationalists. Russian astrologers have also been attracted to Arkhaim. In 1991 a prominent astrologer, Tamara Globa, during the summer solstice at Arkhaim, announced that the memory of the site was preserved by the Indian Magi and its rediscovery was prophesied by the medieval astrologer Paracelsus. Arkhaim attracts up to 15,000 "tourists" during annual holidays, particularly in the spring and summer. They come to pray, tap energy from outer space, worship fire, be cured of disease, dance, meditate, and sing. The thousands of visitors are a ready source of income supporting Dr Zdanovich's research. "We Slavs," he wrote, "consider ourselves to be new arrivals, but that is untrue. Indo-Europeans and Indo-Iranians had been living there [in the southern Urals] since the Stone Age and had been incorporated in the Kazaks, Bashkirs, and Slavs, such is the common thread linking us all" (quoted in Shnirelman 1998: 37, 1999). In a word, the Slavs have been in the southern Urals since time immemorial, they are as primordial as all other modern ethnicities inhabiting the region. Shnirelman (1995: 1) writes in "Alternative Prehistory" that nationalist concerns in the former USSR are creating "an explicitly ethnocentric vision of the past, a glorification of the great ancestors of the given people, who are treated as if they made the most valuable contribution to the culture of all humanity." The wave of nationalism in Russia has given birth to numerous publications of highly dubious merit. Thus, *Kto Oni i Otkuda* (*Who are They and Where From* 1998) is a publication of the Library of Ethnography and sanctioned by the Russian Academy of Sciences. In this monograph one can read that the original homeland of the Vedas was in the Arctic and that the language with the closest affinity to Sanskrit is Russian. The dissolution of the Soviet empire has given rise to a heightened nationalism which, in turn, projects a mythical and majestic Slavic past. The archaeology of Arkhaim is playing an important role in the construction of nationalist myths. Today, wholly unwarranted claims are made for Slavs as the original Aryans, for the Slavic language as closest to Sanskrit, for a Slavic-Aryan origin in the Arctic, for the superiority of the Slavic-Aryans, etc. In discussing ethnic formation Geary states that:

> The second model of ethnogenesis drew on Central Asian steppe peoples for the charismatic leadership and organization necessary to create a people from a diverse following... these polyethnic confederations were if anything more inclusive than the first model [in] which ethnic formation followed the identity of a leading or royal family being able to draw together groups which maintained much of their traditional linguistic, cultural and even political organization under the generalship of a small body of steppe commanders. The economic bases of these confederations was semi-nomadic rather than sedentary. Territory and distance played little role in defining their boundaries, although elements of the confederation might practice traditional forms of agriculture and social organization quite different from those of the steppe leadership.
>
> (1999: 109)

In a similar vein one might imagine the Andronovo consisting of "polyethnic confederations," which took varying archaeological expressions: Alakul, Petrov, Abashevo, "The Country of Towns," etc., each maintaining its "traditional linguistic, cultural, and even political organization." The identification of the Andronovo as a singularity, in both a cultural and linguistic sense, transforms the multiple and the complex into the singular and simple. In considering the history of the peoples of the steppes, whether it be the confederation of the Huns, Goths, or Sarmatians, Patrick Geary is at constant pains to point out that "polyethnicity was obvious" and that "Ethnic labels remained significant... but they designated multiple and at times even contradictory aspects of social and political identity" (Geary 1999: 117, 125). It is difficult to imagine, and there is neither archaeological nor textual evidence to suggest that the Bronze and Iron Age steppe nomads were politically more centralized and/or ethnically more monolithic, than they were when first mentioned by Greek and Roman writers, who were well aware of their diversity.

There are two contending hypotheses for the origins of the SAP culture: (1) it is an indigenous culture, with its roots in the earlier Botai culture of northern Kazakhstan (see Kislenko and Tatarintseva 1999), or (2) its formation is the result of a migration from the west [i.e. from the Abashevo and/or the Mnogovalikovo culture(s) (themselves variants of the Timber Grave culture)]. Kuzmina appears to favor a western origin as forming "the decisive stimulus for the formation of the Andronovo culture" while the Zdanovichs appear to favor indigenous roots. The questions of origins are severely hampered by an inadequate chronological framework. There is a poverty of radiocarbon dates and a plethora of archaeological cultures, all interpreted as variants of the Andronovo culture, spread over a vast distance and extending over a millennium. Recent research in Kazakhstan is able to trace an indigenous series of archaeological cultures from the Mesolithic to the Atbasar culture of the Neolithic; all evident prior to the diffusion of the Andronovo from the west (Kislenko and Tatarintseva 1999).

The hypothesis that the Andronovo culture, or more specifically one of its subtypes, are Indo-Iranians has met with wide acceptance among Russian archaeologists. Arguments focus upon which variant is Indo-Iranian: is it the SAP, or the Alakul, or the Fedorov? If, on the one hand, the SAP culture stems from the indigenous northern Kazakhstan roots (Botai culture), as believed by some, then the Indo-Iranians were present in the region as early as 2900 BC (uncorrected radiocarbon years from Botai). If, on the other hand, the Indo-Iranian culture was introduced from the west, sometime in the first half of the second millennium, as believed by Kuzmina and a majority of Russian scholars, then there is both an absence of evidence for such migrations and an insufficient time period to allow for them to extend over the vast territories that the Indo-Iranians are believed to have occupied.

Before the discovery of the SAP complex the Alakul culture of southern Kazakhstan was thought to be the earliest Andronovo culture, its "classic" expression, and, of Indo-Iranian identity. Alakul settlements are small, usually consisting of no more than 2–4 houses. These houses, however, are on average considerably larger, often in excess of the 200 square meters of the earlier SAP houses. Alakul houses are subdivided into several rooms by interior walls made of logs, wattle, and daub, or sod bricks. There is a considerable difference between SAP mortuary practices and those of the Alakul: large central burials become rare, horse sacrifice declines, and the richness and variety of grave goods diminish. Internment is usually on the left side. Weapons and tools are rarely placed in the graves but decorative items, pendants, bracelets, etc., abound. Burials are frequently accompanied with sheep/goat. And, finally, in the last half of the second millennium, Alakul burials provide evidence of cremation. Distinct similarities between the Alakul (classic Andronovo) and the Timber Grave culture to the west have long been argued (Gimbutas 1965) and continue to be affirmed (Obydennov and Obydennov 1992). The Timber Grave culture is, in turn, seen as descended from the Pit Grave culture which is frequently cited as the "original" Indo-Iranian culture (Anthony 1991). In this view an Indo-Iranian presence is first detected in the Pit Grave culture, continues within the context of the Timber Grave culture, which influences, through migration, the formation of the Andronovo culture. Among the Andronovo variants some scholars identify the Alakul while others offer the SAP as Indo-Iranian. Physical anthropologists add to this confusion.

Alexeev (1967) believes the Andronovo cranial type indicates a common pre-Andronovo origin, probably from the west; while Gerasomov (1955), studying the same materials, concludes that the Andronovo were descended from the Afanasiev culture, suggesting a western Siberian origin.

The identification of the SAP as Indo-Iranian is buttressed by a number of advocates, including Kuzmina (1994) in her highly influential book. Kuzmina offers numerous parallels between the archaeological record and the Rigvedic and Avestan texts. The parallels drawn are, at best, of a most general nature and do not convince, that is, Andronovo houses were large (50–300 square meters), capable of accommodating extended families. A "reading" of the Indo-Iranian texts, the Avesta and Rigveda, attests to the existence of extended families, thus, the Andronovo were Indo-Iranian. For a more thorough reconstruction of the Indo-Iranian world, as reconstructed from the Avesta, see Windfuhr (1999). Kuzmina's perspective is shared by a majority of Russian archaeologists. She advocates a migration of the SAP from the west, bringing with them a complex social order and horse-drawn wagons. The SAP come into contact with an indigenous and more egalitarian culture, the descendants of the Tersek-Botai culture (Kiselenko and Tatarsineva 1999). The Tersek-Botai peoples, it is suggested, spoke Ugrian languages. With the passing of time further migrations coming from the west, combined with regional diversification, led to the formation of the Alakul and Fedorovo cultures (variants of the Andronovo), whose migrations, in turn, impacted upon the peoples of Central Asia and distant Xinjiang (Jianjun and Snell 1999). The extensive migrations of mobile pastoralists throughout the steppes, beginning *c.*2200 BC, is attributed, as noted earlier, to an increase in "desertification" and "steppification." The evidence from phytoliths, soil chemistry, and pollen analyses seem to converge in pointing to an increasing aridity throughout the first half of the second millennium. This resulted in expansive migrations in search of pasturage (the evidence is well summarized by Hiebert 1994).

There is still a great deal of work to be done before the identification of the Indo-Iranians becomes a viable archaeological exercise. The following points are relevant conclusions:

1 There is absolutely NO archaeological evidence for any variant of the Andronovo culture either reaching or influencing the cultures of Iran or northern India in the second millennium. Not a single artifact of identifiable Andronovo type has been recovered from the Iranian Plateau, northern India, or Pakistan.
2 A great deal is made of the horse as an attribute of the Indo-Iranians. There is NO zooarchaeological evidence for the presence of the horse in Iran until the last centuries of the second millennium BC, and even then such finds are exceedingly rare. In South Asia the first appearance of the horse is at Pirak, Pakistan, and dated to *c.*1700 BC (Jarrige and Santoni 1979).
3 There is a tendency to treat the Andronovo as a single monolithic entity, ignoring the chronological and cultural variations. Recent attempts to

differentiate variants of the Andronovo have done much to clarify and much to confuse. It is by no means clear what, for instance, are the specific variants in material culture that differentiate the SAP from the Alakul, or for that matter of any two variants of the Andronovo from each other.

4 The chronological situation is completely out of control. Save for a few carbon-14 dates from Sintashta, the SAP exists in a floating chronology (however see Görsdorf *et al.* 1998 for the beginnings of a radiocarbon chronology). How long was the site of Arkhaim inhabited? What was the chronological duration of the "Country of Towns?" What was the date of the Alakul and/or Fedorov influence in Central Asia, that is, in the BMAC and the later Bishkent culture? The dating of the Andronovo culture, with respect to the chronology of its geographical distribution and cultural variation is simply non-existent.

5 If the chronological sequence is "floating" so is the careful explication of the cultural variants of the Andronovo. Frequently researchers emphasize local, western, and even eastern influences upon the Andronovo by focusing upon a single attribute, that is, burial pattern without considering temporal or typological variations. Typological parallels are drawn in the absence of chronological control and chronological synchronisms made on the basis of assumed typological parallels. The fact that sites appear to be of relatively short duration and are said to rarely overlap offers a considerable challenge in the building of a chronological sequence. A fine, but rare, effort toward establishing a relative chronology in the southern Urals and adjacent eastern steppes, is put forth by Zdanovich (1984). Kuzmina offers a date for the Petrov culture on the basis of parallels to the burial methods and psalia found at Mycenae and in the destruction levels at Troy. On this basis the conventional dates for the Petrov are given as seventeenth to sixteenth century BC. Yet, the carbon-14 dates for the supposedly contemporary Sintashta cemetery cluster *c.*1900 BC. The Sintashta chariots are by no means the earliest ones known. There are several sealing impressions depicting a chariot and driver in a Mesopotamian Early Dynastic III glyptic, *c.*2500 BC (Littauer and Crouwel 1979; Green 1993: 60). Uncalibrated radiocarbon dates for the Petrov culture routinely fall into the end of the third millennium; if calibrated, they would move to the first half of the third millennium. Clearly, the nascent radiocarbon chronology is indicating a substantially greater antiquity for the Andronovo than the present conventional relative chronology. We shall see that an identical situation existed in the initial phases of dating the BMAC in Central Asia. The continued dismissal of mid-third millennium radiocarbon dates for the Andronovo culture, and an insistence on the present relative chronology, is entirely counterproductive (Chernykh 1992).

While it is clear that language, culture, and ethnicity are not isomorphic there are times in which one can offer a reasonably convincing argument for correlations. There is, however, no convincing evidence that allows one to make an ethnic or linguistic, affiliation for any cultural variant of the Andronovo culture. Arguments, one of many "ethnohistoric" proposed by Kuzmina, suggest that the large houses of the Andronovo-Timber Grave cultures are prototypes of large Avestan houses. General similarities in material culture and vague parallels in social behavior (i.e. mortuary ritual and emphasis upon horses), drawn from the Avesta, Rigveda, and other "ethnohistoric" sources typify the manner by which Kuzmina relates the Andronovo with the Indo-Iranians. Even more tenuous are the suggestions advanced by the Genings and Zdanovich. In the Sintashta volume they correlate specific Andronovo subcultures and identify them with Indo-Iranian tribes. With the recognition of Andronovo subcultures the identification of specific ones as Indo-Iranian has become an industry (Vasilyev *et al.* 1995). Needless to say there is no consensus on the ethnicity of any single Andronovo subculture. It has yet to be demonstrated that language expansions can be traced through similarities in material culture or that a widely distributed culture, existing for a millennium and consisting of substantial variation, means that a population shares a common or related ethnicity. There are three conclusions that can be advanced concerning the identity of the Andronovo culture (or any of its specific variants) with the Indo-Iranians: (1) they are "in the right place at the right time." This argument, frequently implied, offers circumstantial evidence but remains thoroughly unconvincing; (2) parallels between the material culture and the environment of the Andronovo are compared to commentaries in the Rigveda and Avesta and are taken to confirm the Indo-Iranian identity of the Andronovo. The parallels are far too general to offer confidence in these correlations; (3) the later Scythians (Saka), known to be Iranian, occupy the same territory and share generalized similarities in material culture with the Andronovo. Thus, the ancestral Andronovo must be Indo-Iranian. Similarity in culture does not necessarily mean identity in language. As often as one recites the mantra that "language, culture, and 'race' are independent variables" as often the mantra is forgotten or ignored. The second chapter of the Indo-Iranian story involves its split into two branches: the Vedic or Indo-Aryan branch, inhabiting India and the Old Iranian, which moved onto the greater Iranian Plateau. Linguists generally place the date for the split of Indo-Aryan and Iranian to the late third millennium and/or the first part of the second millennium BC. Before turning to another archaeological culture identified as Indo-Iranian, one completely different from the Andronovo, it is relevant to identify the presence of the first written texts in an Indo-European language. As we shall see these texts heavily influenced the conceptions of Victor Sarianidi as to the geographical origins and Indo-Iranian identity of the BMAC.

In the fifteenth century BC in a treaty between a Hittite and Mitanni king the latter swears an oath by a series of gods who are major Indic deities: *Mi-it-ra* (Indic Mitra), *Aru-na* (*Varuna*), *In-da-ra* (Indra), and *Na-sa-at-tiya*. In another text a man named Kikkuli, counts from one to nine in Indic numerals and is referred to as an *assussanni* (Sanskrit *asvasani-*), a trainer of horses and chariotry. And, in yet another text, Indo-Aryan words are used to describe the color of horses.

Finally, the Mitanni word "marya" is precisely the same word as the "marya" referred to in the Rigveda and meaning "warrior." This evidence leads to the consensus view, namely, that an Indo-Aryan speaking elite of chariot warriors imposed themselves on a native Hurrian population to form a ruling dynasty that endured for several centuries. The date of the appearance of these Indic speakers bears on the origins and expansion of the Indo-Iranians. By the sixteenth/fifteenth centuries BC, as evidenced in the earlier texts from northern Syria and Turkey, a separate Indo-Aryan language already had diverged from a putative Indo-Iranian linguistic entity. Thus, the split of the Indo-Iranian languages (into Iranian and Indo-Aryan) must predate the fifteenth/fourteenth centuries BC, perhaps by as much as 500 years. Roman Ghirshman (1977) attempted to identify the arrival of the Indo-Aryans in the region of the Hurrians (northern Syria) by affiliating them with a certain type of widely distributed ceramic – Habur Ware, as well as with black and grey wares. This untenable argument was elegantly dispelled by Carol Kramer (1977) in her essay on "Pots and People."

The ethnic and linguistic identity of the Andronovo remains elusive but much discussed. A great deal is made of the importance of the horse within the Andronovo cultural context. But when did they actually begin to ride the horse? Was the development of horse-riding a stimulus to the development of multi-animal (sheep, goat, cattle) pastoralism? What was their relative dependence upon pastoral transhumance compared to sedentary agriculture? And what plants did they harvest? In the absence of settlement archaeology, save for the newly discovered "Country of Towns" we have virtually no understanding of the demographic setting on the steppes. Khazanov (1983: 333) contrasts the dramatic increase in the animals a shepherd can control when riding horseback, up to 2,000 sheep, compared with less than 500 on foot. When did pastoral transhumance on horseback emerge? And to what extent did the fragile environment of the steppes, with such critical factors as severe winters, the relative unavailability of water, and the failure of rainfall in as many as six out of ten years, contribute to the importance of out migration (diffusion)? (Khazanov 1983). These are but several fundamental questions that remain to be answered. High on that list is: When did horseback riding begin? David Anthony (2000) supports an early date, late fourth/early third millennium, while Levine (1999) finds conclusive evidence only in the late second millennium. Interestingly, in Mesopotamia the King of Mari, *c.*1800 BC, is admonished not to ride a horse, lest he jeopardize his status: "You are the King of the Hanaeans and King of the Akkadians. You should not ride a horse. Let my king ride a chariot or on a mule and he will thereby honor his head" (Malamat 1989).

A major contender for Indo-Iranian identity, and a relatively new actor on the archaeological stage of Central Asia, is a cultural complexity of great significance. The BMAC was discovered and named by Victor Sarianidi (1976: 71) following his excavations in Afghanistan in the late 1970s (for a bibliography of significant BMAC publications see Klochkov 1999). Bactria was the name given by the Greeks to the regions of northern Afghanistan, the territory around the

Amu Darya River, while Margiana (Margush) was a Persian province of the Achaemenid empire, whose capital was Merv, in present-day Turkmenistan. Victor Sarianidi (1998a,b) in two important volumes not only has identified the BMAC as Indo-Iranian but isolated, within the archaeological record, what he believes to be distinctive Proto-Zoroastrian cultural characteristics.

In the mid-1970s Soviet archaeologists undertook extensive surveys and excavations in Afghanistan. Following five years of excavation at the important site of Delbarjin (Kushan/Buddhist) a new publication was initiated specifically to report on these excavations and surveys: *Drevnii Baktria* (Ancient Bactria). In the first volume Sarianidi (1976) published his excavations in the Dashly Oasis. In the following year (Sarianidi 1977) he published the first extensive synthesis of his work in Afghanistan. His excavations at Dashly III uncovered a "rotund building" which was interpreted as a temple. The Dashly III culture was reconstructed along Mesopotamian lines; there was a temple community presided over by a "chief priest," which eventually gave way to kingship as the communal sector became privatized. The large round building, which had an outer buttressed wall, was the focus of the community, with radial streets leading to the "temple." The "temple," with dozens of rooms indicating domestic functions, was believed to house 150–200 people. Numerous bronze compartmented seals were recovered but no sealings. The seals were attributed the same function as in Mesopotamia; for securing doors as well as stored and transported goods. Sarianidi concluded that the Dashly III settlements were self-sufficient communities, managed as temple estates. He specifically draws a parallel between them and the Uruk community of Mesopotamia. Already in this first publication he rather cautiously, a caution that will later be abandoned, suggests that at Dashly III there are a few elements that find ready parallel in the Rigveda and Avesta: cattlebreeding, fire temples, circular and rectangular fortresses, animal burials, and the presence of camel (Sarianidi 1984).

There are fundamental differences between Sarianidi's (1990) first book, *Drevnosti Strani Margush* detailing the BMAC, and his most recent publication, *Margiana and Protozoroastrianism* (1998b). In many respects *Drevnosti Strani Margush* is both more extensively illustrated and more fully documented than his later volume. Excavations at Takhirbai (1000–750 BC), Togolok 21 (1250–1000 BC), Gonur [Dashly III/Namazga VI] (1500–1250 BC), and Kelleli [= Hissar III] (1700–1500 BC) offer an extraordinarily rich documentation of material remains, architectural exposure, as well as a chronological sequence. The very extensive horizontal exposure on each of these sites, a signature of Soviet archaeology, is almost as impressive as the monumental architecture discovered on each of the settlements, identified as either a temple, fort, or palace. The site of Gonur, believed by Sarianidi to be the "capital" of the BMAC in Margiana throughout the Bronze Age, contains all three and remains the focus of Sarianidi's archaeological excavations to this day. The palace at North Gonur measures 150 × 140 square meters, the temple at Togolok is 140 × 100 square meters, the fort at Kelleli 3 is 125 × 125 square meters, while the house of a local ruler at Adji Kui is 25 × 25 square meters.

Each of these formidable structures has been fully excavated – plus a great deal more. The temples, forts, and palaces all have impressive fortification walls, gates, and buttresses. It is not always clear why one structure is identified as a temple and another a palace. There is no clear signature, architectural template, within the BMAC. In fact, each building is unique, save for the fact that all are fortified by impressive walls and gates. Although Sarianidi offers ample illustrations he rarely offers specific provenience, room, or feature, in which an object was recovered. However, when a complex feature is excavated, as in the so-called "priestess burial" at Togolok 1, where two bulls and a driver may have been sacrificed, he offers a full contextual analysis. The majority of the objects often are ascribed simply to a major feature, that is, the palace at North Gonur. In *Drevnosti Strani Margush* the author advocates a late second millennium chronology for the BMAC, derives its origin as the result of a migration from southeastern Iran, and identifies it as Indo-Iranian; with objects, beliefs, and rituals ancestral to later Zoroastrianism. An impressive series of illustrations offer specific parallels in the pottery, seals, stone bowls, and metal types found in the BMAC with sites in Baluchistan, as well as with the specific sites, that is, Tepe Yahya, Shahdad, and the Jhukar culture of late Harappan times. There is absolutely no doubt, as amply documented by Pierre Amiet (1984), of the existence of BMAC material remains recovered from Susa, Shahdad, and Tepe Yahya. There is, however, every reason to doubt that because these parallels exist that the BMAC originates in southeastern Iran. This is extremely unlikely for the BMAC materials are intrusive in each of the sites on the Iranian Plateau as they are also on sites of the Arabian Peninsula (Potts 1994).

In *Drevnosti Strani Margush* (p. 62) and *Margiana and Protozoroastrianism* (p. 42) Sarianidi addresses the nature and extent of cultural influence that characterized the BMAC and the steppe cultures, the Andronovo. Even though steppe ceramics have been found on the sites of Togolok 1 and 21, Kelleli, Taip, Gonur, and Takhirbai, Sarianidi is adamant in opposing any significant Andronovo influence on the BMAC. Kuzmina and Lapin (1984) suggest that drought caused the drying up of the delta of the Murghab River, making possible an incursion from the steppes by the Andronovo warrior tribes and an end to the BMAC. By the middle of the second millennium all BMAC sites are abandoned – the reason(s) accounting for this dramatic process and/or event remain entirely elusive. Sarianidi finds neither merit nor evidence for attributing the steppe culture(s) as the agents that brought about the abandonment. In *Drevnosti Strani Margush* he states, "Contrary to the archaeological evidence is the statement that pottery of steppe character was 'plentiful' on the sites of south Turkmenistan. Pottery of the Andronovo type do not exceed 100 fragments in all of south Turkmenistan" (my translation p. 63). As rigorous approaches to data retrieval were not practised such a figure must be merely impressionistic.

The question of the nature and the extent of interaction that characterized the steppic cultures, the generic Andronovo culture, and the sedentary farmers of Central Asia, specifically the BMAC, is of fundamental importance. As we have noted both archaeological entities are distinctive in their material culture, both are chronologically synchronous, and both have been identified as Indo-Iranian. Decades ago, in his excavations at Takhirbai 3, V. M. Masson (1992) suggested that in the first half of the second millennium a high degree of interaction characterized the relations of the steppe nomads and the sedentary farmers of Bactria and Margiana. This has been resoundingly confirmed by the highly productive archaeological surveys undertaken recently by the Turkman–Russian–Italian surveys in Margiana (Gubaev *et al.* 1998). Erdosy (1998: 143) has recently observed that "the greatest desideratum is a clearer understanding of spatial relationships, the one area of archaeological research that has been seriously neglected by Soviet scholarship." The archaeological surveys in the Murghab have documented hundreds of settlements of the BMAC, post-BMAC, and sites containing what the archaeologists refer to as "Incised Coarse Ware" (ICW). The ICW (readily identified as a generic Andronovo ceramic) appears on sites of BMAC, post-BMAC, as well as on settlements exclusively containing ICW. There can be little doubt that the interaction of peoples from the steppes with their sedentary Central Asian neighbors was both extensive and intensive. The fortified settlements of the "Country of Towns" and the well fortified settlements of the BMAC suggest that the interaction was not always peaceful. In a more recent publication Sarianidi (1999) acknowledges this interaction and offers a new slant: "Andronovo type vessels [were found] only in the rooms that were used for the preparation of soma-haoma type drinks in Margiana." Thus, Sarianidi concludes that the BMAC are Indo-Aryan and the Andronovo are Iranian. Both are proto-Zoroastrian sharing common cultic rituals. Clearly, the Turkman–Russian–Italian surveys in the Murghab indicate that the region was what Mary Louise Pratt (1992: 6–7) calls a "contact zone," "the space in which peoples geographically and historically separated come into contact with each other and establish on-going relations, usually involving conditions of coercion, radical inequality, and intractable conflict," relations characterized by "radically asymmetrical relations of power." The relationship that characterized the peoples from the steppes with BMAC, and post-BMAC cultures, remains undefined. The fact that both fortified their settlements is suggestive. Again, the surveys in the Murghab suggest that archaeological cultures, no less than modern ones, are not separated "cultures" or "ethnic groups," or what Geertz (2000: 234) calls "lumps of sameness marked out by limits of consensus" but permeable mosaics of interacting similarities and differences.

The Turkman–Russian–Italian surveys in the Murghab have offered a resounding confirmation of the complex interaction that characterized the region throughout the Bronze Age. Evidence for the interaction of settled farmers and the Andronovo culture also come from the excavations in southern Tadjikistan at the site of Kangurttut (Vinogradova 1994). In this settlement archaeologists recovered Andronovo ceramics, knives, and daggers, including molds for the production of classic Andronovo type daggers. The site is radiocarbon dated to the middle of the second millennium and said to be associated with the Mollali phase of the Sapalli culture, that is the very end of the BMAC. The excavator suggests that the "infiltration process of the Andronovo tribes to the south was relatively slow" and that it was characterized by a peaceful process, such that a "settling down and dissolution of steppe population into that of farming oases could take place" (Vinogradova 1994: 46).

The transition to the Iron Age is one of both continuity and discontinuity. In the second half of the second millennium the Yaz culture emerges, the earliest of Iron Age cultures, and with it an increasing sedentarization of nomads, the emergence of monumental architecture, newly founded settlements, and the emergence of painted pottery with parallels to Susa in Iran and Pirak in Baluchistan. Within the Iron Age, and its widely distributed grey wares, the Yaz culture is frequently cited as a candidate for Indo-Iranian identity (Young 1967; Ghirshman 1977).

The extensive metallurgy of the steppes as well as that of the BMAC is well documented. The types that characterize each of the regions are entirely distinctive. Sarianidi (1990) offers an important analysis of BMAC metals and an appendix on the analysis of specific botanical remains. In her study of the metals, N. N. Terekhova concludes that techniques of casting and forging were utilized in the production of objects manufactured from copper – arsenides, native copper and copper-tin bronze. In the latter category twenty-six objects were analyzed having 1–10 percent tin: N. R. Meyer-Melikyan analyzed floral remains recovered from the monumental complex at Togolok 21. "The samples are floral remains: fragments of stems, often with leaves, pollen grains, anterophors, microsporangia, and scraps of megasporia skin and parts of fruit" (p. 203) which were found in large pithoi in rooms 23 and 34. She concludes that the remains belong to the Ephedra genus. Sarianidi is thus afforded the opportunity of following a number of scholars who believe that ephedra was the essential ingredient in the sacred drink, haoma or soma. This mildly intoxicating drink is referred to in the sacred books of the Indo-Iranians: the Rigveda and the Avesta. As previously noted presence of ephedra at Gonur is taken by Sarianidi as further testimony for both Indo-Iranian and Protozoroastrian identity of the BMAC. On numerous sites Sarianidi identifies altars, fire temples, the importance of fire in mortuary rituals, fractional burials, burials in vessels, cremation, and in chamber 92 at Gonur a "dakhma" is identified. A "dakhma" refers to a communal burial structure, associated with Zoroastrian mortuary practice, in which the dead are exposed.

The use of ephedra to produce haoma, the presence of fire temples, fire altars (which Sarianidi directly compares to "pavi" – Zoroastrian altars), and specific mortuary rituals (animal sacrifice), are all advanced in *Drevni Strani Margush* to bolster the Indo-Iranian and Protozoroastrian identity of the BMAC. This hypothesis underscores Sarianidi's recent book *Margiana and Protozoroastrianism*.

Much of *Margiana and Protozoroastrianism*, in both text and illustration, is derived, if not directly translated, from his earlier work (Sarianidi 1990). There are, however, several important revisions as well as the inclusion of new data, particularly from the excavations at Gonur. Most significantly, in his recent book Sarianidi (1999) accepts, albeit uneasily, the higher chronology for the BMAC, already advanced in the mid-1980s by a number of scholars. A series of radiocarbon dates, collected by Fredrik Hiebert (1994) at Gonur on behalf of the Peabody Museum, Harvard University, offers unequivocal evidence for the dating of the BMAC to the last century of the third millennium and the first quarter of the second millennium. A new series of radiocarbon dates from Tepe Yahya IVB-4, where BMAC imports were recovered, confirms the late third millennium dating for the beginnings of the BMAC (Lamberg-Karlovsky 2001). The BMAC, rather than dating to the second half of the second millennium, is to be dated to the end of the third and beginning of the second millennium. Sarianidi (1999: 78) now writes "that the first colonists from the west appeared in Bactria and Margiana at the transition of the III-II Millennia B.C." (p. 78). However, his insistence upon the late dating of Gonur to 1500–1200 BC continues to fly in the face of his own carbon-14 dates which average 300–500 years earlier.

Of equal significance is Sarianidi's new perspective on the origins of the BMAC. Animal burials, camel and ram, were recovered from Gonur and other BMAC sites. At North Gonur the "Tomb of the Lamb" contained a decorated metal macehead, silver and bronze pins with elaborately decorated heads, an ornamental ivory disc, and numerous "faience" and bone pieces of in-lay. Sarianidi interprets this as evidence for the transition from human to animal sacrifice, even though there is no unequivocal evidence, either on the steppes or in Central Asia, for human sacrifice.

Mortuary rituals, architectural parallels (particularly in what he calls "temples"), and above all, stylistic similarities in cylinder seals, all converge to suggest to Sarianidi that Bactria and Margiana were colonized by the immigrants from the Syro-Anatolian region (1998a: 76, 142). This argument is given greater weight in *Myths of Ancient Bactria and Margiana on its Seals and Amulets* (hereafter, *Myths*). Sarianidi directs a migration of "tribes" from the regions of Syro-Anatolia in two directions: (1) Across the Zagros to Elam and Susa, where there are numerous BMAC parallels (Amiet 1984), and from there to Shahdad and Yahya, where again BMAC materials are found (Hiebert and Lamberg-Kalovsky 1992), and finally toward Baluchistan. (2) A second wave went north of Lake Urmia, skirted the Elburz Mountains, colonized Hissar in Period 111B, and finally went on to settle in the oases of Bactria and Margiana.

There is scant evidence to support the notion of an extensive migration from Syro-Anatolia to Bactria-Margiana at any point in the archaeological record!. Architectural similarities are exceedingly generalized and where parallels are drawn they pay little attention to time/space systematics. Thus, a text from Qumran referring to animal sacrifice is paralleled to the "Tomb of the Lamb" at Gonur, while a "Ligabue vessel," said to come from an illegal excavation at Shahdad, finds a (vague) parallel in the Aegean and "proves the real historical link of the tribes that immigrated from the west with the Mycenean-Minoan world" to Bactria-Margiana (Sarianidi 1998a: 44). For Sarianidi the evidence derived from the BMAC seals is conclusive. He believes that the seals used motifs and subject composition that have an "undisputed Hittite-Mitannian origin" (1998a: 143). One gets the impression that Sarianidi chose the Syro-Anatolian region as the homeland of the BMAC in order to situate it within the geographical region in which the first Indo-Aryan texts, discussed earlier, were recovered. This presumably strengthens his Indo-Aryan claim for the BMAC (1999). His book *Myths* is devoted to convincing the reader that the BMAC seals derive their thematic inspiration and style from the Syro-Anatolian region. For another expansive catalog of BMAC and related seals see Baghestani (1997).

Myths is an extremely important and valuable publication. A total of 1,802 seals are illustrated, describing (1) seal type: cylindrical, flat, three-sided prisms, compartmented; (2) material: stone, copper, silver, shell, faience, gypsum, clay; (3) size; description of scene; and (4) provenience. Of the 1,802 seals less than 250 have an archaeological provenience; the largest provenienced corpus is from Gonur where almost a hundred were recovered. Most of the seals are attributed to their places of sale: the Kabul Bazaar, the Anahita Gallery; or museums: the Louvre, the Metropolitan Museum of Art; or private collectors: Ron Garner, Jonathan Rosen. There are less than two dozen sealings and ten sealed bullae (some baked) listed as coming from Gonur and/or Togolok. Given the extensive areas excavated, with particular attention to elite quarters, this is a very limited number of sealings. Nevertheless, the presence of bullae and sealings does suggest economic functions and security concerns similar, at least in part, to Mesopotamian seal/sealing practices. With reference to writing, I. S. Klotchkov (1998) has made the intriguing suggestion that signs on a potsherd recovered from Gonur contain Elamite linear script. This find remains the only evidence for writing(?) within the BMAC.

The discussion of the seals is divided into Group 1, The Anthropomorpha, including scenes depicting seated deities on thrones, animals, or dragons; the mistress of animals, kneeling deities and heroes in combat; Group 2, serpents and dragons; Group 3, fabulous creatures, including winged lions, griffins; Group 4, animals and birds; Group 5, Arthropoda and Plants, including scorpions, snakes, poppies, tulips, and ephedra; Group 6, Individual Seals and Amulets, seals of such individuality as to defy classification. In discussing each of these groups Sarianidi emphasizes both the general and the specific parallels to seals in Syro-Anatolia. There is no doubt that a few BMAC seals, less than half-a-dozen, find parallel, in theme and/or style with those of Syro-Anatolian type. Sarianidi is relentless in his effort to convince the reader that the origins of the BMAC are to be found in the Hittite-Mitannian world. Generalized parallels are interpreted as evidence for specific BMAC origins. Thus, generic birds appear associated with seated "deities" on seals from the Elamite, Mesopotamian, *and* the Syro-Anatolian world. Yet, Sarianidi emphasizes only the Syro-Anatolian parallels, which have, at best, very generalized similarities. There is nothing in the style of the BMAC seals illustrating birds that privileges its derivation from any of the above regions. Nevertheless, Sarianidi not only derives the birds depicted on BMAC seals as Syro-Anatolian but associates the bird with Varaghna, the symbol of might and victory in the Avesta; "I suppose that this image was generated in the local Indo-Iranian milieu before Zarathustra" (1998b: 23).

The vast majority of the BMAC seals contain motifs, styles, and even material, entirely foreign to the repertoire of seals from Syro-Anatolia, Mesopotamia, the Gulf, and the Indus. The BMAC seals are of a thoroughly distinctive type and are to be seen as indigenous to the Central Asian Bronze Age world and not as derivative from any other region. BMAC seals have been found in the Indus civilization, on the Iranian Plateau, at Susa and in the Gulf. Amiet (1984) and T. Potts (1994) have documented the wide ranging distribution of BMAC materials. It is in the context of a wide ranging distribution of BMAC artifacts that the specific parallels to the Syro-Anatolian region are to be appreciated. The *wide* scatter of a *limited* number of BMAC artifacts does not privilege any area as a "homeland" for the BMAC. An extremely limited number of parallels between the BMAC and Syro-Anatolia signify the unsurprising fact that, at the end of the third and beginning of the early second millennium, interregional contacts in the Near East brought people from the Indus to Mesopotamia and from Egypt to the Aegean into contact.

A distant BMAC "homeland," followed by an expansive migration to Central Asia, is difficult, if not impossible, to maintain. Nevertheless, the origins of the BMAC remains a fundamental issue. Although some scholars advance the notion that the BMAC has indigenous roots, the fact remains that the material culture of the BMAC is not easily derived from the preceding Namazga IV culture, thus suggesting its intrusive nature. The wide scatter of BMAC materials from southeastern Iran to Baluchistan and Afghanistan suggests that the beginnings of the BMAC could lie in this direction, an area of enormous size and an archaeological *terra nullius*. In fact, the BMAC of Central Asia may turn out to be its most northern extension while its heartland might be found in the vast areas of unexplored Baluchistan and Afghanistan.

Ahmed Ali Askarov (1977), and in a later publication with T. S. Shirinov (1993), is responsible for excavating two important BMAC settlements in Uzbekistan: Sapalli depe and Djarkutan. The recent syntheses of these excavations (Askarov and Shirinov 1993) offers an abundance of illustrations of the architecture, ceramics, and material remains recovered from BMAC sites. The walled settlement of Djarkutan covers an area of approximately 100 hectares and features a fortress, almost completely excavated, of more than 3 hectares. The material inventory as well as the architecture firmly places Djarkutan and Sapalli depe within the BMAC cultural context. Askarov follows the late chronology of Sarianidi, placing Djarkutan within the second half of the second millennium BC. He also follows Sarianidi in identifying the presence of palaces, temples, and "fire altars" as having to do with a proto-Zoroastrian world. Special attention is paid to a large structure at Djarkutan, over 50 × 35 square meters, identified as a "fire temple." The structure contains extensive storage facilities with a large paved central room having at its center a raised podium believed to be the seat of the "sacred fire." Other rooms also contained "fire altars." The proto-Zoroastrian nature of this impressive building is explicitly stated. At both Djarkutan and Sapelli depe extensive areas uncovered dozens of structures and numerous graves. There is little attribution of materials to specific rooms and/or structures. One obtains only a vague notion as to how many building levels exist within a single site. My own visits to the sites of Gonur, Togolok, and Djarkutan clearly confirm that each of these sites has multiple building levels. The publications, however, present the data as being essentially from a single period of time. Even though Sarianidi points out that Gonur had 3 meters of accumulation, and Taip 2.5 meters, the stratigraphic complexity and/or periodization of these sites are left unexplored. Thus, the internal development and chronology of the BMAC still awaits definition. Askarov takes the opportunity of reconstructing the social stratification at Djarkutan, from an aristocracy to slavery, all within a state structured society. He identifies both sites as inhabited by Indo-Iranian tribes which, he believes, played an important role in the later formation of Uzbek, Tadjik, and Turkman nationalities.

The settlement pattern around Djarkutan and Sapalli mirrors that of the sites excavated by Sarianidi. A large settlement with impressive "temples" and/or "palaces" is surrounded by smaller agricultural villages. After Sapalli was abandoned, for reasons unknown, the site, particularly the region about the "temple," was utilized as a cemetery. A total of 138 graves were excavated. Raffaele Biscione and L. Bondioli (1988) studied these graves to great benefit. Females outnumber males by 3 : 2. There is also a difference in the amount of wealth placed in the tombs; females are given an average of 15.5 objects while males are given 7.5 objects. There are no differences in the types of materials placed in the tombs; both male and female tombs contain numerous ceramics, metals, and stone vessels. Two male tombs, however, stand out from all the rest. In these the dead are buried in wooden coffins and are accompanied by the greatest number of goods. The authors draw attention to the fact that the general lack of gender distinction, with regard to accompanying grave wealth, mirrors a similar pattern on the steppes where the pattern of gender equality remains a characteristic of Scythian burials of the late first millennium.

Striking evidence for BMAC–Steppe interaction is reported from the salvage excavation of an elite tomb discovered along the upper Zerafshan River, Tadjikistan (Bobomulloev 1999). Excavation of this tomb yielded the burial of a single male, accompanied by a ram, horse bits (psalia), identical to those recovered from Sintashta, a bronze pin, terminating with a horse figurine, and, numerous ceramics of BMAC type. This striking association of steppic and BMAC material in a single tomb underscores the existence of a paradox. On the steppes there is ample evidence for the use of horses, wagons, and chariots but an exceedingly sparse presence of BMAC material remains. While within BMAC communities there is only scanty evidence for the presence of steppic ceramics and a complete absence of the use and/or presence of horses, their equipment, or their depiction. Such an assymetry in the distribution of these highly distinctive cultures would seem to suggest a minimum of contact between the two. The fact that representative communities of both cultures, that is, Arkhaim and Gonur, are heavily fortified suggests the recognition and need within each community to prepare for conflict. The extent of the conflict that existed *within* these distinctive cultures, as well as *between* them, remains an unknown but important question to be addressed. The asymmetry, that is the almost complete absence for evidence of contact between the BMAC and the steppes is made the more enigmatic by the evidence of settlement survey. The Turkman–Russian–Italian surveys indicate that numerous sites of steppe culture are situated near BMAC settlements. The mutually exclusive evidence for the material remains of one culture to be wholly absent from its neighboring "others" suggests intentional avoidance. Clearly this situation, should it be correctly interpreted, requires theoretical insights beyond our present abilities.

In the second century BC Zhang Qian, a Chinese envoy stationed in the western provinces, compared the nature of the agrarian and nomadic polities in Xinjiang. More recently Nicola DiCosmo (2000) suggests that the Iron Age settlements of Xinjiang are similar to the BMAC sites with respect to size, fortifications, oasis environments, subsistence patterns, and processes of nomadic–sedentary interaction. Zhang Qian wrote of twenty-four such "walled towns" in Xinjiang that served as "capitals." DiCosmo (2000), in turn, refers to these nomadic settlements as "city-states." Their size varied greatly. On the one hand, the state of Wutanzli consisted of 41 households: 231 individuals, of which 57 were capable of bearing arms. On the other hand, the state of Yanqi was among the most populous: 4,000 households, with 32,100 individuals and an army of 6,000. Chinese sources identify these political entities as "guo," traditionally rendered in English as "state." Each "guo" was characterized as a political formation with a recognizable head, a bureacratic hierarchy, and a military organization. The Chinese texts indicate that the pastoral-nomads maintained a larger military ratio than their agrarian neighbors. Within Eurasia, pastoral-nomadic states, city-states, and even empires, is a common conceptual framework. In the late Iron Age the scale of nomadic "empire" is attested by the Wusun, who inhabited the Tarim Basin of Xinjiang. They had a population of 630,000 people and an army of 188,800 (quoted in DiCosmo 2000: 398). To the Wusun can be added the pastoral-nomadic Saka, Yuezhi, Xiongnu, and the later Mongol confederations; each of which affected the political organization of Eurasia on a continental scale. The relationships that characterized the nomadic and sedentary communities, as recorded in the Chinese texts, were typically hostile. Why? Chinese sources answer the question: insufficient food supplies resulted in competition and conflict over agricultural resources. When nomadic polities were strong they extracted tribute from their more sedentary neighbors; thus, assuring the need for an extensive miltary presence in return for a sufficient and regular food supply (see also Jettmar 1997).

Skeletal remains from sites of the BMAC have been studied and compared to those of the Harappan civilization. This study has concentrated upon cranial non-metric variations and concluded that the populations of the BMAC and Harappa were "profoundly" different (Hemphill 1999). The authors believe their study documents a "general movement of gene flow from west to east, from western Iran to the oases of Central Asia" (1995: 863). It is the view of these authors that the

BMAC either originated in, or passed through, Iran. The use of "cranial non-metric variation," that is to say the presence or absence of certain non-metric features on the skull, cannot be referred to as "gene flow" and hardly merits the sweeping conclusions advanced. There is absolutely no evidence that genes are involved in governing the presence or the absence of the cranial features studied. There are numerous non-genetic factors that account for cranial features and their variation, that is, diet. To speak of "gene flow" suggests a degree of understanding of the genetic structure of the architecture of the skull that we simply do not have!

5.1 Conclusions

Russian scholars working in the Eurasiatic steppes are nearly unanimous in their belief that the Andronovo, and its variant expressions, are Indo-Iranians. Similarly, Russian and Central Asian scholars working on the BMAC all share the conviction that the BMAC is Indo-Iranian. The BMAC and the Andronovo are contemporary but their archaeological cultures and environmental settings are vastly different. Passages from the Avesta and the Rigveda are quoted by different authors to support the Indo-Iranian identity of both the BMAC and the Andronovo. The passages are sufficiently general as to permit the Plains Indians of North America an Indo-Iranian identity! Furthermore, archaeology offers virtually no evidence for BMAC influence on the steppe and only scant evidence for an Andronovo presence within the settlement of the BMAC. There is little archaeological evidence *within* the settlements to support the notion that the Andronovo and the BMAC experienced a significant and/or sustained contact. Yet, settlement surveys indicate that the distinctive communities were close neighbors, exploiting the same environment. There is certainly no evidence to support the notion that the BMAC and the Andronovo shared a common ancestor. To date the horse has not been identified in the BMAC and the very diagnostic metal inventories that characterize both cultures are entirely absent in the other. There is simply no compelling *archaeological* evidence to support, or for that matter to deny, the notion that either one, both, or neither are Indo-Iranians.

Indo-Iranian is a linguistic construct that formed a shared culture prior to its separation into Iranian and Indic branches. One branch of the Indo-Iranians went to Iran and another to northern India. The date of their arrival in these new homelands is typically taken to be in the second millennium BC. One conclusion can be readily stated: there is not a single artifact of Andronovo type that has been identified in Iran or in northern India! The same cannot be said of the BMAC. There is ample evidence for the presence of BMAC materials on the Iranian Plateau and Baluchistan: Susa, Shahdad, Yahya, Khurab, Sibri, Miri Qalat, Deh Morasi Ghundai, Nousharo, etc. (for a review see Hiebert and Lamberg-Karlovsky 1992). It is impossible, however, to trace the continuity of the BMAC material culture into the first millennium and relate it to the known cultures of Iranian speakers – the Medes or the Achaemenids (or their presumed Iron Age ancestors, see Young 1967; Ghirshman 1977). Within the entirety of the second millennium the only intrusive archaeological culture that directly influences Iran and northern India is the BMAC. However, it remains impossible to link the BMAC with the development of later second and first millennium archaeological cultures on the Iranian Plateau.

The archaeological quest for the identity of the Indo-Iranians remains elusive. When Indo-Iranians are identified in the archaeological record it is by allegation not by demonstration. It is interesting to note that the emphasis in the archaeological (and linguistic) literature has focused entirely upon the Indo-Iranians. What of the other major linguistic families believed to be inhabiting the same regions, the Altaic, Ugric, and Dravidian? The cultural-historical condition becomes inordinately complicated when one introduces the other languages that have an equal claim to be present in the same regions as the Indo-Iranian language. Thus, there is an equally valid quest in searching for the homeland and subsequent migration of the Altaic languages (Turkish, Mongolian), Ugric (Finnish, Hungarian, Estonian) – see Gamkrelidze and Ivanov for a full listings of these language families and Elamo-Dravidian. Each of these three language families have their roots on the Eurasiatic steppes and/or in Central Asia. The fact that these language families, compared to Indo-European, are of far less interest to the archaeologist with regard to the study of homeland(s) and/or subsequent spread, may have a great deal to do with the fact that it is primarily speakers of Indo-European who address this topic in search of their own roots. The archaeologist A. L. Netchitailo (1996) cuts to the chase by referring to all archaeological cultures on the steppes as belonging to what he calls "the European community." Such a view can be interpreted as inclusive, in which Altaic and Ugrian speakers become European, or exclusive, in which case the former played no role on the steppes. Both views are wrong! One of the variants of the Andronovo culture and the BMAC may have spoken Indo-Iranian but they may have just as readily spoken a Dravidian and/or an Altaic language. Contemporary methodologies, be they linguistic or archaeological, are virtually non-existent for determining which language a remote archaeological culture spoke. Simplified notions of the congruence between an archaeological culture and an ethnic group is no more than mere speculation, often one with a political agenda. Archaeology has a long way to go before its methodology allows one to establish which cultural markers, pottery, architecture, burials, etc., are most reliable for designating ethnic identity. Some scholars, both linguists and archaeologists, subscribe to the notion that the Dravidians migrated from the Iranian highlands to South Asia where they came into contact with the Indus civilization (Witzel 1999), others even suggest that the horse and the camel were introduced into Iran by Dravidians (Allchin 1995: 31; Kenoyer 1998: 78). Which archaeological culture in Iran/Central Asia can be identified with the Dravidians? Could the BMAC be Dravidians pushed onto the Iranian Plateau by Altaic and/or Indo-Iranian steppe nomads? Indeed, the BMAC could have been Indo-Iranian as well as Dravidian, or Altaic, or any combination of the three! If, say the BMAC are Dravidians, then where and what archaeological cultures represent the others? There are either too many languages and too few archaeological cultures to permit for a ready fit between archaeology and language, or too few languages and too many archaeological cultures.

Archaeologists and linguists share a difficulty in confronting and identifying processes of convergence and divergence. Migrations result in linguistic and cultural divergence, giving rise to the family tree model of language formation, while seriation, the establishment of a "genetic" relationship between two objects within distinctive material cultures, indicates cultural divergence within the archaeological record. Convergence, that is the coming together of two distinctive languages and/or cultures, is a more recent linguistic concern. Within archaeology, convergence is completely ignored. Archaeological cultures either progress in linear fashion, change due to internal social processes (rarely demonstrated), or more typically are altered by external factors (population pressure, climate change, migration/diffusion, etc.). Migrations, once a fashionable explanation for cultural divergence, have, in recent years, lost their appeal. The Australian linguist R. M. W. Dixon (1997) has given new life to the importance of linguistic convergence, first advocated by Trubetskoy (1939). Dixon convincingly argues that migrations, which trigger linguistic (and cultural) divergence, is a rare "event"; the more normal situation being processes of linguistic (and cultural?) convergence:

> Over most of human history there has been an equilibrium situation. In a given geographical area there would have been a number of political groups, of similar size and organisation, with no one group having undue prestige over the others. Each would have spoken its own language or dialect. They would have constituted a long-term linguistic area, with the languages existing in a state of relative equilibrium.
>
> (1997: 3)

The extract would seem to describe the archaeological cultures of the steppes, from the Pit Grave culture(s) to the Andronovo culture(s). Given the increasingly large number of divisions and subdivisions of the generic Andronovo culture(s), with evidence for "no one group having undue prestige over the others," there is neither reason nor evidence to believe that they all shared an Indo-Iranian language. From the common roots of the millennialong Andronovo culture(s) [and before that the related Timber Grave culture(s)], processes of both convergence and divergence [archaeologically indicated by the eastward migrations of the Andronovo culture(s)] allow for the presence of not only the Indo-Iranian languages but for other language families as well, that is, Altaic and Uralic. Clearly, the convergence of cultures, that is, the assimilation of local populations by an in-coming peoples, is very poorly developed within the archaeological discipline. The variations in distinction between cultural/linguistic and convergence/divergence processes is explained in the diagram below.

		Linguisitic Convergence	Linguisitic Divergence
Cultural	Convergence		
	Divergence		

The problem of identifying cultural and/or linguistic convergence/divergence within an archaeological and/or linguistic framework is highlighted by Henning's (1978) attempt to identify the Guti as the "First Indo-Europeans." At *c.*2200 BC the Guti invade Mesopotamia and bring down the powerful Akkadian Empire. They are identified in the texts as mountain people, probably from northwestern Iran, who ruled Mesopotamia for approximately 100 years. In Mesopotamia archaeologists are unable to identify a single fragment of material culture as belonging to the Guti. Nor do the Akkadian (western Semitic) texts contain any loan words identifiable as Indo-European. Thus, the Guti, save for their name and their activities as recorded in the Mesopotamian texts, are all but invisible. Henning (see also Narain 1987) suggests that the Guti, following their conquest of Mesopotamia, migrated to the east where Chinese texts refer to them as the Yue-chih (the Guti being argued as the phonological equivalent of Yue-chih in Chinese). In the first half of the second millennium there is not a sherd of archaeological evidence for a migration from Mesopotamia to China nor is their a material culture within the realms of the Yue-chih that finds a parallel with a material culture of the Mesopotamian–Gutian world. This does not negate the Guti = Yue-chih identity, it merely underscores the fact that convergence and/or divergence, in a linguistic and/or a cultural context, can almost obliterate the ability to distinguish previously distinctive entities, whether cultural or linguistic.

In an interesting "Afterword" to Sarianidi's *Margiana and Protozoroastrianism* J. P. Mallory confronts the issue, "How do we reconcile deriving the Indo-Iranians from two regions [the steppes (Andronovo) and the Central Asian oases (BMAC)] so different with respect to environment, subsistence and cultural behavior?" (p. 181). He offers three models, each of interest, none supported by archaeological evidence; that is, the BMAC were the Indo-Iranians and they came to dominate the steppe lands, serving as the inspiration for the emergence of the fortified settlements, such as Sintashta, in the southern Urals. Thus, an external source is provided for the development of the "Country of Towns" and with it a linguistic affiliation. The author admits to the unlikely nature of this model. His conclusion is "that the nucleus of Indo-Iranian linguistic developments formed in the steppe lands and, through some form of symbiosis in Bactria-Margiana, pushed southwards to form the ancient languages of Iran and India" (p. 184). It is that "form of symbiosis" that is so utterly elusive! Linguist too frequently and too adroitly, assign languages to archaeological cultures, while archaeologists are often too quick to assign their sherds a language. Dennis Sinor (1999: 396), a distinguished linguist and historian of Central Asia offers advice that more might heed: "I find it impossible to attribute with any degree of certainty any given language to any given prehistoric civilization." The books under review here offer archaeological data of great interest and importance... all authors identify the archaeological cultures with which they are working as Indo-Iranian. Linguists cannot associate an archaeological culture with the words and grammar they deal with and archaeologists cannot make their sherds utter words. Doing either is mere assertion. We need a third arbiter, which may or may not offer degrees of resolution to the relationships between archaeological culture and language. Perhaps that arbiter will be in our genes – the study of DNA. Equally likely is that our biological history is a sufficient mosaic that ambiguity will characterize our DNA "fingerprint" as well.

References

Aklimov, K., N. Boroffka, M. Bubnova, J. Burjakov, J. Cierny, J. Jakubov, J. Lutz, H. Partzinger, E. Pernicka, V. Radililovskij, V. Ruzanov, T. Sirinov, D. Starsinin, and G. Wesigerber, 1998. "Prähistorische Zinnbergbau in Mittelasian, Eurasia Antigua," *Zeitschrift für Archäeologie Eurasiens*, 4: 137–98.

Amiet, P., 1984. *L'äge des echanges inter-iraniens*. Paris: Editions de la Reunion des muses nationaux.

Anthony, D., 1991. "The Archaeology of Indo-European Origins," *Journal of Indo-European Studies*, 19(3/4): 193–222.

——, 2000. "Eneolithic Horse Exploitation in the Eurasian Steppes: Diet, Ritual and Riding," *Antiquity*, 74(283): 75–86.

Askarov, A. A., 1977. *Drevnizemledelichskaj Kulture Epochi Bronzi Ioga Uzbekistana* (Ancient Agricultural Cultures of the Bronze Age in Southern Uzbekistan). Tashkent: Uzbekistan Nauka.

Askarov, A. A. and T. S. Shirinov, 1993. *Ranii Gordskokoj Kultura epochi Bronzi i ioga strednii Azii* (The Early Urban Cultures of Bronze Age Southern Uzbekistan) (in Russian). Samarkand: Uzbek Academy of Sciences.

Baghestani, S., 1997. Metallene Compartimentsiegel aus Ost-Iran Zentralasien and Nord-China. Deutsche Archaeologische Institute, Archäeologie Iranund Turan. Rahden/Westdorf: Marie Leitdorf.

Bar-Yosef, O. and A. Khazanov, 1992. "Introduction." In *Pastoralism in the Levant*, edited by O. Barr-Yosef and A. Khazanov. Monographs in World Archaeology No. 10. Madison, WI: Prehistoric Press.

Biscione, R. and L. Bondioli, 1988. "Sapallitepa." In *Bactria: An Ancient Oasis Civilization from the Sands of Afghanistan*, edited by G. Ligabue and S. Salvatore. Venice: Erizzo.

Bobomulloev, S., 1999. "Discovery of a Bronze Age Tomb on the Upper Zerafshan," Stratum Plus (in Russian), No. 2, pp. 307–14.

Bunker, E., 1998. "Cultural Diversity in the Tarim Basin Vicinity and its Impact on Ancient Chinese Culture." In *The Bronze Age and Iron Age Peoples of Eastern Central Asia*, edited by V. Mair. Philadelphia, PA: The University of Pennsylvania Museum Publications, pp. 604–18.

Chernetsov, V. N., 1973. "The Ethno-Cultural Regions in the Forest and Subarctic Zones of Eurasia in the Neolithic Period" (in Russian), edited by A. P. Smirnov, *Problemv Arkheologi Urala i Sibiri (Archaeology of the Urals and Siberia)*. Moscow: Nauka, pp. 10–17.

Chernykh, S. S., 1992. *Ancient Metallurgy of the USSR*. Cambridge: Cambridge University Press.

——, 1994a. "L'Ancienne Production Miniere et Metallurgique et les Catastrophes Ecologiques," *Trabaijos de Prehistoria*, 51(2): 55–68.

——, 1994b. "Origenes de la metalurgie en Eurasia Central," *Revista de Arqueoliia*, 15 (153): 12–19.

Chesko, S. V., 1998. *Kto Oni i Otkuda*. Biblioteka Russijskogo ethnografa. Moscow: Russian Academy of Sciences.

Childe, V. G., 1926. *The Aryans. A Study of Indo-European Origins*. London: Kegan Paul.

Diakonoff, I., 1995. "Review Article: Whence Came the Indo-Aryans? by E. E. Kuzmina. Russian Academy, Moscow, 1994," *Journal of the American Oriental Society*, 115(3): 37–48.

DiCosmo, N., 2000. "Ancient City-States in the Tarim Basin." In *A Comparative Study of Third Site-State Cultures*, edited by M. H. Hansen. Historisk-filosofiske Skrifter 21. Copenhagen, CA: Reitzels, pp. 393–407.

Dixon, R. M. W., 1997. *The Rise and Fall of Languages*. Cambridge: Cambridge University Press.

Erdosy, G., 1998. "Language, Ethnicity and Migration in Protohistoric Margiana." In A. Gubaev, G. Koshelenko, and M. Tosi. The Archaeological Map of the Murghab Delta. Preliminary Reports 1990–1995. Rome: Istituto Italiano per L'Africa et 1'Oriente.

Gamkrelidze, T. V. and V. V. Ivanov, 1984. Indoevropeiskij Jack i Indoevroneitsv (Indo-European Language and Indo-Europeans). Tbilisi: Izd. TGU.

——, 1995. Indo-European and the Indo-Europeans. New York: Mouton de Gruyter.

Geary, P. J., 1999. "Barbarians and Ethnicity." In *Late Antiquity. A Guide to the Postclassical World*, edited by G. W. Bowersock, P. Brown, and O. Grabar. Cambridge, MA: Harvard University.

Geertz, C., 2000. Available Light. Anthropological Reflections on Philosophical Topics. Princeton, NJ: Princeton University Press.

Gening, V. F., G. B. Zdanovich, and V. V. Gening, 1992. *Sintashta: Arkeologiskiye Pamjianiki Arijs – kick Plemen Uralo-Kazakstanskich St_epii (Sintashta: Archaeological Sites of Aryan Tribes of the Ural Kazak Steppes)*. Chelyabinsk: Russian Academy of Sciences.

Gerasomov, M. M., 1955. *Vosstanovlenie litsa 12o cherenu*. Navaia Seriia, no. 2, Institut Ethnographie.

Ghirshman, R., 1977. *L'Iran et la Migration des Indo-Aryens et des Iraniens*. Leiden: E. J. Brill.

Gimbutas, M., 1965. *Bronze Age Cultures in Central and Eastern Europe*. Hague: Mouton and Co.

Görsdorf, J., H. Partzinger, A. Nagler, and N. Leont'ev, 1998. "Neue 14-C Datierungen für die Sibirische Steppe and ihre Konsequenzen für die regionalen Bronzezeitchronologie," *Eurasia Antigua Zeitschrift für Archäeologie Eurasiens*, 4: 74–80.

Green, A., 1993. *The G Ash-Tip and its Contents: Cultic and Administrative Discard from the Temple? Abu Salabikh Excavations*, Vol. 4. Iraq: British School of Archaeology.

Gubaev, A., G. Koshelenko, and M. Tosi, 1998. *The Archaeological Map of the Murghab Delta, Preliminary Reports 1990–1995*. Rome: Istituto Italiano per L'Africa et 1'Oriente.

Hemphill, B. E., 1999. "Biological Affinities and Adaptations of Bronze Age Bactrians: A Craniometric Investigation of Bactrian Origins," *American Journal of Physical Anthropology*, 18: 173–92.

Henning, W. B., 1978. "The First Indo-Europeans." In *Society and History, Essays in Honor of Karl Wittfogel*, edited by G. L. Ulmen. The Hague: Mouton.

Hiebert, F., 1994. *Origins of the Bronze Age Oasis Civilizations in Central Asia*. American School of Prehistoric Research, Bulletin 42. Peabody Museum, Cambridge, MA: Harvard University.

——, 2000. "Bronze Age Central Eurasian Cultures in their Steppe and Desert Environments." In *Environmental Disasters and the Archaeology of Human Response*, edited by Garth Bawden and R. M. Raycroft. Alburquerque, NM: Maxwell Museum of Anthropology.

Hiebert, F. and C. C. Lamberg-Karlovsky, 1992. "Central Asia and the Indo-Iranian Borderlands," *Iran*, XXX: 1–17.

Jarrige, J.-F. and M. Santoni, 1979. *Fouilles de Pirak*. Paris: Diffusion de Boccard.

Jettmar, K., 1951. "The Altai Before the Turks." *The Museum of Far Eastern Antiquities*, Bulletin no. 23, pp. 135–227.

——, 1997. "Bemerkungen zu Arkaim," *Eurasia Antigua Zeitschrift für Archäeologie Eurasiens*, 3: 249–54.

Jianjun, M. and C. Shell, 1999. "The Existence of Andronovo Cultural Influence in Xinjiang during the Second Millennium," *Antiquity*, 73: 570–8.

Kenoyer, M., 1998. *Ancient Cities of the Indus Valley Civilization*. Oxford: Oxford University Press.

Khazanov, A. M., 1979. "Klassoobrazovaniye: Faktory i Mehanizmy" ("Class Formation: Factors and Mechanisms"), *Issledovaniapo obchei ethnogafii*. Moscow: Nauka, pp. 125–77.

——, 1983. *Nomads and the Outside World*, 2nd edition. Madison, WI: University of Wisconsin Press.

Kislenko. A. and N. Tatarintseva, 1999. "The Eastern Ural Steppes at the End of the Stone Age." In *Late Prehistoric Exploitation of the Eurasian Steppe*, edited by M. Levine, A. Kislenko, and N. Tatarintseva. Cambridge: McDonald Institute Monographs.

Klochkov, I. S., 1998. "Signs on a Potsherd from Gonur (on the Question of the Script used in Margiana)," *Ancient Civilizations from Scythia to Siberia*, 5(2): 165–76.

——, 1999. "Glyptics of Margiana," *Ancient Civilizations From Scythia to Siberia*, 6(2): 41–62.

Koryakova, L., 1996. "Social Trends in Temperate Eurasia during the Second and First Millennia," *Journal of European Archaeology*, 4: 243–80.

Kramer, C., 1977. "Pots and People in Mountains and Lowlands: Essays in the Archaeology of Greater Mesopotamia." In *Bibliotheca Mesopotamica*, Vol. 7, edited by L. Levine and T. Cuyler Young, Jr. Malibu, CA: Undena Publications, pp. 91–112.

Kutimov, Yu. G., 1999. "Cultural Attributes of the Late Bronze Age Steppe Pottery from the Southern Regions of Middle Asia," *Stratum Plus*, (2): 314–23.

Kuzmina, E. E., 1994. *Okuda Prishli Indo Arii (Where did the Indo-Aryans come From?)*. Moscow: Russian Academy of Sciences.

Kuzmina, E. E. and A. Lapin, 1984. "Novie Nechodki Stepnoi keramici na Murgabe." In *Problemi Archeol iii Turkmenistana*. Ashkabad: Nauka.

Lamberg-Karlovsky, C. C. (ed.) 2001. *Excavations at Tepe Yahya: The Third Millennium*. Chapter 1. American School of Prehistoric Research. Peabody Museum. Cambridge, MA: Harvard University.

Levine, M., 1999. "The Origin of Horse Husbandry on the Eurasian Steppe." In *Late Prehistoric Exploitation of the Eurasian Steppe*, edited by M. Levine, Y. Rassamakin, A. Kislenko, and N. Tatterintseva. Cambridge: Cambridge University Press.

Levine, M., Y. Y. Rassamakin, A. M. Kislenko, and N. S. Tatarintseva, 1999. *Late Prehistoric Exploitation of the Eurasiatic Stenoe*. Cambridge: McDonald Archaeological Institute.

Littauer, M. A. and J. H. Crouwel, 1979. *Wheeled Vehicles and Ridden Animals in the Ancient Near East*. Leiden: E.J. Brill.

Malamat, A., 1989. *Mari and the Early Israelite Experience*. London: British Academy.

Mallaspina, P., F. Cruciani, P. Terrenato, P. Santolamazza, and A. Alonso, 1998. "Network Analysis of Y-chromosome Types in Europe, North Africa, and West Asia Reveal Specific Pattern of Geographical Distribution," *American Journal of Human Genetics*, 63: 847–60.

Mallory, J. P., 1989. *In Search of the Indo-Europeans*. London: Thames and Hudson.

Masson, V. M., 1992. "The Bronze Age in Khorassan and Transoxiana." In *History of Civilizations: Central Asia*, edited by A. H. Dani and V. M. Masson. Paris: UNESCO Publishing.

Medvedev, A. P., 1999. "Avestan 'Yima's Town' in Historical and Archaeological Perspective." In *Complex Societies of Central Eurasia in III-II Millennia B.C.*, edited by G. Zdanovich, Chelyabinsk: Chelyabinsk University Press, pp. 285–7.

Mei, J. and C. Shell, 1998. "Copper and Bronze Metallurgy in Late Prehistoric Xinjiang." In *The Bronze Age and Early Iron Age Peoples of Eastern Central Asia*, edited by Victor Mair. Philadelphia, PA: The University Museum Publications, pp. 581–603.

Narain, A. K., 1987. "On the 'First' Indo-Europeans," Papers on Inner Asia, No. 2. Bloomington, IN: University of Indiana, pp. 1–27.

Netchitailo, A. L., 1996. "The European Steppes Community in the Eneolithic," *RossiyskaXa Arkheoloeiva*, 4: 18–31.

Obydennov, A. G. and G. T. Obydennov, 1992. *Severo-Vostochnaia Perifia Srubnoj Kulturno-Istorichneskoj Obshchnosti*. Samara: Samarskij Universitet.

Peng, K., 1998. "The Andronovo Bronze Artifacts Discovered in Toquztara County Ili, Xinjiang." In *The Bronze Age and Iron Age Peoples of Eastern Central Asia*, edited by Victor Mair. Philadelphia, PA: The University Museum Publications, pp. 573–80.

Piggott, S., 1992. *Wagon, Chariot and Carriages*. New York: Thames and Hudson.

Potts, T., 1994. *Mesopotamia and the East* [Monograph 37]. Oxford: Oxford University Committee on Archaeology.

Pratt, M. L., 1992. *Imperial Eyes. Travel Writing and Transculturation*. London: Routledge.

P'yankova, L., 1993. "Pottery of Margiana and Bactria in the Bronze Age," Information Bulletin, International Association for the Study of the Cultures of Central Asia, 19: 109–27.

——, 1994. "Central Asia in the Bronze Age: Sedentary and Nomadic Cultures." *Antiquity*, 68(259): 355–72.

——, 1999. "South Tadjikistan: Synthesis of Settled and Steppe Cultures at the End of the Bronze Age." In *Complex Societies of Central Eurasia in III-II Millennia B.C.*, edited by D. G. Zdanovich. Chelyabinsk University: Chelyabinsk State.

Renfrew, Colin, 1987. *Archaeology and Language*. Cambridge: Cambridge University Press.

——, 1999. "Time Depth, Convergence Theory, and Innovation in Proto Indo-European: Old Europe as a PIE Linguistic Area," *Journal of Indo-European Studies*, 27(3/4): 258–93.

Sarianidi, V. I., 1976. *Issledovanija Pamjatnikov Dashlyiskogo Oazisa* (*Researches on the Sites of the Dashly Oasis*), Drevnii Baktria, Vol. 1. Moscow: Akademia Nauk.

——, 1977. *Drevnii Zemledelichij Afghanistan* (*Ancient Agriculturalists of Afghanistan*), Arkeologiya Sovetskajia. Moscow: Akademia Nauk.

——, 1984. *"Raskoki Monumenta Zdaniij na Dashly III"* (*"Excavations of Monumental Structures at Dashly III"*), Drevnii Baktria, Vol. 3. Moscow: Akademia Nauk.

——, 1990. *Drevnosti Strani Mareush (The Ancient State of Margush).* Ashkabad: Akademia Nauk Turkmenskoi.

——, 1998a. *Myths of Ancient Bactria and Margiana on its Seals and Amulets.* Moscow: Pentagraphic Ltd.

——, 1998b. *Mariziana and Protozoroastrianism.* Athens: Kapon Editions.

——, 1999. "Near Eastern Aryans in Central Asia." *Journal of Indo-European Studies*, 27(3/4): 47–62.

Shnirelman, V. A., 1995. "Alternative Prehistory," *Journal of European Archaeology*, 3(2): 1–20.

——, 1998. "Archaeology and Ethnic Politics: The Discovery of Arkhaim," *Museum International*, 50(198): 33–9.

——, 1999. "Passions about Arkhaim: Russian Nationalism, the Aryans, and the Politics of Archaeology," *Inner Asia*, 67–282.

Sinor, D., 1999. "Some Thoughts on the Nostratic Theory and its Historical Implications." In *Nostratic: Examining a Linguistic Macrofamily*, edited by C. Renfrew and D. Nettle. Cambridge: The McDonald Institute for Archaeological Research.

Stokolos, V. S., 1972. *Kultura Naseleniia Bronzovogo Veka luznoeo Zauralia: Khronologii i Periodizatsiia.* Moscow: Nauka.

Teploukhov, S. A., 1927. "The Ancient Burials in the Minusis Region" (in Russian), *Materialy no Etnografii*, 3(2): 57–112.

Trubetskoy, N. S., 1939 [1968]. "Gedanken fiber das Indogermanenproblem," *Acta Lineuistica* 1: 81–9 (reprinted in A. Scherer (ed.) *Die Urheimat der Indogermanen. Wissenschaftliche Buchgesellschaft.* Darmstadt).

Vasilyev, I. B., P. F. Kuznetsov, and A. P. Semenova, 1995. *Pamyatniki Potapovskogo tipa v lesostepnom Povolzhe. Drevniye Indo-Iranskiye nlemena Volgo-Uralya.* Povolzhya: Samara Institute Historii i Arkheologii, pp. 5–37.

Vinogradova, N. M., 1994. "The Farming Settlement of Tangurttut (South Tadjikistan) in the Late Bronze Age," *Archaeolo$ische Mitteilungen aus Iran*, 27: 29–47.

Windfuhr, G. L., 1999. "A Note on Aryaman's Social and Cosmic Setting." In *Aryan and Non-Aryan in South Asia*, edited by J. Bronkhorst and M. M. Deshpande. Harvard Oriental Studies, Opera Minora, Vol. 3, Cambridge, MA: Harvard University Press, pp. 295–336.

Witzel, M., 1999. "Early Loan Words in Western Central Asia: Indicators of Substrate Populations, Migrations, and Trade Relations," *Mother Tongue* (Extra Number), pp. 1–70.

Young, T. C., 1967. "The Iranian Migration into the Zagros," *Iran*, 5: 11–34.

Zdanovich, G., 1984. "The Relative Chronology of Bronze Age Sites on the Ural Kazakhstan Steppes" (in Russian). In *Bronzovey Vek Uralo-Irt sego Mezhdurechia*, edited by S. I. Zdanovich, V. F. Zaibert, and N. I. Merpert. Chelyabinsk: Chelyabinsk University.

——, 1995. *Arkhaim Isseledovanija. Poiski. Otkritii* (*Investigations, Research, Discoveries*) Chelyabinsk: Centre Arkhaim.

——, 1997. "Arkhaim- kulturnii komplex epokhi srednei Bronzi Iuzhnovo zauralya" (Arkhaim: Middle Bronze Age Cultural Complex in the southern Urals). *Rossiiskaya Arkheologia*, 2: 47–62.

——, 1999a. Arkhaim 1987–1997. Bibliographic Index (in Russian). Chelyabinsk: Chelyabinsk University Press.
——, 1999b. *Complex Societies of Central Eurasia in III-II Millennia B.C.* Chelyabinsk: Chelyabinsk University Press.
——, 2002. "The Country of Towns of Southern Trans-Urals and Some Aspects of Steppe Assimilation in the Bronze Age." In *Ancient Interactions: East and West in Eurasia*, edited by Katie Boyle, Colin Renfrew, and Marsha Levine. McDonald Institute Monographs, Cambridge: Cambridge University Press, pp. 249–65.
Zdanovich, G. and D. Zdanovich, 1995. *Rossiya i Vostok: problemy vzaimodeistviya.* (*Russia and the East: Problems of Interaction*). Chelyabinsk: Chelyabinsk University Press.

Part III

PHILOLOGY AND LINGUISTICS

6

THE DATE OF THE RIGVEDA AND THE ARYAN MIGRATION

Fresh linguistic evidence

*Satya Swarup Misra**

6.1 Structural antiquity of Sanskrit and its impact on the date of the Rigveda and Aryan migration

Nowadays those who have some knowledge of comparative grammar have no doubt about the kinship of languages. A student of Indo-European linguistics will immediately recognize that the following words are cognates of the corresponding languages belonging to the Indo-European language family.

> Skt (= Sanskrit) *asti*, Av (= Avestan) *asti*,
> OP (= Old Persian) *astiy*, Gk (= Greek) *esti*,
> Hittite *estsi*, Lithuanian *esti*, Lat (= Latin) *esti*,
> Old Church Slavic *jesti*, Goth (= Gothic) *ist*.
>
> Skt *bhrātā*, Av *brātā*, OP *brātā*, Gk *phrātē*, Lat *frater*, Goth *broþar*.
>
> Skt *pitā*, Av *pitā*, OP *pitā*, Gk *patēr*, Lat *pater*, Goth *fadar*, Old Irish *athir*.
>
> Skt *trayaḥ*, Av *θrayo*, Gk *treis*, Lat *tres*, Goth *þreis*.

A few centuries back, the kinship of languages was absolutely unknown. But suddenly something so favorable happened that the kinship of languages came to light. This favorable incident was the discovery of Sanskrit by the Europeans. Max Müller has expressed this very beautifully in the following words.

> Languages seemed to float about like islands on the ocean of human speech; they did not shoot together to form themselves into larger continents . . . and if it had not been for a happy accident, which like an electric spark, caused the floating elements to crystallise into regular

* S. S. Misra sadly passed away prior to publication of this book.

> forms, it is more doubtful whether the long list of languages and dialects could have sustained the interest of the student of languages. This electric spark was the discovery of Sanskrit.
>
> (1866: 153–4)

The reason for this emphasis by Max Müller on the discovery of Sanskrit is clear from the oft-quoted speech of Sir William Jones:

> The Sanskrit language, whatever be its antiquity, is of wonderful structure, more perfect than the Greek, more copious than the Latin, and more exquisitely refined than either, yet bearing to both of them a strong affinity. No philologer could examine the Sanskrit, Greek and Latin without believing them to have sprung from some common source, which perhaps no longer exists.
>
> (1788)

The discovery of Sanskrit was responsible not only for the discovery of the Indo-European language family, but also for the birth of comparative grammar, because of which the world now possesses only a few language families, instead of many languages not linked to each other.

Although both William Jones and Max Müller realized the importance of the Sanskrit language and could also see the importance in its structure, which undoubtedly speaks of its antiquity, to a great extent, they did not care to look into its antiquity through its structure. Jones avoided the issue by saying, "Whatever be its antiquity" and Max Müller also, in spite of realizing the great impact of Sanskrit on comparative grammar, proposed a very recent date, the date of the Rigveda (RV) in 1500 BCE, which was considered to be the final verdict for more than a century.

Macdonell also accepted the dating of Max Müller in his history of Sanskrit literature. But in his Vedic Grammar he made some casual remarks which show that he considered the composition of the Rigveda in various stages to be several centuries earlier than its compilation into Rigveda Saṁhitā. "The Saṁhitā text itself, however, only represented the close of a long period in which the hymns, as originally composed by the seers, were handed down by oral tradition. We have thus good reason for believing that the fixity of the text and the verbal integrity of the Rigveda go *several centuries* further back than the date at which the Saṁhitā text came into existence" (1968). If we accept Max Müller's 200-year gap for each stage, this *several centuries* theory will find no place. Thus Max Müller's date was accepted without any serious consideration, even by Macdonell in his history of Sanskrit literature.

Greek, Hittite, Avestan, Old Persian etc., which are important historical languages in the Indo-European language family, have the status of Middle Indo-Aryan from the point of view of linguistic change. It is interesting to quote Lord

Monboddo, who made the following remarks as early as 1774 of the Vedic corpus:

> There is a language, still existing and preserved among the Brahmins of India, which is a richer and in every respect a finer language than even the Greek of Homer. All the other languages of India have great resemblance to this language, which is called the Shanscrit. ... I shall be able to clearly prove that the Greek is derived from the Shanscrit, which was the ancient language of Egypt and was carried by the Egyptians to India with their other arts and into Greece by the colonies which they settled there.
>
> (1774: 97)

Why did Sanskrit have so much impact on Monboddo that without any analysis, even at the first glance, he considered Sanskrit to be the source of Greek? The structure of Sanskrit is responsible.

This can be further understood from Bloomfield's observation on the importance of the structure of Sanskrit

> The descriptive Grammar of Sanskrit, which Panini, brought to its highest perfection, is one of the greatest monuments of human intelligence and (what concerns us more) an indispensable model for description of languages. The only achievement in our field, which can take rank with it is the historical linguistics of the nineteenth century and this indeed owed its origin largely to Europe's acquaintance with the Indian Grammar. One forgot that the Comparative Grammar of the Indo-European languages got its start only when the Paninian analysis of an Indo-European language became known in Europe. ... If the accentuation of Sanskrit and Greek, for instance had been unknown, Verner could not have discovered the Pre-Germanic sound change, that goes by his name. Indo-European Comparative Grammar had (and has) at its service, only one complete description of a language, the grammar of Panini. For all other Indo-European languages it had only the traditional grammars of Greek and Latin woefully incomplete and unsystematic.
>
> (1933: 267–76)

Although Bloomfield gives importance to Sanskrit grammar, he also gives the date of the Rigveda as 1200 BC (1958: 63). This shows that although he understood the importance of Sanskrit grammar, he did not understand the structural antiquity of Sanskrit to be very important for Indo-European comparative grammar and the consequent need for a highly ancient date for the Rigveda.

But Bloomfield rightly pointed out that the scholars of Indo-European comparative grammar were fortunate to get the grammar of Sanskrit at their disposal to work out Indo-European comparative grammar. In effect, Indo-European comparative grammar is nothing but a slightly remodeled Sanskrit grammar. In morphology it depends on Sanskrit grammar 100 percent and in phonology it depends 90 percent on Sanskrit grammar. For example, in morphology Indo-European has eight cases (nominative, accusative, instrumental, dative, ablative, genitive, locative, and vocative), three numbers, three genders, and three tenses (present, aorist, and perfect) like Sanskrit. These are better retained in Sanskrit than in even Greek and Avestan. In phonology the voiced aspirates are retained in Sanskrit only and the voiceless aspirates are more fully retained in Sanskrit than in Greek and other languages, where they show linguistic changes. The main features where Sanskrit is shown to deviate from Indo-European is the merger of IE *a*, *e*, *o* into *a* in Sanskrit and the change of palatal *k* etc. to palatal *ś* etc. in Sanskrit.

Concerning the merger of IE *a*, *e*, *o* into *a* in Sanskrit, it is to be noted that Schleicher, Bopp, Grimm etc. accepted the Sanskrit vowel *a* as showing the original IE vowel and Greek *a*, *e*, *o* as a new development. After the law of palatalization was discovered, Brugmann and subsequent scholars accepted Greek *a*, *e*, *o* to be original IE vowels and Sanskrit *a* as showing the merger of IE *a*, *e*, *o* to *a* in Sanskrit.

The law of palatalization may be critically evaluated here. Let us take IE *e* and *o* as representative of palatal and non-palatal vowels, respectively. The law of palatalization changes Satəm *k* etc. (< IE q/q^w etc.) to *c* etc. in the languages shown in the table, and in Centum q^w etc. (not *q* etc.) show some changes comparable to law of palatalization.

IE	*IIr*	*Skt*	*Av/OP Arm*	*OCS*	*Gk*	*Gme*
$q^w(e)$	*c*	*c*	*c*	*c*	*c*	*t*
$q^w(o)$	*k*	*k*	*k*	*k* (*k*‘)	*k*	*p*
$g^w(e)$	*j*	*j*	*j*	*k*	*dž*	*d*
$g^w(o)$	*g*	*g*	*g*	*k*	*g*	*b*
g^wh (*e*)	*jh*	*h*	*j*	*j* (*ž*)	*dž*	*th*
g^wh (*o*)	*gh*	*gh*	*g*	*g*	*g*	*ph*

Examples:
IE q^we Skt *ca*, Av *ca*, OP *ca*, Gk *te*, Lat *que*
IE g^w*eni* Skt *jāni* ‘wife’, OCS *žena*, Arm *kin*, Goth *qino* ‘queen’, OIrish *ben*
IE g^w*henti* Skt *hanti*, Av *jainti*, OP *ajanam*, OCS *žiny*, Gk *theino*

Several examples of this type may be cited. But there are also many exceptions to the change before *e*.

The exceptions have been explained by analogy; for example, Skt *hataḥ* instead of **ghataḥ* < IE g^w*hn̥tos* is explained as analogical due to the influence of Skt *hand*

< IE *g^w^henti*. Similarly, Gk *sébei* instead of **sédei* < IE *tyeg^w^eti* cp Skt *tyajati* is explained as analogical. Gothic *has* (< IE *q^w^os*) for expected *has* is also considered analogical. The exceptions are too many in various IE languages. Sometimes the same form shows *e* in one IE language and *o* in another, for example, Lat *ped* : Gk *pod*. This is explained as variation in the qualitative ablaut. In this case we have to accept that there was no rule for the qualitative ablaut. The quantitative ablaut, which is based on Sanskrit, is quite systematic and follows a regular morphophonemic pattern. The qualitative ablaut, which is most unsystematic and arbitrary, seems to have been invented simply to accept *a*, *e*, *o* as original. *a* : *e* is not accepted in the qualitative ablaut but Skt *anu* < IE *anu* and Goth *inu* < IE *enu* are comparable. These variations indicate that the reconstruction of *a*, *e*, *o* in IE instead of *a* created much confusion.

Moreover, Sanskrit has doublets like *vākya* : *vācya* with both *k* and *c* before *y*. Besides, Sanskrit shows *cukopa*, *jugopa* etc. without a palatal vowel. Moreover, there is no explanation as to why Greek presents a dental instead of a palatal when followed by a palatal vowel.

In reduplications it is easy to explain that a palatal appears for a velar in Sanskrit by dissimilation. Similarly, the dentals in Greek can also be explained as due to dissimilation.

Recent researches on the Gypsy languages show that Indo-Aryan *a* remains *a* in Asiatic Gypsy but becomes *a*, *e*, *o* in European Gypsy. This confirms that original IE *a* was the same as Skt *a* and remained *a* in the Indo-Iranian languages, but changed to *a*, *e*, *o* in their sister languages. This is elaborated in Section 6.5.

That IE palatal *k* becomes *ś* in Sanskrit is also questionable, because in Sanskrit itself *ś* becomes *k* before *ṣ*. Thus, the *k* which was allophonic to *ś* in Sanskrit might have been generalized in the Centum languages. Some Satəm languages also sporadically present *k* instead of a sibilant, for example, Lithuanian *klausaū* < IE *kleu-*, Skt *śru-*, Av *sru-*, Gk *klu-*.

This shows that the allophonic nature of *ś* : *k* as shown by Sanskrit was partly disturbed in some Satəm languages and was fully lost in the highly innovating Centum languages, and that the allophone *k* has become a phoneme, replacing *ś* completely.

A question may be raised here. If we do not accept that IE *k* > *ś* in Skt should we drop the entire palatal series, that is, *k*, *kh*, *g*, *gh*? I do not want to discuss in detail the reconstruction of the three guttural series in IE. This has always been accepted simply because it is a convenient formula to explain the various developments in various Satəm and Centum languages. All of us are aware of the gaps in the three-series system. It is sufficient to say here that evidence of IE *kh* is almost nil in Sanskrit. The developments of IE *kh*, *g*, *gh*, as, *ch*, *j*, *h* in Sanskrit can otherwise be mostly proved, as *ch*, *j*, *h* came from velars by palatalization. If we do not accept palatalization by *e* etc., there are other explanations. If the origin of *ś* < *k* is not accepted, the palatal series is 80 percent doomed.

If the Centum velars from the IE palatal series are accepted as innovation by changing the allophonic *k* (< *ś*) to a phoneme in the Centum languages, the three-series system of IE gutturals almost vanishes, because the labiovelars are conjectured simply to explain certain innovations in the Centum languages. Brugmann in the first edition of his comparative grammar did not reconstruct a labiovelar series, but explained this as a special development in Centum (Brugmann 1972: 259–321).

Thus, apart from these two reconstructions – namely, IE *a*, *e*, *o* for Skt *a* and IE *k* etc. for Skt *ś* etc. – which are, as shown earlier, controversial reconstructions, Skt shows archaic features in almost all other cases. In another reconstruction, according to which IE *r* and *l* have become Indo-Iranian *r*, which further becomes *r* and *l* in Skt, it seems that Skt has some innovations.

The theory is that in earlier portions of the Rigveda Saṃhitā *r* prevails and gradually *l* prevails more and more in later languages, that is, in later Saṃhitās, Āraṇyaka, Upaniṣad, Classical Sanskrit and finally in Middle Indo-Aryan (MIA). But in fact distribution of *r* and *l* is universal across dialects. Some languages show a preference for *r* (e.g. the Old Iranian languages) and some show a preference of *l* (e.g. Chinese). If historically *l* replaced *r* in Indo-Aryan then all New Indo-Aryan languages should show a preference for *l*, which is not the case. Some show a preference for *r* and others show a preference for *l*. If we take a single IE standard for distribution of *r* and *l*, we find confusion of distribution of *r* and *l* to some extent even in the languages considered to represent the original distribution. For this reason, the Sanskrit grammarians have accepted *ralayor abliedaḥ*.

In all other aspects Sanskrit shows archaism and, therefore, IE reconstruction is based mainly on Sanskrit. The linguistic changes found in India in the Middle Indo-Aryan stage are found amply in Greek, Iranian, and Hittite, which are stamped as very old historical forms of IE.

Greek presents many linguistic changes comparable to Middle Indo-Aryan. Some of them may be taken up here:

1 All voiced aspirates are devoiced in Greek, for example, IE *bhrātēr* > Gk *phrātēr* cp Skt *bhrātā*. Similar change is found in Paiśācī Prakrit, for example, Skt *megha* > Paiśācī *mekha*.
2 All final consonants except *n*, *r*, *s* are lost in Greek, for example, IE *ebheret* > Gk *éphere*. Similarly, all final consonants except *m* are dropped in MIA.
3 Heterogeneous conjunct consonants are often assimilated in Greek, for example, Homeric *hóppōs* < *hód-pōs*, Gk *gramma* < **graphma*, Gk *eimi/ emmi* < IE *esmi* etc. This is quite frequent in MIA.
4 Greek shows syncretism like MIA. In Greek the dative, locative and instrumental have merged. In MIA the dative and genitive have merged.
5 Greek shows vowel sandhi like MIA, for example, *stemmata* + *ekhōn* > *stemmat'ekhōn*. This type of sandhi is normal in MIA.

Thus, Sanskrit deserves attribution of a much more archaic status than Greek. Hittite is another IE Centum language discovered in the twentieth century, which claims archaism superseding Sanskrit and Greek. For this language two new theories were developed, namely the Laryngeal theory and the Indo-Hittite theory. I have refuted both the theories elsewhere (1975, 1977). Thus, Hittite no longer enjoys archaic status, because it shows a lot of linguistic change. Nowadays very few scholars believe in the Laryngeal theory and nobody believes in the Indo-Hittite theory.

Hittite also shows linguistic changes comparable to MIA. Some may be taken up here:

1 All aspirates have been deaspirated in Hittite, for example, IE *dḷghos* > Ht *dalugas*, Gk *dolikhós* cp Skt *dīrghaḥ*. Such changes are not attested in Sanskrit. They start only from the MIA stage.
2 Hittite also shows assimilation like MIA, for example, Ht *luttai* < **luktai*, Ht *apanna* < **apatna*; Ht *gwemi* < **gwenmi* < IE g^w*henmi* cp Skt *hanmi*.
3 Hittite also shows syncretism like MIA. The dative and locative have merged in Hittite in the singular. In the plural Hittite has lost most of the cases.

From the outset Sanskrit was the top ranking language for the reconstruction of IE comparative grammar. And in spite of the effort of some scholars to downgrade the position of Sanskrit, Sanskrit still enjoys the position of the most important language for comparison with the newly discovered IE languages like Hittite, Luwian, Palaic, and Hieroglyphic Hittite (S. S. Misra 1968, 1983a, 1985, 1986). Even now scholars who attempt a comparison of IE with any other language family use Skt forms to represent IE.

Therefore, on the basis of linguistic archaism, Sanskrit deserves a much earlier date than 1500 BC, based on Max Müller's hypothesis which was accepted by most of the linguists in Europe as well as India. But as we will see in subsequent sections, on the basis of fresh linguistic evidence the Rigveda deserves a very early date such as 5000 BC, which will match the linguistic archaism of Sanskrit.

If 5000 BC is accepted as the date of the Rigveda, then we also have to accept that India was probably the original home of the Aryans (or Indo-Europeans) and that they went to the other parts of Asia and Europe from India, because no other IE language can be traced to such an early date on any basis.

6.2 Indus civilization, a continuation of Vedic culture

A proper analysis of the language and culture of the Indus civilization is also of considerable importance to determine the date of Rigveda and whether Aryans came from outside or not.

The discovery of the Indus civilization challenged three major hasty conclusions of Western scholars, namely, (1) the writing system was borrowed from the Iranians; (2) the date of Rigveda is 1500 BC; and (3) the Aryans came from elsewhere to India.

The argument that there was no script in India and they borrowed the writing system from the Iranians is based on the evidence of the word *lipi*..., a term for writing, which is a loan word, thereby suggesting to some scholars that writing itself was a foreign import and thus not indigenous to the Vedic culture. After the Indus civilization was discovered Western scholors did not discuss this issue, as if it had never been raised. The word *lipi* may be a loan word. But in India the root *likh* is used for writing. The older form *rikh* is found in the Rigveda, meaning 'scratch, write.' Originally *rikh* and *likh* were both used for scratching or writing. The word *kāru* (< √ *kṛ*) means poet, writer. And √ *kṛ* is used several times in the Rigveda in the sense of writing (S. S. Misra 1992a): *akāri te navyam brahma* (RV 4.16.2) 'I have made new hymns for you.' Here 'made' means 'composed/wrote'. This meaning is further strengthened by a similar use of √ *takṣ* 'fashion': *navyam atakṣat brahma* '[he] fashioned [= composed, wrote] new hymns for you'.

The date of the Rigveda as 1500 BC based on the suggestion of Max Müller was widely accepted by Western as well as Indian scholars and continued smoothly until the Indus Valley civilization came to light. Since the date of the Indus civilization is based on archaeological evidence, it cannot be challenged and the Indus civilization cannot be more recent than 2500 BC. To reconcile the 1500 BC date of the Rigveda and the 2500 BC date of the Indus civilization with the theory of Aryans coming from outside, a new theory was advanced that Aryans came in 1500 BC and destroyed the urban civilization of the Indus and established a rural civilization of the Vedic type. One basis for this theory was the name of *Indra* being given as *Purandara*. What did the Aryans destroy? They destroyed the Indus Civilization of the Dravidians. I fail to understand how such theories develop and continue, and remain followed for decades. Even the theory that Dravidians are different from Aryans is not confirmed by any ancient literature or any archaeological evidence or by any cultural difference. Some linguistic difference is proposed, as by Caldwell, and accordingly, following him, Dravidian is taken as an independent language family. But nobody has attempted to institute a comparison of Dravidian and Indo-Aryan. We will take up this issue in Section 6.3. Dravidian literature is not older than Vedic literature, nor is there any other evidence in any form that the Dravidians were in India before the Aryans came. Thus, the theory of Aryans destroying the Dravidian civilization was merely a policy-based theory to undermine Indian national integration.

A few years back B. B. Lal, an Indian archaeologist of international fame, strongly asserted without any special new evidence that the Indus civilization was not Aryan, although he agrees that "In so far as the space factor is concerned, the Indus civilization covers most of the areas, associated with the Rigvedic Aryans"

(1981: 286).[2] Still, Lal does not take Indus Valley civilization as Indo-Aryan because he appears to be sure that the Indus Valley civilization antedates the Vedic civilization, since the date of Rigveda, according to him, cannot be beyond 1500 BC. Nobody except Lal, as far as I know, puts an upper limit for the date of Rigveda. In addition, he is fully convinced that John Marshall finally solved the problem as early as 1931: "John Marshall made a comprehensive survey of this issue way back in 1931 and demonstrated unambiguously that Indus civilization could not be associated with the Aryans. Thus, one need not go all over this issue again" (285).

Lal then compares the contents, namely, the rural civilization of RV and the urban one of the Indus, the uniconic of RV and the iconic of the Indus, the absence of the mother goddess cult in RV and its presence in the Indus. But if the date of the Rigveda is accepted as earlier than the Indus Valley civilization then the changes found in the Indus Valley civilization are quite natural late developments, like the *Purāṇic* civilization, which is a later development of the Vedic civilization.

Lal finally uses the evidence of the horse, and attempts to prove that horses were absent from the Indus civilization, although he is aware of the evidence for horses in Lothal (from late levels, even if the evidence for horses from Mohenjodaro is ruled out as belonging to surface levels). His argument is that the evidence is meager. But meager evidence rules out the possibility of non-existence. F. R. Allchin has also taken up the problem of the association of the Indo-Aryans with the Indus civilization. After discussing the various issues, Allchin admits in his conclusion that the problem is highly complicated and confusing. He accepts the cemetery culture as that of Vedic Aryans and accepts several objects to be purely Vedic. Allchin has also examined the question of a fire cult at Kalibangan.

Finally he says, "Probably the first settlers arrived in the region around 1750–1600 BC and their numbers grew steadily during the following centuries. We would expect this early Vedic period to come to an end around 1500 BC and the first compilation of the Rigveda Saṁhitā, i.e. Maṇṇals II–VII, to be made during the next two or three centuries" (1981: 344). Here it is worth noting that, although there is concrete proof that the Indus civilization is an Aryan civilization, Allchin has apparently advanced his theory to protect the date of the Rigveda as 1500 BC based on Max Müller's chronology.

Allchin, along with many others, accepts the Indus civilization as preceding the Vedic period, and this poses many problems. If the Vedic period is proved to precede the Indus civilization, many of the confusions will be automatically removed.

Some Indian scholars have attempted the decipherment of the Indus script and have shown it to be Indo-Aryan. Out of several such attempts, that made by S. R. Rao is comparatively more successful. Before him S. K. Roy also made a good attempt. Perhaps Roy rightly guessed the apparent pictographs to be compound syllabic signs. But his readings of the script have given us forms comparable to NIA or at best comparable to Apabhraṁśa, for example, *kāma* 'work', cp Skt *karma*, MIA *kamma*, NIA *kāma*; pāna 'leaf', cp Skt *parṇa*, MIA *panna*, NIA *pāna*. Therefore, his reading could not attract the attention of scholars. S. R. Rao has similarly taken the apparent pictographs as compound syllabic signs. But his readings, if accepted, present a language which is transitional between Old Indo-Aryan and Middle Indo-Aryan. S. R. Rao himself considers the language to be pre-Vedic by a misunderstanding of the laryngeal theory (S. S. Misra 1983b).

The language presented by the decipherment of Rao is linguistically analysed next:

1 It does not present any final consonant, like MIA. Exceptional forms with final consonants like *pat/pt* 'lord' may be abbreviations for *pati*, like OP *bg* for *baga*.
2 *ś*, *ṣ*, *s*, are confused like BHS (= Buddhist Hybrid Sanskrit), for example, *śāśa-kka* = Skt *śāsaka* 'ruler'.
3 *ṛ* represents BHS *ri/ru* with hyper-Sanskritism, for example, *tṛka* = *trika* 'triad'.
4 Conjuncts have started to be assimilated or simplified, like MIA *gavva* = *gavya* 'bovine' (assimilated); *karka* (= *karikal karuka*) = *karka* 'white' (simplified). Apparent conjuncts like *pt* etc. are abbreviations for *pati* etc.
5 It shows voiceless for voiced and aspirate for non-aspirate etc. like MIA, for example, *phadra* beside *bhadra* = Skt *bhadra*; *paka* beside *baga*, *bhaga* = Skt *bhaga*; *dhaksa* beside *dakṣa* = Skt *dakṣa.*
6 It shows nasal aspirates *mh*, *nh* etc. like MIA.
7 An *a*-stem influences other stems like MIA, for example, *catus-ha* 'of four' beside *bhagaha* 'of bhaga'.
8 The ablative ends in *ā* (< *āt*), for example, *baka-a* 'from baka'.
9 The dative is sporadically retained as in first MIA, for example, *sakae* = Skt *sakāya*, cp Aśokan *supathāye* = Skt *supārthāya.*

Thus, the language as deciphered by S. R. Rao presents a language that is transitional between OIA and MIA and thus is comparable to Buddhist Hybrid Sanskrit. This is not at all pre-Vedic. This presents a language which represents a continuation of Vedic culture. Buddhist Hybrid Sanskrit, which was named by F. Edgerton, is not actually a hybrid language but represents a transitional stage between OIA and MIA.

This analysis of the language of the Indus seals demands an earlier date for the Rigveda, since the language needs many centuries to have reached this stage from the Rigvedic type. This analysis also further sheds light on the fact that the theory of Aryans coming from outside India is to be fully abandoned, since we find no such archaeological nor literary evidence from India, or from outside.

The *Purāṇic* culture, which is a late development of the Vedic civilization, is found in both Aryan and Dravidian culture. Thus, the Indus civilization, which presents the *Purāṇic* civilization, can easily be taken as a later phase of the Vedic civilization even though the linguistic interpretation of the Indus seals remains somewhat uncertain.

6.3 Relationship of Dravidian and Indo-Aryan and its impact on the date of the Rigveda and Aryan migration

Indo-Aryans and Dravidians were neighbors for centuries. Indian tradition has never spoken about either of them as not related to the other. Both have the Vedic tradition as their oldest tradition. Both equally show inheritance of the Vedic culture. In the Mahabharata and other *Purāṇās*, Dravidians are often referred to as persons belonging to a particular region or province of India like Aṅga, Baṅga, Kaliṅga or Magadha.

After European scholars came into contact with India, the Sanskrit language was discovered in Europe, and Western scholars, mostly Germans, made comparative studies of Sanskrit with various Indo-European languages and consequently the Indo-European language family was discovered. But none of them made any effort to compare Sanskrit with the Dravidian languages. This may be because Dravidian was not taken to be a separate language family at that time. Bishop Caldwell was first to present the hypothesis that Dravidian is an independent language family. This was accepted because the Dravidian languages differ from Indo-Aryan much more than the Indo-Aryan languages differing from each other. But there are many common words which occur in Dravidian and Indo-Aryan. After Caldwell's hypothesis was accepted these words were taken as borrowed words, in some cases from Indo-Aryan to Dravidian, in other cases from Dravidian to Indo-Aryan. Gradually the effort increased to prove that most of the loans are borrowings from Dravidian to Indo-Aryan. A few years back one scholar, namely, F. B. J. Kuiper in his book *Aryans in the Rigveda*, tried to show that many words which have been accepted to be of Indo-European origin are in fact loans from Dravidian into Indo-Aryan. In his book there are several generalizations, which claims to present some new and revolutionary theory, and scholars are called outdated. Apparently nothing new is proved by this enthusiastic scholar except the addition of some more Dravidian loan words in Sanskrit, based on a wrong analysis.

Dravidian chronologically belongs to a much later date than the Rigveda in linguistic structure. From the point of view of linguistic changes the structure of Dravidian is comparable to an early phase of New Indo-Aryan.

Recent researches propose a revised date for NIA of the first century BC (S. S. Misra 1980: 86), on the basis of the linguistic development of NIA stage by stage into independent NIA languages. NIA is now taken to date to the third or fourth century BC, using evidence of the migration of gypsies with an NIA language from India to parts of Europe and Asia, on the basis of the date of their migration assigned by Turner (S. S. Misra 1992b: 78).

The earliest date of Dravidian is now known to be the third century BC, and therefore, chronologically, it is also now comparable to NIA. I quote I. J. S. Taraporewala and T. P. Meenakshi Sundaram for the chronology of Dravidian: "among all the Dravidian languages Tamil is the oldest . . . It has works going back to the third Century BC" (Taraporewala 1982: 226). "Short inscriptions in Brāhmi script have been found in the caves of the Southern District of the Tamil land . . . assigned by epigraphists to the third and second centuries BC" (Sundaram 1965: 7).

New Indo-Aryan differs from Old Indo-Aryan significantly, but because we have records of the intervening linguistic changes in Middle Indo-Aryan, we non-controversially accept NIA languages as having developed from OIA. For the Dravidian languages, however, the intermediate stage is not yet traceable and linguistic changes appear to be much different from OIA; hence, Dravidian could easily be dismissed as not belonging to Indo-Aryan.

Now let us see how far New Indo-Aryan and Dravidian are comparable. For this purpose some of the linguistic changes shared by the two languages are given:

1 In OIA cerebral consonants normally do not occur initially. This tendency is inherited by MIA and NIA, with a few exceptions of initial occurrences which are later developments. Similarly, retroflexes do not occur in word initial position in Proto-Dravidian (Subrahmanyam 1983: 334).

2 OIA intervocal single stops became voiced and were lost in the MIA stage, leaving the preceding and following vowels in contact (Chatterji 1970: 82). Subsequently, these contact vowels were contracted (345).

The disappearance of intervocalic plosives and subsequent contraction of vowels is found in Tolkappiyam (Sundaram 1965: 66) and in the language of the Pallava, Chola and Nayaka Ages (p. 135).

Medial *-k-* in certain languages and *-c-* in many are often weakened to *-y-*, and medial *-y-* either from **-c-* or original is often lost giving rise to contraction of the preceding and the following vowels in many languages (Subrahmanyam 1983: 391).

This may be better explained as follows: the hiatus created by the loss of *-k-* or *-c-* was maintained by introducing a *-y-* glide; later on this *y* glide was also lost, followed by contraction. In the case of original *y* also, loss of *y* was followed by contraction. Intervocal alveolar plosives have changed to a trill in most of the Dravidian languages, which is in consonance with the general process of weakening and spirantization of plosives in the intervocalic position (Subrahmanyam 1983: 345).

3 OIA intervocal cerebrals were not elided in MIA, but were changed either to *ḷ*, *l* or *r* (Pischel 1965: 226). These are represented as *ḷ*, *l*, *ṛ* or *r* in NIA

(Turner 1975: 241). In South Indian manuscripts, OIA *-ṭ-*, *-ḍ-* is represented by *-ḷ-* or *-l-* (Pischel 1965: 226).

Among the Dravidian languages these *-ḷ-* or *-l-* are split into *ḷ*, *l*, *r*, *ḍ*, *L*, just like the NIA *-ḷ-* is preserved in Tamil and Malayalam etc. It has become *r* in Telugu, Naiki, Kurux, Kuwi etc. and *l*, *ḍ* in Kui (Subrahmanyam 1983: 441).

4 OIA conjunct consonants were assimilated in MIA (Pischel 1965: 268) and the preceding vowel, if long, was shortened following the law of mora.

Shortening of a long vowel before geminates was dialectal (Turner 1975: 405). In proto-NIA these double consonants were reduced to single consonants and the preceding vowel was lengthened in compensation. It affected the whole of IA except the North-Western group. In Lahnda and some areas of Panjabi, the length of both consonant and vowel has been preserved; in Sindhi, the consonant has been shortened. In the region between Panjabi and western Hindi the vowel has been shortened but the double consonants remain.

Dravidian languages likewise do not contain consonant clusters (Subrahmanyam 1983: 224). Double consonants are retained in Tamil and Malayalam. In Tamil shortening of a vowel before double consonants is found from the Pallava period (Sundaram 1965: 122). Proto-Dravidian *-kk-*, *-cc-*, *-tt-*, *-pp-* are retained after a short vowel in Kannada, Kodagu, Tullu and Telugu etc., but are reduced to *-k-*, *-c-*, *-t-*, *-p-* after a long vowel (Subrahmanyam 1983: 22.3.1, 23.3.1, 26.3.1, 27.3.1).

5 OIA consonant groups of a nasal plus homorganic stops were best preserved in MIA, with a few exceptions (Pischel 1983: 272, 273). In NIA these sound groups have undergone modification. In the case of a nasal plus a voiceless stop, the nasal is lost and the preceding vowel is lengthened and nasalized in the majority of NIA languages, except in the North-Western group, where the nasal is retained and the voiceless stop becomes voiced. Oriya shows partial nasalization.

Examples:

ṅk:

Old Indo-Aryan (OIA) *aṅka-*, Middle Indo-Aryan (MIA) *aṅka* cp Bengali (Beng) *āk*, Orissa (Or) *aṅka*, Assamesse (Ass) *āk*, Bhojpuri (Bhoj) *āk*, Awadhi *āk*, Maithili (Maith) *āk*, Gujarati (Guj) *āk*, Marathi (Mar) *āk*, (North-Western) Sindhi *aṅgu*.

ñc:

OIA *þañca*, MIA *þañca* cp Beng *þāc*, Ass *þās*, Guj *þāc*, Awadhi *þāc*, Bhoj *þāc*, Or *þañca*, (North-Western) Panjabi (Panj) *þañj*, Sindhi *þañja*, Lah *þañj*.

ṇṭ:

OIA *kaṇṭaka-*, Beng *kāṭā*, Braj *kāṭā*, Awadhi *kāṭā*, Maith *kāṭā*, Guj *kāṭā*, Or *kaṇṭā*, (North-Western) Panj *kaḍā*, Sindhi *kāḍǐ*.

nt:

OIA *danta-*, Beng *dā̃t*, Braj *dā̃t*, Bhoj *dā̃t*, Maith *dā̃t*, Guj and Mar *dā̃t*, Panj and Lah *dand*, Sindhi *ḍandŭ*, Or *dā̃nta*.

Nasal plus voiced stop – threefold treatment:

(i) The nasal is lost and the preceding vowel is lengthened and nasalized in languages like Gujarati and Marathi.
(ii) The stop is assimilated to the nasal and lost after lengthening of the preceding vowel in the Eastern group of languages.
(iii) Nasals plus voiced stops become double nasals generally in the North-Western group of languages.

Examples:

ṅg:

OIA *aṅguli*, MIA *aṅguli*, Beng *aṅali*, Braj *aṅuri*, *ā̃guli*, Bhoj *aṅuri*, Maith *aṅuri*, Mar *ā̃goli*, Guj *ā̃gli*, Or *ā̃ṅguḷi*, Panj *ũggali*, Sindhi *aṅuri*.

ñj:

OIA *piñjara*, Hindi *pĩjarā*, Guj *pĩjrũ*, Mar *pĩjrā*, Panj *piñjar*, Sindhi *piñiro*.

ṇḍ:

OIA *Kuṇḍa-*, Beng *Kũri*, Bhoj *Kũr*, Guj *kũdi*, Mar *kũḍi*, Kum *kuno*, Or *kuṇḍa*, Panj and Lah *kunni*, Sindhi kuno.

nd:

OIA *sindura*, Or *sindura*, Beng *sĩdur*, Braj *senur*, Bhoj *senur*, Mar *sedur*, Guj *sindur*, Sindhi *sindhurũ*, Ass *Xindur*, Nep *sĩdur*, *sinur*.

Among the Dravidian languages, in the case of nasal plus voiceless stop, the nasal has been assimilated by the stop in Tamil and the group becomes a double stop. Tamil has retained voiced stops after homorganic nasals. Because Tamil forms have been taken as the model for the reconstruction of Proto-Dravidian (PDr), some scholars assumed that Proto-Dravidian had no voiceless stop after homorganic nasals. K. Kushalappa Gouda has expressed his discontent concerning the manner of the reconstruction of PDr forms:

> There are quite a number of examples where the reconstructed form of PDr may differ from what is found in Tamil. But mostly, there is little difference between the PDr and Tamil reflex. In the absence of literary records in the other languages as ancient as that of Tamil, and in the situation where the majority of languages are merely spoken ones, nobody would be able to say whether such reconstructed forms are really the PDr ones, or simply the ancient Tamil forms for which the PDr forms will be entirely different.

> It is possible that the PDr reconstructed forms could be entirely different from what is known now, had the other languages also possessed equally ancient records, or if the records of ancient Tamil had not been taken into account. The non-availability of certain items in some languages does not mean that those languages did not possess them at all.
>
> (1972: 82)

Thus, the non-availability of nasal plus voiceless stop in Tamil and Malayalam does not prove that there were no voiceless stops after homorganic nasals in Proto-Dravidian. Further the nasal plus voiceless stop of Old Telugu and (Old) Kannada corresponds to the double stop of Tamil, as in the following etyma:

Tel *anta* 'that such'	Tam *aṉaittu*
Tel *anipa-kādu* 'archer'	Tam *appu* adj.
Tel *t* 'date palm'	Tam *iccam* adj.
(-*cc*- instead of -*tt*- due to the palatalization)	
Tel *kalãka* 'turbidity'	Tam *kalakka*
Tel *koṅki* 'hook'	Tam *kokki*
Tel *vēta* 'hunting'	Tam *vettam*
Tel *onti* 'an ear ring'	Tam *oṭṭuk*
Kan *eṇṭu* 'eight'	Tam *eṭṭu*, *eṇ*
Kan *kalaṅku* 'make something turbid'	Tam *kalakku*
Kan *koñce* 'inferiority'	Tam *koccai*
Kan *maṅku* 'sluggishness'	Tam *makku*

It is evident from the above examples that there were voiceless plosives after homorganic nasals in Proto-Dravidian which were assimilated to the following stops in Tamil. Malayalam follows Tamil in this respect. In the case of nasal plus voiced stop, the group is retained in Tamil. In Malayalam it often becomes a double nasal. In Old Telugu the nasal was retained after a short vowel, but it was lost after a long vowel nasalizing the preceding vowel. Homorganic nasals were retained in Old Kannada only after short vowels. Even here a voiceless stop often became voiced, thus reducing the distinction between voiced and voiceless plosives in Kannada also. Sporadic loss of a homorganic nasal is found in medieval Kannada, which became a regular feature of Modern Kannada (Subrahmanyam 1983: 22.8.1).

6 The OIA inflectional system was simplified in MIA to some extent owing to the phonetic modification of forms. Out of eight cases in OIA, NIA had only two: nominative and oblique. The nominative represents the old nominative and oblique is the representative of the other case inflections of OIA (Chatterji

> 1970: 481), to which post-positions are added to show the case relation. Similarly, Dravidian languages also show two types of stems, namely, nominative and oblique (Shanmugam 1971: 196).

It is true that Caldwell's theory of Dravidian being an independent family has had a long-lasting effect. Because of his theory several foreign and Indian scholars have compared Dravidian with other language families but never with Indo-Aryan or Indo-European. It is also to be noted that some scholars have compared Indo-European with other language families, taking Sanskrit forms as representative of IE. Even sometimes, strangely, for one and the same language family (e.g. Uralic), some have compared it with Indo-European, others have compared it with Dravidian. But almost no linguist has ever dared nor cared to institute a comparison of Indo-European (or Indo-Aryan) and Dravidian, as if this was a forbidden field.

But R. Swaminath Aiyar was an exception. He wrote a book entitled *Dravidian Theories* (published posthumously, 1975) in which he tried to prove that Dravidian and Indo-Aryan have linguistic affinity and are genetically related. He refuted Caldwell and quoted G. U. Pope in support, who said that several Indo-European languages are linguistically further away from Sanskrit than Dravidian.

Aiyar illustrated his case by showing that many forms where Caldwell compared Sanskrit with Dravidian to show disagreement actually agree with another Sanskrit form supplied by Aiyar. Some of Aiyar's examples are given here (Aiyar 1975: 18–19).

Object	*Sanskrit*	*Tamil*	*Proposed Sanskrit forms of Aiyar*
hair	*keśa*	*mayir*	*śmaśru*
mouth	*mukha*	*vāya*	*vāc*
ear	*karṇa*	*śevi*	*śrava*
hear	*śru*	*kēḷ keṇ* (*Tulu*)	*karṇa*
eat	*bhakṣa t*	*intu*	*tṛṇu, tṛ*
walk	*car*	*gu, śel*	*yā, car*
night	*nak*	*ira, irabu*	*rātri*
mother	*mātṛ*	*āyi*	*yāy* (*Paiśācī*)

J. Harmatta has shown that there was contact between the Proto-Indo-Aryans and Proto-Dravidians in the fourth millennium BC (1981). His conclusion for the date of contact is based on linguistic evidence. Instead of using the terms Dravidians and Indo-Aryans, he called them Proto-Dravidians and Proto-Indo-Aryans because, on linguistic evidence, he needed a very early date for the contact, although at that time (i.e. the fourth millennium BC), according to the theory of some Western scholars, Indo-Aryans were supposed not to have been in India. This might have been a problem to Harmatta. Therefore, he suggested that both Indo-Aryans and Dravidians came to India, and that on the way to India they had linguistic contact. But it is simpler to assume that both were in India at that time and had linguistic contact there. It is still more simple and sound to assume that the words which need a date of contact of the fourth millennium BC on linguistic grounds as loan words in Dravidian might be words originally inherited in Dravidian from the Proto-speech which was the common ancestor of both Dravidian and Indo-Aryan.

The following are some of the Dravidian words illustrated by Harmatta as loans from Sanskrit: *cāy* 'to incline, lie down' (Skt *śete*), *cāntan* 'pleasure' (Skt *śānta, sānti*), *cāti* 'to destroy' 'to kill' (Skt *śātayati*). Such words were traced by Harmatta as borrowings into Dravidian from Indo-Aryan in the fourth millennium BC and he himself was surprised as to how this was possible. Harmatta's surprise will be answered perfectly if the date of the Rigveda goes beyond the fourth millennium BC – that is, to (approximately) the fifth millennium BC – and India is taken as the original home of both Indo-Aryans and Dravidians. It will be simpler to explain the situation if both Indo-Aryan and Dravidian are traced to a common language family. In vocables they show significant agreement. In phonology and morphology the linguistic structures agree significantly. It requires a thorough comparative study of the two language families to conduct a fuller study. The real problem is that Dravidian in its oldest available structure is comparable to New Indo-Aryan in phonological and morphological developments, as shown earlier. A comparative study of the structure of Dravidian should be made with that of NIA since both belong to almost the same chronological level according to contemporary research.

NIA, which without controversy is accepted as a development from Sanskrit, is known because of the intermediate stage MIA. If MIA were not there, it would not have been possible to link the NIA languages with Sanskrit because there are so many linguistic peculiarities within NIA which distance it from Sanskrit; for example, Hindi second causative *kar(a)vānā* is derived from Skt **karāpayati* instead of Skt regular *kārayati*, which is the source of Hindi *karānā*, the first causative. The derivation of Hindi *-avā-* from Skt *āpaya* is known through the MIA form *-āva-*, which was extended in MIA to all causative formations. It is probable that for Dravidian such an intermediate link is lost, for which reason it appears as though the language is of another family. But its affinity with Indo-Aryan (or Indo-European) should be explored and not ignored. Although the history of the Albanian language has not yet been properly worked out because of the non-availability of an intermediate stage, its Indo-Europeanness is not challenged.

Caldwell also said that the Dravidian languages occupy a position of their own between the languages of the Indo-European language family and those of the Turanian or Scythian (= Ural-Altaic) group – not a midway position, but considerably nearer the latter than the former (Taraporewala 1982: 220).

In this way, Caldwell wanted to prove that Dravidian is nearer to Ural-Altaic than to IE, but he unwittingly opened up the fact that Dravidian and Indo-European are comparable; therefore, it is high time that they were compared and it would be better still if the three languages – Dravidian, Indo-European, and Ural-Altaic – are grouped together after a thorough comparison, which will enrich the grouping of languages. For all these comparisons, Sanskrit is always ready to help us with its ocean of linguistic material, which scholars use for comparing IE with other language families.

Therefore, a serious effort to compare Dravidian and Indo-Aryan (or Indo-European) should now be made. This research will be successful and will conclusively prove that Dravidian and Indo-Aryan belong to one common source; there will be no scope to assume that Aryans came from outside and drove the Dravidians away to the South.

6.4 Evidence from the Uralic languages for the date of the Rigveda and Aryan migration

The Uralic languages contain many loan words from Indo-Aryan, beginning from the Rigvedic stage. Many scholars have worked on these loan words. The oldest loan words have been shown by most of them to be Indo-Iranian. But often these so-called Indo-Iranian words are attested in Sanskrit, and such words should be taken to be Indo-Aryan. Loan words, when traceable in an attested language, should preferably be accepted as loans from the attested language rather than an hypothetical earlier stage. It will be seen below that most of the loan words attested in the Uralic languages are borrowed from various stages of Indo-Aryan, namely, Vedic, Classical Sanskrit, Middle Indo-Aryan, and New Indo-Aryan.

Of the scholars who have taken an interest in these loan words, we may mention a few important names here, namely, T. Burrow, J. Harmatta and V. I. Abayev.

Burrow, in his *Sanskrit Language*, discussed only twenty-three loan words, and he derived them from Indo-Iranian even when they are clearly Indo-Aryan loans (1955: 23–5). His discussion is not of much use for us since he does not talk about chronology. But that he stamped these words as Indo-Iranian instead of Indo-Aryan shows that he also might have accepted that these borrowings were made by the Uralic languages at very early dates, which indirectly confirms an early date of the loan words proposed by Harmatta.

Harmatta's work is very important for its chronological estimate (1981: 75–9). He classified the loan words into eleven periods, with the linguistic changes of each stage accompanied by examples.

The examples of the Uralic forms are cited by him in reconstructed forms. He cited fifty-three examples. In the first stage, which he assigns to 5000 BC, he cites only one example, *aja*, as an Indo-Iranian borrowing, which is actually a borrowing from the Rigvedic language. Elsewhere, I have critically evaluated Harmatta's linguistic analysis (1992a: 18–24). I cite some examples from Harmatta's work stage by stage. In conclusion Harmatta showed that the 11th Period of borrowing was in 1500 BC and that the 1st Period belongs to 5000 BC. He assumes about 300 years for each of the eleven stages. The Sanskrit forms given in brackets in the following list are supplied by me.

1st Period:
FU (= Finno Ugric = Uralic) **aja-* 'to drive' < PIr **aja* (cp Skt < *aj* 'drive', this is a Rigvedic verb).

2nd Period:
FU **orpas* **orwas* 'orphan' < PIr **arbhas* (cp Skt *arbha-(ka)* 'child').
FU **pakas* 'god' < PIr **bhagas* (= Skt *bhagaḥ*).
FU **martas* 'dead' < PIr **mṛtas* (= Skt *mṛtaḥ*).
FU **taiwas* 'heaven' < PIr **daivas* (= Skt *daivaḥ*).

3rd Period:
FU **oćtara* 'whip' < PIr **aćtra* (Skt *aṣṭrā*).
FU **caka* 'goat' < PIr **ćāgaḥ* (Skt *chāgaḥ*).

4th Period:
FU **arwa* 'present given or received by the guest' < PIr **arg*^{w}*haḥ* (cp Skt *arghaḥ*).

5th Period:
FU **tajine* 'cow' < PIr **dheinuḥ* (Skt *dhenuḥ*).
FU **ta e* 'milk' < PIr **dedhi* (cp Skt *dadhi*).
FU **sasar* 'younger sister' < PIr **svasar* (cp Skt *svasā*).

6th Period:
FU **warsa* 'foal, Colt' < PIr **vṛṣaḥ* (cp Skt *vṛṣaḥ* 'bull').
FU **sapta* 'seven' < PIr **septa* (Skt sapta).
FU **teśe* 'ten' < PIr **deśa* (cp Skt *daśa*).
FU **sata* 'hundred' < PIr **śata* (cp Skt *śata*).
FU **reśme* 'strap, cord' < PIr **raśmiḥ* (cp Skt *raśmiḥ*).

7th Period:
FU **mekše* 'honey bee' < PIr **mekši* (cp Skt *makṣi*).
FU **mete* 'honey' < PIr **medhu* (cp Skt *madhu*).
FU **jewä* 'corn' < PIr **yevaḥ* (cp Skt *yavaḥ*).

8th Period:
FU **asura* 'lord' < PIr **asuraḥ* (cp Skt *asuraḥ*).
FU **sara* 'flood' < PIr **saraḥ* (cp Skt *saraḥ*).
FU **sura* 'beer, wine' < PIr **surā* (cp Skr *surā*).
FU **sasra* 'thousand' < PIr **zhasra* (cp Skt *sahasra*).

9th Period:
FU **sas, soś* 'to become dry' < PIr **sauś* (cp Skt *śoṣah*).
FU **sare* 'booklet, rill' < PIr **kṣaraḥ* (cp Skt *akṣaraḥ*).

10th Period:
FU **wisa* 'anger, hatred, hate' < PIr **viš-višam* (cp Skt *viṣam*).
FU **ora* 'bowl' < PIr **ārā* (cp Skt *ara*).

11th Period:
FU *onke* 'hook' < PIr **aṅkaḥ* (cp Skt *aṅkaḥ*).

Harmatta constructed the chronology by taking the separation of Indo-Iranian from Balto-Slavic as occuring in the first half of the fifth millennium BC. The loan word he assigns to 5000 BC is a Rigvedic form. Hence, his chronology indirectly puts the date of the Rigveda in 5000 BC.

Abayev does not discuss chronology by so thoroughly showing linguistic changes stage by stage (1981: 84–9). He puts the date for the oldest period (i.e. IIr, where actually he cites Sanskrit forms as IIr) as 3000 BC and the last period as the first century AD, where we find NIA borrowings. By this he also confirms the date of NIA as the first century BC (Abayev 1980: 98). Now of course, from gypsy evidence, the date of NIA has been placed further back, to the fourth century BC (Section 6.6 below).

But Abayev's classification of stages is in the normal, accepted formula: Aryan (= Indo-Iranian), Indo-Aryan etc. He cites many examples – around a hundred in all. His examples are very important as they illustrate loans from Old Indo-Aryan, Middle Indo-Aryan, and even New Indo-Aryan. Some of his illustrations are given by stage:

A. Proto-Aryan borrowings (= Proto-Indo-Iranian borrowings):
Saami *åriel*, *årjän* 'southern, south-western' cp Indo-Iranian (= IIr) *arya-*, 'Aryan', Av *arya-* 'id.' (actually Av *airya*: but Skt *arya*, present author).
Mansi *sāt* 'seven', Hung *het* 'id.', cp IIr *sapta*, Skt *sapta* 'id.', Av *hapta* 'id.'
Finn (= Finnish) *jyva* 'corn', Ost (= Ostya) *jüvä* 'id.', cp IIr *yava*, Skt *yava*, 'id.', Av *yava* 'id.'
Mord (= Mordvian) *ažja* 'connecting pole', cp IIr *atšā-*, Skt *iṣā* 'id.', Av *aeša-* 'plough'.
Mord *sazor*, *sazər* (< *sasar*) 'younger sister', Udm (= Udmurt) *sazer* 'id.', cp Skt *svasar* 'sister'.
Finn *parsas*, Mord *purtsos*, *purts* 'suckling pig', Komi *pors* 'swine', Udm *pars* 'id.', IIr *parsa*, Saka *pā'sa* 'swine'.
Komi *sur*, Udm *sura* 'beer', cp Skt *surā-* 'intoxicating drink'.
Komi, Udm *surs* (< *sasr*) 'thousand', Skt *sahasra* 'id.'
Finn, Ost *udar*, Mord *odar*, Mari *woδar* 'udder', cp Skt *udhar* 'id.'
Finn *vermen* 'thin skin', *vermeet* 'clothes', cp Skt *varman* 'cover', 'armour'.
Finn *marras* 'dead', cp IIr *mṛtas*, Skt *mṛtas* 'dead'.

B. Borrowings which may be Indo-Iranian or Old Indo-Aryan or Old Iranian:
Finn *muru* 'crumb', Mansi *mur*, *mor-* 'crumble', cp Skt *mur* 'crumble', *murṇa-* 'shattered', Saka *murr* 'crumble', Osset *mur-* 'crumb'.
Komi *karni* 'to make', Udm *karni*, cp Skt, Av *kar-* 'to make'.
Finn *arvo* 'price', Skt *argha* 'price', Av *arγa* 'price', Osset *arg* 'price'.
Hanti *pănt* 'road', cp Skt *panthā* 'road', Av *pantā* 'road'.
Komi *pod* 'foot', Skt, Ir *pada-* 'foot'.
Komi *ram* 'rest, peace', Skt *rama*, Av *raman*, Pahlavi, Persian *ram* 'rest, peace'.

Komi, Udm *das* 'ten', Skt *daśa*, Av *dasa*, Osset *dæs* 'ten'.
Finn *sata* 'hundred', Osset *sada*, Mansi *sat*, Hanti *sot*, Mord *sada*, Mari *süδə*, cp Skt *śata* 'id.', Av *sata*, Osset *sædæ*.
Finn, Ost *asa* 'portion', Skt *aṃśa*, Av *sa-* 'id.'
Finn *orja* 'slave', Skt, Av *arya* 'Aryan' (actually Skt *arya*, Av *airya* cp also OP *ariya*).
Mord *sava* 'goat', cp Skt *chāga*, Osset *sæv* (*g* > *v*, cp *bhanga* > *pavas*).
Hanti *wāt*, *wōt* 'wind', Mansi *wāt*, cp Skt, Av *vāta* 'id.', Osset *wad*.
Hung *var* 'fortress', cp OP *var*, Av *vara-*, Pahl *war*.

C. Borrowings from Proto Indo-Aryan:
Hung *tehen* 'cow', cp Skt *dhenu* 'id.', Av *dainu* (actually *daenu*), IIr *dhainu*.
Hung *tei* 'milk', cp Hindi *dhai* (actually *dahi*), Nep *dai*, Kashmiri *dai*, Pkt *dahi*, Skt *dadhi*, 'soured milk'.
Mansi *śiś* 'child', cp Skt *śiśu*.
Komi, Udm *med* 'pay, fee', cp Skt *mīḍha-*, Av *mižda*.
Mord *śed*, *sed*, Komi *sod* 'bridge', cp Skt *setu*, Av *haetu* 'id.'
Mansi *sänkwa* 'stake', cp Skt *śaṅku* 'id.'
Mansi *mant* 'bucket', cp Skt *mantha*, *manthana*, Pali *mantha*.
Hung *szeker* 'carriage', cp Bihari *sagar*, Hindi *sagar*, Punj *chakrā*, Or *chakaṛa* (actually *sagaḍa*), cp Skt *śakaṭa*.
Komi *dom* 'briddle', *domavna*, Udm *dum n*, cp Skt *dāman* 'rope'.
Komi *dar*, Udm *dur* 'ladle', cp Skt *darvi-* 'ladle', Kafir dur.

D. Borrowings from Iranian:
Mari *marij* 'man', cp OIr *marya*, Av *mairya*, OP *marika*, Skt *marya*.
Komi *mort* 'man', Udm *murt* 'man', Mord *mirde*, cp OIr, OP *martya* 'id.', Persian *mard* (but actually Skt *martya* is also comparable).
Finn *oras*, Mord *urozi* 'wild boar', cp Av *varaza*, Pahl *waraz*, Oset *wæraz* (but cp also Skt *varāha*).
Finn *sarvi* 'horn', Oset *sarv*, Mord *suro*, Komi and Udm *sur*, Mari *sur*, cp Av *sru*, *srva* (but cp also Skt *śṛṅga-*).
Komi *varnös* 'sheep', cp Skt **varṇa*, Pahl *warrak*, Komi *vurun* 'wool', cp Skt *ūrṇa*.
Finn *vasa*, Ost *vasik*, Mansi *vasir*, Hung *üszo* 'bull', cp OIr *vasa*, Oset *wæs*, Skt *vatsa* 'calf' (but better cp also MIA *vasa* 'bull', Skt *vṛṣa* 'bull').
Komi *kurög*, Udm *kureg* 'hen', cp Av *kahrka*, Oset *kark* (but cp also Skt *ṛja-pya-* 'stretching oneself'), Arm *arciv*.
Hanti *wärəs* 'horse hair', cp Av *varasa* Sogd, Pahl *wars* 'hair' (but cp also Skt *vāra-*, *vāla-* 'hair').
Mansi *aṅśer* 'fang, tusk', Hanti *aṅźar*, Hung *agyar*, Sogd **ansur* (*'nswr*), cp Tokh *āṅkar* 'fang, tusk' (but cp also Skt *aṃśu* 'filament, point').
Komi *buriś*, *burśi* 'mane', cp Av *barəsa-*, Osset *bars* 'mane'.
Komi, Udm *majeg* 'stake', OP *mavuχa*, *Skt mayukha*, Sogd *meχk*, Osset *meχ*.

Finn *wasara*, Ost *vasar* 'hammer', Mord *uzer*, cp Av *vazra-* (but cp Skt *vajra*).
Mord *spanst* 'briddle belt', cp Afgan *spansai*, Osset *fsonz* (**spanti*) 'yoke'.
Mansi *rāsn* 'rope', cp *Pers rasan*, OIr *rasana-*, Skt *rasana-* 'rope'.
Hung *ostor* 'whip' *dialectal aštar*, Mansi *aštər*, *oštər*, cp Av *aštra-*, Pahl *aštar* (cp also Skt *aṣṭrā*).
Komi *gort* 'house', Udm *gurt*, Hanti *kort*, *kurt*, Ir **gṛda*, Av *gra-*, Skt *gṛha* 'id.'
Komi, Udm *zarni*, Hung *arany* 'gold', cp Av *zaranya* 'gold', Osset *zærin* (but cp also Skt *hiraṇya*).
Hung *nad* 'reed', cp Av *nada* 'reed' (cp also Skt *nada*, *nala* 'id.').
Mansi *šat* 'happiness, luck', Komi Udm *šud*, cp Av *šāti-*, OP *šyāti*, Pers *sād*.
Southern Samoed *ārda* 'right', cp OIr *arta-* (but cp also Skt *ṛta* 'right' whereas Av has *aša-*).
Mord *erva* 'every', cp Av *harva* 'every' (actually Av *haurva*, cp Skt *sarva*).
Mori *rakš* 'dark horse', cp Pers *raχš* 'id.' Skt *lākṣā* 'lac'.
Hung *tart* 'to hold', cp OP *dar-*, Av *dar-*, Osset *daryn* 'to hold' (cp also Skt *dhār-aṇa*, *dhṛta* 'hold').
Mansi *kõn*, Hand *kiṇṭa* 'dig', Hung *hany*, Komi *kund*, cp Av *kan*, OP *kan-* 'dig' (cp also Skt *khan* 'dig').
Hung *kincz* 'treasure', cp OP *granza-*, Arm (< Iranian) *gandza* 'treasure'.
Hung *nemez* 'thick felt', Hanti *namat*, Komi *namət*, *namot*, cp Av *nimata*, Skt *namata*, Sogd *namat*, Osset *nymæt* 'thick felt'.
Finn *suka* 'brush', cp Av *sukā* 'thorn', Osset *sug* 'beard', 'awn', Skt *šuka* 'beard', 'awn'.
Finn *tarna* 'grass', Ost *tarn*, Komi, Udm *turin*, cp Skt *tṛṇa* 'grass', Saka *tarna* (< **tarna*) 'grass'.

E. Borrowings from Late Iranian (or Northern Iranian):
Mari *kərtni*, Komi *kört*, Udm *kort*, Hanti *kārtə* 'iron', cp Osset *kard* 'knife', 'sword', Av *kart*, Av *karəta-* 'knife' (cp also Skt *kartari* 'knife').
Komi *tarźənə* 'shiver', cp Osset *tærsyn* 'to be afraid' (cp Skt *tarjana* 'to shout with anger').
Hanti *tegər*, Mari *torkek* 'fire (tree)', cp Osset *tægær* 'maple (tree)'.
Mansi *sirej (sirj)* 'sword', cp Osset *cirq* 'a kind of sword'.
Komi *jenden*, Udm *andan* 'steel', cp Osset *ænden* 'steel' < OIr *handāna* 'steel fish plate'.
Komi, Udm *pod* 'crossing, cross road', cp Osset *fæd* 'track, foot print' (cp Skt *pad* 'foot', *path* 'path').
Mari *kańe* 'hemp', cp Osset *gæa* (< *kana-*) 'hemp' (cp also Skt *kanīci* 'a creeper').
Kom *gön*, Udm *gon* 'hair', cp Osset *qun* 'hair', 'wool', Av *gaona*.
Finn *varsa*, Ost *vars* 'stallion, foal', cp Osset *wyrs* 'stallion' < Iranian *vṛšan* (cp Skt *vṛṣan-* 'bull').

Finn *ternikko* 'young animal', Osset *tærna* 'boy', Av *tauruna* (cp Skt *taruṇa* 'young').
Komi *vurd* 'otter', cp Osset *uyrd, urd* 'otter', OIr *udra* (cp Skt *udra*).
Hung *keszeg* 'name of a fish', Mansi *kāseuw*, Hanti *kosə*, cp Osset *kæsag*.
Mari *ängər* 'fishing hook', Osset *ængur* 'id.' (cp Skt *aṅkura*, 'shoot', *aṅkuśa* 'hook').
Mansi *šerkeš čargeš* 'eagle', cp Osset *cærgæs*, Av *kahrkasa* (cp Skt *kṛkalāsa*).
Mord *loman* 'man', cp Osset *lymæn* 'friend' (cp Skt *ramaṇa* 'husband').
Udm *äksej* 'prince', Osset *æksin* 'lady', Av *χšaya-*, OP *χšāyaθiya* (cp Skt *kṣayati* 'rules').
Komi *idög* 'angel', Osset *idawæg* 'deity' < OIr **witawaka*.
Mari *werg* , Komi *vörk-* 'kidney', Osset *wərg* 'id.', Skt *vṛkkau*, Av *vərəδka*.
Komi *gor* 'sound', Udm *gur* 'tone', Osset *qær, γær* 'sound', cp Skt *gīr* 'sound'.
Udm *ana* 'without', 'minus', Osset *ænæ* 'id.', Av *ana* 'preposition', cp Skt *an-* 'negative prefix'.
Udm *bad'zim, bad'zin* 'big' Osset *badzin* 'id.'
(Note: The Sanskrit forms given in brackets are supplied by me.)

Although I do not agree fully with Abayev's classification of the forms, I accept the importance of his classification. The forms given in the first stage of borrowing which he calls Proto-Aryan (= Indo-Iranian) actually include clearly Sanskrit forms, and thus the date of the Rigveda must precede this earliest stage of borrowing. Abayev's forms for other stages actually present borrowings sometimes from Middle Indo-Aryan and sometimes from New Indo-Aryan. Therefore, Abayev's examples very clearly indicate that there are forms from various stages of Indo-Aryan, that is, Old Indo-Aryan (Vedic and classical), Middle Indo-Aryan (including various stages), and New Indo-Aryan. By way of example a few forms borrowed in Uralic from various stages of Indo-Aryan may be cited next. I have classified these after analyzing the examples given by Abayev.

Borrowings from the Vedic stage:
Saarni *ariel, arjan*, cp Skt *arya*.
Mord *sazor, sazer*, Udm *sazer*, cp Skt *svasar*.
Mari *marij* 'man', cp Skt *marya*.
Komi Udm *med* 'pay', cp Skt *mīdha*.
Komi *dar* 'ladle', cp Skt *darvi*.

Borrowings from the Vedic or classical stage:
Komi *sur-*, Udm *sunt* 'beer', cp Skt *surā*.
Komi Udm *surs* 'thousand', cp Skt *sahasra*.
Finnish *vermen* 'thin skin', *vermeet* 'clothes', cp Skt *varman* 'cover', 'armour'.
Mansi *śiś* 'child', cp Skt *śiśu*.
Mansi *sankw* 'stake', cp Skt *ṣaṇku*.
Finnish *tarna*, Osty *tarn* 'grass', cp Skt *tṛṇa*.

Borrowings from the Middle Indo-Aryan stage:
Finnish *vasa*, Osty *vasik*, Mansi *vasir*, Hung *uszo* 'bull', cp MIA *vasa* < *vṛṣa*.
Mord *sed*, Komi *sod* 'bridge', cp MIA *sedu* < Skt *setu*.

Borrowings from the New Indo-Aryan stage:
Mansi *sat* 'seven' < NIA *sāta* < MIA *satta* < Skt *sapta*.
Finnish *marras* 'dead' < NIA *marā* 'dead'.
Hung *szeker* 'carriage', cp Hindi *sagar*, Or *sagaḍa*.
Hung *tei* 'milk', cp Hindi *dahī*, Or *dahi*, Beng *dai*.

Therefore, Indo-Aryan loan words in Uralic present evidence for the date of the Rigveda as being before 5000 BC, in accordance with Harmatta's chronology, since the Uralic forms show the source as being the Rigveda.

Thus, the evidence of loan words from Indo-Aryan in the Uralic languages as given by T. Burrow, J. Harmatta, and V. I. Abayev helps us in coming to the following conclusions.

1 The loans belong to a very early age, and although the loan words often clearly present Old Indo-Aryan or Vedic forms, the scholars prefer to take them as Indo-Iranian in view of their earliness. But since in form they are clearly Indo-Aryan words, they should be taken as Indo-Aryan and not Indo-Iranian and also not as Iranian, when a form is phonetically nearer to Indo-Aryan.
2 In this way of taking the forms as Indo-Aryan, the earliest loan ascribed by Harmatta to 5000 BC is to be accepted as a Rigvedic form and, therefore, the date of the Rigveda goes beyond 5000 BC.
3 Since loan words found in Uralic are borrowed from various periods of Indo-Aryan including OIA, MIA and NIA, it is to be accepted that the Indo-Aryans were present in the Uralic area at various times as a result of which there was linguistic contact, which indirectly helps us to assume that Indo-Aryans (who were the original Aryans, i.e. Indo-Europeans) might have gone out in prehistoric times to other places of historical IE languages like Greek, etc.

6.5 Evidence from Gypsy languages for Aryan migration

The Gypsy languages also present some indirect but very strong evidence for Aryan migration. Many scholars have worked on these languages, and now nobody has any doubt about their origin. These Gypsy languages are now included under New Indo-Aryan without any controversy. Their characteristics are the same as Modern Indo-Aryan languages, with natural dialectal variations. There is also no controversy about their homeland being India. From India they went to various parts of Europe and Asia. Accordingly, they are broadly classified as Asiatic Gypsies and European Gypsies, not merely geographically but also on the basis of some linguistic differences which will be taken up next. Besides, the Gypsy languages are more locally distributed, with local names in different parts of Europe and Asia. Accordingly they are called Armenian Gypsy, Bohemian Gypsy, English Gypsy, German Gypsy, Greek Gypsy, Hungarian Gypsy, Romanian Gypsy, Spanish Gypsy etc. on the basis of the places where they have settled.

There is some controversy regarding the exact region of India from which they originated. Turner discussed the controversy about their region of origin and concluded that Gypsy belongs to the Central group of Indo-Aryan, but that the Gypsies severed connections with the Central group before the time of Moka. Thus, Turner considers their original homeland to be Central India and the date of their migration to be earlier than the third century BC. The route of their migration has also been hinted at by Turner, "Where did they go? Since later on they appeared in Persia, it is reasonable to suppose that they migrated through the North West" (1975: 269). Thus, it is perfectly clear that the Gypsies went outside India via the north-west around the fourth century BC. On the authority of Turner we may take it as concrete evidence of the migration of the Indo-Aryans from India to Iran around the fourth century BC. Subsequently, from Iran they went on to other parts of Asia and Europe. Therefore, it is quite likely that in the remote past, say in about 5000 BC or earlier, the same thing might have happened, that is, the Indo-Aryans (or Aryans, i.e. the Indo-Europeans) migrated from India via the north-west, first to Iran and then to other parts of Asia and Europe. This will be better established when we examine the linguistic changes which have happened in Gypsy in comparison with the other New Indo-Aryan languages in India and compare the changes with the linguistic changes of other historical Indo-European languages in comparison with Sanskrit. Two very important features may be cited here: (1) New Indo-Aryan *a* is found as *a*, *e*, *o* in European Gypsy (examples are cited later). Sanskrit *a* is found as *a*, *e*, *o* in Greek and with further modification in other Indo-European languages. (2) New Indo-Aryan voiced aspirates are not retained as voiced aspirates in any dialect of Gypsy. They have become devoiced or deaspirated in various Gypsy languages (examples are cited below). Sanskrit voiced aspirates are the same as Indo-European voiced aspirates but in Greek they are devoiced and in several other Indo-European languages they are deaspirated.

The change of NIA *a* to European Gypsy *a*, *e*, *o* is to some extent guided by the following situation, as studied by me from the examples cited by Turner (1975: 272ff.) It normally becomes *e*, but in final syllables often becomes *o* and in forms which had closed syllable in Sanskrit remains *a* in European Gypsy.
Examples:

Eur Gyp *kher* 'donkey', Arm Gyp *χari*, Syr Gyp *kăr*, cp Skt *khara* (Av *χara-*) etc.
Eur Gyp *gelo* 'went', Syr Gyp *gara*, cp Beng *gelo*, Or *galā*, Skt **gatala*.
Eur Gyp *kher* 'house', Arm Gyp *khar*, cp Hindi *ghar*, Or *ghara*, Pali *gharaṃ*.

Eur Gyp *ciken* 'fat', cp Or *cikkaṇa*, Bhoj *cikkan*, Hindi *ciknā*, Skt *cikkaṇa*.
Eur Gyp *jena* 'person', cp Or *jaṇa*, Hindi *janā*, Skt *janaḥ*.
Eur Gyp *terna* 'youth', Syr Gyp *tanta*, Or *taruṇa*, Skt *taruṇa*.
Eur Gyp *tele* 'under', cp Hindi *tal*, Or *tala*, Skt *tala*.
Eur Gyp *dives* 'day', Or *dibasa*, Skt *divasa*.
Eur Gyp *des* 'ten', Arm Gyp *las*, Syr Gyp *das*, cp Skt *daśa*, Hindi *das*, Or *daśa* (= *dasa*), Bhoj *das*.
Eur Gyp *devel* 'god', Arm Gyp *leval*, Skt *devatā*, Or *debatā*, Bhoj *devatā*.
Eur Gyp *therel* 'holds', Arm Gyp *thar-*, *cp* Skt *dhar*, MIA and NIA *dhar*.
Eur Gyp *len* 'river', cp Skt, MIA and NIA *nadī*.
Eur Gyp *nevo* 'new', Syr Gyp *nawa*, cp Skt *nava-*, Or *naba*, Hindi, Bhoj *nayā*.
Eur Gyp *perel* 'falls', Arm Gyp *par-*, cp MIA *paḍai* (Skt *patati*), NIA *pad*.
Eur Gyp *phenel* 'speaks', cp Skt *bhaṇ-*, Or *bhaṇ*.
Eur Gyp *pherel* 'fills', Arm Gyp *phar-* 'ride', cp Skt *bhar* 'bear', Or *bhar* 'fill', Hindi *bhar-* 'fill', Bhoj *bhar*.
Eur Gyp *merel* 'dies', Syr Gyp *murar* 'dies', cp Skt, MIA and NIA *mar-* 'die'.
Eur Gyp *juvel* 'young woman', Syr Gyp *juar*, cp Skt *yuvatiḥ*, Or *jubati*.
Eur Gyp *šel* 'hundred', Syr Gyp *sai*, cp Skt *śatam*, Hindi sau.

In closed syllables European Gypsy retains *a*, for example,

Eur Gyp *aṅgušt* 'finger', cp Skt *aṅguṣṭha*, Hindi *aṅgūthā*.
Eur Gyp *ame* 'we', Syr Gyp *ame* 'we', cp Or *āme* 'we', Skt *asma*.
Eur Gyp *katel* 'spin', Hindi *kāt* 'spin', Skt **kartati* = *kṛṇatti*.
Eur Gyp *kham* 'sun', Hindi *ghām* 'heat', Skt *gharma*.

Sometimes *ā* and *ō* occur in other circumstances owing to analogy and other factors:

Eur Gyp *na* 'not', Skt *na*.
Eur Gyp *šoša* 'moustache', cp Skt *śmaśru*.
Eur Gyp *sosai* 'hare', cp Skt *śaśa*.

Well known is the equation of Skt *a* to Greek *a*, *e*, *o*. A few examples may be cited for comparison:

Skt *dadarśa*, Gk *dédorka*.
Skt *apa*, Gk *apo*.
Skt *bharāmi*, Gk *pherō*.
Skt *asti*, Gk *esti*.

Comparison of the examples of the linguistic change of Indo-Aryan *a* to Gypsy *a*, *e*, *o* suggests that, similarly, original IE *a* (= Skt *a*) has become *a*, *e*, *o* in Greek, and other IE languages show further changes.

Some examples show that NIA voiced aspirates have become devoiced and deaspirated in various Gypsy dialects:

> Eur Gyp *kher* 'house', Arm Gyp *khar-*, Pali *gharaṃ*, Hindi and Beng *ghar*, Or *ghara*, Bhoj *ghar*.
> Eur Gyp *kham* 'sun', Syr Gyp *gam*, Skt *gharma*.
> Eur Gyp *ǝranth-* 'to cook', Skt *randh-* 'to cook'.
> Eur Gyp *phenel* 'speaks', Arm Gyp *phan-*, cp Skt *bhaṇati*.
> Eur Gyp *phago* 'broken', Syr Gyp *bagar* 'breaks', cp Skt *bhagnaḥ*, Or *bhaṅgā*.

Well known is the devoicing of IE voiced aspirates in Greek and the deaspiration in several IE languages like Avestan, Gothic, Hittite etc.

> Skt *bharāmi*, Gk *pherō* 'I bear', Goth *baira*, Av *barāmi*.
> Skt *dadhāmi*, Gk *dolikhós* 'I hold, put', Av *dadāmi*.
> Skt *dīrghaḥ*, Gk *dolikhós* 'long', Ht *daluga*, Av *darǝγo*.

In this manner Gypsy languages present evidence of linguistic changes that repeat what had happened several thousand years back. Thereby they also prove that IE *a* (= Skt *a*) becoming *a*, *e*, *o* in Greek is a quite natural change, as it happened with the European dialects of the Gypsy language several thousand years later.

Further to confirm that the original IE vowel was *a* (as in Skt) instead of *a*, *e*, *o* as in Greek, let us see the position of *a* : *a*, *e*, *o* in the Indo-European historical languages. For IE *a* (or *a*, *e*, *o*) Skt has *a*, Iranian *a* (where Old Persian has *a* but Avestan changes Iranian *a* to *a*, *ǝ*, *e*, *i*, *o* under certain circumstances, for which see Section 6.6). Greek has *a*, *e*, *o*, Latin has *a*, *e*, *o* (but sometimes *e* changes to *i*, and *o* changes to *u* in Latin), Baltic *a*, *e*, Slavic *o*, *e*, Gothic *a*, *e*, Hittite *a*, *e*, Luw *a*, Palaic *a*, Hieroglyphic Hittite *a*, Lycian *a*. Some examples may be cited here to illustrate the distribution of *a* : *a*, *e*, *o* in various IE historical languages. IE *esti* > Skt *asti*, Av *asti*, OP *astiy*, cp HHt *astu*, Luw *astu* (*as-du*), Pal *astu* (*asdu*), Gk *esti*, Lat *est*, Goth *ist*, OCS *jestĭ*, Lith *esti*, Ht *estsi* (*es-zi*). IE *apo* > Skt *apa*, Av *apa*, OP *apa*, Lat *ab*, Goth *af*, Ht *apa*, Luw *apa*(*n*), HHt *apan*, Lyc *epn* (here Lyc shows *e* for IE *a* reconstructed on the basis of Gk *a*). JE *osih* > Luw *hassa* (= *has-* < *hasi*) 'bone', Ht *hasti-*, Skt *asthi*, Av *ast-*, Gk *ostéon*, Lat *os* < * *ost*.

This shows that *a*, *e*, *o* as three vowels are found only in Greek and with further changes as five vowels in Latin. Some other languages show only two vowels (*a and e*); most languages show one vowel, *a*. If we accept the changes shown in Gypsy as model, then it will be clear that changes in IE historical languages were also independent developments in each, as in case of *ped* in Latin and *pod* in Gk from IE *pad*, which is *pad* in Sanskrit, Avestan, Old Persian, Hieroglyphic Hittite, Luwian etc.

Reviewing the position of the distribution of *a*, *e*, *o* in various IE historical languages, it is now clear that the reconstruction of *a* as made by Schleicher,

Bopp and Grimm is more appropriate than the later reconstruction of *a*, *e*, *o* as made by Brugmann etc. (followed by many including myself [1968, 1975, 1979, 1983, 1985, 1986, 1991, 1993]) if the Aryans had India as their original home and went out to different parts of Europe and Asia via Iran. The original *a* (= Skt *a*) is retained in Old Iranian (with changes in Avestan under different circumstances [Section 6.6]) and gradually changes in various historical languages for which the change of climate might also have been partly responsible.

Similarly, the IE voiced aspirate became mostly deaspirated and sometimes devoiced under similar climatic variation. Therefore, the Gypsy evidence is helpful for the conclusion that the Centum languages, of which Greek is the most archaic, are all innovators and have changed significantly in comparison with the proto-speech; moreover Sanskrit antedates Greek etc. in archaism. Therefore, the original area of Sanskrit, that is, India, is more likely to be the original home of the Aryans (i.e. Indo-Europeans).

6.6 Evidence from Iranian for Aryan migration

In Section 6.1 I showed that Sanskrit is the most archaic language in the Indo-European language family. Iranian is next in order of archaism, from the point of view of its structure.

Iranian agrees significantly with Indo-Aryan. Therefore, Sanskrit and Iranian are well known to be very close to each other, on which basis they are put by the Indo-Europeanists into the Indo-Iranian branch without any controversy. A similar effort to link Italic and Celtic into an Italo-Celtic branch has not been successful. The Baltic and Slavic branches were similarly linked into Balto-Slavic, but this, too, was not highly successful. Iranian is closest to Sanskrit. Sanskrit is very close to Proto-Indo-European, if not identical. Iranian is second in order of closeness to Indo-European. Formerly, Greek was accepted as the second-most archaic language in as it retains IE *a*, *e*, *o* as against Sanskrit (or Indo-Iranian) *a*. But the Gypsy evidence presented in Section 6.5 conclusively proves that the Sanskrit (or Indo-Iranian) *a* is the original IE vowel, and this takes away the second position of archaism formerly allotted to Greek.

Although Indo-Iranian *a* (or Skt *a*) was retained in Old Iranian and subsequently also in Old Persian, it has changed considerably in Avestan. The change of Iranian *a* in Avestan may be shown by the following examples (S. S. Misra 1979: 16–18):

1. *a* > *ə* when followed by *m*, *n*, *v* but preceded by any sound except *y*, *c*, *j*, *ž*. Av *kəm*, cp Skt *kam*: Av *barən*, cp Skt (*a*) *bharan*; Av *səvišto*, cp Skt *śaviṣṭhaḥ*.
2. *a* > *i* when followed by *m*, *n*, *v* and preceded by *y*, *c*, *j*, *z*. Av *yim*, cp Skt *yam*: Av *vācim*, cp Skt *vācam*; Av *drujim* < Iranian *drujam*, cp Skt *druham* < **dru-jham;* Younger Av *druzinti* < Iranian *drujanti*, cp Skt *druhyanti*.

3 *a* > *e* after *y* when the next syllable had *e*, *y*, *c*, *j* or *ŋ́h* (= Skt *sy*). Av *yeidi/yedi*, cp Skt *yadi*; Av *yehe/yeŋ́he*, cp Skt *yasya*; Av *iθyajah-*, cp Skt *tyaj*; Av *yesnya*, cp Skt *yajñiya*.
4 *a* > *o* sometimes after labial sounds when the next syllable had *u/o*. Rarely also *a* > *o* when the next syllable had a conjunct preceded by *r*. Av *vohu*, cp Skt *vasu*; Av *mosu*, cp Skt *makṣu*; Av *pouru* < **poru* (< Iranian *paru* < IIr *pṛru*), cp Skt *puru*; Gothic Av *corət* < **cort* < **cart*, cp Skt *kaḥ* < *kart*.
5 *a* > *a* in all other situations. Av *apa*, cp Skt *apa*; Av *asti*, Skt *asti*.

The change of *a* to several vowels *a*, *e*, *o* etc. in Avestan was conditioned by definite situations. But the change of *a* to *a*, *e*, *o* in Greek, Latin and to *a*, *e* in several other languages was a change for which no condition can be determined. This shows that these languages belong to a much later date, when there were generalizations and several other phonological and morphological changes.

The Middle Indo-Aryan languages are characterized by a lot of linguistic change in comparison to Old Indo-Aryan, in phonology and morphology. They show changes in vowel quality (e.g. Skt *candramā* > Pali *candimā*), assimilation of consonants (e.g. Skt *yukta* < MIA *yutta*), dropping of final consonants (e.g. all final consonants except *m* are dropped in MIA), syncretism (e.g. the dative is replaced by the genitive, Skt *rāmāya dehi* > MIA *rāmassa dehi*) and several other changes.

Similarly, important Indo-European languages other than Sanskrit show several linguistic changes in comparison to Sanskrit. The Old Iranian languages (Avestan and Old Persian), Greek, Latin, and the Anatolian languages are some of the most important IE historical languages. But they present many linguistic changes comparable to Middle Indo-Aryan. Comparatively, Iranian proves to be more archaic than Greek, Latin, and Anatolian as far as the linguistic changes are concerned. Therefore Iranian may be placed as next to Sanskrit in archaism.

Nevertheless, Iranian is much less archaic than Sanskrit and deserves a much later date than Sanskrit, in spite of being placed earlier than Greek etc. Iranian also presents several linguistic changes and, thus, is comparable to Middle Indo-Aryan to some extent.

Avestan has several developments from *a*, as shown earlier. Moreover, it shows other linguistic changes, some of which may be taken up here.

1 Avestan shows spirants for voiceless aspirates, for example, Skt *sakhā*, Av *haχā*.
2 Av deaspirates the voiced aspirates, for example, Skt *brātā*, Av *brātā*.
3 Final vowels are lengthened in Gothic Avestan and shortened in Younger Avestan; hence the quantity of final vowels cannot be determined in Avestan.
4 The *a*-stem influences other stems in Av as in MIA. Thus the ablative singular is extended to other forms, for example, Av *χraθvat* (of *u*-stem) after *mašyāat* (of *a*-stem).

Old Persian retains original *a* as *a*, but it also has many linguistic changes comparable to MIA.

1 OP drops all final consonants except *m*, *r*, *š*. MIA drops all final consonants except *ṃ*.
2 OP shows spirants for voiceless aspirates like Avestan, for example, Skt *sakhā*, OP *haXā-*. In MIA Niya Prakrit sometimes shows spirants; Niya *aneǵa* (= *aneγa*) < Skt *aneka.*
3 OP also deaspirates all voiced aspirates like Avestan, for example, Skt *bhrātā*, OP *brātā*. In MIA Niya shows deaspiration, for example, *buma* < *bhūmi.*
4 The dative is lost and replaced by the genitive in OP as in MIA.
5 The alternative instrumental plural ending *-ais* of *-a*-stems is fully replaced by *-bhis* in OP as in MIA.
6 In OP the imperfect and aorist tenses have merged to form a preterite as in MIA.
7 The perfect tense is almost lost in OP as in MIA.
8 The passive voice often takes active endings in OP as in MIA, replacing the original middle endings.

In this way Iranian, although more archaic than other IE languages, is much less archaic than Sanskrit and is akin to the eldest daughter of Sanskrit from the point of view of archaism.

Therefore, if India was the original home of the Aryans (or Indo-Europeans) and the migration started from India via the north-west, then Iran was the first destination. This is proved by the movement of the Gypsies, who first reached Iran going via the north-west, as shown in Section 6.5.

In Indian tradition there is no hint even about the Indo-Aryans coming to India from outside. But in Avestan we have evidence of the Iranians coming from outside. Iranian presents evidence by means of the words naming several rivers in the Rigveda, for example, Sindhu (Av, OP, Hindu), Sarayu (Av Haroyu, OP Harayu), Sarasvati (Av Haraχv aiti, OP Harauvatiy). These are often shown in Iranian evidence as names of areas. The Rigveda does not speak of any such place as Iran. Thus, although the Iranians refer to the Vedic areas, Vedic people never refer to the Iranian areas, which shows that Iranian culture is a later phase of the Vedic culture. In other words, the original homeland of the Iranians must have been the Vedic lands.

P. L. Bhargava came to the same conclusion on the basis of other important evidence (1979: 59–61). He showed that the first section of the Vendidad enumerates sixteen holy lands, created by Ahuramazda, which were later rendered unfit for the residence of men (i.e. the ancestors of the Iranians) on account of different things created therein by Angra Mainyu, the evil spirit of the Avesta. This clearly means that the ancestors of the Iranians had lived turn by turn in all these lands. One of these lands was a land of severe winter and snow. This may be a reference to the north-west Himalayan pass by which they went to Iran. Another was

HaptaHindu the land of seven rivers. Excessive heat created in this region by Angra-Mainyu was the reason the ancestors of Iranians left this country. Thus, the Iranians lived in the region of Sapta-Sindhu of the Rigveda before going to Iran.

This gives us sufficient evidence that India was the original home of Iranians and also of Indo-Aryans. Avestan also refers to Airyana Vaeja, which means the original land of the Aryans; this indicates that Iran was not their original home and thus indirectly shows that India was their original home.

In Sanskrit *deva* means 'god' and *asura* means 'demon'. But in the Rigveda *asura* is also used as an epithet of some gods. In Iranian *deva* (Av *daeva*, OP *daiva*) means 'devil/demon' and *asura* (Av and OP *ahura*) is used for 'god'. The word *deva* originally signifies god in Indo-European, cp Lat *deus* 'god', Lith *devas* 'god' etc. The Iranian use of *deva* 'devil' is definitely an innovation. It is quite natural that when the Indo-Aryan and Iranians differed from each other dialectally and could not remain amicable, the Iranians left for Iran and settled there. There they might have developed an extremely antagonistic attitude toward the Indo-Aryans (who remained in India) and consequently in Iranian the use of the words *deva* and *asura* was reversed, which resulted in special sets of words called *ahura* and *daeva* words in Avestan.

R. Ghirshman showed on the basis of archaeological evidence that the Indo-Aryans were present in the lower reaches of the Volga in 4000 BC and the Iranians came there in 2000 BC (1981: 140–4). He, however, takes the lower reaches of the Volga as the original home of the Indo-Iranians. But there is no evidence in his analysis for this being the original home. On the basis of archaeological evidence a date can be decided showing the presence of some people or certain things in an area. But the place from which they came to that place cannot be decided. Therefore it is likely that the Indo-Aryans went to the Volga from India, since their presence in the Volga is attested by the archaeological evidence of chariots, equine bones and signet horns etc., as shown by Ghirshman. Iranians reached there 2,000 years later, in 2000 BC, after they were separated from Indo-Aryans in language and culture. This evidence of the date of the Indo-Aryans being outside India in 4000 BC also confirms further the date of the Rigveda as beyond 5000 BC, already known on the basis of the Uralic evidence (Section 6.5). It also indirectly confirms India as the original home of the Indo-Aryans (and of the Indo-Iranians and further also of the Indo-Europeans) and also confirms other evidence which suggests that Indo-Aryans were migrating to various places in different periods beginning from 5000 BC, as the Uralic and other evidence reveals.

6.7 Evidence from the Anatolian languages for the date of the Rigveda

Even when it was assigned a recent date like 1500 BC, the Rigveda was considered to be the oldest document of the Indo-European language family until the discovery of the Hittite inscriptions. The date of Hittite was fixed by archaeology and there was no controversy. It was considered to be earlier than the Rigveda, since some of the inscriptions are said to belong to the nineteenth century BC, although most of them belong to the thirteenth or fourteenth century BC. Soon two new theories developed. One is the Indo-Hittite theory, which proposed that Hittite is a sister of Indo-European, and other historical languages like Sanskrit or Greek etc. are like nieces to Hittite. We will see later that it was too hasty a conclusion based on no evidence, and therefore it is almost buried now. The other theory was the laryngeal theory. This proposes that there were some laryngeal sounds in the proto-speech, which are retained only in Hittite and lost in all other historical languages including Sanskrit, Greek, etc. This was also a hasty theory based on a shaky foundation.

Before we take up the two theories let us give a brief sketch of the Anatolian languages. Several other languages were discovered along with Hittite. They are Luwian, Palaic, Lycian, Lydian, and Hieroglyphic Hittite. These along with Hittite are grouped together as Anatolian. Hittite is distinguished from the rest in some respects. Accordingly, the other Anatolian languages are classified as ti-Anatolian, since they retain IE *ti* as *ti*. But Hittite is called tsi-Anatolian, as it changes IE *ti* to *tsi* (written zt).

The following are some of the special characteristics of Anatolian.

1 Anatolian presents a laryngeal, borrowed orthographically from Semitic, because Anatolian is written in a Semitic script.
2 Vowel length is lost, at least orthographically.
3 Aspirates have lost aspiration.
4 Voiced stops are distinguished from voiceless orthographically by single writing and double writing, wherever possible.
5 The distinction between masculine and feminine forms is lost due to perhaps loss of vowel length. But according to Meriggi, Lydian presents evidence of a feminine (Sturtevant 1951: 8). Hittite shows a feminine formative *-sara* (cp Skt *-sra* in *tisraḥ*, *catasraḥ*, feminine formative in numerals).
6 The Dual is almost lost in Anatolian languages, as in Middle Indo-Aryan.
7 Syncretism is found in the plural.
8 The perfect tense is lost, as in MIA.
9 The imperfect and aorist tenses have merged to form a preterite, as in MIA.
10 Out of the five moods of IE, only the indicative and imperative are retained, as in NIA. Even MIA retains the optative along with the indicative and imperative.
11 The middle voice is partly retained, as in first MIA.

Let us now take up the laryngeal theory. This theory is more popular than the Indo-Hittite theory, as many scholars think that it explains many unsolved problems of Indo-European comparative grammar. I have refuted the laryngeal theory and have shown, successfully, that it is not useful to explain anything; in fact, it is an unnecessary burden on Indo-European grammar (1977). Here a brief exposition may be presented.

The Anatolian languages were written in a Semitic script and the laryngeal symbol of the Semitic script was frequently used in writing the Anatolian languages.This might have entered first as an orthographic inaccuracy but subsequently have been phonetically established in the Anatolian languages. Scholars reconstruct several laryngeals in the proto-speech, from two to twelve. The widely accepted number of laryngeals in proto-IE was four, as reconstructed by Sturtevant, out of which two are said to be retained in Anatolian and none is retained in any other IE language. Scholars of laryngeal theory have explained certain linguistic changes in non-Anatolian IE languages as being due to the loss of laryngeals. Let us take here some such features one by one. For convenience of description let us call the four laryngeals *H1*, *H2*, *H3* and *H4*.

Laryngealists like Sturtevant have cited examples from Hittite only. Accordingly *H3* and *H4* are retained in Hittite. *H1* and *H2* are lost even in Hittite. Hittite shows only one symbol for the laryngeals, namely, *h*, which is often written doubled *hh*. Sturtevant takes *hh* as voiceless coming from *H3* and *h* as voiced coming from *H4*, on the model of the stops, which show double writing for voiceless. But that *h* is voiced and *hh is* voiceless cannot be proved by cognates from other IE languages, whereas other stops such as *kk/gg* being voiceless and *k/g* being voiced can be proved by cognates. And even if we accept two laryngeals as being retained in Hittite to prove some phonological change in the other IE historical languages caused by the loss of laryngeals, that also cannot be established by these two only. They are supplemented by *H1* and *H2*, and for these laryngeals there is no evidence even in Hittite or any other Anatolian language. Some examples of the treatment of the Laryngeals are cited here.

1 *eH4* > Ht *eh* and *ē* in others, for example, *meH4* > Ht *mehur* 'time' but Skt *mā* (< IE *mē*) 'measure', Gk *metis* 'skill', Goth *mel* 'time'.

1a But *eH2* > Ht *e* and *ē* in others: *eH2s* > Ht *estsi* 'sits', Gk *hestai*, Skt *āste* 'sits'. Here to prove long *ē* from *e* plus a laryngeal, *H2* is conjectured, for which there is no evidence in Ht. This conjecture has been made just to make *eH4* > *ē* acceptable.

2 *H3e* > Ht *ha* and *a* in others: *H3enti* > *hanti* 'in front', Skt *anti* 'near', Gk *anti* 'in front'.

2a *H1e* > Ht *a* and *a* in others: *H1epo* > Ht *apa* 'back', Skt *apa* 'away', Gk *apo* 'away'. Here to prove laryngeal plus *e* > *a*, *H1* is conjectured without any evidence from any Anatolian language, when *H3* is not attested in Hittite.

The laryngeal theory. The main utility of the laryngeal theory was to explain the laryngeals found in the Anatolian languages. But the laryngeal in

Anatolian is merely an orthographic borrowing from Semitic, since these Anatolian languages used a Semitic script. The laryngeal is also not always fully systematic in orthography, for example, Ht *eshar* : *esar* 'blood', Ht *walh* 'beat': Hieroglyphic Ht *wal* 'die', Ht *ishiyanzi* 'they bind': Luwian *hishiyanti* 'they bind', Ht *mahhan* 'when' : Ht *man* 'when': Hieroglyphic Ht *man* 'when'. I have refuted this theory in greater detail in my *The Laryngeal Theory, A Critical Evaluation* and *New Lights on Indo-European Comparative Grammar.*

Now let us take up the Indo-Hittite theory, which owes its inception to Emil Forrer and cradling to E. H. Sturtevant. This theory was advanced merely with the intention of proving that Hittite was more archaic than other Indo-European languages including Sanskrit. But once the laryngeal theory is refuted, nothing remains in Hittite to prove its archaism. The Indo-Hittite theory has been discussed in detail and thoroughly refuted in my *New Lights on Indo-European Comparative Grammar.* I present a few important features of the theory here.

1 Indo-Hittite (IH) had no long vowel. Long vowels developed later by the merger of a laryngeal with short vowels. This is automatically refuted by refuting the laryngeal theory, as the evidence for laryngeals is not fully available to prove this assumption. Besides, Hittite and other Anatolian languages distinguish the development of short and long diphthongs, which proves that length was there in the proto-speech. Hittite itself needs a long *ē* in the proto-speech to explain the change of *t* to *ts*, for example, IE *te* > Ht *tseg* 'you'; but IE *te* remains *te* in Hittite; for example Ht *esten*. The short vowels in Anatolian may be orthographic or new developments and do not present any archaism.
2 IH did not have aspirates. Aspirates developed later in combination with the laryngeals. In fact in Anatolian languages, as in several other IE languages, aspiration of aspirates is lost. This is not an archaism: loss of aspiration is a late development, as in Iranian, Germanic etc.
3 IH had laryngeals, retained in Anatolian languages, and other IE languages have lost them. The laryngeal theory has been refuted earlier. Thus, the proto-speech had no laryngeal.
4 IH did not have a feminine gender. The feminine is a late development. The lack of a feminine in Anatolian may be due to the loss of length of vowels, since most feminines had long vowels. Besides, Hittite shows feminine formative *-saras* as in *supi-saras* 'virgin', which indicates that the feminine was also there in Anatolian.
5 IH had a restricted use of the dual, and the plural also lacked a full development in IH. In fact Hittite also presents evidence of a dual, as in *hasa hantsasa* 'children and grandchildren'. The IE dual is lost in many IE languages, and loss of the dual in Anatolian is quite natural.

6 IH did not develop all tenses and moods found in IE. In fact the Anatolian languages, which are now known to belong chronologically to the Middle Indo-Aryan period, show many changes in common with MIA, and as in MIA many tenses and moods are lost in Anatolian.

Thus, the Indo-Hittite theory was a hasty conjecture based on no evidence.

Therefore, since both the Indo-Hittite theory and the laryngeal theory are no longer valid, the claim of Hittite to be more archaic than Sanskrit is no more acceptable. On the other hand, a thorough linguistic study of Hittite gives Sanskrit a more archaic status than Hittite, since Hittite is comparable chronologically to Middle Indo-Aryan on the basis of several linguistic changes. A few such linguistic changes may be listed here.

1 It shows assimilation as in MIA:

kt > *tt*, for example, **luktai* > Ht *hatai* 'window', cp MIA *jutta* < Skt *yukta*. *mn/nm* > *mm* (also written *m*), for example, **memnai* > Ht *memai*. **gwenmi* (< IE *g*^{w}*henmi*) > Ht *gwemi* 'I strike', cp Skt *hanmi*, cp MIA *jamma* < Skt *janma*. **dwan* (< IE *dwom*) > Ht *dan* 'two', cp Skt **dvam* as in *dvandva*, cp MIA *do* < Skt *dvau*. *tn* > *nn*, for example, Ht *apanna* < **apatna*, cp MIA *raṇṇa* < Skt *ratna*.

2 Prothesis, for example, Ht *ararantsi* < Ht (rare) *rarantsi* 'washes', cp MIA, Aśokan *istrī*, Saurseni *itthī* < Skt *strī*.
3 Anaptyxis, for example, Ht *arunas* 'sea' < IE *ornos*, cp Skt *arṇas* 'water', cp MIA *radaṇa/raaṇa* < **ratana* < Skt *ratna*.
4 Metathesis, for example, Ht *degan* < **dgan* < **gdan* < IE *ĝhδom*, cp Skt *kṣam*, cp MIA (Pali) *makasa* < Skt *maṣaka*.
5 Syncretism: in Hittite, the singular and the dative and locative have merged; in the plural the instrumental, ablative, genitive, and locative have merged. In MIA the dative and genitive have merged.
6 The dual is lost in Hittite except in one example of a compound, *hasa hantsasa* 'children and grandchildren'. The dual is lost in MIA except in two words, *do* (< Skt *dvau*) and *ubho* (< Skt *ubhau*).
7 The aorist and imperfect have merged to form the preterite in Hittite as well as in MIA.
8 The perfect is lost in Hittite as well as in MIA.

The other Anatolian languages are less archaic than Hittite.

Of greater importance are the Indo-Aryan borrowings in Anatolian documents, which present conclusive evidence on the date of Rigveda as being much beyond 2000 BC. These borrowings include the names of Vedic gods, Indo-Aryan numerals, the names of kings, and several other words. But the language when analyzed indicates a transitional stage between Old Indo-Aryan and Middle Indo-Aryan which is comparable to Buddhist Hybrid Sanskrit and the language of the Indus seals as deciphered by S. R. Rao.

When these words were discovered, scholars initially took them to be Indo-Iranian loan words, perhaps because the date of Anatolian was accepted to be earlier than the date of the Rigveda, assigned at that time as 1500 BC. But now all accept these loan words as Indo-Aryan.

The following names of Vedic gods are available in a treaty between the Hittite king Suppiluliuma and the Mitanni king Matiwaza (*c.*1300 BC). The Vedic gods mentioned here are Indara (= Indra), Mitrašil (= Mitra), Našatianna (= Nāsatyā, the Asvins), Uruvanaššil (= Varuṇa). Since Indra is an evil spirit in Avesta and an important god in the Rigveda, these names are definitely taken from the Rigvedic pantheon.

The Indo-Aryan numerals are found in the treatise on horse training composed by Kikkulis of Mitanni (Section 6.9). They are *aikawartanna* (= Skt *ekavartana*) 'one turn of the course', *terawartanna* (= Skt *tre-vartana*) 'three turns of the course', *sattawartanna* (= Skt *sapta-vartana*) 'seven turns of the course', *nawartana* with haplology for *nawawartana* (= Skt *nava-vartana*) 'nine turns of the course'. The forms of numerals in these words are clearly Indo-Aryan. The form *aika-* is especially confirmatory. The form *satta* for Skt *sapta-* is a clearly Middle Indo-Aryan form.

T. Burrow also tried to prove that the names of gods and numerals are not Indo-Aryan but Indo-Iranian. After it was finally proved that these words are Indo-Aryan beyond doubt, T. Burrow in a revised edition of his book (1977) tried rather unconvincingly to propose a third branch of Indo-Iranian from which these loan words were taken. His statements in both editions of *Sanskrit Language* have been criticized by me elsewhere (Burrow 1992: 5–8).

Besides the names of the Vedic gods and the treatise on horse training showing Indo-Aryan numerals, the Anatolian documents present the following forms also borrowed from Indo-Aryan. It will be observed that in several forms the Hurrian suffix *-ni*/*-nu* is appended. Sanskrit cognates are given in parentheses.

wašannašaya 'of stadium' (Skt *vasanasya*).
aratiyanni 'part of cart' (Skt *rathya*).
ašuwaninni 'stable master' (Skt *aśva-nī*).
babrunnu 'red brown' (Skt *babhru*).
baritannu 'golden yellow' (Skt *bharita*).
pinkarannu 'red yellow, pale' (Skt **piṅgara*), cp Skt *piñjara* + *piṅgala*.
urukamannu 'jewel' (Skt *rukma*).
zirannu 'quick' (Skt *jira*).
Makanni 'gift' (Skt *magha*).
maryannu 'young warrior' (Skt *marya*).
matunni 'wise man' (cp Skt *mati* 'wisdom').

Besides, the following names are also of Indo-Aryan origin: *Šutarna* (Skt *sutarṅa* or *Sutrāṅa*), *Paršašatar* (Skt *praśastra*), *Šuššatar* (Skt *saśastra* or *sauśastra*),

Artadāma (Skt *ṛtadhāma*), *Tušratha* (Skt *tuṣ-ratha*), *Mativāza* (Skt *mativāja*), *Artamna* (Skt *ṙtamna*), *Bardašva* (Skt *vṛdh-aśva*), *Biryašura* (Skt *vīrya-śura* or *vīrya-sura*), *Puruš* (Skt *Puruṣa*), *Šaimašura* (Skt *sima-sūra* or *saimasūra*), *Satavāza* (Skt *śatavāja*). A linguistic analysis of all the Indo-Aryan names borrowed into Anatolian, as quoted above, depicts a language with the following characteristics.

1 The language is conclusively Indo-Aryan. It is neither Iranian nor Indo-Iranian.
2 The following linguistic features reveal that the language belongs to an early Middle Indo-Aryan stage or to a transitional stage between Old Indo-Aryan and Middle Indo-Aryan.

   (i) Dissimilar plosives have been assimilated, for example, *sapta* > *satta*. Gray quotes the MIA form for comparison, but he is silent about the fact that the borrowing in Anatolian is from MIA (1950: 309).
   (ii) Semi-vowels and liquids were not assimilated in conjuncts with plosives, semi-vowels or liquids as in 1st MIA, for example, *vartana* > *wartana*, *rathya* > *aratiya-*, *vīrya* > *Birya-*, *Vṛdhašva* > *Bardašva.*
   (iii) Nasals were also not assimilated to plosives/nasals, unlike in 1st MIA and like in OIA. This characteristic places the language of these documents earlier than 1st MIA, for example, *rukma* > *urukmannu*, *ṛtanma* > *artamna.*
   (iv) Anaptyxis was quite frequent, for example, *Indra* > *Indara smara* > *šumara.*
   (v) *v* > *b* initially, for example, *vīrya* > *birya*, *vṛdhasva* > *bardašva.*
   (vi) *ṛ* > *ar*, for example, *ṛta* > *arta*, *vṛdh* > *bard-*.

Thus, a linguistic study of the borrowed Indo-Aryan forms in the Anatolian records shows that they are definitely Indo-Aryan and not Iranian nor Indo-Iranian. This also shows that this language belongs to a transitional stage between OIA and MIA. Further, this language is comparable to the language of the Indus seals as deciphered by S. R. Rao. And this language is the base for Buddhist Hybrid Sanskrit, which was wrongly named Hybrid because of a misconception that it was a mixed language.

Thus, the language of Middle Indo-Aryan is much before the Aśokan Prakrit. And on the basis of the borrowed words in Anatolian records and the language of the Indus seals as deciphered by S. R. Rao the date of MIA may go beyond 2000 BC. The transitional stage between OIA and MIA might have started in 2500 BC.

These loan words are also important in showing that Indo-Aryans were going to the Anatolian area in such ancient times. This is fully confirmed by the borrowed words. Further if India is taken as the original home of Indo-Aryans, then the Anatolians, including Hittites, Luwian, Lycians, Lydians etc., also have their original home in India. These borrowed words point out the possibility that because the Anatolians were originally Indo-Aryans, there was a link with the Indo-Aryans, and the Indo-Aryans could reach the Anatolian area even in the transitional MIA period.

6.8 Evidence from Pamir and the shore of the Caspian Sea for Aryan migration

After the IE language family was discovered, it was felt by scholars that India was definitely the original home of Indo-Europeans, because Sanskrit, which was almost like Proto-IE, was the language of India. This is indirectly expressed by H. L. Gray. "The earliest investigators were quite certain that it was in Asia, the continent which was the source of oldest civilization, the traditional site of the garden of Eden, and where Sanskrit was spoken" (1950: 304–5). Here Gray has used "Asia" instead of "India". This shows how scholars were wary of using the name of India, which was enslaved by the British.

Therefore, after rejecting India, they first considered Pamir to be the original home of the Aryans, because Pamir was very close to India. But subsequently they preferred to shift the original home farther from Pamir to the shore of the Caspian Sea.

Now let us examine the fresh evidence from Pamir and the shore of the Caspian Sea in terms of how far these places deserve to be termed the original home of the Aryans in the light of recent linguistic and archaeological researches.

First of all let us take up the case of Pamir. Several scholars have studied the Pamiri dialects in detail. D. Karamshoyev has shown that the Pamiri dialects belong to the Indo-Iranian branch. Some forms are quoted from Karamshoyev's analysis (1981: 230–7). The Sanskrit forms given in parentheses are added by me.

Shugn *maγ*, Rush *mēw*, Yazg *mů̄w*, Tadzh *meš* 'sheep', Av *maeši* (cp Skt *meṣa*).

Shugn, Rush *žōw*, Bart *žāw*, Yazg *γew*, Baχ *γiw*, Tadzh *gow*, Av *gav-*, *gāuš*, Skt *gav-*, *gauḥ* 'cow'.

Shugn *χij*, Rush *χöj*, Bart *χöj*, Av *uχšab*, Skt *ukṣan* 'bull'.

Shugn, Rush, Bart *vaz* 'goat', Tadzh *buz*, Av *buza-*.

Shugn, Rush, Bart *pōc* 'protection of cattle', Av *paθra* (not in Bartholomae 1960).

Shugn *χūvd*, Rush, Bart *χuvd-* 'milk', Tadzh *šir*, Av *χšvipta-* 'milked', *χšvid-* 'milk', Sogd *χšypt-* (cp Skt *kṣīra-* 'milk', *kṣipta* 'spilled').

Shugn *χεδ-*, Rush *χeδ*, Bard *χod*, Yazg *χād*, Vaχ *šad-* 'summer sheepfold for cattle'.

Shugn *χoδ*, Rush *χůδ* 'house garden', Tadzh *saroy*, Av *say-* (cp Skt *kṣiti*, *kṣetra*).

Shugn *wūn*, Rush *wāwn*, Bart *wown* 'sheep wool', Av *varəna-*, Skt *ūrṇa-*.

Shugn, Rush *zimc*, Vanc *zamc*, Av *zam* 'land' (cp Skt *jmā*, 'earth', 'land').
Shugn *yaw*, Sogd *yw*, Mundzh *you*, Yazg *zuw*, Osset *yoew* 'millet', Av *yava-* (cp Skt *yava*).
Shugn *pinj*, Rush *pinj* 'millet', Kashmiri *piṅga*, Skt *priyaṅgu*, Lat *panicum*.
Shugn, Rush *kaχt*, Rush *kaχtā* 'seed', Tadzh *kišt*, Av *Karšta* (cp Skt *kṛṣṭa*).
Shugn *sɛr*, Rush *sēr*, Bart, Rosh *sōr*, Baχ *sor* 'yield'.
Shugn, Rush *piχt*, Yazg *paχt*, Tadzh *pist* 'oat flour', Skt *piṣṭa* 'pound'.

A study of Pamiri dialects brings us to assume the following assumption: some of the Indo-Aryans left their homeland India and went to Iran and became Iranians and some of them went subsequently to Pamir. Thus, Pamir was not the original homeland of Aryans; rather India was the original homeland, from which Aryans went to Pamir, through Iran, and settled.

A study of the Pamiri dialects shows that they belong to the Indo-Iranian branch. They show significant linguistic change and it is quite likely that the Aryans went from India to Iran, and that they might have gone to Pamir from Iran or might have gone to Pamir directly from India and settled there. The Pamiri dialects present much later forms. They give us no linguistic evidence that Pamir was the original homeland of the Aryans. On the other hand, the linguistic changes which they exhibit clearly show that they represent dialects which belong to a later stage of Iranian or Indo-Aryan.

Now let us discuss the case for the shore of the Caspian Sea being the original home of the Aryans on the basis of older and recent linguistic and archaeological studies. After India and Pamir were discarded, the northern shore of the Caspian Sea, as suggested by Schrader, was widely accepted as the original home of the Aryans. The linguistic basis utilized by Schrader was applicable to this area to a great extent. Comparative evidence was taken from various IE languages and some common objects were considered to be items existing in the IE speech community, but one point was perhaps ignored. When people migrate from their original home and spread over a big area they may acquire several new things common in this area, and thus found in all the dialects spread here. The linguistic chronology of forms should also be taken into account while selecting the items to attribute to the original homeland. From this point of view, the following items are the most important and deserve special attention:

1 They knew the following animals:
Horse: cp Skt *ašva*, Av *aspa*, Tokh *yakwe*, *yuk*, Gk *-hippos*, Venetic *ecupeθaris* (= 'charioteer'), Lat *equus*, OIrish *ech*, OE *ech*, Lith *aszva* 'mare'.
Bear: cp Skt *ṛkṣa*, Av *arəša*, Arm *arj*, Gk *árktos*, Alb *ari*, Lat *ursus*, Mid Irish *art*.
Hare: cp Skt *śaśa*, Afgan *soya*, *soe*, Welsh *Ceinach*, OHG *haso*, NE *hare*, O Pruss *sasins*.
Wolf: cp Skt *vṛka*, Av *vəhrka-*, Arm *gayl*, Gk *lúkos*, Lat *lupus*, Goth *wulfs*, NE *wolf*, Lith *vilkas*, OCS *vlŭkŭ*.

2 They knew the following trees:
Birch: cp Skt bhūrja, Ossetic bärz, NE *birch*, Dacian (place name) *bersovia*, Lat *froχinus* 'ash', OHG *bircha*, NHG *birke*, OE *birce*, Lith *berzas*, Russ *berëza*.
Willow: cp Av *vaetay-*, Gk *ītea*, Lat *vitis* 'vine', OHG *wida*, Lith *výtis*.
Pine: cp Skt *pīta-dāru*, Gk *pitus*, Alb *pishë*, Lat *pīnus*.

3 They knew the following metals:
Gold: cp Skt *hāṭaka*, *hiraṇya*, Av *zaranya*, NE *gold*.
Silver: cp Skt *rajata*, Av *ərəzata*, Gk *arguros*.
Iron: cp Skt *ayas*, Av *ayah-*, Lat *aes* 'copper', Gaulish *īsarno*, OHG *îsarn*, NHG *eisen*, NE *iron*.
Copper: cp Skt *lauha* (later 'iron'), Middle Persian *rod*, Lat *raudus*.

4 They knew snow:
cp Skt *hima*, Av *zima*, Gk *kheīma*, Lat *hiems*, Lith *sziema*, OCS *zim*, Arm *jiwn*.

On the basis of these important items, India equally deserves to be considered the original home of Aryans and the shore of the Caspian Sea, the place where Aryans came to from India and where they settled for some time, may be accepted as the original home of the Centum branch of Indo-European. The original Indo-European proto-speech, which was very close to Sanskrit, might have undergone several changes here.

The shore of the Caspian Sea was most probably the area where the innovating Centum group was separated from the more original Satəm group by many linguistic changes such as *a* > *a*, *e*, *o*; *ś* > *k* etc. From this place Centum speakers might have traveled to different parts of Europe and Anatolia etc. But before the Satəm–Centum distinction went beyond the dialect level, there was mutual intelligibility, and the Indo-European speakers might have traveled to this place from India (their original home). This hypothesis is based on the fact that the Indo-Aryans returned to this area repeatedly in both very early periods and later periods, for which there is some archaeological and linguistic evidence.

Caucasus, which is on the shore of the Caspian Sea, presents archaeological evidence which shows traces of the horse cult in the late second and early first millennium BC in the vicinity of the Mingechaur reservoir, as shown by Igrar Aliyer and M. N. Pogrebova (1981: 126–36).

The horse cult is equally Indo-Aryan and Iranian. In fact we have more Indo-Aryan evidence for it. Thus, the horse cult speaks of Indo-Aryan presence in the second millenium BC and Iranian presence at a later period in the Caucasus area. This makes it probable that the original home of the Indo-Aryans was the original home of the Indo-Europeans. On the basis of the evidence cited above, it is quite likely that India was the original home of the Indo-Europeans, from which they traveled toward the Caspian Sea, where the innovating Centum group was separated with generalization of *k*, which developed from *ś* before *s*.

Linguistic evidence as presented by Harmatta confirms the above archaeological evidence (1981: 79–80). Harmatta showed the word for horse found in Caucasian languages as being borrowed from Indo-Iranian in various early and late periods, for example, Udi *ek* 'horse' (this is borrowed according to Harmatta in 4000 BC). Other evidence also is found in different phases of borrowing. In NW Caucasian languages the examples are Circassian *šə*, Kabardian *šə* 'horse', Abkaz *a-čə* 'the horse'. In the SW Caucasian languages the following loan words are available Lak *ču*, also cp Khinalug *spa* 'ass, colt' (maybe from Iranian *aspa*), but khinalug *pša* (<**b-sə*), cp also Chechen *gaur*, Ingush *gaur* 'horse' < IIr *gaura*, cp Vedic *gaura* 'wild cow', Persian *gor* 'wild ass'.

The loan word for horse affirms that the horse cult was taken from India at a very early period (Harmatta's date is 4000 BC). Harmatta cited other loan words as well, for example, Kurin *γab* 'handful' < Skt *gabha*, cp also *gabhasti* 'ray', Batsian *həč* 'to see' < Proto-Indian/Proto-Iranian *kać* 'to see' (4000 BC), Chechen, Ingush *mār* 'husband' (<Skt *marya*). Harmatta concludes: "In spite of the paucity of this linguistic evidence, these ancient Proto-Iranian or Proto-Indian loan words to be found in the Caucasian languages offer a valuable testimony of the advance of Proto-Iranian or Proto-Indian tribes toward Caucasus at a very early date." Thus, it is clear that the Aryans moved from India through Iran to the Caucasus in several waves in very early periods as well as in later periods, and in some later phases Iranians also might have gone there, and the horse cult was introduced into the Caucasus by the Aryans (i.e. the Indo-Aryans) as early as 4000 BC.

This evidence also confirms that the date of the Rigveda is before 5000 BC. This also sheds light on the fact that Indo-Aryans were migrating toward these areas beginning from 4000 BC and continuing in subsequent periods, which strengthens our hypothesis that India was the original home of the Aryans.

6.9 Evidence from the horse for the date of the Rigveda and Aryan migration

'Horse' was well known to the Indo-European language family and we have cognates of this word in almost all the IE languages, cp Skt *aśva*, Av *aspa*, OP *asa* also OP *aspa* (< Median), Lith *aszva*, Gk *híppos*, Lat *equus*, call *epo*, OIrish *ech*, Goth *aihva* etc.

But domestication of the horse was in a way a monopoly of the Indo-Aryans. The horse was used for several domestic purposes like cultivation etc. Besides, the horse was also yoked to the chariot. Wherever we find archaeological evidence of the Indo-Aryans we often find equine bones. That Indo-Aryans were going to different places is often proved by the availability of equine bones in some areas as archaeological evidence and the loan words for horse found in some areas as linguistic evidence.

The Indus civilization is now claimed to be Indo-Aryan on the basis of the linguistic evidence and the archaeological evidence in terms of the availability of equine bones.

Harmatta showed loan words for horse taken from Indo-Aryan (which he named Indo-Iranian) found in many languages outside India. Harmatta's examples of loan words of horse from Indo-Aryan, were given earlier (Section 6.8) and are repeated here:

> NW Caucasian languages:
> Udi *ek* 'horse' (4000 BC – chronology by Harmatta), Circassion *šə*, Kabardian *šə*, 'horse', Abkhaz *a-čə* 'the horse'.
>
> SE Caucasian languages:
> Lak *ču*, Khinalug *pšə* (< *b-šə*).
> Khinalug *spa* 'ass', 'colt'.
> Chechen *gaur*, Ingush *gour* 'horse' < Pers *gor* 'wild ass' (cp RV *gaura* 'wild cow').

The loan words in various Caucasian languages prove that the Indo-Aryans were coming to these areas in various periods beginning from 4000 BC, and that the horse cult came to these areas with them.

Although there is no controversy that Indo-Aryans were responsible for domesticating the horse, Malati J. Shendge attempted to show that Indo-Aryans or Indo-Europeans were not responsible for the domestication of the horse. In the Anatolian loan words connected with horse training, we clearly find Indo-Aryan loan words, even though the person who wrote them, Kikkuli of Mitanni, may not have been Indo-Aryan: *aika-wartana*, *panza-wartana*, *tetawartana*, *sattawartana*, and *nawartana* (= *nava-vanana*) are definitely more important than the person who used them. The controversy is resolved, and now nobody takes them to be anything other than Indo-Aryan.

But Shendge has tried to prove that the word for horse is not IE and is a loan available in almost all IE languages. The Greek word *hippos* shows further linguistic change. The expected form in Greek should have been **eppos*. In a few other, rare forms *e* has become *i* in words in Greek, for example, Gk *isthi* <**esthi* < IE *ezdhi*. The initial aspiration may be analogical. On the basis of a slight defective cognate, Shendge rejects it. Taking a rather rare and obscure word, *sisa*, he interprets it as 'horse' and takes the word as a loan word from Akkadian *sisu*, which means 'horse', concluding that the Indo-Aryans learnt domestication of the horse from the Akkadians.

There are many new facts which were unknown to Shendge. The date of the Rigveda now has gone beyond 5000 BC. The Indus Valley civilization is now known to be preferably Indo-Aryan. There is also the probability that Dravidian and Indo-Aryan belong to one language family. The date of the Rigveda on the basis of the present estimate antedates many other civilizations. And evidence of the domestication of the horse is fully attested in the Indian literature from Vedic to Puranic times. The knowledge of Indo-Aryans being responsible for the domestication of the horse is found in loan words for horse in many languages, as shown earlier.

Many scholars, including Harmatta and Ghirshman, on the basis of the former theory of the original home of the Aryans have proposed that the Indo-Aryans/ Iranians came from the shore of the Caspian Sea while going toward Iran and India. But the loan words cited as evidence belong to various periods; therefore, it is more plausible to assume that their original home was India and they went to these places repeatedly in various periods, and thus that the loan words for horse show linguistic changes of various periods both in the source language (Indo-Aryan) and the borrowing languages.

It may be worthwhile here to give an example of how scholars without knowing the true context of a fact often misunderstand it and feel happy that they have created unanswerable questions. The following is quoted from Shendge:

> If Kikkuli's treatise on horse training is made the basis of the conclusion that the Indo-Europeans were the original horse domesticators, it raises several unanswerable questions. For example, it is curious that if the Indo-Europeans had the knowledge of horse breedings, why should the Hittites not have known it as a matter of course? But instead we find them looking to Mitannian Hurrain, not even an Indo-Aryan proper or his ancestor, for being initiated into the technique! And it's all the more curious that this Mitannian Hurrian should use only a few technical terms, probably four of five, from Proto Indo-Aryan and the terms for horse etc., from Sumerian and Akkadian (that's what we have to say for lack of better evidence) – this situation seems to arise because the available evidence is somewhere wrongly oriented. And that point lies in the assumption that the horse-breeders were Proto-Indo-Aryans.
>
> The linguistic evidence in Sanskrit for the purposes of comparison is mainly the term *aśva*, horse. It has been compared with Lat *equus*, despite the intervening centuries between the two words, and several continents. Skt *aśva* is treated as a primary root without any prehistory. It is also assumed that the Hurrian *iss* (*ia*) 'horse' is derived from *aśva*. Even Akkadian *sisu* 'horse' is derived from the Indo-Aryan *aśva* is said to be a loan from the Aryan branch. *Aśva* does not occur in Kikkuli's work, but 5± Indic words are found used. On the basis of these 5± words, the originators of the art of horse breeding in the ancient world are said to be the migrating Indo-Aryan clans. If this is the criterion, the Sumerians and the Akkadians should be given a chance. More than these,

Kikkuli being a Mitannian-Hurrian, the Hurrians should really be the horse breeders.

(1977, 1996)[1]

Shendge, not knowing the five Indo-Aryan words *aikavartana* etc., has toiled hard without any evidence to prove that horse training was taken from Akkadian or Sumerian, citing the Indo-Europeans and at other times the Indo-Aryans as horse breeders. The cognates for Sanskrit *aśva* 'horse' are found in the IE languages, as shown earlier. The Indo-Aryans were the domesticators of the horse. And the Anatolians are definitely Indo-European, but they had left their original home, India, without knowledge of horse breeding or horse training and hence, they borrowed it from the Indo-Aryan source through Kikkuli of Mittani. Other branches of IE might have learnt horse domestication from the Indo-Aryans, since the Indo-Aryans were masters in this art. It is easy to explain Hurrian *issi(a)* and Akkadian *sisu* as loan words from Indo-Aryan, since Middle Indo-Aryan has already started by that time. The word *satta* (<Skt *sapta*) is evidence for this. Similarly, MIA *assa* (<Skt *aśvai*) might have become Hurrian *issia* and Akkadian *sisu*.

Thus, the evidence of the horse proves the antiquity of Sanskrit as well as the fact that Indo-Aryans were going to various parts of the world in different periods of prehistory.

6.10 Concluding observations

The linguistic structure of Sanskrit demands an archaic status for it in the IE language family. Other historical IE languages such as Avestan or Greek are like daughters of Sanskrit on the basis of linguistic changes. Greek was given an archaic status on the basis of the retention of the *a*, *e*, *o* of IE, but evidence from the Gypsy languages conclusively proves that the *a* of Indo-Aryan was changed into *a*, *e*, *o* in European Gypsy. A similar change of *a* to *a*, *e*, *o* is quite likely in an earlier period. The change of IE palatal *k* to palatal *ſ* in Sanskrit is also doubtful because Sanskrit itself shows change of palatal *d* to *k* as a positional variation. Thus, Sanskrit deserves a highly archaic status and on the basis of the archaic linguistic structure a much earlier date than the date given by European scholars.

The Uralic languages show loan words from the early Vedic stage up to the New Indo-Aryan Stage. Harmatta ascribed 5000 BC as the date for the earliest loan words, which he worked out on the basis of linguistic changes. He showed the oldest form to be IIr. But I have shown that the earliest loan words belong to the Rigvedic stage. Therefore, the date of Rigveda must go beyond 5000 BC.

The Indus civilization culturally and linguistically presents a continuation of the Vedic civilization. The apparent non-similarity of the rural civilization of the

Rigveda and the urban civilization of the Indus Valley can be solved by taking Indus civilization as a later development of the Vedic civilization.

The language of the Indus seals as deciphered by S. R. Rao (if accepted) presents the language of a very early stage of MIA which belongs to a transitional stage between OIA and MIA. But until a bilingual seal is available the decipherment may remain controversial.

The study of the Indo-Aryan loan words in Anatolian shows a similar language, which is also early MIA, belonging to a transitional stage between OIA and MIA. Therefore, we may ascribe 2500–2000 BC as a date for the transitional stage between OIA and MIA and 2000 BC as the starting point of MIA proper.

Epic Sanskrit, which is the earliest stage of classical Sanskrit may be tentatively placed between 5000 BC (the date of RV) and 2000 BC (the date of MIA), that is, about 3500 BC. Tentatively we date the *Rāmāyaṇa* of *Vālmīki* to 3500 BC and the *Mahābhārata* of *Kṛṣṇadvaipāyana Vyāsa* to about 3000 BC, since the language of the two does not differ much. The theory that the *Mahābhārata* precedes the *Rāmāyaṇa* is baseless.

The archaic structure of Sanskrit and the dating of the Rigveda as beyond 5000 BC demand that India, the place of composition of the Rigveda, must be the original home of the Indo-Aryans as well as the Iranians. Iranian literature refers to an earlier place of residence, namely, Haptahindu, which is the Saptasindhu of the Rigveda. Thereby their original home in India is also confirmed. Indo-Aryans in their earliest literature of the Vedas and Purāṇas never speak of any original home and there is no literary or archaeological evidence nor any tradition in India which refers to any former place. Therefore, we are sure that India is the original home of the Indo-Aryans and the Iranians. I have shown above that Iranian is the second most archaic language in the IE language family. If India is the original home of the Indo-Iranians, there is a fair chance that it is the original home of the Indo-Europeans.

Although there is no evidence that Indo-Aryans came to India from outside, there is enough evidence that they went outside India again and again in prehistoric times. The loan words in the Uralic languages provide evidence of Indo-Aryans going to the Uralic area from 5000 BC (i.e. Rigvedic times) up to the New Indo-Aryan period. The Caucasian languages also speak of the going of the Indo-Aryans to this place several times.

Indo-Aryan loan words in Chinese and Korean also give some evidence that Indo-Aryans were migrating to various other places in prehistoric times. The Indo-Aryan loan words attested in Chinese and Korean are placed in the second–third millennium BC by Harmatta, who, however, wrongly calls them proto-Iranian (1981: 81). He says, "Finally we still have to give some hints about the migration of Proto-Iranians (= Indo-Aryans) toward Eastern Asia." The loan words, although few in number, are significant enough to attest the presence of Indo-Aryan speakers in those areas. The loan words from Chinese and Korean taken from Harmatta are cited next. The Sanskrit forms are supplied by me, to show they are more Indo-Aryan than Iranian.

Chinese:
Forms shown here are archaic Chinese forms reconstructed by Harmatta.
**k'an* 'cut', cp Skt *khan* 'dig', Av *χan.*
**g'wan* 'martial', cp Skt *han/ghan-*, Av *γan-/jan.*
**dz'cwan* 'create', cp Skt *jan* 'create', Av *zan.*
**swən* 'grandson', cp Skt *sūnu*, Av *hunu.*
**akk* 'bad, evil, wrong', cp Skt agha 'evil, bad', Av *aγa.*

Korean:
pad- 'field', cp Skt *pada-*, Av *pada-* 'foot', 'place'.
yoka 'bind', cp Skt *yukta* 'bound', Av *yaoχta.*
sul 'wine', cp Skt *surā* 'id.', Av *hurā.*
sena 'old', cp Skt *sana-* 'id.'

Although Harmatta took the source of borrowing to be Proto-Iranian and Proto-Indian (= Indo-Aryan), actually the forms are mostly Indo-Aryan and a few forms may be Iranian. Of these, Indo-Aryan forms may be early borrowings and Iranian forms may be late borrowings.

These loan words clearly show that Indo-Aryans were going out to various places in various periods. Thus, this helps us in taking India as the original home of Aryans, by supplying evidence of people going out to other distant places like China and Korea in ancient times.

In this way Indo-Aryans migrated to several parts of Europe and Asia in prehistoric times. In the historical period, which is linguistically the starting period of NIA, the Gypsies had gone out to Asia and Europe in the fourth century BC. Therefore, we have enough evidence that Indo-Aryans were migrating in pre-historical and historical periods, but we have no evidence which shows that they had come from outside. The story coined by some Western scholars that Aryans came from outside and destroyed the Indus civilization is now altogether to be dropped. The Indus civilization is now accepted as a continuation of the Vedic civilization, especially since the fire altars were discovered. Another, older theory that the Indo-Aryans drove away the Dravidians to the South is also a totally false assumption. There is no such archaeological or literary evidence nor tradition anywhere in India.

Classification of Dravidian as a separate race or as a separate language family is a hasty conclusion, because no proper linguistic comparison of Indo-Aryan and Dravidian has ever been attempted. The Dravidians are also Aryans.

There are many common words in Dravidian and Indo-Aryan which are taken as loan words from one to the other, since no proper comparison has been made as yet. There are phonological and morphological similarities. The structure of Dravidian as examined by me is to a great extent of the New Indo-Aryan type.

Therefore, there is no question of the Indo-Aryans driving away the Dravidians. Thus, there is no doubt that India was the original home of the Indo-Aryans (including the Dravidians) and the Iranians and it is wholly possible that it was the original home of the Aryans, that is, Indo-Europeans, since there is enough evidence that Indo-Aryans were migrating in historic and prehistoric times. Other branches of Indo-European, in contrast, present sufficient evidence that they have come from outside.

The Greek people came to Greece from outside: "The invading Greek tribes were rude Barbarians, they destroyed the Minoan-Mycenean civilisation" (Ghose 1979: 33). "Numerous inscriptions in non-Greek languages prove beyond every doubt the existence of an older civilisation in the Aegean World" (p. 35).

The Hittites also went to the later Hittite empire from outside. "The original Hatti were a people of Central Asia Minor, whose name and some of whose gods the Hittites adopted along with capital city Hattus (Ht *hattusas*)... conqueror and conquered had been completely amalgamated" (Sturtevant 1951: 4).

The Germanic people also show evidence of coming from outside. "The earliest known home of Germanic was South Scandinavia and North Germany. But at the beginning of the historical period, it was decidedly expansive. In the first century BC the Suevi are seen to have moved southwards and to have crossed to the left bank of the Rhine. To the east, other tribes were taking possession of land in Central and South Germany and in Bohemia. All these gains were, it is believed, on the territory previously in the hands of celts" (Lockwood 1972: 95). From this it is quite likely that the Germanic people first of all reached South Scandinavia and North Germany and spread into other parts at the expense of the Celts.

But the Celtic people were in turn also outsiders. "Judging by references in Greek writings and by archaeological evidence, Celtic tribesmen began to move into the Balkan area and settle among Illyrians and Thracians during the course of the fourth century BC. They burst into Greece, but were repulsed..." (Lockwood 1972: 95).

The Slavs also reached the Slavonic area coming from outside. "The Slavs have expanded enormously at the expense of the speakers of Finno-Ugrian and Baltic languages. The Volga was Finnish, and so also the Don area and Moscow. In the north the Baltic Lithuanians held the basins of the Niemen and the Dvino. None of these wild tracts could have been included in the original habitat of the Slavs" (Ghose 1979: 148).

The Iranian people were not originally from Iran. They went to Iran from India (Section 6.6). Other Indo-European languages present records of a recent date. They must have gone to those places much later. There is no basis for these places to be treated as original home of Aryans.

India presents the oldest record of the Indo-European language family. The language of the Rigveda shows archaism unparalleled by any other branch of Indo-European. India is also considered by several scholars as the best place for the origin of human beings. Taking all these factors into account, it seems quite likely that India was the original home of the Aryans (or Indo-Europeans). The date of the Rigveda, as shown earlier, must be beyond or much beyond 5000 BC.

Abbreviations

Alb	Albanian
Arm	Armenian
Ass	Assamese
Av	Avestan
Beng	Bengali
Bhoj	Bhojpuri
BHS	Buddhist Hybrid Sanskrit
Braj	Braj bhasa
Eur	European
Finn	Finnish
FU	Finno-Ugric
Gk	Greek
Goth	Gothic
Guj	Gujarati
Gyp	Gypsy
HHt	Hieroglyphic Hittite
Ht	Hittite
Hung	Hungarian
IA	Indo-Aryan
IE	Indo-European
IH	Indo-Hittite
IIr	Indo-Iranian
Ir	Iranian
Kan	Kannada
Kum	Kumaoni
Lat	Latin
Lith	Lithuanian
Luw	Luwian
Maith	Maithili
Mar	Marathi
MIA	Middle Indo-Aryan
Mord/Mordv	Mordvian
NE	New English
Nep	Nepali
NHG	New High German
NIA	New Indo-Aryan
OCS	Old Church Slavic
OHG	Old High German

OIA	Old Indo-Aryan
OIr	Old Iranian
OP	Old Persian
Or	Oriya
Osset	Ossetic
Ost/Osty	Ostyak
Pahl	Pahlavi
Panj	Panjabi
PDr	Proto-Dravidian
PIr	Proto-Iranian
Pkt	Prākrit
Russ	Russian
RV	Rigveda
Skt	Sanskrit
Sogd	Sogdian
Tam	Tamil
Tel	Telugu
Tokh	Tokharian
Udm	Udmurt

Acknowledgments

The present work is a revised and enlarged version of ten lectures delivered by me in the Centre of Advanced Study in Sanskrit, University of Pune, during August 1997.

Two decades earlier, in 1977, I had visited the USSR as a delegate of the Government of India, where I had to attend a symposium on the Aryan problem, held in Dushanbe, the capital of the then Soviet Tajikistan. I was asked to present a paper on "The Bearing of the Indo-European Comparative Grammar on the Aryan Problem". I am chiefly a scholar of Indo-European comparative linguistics and I have written comparative grammars of several Indo-European languages. The Aryan problem was untouched by me as a researcher. While collecting material for my paper, I realized that many of the existing theories were rather blindly accepted by scholars. While taking part in the discussions of the symposium, I was convinced that I should work more diligently in this line and contribute some of my busy hours to solving some of the questions of the Aryan problem. The result of my further research was published in 1992, with the title *The Aryan Problem: A Linguistic Approach*, where I have dealt with several aspects of the problem like the date of the Rigveda, the original home of the Aryans, as well as iron, cotton, and several other items related with the problems of the Aryans.

Since I remained interested in this problem I was automatically making further studies on the date of the Rigveda and the original home of the Aryans, along with my research on the comparative grammar of Indo-European.

When I was asked to deliver lectures on this topic by the Director of the Centre of Advanced Study in Sanskrit, I decided to include all my further researches in my lectures. By this time, I was convinced that languages like Greek, Hittite, Avestan, etc. are, from the point of view of linguistic structure, comparable to Middle Indo-Aryan, as they show many linguistic changes like loss of final consonants, assimilation of heterogeneous consonants, syncretism etc. Therefore, on the basis of antiquity in structure, Sanskrit deserves a much more ancient date than Greek, Hittite, Avestan, Old Persian etc. Formerly Greek was given the second place from the point of view of the antiquity of structure for retention of IE *a*, *e*, *o* but in this work I have conclusively shown that *a*, *e*, *o* are late developments in Greek and other languages, and Sanskrit *a* as proposed by Schleicher, Bopp, Grimm etc. presents the original picture of the Indo-European vowel. Thus, now, Iranian gets the second position in antiquity. Other evidence is also presented as complementary.

K. C. Verma, an Indologist, drew my attention to the comparison of Dravidian and Indo-Aryan made by R. Swaminath Aiyar.

In my *Aryan Problem: A Linguistic Approach* I devoted some pages to the common origin of Dravidian and Indo-Aryan, my studies for which were based chiefly on the researches of R. Swaminath Aiyar and J. Harmatta. After studying that part of my book, one young American scholar, Edwin F. Bryant, asked me to make a full-fledged study of this area. As I was busy with several other researches, I asked Dr Sushila Devi, my former student, to work in this line. She has done a lot of work, constantly consulting me and discussing issues with me. I have taken some points from this unpublished material and added them here to bring to the notice of scholars that Dravidian is comparable to New Indo-Aryan, both chronologically and structurally.

Lastly, I must thank some scholars who have helped me considerably by sending some books and articles/photocopies of books and chapters which made my research more complete than it could have been. They are K. C. Verma, Kṛṣṇa Deva and Edwin F. Bryant.

I am grateful to Professor V. N. Jha, Director, Centre of Advanced Study in Sanskrit, who invited me to give this lecture and who expressed his keen interest in its publication. I will be happy if my humble effort is useful for the enrichment of the knowledge of Proto-Indo-European language and culture.

Notes

1 Misra passed away prior to editing his paper in which he did not provide the full bibliographic specifics of this quote from Shendge. Since neither of the latter's two books were available to the editors, both publications have been noted here, unfortunately without the relevant page number.

2 As is clear from Lal's paper in this volume, Lal no longer upholds the views he held in 1981, to which Misra is here referring, and now critiques the very views to which he once subscribed. Unfortunately, as we noted, Misra has passed away and can thus not update his paper, but we have retained this section since Lal's views in 1981 are still widely held by others and, moreover, since the development of Lal's published statements on this issue exemplifies the change in paradigm which considerable numbers of South Asian archaeologists and historians of ancient India have undergone since the 1980's – Editors.

References

Abayev, V. I., 1981. "Prehistory of Indo-Iranians in the Light of Aryo-Uralic Contacts." In *Ethnic Problems of the History of Central Asia in the Early Period (EPHCA)*, edited by M. S. Asimov, *et al.* Moskva: Izd-vo "Nauka."

Aiyar, R. S., 1975. *Dravidian Theories*. Madras: Madras Law Journal Office.

Aliyer, I. and M. N. Pogrebova, 1981. "On the Processes in Some Areas of the East Trans-Caucasus and Western Iran in the Late 2nd and Early 1st Millenium BC." In *EPHCA*, edited by M. S. Asimov *et al.* Moskva: Izd-vo "Nauka."

Allchin, F. R., 1981. "Archaeological and Language – Historical Evidence for the Movement of Indo-Aryan Speaking Peoples into South Asia." In *EPHCA*, edited by M. S. Asimov *et al.* Moskva: Izd-vo "Nauka."

Asimov, M. S. *et al.*, eds. 1981. *Ethnic Problems of the History of Central Asia in the Early Period (EPHCA)*. Moskva: Izd-vo "Nauka."

Bartholomae, Ch., 1960 (reprint). *Altiranisches Wörterbuch*. Berlin: W. de Gruyter.

Bhargava, P. L., 1979. "The Comparative Antiquity of Mitra and Varuṇa," *Ludwick Sternback Felicitation Volume*, edited by J. P. Sinha. Lucknow: Akhila Bharatiya Sanskrit Parishad, pp. 59–61.

Bloomfield, L., 1933. *Language.* New York: Holt, Rinehart and Winston.

——, 1958 (1920). "Language," "Review of Konkordanz Panini-Chandra von Dr. Breeno, Language," *Journal of the Linguistic Society of America*, 5. London.

Brugmann, K., 1972. *Comparative Grammar of the Indo-Germane Languages*. Varanasi: Chowkhamba Sanskrit Series Office.

Burrow, T., 1970. *The Sanskrit Language*. London: Faber, 1955 and revised edition. London: Faber.

Chatterji, S. K., 1970 (reprint). *Origin and Development of the Bengali Language*. London: Allen and Unwin.

Devi, S., "A Historical and Comparative Study of Eastern Hindi Phonology," Thesis, B. H. U. (unpublished).

Gauda, K., 1972. "The Other Side of Comparative Dravidian," The Third Seminar on Dravidian Linguistics. Annamalainagar: Annamalai University.

Ghirshman, R., 1981. "Iran and Migration of Indo-Aryans and Iranians." In *EPHCA*, edited by M. S. Asimov *et al.* Moskva: Izd-vo "Nauka."

Ghose, B. K., 1979. *A Survey of Indo-European Languages*. Calcutta: Sanskrit Pustak Bhandar.

Gray, L. H., 1950. *The Foundations of Language*. New York: Macmillan.

Harmatta, J., 1981. "Proto Iranians and Proto Indians in Central Asia in the 2nd Millenium BC, Linguistic Evidence." In *EPHCA*, edited by M. S. Asimov *et al.* Moskva: Izd-vo "Nauka."

Jones, W., 1788. "On the Gods of Greece, Italy and India." *Asiatic Researches*, 1: 221–75.

Karamshoyev, D., 1981. "The Importance of Pamiri Language Data, for the study of Ancient Iranians Ethnic Origin." In *EPHCA*, edited by M. S. Asimov *et al.* Moskva: Izd-vo "Nauka."

Kuiper, F. B. J., 1991. *Aryans in the Rigveda*. Leiden Studies in Indo-European 1 Atlanta: Rodopi.

Lal, B. B., 1981. "The Indo-Aryan Hypothesis vis-a-vis Indian Archaeology." In *EPHCA*, edited by M. S. Asimov *et al.* Moskva: Izd-vo "Nauka."

Lockwood, W. B., 1972. *A Panorama of Indo-European Languages*. London: Hutchinson.

Macdonell, A. A., 1971 (reprint). *History of Sanskrit Literature*. New Delhi.

——, 1968 (reprint). *Vedic Grammar*. Varanasi: Indological Book House.

Misra, H., 1984a. "A Comparative Study of Assimilation of Conjuct Consonants in Prakrit and Greek." In *Linguistic Researches, Vol. IV*. Varanasi.
——, 1984b. *A Historical Grammar of the Hindi Language*. Varanasi.
——, 1985. "A Comparative Study of the vowel contraction in Greek and Middle Indo-Aryan." In *Historical and Comparative Linguistics*, Vol. I. Varanasi: Ashutosh Prakashan Sansthan.
——, 1986. *Linguistic Chronology of Middle Indo-Aryan Ṛtambharā*. Gaziabad.
——, in press. *A Historical Grammar of the Oriya Language*. Orissa Sahitya Akadami.
Misra, S. S., 1968. *A Comparative Grammar of Sanskrit, Greek and Hittite*. Calcutta: World Press.
——, 1975. *New Lights on Indo-European Comparative Grammar*. Varanasi: Manisha Prakashan.
——, 1977. *The Laryngeal Theory, A Critical Evaluation*. Varanasi: Chaukhambha Orientalia.
——, 1979. *The Avestan, A Historical and Comparative Grammar*. Varanasi: Chaukhambha Orientalia.
——, 1980. *Fresh Light on Indo-European Classification and Chronology*. Varanasi: Ashutosh Prakashan Sansthan.
——, 1983a. *The Luwian Language, A Historical and Comparative Grammar*. Varanasi: Larina.
——, 1983b. "Linguistic Assessment of the Indo-Aryans' of the Language of Indus seals." In *Gharati, New Series No. 1*, Varanasi.
——, 1985. *The Palaic Language, A Historical and Comparative Grammar*. Varanasi.
——, 1986. *The Hieroglyphic Hittite, A Historical and Comparative Grammar*. Varanasi: Ashutosh Prakashan Sansthan.
——, 1987. *Sound Synthesis in Indo-European, Indo-Iranian and Sanskrit*. Varanasi: Ashutosh Prakashan Sansthan.
——, 1991. *The Old Indo-Aryan, A Historical and Comparative Grammar*, Vol. I. Varanasi: Ashutosh Prakashan Sansthan.
——, 1992a. *Evidence of Writing in the Rigveda, Saṃskriti Sandhan*, Vol. 5. Varanasi.
——, 1992b. *The Aryan Problem, A Linguistic Approach*. New Delhi: Munshiram Manoharlal Publishers.
——, 1993a. *The Old Indo-Aryan, A Historical and Comparative Grammar*, Vol. II. Varanasi: Ashutosh Prakashan Sansthan.
——, *The Old Persian, A Historical and Comparative Grammar* (unpublished).
——, *The Albanian, A Historical and Comparative Grammar*, Vol. I (unpublished).
——, *A Comprehensive Comparative Grammar of the Indo-European Languages* (in preparation).
Misra, S. S. and S. Devi, *Dravidian and Indo-Aryan. A Comparative Study* (in preparation).
Misra, S. S. and H. Misra, 1982. *A Historical Grammar of Ardhamagadhi*. Varanasi.
Monboddo, Lord, 1774. *Of the Origin and Progress of Language*, 2nd edition. Edinburgh: J. Balfour.
Müller, M., 1873 (1866). *The Science of Language*. London: Longman, Green, and Co., pp. 153–4.
——, 1886. *Lectures on the Science of Language*. London: Longman, Green, and Co.
Pischel, R., 1965. *Comparative Grammar of the Prakrit Languages* (trans. by S. Jha) 2nd edition. Varanasi.
Rao, S. R., 1973. *Lothal and The Indus Civilisation*. Bombay: Asia Publishing House.

——, 1982. *The Decipherment of the Indus Script*. Bombay: Asia Publishing House.
Schleicher, 1876. *Compendum der vergleichenden Grammatic der Indogermanischen sprachen* by Bendal (trans.), London.
Shanmugam, S. V., 1971. *Dravidian Nouns, A Comparative Study*. Annamalainagar: Annamalai University.
Shendge, M. J., 1977. *The Civilized Demons: The Harappans in the Rgveda*. New Delhi: Abhinava Publications.
——, 1996. *The Aryans: Facts Without Fancy and Fiction*. New Delhi: Abhinava Publications.
Steblin-Kemensky, I. M., *Pamiri Language Data on the Mythology of Ancient Iranians* [Other information not available].
Sturtevant, E. H., 1951. *Comparative Grammar of the Hittite Language*, revised edition. New Haven, CT: Yale University Press.
Subrahmanyam, P. S., 1983. *Dravidian Comparative Phonology*. Annamalainagar: Annamalai University.
Sundaram, T. P. M., 1965. *A History of Tamil Language*. Poona: Deccan College Post-graduate Research Institute.
Taraporewala, I. J. S., 1982. *Elements of the Science of Language*. Calcutta.
Turner, R. L., 1975. *Collected Papers (1912–1973)*. London.

7

LINGUISTIC ASPECTS OF THE ARYAN NON-INVASION THEORY

Koenraad Elst

7.1 Summary

It is widely assumed that linguistics has provided the clinching evidence for the Aryan invasion theory (AIT) and for a non-Indian homeland of the Indo-European (IE) language family. Defenders of an "Out of India" theory (OIT) of IE expansion unwittingly confirm this impression by rejecting linguistics itself or its basic paradigms, such as the concept of IE language family. However, old linguistic props of the AIT, such as linguistic paleontology or glottochronology, have lost their persuasiveness. On closer inspection, currently dominant theories turn out to be compatible with an out-of-India scenario for IE expansion. In particular, substratum data are not in conflict with an IE homeland in Haryana–Panjab. It would, however, be rash to claim positive linguistic proof for the OIT. As a fairly soft type of evidence, linguistic data are presently compatible with a variety of scenarios.

7.2 Preliminary remarks

7.2.1 Invasion versus immigration

The theory of which we are about to discuss the linguistic evidence, is widely known as the "Aryan invasion theory" (AIT). I will retain this term even though some scholars object to it, preferring the term "immigration" to "invasion." They argue that the latter term represents a long-abandoned theory of Aryan warrior bands attacking and subjugating the peaceful Indus civilization. This dramatic scenario, popularized by Sir Mortimer Wheeler, had white marauders from the northwest enslave the black aboriginals, so that "Indra stands accused" of destroying the Harappan civilization. Only the extremist fringe of the Indian Dalit (ex-Untouchable) movement and its Afrocentric allies in the USA now insist on this black-and-white narrative (vide Rajshekar 1987; Biswas 1995).

But, for this once, I believe the extremists have a point. North India's linguistic landscape leaves open only two possible explanations: either Indo-Aryan was native, or it was imported in an invasion. In fact, scratch any of these emphatic "immigration" theorists and you'll find an old-school invasionist, for they never fail to connect Aryan immigration with horses and spoked-wheel chariots, that is, with factors of military superiority.

Immigration means a movement from one country to another, without the connotation of conquest; invasion, by contrast, implies conquest or at least the intention of conquest. To be sure, invasion is not synonymous with military conquest; it may be that, but it may also be demographic *Unterwanderung*. What makes an immigration into an invasion is not the means used but the end achieved: after an invasion, the former outsiders are not merely *in*, as in an immigration, but they are also *in charge*. If the newcomers end up imposing their (cultural, religious, linguistic) identity rather than adopting the native identity, the result is the same as it would have been in the case of a military conquest, namely that outsiders have made the country their own, and that natives who remain true to their identity (such as Native Americans in the USA) become strangers or second-class citizens in their own country.

In the case of the hypothetical Aryan invasion, the end result clearly is that North India got aryanized. The language of the Aryans marginalized or replaced all others. In a popular variant of the theory, they even reduced the natives to permanent subjugation through the caste system. So, whether or not there was a destructive Aryan conquest, the result was at any rate the humiliation of native culture and the elimination of the native language in the larger part of India. It is entirely reasonable to call this development an "invasion" and to speak of the prevalent paradigm as the "Aryan invasion theory."

As far as I can see, the supposedly invading Aryans could only initiate a process of language replacement by a scenario of *elite dominance* (that much is accepted by most invasionists), which means that they first had to become the ruling class. Could they have peacefully immigrated and then worked their way up in society, somewhat like the Jews in pre-War Vienna or in New York? The example given illustrates a necessary ingredient of peaceful immigration, namely, linguistic adaptation: in spite of earning many positions of honor and influence in society, the Jews never imposed their language like the Aryans supposedly did, but became proficient in the native languages instead. So how could these Aryan immigrants first peacefully integrate into Harappan or post-Harappan society yet preserve their language and later even impose it on their host society? Neither their numbers, relative to the very numerous natives, nor their cultural level, as illiterate cowherds relative to a literate civilization, gave them much of an edge over the natives.

Therefore, the only plausible way for them to wrest power from the natives must have been by their military superiority, tried and tested in the process of an actual conquest. Possibly there were some twists to the conquest scenario, making it more complicated than a simple attack, for example, some Harappan faction in a civil war may have invited an Aryan mercenary army which, after doing its job, overstayed its welcome and dethroned its employers. But at least *some* kind of military showdown should necessarily have taken place. As things now stand, the Aryan "immigration" theory necessarily implies the hypothesis of military conquest.

7.2.2 The archaeological argument from silence

This chapter will give a sympathizing account of the *prima facie* arguments in favor of the OIT of IE expansion. I am not sure that this theory is correct, indeed I will argue that the linguistic body of evidence is inconclusive, but I do believe that the theory deserves a proper hearing. In the past, it didn't get one because the academic establishment simply hadn't taken serious notice. Now that this has changed for the better, it becomes clear that the all-important linguistic aspect of the question has never been properly articulated by "Out of India" theorists. The OIT invokes archaeological and textual evidence, but doesn't speak the language of the IE linguists who thought up the AIT in the first place. So, now, I take it upon myself to show that the OIT need not be linguistic nonsense.

But first a glimpse of the archaeological debate. In a recent paper, two prominent archaeologists, Jim Shaffer and Diane Lichtenstein (1999), argue that there is absolutely no archeaological indication of an Aryan immigration into northwestern India during or after the decline of the Harappan city culture. It is odd that the other participants in this debate pay so little attention to this categorical finding, so at odds with the expectations of the AIT orthodoxy, but so in line with majority opinion among Indian archaeologists (e.g. Rao 1992; Lal 1998).

The absence of archaeological evidence for the AIT is also admitted, with erudite reference to numerous recent excavations and handy explanations of the types of evidence recognized in archaeology, by outspoken invasionist Shereen Ratnagar (1999). It then becomes her job to explain why the absence of material testimony of such a momentous invasion need not rule out the possibility that the invasion took place nonetheless. Thus, she mentions parallel cases of known yet archaeologically unidentifiable invasions, for example, the Goths in late-imperial Rome or the Akkadians in southern Mesopotamia (Ratnagar 1999: 222–3). So, in archaeology even more than elsewhere, we should not make too much of an *argumentum e silentio*.

To quote her own conclusion:

> We have found that the nature of material residues and the units of analysis in archaeology do not match or fit the phenomenon we wish to investigate, viz. Aryan migrations. The problem is exacerbated by the strong possibility that simultaneous with migrations out of Eurasia there were expansions out of established centres by metallurgists/prospectors. Last, when we investigate pastoral land use in the Eurasian steppe, we can make informed inferences about the nature of Aryan emigration thence, which is a kind of movement very unlikely to have had artefactual correlates.
>
> (Ratnagar 1999: 234)

It is against the stereotype of overbearing macho invaders, but the Aryans secretively stole their way into India, careful not to leave any traces.

7.2.3 Paradigmatic expectation as a distortive factor

If the Aryan invasion does not stand disproven by the absence of definite archaeological pointers, then neither does an Aryan emigration from India. However, there is one difference. Because several generations of archaeologists have been taught the AIT, they have in their evaluation of new evidence tried to match it with the AIT; in this, they have failed so far. However, it is unlikely that they have explored the possibility of matching the new findings with the reverse migration scenario. Psychologically, they must have been much less predisposed to noticing possible connections between the data and an out-of-India migration than the reverse.

This predisposition is also in evidence in the debates over other types of evidence. Thus, in a recent internet discussion about the genetic data, someone claimed that one study (unlike many others) indicated an immigration of Caucasians into India in the second millennium BC. To be sure, archaeo-genetics is not sufficiently fine-tuned yet to make that kind of chronological assertion, but even if we accept this claim, it would only prove the AIT in the eyes of those who are already conditioned by the AIT perspective. After all, a northwestern influx into India in the second millennium, while not in conflict with the AIT, is not in conflict with the OIT either: the latter posits a northwestern emigration in perhaps the fifth millennium BC, and has no problem with occasional northwestern invasions in later centuries, such as those of the Shakas, Hunas, and Turks in the historic period.

Likewise, linguistic evidence cited in favor of the AIT often turns out to be quite compatible with the OIT scenario as well (as we shall see), but is never studied in that light because so few people in the twentieth century even thought of that possibility. And today, even those who are aware of the OIT haven't thought it through sufficiently to notice how known data may verify it.

7.2.4 The horse, argument from silence

In a recent paper, Hans Hock gives the two arguments which had, all through the 1990s, kept me from giving my unqualified support to the OIT. These are the dialectal distribution of the branches of the IE language family, to be discussed later, and the sparse presence of horses in Harappan culture. About the horse, he summarizes the problem very well:

> no archaeological evidence from Harappan India has been presented that would indicate anything comparable to the cultural and religious significance of the horse (. . .) which can be observed in the traditions of the early IE peoples, including the Vedic Aryas. On balance, then, the "equine" evidence at this point is more compatible with migration into India than with outward migration.
>
> (Hock 1999: 13)

B. B. Lal (1998: 111) mentions finds of true horse in Surkotada, Rupnagar, Kalibangan, Lothal, Mohenjo-Daro, and terracotta images of the horse from

Mohenjo-Daro and Nausharo. Many bones of the related onager or half-ass have also been found, and one should not discount the possibility that in some contexts, the term *ashva* could refer to either species. Nevertheless, all this is still a bit meager to fulfill the expectation of a prominent place for the horse in an "Aryan" culture. I agree with the OIT school that such paucity of horse testimony may be explainable (cfr. the absence of camel and cow depictions, animals well-known to the Harappans, in contrast with the popularity of the bull motif, though cows must abound when bulls are around), but their case would be better served by more positive evidence.

On the other hand, the evidence is not absolutely damaging to an Aryan–Harappa hypothesis. Both outcomes remain possible because other, reputedly Aryan sites are likewise poor in horses. This is the case with the Bactria-Margiana Archaeological Complex (BMAC), surprisingly for those who interpret the BMAC as the culture of the Indo-Aryans poised to invade India (Sergent 1997: 161ff.). It is also the case for Hastinapura, a city dated by archaeologists at *c.* eighth century BC, when that part of India was very definitely Aryan (Thapar 1996: 21). So, the argument from near-silence regarding horse bones need not prove absence of Aryans nor be fatal to the OIT, though it remains a weak point in the OIT argumentation.

7.2.5 Evidence sweeping all before it

When evidence from archaeology and Sanskrit text studies seems to contradict the AIT, we are usually reassured that "there is of course the linguistic evidence" for this invasion, or at least for the non-Indian origin of the IE family. Thus, F. E. Pargiter (1962: 302) had shown how the *Puranas* locate Aryan origins in the Ganga basin and found "the earliest connexion of the Vedas to be with the eastern region and not with the Panjab," but then he allowed the unnamed linguistic evidence to overrule his own findings (1962: 1): "We know from the evidence of language that the Aryans entered India very early." His solution is to relocate the point of entry of the Aryans from the western Khyber pass to the eastern Himalaya: Kathmandu or thereabouts.

A common reaction among Indians against this state of affairs is to dismiss linguistics altogether, calling it a "pseudo-science." Thus, N. S. Rajaram describes nineteenth-century comparative and historical linguistics, which generated the AIT, as "a scholarly discipline that had none of the checks and balances of a real science" (1995: 144), in which "a conjecture is turned into a hypothesis to be later treated as a fact in support of a new theory" (1995: 217).

Along the same lines, N. R. Waradpande (1989: 19–21) questions the very existence of an Indo-European language family and rejects the genetic kinship model, arguing very briefly that similarities between Greek and Sanskrit must be due to very early borrowing. He argues that "the linguists have not been able to establish that the similarities in the Aryan or Indo-European languages are genetic, i.e. due to their having a common ancestry." Conversely, he also (1993: 14–15) rejects the separation of Indo-Aryan and Dravidian into distinct language families, and alleges that "the view that the South-Indian languages have an origin different from that of the North-Indian languages is based on irresponsible, ignorant and motivated utterances of a missionary" (meaning the nineteenth-century pioneer of Dravidology, Bishop Robert Caldwell).

This rejection of linguistics by critics of the AIT creates the impression that their own pet theory is not resistant to the test of linguistics. Indeed, nothing has damaged their credibility as much as this sweeping dismissal of a science praised in the following terms by archaeologist David W. Anthony:

> It is true that we can only work with relatively late IE daughter languages, that we cannot hope to capture the full variability of PIE, and that reconstructed semantic fields are more reliable than single terms. It is also true that both the reconstructed terms and their meanings are theories derived from systematic correspondences observed among the daughter IE languages; no PIE term is known with absolute certainty. Nevertheless, the rules that guide phonetic (and to a lesser extent, semantic) reconstruction are more rigorous, have been more intensely tested, and rest upon a more secure theoretical foundation than most of the rules that guide interpretation in my own field of prehistoric archaeology. Well-documented linguistic reconstructions of PIE are in many cases more reliable than well-documented archaeological interpretations of Copper Age material remains.
>
> (1991: 201–2)

However, the fact that people fail to address the linguistic evidence, preferring simply to excommunicate it from the debate, does not by itself validate the prevalent interpretation of this body of evidence. Rajaram's remark that scholars often treat mere hypotheses (esp. those proposed by famous colleagues) as facts, as solid data capable of overruling other hypotheses and even inconvenient new data, is definitely valid for much of the humanities.

But then, while some linguists have sometimes fallen short of the scientific standard by thus relying on authority, it doesn't follow that linguistics is a pseudo-science. Nobody can observe the Proto-Indo-Europeans live to verify hypotheses, yet comparative IE linguistics does sometimes satisfy the requirement of having predictions implicit in the theory verified by empirical discoveries. Thus, some word forms reconstructed as the etyma of terms in the Romance languages failed to show up in the classical Latin vocabulary, but were finally discovered in the vulgar-Latin graffiti of Pompeii. The most impressive example of this kind is probably the identification of laryngeals, whose existence had been predicted *in abstracto* decades earlier by Ferdinand de Saussure, in newly discovered texts in the Hittite language. We will get to see an important sequel to the laryngeal verification later.

At the same time, some linguists are aware that the AIT is just a successful theory, not a proven fact. One of them told me that he had never bothered about a linguistic justification for the AIT framework, because there was, after all, "the well-known archaeological evidence"! But for the rest, "the linguistic evidence" is still the magic mantra to silence all doubts about the AIT. It is time that we take a look at it for ourselves.

7.3 The Indo-European landscape

7.3.1 Intuitive deductions from geography

There is, *pace* Misra 1992, absolutely no reason to doubt the established refutation of the Indian (and turn-of-the-nineteenth-century European) belief that Sanskrit is the mother of all IE languages, though Sanskrit remains in many respects closest to PIE, as a standard textbook of IE testifies:

"The distribution [of the two stems *as/s* for 'to be'] in Sanskrit is the oldest one" (Beekes 1990: 37); "PIE had 8 cases, which Sanskrit still has" (Beekes 1990: 122); "PIE had no definite article. That is also true for Sanskrit and Latin, and still for Russian. Other languages developed one" (Beekes 1990: 125); "[For the declensions] we ought to reconstruct the Proto-Indo-Iranian first, . . . But we will do with the Sanskrit because we know that it has preserved the essential information of the Proto-Indo-Iranian" (Beekes 1990: 148); "While the accentuation systems of the other languages indicate a total rupture, Sanskrit, and to a lesser extent Greek, seem to continue the original IE situation" (Beekes 1990: 187); "The root aorist . . . is still frequent in Indo-Iranian, appears sporadically in Greek and Armenian, and has disappeared elsewhere" (Beekes 1990: 279).

All the same, Sanskrit has moved away from PIE and the path can be mapped. Thus, you can explain Skt *jagâma* from PIE **gegoma* as a palatalization of the initial velar (before *e/i*) followed by the conflation of *a/e/o* to *a*, but the reverse is not indicated and is close to impossible: palatalization is a one-way process, attested in numerous languages on all continents (including English, e.g. *wicca* > *witch*), while the opposite shift is practically unknown. The Kentum forms and the forms with differentiated vowels as attested in Greek represent the original situation, while the Sanskrit forms represent an innovation. This means that Sanskrit is not PIE, that it has considerably evolved after separating from the ancestor-languages of the other branches of IE.

However, accepting the conventional genealogical tree of the IE languages does not imply acceptance of their conventional geography. When Sanskrit was dethroned in the nineteenth century and the putative linguistic distance between PIE and Sanskrit progressively increased, there was a parallel movement of the PIE homeland away from India. Apart from linguistic considerations (chiefly linguistic paleontology) and the political background (increased Eurocentrism at the height of the colonial period), this was certainly also due to a more or less conscious tendency to equate linguistic distance from PIE with geographical distance from the *Urheimat*. That tendency has persisted here and there all through the twentieth century, for example, Witold Manczak (1992) deduces that the Urheimat must be in or near Poland from his estimate that lexically, Polish is closest to PIE in that it is the IE language with the fewest substratal borrowings.

Obviously, that type of reasoning must be abandoned. It is perfectly possible for the most conservative language to be spoken by a group of emigrants rather than by those who stayed behind in the homeland. Indeed, according to the so-called Lateral Theory, it is precisely in outlying settlement areas that the most conservative forms will be found, while in the metropolis the language evolves faster. That exactly is what the OIT posits regarding palatalization.

7.3.2 Kentum/Satem

The first innovation acknowledged as creating a distance between PIE and Sanskrit was the Kentum > Satem shift. It was assumed, in my view correctly (*pace* Misra 1992), that palatalization is a one-way process transforming velars (*k,g*) into palatals (*c,j*) but never the reverse; so that the velar or "Kentum" forms had to be the original and the palatal or "Satem" forms the evolved variants.

However, it would be erroneous to infer from this that the homeland was in the Kentum area. On the contrary, it is altogether more likely that it was in what became Satem territory, for example, as follows: India originally had the Kentum form, the dialects which emigrated first retained the Kentum form and took it to the geographical borderlands of the IE expanse (Europe, Anatolia, western China), while the last-emigrated dialects (Armenian, Iranian) plus the staybehind Indo-Aryan languages had meanwhile adopted the Satem form.

Moreover, the discovery of a small and extinct Kentum language inside India (Proto-Bangani, with *koto* as its word for 'hundred'), surviving as a sizable substratum in the Himalayan language Bangani, tends to support the hypothesis that the older Kentum form was originally present in India as well. This discovery was made by the German linguist Claus Peter Zoller (1987, 1988, 1989). The attempt by George van Driem and Suhnu R. Sharma (1996) to discredit Zoller has been overruled by the findings made on the spot by Anvita Abbi (1997) and her students. She has almost entirely confirmed Zoller's list of Kentum substratum words in Bangani. But as the trite phrase goes: this calls for more research.

Zoller does not explain the presence of a Kentum language in India through an Indian Homeland Theory but as a left-over of a pre-Vedic Indo-European immigration into India. He claims that the local people have a tradition of their immigration from Afghanistan. If they really lived in Afghanistan originally, their case (and their nuisance value for the AIT) isn't too different from that of the Tocharians, another Kentum people showing up in unexpected quarters. But if even the Vedic poets could not recall the invasion of their grandfathers into India (Vedic literature doesn't mention it anywhere, vide Elst 1999: 164–71), what value should we attach to a tradition of this mountain tribe about its own immigration many centuries ago? Could it not rather be that they have interiorized what the school-going ones among them picked up in standard textbooks of history? Their presence in Afghanistan or in Garhwal itself is at any rate highly compatible with the OIT.

7.3.3 Indo-Hittite

Another element which increased the distance between reconstructed PIE and Sanskrit dramatically was the discovery of Hittite. Though Hittite displayed a very large intake of lexical and other elements from non-IE languages, some of its features were deemed to be older than their Sanskrit counterparts, for example, the Hittite *genus commune* as opposed to Sanskrit's contrast between masculine and feminine genders, or the much-discussed laryngeal consonants. Outside Hittite, some phonetic side effects are the only trace of these supposed laryngeals, for example, Greek *odont-*, 'tooth', shows trace of an initial H-, which Latin lost to yield *dent-*. Greek *anêr*, 'man', would come from **Hnr*, whereas Sanskrit has *nr/nara*, only preserving the laryngeal in the form of vowel-lengthening in a prefix, as in *sû-nara* from *su + *Hnara*. In meter, we find traces of an original laryngeal consonant marking a second syllable which was later contracted with the preceding syllable: "In Indo-Iranian such forms are often still disyllabic in the oldest poetry: *bhâs*, 'light', = */bhaas/ < /bheH-os/*" (Beekes 1990: 180). This fact has gone unnoticed in all pro-OIT writing so far. The laryngeal came in three varieties, and these later yielded the three vowels *a/e/o*, which in the Greek alphabet happen to be derived from the three more or less laryngeal consonants in Northwest-Semitic: *aleph*, *he*, and *ayn*.

The laryngeal theory has been attacked by both OIT and mainstream circles. Misra (1992: 21) claims to have "refuted" it, Décsy (1991: 17) calls it "the infamous laryngeal theory." When scholars claim proof of the laryngeals in Caucasian loanwords from IE, Décsy (1991: 14, w. ref. to Wagner 1984) counters that it is the other way around: "Hittite lost its Indo-European character and acquired a large number of Caucasian areal features in Anatolia. These Caucasian-type features can not be regarded as ancient characteristics of the entire PIE." Likewise Jonsson (1978: 86), though accepting that the laryngeals may offer a "more elegant explanation of certain cases of hiatus in Vedic, of certain suffixal *î*'s, *û*'s," presents as "an acceptable alternative" the scenario that the laryngeal in IE-inherited Anatolian words "comes from the unknown non-IE language or languages that are responsible for the major part of the [Anatolian] vocabulary."

But we need no dissident hypotheses here: even in the dominant theory, there is no reason why the Urheimat should be in the historical location of Hittite or at least outside India. As the first emigrant dialect, Hittite could have taken from India some linguistic features (*genus commune*, laryngeals) which were about to disappear in the dialects emigrating only later or staying behind.

As for the shift from *genus commune* to a differentiation of the "animate" category in masculine and feminine, this has been used to illustrate a theory of fast-increasing complexity of post-PIE grammar, which Zimmer (1990b) interprets as a typical phenomenon of Creole languages. He sees early IE as the language of a *colluvies gentium*, a synthetic tribe of people from divergent ethnic backgrounds, which developed its makeshift link language into a complex language, with

Hittite splitting off in an early stage of this evolution. This is an interesting hypothesis, but so far the evidence for it is lacking. Thus, there is no proof that the simpler verbal tense system of Germanic and Hittite came first while the more elaborate tense system of Aryan or Greek was a later evolution; more likely, the aorist which exists in the latter two but not in the former two is a PIE tense which some retained and some lost. The theories that PIE grammar was Hittite-like simple and that PIE was a Creole developed by a *colluvies gentium* are mutually supportive, but there is no outside proof for either. And if there were, it would still not preclude northwestern India as the habitat of this *colluvies gentium*.

7.3.4 Dialect distribution

One consideration which has always kept me from simply declaring the AIT wrong concerns the geographical distribution of the branches of the IE family. This argument has been developed in some detail by Hans Hock, who explains that

> the early Indo-European languages exhibit linguistic alignments which cannot be captured by a tree diagram, but which require a dialectological approach that maps out a set of intersecting "isoglosses" which define areas with shared features (...) While there may be disagreements on some of the details, Indo-Europeanists agree that these relationships reflect a stage at which the different Indo-European languages were still just dialects of the ancestral language and as such interacted with each other in the same way as the dialects of modern languages.
>
> (1999: 13)

Isoglosses, linguistic changes which are common to several languages, indicate either that the change was imparted by one language to its sisters, or that the languages have jointly inherited or adopted it from a common source. Within the IE family, we find isoglosses in languages which take or took geographically neighboring positions, for example, in a straight Greece-to-India belt, the Greek, Armenian, Iranian, and some Dardic and western Indo-Aryan languages, we see the shift *s* > *h*, for example, Latin *septem* corresponding to Greek *hepta*, Iranian *hafta*. In the same group, plus the remaining Indo-Aryan languages, we see the "preterital augment": Greek *e-phere*, Sanskrit *a-bharat*, 'he/she/it carried'. Does this mean that the said languages formed a single branch for some time after the disintegration of PIE unity, before fragmenting into the presently distinct languages?

Not necessarily, for this group is itself divided by separate developments which the member languages have in common with nonmember languages. Best known is the Kentum/Satem divide: Greek belongs to the Kentum group, while Armenian and Indo-Iranian share with Baltic and Slavic the Satem isogloss (as well as the related '*ruki* rule', changing *s* to *sh* after *r, u, k, i*). So, like between the dialects of any modern language, the IE languages share one isogloss with this neighbor, another isogloss with another neighbor, which in turn shares isoglosses with yet other neighbors.

The key factor in Hock's argument seems to be *neighbor*: the remarkable phenomenon which should ultimately support the AIT is that *isoglosses are shared by neighboring branches of IE*. Thus, the Kentum languages form a continuous belt from Anatolia through southern to western and northern Europe (with serious exceptions, namely, Tocharian and proto-Bangani), and the Satem isogloss likewise covers a continuous territory, only later fragmented by the intrusion of Turkic, from central Europe to India. Hock provides (1999: 15) a map showing ten isoglosses in their distribution over the geographically placed IE language groups, and we do note the geographical contiguity of languages sharing an isogloss.

Why is this important?

> What is interesting, and significant for present purposes, is the close correspondence between the dialectological arrangement in Figure 2 (based on the evidence of shared innovations) and the actual geographical arrangement of the Indo-European languages in their earliest attested stages. (...) the relative positions of the dialects can be mapped straightforwardly into the actual geographical arrangement if (...) the relative positions were generally maintained as the languages fanned out over larger territory.
>
> (Ibid.: 16)

In other words: the geographical distribution of IE languages which actually exists happens to be the one which would, at the stage when the proto-languages were dialects of PIE, be best able to produce the actual distribution of isoglosses over the languages.

So, the relative location of the ancestor-languages in the PIE homeland was about the same as their location at the dawn of history. This, Hock proposes, is best compatible with a non-Indian homeland. And indeed, if the homeland was in the Pontic region, the dialect communities could spread out radially, with the northwestern proto-Germanic tribe moving further northwest through what is now Poland, the western proto-Celtic tribe moving further west, the southwestern proto-Greek and proto-Albanian tribes moving further southwest through the Balkans, the southeastern proto-Indo-Iranians moving southeast, etc. (One reason given by the early Indo-Europeanists for assuming such radial expansion is that they found little inter-borrowing between IE language groups, indicating little mutual contact, this in spite of plenty of Iranian loans found in Slavic, some Celtic loans in Germanic, etc.) This way, while the distances grew bigger, the relative location of the daughters of PIE *vis-à-vis* one another remained the same.

If this is a bit too neat to match the usual twists and turns of history, it is at least more likely than an Indocentric variant of Hock's scenario would be:

> To be able to account for these dialectological relationships, the "Out-of-India" approach would have to assume, first, that these relationships reflect a stage of dialectal diversity in a Proto-Indo-European ancestor

> language located *within India*. While this assumption is not in itself improbable, it has consequences which, to put it mildly, border on the improbable and certainly would violate basic principles of simplicity. What would have to be assumed is that the various Indo-European languages moved out of India in such a manner that they maintained their relative position to each other during and after the migration. However, given the bottle-neck nature of the route(s) out of India, it would be immensely difficult to do so.
>
> (Ibid.: 16–17, emphasis Hock's)

I believe there is a plausible and entirely logical alternative. The geographical distribution of PIE dialects in the PIE homeland is unrelated to the location of their daughter languages; the isoglosses are the result of a twofold scenario, part areal effect and part genealogical tree, as follows. In part, they reflect successive migrations from the heartland where new linguistic trends developed and affected only the dialects staying behind. Gamkrelidze and Ivanov (1995: 348–50) have built an impressive reconstruction of such successive migrations on an impressive survey of the linguistic material. To summarize:

1. Initially, there was a single PIE language.
2. The first division of PIE yielded two dialect groups, which will be called A and B. Originally they co-existed in the same area, and influenced each other, but geographical separation put an end to this interaction.
3. In zone A, one dialect split off, probably by geographical separation (whether it was its own speakers or those of the other dialects who emigrated from the Urheimat, is not yet at issue), and went on to develop separately and become Anatolian.
4. The remainder of the A group acquired the distinctive characteristics of the Tocharo-Italo-Celtic subgroup.
5. While the A remainder differentiated into Italo-Celtic and Tokharic, the B group differentiated into a "northern" or Balto-Slavic-Germanic and a "southern" or Greek-Armenian-Aryan group; note that the Kentum/Satem divide only affects the B group, and does not come in the way of other and more important isoglosses distinguishing the northern group (with Kentum Germanic and predominantly Satem Baltic and Slavic) from the southern group (with Kentum Greek and Satem Armenian and Aryan).

The second part is that the isoglosses not explainable by the former scenario are post-PIE areal effects, which is why they affect historically neighboring languages, regardless of whether these had been neighbors when they were dialects of PIE. Archaeologists (mostly assuming a North-Caspian homeland) have said that the North-Central-European Corded Ware culture of *c.*3000 BC was a kind of secondary homeland from which the western branches of PIE spread, again more or less radially, to their respective historical locations; the OIT would allot that role of secondary western-IE homeland to the Kurgan culture. In such a secondary homeland, IE-speaking communities would, before their further dispersal, be close enough to allow for the transmission of lexical innovations or common substratal borrowings (e.g. *beech*, cfr. Latin *fagus*; or *fish*, cfr. Latin *piscis*, unattested in eastern IE languages). Communities in truly close interaction, at whichever stage of the development of IE, would also develop grammatical isoglosses.

Hock (1999: 14) himself unwittingly gives at least one example which doesn't easily admit of a different explanation: "The same group of dialects [Germanic, Baltic, Slavic] also has merged the genitive and ablative cases into a single 'genitive' case. But within the group, Germanic and Old Prussian agree on generalizing the old genitive form (...) while Lithu-Latvian and Slavic favor the old ablative."

But clearly, Old Prussian and Lithu-Latvian lived in close proximity and separate from Germanic and Slavic for centuries, as dialects of proto-Baltic, else they wouldn't have jointly developed into the Baltic group, distinct in many lexical and grammatical features from its neighbors. So, if the Baltic language bordering on the Germanic territory happens to share the Germanic form, while the languages bordering on Slavic happen to share the Slavic form, we are clearly faced with a recent areal effect and not a heirloom from PIE days. The conflation of cases has continued to take place in many IE languages in the historical period, so the example under consideration may well date to long after the fragmentation of PIE.

A second example mentioned by Hock may be the split within the Anatolian group, with Luwian retaining a distinction between velar and palatal but Hittite merging the two, just like its Greek neighbor. Positing an areal influence at the stage of PIE dialectal differentiation on top of an obviously existing areal influence in the post-PIE period seems, in this context, like a "multiplication of entities beyond necessity": neighboring languages need not also have been neighbors at the dialectal PIE stage in order to transmit innovations, because their present or recent neighborliness already allows for such transmissions.

As far as I can see from Hock's presentation, the twofold scenario outlined earlier is compatible with all the linguistic developments mentioned by him. For now, I must confess that after reading Hock's presentation, the linguistic problem which I have always considered the most damaging to an Indo-centric hypothesis, doesn't look all that threatening anymore. The isoglosses discussed by him do not necessitate the near-identity of the directional distribution pattern of the PIE dialects with that of their present-day daughter languages, which would indeed be hard to reconcile with an out-of-India hypothesis. But I cannot as yet exclude that Hock's line of argument could be sharpened, namely, by proving that certain isoglosses *must* date back to PIE times, making it tougher to reconcile the distribution of isoglosses with an Indian homeland hypothesis.

7.3.5 Distribution of large and small territories

Another aspect of geographical distribution is the allocation of larger and smaller stretches of territory to the different branches of the IE family. We find the Iranian (covering the whole of Central Asia before AD 1000) and Indo-Aryan branches each covering a territory as large as all the European branches (at least in the pre-colonial era) combined. We also find the Indo-Aryan branch by itself having, from antiquity till today, more speakers on the Eurasian continent (now nearing 900 million) than all other branches combined. This state of affairs could help us to see the Indo-Aryan branch as the center and the other branches as wayward satellites; but so far, philologists have made exactly the opposite inference.

It is said that this is the typical contrast between a homeland and its colony: a fragmented homeland where languages have small territories, and a large but linguistically more homogeneous colony. Thus, English, shares its little home island with some Celtic languages, but has much larger stretches of land in North America and Australia all to itself, and with less dialect variation than in Britain. By that criterion, it may be remarked at once, the Pontic region too would soon be dismissed as an IE homeland candidate, for it has been homogeneously Slavic for centuries, though it was more diverse in the Greco-Roman period.

It is also argued that Indo-Aryan must be a late-comer to India, for otherwise it would have been divided by now in several subfamilies as distinct from each other as, say, Celtic from Slavic.

To this last point, we must remark first of all that the linguistic unity of Indo-Aryan should not be exaggerated. The difference between Bengali and Sindhi may well be bigger than that between, say, any two of the Romance languages, especially if you consider their colloquial rather than their high-brow (sanskritized) register. Further, to the extent that Indo-Aryan has preserved its unity, this may be attributed to the following factors, which have played to a larger extent and for longer periods in India than in Europe: a geographical unity from Sindh to Bengal (a continuous riverine plain) facilitating interaction between the regions, unlike the much more fragmented geography of Europe; long-time inclusion in common political units (e.g. Maurya, Gupta, and Moghul empires); and continuous inclusion in a common cultural space with the common stabilizing influence of Sanskrit.

As for the high fragmentation of IE in Europe when compared to its relative homogeneity in North India: from the viewpoint of an Indian homeland hypothesis, the most important factor explaining it is the way in which an emigration from India to Europe must have taken place. Tribes left India and mixed with the non-IE-speaking tribes of their respective corners of Central Asia and Europe. This happens to be the fastest way of making two dialects of a single language grow apart and develop distinctive new characteristics: make them mingle with different foreign languages.

Thus, in the Romance family, we find little difference between Catalan, Occitan, and Italian, three languages which have organically grown without much outside influence except for a short period of Germanic influence which was common to them; by contrast, Spanish and Rumanian have grown far apart (lexically, phonetically, and grammatically), and this is largely due to the fact that the former has been influenced by Germanic and Arabic, while the latter was influenced by Greek and Slavic. Similarly, under the impact of languages they encountered (now mostly extinct and beyond the reach of our searchlight), and whose speakers they took over, the dialects of the IE emigrants from India differentiated much faster from each other than the dialects of Indo-Aryan.

To be sure, expanding Indo-Aryan communities have likewise merged with communities speaking now-extinct non-IE languages, but they remained continually in touch with neighboring speakers of "pure" Indo-Aryan, so that they maintained the original standards of their language better. It is widely assumed that the Bhil tribals of Gujarat and Madhya Pradesh originally spoke a non-IE language, probably Nahali, yet: "No group of Bhils speak any but an Aryan tongue. (...) it is unlikely that traces of a common non-Aryan substratum will ever be uncovered in present-day Bhili dialects" (von Fürer-Haimendorf 1956: x, quoted in Kuiper 1962: 50). One can still witness this process today: when tribals in Eastern and Central India switch over to Hindi, they retain at most only a handful of words from their Austro-Asiatic or Dravidian mothertongues, because the influence of standard Hindi is continually impressed upon them by the numerous native Hindi speakers surrounding them and by the media.

By contrast, upon arrival on the North-European coasts, the speakers of proto-Germanic merged completely with the at least equally numerous natives. Having covered greater distances and in smaller numbers than the gradually expanding Indo-Aryan agriculturalists in India, they lost touch with the language standards of their fathers because they were not surrounded by a compact and numerically overwhelming environment of fellow IE-speakers. This allowed a far deeper impact of the native language upon their own, differentiating it decisively from IE languages not influenced by the same substratum.

7.3.6 Go west

A seemingly common-sense objection to an Indian homeland is that it implies an IE expansion almost entirely in one direction: east to west, with the homeland lying in the far corner of the ultimate IE settlement area rather than in the center. Isn't this odd?

Well, no: it is the rule rather than the exception. Chinese spread from the Yellow River basin southward, first assimilating Central and then South China. Arabic spread from Arabia a little northward and mostly westward. The circumstances in north and south, or in east and west, are usually very different, making the prospects of expansion very attractive on one side but much less promising on the other. Spanish and English could expand westward, in the Americas, because of their steep technological-military edge over the natives; this did not apply in the equation of forces to their east, in Europe.

Assuming the OIT with Panjab–Haryana as the center, we can safely surmise that a similar number of migrants went southeast and northwest, yet their destinies were quite different. The first didn't have far to go: they colonized the rain forests of India's interior, where soil and climate allowed for the settlement of large populations on a relatively small surface. It was always easier to chop down another stretch of forest and expand locally than to leave the material security of interior India for a dangerous and probably pointless mountain trek into China or a sea voyage to Indonesia. By contrast, the second group going to Central Asia found itself challenged by more uncomfortable conditions: a variable climate, large stretches of relatively useless land, a crossroads location with hostile nomads or migrating populations passing through. They had to cross far larger distances in order to settle comfortably, mixing with many more people along the way, thus losing their physical Indianness and linguistically growing away from PIE fast and in different directions.

As an economic and demographic outpost of India, Bactria was, along with Sogdia, a launching-pad for the most ambitious migration in premodern history; the first Amerindians and Austronesians covered even larger distances but settled empty lands, while the Indo-Europeans assimiliated large populations in a whole continent. This followed (or rather, set) a pattern: recall how the Mongols conquered this region, then proceeded to conquer the western half of Asia and Eastern Europe; in the preceding centuries, the Turks; before that, the Iranians or (*pars pro toto*) Scythians; and first of all, the Indo-Europeans undertook similar expansions. Nichols 1997 (see later) adds Kartvelian to this list, as one case of a language spread westward through the Central-Asian "spread zone" but entirely losing its foothold there, only to survive in a South-Causasian backwater; and points to the parallel westward movement of the Finno-Ugrians from Siberia to Northeastern Europe. Until the eastward expansion of Russia, Central Asia was subject to an over-arching dynamic of east-to-west migration. This may have started as early as the end of the Ice Age, when a depopulated Europe became hospitable again, and lasted until the reversal of the demographic equation, when European population pressures forced an eastward expansion.

7.4 Loans and substratum features

7.4.1 How to decide on the foreign origin of a word?

One widely accepted criterion for deciding whether a word attested in ancient Sanskrit is IE or not, is the presence of sound combinations which do not follow the standard pattern. It is argued that a word in a given language cannot take just any shape, for example, a true English word cannot start with *shl-, shm-, sht-*. Consequently, when a word does contain such irregular sounds, it must be of foreign origin, that is, German or Yiddish, such as in loans like *schnitzel, schmuck, schlemiel*. Likewise, a Sanskrit word cannot contain certain sound combinations, which would mark it as a foreign loan.

However, there are problems with this rule. First, and invasionists should welcome this one, if a sound is too strange, chances are that people will "domesticate" it into something more manageable. This will result in a loan which differs in pronunciation from its original form, but which is no longer recognizable as a loan by the present criterion. Thus, in Sino-English, a boss or upper-class person is called a *taiban*, Chinese for "big boss"; there is nothing decisively un-English about this string of consonants and vowels. The one feature of this Chinese word which could have marked it as un-English, is its tones (*tai* fourth tone, *ban* third tone), – but precisely that typically foreign feature has been eliminated from the English usage of the word. The same is true in Japanese, which has adopted hundreds of Chinese words after stripping them of tones and other distinctively Chinese phonetic characteristics. Likewise, Arabic has a number of sounds and phonemic distinctions unknown in European languages, which are systematically eliminated in the Arabic loans in these languages, for example, *tariff* from *ta'rîfa* with laryngeal *'ayn*, or *cheque* from *Sakk* with emphatic *Sâd*.

Another point is: how do you decide what the standard shape of a word in a given language should be? Witzel (1999a: 364) calls *bekanâṭa* "certainly a non-IA name" citing as reason the retroflex *ṭ* and the initial *b*-. It may be conceded that the suffix *-ṭa* is common in seemingly non-IA ethnonyms (*kîkaṭa* etc.), but the phonetic exceptionalism, by contrast, cannot be accepted as a valid ground for excluding an IA etymology. The dental/retroflex distinction must initially have been merely allophonic, representing a single but phonetically unstable phoneme; and at any rate, numerous purely IE words have acquired the retroflex pronunciation, for example, *Saḍ*, 'six', or *aṣṭa*, 'eight'. While *b*- may be rare in Old IA, there is no good reason to exclude it altogether from the acceptable native sounds of the language. It is also attested in *bala*, 'strength', related to Greek *bel-tiôn*, 'better', and Latin *de-bil-is*, 'off-strength', 'weak', a connection which Kuiper (1991: 90) admits to be "attractive" though he would prefer to "accept the absence of /b/ in the PIE consonant system," it being otherwise only attested in the Celtic-Germanic-Slavic (hence probably Euro-substratal) root **kob*, 'to fall'.

What threatens to happen here, is that the minority gets elbowed out by the majority, such that the majoritarian forms are imposed as the normative and only permissible forms. Compare with the argument by Alexander Lehrmann (1997: 151) about accepting or excluding the rare sequence "e + consonant" as a possibly legitimate root in Hittite: "There is absolutely no reason why a lexical root of Proto-Indo-European (or Proto-Indo-Hittite) cannot have the shape *eC-, except *the wilful imposition by the researching scholar of the inferred structure of a majority of lexical roots on a minority of them*" (emphasis mine). The same openness to exceptions to the statistical rule is verifiable in other languages, for example, Chinese family names are, as a rule, monosyllabic (the *Mao* in Mao Zedong), yet two-syllable names have also existed, though now fallen in disuse (the *Sima* in Sima Qian). As a rule, Semitic verbal roots have a "skeleton" of three consonants, yet a few with two or four consonants also exist. Admittedly, both examples also illustrate a tendency of the exception to disappear in favor of (or to conform itself to) the majoritarian form; but their very existence still provides an analogy for the existence of atypical minoritarian forms in IE.

Another point is that there may be a covert *petitio principii* at work here. Many assertions on what can or cannot be done in Indo-Aryan are based on the assumption that Vedic Sanskrit is more or less the mother of the whole IA group, it being the language of the entry point whence the Aryan tribes populated a large part of India. In an OIT scenario (e.g. Talageri 1993: 145) of ancient Indian history, Sanskrit need not be the mother of IA at all, there being IA dialects developing alongside Vedic Sanskrit. Just as Vedic religion was but one among several Indo-Aryan religious traditions, the traces of which are found in the *Puranas* and *Tantras*, Vedic Sanskrit is but one among a number of OIA dialects. The eastward expansion of Vedic culture attested in the *Atharva Veda*, *Shatapatha Brâhmana* etc. may have vedicized regions which were already IA-speaking though religiously non-Vedic.

Thus, the *sh/ṣ* > *s* shift in eastern Hindi and Bengali, for example, *subhâṣa* > *subhâs*, *ghoṣa* > *ghos*, may be due to substratum influence (cfr. the case of Kosala in Section 7.4.2), but then again, what is more ordinary than this inter-sibilant shift in dialectal variation? Remember Semitic *salâm/shalom*, or the Biblical test of pronouncing *sibboleth/shibboleth*. This could be a substratum influence, but it could also simply be a spontaneous variation in a non-Vedic dialect of IA. More generally, one should not jump to conclusions of foreign origins without a positive indication. Mere oddities may come into being without adstratal or substratal influence (cfr. French phonetic oddities like nasalization or uvular *[r]*); they are not proof enough that IA was an intruding language replacing a native one.

7.4.2 ***River names in Panjab***

If a word looks Sanskritic, it may still be of foreign origin, but thoroughly assimilated. With historical languages, the assimilation into Sanskrit sound patterns is well-attested, for example, Greek *dekanos* becoming *drekkâṇa*, Altaic *turuk* becoming *turuṣka*, Arabic *sultan* becoming *suratrâṇa*, etc. Sometimes this phonetic adaptation gives rise to folk-etymological reinterpretation, often with hypercorrect modification of the word, for example, the *râṇa*, 'king', in *suratrâṇa*. Such adaptation can also take place even without etymological interpretation, just for reasons of "sounding right." Thus, it is often said (e.g. Witzel 1999a: 358) that *yavana*, vaguely "West-Asian," is a hypersanskritic back-formation on *yona*, Ionia, that is, the name of the Asian part of Greece. This principle underlies the Sanskrit look of many foreign loans in Sanskrit.

Witzel uses this phenomenon to explain the Sanskrit looks of no less than thirty-five North-Indian river names: "Even a brief look at this list indicates that in northern India, by and large, only Sanskritic river names seem to survive" (1999a: 370). He quotes Pinnow 1953 as observing that over 90 percent don't just look IA but "are etymologically clear and generally have a meaning" in IA. He attributes this unexpectedly large etymological transparency to "the ever-increasing process of changing older names by popular etymology." This hypothesis of a very thorough assimilation of foreign names with pseudo-etymology is a possibility but quite unsubstantiated, a complicated explanation satisfying AIT presumptions but not Occam's razor. It has no counterpart in any other region of

IE settlement, for example, in Belgium most river names are Celtic or pre-Celtic and make no sense at all in Dutch or French; yet in their present forms no attempt is in evidence of semantically romanizing or germanicizing them. In the USA, there are plainly native river names like Potomac, and plainly European ones like Hudson, but no anglicized native names. So, most likely, the Sanskrit-looking river names are simply Sanskrit.

This may be contrasted with the situation farther east in the Ganga plain, where we do find many Sanskrit-sounding names of rivers and regions which however do not have a transparent etymology, for example, *kaushikî* or *koshala*, apparently linked to Tibeto-Birmese *kosi*, 'water', and the name of the river separating *Koshala* from *Videha*. In that case, we also see the ongoing sanskritization: *kaushikî* evolved from *kosikî* (attested in Pali), and *koshala* from *kosala*, which Witzel (1999a: 382) considers as necessarily foreign loans because the sequence *-os-* is "not allowed in Sanskrit." But while the phonetic assimilation can be caught in the act, we can see no semantic domestication through folk etymology at work. The name *koshala* doesn't mean anything in Sanskrit, and that is a decisive difference with the western hydronyms *gomatî*, 'the cow-rich one', or *asiknî*, 'the dark one'. While the occurrence of *some* folk-etymological adaptation among the Panjabi river names can in principle be conceded, it is highly unlikely to be the explanation of all thirty-five names. Until proof to the contrary, the evidence of the Northwest-Indian hydronyms goes in favor of the absence of a non-IE substratum, hence of the OIT.

7.4.3 Exit Dravidian Harappa

The European branches of IE are all full of substratum elements, mostly from extinct Old European languages. For Germanic, this includes some 30 percent of the acknowledged "Germanic" vocabulary, including such core lexical items as *sheep* and *drink*; for Greek, it amounts to some 40 percent of the vocabulary. In both cases, extinct branches of the IE family may have played a role along with non-IE languages (vide Jones-Bley and Huld 1996: 109–80 for the Germanic case). The branch least affected by foreign elements is Slavic, but this need not be taken as proof of a South-Russian homeland: in an Indian Urheimat scenario, the way for Slavic would have been cleared by other IE forerunners, and though these languages would absorb many Old European elements as substratum features, they also eliminated the Old European languages as such and prevented them from further influencing Slavic.

Even if we accept as non-IE all the elements in Sanskrit described as such by various scholars, the non-IE contribution is still smaller than in some of the European branches of IE, which bear the undeniable marks of "Aryan" invasions followed by linguistic assimilation of large native populations. Among the highest estimates is the 5–9 percent of loans in Vedic Sanskrit proposed by Kuiper 1991: 90–3, in his list of 383 "foreign words in the Rigvedic language." A number of these words are certainly misplaced: some have no counterpart in Dravidian or

Munda, or when they do, there is often no reason to assume that the direction of borrowing was into rather than out of Indo-Aryan.

To take up one example, the name *agastya* is a normal Sanskritic derivative of the tree name *agasti*, "Agasti grandiflora" (Kuiper 1991: 7 sees the derivation as a case of totemism). This word is proposed to be a loanword, related to Tamil *akatti, acci*, as if the invaders borrowed the name from Dravidian natives. That non-Indian branches of IE do not have this word, says nothing about its possible IE origins: they didn't need a word for a tree that only exists in India, so they may have lost it after emigrating. It is perfectly possible that the Tamil word was derived from Sanskrit *agasti*, and by looking harder we just might discern an IE etymon for it, for example, Pirart (1998: 542) links *agastya* with Iranian *gasta*, "foul-smelling, sin."

But let us accept that some 300 words in Kuiper's list are indeed of non-IE origin. Even then, the old tendency to impute Dravidian origins to IA words of unclear etymology must be abandoned because the underlying assumption of a Dravidian-speaking Harappan civilization has failed to get substantiated. Likewise, the relative convergence of Indo-Aryan and Dravidian (as well as Munda and to an extent Burushaski) in phonetic, lexical, and grammatical features, forming a pan-Indian linguistic zone (vide e.g. Abbi 1994), is no longer explained as the substratal effect of an India-dominating Dravidian culture.

That the Dravidians are not native to their present habitat, had already been accepted: "Arguments in favour of the South Indian peninsula being the original home of the Dravidian language family, very popular with Tamil scholars at one time, cannot resist the weight of the evidence, both archaeological and linguistic" (Basham 1979: 2). Now, even Harappa is being lifted out of their claimed heritage. Bernard Sergent (1997: 129) and Michael Witzel (1999a: 385) are among the latest experts to bid goodbye to the popular assumption that Harappa was Dravidian-speaking. Indeed, the most important shift in scholarly opinion in recent years is the realization that, when all is said and done, there is really not a shred of evidence for the identification of the Harappans as Dravidian, even though several elaborate attempts at decipherment of the Indus "script" (Fairservis 1992; Parpola 1994) have been based on it.

Some of the arguments classically used against Vedic Harappa equally stand in the way of Dravidian Harappa, for example, like Vedic culture, the oldest glimpsable Dravidian culture was not urban: according to McAlpin (1979: 181–2), the Dravidians "were almost certainly transhumants practising both herding and agriculture, with herding the more unbroken tradition." Of course, in both cases, a chronological shift placing them in the pre-urban pre-Harappan period could solve this problem. More importantly, the Dravidian contribution to the Indo-Aryan languages is not such as one would expect if Indo-Aryan newcomers had incorporated a prestigious Dravidian-speaking city culture. Even linguists eager to discover Dravidian words in IA are surprised to find how small their harvest is: "Dravidian influence is less than has been expected by specialists" (Wojtilla 1986: 34).

Judging from the substratum of place-names, Dravidians once were located along the northwestern coast (Sindh, Gujarat, Maharashtra) in the southern reaches of the Harappan civilization. Parpola points out the presence of a Dravidian substratum, starting with the place-names:

> *palli*, 'village' (when *valli* and modern *-oli, -ol* in Gujarat), corresponding to South-Dravidian *paḷḷṙ*; and *pâṭa(ka)* or *pâṭi* (when *vâṭa, vâṭi*, etc., modern *-vâḍâ, vâḍ* etc. in Gujarat) as well as *paṭṭana* (Gujarati *paṭṭan*), all originally 'pastoral village' from the Dravidian root *paṭu*, 'to lie down to sleep'. In addition to place-names, other linguistic evidence suggests that Dravidian was formerly spoken in Maharashtra, Gujarat and, less evidently, Sind, all of which belonged to the Harappan realm. It includes Dravidian structural features in the local Indo-Aryan languages Marathi, Gujarati, and Sindhi, such as the distinction between two forms of the personal pronoun of the first person plural, indicating whether the speaker includes the addressee(s) in the concept "we" or not. Dravidian loanwords are conspicuously numerous in the lower-class dialects of Marathi.
>
> (1994: 170)

Add to this the cultural influence, for example, the Dravidian system of kinship (Witzel 1999a: 385).

So, that is how a Dravidian past perpetuates itself along the presently IA-speaking coastline, but it is conspicuous by its absence in Panjabi and Hindi. The latter has much fewer Dravidian elements than the link language Sanskrit, for example, the Dravidian loan *mîna*, 'fish', caught on in Sanskrit but never in Hindi. There is no reason to assume a Dravidian presence in North India at any time. The main part of the Harappan civilization was definitely not Dravidian if we may judge by the substratum evidence there, for example, the lack of Dravidian hydronyms. There are also no indications that South-Indian Dravidian culture is a continuation of Harappan culture.

The Dravidians may have entered Sindh through the Bolan Pass from Afghanistan (Samuel *et al.* 1990: 45), possibly as late as the third millennium BC (McAlpin 1979), though I am not aware of any firm proof against their indigenous origins. Vedic culture was established in the Panjab for quite some time before encountering Dravidian, considering that the oldest layers of Vedic literature do not contain loans from Dravidian: according to Witzel (1999b: section 1.1), "RV level 1 has no Dravidian loans at all." Dravidian loans appear only gradually in the next stages (i.e. when Indo-Aryan culture penetrates Dravidian territory) and are typically terms used in commercial exchanges, indicating adstratum rather than substratum influence. With that, Dravidian seems now to have been eliminated from the shortlist of pretenders to the status of Harappan high language.

7.4.4 Pre-IE substratum in Indo-Aryan: para-Munda

Unlike Dravidian, other languages seem to have exerted an influence on Sanskrit since the earliest Vedic times: chiefly a language exhibiting Austro-Asiatic features, hence provisionally called para-Munda, not the mother but at least an aunt of the Munda languages still spoken in Chhotanagpur. Where IA–Dravidian likenesses in words without apparent IE etymology were hitherto often explained as Dravidian substratum in IA, the favorite explanation now is that Dravidian borrowed from IA what IA itself had borrowed from para-Munda, for example, *mayûra*, 'peacock' was derived from Munda **mara* and in its turn yielded Tamil *mayil*. A second influence is attributed to an unknown language, nonetheless discernible through consistent features, and provisionally called Language X.

Indian non-invasionists strongly dislike the alleged fondness of Western linguists for "ghost languages," for example, Talageri (1993: 160) dismisses "purely hypothetical extinct languages" thus: "We cannot proceed with these scholars into the twilight zone of non-existent languages." But the simple fact remains that numerous languages *have* died out, and that the ghost of some of them can be seen at work in anomalous elements in existing languages. Thus, the first Sumerologists noticed an un-Sumerian presence of remnants of an older language typified by reduplicated final syllables, hence baptized "banana language." Today, much more is known about a pre-Sumerian Ubaidic culture, which has become considerably less ghostly.

In the para-Munda thesis, the hypothetical para-Munda language seems to be the main influence, reaching far northwest to and even beyond the entry point of the Vedic Aryans in India, and definitely predominant in the whole Ganga basin. The word *gangâ* itself has long been given an Austro-Asiatic etymology, especially linking it with southern Chinese *kang/kiang/jiang*, supposedly also an Austro-Asiatic loan. The latter etymology has recently been abandoned, with the pertinent proto-Austro-Asiatic root being reconstructed as **krang* and the Chinese word having a separate Sino-Tibetan origin (Zhang 1998). Witzel (1999a: 388) now proposes to explain Ganga as "a folk etymology for Munda **gand*," meaning 'river', a general meaning it still has in some IA languages. The folk etymology would be a reduplication of the root **gam/ga*, 'moving-moving', 'swiftly flowing', which only applies meaningfully to the river's upper course, nearest to the Harappan population centers. But there is no decisive reason why the folk etymology could not be the real one, nor why some other IE etymology could not apply. For the sake of argument, we might propose a phonetically impeccable kinship with Middle Dutch *konk-elen*, 'twist and turn', related to English *kink*, 'torsion'.

In some cases, a Munda etymology is supported by archaeological evidence. Rice cultivation was developed in Southeast Asia (including South China), land of origin of the Austro-Asiatic people, who brought it to the Indus region by the Late Harappan age at the latest. Therefore, it is not far-fetched to derive Sanskrit *vrihi* from Austro-Asiatic **vari*, which exists in practically the same form in Austronesian languages like Malagasy and Dayak, and reappears even in Japanese (*uru-chi*), again pointing to Southeast-Asia as the origin and propagator in all directions of both the cultivation of rice and its name **vari*.

All this goes to confirm that at least linguistically, the Munda tribals are not "aboriginals" (or with a pseudo-native modern term, *âdivâsî*s), but carriers and importers of Southeast-Asian culture. Witzel himself acknowledges that "Munda speakers immigrated," as this should explain why in Colin Masica's list of agricultural loans in Hindi (1979), which in conformity with the invasionist paradigm is very generous in allotting non-IE origins to Indo-Aryan words, Austro-Asiatic etymologies account for only 5.7 percent. In borrowing so few Munda words, the Vedic Aryans clearly did not behave like immigrants into Munda-speaking territory.

This paucity of Munda influence in the agricultural vocabulary, soil-related par excellence, should also caution us against reading Munda etymologies into the equally soil-bound hydronyms, which are overwhelmingly Indo-Aryan from the *kubhâ* to the *yamunâ*. Witzel (1999a: 374) diagnoses the usual Sanskritic interpretations as artificial "popular etymology," but in most cases does not produce convincing Munda alternatives. The one plausible Munda etymology is for *shutudrî* (prefix plus **tu-*, 'to drift', plus **da*, 'water', Witzel 1999b: section 1.4), if only because the Vedic Aryans themselves showed their unfamiliarity with it by devising folk etymologies like *shata-drukâ*, 'hundred streams'; even there, the step from *-da* to *-drî*, though possible, does not impress itself as compelling.

Numerous words have wrongly or at least prematurely been classified as foreign loans. Talageri (1993: 169–70) gives the examples of animal-names like *khaḍgin* ('breaker', rhinoceros), *mâtaṃga* ('roaming at will', elephant), *gaja* ('trumpeter', elephant), which Suniti Kumar Chatterji had cited as loans from Dravidian or Munda but which easily admit of an IE etymology. Likewise, there may well be an IA explanation for terms commonly given non-IE etyma, for example, exotic-sounding *ulûkhala*, 'mortar (for *soma*)', may well be analyzed, following Paul Thieme, into IA *uru*, 'broad', plus *khala*, 'threshing-floor', or even *khara*, 'rectangular piece of earth for sacrifices' (with Greek cognate, *eschara*). The word *mayûra*, "peacock", is often given a Dravidian or (by Witzel 1999a: 350) Munda etymon, but Monier Monier-Williams (1899: 789) already derived it from an onomatopoeic IA root **mâ*, 'bleat', and the related words in non-IA languages may very well be derived from IA forms (but in this case, the suffix *-ûr-*, unknown in Indo-Aryan, pleads in favor of a foreign origin).

As a rule, one should not allot Dravidian or Munda origins to an IA word unless the etymon can actually be pointed out (at least indirectly) in the purported source language. It is therefore with great reservation that we should consider the list of para-Munda words "in the RV, even if we cannot yet find etymologies" (Witzel 1999b: section 1.2). On the other hand, many hypothetical etyma which do not exist in Munda in full, and which should at first sight be rejected, may be analyzed as composites with components which do exist in Munda.

The main pointer to a Munda connection seems to be a list of prefixes, now no longer productive in the Munda languages, and not recognized or used as prefixes by Vedic Sanskrit speakers. Thus, the initial syllable of the ethnonym *kî-kaṭa* seems to be one in a series of non-IA and probably para-Munda prefixes *ka/ke/ki* etc. (Witzel 1999a: 365), some of which look like the declension forms of the definite article in Khasi, an Austro-Asiatic language in the Northeast. On this basis, very common words become suspected loans from "para-Munda," for example, *ku-mâra*, 'young man', a term not explainable in IE, but plausibly related to a Munda word *mar*, 'man' (Witzel 1991b: section 1.2).

Between Sanskrit *karpâsa*, 'cotton', and Munda *ka-pas* (cfr. Sumerian *kapazum*), it may now be decided that the latter was first while the former, with its typical cluster *-rp-*, is but a hypersanskritized loan. This also fits in with the archaeological indications of textile-manufacturing processes pioneered by the Southeast-Asians, and with an already-established Austro-Asiatic etymon **pas* (without the prefix) for Chinese *bu*, 'cotton cloth'. Incidentally, this does not affect the argument by Sethna that the appearance of this word in late-Vedic, regardless of its provenance, should be synchronous with the appearance of actual cotton cloth in the Panjab region, namely, in the mature Harappan phase (implying that early Vedic predated the mature Harappan phase); indeed, Sethna (1982: 5) himself accepts the Austro-Asiatic etymology.

An interesting idea suggested by Witzel concerns an alleged alternation *k/zero*, for example, in the Greek rendering of the place-name and ethnonym *Kamboja* (eastern Afghanistan) as *Ambautai*, apparently based on a native pronunciation without *k-*. Citing Kuiper and others, Witzel (1999a: 362) asserts that "an interchange *k : zero* 'points in the direction of Munda' " though this "would be rather surprising at this extreme western location." Indeed, it would mean that not just Indo-Aryan but also other branches of Indo-Iranian have been influenced by Munda, for *kam-boja* seems to be an Iranian word, the latter part being the de-aspirated Iranian equivalent of Skt *bhoja*, 'king' (Pirart 1998: 542). At any rate, if the Mundas could penetrate India as far as the Indus, they could reach Kamboja too.

But the interesting point here is that the "interchange k : zero" is attested in IE vocabulary far to the west of India and Afghanistan, for example, English *ape* corresponding to Greek *kepos*, Sanskrit *kapi*, 'monkey', or Latin *aper*, 'boar', corresponding to Greek *kapros*. Gamkrelidze and Ivanov (1995: 113, 435) have tried to explain this through a Semitic connection, with the phonological closeness, somewhere in the throat, of *qof* and *'ayn*. But if the origin of this alternation must be sought in an Afghano-Munda connection, what does that say about the geographical origin of English, Latin, and Greek?

Given the location of the different language groups in India, it is entirely reasonable that Munda influence should appear in the easternmost branch of IE, namely, Indo-Aryan. If both IE and Munda were native to India, we might expect Munda influence in the whole IE family (though India is a big place with room for nonneighboring languages), but since Munda is an immigrant language, we should not be surprised to find it influencing only the stay-behind IA branch of IE. This merely indicates a relative chronology: first Indo-Aryan separated from the other branches of IE when these left India, and then it came in contact with para-Munda. So, if we accept the presence of para-Munda loans in Vedic Sanskrit, we still need not accept that this is a native substratum influence in a superimposed invaders' language.

7.4.5 Pre-IE substratum in Indo-Aryan: language X

The mysterious language X has possibly not left this earth without a trace, for it is tentatively claimed to be connected with the nearly vanished but known Kusunda language of Nepal (Witzel 1999a: 346). Masica (1979) had found no known etymologies for 31 percent of agricultural and flora terms in Hindi, and Witzel credits these to language X (1999a: 339). I would caution, with Talageri (1993: 165ff.), against prematurely deciding on the non-IE origin of a word not having parallels in other IE languages, especially in the case of terms for indigenous flora and fauna. Though Sanskrit *kukkura* or Hindi *kuttâ*, both 'dog', have no IE cognates outside India, we cannot expect the Aryans to have been ignorant of this animal and to have learned about it from the Indian natives upon invading. Onomatopoeic or otherwise slang formations just come into being and sometimes replace the original standard terms, without implying foreign origin or a substratum effect.

The OIT has no objection to the impression that Vedic Sanskrit has absorbed some foreign words, for example, from immigrants into their metropolis, just like the Romance languages borrowed many Germanic words from the Gothic invaders. All that the OIT requires is merely that this absorption should have taken place after the emigration of the other branches of IE from India. Also, it is accepted that some substratal effects may have taken place during the Aryan "colonization" of the non-Aryan lower Ganga plain, in which the western IE languages took no part.

One discernible trait of this ghost language X is claimed to be the "typical gemination of certain consonants" (Witzel 1999b: section 1.1), for example, in the name of the *malla* tribe/caste. Often these geminates are visible upon first borrowing but are later masked by hypersanskritic dissimilation, for example, *pippala* becoming *pishpala*, or *guggulu* becoming *gulgulu* (Witzel 1999b: section 2.4). However, the geminated *-kk-* in *kukkura* or the *-tt-* in *kuttâ*, though atypical of the IE word pattern, can perfectly come into being as onomatopoeic formations within a purely IE milieu: in imitating the sound of a dog, even IE-speakers need not have assumed that barking sounds follow the IE pattern.

The assumption of a language X in North India will be welcomed by many as the solution to the vexing question of the origin of retroflexion in the Indian languages. Weak in Burushaski and Munda, strong yet defective (never in initial position) in Dravidian, strong in Indo-Aryan but unattested among its non-Indian sister-languages, retroflexion in its origins is a puzzling phenomenon. So, language X as the putative language of the influential Harappan metropolis, or as the native substratum of the later metropolitan region, namely, Eastern Uttar Pradesh and Bihar, might neatly fit an invasionist scenario for the genesis of retroflexion in Indo-Aryan as well as its spread to all corners of India.

Still, there is no *positive* reason yet for locating the origin of retroflexion in this elusive language X. An entirely internal origination of retroflexion within early Indo-Aryan, which then imparted it to its neighbors, has always had its defenders even among linguists working within the invasionist paradigm (e.g. Hamp 1996). And consider the following possibility.

The Vedic hymns may well be somewhat older than the language in which they have come down to us. We need not exclude a phonetical evolution between the time of composition and the time when the Veda was given its definitive shape, traditionally by *vyâsa*, 'compiler'. Strictly speaking, it is not even impossible that a hymn composed in a language phonetically close to PIE, pre-proto-Indo-Iranian, subsequently underwent the Kentum/Satem shift and the vowel shift from IE /a/e/o/ to Sanskrit /a/, somewhat like the continuity of living Latin across centuries of phonetic change: *Caesar* evolving from [kaisar] to [cezar] or [sezar], *agnus* (lamb) from [agnus] to [anyus], *cyclus* from [küklus] to [ciklus] or [siklus], *descendere* from [deskendere] satemized to [deshendere], the vowels *ae/oe/e* coinciding as [e], etc. In the Middle Ages, Virgil's verses were still recited, but with a different pronunciation, just as in China, children memorized the Confucian Classics in the pronunciation of their own day, without knowing what the ancient masters' own pronunciation must have sounded like. Similarly, the Vedic hymns may well be older than the language form in which they have been preserved till today.

A very modest application of this line of thought is the hypothesis that the differentiation between dental and retroflex or cerebral consonants was not yet present in the original Vedic, and only developed by the time Sanskrit reached its classical form. Deshpande (1979) argues that the cerebral sounds crept in when the center of Brahminical learning had shifted from Sapta-Sindhu to the Ganga basin, where the Indo-Aryan dialects had developed the dental–cerebral distinction. In that case, the Veda recension which we have today (the *mâṇḍûkeya* and *shâkalya* recensions, which Deshpande dates to 700 BC), was established in Videha-Magadha (Bihar), where native speakers imposed their pronunciation on the Veda.

Deshpande also mentions a Magadhan king Shishunaga (fifth century BC?) who prohibited the use of the retroflex sounds *ṭ/ṭh/ḍ/ḍh/ṣ/kṣ* in his harem. But this seems to indicate that retroflexion was an intrusive new trend in Magadha, not at all a native tendency which was so strong and ingrained that it could impose itself on the liturgical language. Something may be said for Kuiper's (1991: 11–14) rebuttal to Deshpande's thesis, namely, that *mâṇḍûkeya*'s insistence on retroflex pronunciation was a case of upholding ancient standards against a new and degenerative trend, implying that retroflexion was well-established by the time the Vedas were composed, and was being neglected in the new, eastern metropolis. That puts us back at base one: Munda (probably the main influence in Bihar) is clearly not the source of retroflexion, and that elusive language X didn't have much lexical impact on Vedic yet, making phonological influence even less likely. So if retroflexion was already present in Vedic, and otherwise too, the search for its origin continues.

7.4.6 The peculiar case of "Sindhu"

Among IA-looking river names, a case can be made for surprising IE etymologies of names usually explained as loans. In particular, *sindhu* might be an "Indo-Iranian coinage with the meaning 'border river, ocean' and fits Paul

Thieme's etymology from the IE root **sidh*, 'to divide' " (1999a: 387). Now, if the Vedic Aryans only entered India in the second millennium BC, the name Sindhu cannot be older than that.

According to Oleg Trubachov (1999), elaborating on a thesis by Kretschmer (1944), Indo-Aryan was spoken in Ukraine as late as the Hellenistic period, by two tribes knows as the *Maiotes* and the *Sindoi*, the latter also known by its Scythian/Iranian-derived name *Indoi* and explicitly described by Hesychius as "an Indian people." They reportedly used a word *sinu*, from *sindhu*, for 'river', a general meaning which it also has in some Vedic verses. Trubachov lists a number of personal and place-names recorded by Greek authors (e.g. *Kouphes* for the *Kuban* river, apparently a re-use of *kubhâ*, the *Kabul* river, Greek *Kophes*), and concludes that the Maiotes and Sindoi spoke an Indo-Aryan dialect, though often with *-l-* instead of *-r-*, as in king *Saulios*, cfr. *sûrya* (just the opposite from Mitannic, where *palita*, 'grey', and *pingala*, 'reddish', appear as *parita* and *pinkara*) and with *-pt-* simplified to *-tt-* (so that, just like in Mitannic, *sapta* appears as *satta*, a feature described by Misra 1992 as "Middle IA").

Working within the AIT framework, Kretschmer saw these Sindoi as a left-over of the Indo-Aryans in their original homeland, and even as a splendid proof of the Pontic homeland theory (Trubachov is less committed to any particular homeland hypothesis). In that case, again, the name *sindhu* (and likewise *kubhâ*) would be an Indo-Aryan word brought into India by the Vedic-Aryan invaders.

However, Witzel himself (1999b: section 1.9) notes that the Sumerians (who recorded a handful of words from "Meluhha"/Sindh, which incidentally seem neither IA nor Dravidian) in the third millennium already knew the name *sindhu* as referring to the lower basin of the Indus river, then the most accessible part of the Harappan civilization, when they imported "*sinda*" wood. If this is not a coincidental look-alike, then either *sindhu* is a word of non-IE origin already used by the non-IE Harappans, in which case the Pontic Sindoi were migrants from India (demonstrating how earlier the Kurganites might have migrated from India?); or *sindhu* was an IE word, and proves that the Harappan civilization down to its coastline was already IA-speaking.

7.5 Linguistic paleontology

7.5.1 Hot and cold climate

One of the main reasons for nineteenth-century philologists to exclude India as a candidate for Urheimat status was the findings of a fledgling new method called *linguistic paleontology*. The idea was that from the reconstructed vocabulary, one could deduce which flora, fauna, and artifacts were familiar to the speakers of the proto-language, hence also their geographical area of habitation. The presence in the common vocabulary of words denoting northern animals like the bear, wolf, elk, otter, and beaver seemed to indicate a northern Urheimat; likewise, the absence of terms for the lion or elephant seemed to exclude tropical countries like India.

It should be realized that virtually all IE-speaking areas are familiar with the cold climate and its concomitant flora and fauna. Even in hot countries, the mountainous areas provide islands of cold climate, for example, the foothills of the Himalaya have pine trees rather than palm trees, apples rather than mangoes. Indians are therefore quite familiar with a range of flora and fauna usually associated with the north, including bears (Sanskrit *ṛksha*, cfr. Greek *arktos*), otters (*udra*, Hindi *ûd*/*ûdbilâw*), and wolves (*vṛka*). Elks and beavers do not live in India, yet the words exist, albeit with a different but related meaning: *ṛsha* means a male antelope, *babhru* ('brownie') a mongoose. The shift of meaning may have taken place in either direction: it is perfectly possible that emigrants from India transferred their term for 'mongoose' to the first beavers which they encountered in Russia.

7.5.2 Early Vedic flora terms

When the Hittites settled in Anatolia, they found an advanced civilization and adopted numerous lexical and grammatical elements from it. By contrast

> It was different with the Indo-Aryan tribes arriving in India: with the Harappan civilization probably already in decline, they could very well preserve the full range of their traditions including their remarkably archaic language. The influence of non-Indo-European languages is just beginning to be visible (e.g. the retroflex series). The Aryan ideology of "hospitality" and "truth" is very vivid, as in Ancient Iran.
>
> (Zimmer 1990a: 151)

The same conservation of IE heritage seems to be in evidence in their vocabulary. As we saw, Austro-Asiatic is plausibly argued to have contributed many words to IA, yet only little in the semantic range where substratum influence is usually the largest, namely, indigenous flora. In that field, the early Vedic vocabulary has been screened for linguistic origins by Jean Haudry (2000: 148), who argues that the foreign origin of IA is indicated not just by non-IE etymologies but also by artificial IA coinages based on IE vocabulary. Admittedly, a few are simply IE:

- *bhûrja*, birch;
- *parkatî*, *ficus infectoria*, cfr. Latin *quercus*, 'oak';
- *dâru*, 'wood', cfr. Gk. *doru*, Eng. *tree*;
- *pitu-dâru*, a type of pine, cfr. Lat. *pituita*, a type of pine.

A few (but here, Haudry is apparently not trying for exhaustiveness) are loans:

- *shimshapa*, dalbergia sisa ("from a West-Asian language");
- *pîlu*, an unspecified tree ("probable loan from Dravidian").

But all the others are Indian coinages on an IE base:

- *nyagroha, ficus indica*, 'downward-growing';
- *ashvattha, ficus religiosa*, 'horse food' (at least "probably", according to Haudry);
- *vikankata, flacourtia sapida*, 'stinging in all directions';
- *shamî, prosopis spicigera*, 'hornless';
- *ashvaghna, nerium odoratum*, 'horse-slayer';
- *târshtâghna*, an unidentified tree, 'evil-killer';
- *spandana*, an unidentified tree, 'trembler';
- *dhava, grislea tomentosa* or *anogeissus latifolia*, 'trembler';
- *parna, butea frondosa*, 'feather', hence 'leaf' (metonymic);
- *svadhiti*, an unidentified tree, 'hatchet' (metaphoric).

It is of course remarkable that they didn't borrow more terms from the natives, as if they had invaded an uninhabited country and had to invent names from scratch. But the main question here is: does "artificial coinage" indicate that the referents of these words were new to the Indo-Aryans? It would seem that, on the contrary, artificial coinage pervades the whole IE vocabulary.

It is true that new phenomena are often indicated with such descriptive terms, for example, French *chemin de fer* ('iron road') for 'railway'; or in classical Sanskrit, *loha*, 'the red one', to designate the then new metal 'iron'. Yet, far from being confined to new inventions, "artificial" coinage is the typical PIE procedure for creating names for natural species. Thus, PIE **bheros*, 'brown', has yielded the animal names Skt *bhâlu*, Eng. *bear*, and with reduplication, **bhebhrus*, Eng. *beaver* (perhaps also Gk. *phrunos*, 'toad'), all meaning simply 'the brown one'. Similarly, **kasnos*, Eng. *hare*, Skt *shasha*, means 'the grey one'; **udros*, Eng. *otter* (when also Gk. *hydra*, water-snake) means 'the water-animal' (a general meaning which it has at least partly preserved in Skt *udra*); *lynx* is from **leukh*, 'to be bright'; *frog* from **phreu-*, 'to jump'. The deer, Lat. *cervus*, Dutch *hert*, is 'the horned one', cfr. Lat. *cornu*, 'horn'. The bear, Slavic *medv-ed*, Skt *madhv-ad*, is also the 'honey-eater'. Some of the said animals known by descriptive terms are inhabitants of the northern zone; following the AIT argument that such coinages indicate immigration, we would have to conclude that the Urheimat definitely did not know otters, beavers, bears, hares, and lynxes.

The Indo-Europeans certainly knew the species *homo*, and had no need to be told about its existence by natives of some invaded country. Well, Latin *homo/hom-in-is* is an artificial derivative of *hum-u-s*, 'soil', hence 'earth-dweller' (cfr. Hebrew *adam*, 'man', and *adamah*, 'earth'), as opposed to the heaven-dwellers or gods, which gives us a glimpse of the philosophy of the PIE-speaking people. The Iranian-Armenian term for this species, *mard*, is another philosophical circumlocution, 'mortal'. The Sanskrit term *manuṣa*, and possibly even *puruṣa*, is a patronym: 'descendent of Manu' and 'descendent of Puru' (cfr. Urdu *âdmî*, 'man', i.e. 'son of Adam'), with *manu* itself apparently derived from **man-*, 'mind'. Not one of these is a truly simple term, all are artificially coined from more elementary semantic matter.

In so basic a vocabulary as the numerals, we encounter artificial coinages: PIE **oktou* is a dual form meaning 'twice four' (cfr. Avestan *ashti*, 'four fingers', and perhaps Kartvelian **otxo*, 'four'); **kṃtom*, 'hundred', is a derivative of **dkṃ*, 'ten', through **dkṃtom*. And there are connections between the numerals and the real world: *five* is related to *finger; nine* is related to *new*; **dkṃ*, 'ten' is related to *in-dek-s*, 'pointing finger', Greek *deik-numi*, 'to point out', etc.

Likewise for family terminology. The *daughter*, according to a popular etymology, is the 'milkmaid', cfr. Skt *dugdha*, 'milk' (though the semantic connection could also be through 'suckling' > 'child' > 'girl', cfr. the trendy use of 'babe'). The Roman children, *liberi*, were the 'free ones', as opposed to the serf section of the extended household (cfr. conversely Persian: *â-jâta*, 'born unto', 'own progeny' > *âzâd*, 'free'). Even the word **pa-ter*, 'father', usually interpreted as 'protec-tor' is a more artificial construction than, for example, Gothic *atta* (best known through its diminutive *Attila*), a primitive term present in very divergent languages (as in the *pater patriae* epithets *Ata-türk* and *Keny-atta*).

Such descriptive formations are common in IE, but Sanskrit is often the only IE language in which the descriptive origin of words is still visible, which may indicate its high age. In all other IE languages, 'wolf' is exclusively the name of this animal; in Sanskrit, *vṛka* is treated as part of a continuum with the verb *vṛk*, "to tear" (likewise for *pṛdâku*, later). Very primitive even seemingly pre-PIE, would be the nonuse of a suffix, as in the 'tear-*er*', with the root itself is both verbal root and nominal stem.

Not the descriptive term, but rather the etymologically isolated term, which only appears in the lexicon to designate a species, is an indicator of the newness and strangeness of the species to the speakers of the language concerned, because it would probably be borrowed by newcomers from the natives of the habitat of the species. Thus, *tomato* has no descriptive value and no etymological relatives in the IE languages, because it was borrowed wholesale as the name of this vegetable from the Amerindian natives of the tomato-growing regions. That Sanskrit *matsya*, 'fish', is derivable from an IE root *mad*, 'wet', while Greek *ichthys* and Italo-Germanic *piscis/fish* have no PIE etymology, indicates a substratum influence on the European branches of IE, not on the Indian one. Proposals of a link between *ichthys* and Greek *chthôn*, PIE **dhghom*, 'earth' (hence 'nether world', including the submarine sphere?) are doubtful, and even if valid, they would only confirm our finding that description, that is, of the fish as a 'netherworlder', is a common formula for coining words in IE.

In Haudry's own list of simple inherited IE words, *bhûrja* is an artificial coinage, meaning 'the bright one', the birch being exceptional in color, namely, white. The same may hold for *parkatî/quercus*, which seems related to the word for 'lightning', cfr. the personified lightning-god, Baltic *Perkunas*, Skt *Parjanya*. It is certainly true of a general Vedic word for 'tree', which Haudry also mentions: *vanaspati*, 'lord of the jungle'. Such metaphoric circumlocution is what the Nordic poets called a *kenning*, and it is omnipresent not only in the earliest known IE poetry traditions, but even in the formation of IE words themselves.

7.5.3 The linguistic horse

The word **ekw-o-s*, 'horse', is a later formation in PIE. The oldest vocabulary had athematic stems (e.g. Latin *lex* from *leg-s*), the thematic stems (e.g. Latin *cerv-u-s*), belong to a later generation of PIE words. Simple roots are older than roots which have been lengthened with an extra (mostly gender-specific) vowel *-a* or *-o*; the development of the latter category, with its own declension, had also been completed before the disintegration of PIE. To take two momentous inventions, the IE words for 'fire' (**egnis*, **pûr*, **âter*) belong to the older category, while the words for 'wheel' (**rot-o-s*, **kwekwl-o-s*) belong to the younger type, which indicates that the wheel was newly invented or newly adopted from neighboring peoples by the Proto-Indo-Europeans, whereas the use of fire was already an ancient heritage.

Coming to livestock: **gwou-s*, 'cow', and **su-s*, 'pig' (with the younger diminutive **su-in-o*, 'swine') belong to the older category, while **ekw-o-s*, 'horse', belongs to the younger category. Some scholars deduce from this that the pig and the cow were domesticated earlier than the horse, which happens to tally with the archaeological data. But it might just as well be interpreted as an indication that the horse was not only not domesticated by the earliest Proto-Indo-Europeans, but was simply not known to them; after all, the inhabitants of the areas where horses were available for domestication, must have known the horse since much earlier, as a wild animal on par with the wolf and the deer. We shouldn't give too much weight to this, but if it matters at all that the term for 'horse' is a younger formation, it would indicate that the horse was not native to the Urheimat, and that the Proto-Indo-Europeans only got acquainted with it, as with the wheel, shortly before their dispersal. In that case, India was a better candidate for Urheimat status than the horse-rich steppes.

This cannot be taken as more than a small indication that the horse was not part of the scenery in the PIE homeland. There are many newer-type formations for age-old items, for example, the species *lup-u-s*, 'wolf', and *cerv-u-s*, 'deer', were most certainly known to the first PIE-speakers, wherever their homeland. But in the present case, another argument for the late origin of *ekw-o-s* has been added (by Lehmann 1997: 247), namely, its somewhat irregular development in the different branches of IE, for example, the appearance from nowhere of the aspiration in Greek *hippos*.

The only convincing attempt to give **ekwos* roots in the basic PIE vocabulary, is through the Greek word *ôkus*, from **oku/eku*, 'fast', interpreting the name of the horse as 'the fast one'. Another cognate word, mentioned by Lehmann (1997: 247), could be Balto-Slavic **ashu*, 'sharp'. If this is so, those who see artificial coinage of Indian tree names in Sanskrit as proof of the speakers' unfamiliarity with the trees in question, should also deduce that this artificial coinage indicates the foreignness of the horse to the original PIE-speakers in their Urheimat. Conversely, if the irregularities in the various evolutes of **ekwos* are taken to indicate that it 'was borrowed, possibly even independently in some of the dialects' (Lehmann 1997: 247), this would again confirm that the horse was a newcomer in the expanding PIE horizon. Could this be because the PIE horizon started expanding from horseless India?

If this is not really a compelling argument, at least the converse is even more true: any clinching linguistic evidence for a horse-friendly Urheimat is missing. We should now consider the possibility that the Proto-Indo-Europeans only familiarized themselves with the horse toward the time of their dispersion. A possible scenario might be during some political or economic crisis, adventurers from overpopulated India, speaking PIE dialects, settled in Central Asia where they acquainted themselves with the horse. More than the local natives, they were experienced at domesticating animals (even the elephant, judging from RV 9.47.3 which mentions an elephant decorated for a pageant), and they domesticated the horse. While relaying some specimens back to the homeland, they used the new skill to speed up their expansion westward, where their dialects became the European branches of the IE family. The horse became the prized import for the Indian elite, which at once explains both its rarity in the bone record and its exaltation in the Vedic literary record.

The terms for cart and the parts of a cart (wheel, axle) famously belong to the common PIE vocabulary, giving linguistic-paleontological support to the image of the PIE-speaking pioneers leaving their homeland in ox-drawn carts and trekking to their Far West. This cart was also known in Harappa. But unlike the wheel and its parts, the spoked wheel seems to be a later invention, at least according to the same criterion: felloe and spoke are not represented in the common PIE lexicon. The fast horse-drawn chariot with spoked wheels was a post-PIE innovation; its oldest available specimen was reportedly found in Sintashta in the eastern Urals and dated around the turn of the second millennium BC, synchronous with the declining years of Harappa. It remains possible that the 99 percent of non-excavated Harappan sites will also yield some specimens, but so far no Harappan chariots have been found; nor has any identifiably Vedic chariot, for that matter.

Yet, the Ṛgveda does mention chariots, though not everywhere and all the time. If the internal chronology of the Ṛgveda developed by Shrikant Talageri (2000) is approximately right (and much of it is uncontroversial, e.g. putting books 8 to 10 later than the "family books", 2 to 7), we can discern an Early Vedic period in which the spoked wheel was unknown, or at least unmentioned, and a later period when it was very much present in the Vedic region and culture. In that case, the Vedic Aryans had lived in India well before the chariot was imported there (if not locally invented, so far unattested but not unlikely given Harappa's edge in technology). This implies that they either invaded India in an earlier period, without the aid of the horse-drawn spoked-wheel chariot, the tank or *Panzer* of antiquity; or that they were native to India.

7.5.4 Positive evidence from linguistic paleontology

In assessing the linguistic-paleontological evidence, it has been shown earlier that the fauna terms provide no proof for a northern Urheimat. Thomas Gamkrelidze and Vyaceslav Ivanov (1995: 420–31 and 442–4), in their bid to prove their Anatolian Urheimat theory, have gone a step further and tried to find positive proof, namely, terms for hot-climate fauna in the common IE vocabulary.

Thus, they relate Sanskrit *pṛdâku* with Greek *pardos* and Hittite *parsana*, all meaning 'leopard', an IE term lost in some northern regions devoid of leopards (note that the meaning in Sanskrit is still transparent, namely, 'the spotted one', and that this description is also applied to the snake, while a derivative of the same root, *pṛshati*, means 'spotted deer'). The word *lion* is found as a native word, in regular phonetic correspondence, in Greek, Italic, Germanic, and Hittite, and with a vaguer meaning 'beast' in Slavic and Tocharian. It could be a Central Asian acquisition of the IE tribes on their way from India; alternatively, it is not unreasonable to give it deeper roots in IE by linking it with a verb **reu-*, Skt *rav-*, 'howl, roar', considering that alternation *r/l* is common in Sanskrit (e.g. the double form *plavaga/pravaga*, 'monkey', or the noun *plava*, 'frog' related to the verb *pravate*, 'jump').

A word for 'monkey' is common to Greek (*kepos*) and Sanskrit (*kapi*), and Gamkrelidze and Ivanov argue for its connection with the Germanic and Celtic word 'ape'. For 'elephant', they even found two distinct IE words (1995: 443): Sanskrit *ibha*, 'male elephant', corresponding to Latin *ebur*, 'ivory, elephant'; and Greek *elephant-* corresponding to Gothic *ulbandus*, Tocharian **alpi*, 'camel'. In the second case, the 'camel' meaning may be the original one, if we assume a migration through camel-rich Central Asia to Greece, where trade contacts with Egypt and India made the elephant known once more; the word may be a derivative from a word meaning 'deer', Greek *elaphos*. In the case of *ibha/ebur*, however (which Gamkrelidze and Ivanov connect with Hebrew *shen-habbim*, 'tusk-of-elephant', "ivory"), we have a straightforward linguistic-paleontological argument for an Urheimat with elephants. Though the alternative of a later borrowing through trade should not be discounted.

To be sure, linguistic paleontology is no longer in fashion: "The long dispute about the reliability of this 'linguistic paleontology' is not yet finished, but approaching its inevitable end – with a negative result, of course" (Zimmer 1990a: 142). Yet, to the extent that it does retain some validity, it no longer militates against the OIT, and even provides some modest support to it.

7.6 Exchanges with other language families

7.6.1 Souvenirs of language contacts

One of the best keys to the geographical itinerary of a language is the exchange of lexical and other elements with other languages. Two types of language contact should be distinguished. The first type of language contact is the exchange of vocabulary and other linguistic traits, whether by long-distance trade contact, by contiguity, or by substratum influence, between languages which are not necessarily otherwise related.

Perhaps more than by proven contact, a language can also be "rooted" in a region by a second type of "contact," namely, genetic kinship with a local language. To be sure, just like languages with which contacts were established, cognate languages may have moved, and their place of origin overwhelmed by newcomers. Still, in the present discussion it would count as a weighty argument if it could be shown that IE was genetically related to either a West-European or an East-Asian language. This would "pull" the likely Homeland in a westerly or easterly direction. In Europe, the kinship would have to be with Basque, but this remains a language isolate, so this solid proof for a westerly homeland is missing. How about the Asian connection?

7.6.2 Sumerian and Semitic

If we discount coincidence, a few look-alikes between Sumerian and PIE may be assumed to be due to contact, though in the first millennium of writing, "Indo-European is not documented in the earliest Mesopotamian records" (Anthony 1991: 197, contra the Anatolian homeland theory of Renfrew 1987 and others). Also, these look-alikes are so few and phonetically so elementary that sheer coincidence might really be sufficient explanation. To borrow some examples from Gamkrelidze and Ivanov (1995), Sumerian *agar*, 'irrigated territory', may be related to PIE **agr-o* (Lat. *ager*, Skt *ajraḥ*), and may have been borrowed in either direction. Sumerian *tur*, 'yard, enclosure for cattle', could be related with PIE **dhwer*, Grk *thyra*, English *door*. Sumerian *ngud/gud/gu*, 'bull, cow' (cfr. Skt *go*, English *cow*), should be seen together with the Egyptian word *ng3w*, 'a type of bull'; the latter type of semantic relation from 'bull' to 'type of bull', narrowing down from the general to the particular, is often indicative of borrowing (cfr. from French *chauffeur*, 'a driver' to English *chauffeur*, 'the driver in your employ', or later, from PIE **ḥster-* 'star', to Akkadian *Ishtar*, 'planet Venus'): Egyptian borrowed from Sumerian, which in turn borrowed from IE. Sumerian *kapazum*, 'cotton', already mentioned, may be from Austro-Asiatic **kapas* as well as from Skt *karpâsa*.

Kinship of Sumerian with IE is practically excluded (though there are vague indications of Sumerian-Munda kinship, fitting into the theory of the migration of both Sumerian and Austro-Asiatic from 'Sundaland', the Sunda shelf to the south and east of Vietnam, when it was submerged by the post-Glacial rising tide in *c.*6000 BC, cfr. Oppenheimer 1998), because there is just no above-coincidence similarity in phonetic or grammatical features. If some words are related, it must be due to borrowing in the context of trade relations. The main geographical candidates for PIE regions trading with Sumer would be Anatolia and the Indus basin. Then again, being the main language of civilization in *c.*3000 BC, some Sumerian terms may have been used in long-distance trade with the Pontic area, the more conventional Urheimat candidate. Note however that the trade links between Sumer and the Harappan civilization ('Meluhha' in Mesopotamian texts) are well-attested, along with the presence of Indo-Aryans in Mesopotamia, for example, the names *Arisena* and *Somasena* in a tablet from Akkad dated to *c.*2200 BC (Sharma 1995: 36 w. ref. to Harmatta 1992: 374). It doesn't follow that these Indo-Aryans in Mesopotamia originated in the Indus Valley, but it is not excluded either.

Far more important is the linguistic relation between IE and Semitic (and, if genetic, hence also with the Chadic, Kushitic, and Hamitic branches of the Afro-Asiatic family, assumed to be the result of a pre-fourth-millennium migration of early agriculturists from West Asia into North Africa). Semitic has frequently been suspected of kinship with IE, even by scholars skeptical of "Nostratic" mega-connections. Most remarkable are the common fundamental grammatical traits: Semitic, like IE, has grammatically functional vowel changes, grammatical gender, three numbers (singular, plural, and a vestigial dual), declension, and conjugational categories including participles and medial and passive modes. Many of these grammatical elements are shared only by Afro-Asiatic and IE, setting them off as a pair against all other language families. The two also share most of their range of phonemes, even more so if we assume PIE laryngeals to match Semitic *aleph, he* and *'ayn*, and if we take into account that the fricatives seemingly so typical of Semitic are often evolutes of stops (e.g. modern Hebrew *Avraham* from Abraham, thus transliterated in the Septuagint), just like Persian or Germanic developed fricatives from PIE stops (e.g. *hafta* c.q. *seven* from **septṃ*). Moreover, if we count PIE laryngeals as consonants, two-consonant IE roots come closer to the typical three-consonant shape of Semitic roots.

One way to imagine how Semitic and IE went their separate ways has been offered by Bernard Sergent (1995: 398 and 432), who is strongly convinced of the two families' common origin. He combines the linguistic evidence with archaeological and anthropological indications that the (supposedly PIE-speaking) Kurgan people in the North-Caspian area of *c.*4000 BC came from the southeast, a finding which might otherwise be cited in support of their ultimate Indian origin. Thus, the Kurgan people's typical grain was millet, not the rye and wheat cultivated by the Old Europeans, and in *c.*5000 BC, millet had been cultivated in what is now Turkmenistan (it apparently originates in China), particularly in the mesolithic culture of Jebel. From there on, the archaeological traces become really tenuous, but Sergent claims to discern a link with the Zarzian culture of Kurdistan, 10000–8500 BC. He suggests that the Kurgan people had come along the eastern coast of the Caspian Sea, not from the southeast (India) but the southwest, near Mesopotamia, where PIE may have had a common homeland with Semitic.

However, those who interpret the archaeological data concerning the genesis of agriculture in the Indus site of Mehrgarh as being the effect of a diffusion from West Asia, may well interpret an eventual kinship of IE with Semitic as illustrating their own point: along with its material culture, Mehrgarh's language may have been an offshoot of a metropolitan model, namely, a Proto-Semitic-speaking culture in West Asia. This would mean that the Indus area was indeed the homeland of the original PIE, but that in the preceding millennium, PIE had been created by the interaction of Proto-Semitic-speaking colonists from West Asia with locals.

A less heady theory holds that there is no genetic kinship between IE and Semitic, the lexical connection being too meagre, and that there has only been some contact. Oft-quoted is the seeming Semitic origin of the numerals 6 and 7 (Hebrew *shisha, shiva*, Arabic *sitta*, *sab'a*), conceivably borrowed at the time when counting was extended beyond the fingers of a single hand for the first time. Contact with Akkadian and even Proto-Semitic is attested by a good handful of words, especially some terms for utensils and animals. Examples of borrowing in the opposite direction, from PIE/IE to Semitic, include Semitic **qarn*, 'horn' (e.g. Hebrew *qeren*), from PIE *khr-n* (cfr. Latin *cornu*, Sanskrit *shṛnga*), derived within PIE from a root *kher-*, 'top, head' (Greek *kar*); and the well-known Semitic names of the planet Venus, *Ishtar/'Ashtoret/'Ashtarte*, from PIE **ḥster-*, 'star' (with Semitic feminine suffix *-t*), derived within PIE from the root **as*, 'to burn, glow'.

Some terms are in common only with the Western IE languages, for example, Semitic *gedi* corresponding to IE **ghed-*, still recognizable in Latin *haedus*, English *goat*; IE **taur-o-s*, 'bull', Semitic **ṭaur-*, from Proto-Semitic *cu-r-*; and IE *woi-no-/wei-no*, 'wine', West-Semitic *uain-*, Hebrew *yayin*. In this case we should count with a common origin in a third language, possibly Hattice or the language of the Old-European culture or its last stronghold, Minoic Crete. The transformation of demonstratives into the definite article in most Western IE languages has also been related, vaguely and implausibly, to Semitic influence. However, all this testimony is a bit too slender for concluding that the Western Indo-Europeans had come from the East and encountered the Semites or at least Semitic influence on their way to the West. Meanwhile, the word **peleku*, 'axe', apparently related to Semitic (Arabic) *falaqa*, 'to split', is only attested in the Eastern Greek-Armenian-Aryan subgroup of PIE, possibly a later loan to that group in its homeland after the northwestern branches had left it.

The very fact of IE-Semitic contact, like in the case of Sumerian, dimly favors an IE homeland with known trade relations with the Middle East, especially Anatolia or India, over a Russian or European one. But given the very early civilizational lead of Semitic-speaking centers (e.g. Ebla, Syria, 3200 BC), the effect of truly long-distance trade to northern backwaters cannot be excluded. So, the evidence of Semitic or Sumerian contacts is inconclusive, though it does not preclude an Indian homeland for PIE.

More promising though far more complicated is the analysis by Nichols (1997) of the transmission of loans in and around Mesopotamia, also taking the three Caucasian families into account. Of the latter, the two northern ones show little lexical exchange with IE, which pleads against a Pontic homeland. On the basis of these "loanword trajectories" through different languages, especially of Mesopotamian cultural terms including those discussed earlier, Nichols (1997: 127) finds that in the fourth millennium BC, "Abkhaz-Circassian and Nakh-Daghestanian are in approximately their modern locations, and Kartvelian and IE are to the east." More precisely, Kartvelian is "likely to have emanated from somewhere to the south-east of the Caspian" while the "locus of IE was farther east and farther north" (1997: 128) – which can only be Bactria.

Whether Bactria was the homeland in its own right or merely a launching-pad for Indians trekking west remains to be seen. But if Nichols' findings, as yet based on a limited corpus of data, could be corroborated further, it would generally help the OIT.

7.6.3 Uralic

A case of contact on a rather large scale which is taken to provide crucial information on the Urheimat question, is that between early IE and Uralic. It was a one-way traffic, imparting some Tocharian, dozens of Iranian and also a few seemingly Indo-Aryan terms to either Proto-Uralic or Proto-Finno-Ugric (i.e. mainstream Uralic after Samoyedic split off). Among the loans from Indo-Iranian or Indo-Aryan, we note *sapta*, 'seven, week', *asura*, 'lord', *sasar*, 'sister', *shata*, 'hundred' (Rédei 1988). The Iranian influence is uncontroversial and easily compatible with any IE Urheimat scenario because for long centuries Iranian covered the area from Xinjiang to Eastern Europe, occupying the whole southern frontier of the Uralic speech area. But how do the seemingly Indo-Aryan words fit in?

At first sight, their presence would seem to confirm the European Urheimat theory: on their way from Europe, the Indo-Iranian tribes encountered the Uralic people in the Ural region and imparted some vocabulary to them. This would even remain possible if, as leading scholars of Uralic suggest, the Uralic languages themselves came from farther east, from the Irtysh river and Balkhash lake area.

The question of the Uralic homeland obviously has consequences. Karoly Rédei (1988: 641) reports on the work of a fellow Hungarian scholar, Peter Hajdu (1950s and 1960s): "According to Hajdu, the Uralic Urheimat may have been in western Siberia. The defect of this theory is that it gives no explanation for the chronological and geographical conditions of its contacts between Uralians (Finno-Ugrians) and Indo-Europeans (Proto-Aryans)." Not at all: Hajdu's theory explains nicely how these contacts may have taken place in Central Asia rather than in Eastern Europe, and with Indo-Iranian rather than with the Western branches of IE. V. V. Napolskikh (1993) has supported the Irtysh/Balkhash homeland theory of Uralic with different types of evidence from that given by Hajdu, and now that the genetic aspect of population movements is being revaluated (Cavalli-Sforza 1996), the Asiatic physical features of isolated Uralic populations like the Samoyeds could also be included as pointers to an easterly homeland.

In that case, three explanations are equally sustainable. One rather facile scenario is the effect of long-distance trade between an Indian metropolis and the northerly backwaters, somewhat like the entry of Arabic and Persian words in distant European languages during the Middle Ages (e.g. *tariff*, *cheque*, *bazar*, *douane, chess*). More interesting is the possibility that these words were imparted to Uralic by IA-speaking emigrants from India.

One occasion for mass emigration, which the OIT sees as a carrier of IA languages, was the catastrophe which led to the abandonment of the Harappan cities in *c.*2000 BC. This must have triggered migrations in all directions: to

Maharashtra, to India's interior and east, to West Asia by Mitannic true Indo-Aryans as well as by the "sanskritized" non-IA Kassites. (I disagree with R. S. Sharma 1995: 36 that Mesopotamian inscriptions from the sixteenth century BC "show that the Kassites spoke the Indo-European language," though they do mention the Vedic gods "Suryash" and "Marutash"; for samples of the non-IE Kassite lexicon, vide Van Soldt 1998.) And so, one of these groups went to the Pontic region. Along the way, some members ended up in an Uralic-speaking environment, imparting a bit of IA terminology but getting assimilated over time, just like their Mitannic cousins. The Uralic term *orya*, 'slave', from *ârya*, may indicate that their position was not as dignified as that of the Mitannic horse trainers. Incidentally, it also indicates that at some point, *ârya* did serve as an ethnic term, a hypothesis hotly dismissed by OTI spokesmen (who claim it is purely relegio-cultural: "Vedic", or sociological-ethical: "noble") as a "colonial racist construct."

A third possibility is that the linguistic exchange which imparted Sanskrit-looking words to Uralic took place at a much earlier stage, that of Indo-Iranian, that is, before the development of typical Iranianisms such as the softening of [s] to [h]. Even the stage before Indo-Iranian unity, namely, when Indo-Iranian had not yet replaced the PIE Kentum forms with its own Satem forms and the PIE vowels *a/e/o* with its own uni-vowel *a*, may already have witnessed some lexical exchanges with Uralic. As Asko Parpola (1995: 355) has pointed out, among the IE loans in Uralic, we find a few terms in Kentum form which are exclusively attested in the Indo-Iranian branch of IE, for example, Finnish *kehrä*, 'spindle', from PIE **kettra*, attested in Sanskrit as *cattra*. While it is of course also possible that words like **kettra* once did exist in branches other than Indo-Iranian but disappeared in the intervening period, what evidence we do have points to pre-Satem proto-Indo-Iranian.

The continuous IE-Uralic contact may stretch back even further: to the stage of PIE. Thus, there is nothing pointing to any specifics of the Indo-Iranian branch in the Uralic loan **nime*, 'name', **wete*, 'water', or **wige*, 'to transport' (cfr. Latin *vehere*): these may have been borrowed from united PIE or from other proto-branches, for example, from proto-Germanic. Even more intimate common items concern the pronominal system, for example, **m-* marking the first and **t-* the second person singular, **t-* the demonstrative, **ku/kw* the interrogative.

And the process of borrowing stretches back even farther than that: to the stage of laryngeal PIE. No less than twenty-seven Uralic loans from IE have been identified where original PIE laryngeals are in evidence, mostly adapted as [k], for example, Finnish *kulke*, 'go, walk' (Koivulehto 1991: 46) from PIE *kwelH-*, whence Skt *carati*, 'goes, walks'. Sometimes the resulting sound is [sh], in most cases weakened later on to [h], for example, Finnish *puhdas*, 'clean', from PIE *pewḥ-*, 'to clean', with perfect participle suffix *-t-*, cfr. Skt *pûta*, 'cleaned' (Koivulehto 1991: 93). If this is correct, PIE and proto-Uralic have come in contact even before they got fragmented, that is, in their respective homelands. In that case, PIE cannot have been located far from Central Asia, and probably Northwest India could do the job, especially if the Uralians ultimately arrived in the Ob-Irtysh basin from a more southerly region such as Sogdia.

A third partner in this relationship must also be taken into account, though its connection with Uralic looks older and deeper than that of PIE: Dravidian. Witzel (1999a: 349) acknowledges the "linguistic connections of Dravidian with Uralic." Both are families of agglutinative languages with flexive tendencies, abhorring consonant clusters and favoring the stress on the first syllable. Sergent (1997: 65–72) maps out their relationship in some detail, again pointing to the northwest outside India as the origin of Dravidian. We may ignore Sergent's theory of an African origin of Dravidian for now, and limit our attention to his less eccentric position that a Proto-Dravidian group at one point ended up in Central Asia, there to leave substratum traces discernible even in the IE immigrant language Tocharian. The most successful lineage of Dravidians outside India was the one which mixed its language with some Palaeo-Siberian tongue, yielding the Uralic language family. Looking around for a plausible location for this development, we find that Siberia may have been a peripheral part where the resulting language could survive best in relative isolation, but that its origins may have been in a more hospitable and crossroads-like region such as Bactria-Sogdia. In the OIT scenario, the Dravidians moved south to Baluchistan and then east into Sindh and Gujarat (avoiding confrontation with the Proto-Indo-Europeans in Panjab), while the Uralians moved north, and those who stayed behind were absorbed later into the expanding PIE community. The interaction of the three may perhaps be illustrated by the word **kota/koṭa*, 'tent, house' in Uralic and in Dravidian, and also in Sanskrit and Avestan but not in any other branch of IE: perhaps Dravidian gave it to Uralic as a birth gift, and later imparted it to those IE languages it could still reach when in India. If this part of the evidence leaves it as conjectural that India was the habitat of the Proto-Indo-Europeans, it does at least argue strongly for some Central-Asian population center, most likely Bactria-Sogdia, as the meeting-place of Proto-Uralic, Proto-Dravidian and PIE, before IE and Uralic would start their duet of continuous (one-way) linguistic interaction on their parallel migrations westward.

7.6.4 Sino-Tibetan

To prove an Asian homeland for IE, it is not good enough to diminish the connections between IE and more westerly language families. To anchor IE in Asia, the strongest argument would be genetic kinship with an East-Asian language family. However, in the case of Sino-Tibetan, all we have is loans, early but apparently not PIE. The early dictionaries suggested a connection between Tibetan *lama*, written and originally pronounced as *blama*, and Sanskrit *brahma* (S. C. Das 1902: 900); *blama* is derived from *bla-*, 'upper, high' (as in *(b)ḷa-dakh*, 'high mountain-pass'), and doesn't Sanskrit *bṛh-*, root of *brahma*, mean 'to grow', that is, 'to become high', close enough to the meaning of Tibetan *bla-*? But more such look-alikes to build a case for profound kinship were never found.

On the other hand, early contact between members of the two families is well-attested, though not in India. A well-known set of transmitted terms was in the sphere of cattlebreeding, all from IE (mostly Tocharian) to Chinese: terms for horse (*ma* < **mra*, cfr. *mare*); hound (*quan*, cfr. Skt *shvan*); honey (*mi*, cfr. *mead*, Skt *medhu*); bull (*gu*, cfr. Skt *go*); and, more recently, lion (*shi*, Iranian *sher*). This does not add new information on the Urheimat question, for the IE-speaking cattle-breeders in Northwest China could have come from anywhere, but it confirms our image of the relations between the tea-drinking Chinese farmers (till today, milk is a rarity in the Chinese diet) and the milk-drinking "barbarians" on their borders.

The first one to point out some common vocabulary between IE and Chinese was Edkins (1871). Since then, the attempt has become more ambitious. The old racial objection has been overruled: there is no reason why the Early Indo-Europeans should have been fair-haired Caucausians (the mummies and skeletons of such types found in large numbers in Xinjiang have been dated to well after the PIE age range), and at any rate languages are known to cross racial frontiers, witness the composition of the Turkish language community, from Mongoloid in pre-Seljuq times to indistinguishable from Armenians or Syrians or Bulgarians today. Also, unlike modern Chinese, archaic Chinese was similar to IE in the shape of its words: monosyllabic roots with consonant clusters, and probably not yet with different tones except for a pitch accent, traces of which also exist in Sanskrit and Greek.

Pulleyblank (1993) claims to have reconstructed a number of rather abstract similarities in the phonetics and morphology of PIE and Sino-Tibetan. Though he fails to back it up with any lexical similarities, he confidently dismisses as a "prejudice" the phenomenon that "for a variety of reasons, the possibility of a genetic relationship between these two language families strikes most people as inherently most improbable". He believes that "there is no compelling reason from the point of view of either linguistics or archaeology to rule out the possibility of a genetic connection between Sino-Tibetan and Indo-European. Such a connection is certainly inconsistent with a European or Anatolian homeland for the Indo-Europeans but it is much less so with the Kurgan theory," especially considering that the Kurgan culture "was not the result of local evolution in that region but *had its source in an intrusion from an earlier culture farther east*" (1993: 106, emphasis mine).

This is of course very interesting, but: "It will be necessary to demonstrate the existence of a considerable number of cognates linked by regular sound correspondences. To do so in a way that will convince the doubters on both sides of the equation will be a formidable task" (1993: 109). That lexical common ground has been mapped rather daringly by Chang Tsung-tung (1988), who offers a rich harvest of common Sino-IE words of *c.*1500 BCE.

Among Chang's findings, we may note, for example, Chinese *sun*, 'grandson', cfr. *son*; *pi* (archaic **peit*), 'must, duty', cfr. *bid*, Lat. *fides*, 'trust', Grk *peithô*, 'persuade'; *gei* (**kop*), 'give', cfr. *give*; *gu* (**kot*), 'bone', cfr. Lat. costa, 'rib'; *lie* (**leut*), 'inferior', cfr. *lit-tle*; *ye* (**lop*), 'leaf', cfr. *leaf*; *bao* (**bak*), 'thin', cfr. *few*, Latin *paucus*, 'few'; *zhi* (**teig*), 'show, point at', cfr. *in-dex*, Grk *deiknumi*; *shi* (**zieg*), 'see', cfr. *see, sight*.

Most remarkable in Chang's list is the high number of Northwest-IE and specfically Germanic cognates: "Germanic preserved the largest number of cognate words" (1988: 32). Eurocentric expansion models would explain this rather simply by letting some Germanic warriors, after their ethnogenesis in Europe, strike east all through Central Asia, a scenario already widely accepted for Tocharian and implemented in recent centuries by the Russians. A more contrived alternative is offered by Gamkrelidze and Ivanov (1955: 832), who trace a Germanic itinerary from their preferred homeland in Anatolia all through Central Asia (and then back west to Europe), leading to contact with at least Yeniseian, the northwesternmost branch of Sino-Tibetan. Their proof amounts to little more than a very tenuous etymology: "And in some Ancient European dialects, in particular Germanic, borrowings from Yeniseian must be assumed in such word as **hus*, 'house' (...), cfr. Yeniseian *qus*, 'tent, house'."

The OIT would let it all fall into place a little better but still require some special pleading: on their way from India, somewhere near the Aral Lake, the Proto-Germanic tribe lost one adventurous clan branching off to the east and settling in China. This would imply that the ethnogenesis of the Germanic tribes, included their distinctive vocabulary, took place in Central Asia rather than in their historic North-European habitat. This is counterintuitive though not strictly impossible. But then, Chang may simply have been wrong about the large Germanic input.

However, the main point remains that Chang's scenario, spectacular though it may be, is not fundamentally different from what we already knew. It claims that some Indo-Europeans imparted some vocabulary to Chinese, but this was a process of contact, not of common origin. Chang does not posit a genetic kinship but the effect of IE superstratum influence imparted to a native dialect when the first Chinese state was "established by IE conquerors" (1988: 34), identified by tradition with the culture heroes, especially the Yellow Emperor, said to have been enthroned in 2697 BC. Chang's list, even if ever verified, does not decide the IE homeland question, except to confirm trivially that it was not China, since the IE input was brought there by foreign invaders. So, Chang's vocabulary does not fill the gaping need of Pulleyblank's hypothesis for a lexico-genetic common ground to complement the purported structural similarity between Sino-Tibetan and IE. Thus far, we still have no East Asian anchor for IE.

7.6.5 Austronesian

Even more unexpected and eccentric than the Chinese connection is the case for early contact or kinship between IE and Austronesian. According to Southworth:

> The presence of other ethnic groups, speaking other languages [than IE, Dravidian or Munda], must be assumed (...) numerous examples can be found to suggest early contact with language groups now unrepresented in the subcontinent. A single example will be noted here. The word for "mother" in several of the Dardic languages, as well as in Nepali, Assamese, Bengali, Oriya, Gujarati, and Marathi (...) is *âî* (or a similar form). The source of this is clearly the same as that of classical Tamil *ây*,

> "mother." These words are apparently connected with a widespread group of words found in Malayo-Polynesian (cf. Proto-Austronesian **bayi*...) and elsewhere. The distribution of this word in Indo-Aryan suggests that it must have entered Old Indo-Aryan very early (presumably as a nursery word, and thus not likely to appear in religious texts), before the movement of Indo-Aryan speakers out of the Panjab. In Dravidian, this word is well-represented in all branches (though *amma* is perhaps an older word) and thus, if it is a borrowing, it must be a very early one.
>
> (1979: 205)

Next to *âyî*, 'mother', Marathi has the form *bâî*, 'lady', as in *ṭârâ-bâî, ḷakṣmî-bâî.* etc.; the same two forms are attested in Austronesian. So, we have a nearly pan-Indian word, attested from Nepal and Kashmir to Maharashtra and Tamil Nadu, and seemingly related to Austronesian. For another example: "Malayo-Polynesian shares cognate forms of a few [words which are attested in both Indo-Aryan and Dravidian], notably Old Indo-Aryan *phala-* ['fruit'], Dravidian *palam* ['ripe fruit'], etc. (cf. Proto-Austronesian **palam*, 'to ripen a fruit artificially'...), and the words for rice" (Southworth 1979: 206).

Austronesian seems to have very early and very profound links with IE. In the personal pronouns (e.g. Proto-Austronesian **aku*, cfr. *ego*), the first four numerals (e.g. Malay *dua* for 'two', though one theory holds that the proto-Austronesian form is **dusa*, whence *duha, dua*; but then why not consider the possibility that the similar IE form is likewise the evolute of some older form **dusa*?) and other elementary vocabulary including the words for 'water' and 'land', the similarity is too striking to be missed. Remarkable lexical similarities had been reported since at least the 1930s, and they have been presented by Isidore Dyen (1970), whose comparisons are sometimes not too obvious but satisfy the linguistic requirement of regularity.

However, this lexical similarity or exchange is not backed up by grammatical similarities: in contrast with the elaborate categories of IE grammar, Austronesian grammar looks much less complicated, or at least much less orderly, the textbook example being the "childlike" plural by reduplication, as in Malay *orang*, 'man', *orang-orang*, 'men'. If the connection is real, we may be dealing with a case of heavy creolization: a mixed population (*colluvies gentium*) adopting lexical items from another language but making up a grammar from scratch. Then again, genetically related languages may become completely different in language structure (e.g. English versus Sanskrit, Chinese versus Tibetan): Dyen therefore saw no objection to postulating a common genetic origin rather than an early large-scale borrowing.

Dyen cannot be accused of an Indian homeland bias either for IE or for Austronesian. For the latter, "Dyen's lexicostatistical classification of Austronesian suggested a Melanesian homeland, a conclusion at variance with all other sources of information (...) heavy borrowing and numerous shifts in and around New Guinea have obviously distorted the picture," according to Bellwood (1994). For IE, he didn't feel qualified to question the AIT consensus. It is *in spite of* his opinions about the Austronesian and IE homelands that he felt forced to face facts concerning IE–Austronesian similarities. It just happens to be difficult to rhyme these data together otherwise, except for their unsportsmanlike dismissal as "probably coincidence."

The dominant opinion as reported by Bellwood is that Southeast China and Taiwan (ultimately "Sundaland"?) are the homeland from where Austronesian expanded in all sea-borne directions. Hence its adstratum presence in Japanese, which may yet prove to be a rather hard nut to crack for an Indian homeland theory of Austronesian. Talageri (1993: 129) predictably incorporates Dyen's suggestion of linguistic kinship into a defense of an Indian common homeland for IE and Austronesian. But meanwhile, to my knowledge, ever since Dyen's publication, no expert has come forward to corroborate his hypothesis or develop it further. That's only an argument from opinion trends, possibly even reflecting mere inertia and conformism, but it cannot be ignored altogether.

Incidentally, even a common linguistic origin of IE and Austronesian need not prove that they originated in India. Indian Puranic tradition teaches that Manu Vaivasvata trekked inland to North India after washing up on the shore during the Flood. Suppose the Indo-Europeans and the Austronesians shared a homeland somewhere in Southeast Asia? An arrival of the Indo-Europeans into India by boat from Southeast Asia, is an interesting thought experiment, if only to free ourselves from entrenched stereotypes. Why not counter the Western AIT with an Eastern AIT?

7.7 Glottochronology

Among the methods once used to map out the history of IE, one which has gone out of fashion is glottochronology, that is, estimating the rate of change in a language, and deducing a given text corpus's age from the amount of difference with the language's present state (or state at a known later time) divided by the rate of change. In a few trivial cases, the assumption remains valid, for example, it is impossible for the Ṛgveda to have been composed over a period of a thousand years, because no language remains that stable for so long, that is, no language has a rate of change approximating zero (*unless* it is a classical language artificially maintained, like classical Sanskrit or classical Chinese, or alternatively, unless the Vedic hymns were linguistically updated at the time of their final compilation and editing).

Likewise, trivial glottochronology allows us to say that the time-lapse between Ṛgveda and Avesta must be longer than approximately zero. It is often said that with a few phonetic substitutions, an Avesta copy in Devanagari script (as is effectively used by the Parsis: Kanga and Sontakke 1962) could be read as if it were Vedic Sanskrit. But in fact, there is already a considerable distance between the two languages, including a serious morphological recrudescence in Avestan as compared to Vedic. Indeed, in the introduction to his authoritative translation of Zarathushtra's *Gâthâ*s, Insler writes: "The prophet's hymns are laden with ambiguities resulting both from *the merger of many grammatical endings* and from the intentionally compact and often elliptical style..." (1975: 1, emphasis mine). Having evolved from a common starting-point, the Avestan language represents a younger stage of Indo-Iranian, a linguistic fact matched by the religious difference between the Ṛgveda, which initially knows nothing of a *Deva/Asura* conflict, and the Avesta where this conflict has come center-stage, just as it has in younger Vedic literature.

Though a glottochronological intuition remains legitimate, the attempt to define a universal rate of change has been abandoned. A test of the common assumptions behind much glottochronological reasoning has been carried out on a group of languages with a well-known history: the Romance languages. It was found that according to the glottochronological assumptions, Italian and French separated to become different languages in AD 1586, Romanian and Italian in AD 1130, etc.: nearly a millennium later than in reality (Haarmann 1990: 2). If this is an indication of a general bias in our estimates, the intuitive or supposedly scientific estimates of the age at which PIE split (3000 BC), at which Indo-Iranian split (1500 BC) etc., are probably too low as well. And it so happens that the OIT tends to imply a higher chronology, with the Ṛgveda falling in the Harappan or even the pre-Harappan period.

The AIT itself gets into difficulties, having to cram a lot of Old IA history into the period between the decline of Harappa and the life of the Buddha, especially if both the Vedic period and the invasion-to-Veda period have to be lengthened. And they may really have to. Winternitz already wrote (1907: 288): "We cannot explain the development of the whole of this great literature if we assume as late a date as round about 1200 BC or 1500 BC as its starting-point." He consequently opted for "2000 or 2500 BC" as the beginning of Vedic literature. And this beginning came a long while after the invasion, for according to Kuiper (1967, 1997: xxiv, quoted with approval by Witzel 1999a: 388), "between the arrival of the Aryans (...) and the formation of the oldest hymns of the RV a much longer period must have elapsed than normally thought."

On the other hand, one is struck by the living presence of the Iranian ethnic groups first mentioned in the Ṛgveda (*dâsa*s, *dasyu*s and *paṇi*s, who were not "dark-skinned pre-Aryan aboriginals" but Iranians, as shown e.g. by Parpola 1995: 367ff.) as late as the Greco-Roman period. Herodotos, Strabo, and others know of such Iranian peoples as the *Parnoi* and the *Dahae*. Alexander encountered an Indian king called *Poros*, apparently the same name as carried by the Vedic patriarch *Puru*, a very rare name in classical Hinduism. As a matter of intuitive glottochronology, one wonders: at a thousand years after their mention in the Ṛgveda, isn't this stability of nomenclature already a sign of unusual conservatism, given that cultures and names change continually? For the Iranian tribes, isn't staying around to be noted by Herodotos already a big achievement, considering that nations continually disappear, merge, change names, move out, or otherwise disappear from the radar screen? Isn't it consequently unlikely that the Ṛgveda be, say, another thousand years older, making the lifespan of these names and tribes even more exceptional?

In fact, tribal identities can last even longer, and it is again the Ṛgveda which provides ethnonyms which have remained in use till today, that is, 3200 years later by even the most conservative estimate. The Vedic king *sudâs* faced and defeated a coalition of tribes among which we recognize Iranian ethnonyms still in use, including the *paktha*, *bhalâna* (both 7.18.7), and *parshu* (RV 7.83.1, 8.6.46). The first is *Pakhtoon*, *Pashtu* or *Pathan*, the second is still found in *Bolan*, the mountain pass in *Baluchistan*; and these two embolden us to identify the third as the eponymous founders of the *Persian* province of *Fars*. Whichever the date of the Ṛgveda, if the Pathans could retain their tribal name and identity till today, the *dâsa*s and *paṇi*s could certainly do so until the Greco-Roman period. Glottochronology is no longer an obstacle standing in the way of the higher chronology required by most versions of the OIT.

7.8 Conclusion

We have looked into the pro and contra of some *prima facie* indications for an OIT of IE expansion. Probably none of these can presently be considered as decisive evidence against the AIT. But at least it has been shown that the linguistic evidence surveyed does not necessitate the AIT either. One after another, the classical proofs of a European origin have been discredited, usually by scholars who had no knowledge of or interest in an alternative Indian homeland theory.

It is too early to say that linguistics has proven an Indian origin for the IE family. But we can assert with confidence that the oft-invoked linguistic evidence for a European Urheimat and for an Aryan invasion of India is wanting. We have not come across linguistic data which are incompatible with the OIT. In the absence of a final judgment by linguistics, other approaches deserve to be taken more seriously, unhindered and uninhibited by fear of that large-looming but in fact elusive "linguistic evidence for the AIT."

Bibliography

Abbi, A., 1994. *Semantic Universals in Indian Languages*. Shimla: Institute of Advanced Study.

——, 1997. "Debate on Archaism of Some Select Bangani Words," *Indian Linguistics*, 58: 1–14.

Anthony, D. W., 1991. "The Archaeology of Indo-European Origins," *Journal of Indo-European Studies* (Fall): 193–222.

Basham, A. L., 1979. "Foreword." In *Aryan and Non-Aryan in India*, edited by Deshpande and Hook. Ann Arbor, MI: Centre for South and Southeast Asian Studies.

Beekes, R. S. P., 1990. *Vergelijkende Taalwetenschap. Tussen Sanskrit en Nederlands*. Utrecht: Het Spectrum.

Bellwood, P., 1994. "An Archaeologist's View of Language Macrofamily Relationships," *Oceanic Linguistics* (December): 391–406.

Biswas, S. K., 1995. *Autochthon of India and the Aryan Invasion*. Delhi: Genuine Publications & Media.

Cavalli-Sforza, L. L., 1996. *Gènes, Peuples et Langues*. Paris: Odile Jacob.

Chang, T., 1988. "Indo-European Vocabulary in Old Chinese," *Sino-Platonic Papers*, no. 7, Philadelphia, PA.

Das, S. C., 1902 [1991]. *Tibetan-English Dictionary*. Delhi: Gaurav Publishers.

Décsy, G., 1991. *The Indo-European Protolanguage. A Computational Reconstruction*. Bloomington, IN: Eurolingua.

Deshpande, M. M., 1979. "Genesis of Rgvedic Retroflexion. A Historical and Sociolinguistic Investigation." In *Aryan and Non-Aryan in India*, edited by M. Deshpande and P. E. Hook. Ann Arbor, MI: Center for South and Southeast Asian Studies, University of Michigan, pp. 235–315.

Dyen, I., 1970 [1966]. "Background 'noise' or 'evidence' in Comparative Linguistics: the Case of the Austronesian-Indo-European hypothesis." In *Indo-European and Indo-Europeans*, edited by G. Cardona. Philadelphia, PA: Proceedings of the Third Indo-European Conference.

Edkins, J., 1871. *China's Place in Philology. An Attempt to Show that the Language of Europe and Asia Have a Common Origin*. London: Trübner.

Elst, K., 1999. *Update on the Aryan Invasion Debate*. Delhi: Aditya Prakashan.

Fairservis, W., 1992. *The Harappan Civilization and its Writing. A Model for the Decipherment of the Indus Script*. Delhi: Oxford & IBH Publishers.

Gamkrelidze, T. and V. Ivanov, 1995. *Indo-European and the Indo-Europeans. A Reconstruction and Historical Analysis of a Proto-Language and a Proto-Culture* (Vol. 1: Text). Berlin: Mouton de Gruyter.

Haarmann, H., 1990. " 'Basic vocabulary' and Language Contacts: the Disillusion of Glottochronology." *Indogermanische Forschungen*, 95: 1–37.

Hamp, E., 1996. "On the Indo-European Origins of the Reflexes in Sanskrit," *Journal of the American Oriental Society*, 116(4): 719–23.

Harmatta, J., 1992. "The Emergence of the Indo-Iranians: the Indo-Iranian Languages." In *History of Civilizations*, edited by A. H. Dani and V. M. Masson. Paris: UNESCO Publishers.

Haudry, J., 2000. "Les Aryens sont-ils autochtones en Inde?" *Nouvelle Ecole*, 51: 147–53.

Hock, H. H., 1999. "Out of India? The Linguistic Evidence." In *Aryan and Non-Aryan in South Asia. Evidence, Interpretation and Ideology*, edited by J. Bronkhorst and M. Deshpande. Cambridge, MA: Harvard University Press, pp. 1–18.

Insler, S., 1975. *The Gathas of Zarathustra*. In *Acta Iranica*, troisième série, Vol. 1. Teheran: Bibliothèque Pehlevi.

Jones-Bley, K. and M. Huld, 1996. *The Indo-Europeanization of Northern Europe, Journal of Indo-European Studies*, Monograph no. 17. Washington DC.

Jonsson, H., 1978. *The Laryngeal Theory. A Critical Survey*. Lund: Publications of the New Society of Letters at Lund.

Kanga, E. and N. S. Sontakke, 1962. *Avestâ, the Sacred Scripture of the Parsees*. Pune: Vaidika Samshodhana Mandala.

Koivulehto, J., 1991. *Uralische Evidenz für die Laryngaltheorie*. Vienna: Verlag der Oesterreichischen Akademie für Wissenschaften.

Kretschmer, P., 1944. *Inder am Kuban*. Vienna.

Kuiper, F. B. J., 1962. *Nahali, a Comparative Study*. Amsterdam: Noord-Hollandsche Uitgeversmaatschappij.

——, 1967. "The Genesis of a Linguistic Area," *Indo-Iranian Journal*, 10: 81–102.

——, 1991. *Aryans in the Rigveda*. Amsterdam: Rodopi.

——, 1997. In *Selected Writings on Indian Linguistics and Philology*, edited by A. Lubotsky *et al.* Amsterdam/Atlanta: Rodopi.

Lal, B. B., 1998. *New Light on the Indus Civilization*. Delhi: Aryan Books.

Lehmann, W. P., 1997 [1993]. *Theoretical Bases of Indo-European Linguistics*. London: Routledge.

Lehrmann, A., 1997. "Hitt. ga-ne-esh-+ and the Laryngeal Theory." *Indogermanische Forschungen*, 102: 151.

McAlpin, D., 1979. "Linguistic Prehistory: the Dravidian Situation." In *Aryan and Non-Aryan in India*, edited by M. Deshpande and P. Hook. Ann Arbor, MI: University of Michigan Press.

Manczak, W., 1992. *De la Préhistoire des Peuples Indo-Européens*. Krakow: Uniwersytet Jagiellonski.

Masica, C., 1979. "Aryan and non-Aryan elements in North-Indian agriculture." In *Aryan and Non-Aryan in India*, edited by M. Deshpande and P. Hook. Ann Arbor, MI: University of Michigan Press.

Misra, S. S., 1992. *The Aryan Problem. A Linguistic Approach*. Delhi: Munshiram Manoharlal.

Monier-Williams, Sir M., 1984 [1899]. *A Sanskrit-English Dictionary*. Varanasi: Motilal Banarsidass.

Napolskikh, V. V., 1993. "Uralic Fish Names and Original Home." *Ural-Altaische Jahrbücher*, Neue Folge Band 12: 35–57.

Nichols, J., 1997. "The Epicentre of the Indo-European Linguistic Spread." In *Archaeology and Language I: Theoretical and Methodological Orientations*, edited by R. Blench and M. Spriggs. London: Routledge, pp. 122–48.

Oppenheimer, S., 1999 [1998]. *Eden in the East. The Drowned Continent of Southeast Asia*. London: Phoenix.

Pargiter, F. E., 1962. *Ancient Indian Historical Tradition*. Delhi: Motilal Banarsidass.

Parpola, A., 1994. *Deciphering the Indus Script*. New York: Cambridge University Press.

——, 1995. "The Problem of the Aryans and the Soma: Textual-linguistic and Archaeological Evidence." In *The Indo-Aryans of Ancient South Asia: Language, Material Culture, and Ethnicity*, edited by G. Erdosy. Berlin: Walter de Gruyter.

Pinnow, H.-J., 1953. "Zu den altindischen Gewässernamen," *Beiträge zur Namensforschung*, 4: 217–34.

Pirart, E., 1998. "Historicité des forces du mal dans la Rgvedasamhita," *Journal Asiatique* 286(2).

Pulleyblank, E. G., 1993. "The Typology of Indo-European," *Journal of Indo-European Studies* (Spring): 63–118.

Rajaram, N. S., 1995. *The Politics of History: Aryan Invasion Theory and the Subversion of Scholarship*. New Delhi: Voice of India.

Rajshekar, V. T., 1987. *Dalit. The Black Untouchables of India*. Atlanta: Clarity Press.

Rao, S. R., 1992. *Dawn and Devolution of the Indus Civilisation*. Delhi: Aditya Prakashan.

Ratnagar, S., 1999. "Does Archaeology Hold the Answers?" In *Aryan and Non-Aryan in South Asia*, edited by J. Bronkhorst and M. Deshpande, Harvard Oriental Series. Opera Minora, Vol. 3, Cambridge, MA: Harvard University Press, pp. 207–38.

Rédei, K., 1988. "Die ältesten indogermanischen Lehnwörter der Uralischen Sprachen." In *The Uralic Languages: Description, History and Foreign Influences* (*Handbuch der Orientalistik*, Achte Abteilung, Vol. 1), edited by Denis Sinor. Leiden: Brill, pp. 638–64.

Renfrew, C., 1987. *Archaeology and Language: the Puzzle of Indo-European Origins*. London: J. Cape.

Samuel, G. J., *et al.* eds, 1990. *Encyclopedia of Tamil Literature*. Madras: Institute of Asian Studies.

Sergent, B., 1995. *Les Indo-Européens. Histoire, Langues, Mythes*. Paris: Payot.

——, 1997. *Genèse de l'Inde*. Paris: Payot.

Sethna, K. D., 1982. *Karpasa in Prehistoric India. A Chronological and Cultural Clue*. Delhi: Biblia Impex.

Shaffer, J. and D. Lichtenstein, 1999. "Migration, Philology and South Asian Archaeology." In *Aryan and Non-Aryan in South Asia: Evidence, Interpretation and Ideology*, edited by J. Bronkhorst and M. Deshpande. Cambridge, MA: Harvard University Press.
Sharma, R. S., 1995. *Looking for the Aryans*. Madras: Orient Longman.
Southworth, F., 1979. "Indo-Aryan and Dravidian." In *Aryan and Non-Aryan India*, edited by M. Deshpande and P. Hook. Ann Arbor, MI: Center for South and Southeast Asian Studies, University of Michigan.
Talageri, S., 1993. *The Aryan Invasion Theory. A Reappraisal*. Delhi: Aditya Prakashan.
——, 2000. *The Rg-Veda, a Historical Analysis*. Delhi: Aditya Prakashan.
Thapar, R., 1996. "The Theory of Aryan Race and India", *Social Scientist*, January–March: 3–29.
Trubachov, O., 1999. *Indo-Arica: Indo-arijcy v Severnom Princhernomor'e* (partly translated as *Indoarica in the North Black Sea Region*). Moscow: Nauka.
van Driem, G. and S. R. Sharma, 1996. "In Search of Kentum Indo-Europeans in the Himalayas," *Indogermanische Forschungen*, 101: 107–46.
Van Soldt, W., 1998. "Het Kassitisch." *Phoenix*, 44: 90–3.
von Fürer-Haimendorf, C., 1956. "Foreword." In *The Bhils*, edited by T. B. Naik. Delhi: Bharatiya Adimjati Sevak Sangh.
Wagner, H., 1984. *Das Hethitische vom Standpunkte der typologischen Sprachgeographie*. Pisa: Giardini.
Waradpande, N. R., 1989. *The Aryan Invasion, a Myth*. Nagpur: Babasaheb Apte Smarak Samiti.
——, 1993. "Fact and Fiction about the Aryans." In *The Aryan Probem*, edited by S. B. Deo and Suryanath Kamath. Pune: Bharatiya Itihasa Sankalana Samiti.
Winternitz, M., 1907 [1987] (reprint). *History of Indian Literature*. Delhi: Motilal Banarsidass.
Witzel, M., 1995. Early Indian History: Linguistic and Textual Parameters. In *The Indo-Aryans of Ancient South Asia: Language, Material Culture and Ethnicity*, edited by G. Erdosy. Berlin: Walter de Gruyter.
——, 1999a. "Aryan and Non-Aryan names in Vedic India. Data for the Linguistic Situation, *c*.1900–500 BC." In *Aryan and Non-Aryan in South Asia*, edited by J. Bronkhorst and M. Deshpande, Harvard Oriental Series. Opera Minora, Vol. 3, Cambridge, MA: Harvard University Press, pp. 337–404.
——, 1999b. "Substrate Languages in Old Indo-Aryan," *Electronic Journal of Electronic Studies*, September: 1–67.
Wojtilla, G. J., 1986. "Notes on Indo-Aryan Terms for 'ploughing' and 'the plough'," *Journal of Indo-European Studies*, Spring: 27–38.
Zhang H., 1998. "Chinese Etyma for River," *Journal of Chinese Linguistics*, January: 1–47.
Zimmer, Stefan, 1990a. "On Indo-Europeanization," *Journal of Indo-European Studies*, Spring.
——, 1990b. *Ursprache, Urvolk und Indogermanisierung*, Universität Innsbruck.
Zoller, C. P., 1987. "On the Vestiges of an Old Kentum Language in Garhwal (Indian Himalayas)." Paper read at Leiden University Conference.
——, 1988. "Bericht über besondere Archaismen im Bangani, einer Western Pahari-Sprache," *Münchener Studien zur Sprachwissenschaft*, 49: 173–200.
——, 1989. "Bericht über grammatische Archaismen im Bangani", *Münchener Studien zur Sprachwissenschaft*, 50: 159–218.
Zvelebil, K. V., 1990. *Dravidian Linguistics. An Introduction*. Pondicherry: Pondicherry Institute of Linguistics and Culture.

8

PHILOLOGY AND THE HISTORICAL INTERPRETATION OF THE VEDIC TEXTS

Hans Henrich Hock

etaddhastidarśana iva jātyandhāḥ
That is like people blind by birth in/when viewing an elephant.
(*Śaṅkarācārya's bhāṣya* on *Chāndogya-Upaniṣad* 5.18.1)

. . . we are all more or less in the position of the Blind Men with the Elephant in the Indian parable . . .
(Thomas 1904: 461)

8.1 Introduction

The two citations at the beginning of this chapter characterize two very different approaches to the study of the Vedic tradition, or of any tradition – whether in India/South Asia or anywhere else. That of Śaṅkarācārya expresses the reaction of somebody who already knows the truth, for religious/philosophical or ideological reasons, and therefore is able to characterize all those who do not agree as being blind to that truth. That of Thomas represents a common view among philologers and other scholars who consider truth to be their ultimate goal, but realize that truth is always conditional, to be superseded by better evidence or interpretation of evidence. The problem with the first view as applied to scholarship is that its goal is to forestall all dissenting voices and that it therefore does not invite meaningful debate. The potential problem with the second approach is that it may accept all competing views as equally conditional and therefore, in its own way, fails to invite the scholarly challenges and ensuing debate that can lead to better insights and closer approximation of the truth.

To avoid the pitfalls of both approaches it is useful to remind ourselves that blind people are just as capable of producing scholarship as anyone else, by challenging each other and themselves – as well as sighted people – to go beyond what can be grasped at first contact and, as a consequence of having to defend their perceptions against competing views, to investigate matters more thoroughly. In so doing they – we all – can approximate truth more closely. It is in this sense that Thomas's statement should be read and it is in this sense that philology and related fields can be truly defined by the German term "Geisteswissenschaft," that is, science of the mind, *manaḥśāstra*. Stated differently, to yield results that go beyond initial impressions and beyond the validation of preconceived interpretations, philology must embrace the scientific approach of being *transparent* and *vulnerable* – transparent by being open to verification in terms of providing supporting evidence and discussing potentially conflicting evidence, and vulnerable by being open to challenge and potential falsification. This, I believe, is the only way that we can establish a common ground for those working in Vedic studies. Without this common ground, there is nothing that permits us to evaluate the very different perspectives that are current and thus to reach beyond the differences in perspective, ideology, or bias which some of our friends in Cultural Studies claim are inherent in any scholarly activity.

In this chapter I discuss five different cases of Vedic interpretation and a related case of Avestan interpretation which have been taken as supporting either the view that the Aryans, here defined as speakers of Indo-Aryan (Vedic or Pre-Vedic Sanskrit), invaded or migrated into India/South Asia and subjugated a linguistically and racially different indigenous population, or the opposing view that considers Vedic speech to have been established in India/South Asia long before the assumed Aryan invasion or immigration.

Before going into the details, let me say a few words of caution, however. Although, as I show, the passages in question and their interpretation do not provide cogent support for the hypotheses they are supposed to support, this does not mean that either of the two theories is therefore invalidated. It merely means that the evidence in question is not sufficiently cogent to provide support for the respective hypothesis and therefore must be considered irrelevant. First of all, neither hypothesis rests solely on the evidence here examined; and it is in principle perfectly possible that other evidence can show one hypothesis to be superior to the other. But to do so would require a similar thorough sifting of the evidence and its interpretation; and moreover, any new evidence or better interpretation would, in true scientific spirit, be able to overturn the so far victorious hypothesis. It is also possible in principle that none of the currently available evidence stands up under scrutiny and that nevertheless, one or the other hypothesis was historically correct, except that the evidence in its favor has not been preserved for us. Here as elsewhere it is important to keep in mind the statement attributed to the American linguist Paul Postal that "You can't prove that the platypus doesn't lay eggs by showing a picture of a platypus not laying eggs."

8.2 Case I: dialectal variation due to Dravidian influence?[1]

The first case I examine concerns two passages that have been considered evidence that the easterners had less correct speech in Vedic times, that this speech was closer to Prakrit, and/or that all of this was the result of the linguistic influence of the indigenous Dravidians. (Compare for instance the discussion and references in Macdonell and Keith 1912: 1.87, 168, 2.279–80, as well as Renou 1956: 10, 103, Chatterji 1960, and more recently, Deshpande 1978.) Let us refer to this view as "dialectal Dravidian influence."

One of the passages comes from the *Śatapatha-Brāhmaṇa* and is cited in example [1]. What is significant here is that the expression *he 'lavo he 'lavaḥ* for more correct *he 'rayo he 'rayaḥ* or *he arayo he arayaḥ* 'Oh enemies, oh enemies' exhibits the substitution of *l* for *r* which later is associated with eastern, Magadhi speech and is at that stage considered inferior. In addition, of course, the present passage condemns the Asuras' expression as a barbarism.

[1] *te 'surā āttavacaso he 'lavo he 'lava iti vadantaḥ parābabhūvuḥ // tatrainām api vācam ūduḥ / upajijñāsyāṁ sa mlechas tasmān na brāhmaṇo mleched asuryā haiṣā vāg*

(*Śatapatha-Brāhmaṇa* 3.2.1.23–4)

The *Asuras*, deprived of (proper) speech, saying *he 'lavo he 'lavaḥ* [instead of *he 'rayo he 'rayaḥ* or the like] were defeated. At that time they spoke this speech, (which was) unintelligible. That is a barbarism. Therefore a brahmin should not speak like a barbarian. That speech is of the *Asuras*.

A second passage which has been cited in support of dialectal Dravidian influence is given in example [2]. The assumption is that *aduruktavākya* refers to the more complex consonant groups characteristic of Sanskrit (as in *ukta* 'spoken') which in Prakrit were simplified (as in *utta* 'spoken') and thus would be considered by speakers of Prakrit to be *durukta* – or rather *durutta* – 'difficult to pronounce'. The Prakrit simplification, in turn, is attributed to Dravidian influence.

[2] *aduruktavākyaṁ duruktam āhur*...

(*Pañcaviṁśa-Brāhmaṇa* 17.9)

Speech that is not difficult they consider difficult...

Although, as noted, many scholars have accepted the view that these two passages establish dialectal Dravidian influence, closer examination reveals a number of difficulties. One of these is the obvious one that passage [2] does not contain any explicit or even implicit reference to eastern speech; and neither of the two passages contains a reference to Dravidian. But the difficulties do not end here.

Consider first the fuller version of [2], given as [2′]. Evidently, the thrust of the passage is not just language use, and certainly not ordinary language use, but general incorrect behavior, and the final sentence, *adīkṣitā dīkṣitavācaṃ vadanti*, whatever its precise interpretation, localizes this behavior in the realm of the ritual. Given that correct use of language in ritual is a recurrent concern of the Vedas, the default interpretation should be that the *durukta* and *adurukta* of our passage refer to improper and proper language use in the ritual; *durukta* thus contrasts with the *sūkta* 'well-spoken' which underlies the term *sūktha* 'mantra, hymn'. This interpretation finds further support in a near-parallel passage of the *Jaiminīya-Brāhmaṇa* [3] which explicitly refers to ritual purity or impurity. The passage in [2/2′], thus, does not offer clear and unambiguous evidence for dialectal Dravidian influence.

[2′] *garagiro vā ete ye brahmādyaṁ janyam annam adanty (|) aduruktavākyaṁ duruktam āhur (|) adaṇḍyaṁ daṇḍena ghnantaś caranty (|) adīkṣitā dīkṣitavācaṁ vadanti*

(*Pañcaviṁśa-Brāhmaṇa* 17.9)

They who eat foreign (or people's) food (?) as brahmin food are eaters of poison. Speech that is not badly spoken they consider badly spoken. They go around punishing what/who is not to be punished. Even though not consecrated, they (dare to) speak the language of the consecrated.

[3] *vācā hy avratam amedhyaṁ vadanti*

(*Jaiminīya-Brāhmaṇa* 2.222)

By means of speech they speak something not in accordance with religious duties, something ritually impure.

That the passage in [1] is similarly concerned more with ritually correct speech than with dialectal features in pronunciation is shown by the fuller context, given in example [1′]. Note especially the passage *tā́ṁ svīkṛ́tyāgnā́v eva parihṛ́tya sarvahutam ajuhavur āhutir hí devā́nā́ṁ* 'Having obtained her and having enveloped her in fire, they sacrificed her as a burnt offering, for she is an offering of/for the Gods'.

[1′] *...devā́ś ca vā́ āsurā́ś cobhaye prājāpatyā́ḥ prajā́pateḥ pitur dāyam upeyur mana eva devā́ upā́yan vā́cam asurā... ||... tāṁ devā́ḥ | āsurebhyo 'ntarāyaṁs tā́ṁ svikṛ́tyāgnā́v eva parihṛ́tya sarvahutam ājuhavur āhutir hí devā́nā́ṁ sa yā́m evā́mū́m anuṣṭubhā́ juhavus tad evaīnāṁ tad devā́ḥ svyakurvata te 'surā āttavacaso he 'lavo he 'lava iti vadantaḥ parābabhūvuḥ || tatraināṁ api vā́cam ūduḥ | upajijñā́syā́ṁ sa mlechas tasmān na brāhmaṇo mleched asuryā́ haiṣā́ vā́g*

(*Śatapatha-Brāhmaṇa* 3.2.1.18–24)

Now, the Gods and the *Asuras,* both descended from *Prajāpati*, entered upon the inheritance of their father, *Prajāpati*. The Gods inherited mind, the *Asuras*, speech... The Gods wrested her (= speech) from the *Asuras*. Having obtained her and having enveloped her in fire, they sacrificed her as a burnt offering, for she is an offering of/for the Gods. Now, in that they sacrificed her with an *anuṣṭubh* verse, thereby they obtained her for themselves. The *Asuras*, [thus] deprived of (proper) speech, saying *he 'lavo he 'lavaḥ* [instead of *he 'rayo he 'rayaḥ*] were defeated. At that time they spoke this speech, (which was) unintelligible. That is a barbarism. Therefore a brahmin should not speak like a barbarian. That speech is of the *Asuras*.

Finally, a famous passage of *Patañjali's* (see [4]), containing a near-quotation of [1], quite overtly argues for an interpretation of [1] as being primarily concerned with ritually correct speech, not with dialectal differences.

[4] *te 'surāḥ / te 'surā helayo helayaḥ kurvantaḥ parābabhūvuḥ / tasmād brāhmaṇena na mlecchitavai nāpabhāṣitavai / mleccho ha vā eṣa yad apaśabdaḥ / mlecchā mā bhūmety adhyeyaṁ vyākaraṇam // te 'surāḥ // duṣṭaḥ śabdaḥ / duṣṭaḥ śabdaḥ svarato varṇato vā mithyā prayukto na tam artham āha / sa vāgvajro yajamānaṁ hinasti yathendraśatruḥ svarato 'parādhād iti // duṣṭāñ śabdāṇ mā prayukṣmahīty adhyeyaṁ vyākaraṇam // duṣṭaḥ śabdaḥ //*
(*Mahābhāṣya* on Pāṇ. 1.1.1, Kielhorn ed. p. 2.7–13)

The *Asuras*: The *Asuras*, saying *helayo helayaḥ* were defeated. Therefore a brahmin must not speak like a barbarian nor use incorrect speech. For incorrect speech is barbaric speech. Because we do not want to be barbarians, therefore we must study grammar. (So much on) the Asuras. Incorrect word: A word incorrect because of the accent or a sound, used wrongly, does not convey the (proper) sense. (Being) a thunderbolt of speech, it injures the sacrificer just as did (the use of) *indraśatruḥ* because of a wrong accent. Because we do not want to use incorrect words, therefore we must study grammar. (So much for) the incorrect word.

We can thus conclude that the passages in [1] and [2] do not provide cogent evidence for dialectal Dravidian influence. To establish such influence, it would be necessary to draw on other, more cogent evidence. (In numerous publications I have questioned whether any such evidence exists; see Hock 1975, 1984, 1993 but see also 1996a,b.)

8.3 Case II: racial differences between *āryas* and *dāsas/dasyus?*

Since at least the time of Zimmer (1879), the conflict between *ārya* and *dāsa/dasyu* in the earliest Vedic texts has been widely interpreted as one between two racially distinct groups, whose differences are characterized especially in terms of white or light versus black or dark skin color. Basham's summary of the racial characterization of the *dāsas* is representative of this perspective: "The Dāsas are described as dark and ill-favoured, bull-lipped, snub-nosed, worshippers of the phallus, and of hostile speech..." (1954: 32). Similar views are found in Chatterji (1960: 7 and

32),[2] Childe (1926), Elizarenkova (1995: 36), Geldner (1951: *passim*), Gonda (1975: 129), Hale (1986: 147, see also 154), Kuiper (1991: 17 versus a different view on 3–4), Kulke and Rothermund (1986: 35), Macdonell and Keith (1912: s.vv. *dāsa* and *várṇa*), Mansion (1931: 6), Parpola (1988: 104–6, 120–1, 125), Rau (1957: 16). See also Deshpande (1978: 260) and Sjoberg (1990: 47, 62).

Evidence for this interpretation comes first of all from the Rig-Vedic passages cited in [5]–[13], in which words meaning 'black' or 'dark' appear in reference to the opponents of the Aryas.

[5] *ā́ryaṁ prā́vad*... svàr*miḷheṣv*... / ... ***tvácaṁ kṛṣṇā́m*** *arandhayat*
(RV 1.130.8)

Geldner: 'Indra helped the Aryan in the battles for the *sunlight*... he made the **black skin** subject...'[3]
(Geldner's note: 'the black skin'[4] refers to 'the black aborigines'[5])

[6] (a) *pañcāśát* ***kṛṣṇā́*** *ní vapaḥ sahásrā͜ átkaṁ ná púro jarimā́ ví dardaḥ*
(RV 4.16.13cd)

Geldner: 'Fifty thousand Blacks you defeated. You slit up the forts like age [slits up] a garment.'[6]

(b) sū́ra *upāké tanvàṁ dádhāno ví yát te céty amṛ́tasya várpaḥ* /
(RV 4.16.14ab = continuation of 13cd)

Geldner: 'Taking your stand next to the *sun* so that the figure of you, the immortal, strikes one's eyes...'[7]

[7] (a) *tvád bhiyā́* ***víśa*** *āyann* ***ásiknīr*** *asamanā́ jáhatīr bhójanāni*
(RV 7.5.3ab)

Geldner: 'Out of fear of you the **black tribes** moved away, leaving behind their possessions without fight...'[8]

(b) *tvám dásyūm̐r ókaso agna āja* urújyótir *janáyann ā́ryāya*
(Ibid. 6cd)

You, Agni, drove out the *Dasyus* from their home, making *broad light* for the 'Arya.'

[8] (a) *antáḥ* ***kṛṣṇā́m*** aruṣaír *dhā́mabhir gāt*
(RV 3.31.21b)

Geldner: 'He excluded the **Blacks** with the *fiery* beings (...)'[9]
(Geldner's note: 'The Blacks probably are the black race and, in the mythological background, the Paṇis or the powers of darkness; the ruddy beings or powers... [are] the powers of light... *aruṣá* and *kṛṣṇá* elsewhere are the contrast between morning and night...'[10])

(b) *drúho ví yāhi bahulā́ ádevīḥ* svàś *ca no maghavan sātáye dhāḥ* ||

(Ibid. 19cd)

Geldner: 'Thwart the many godless malices, and let us win the *sun*, O you who are rich in gifts.'[11]

[9] (a) *ghnántah **kṛṣṇā́m** ápa **tvácam***

(RV 9.41.1c)

Geldner: 'driving away the **black skin**'[12]
(Geldner's note: the "black skin" refers to "the demons or the un-Aryan race"[13])
Graßmann: 'the black cover, i.e. darkness'[14]

(b) *sá pavasva vicarṣaṇa ā́ mahī́ ródasī pṛṇa / uṣā́ḥ* sū́ryo *ná raśmībhiḥ*

(Ibid. 5)

Geldner: 'Clarify yourself, you excellent one, fill both great worlds, (like) *Uṣas*, like *Sūrya* [i.e. the sun] with your beams.'[15]

[10] *sá vṛtrahéndraḥ **kṛṣṇáyonīḥ** puraṁdaró dā́sīr airayad ví / ájanayan* mánave kṣā́m…

(RV 2.20.7ac)

Geldner: 'The killer of Vṛtra, Indra, broke open the dasic (forts) which protected the **Blacks** in their wombs, he, the breaker of forts. He created *land for Manu…*'[16]

[11] *yáḥ **kṛṣṇágarbhā** niráhann…*

(RV 1.101.1b)

Geldner: '…who made the ones who were **pregnant with the Blacks** abort (their embryos)…'[17]

[12] *índradviṣṭam ápa dhamanti māyáyā **tvácam ásiknīṁ** bhū́mano divás pári*

(RV 9.73.5cd)

Geldner: 'the pressing stones, through magical power, blow away from earth and heaven the **black skin** hateful to *Indra*.'[18]
(Geldner's note: the 'black skin' refers to the 'black aborigines')
Graßmann: 'the black cover, i.e. darkness'[19]

[13] ***aruśahā́*** (10.116.4d)
Geldner: 'The killer of the **Blacks**'[20]
(Geldner's note: The non-White is the dark-colored non-Aryan…'[21])
Graßmann: 'slaying the non-shining one, i.e. the dark (cloud)…'[22]

Closer examination suggests an alternative interpretation of the terms 'black' or 'dark' as referring to the dark world of the *dāsas/dasyus* in contrast with the light world of the *āryas*, an interpretation which is in perfect agreement with the contrast between good/light and evil/dark forces that pervades the Vedas (and has parallels in many, perhaps most other traditions around the world). First, wherever there is sufficient context for interpretation (which excludes [11], [12], and [13]), either the same line or verse or a closely neighboring one contains a reference to the 'sun' [5], [6], and [9], to 'broad light' [7], or to 'red' or 'fiery' beings [8].[23] These references are marked in roman. Further, elsewhere in the Rig-Veda the word *tvac-* 'skin', which occurs in [5], [9], and [12], does not necessarily designate human or animal skin, but may refer to the surface of the earth. Examples of this use occur at RV 1.79.3, 1.145.5, 10.68.4, and possibly 4.17.14. The expression *rómā pṛthivyā́ḥ* (1.65.8) 'the body-hair of the earth' = 'the plants', suggests that the metaphor of *tvac-* as the 'skin' or surface of the earth was well established in the poetic language of the Rig-Veda. In [5], [9], and [12], therefore, the reference may well be to the 'dark earth' or 'dark world' of the *dāsas/dasyus* that contrasts with the *urújyótiḥ* 'broad light' of the *āryas*, which is lit up by the sun or by 'fiery beings'. In this regard note the close similarity between the expressions *ájanayan mánave* ***kṣā́m*** 'he created **land** for Manu' in [10] and ***urújyótir*** *janáyann ā́ryāya* 'making **broad light** for the *ārya*'. (For further discussion see Hock 1999.) Kennedy (1995: 56) argues for a similar interpretation, but without detailed philological support; the situation is similar in publications such as Frawley (1994).

The case is even weaker for the "noseless" and "bull-lipped" characterizations of the *dāsas/dasyus*. Both characterizations rest on a *single* passage each ([14] and [15]); and in both cases it was soon realized that the "racially" tinted interpretation is problematic at best. Nevertheless, as Trautmann (1999) points out, the single occurrence of the "noseless" passage gave rise to an elaborate "racial" account by Risley (1891: 249–50), which claims that there are "*frequent* references to the noses of the people whom the Aryans found in possession of the plains of India" [emphasis supplied].

[14] ***anā́so*** *dásyūm̐r amṛṇo vadhéna*
ní duryoṇá āvṛṇaṅ ***mṛdhrávācaḥ***

(RV 5.29.10cd)

You destroyed the **noseless** (*anā́s-* = *a-* 'negative' + *nā́s-* 'nose'?) dasyus with your weapon; you smashed those of **evil speech** in their abode.

[15] *dā́sasya cid* ***vṛṣaśiprásya*** *māyā́ jaghnátur narā pṛtanájyeṣu*

(RV 7.99.4cd)

You have destroyed the tricks even of the *dāsa* "bull-lipped" (?) in the battles, O lords.

A very different interpretation of [14] has been available since *Sāyaṇa*, has been accepted by most Indologists, and is supported by the use of *mṛdhrávāc-* in the same verse, which can only mean 'of evil or bad speech'. This is the analysis of *anās-* as *an-* 'negative' + *ā́s-* 'mouth' – that is 'mouthless' = 'speechless; barbarian'. Given the limited context, it is I believe impossible to judge whether this characterization refers to a linguistic difference such as Dravidian versus Aryan, or whether it should be interpreted as referring to ritually incorrect speech, along the same lines as in examples [1] and [2].

As for the word glossed as "bull-lipped," the problem is that, as acknowledged for example, by Macdonell and Keith (1912, s.v. śiprā), the element *śiprá* in this compound is of rather uncertain interpretation and that there are numerous other problems of a formal nature. Moreover, it must be kept in mind that words meaning 'bull' do not have negative connotations in early Sanskrit, as they tend to have in Modern English, but are used widely to indicate male or masculine strength. The correct interpretation of *vṛṣaśiprá* therefore is anybody's guess.

The evidence of the Rig-Vedic passages just examined thus does not establish a difference in "race" or phenotype between *āryas* and *dāsas/dasyus*. Whether there was such a difference or not will have to be argued out on the basis of other evidence which, of course, must likewise be subjected to close scrutiny. (The archaeological evidence at this point does not support an in-migration of a different racial group in the entire second millennium BC; but then it also fails to furnish evidence for the well-established later in-migrations of Sakas, Hunas, and many other groups. So this evidence, too, fails to yield reliable results. See Hock 2002 for further discussion.)

8.4 Case III: textual evidence for Aryan in-migration?

Some publications claim that the Rig-Veda contains actual textual evidence for an Aryan in-migration; see for example, Biswas 1995, Witzel 1995. In support of this claim they refer to passages such as RV 6.45.1, 10.63[.1], 10.108.1–10 (the *Saramā*-episode) which are said to mention travel or arrival from afar; 6.20.12 = 1.174.9, 2.13.12;[24] 4.19.6, 10.53.8 which supposedly deal with the often difficult crossing of rivers; 6.47.20–21 which is considered to refer to traversing through narrow passages; and the like. A detailed exemplification of these and other similar passages can be dispensed with; suffice it to state that none of them provide unambiguous clues that the point of origin for these travels was further (north-)west or *outside* of India/South Asia, or that the direction of travel was to the east or further *into* India/South Asia.[25] In fact, Witzel weakens his own case by mentioning (1995: 322) that "several tribes on the Indo-Iranian Borderlands undergo this ordeal twice a year: they descend to the plains of the Panjab in the winter, only to return to the highlands of Afghanistan in the spring, in each case passing through hostile territory." Given this modern-day parallel, what is to prevent us from looking at the passages cited by Biswas and Witzel as referring to similar, fairly local movements back and forth within the larger South Asian area, rather than a movement of new immigrants?

Witzel, to be sure, believes to have found Rig-Vedic evidence that does support an eastward movement of the Aryans; see [16]. Witzel gets this interpretation by claiming that *savyatáḥ* 'on the left' can also mean 'to the North', and indicates once again that Vedic poets faced the east – their presumed goal – in contemplating the world.

[16] *ápāvṛṇor jyótir ā́ryāya ní savyatáḥ sādi dásyur…*

(RV 2.11.18cd)

for the *Ārya* you opened the light; the Dasyu was left behind, on the left…

While *uttara* certainly can mean both 'left' and 'north', for the *savya* of this passage the meaning 'left' is normal, and 'north' seems to be quite uncommon (Böthlingk-Roth give no attestation). Moreover, there is nothing in this passage which requires the meaning 'north'. At best, then, the passage is ambiguous – which means that it cannot be used in support of *any* hypothesis. What is more serious is Witzel's claim that the Vedic poets' orientation to the east reflects their "goal," presumably of their migration. A much simpler explanation is possible, namely that the orientation to the east reflects a ritual or religious orientation to the rising sun. This explains not only the eastern orientation of Vedic society and ritual in general [17a], but also the similar orientation in Old Irish [17b] (where an eastward migration can be safely excluded), the fact that English *north* and its Germanic cognates are related to words meaning 'left' elsewhere in Indo-European [17c]; and the very etymology of the words *orient*, *orientation*, which derive from Lat. *oriri* 'to rise', and similar words such as *Levante* and *Anatolia* [17d]. (See Hock and Joseph 1996: 245–8 with parallels elsewhere.)

[17]	(a)	Skt	*prāñc-*	'east' (lit. 'forward')
			uttara-	'north' (lit. 'left')
			dakṣiṇa-	'south' (lit. 'right')
			paścima-	'west' (lit. 'behind')
	(b)	OIr.	*airther*	'east' (lit. 'directed forward')
			tuascert	'north' (lit. 'left direction')
			descert	'south' (lit. 'right direction')
			iarthar	'west' (lit. 'directed to behind')
	(c)	Engl.	*north*	Compare Oscan-Umbrian *nertro-* 'left'
	(d)	Lat.	*oriens*	'east' (lit. 'rising')
		Ital.	*levante*	'east' (lit. 'rising')
		Gk	*anatolē*	'east' (lit. 'rising')

An investigation of the Vedic texts that follows the strict philological principles which this chapter advocates then must conclude that the passages cited by Biswas and Witzel do not provide cogent evidence for Aryan in-migration and thus cannot be used to counter the claim of opponents of the so-called "Aryan Invasion Theory" (e.g. Rajaram and Frawley 1997: 233) that there is no indigenous tradition of an outside origin. (But note that with the claimed exception of Avestan, for which see Section 8.5, and the fanciful dynastic self-derivation of the Romans from Troy, none of the other ancient Indo-European traditions are aware of an origin outside their settlement areas either; see Hock 2002.)

8.5 Case IV: Avestan evidence for out-migration from India?

Like many opponents of the "Aryan Invasion Theory," Rajaram and Frawley (1997) maintain that there is no textual evidence for in-migration to India, but that the *purāṇas* offer references to an out-migration. Following Talageri (1993a,b) they further suggest that in spite of their late attestation the *purāṇas* preserve Vedic tradition. While it is in fact possible that the *purāṇas* preserve much older traditions, it is also possible that only some of their information is old and other information is quite recent. To keep Rajaram and Frawley's from remaining a mere assertion, it would be necessary to furnish supporting evidence or, failing that, criteria that make it possible to distinguish ancient from recent textual material regardless of one's ideological persuasion.

Rajaram and Frawley (1997: 233) further argue that, by contrast to the Vedic tradition, the Avestan/Zoroastrian tradition recognizes an outside origin, the *airiianəm vaējah*. The latter suggestion goes back to Bhargava (1956) via Talageri (1993a: 180–1, 1993b: 140–1), and is also advocated by Elst (1999: 197–8).[26] In the interest of transparency I give an extensive citation of Bhargava's claim and Talageri's interpretation of that claim, with just some minor omissions (indicated as [. . .]):

> . . . Bhargava points out: The evidence of the Avesta makes it clear that sections of these Aryans in course of time left Sapta Sindhu and settled in Iran. The first chapter of the Vendidad [. . .] enumerates sixteen holy lands created by Ahura Mazda which were later rendered unfit for the residence of man (i.e. the ancestors of the Iranians) on account of different things created by Angra Mainyu, the evil spirit of the Avesta . . . [Talageri's omission]. The first of these lands was of course *Airyana Vaejo* which was abandoned by the ancestors of the Iranians because of severe winter and snow; of the others, one was *Hapta Hindu*, i.e. *Saptasindhu*. This is the clearest proof that the Aryan ancestors of the Iranians were once part and parcel of the Aryans of Sapta Sindhu before they finally settled in Iran. Excessive heat created in this region by Angra Mainyu was, according to the Vendidad, the reason why the ancestors of the Iranians left this country.
>
> (Talageri 1993a: 180–1)

> [. . .] The Hapta Hindu mentioned in the Vendidad is obviously the Saptasindhu (the Punjab region), and the first land, "abandoned by the ancestors of the Iranians because of severe winter and snow" before they

> came to the Saptasindhu region and settled down among the Vedic people, is obviously Kashmir.
>
> (Ibid. 1993b: 140–1)

Let us contrast this "Out-of-India" account with a summary of the textual evidence, focusing on the sixteen different regions mentioned in *Vidēvdād* 1,[27] with indications in the right column of the geographical identification where such an identification is possible. (A blank indicates that the location is uncertain.)

First, there is the *Airiianəm Vaējah* of the Good *Dāitiiā* River.
Second, there is the progression:

1	*Airiianəm Vaējah*	
2	*Gǟva* inhabited by the Sogdians	(NE, north of the Oxus)
3	*Margiana*	S. of the Oxus
4	*Bakhtria/Balkh*	
5	*Nisāy* between Margiana and Bakhtria	
6	*Harōiiūm*	(Modern Herat)
7	*Vaēkərəta*	
8	*Urva*	
9	*Xnanta*, inhabited by Hyrcanians	
10	*Harax^{v}aitī* = Arachosia	The area around the modern Helmand
11	*Haētumənt*	
12	*Raga*	
13	*Caxra*	
14	*Varəna*	
15	*Hapta Həndu*	*Ved. Sapta Sindhavaḥ*
16	*Raŋhā*	*Ved. Rasā* (exact location unclear)

Even a cursory examination of the order in which the different regions appear shows that there is no direct link between the starting point, the *airiianəm vaējah*, and *hapta həndu*, which is the next-to-last mentioned region.

A closer look reveals other, even more damaging problems for the Bhargava–Talageri hypothesis. First, there is the question of where to locate the starting point, the *airiianəm vaējah*. Skjærvø (1995) is no doubt correct in concluding that if an identification is possible at all, it would at best be Khwarezmia.[28] Such a location north of the river Oxus would be suggested by the geographic logic of the listing of regions 2–11. To the extent that the regions can be identified, they present a progression from north of the Oxus (region 2) to between Oxus and *Hārī Rud* (3–5), to Herat (6), and ending at what appears to be a southern-most area, that around the modern Helmand (10–11) which, like the *airiianəm vaējah* has special religious significance: The Hamun-i-S(e)istan into which the Helmand empties, identified with the Avestan Lake Kąsaoiia, is the place where bathing maidens will receive Zarathushtra's seed (deposited there by

Arədvī = *Arədvī Sūrā Anāhitā* 'Fertile, powerful, spotless', a deified river) and will give birth to the future saviors, the *Saošiiants*.

What is especially remarkable is the fact that, to judge by the identifiable regions, there is a clear north-to-south progression from region 2 to regions 10–11; and this progression is to be situated to the *west* of the mountain ranges that (roughly) separate present-day Iranian and Indo-Aryan territory. The *Hapta Həndu* of region (15), on the other hand, clearly is on the *eastern* side and, together with the last region, the *Raŋhā*, overlaps with the Vedic geographical horizon (even though the exact location of the *Raŋhā*, Ved. *Rasā*, is not clear). See Figure 8.1, where the different regions are identified by their numbers.

One possible interpretation of this evidence is that we are simply dealing with an outline of a core Iranian or Zoroastrian territory (probably idealized), with the different regions defining its boundaries on the north (region 2; also 1?), west (3–6, also 7–8?), south (10–11),[29] and east (region 15; also region 16?). The purpose of the listing, in that case, would be similar to the various Indo-Aryan definitions of *Āryāvarta*.

In this case, the overlap of regions (15) and (16) with the Vedic geographical horizon would of course raise interesting questions. Was the overlap not just geographical but also chronological? In that case, did Indo-Aryans and (Zoroastrian) Iranians live in close proximity to each other in this area? Since the *Vidēvdād* is a late text, no doubt postdating the Vedic period, this is at best a possibility, not a necessary conclusion. Or does the overlap reflect the well-known Vedic shift from the northwest to *Madhyadeśa*, accompanied (or caused?) by an in-migration of Iranians to the northwest? The fact that the Sindhu tends to become the border river between Iranians and Indo-Aryans might provide further

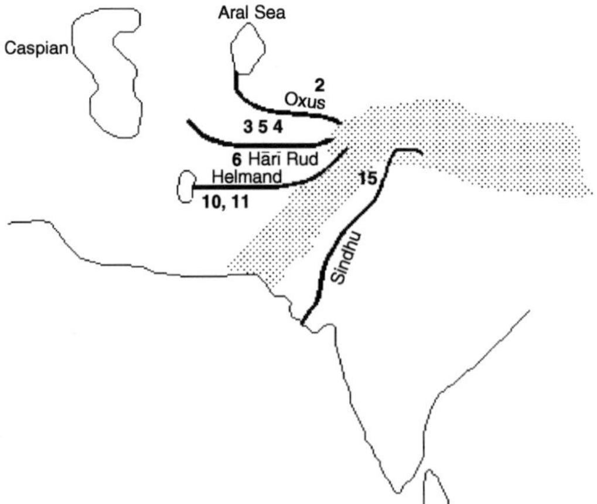

Figure 8.1 The geography of regions listed in Vidēvdād 1.

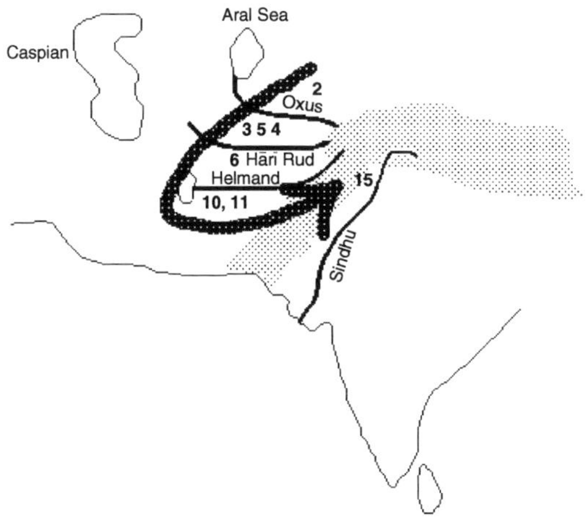

Figure 8.2 A migration interpretation of Vidēvdād 1 (?).

support for such an "Iranian In-Migration" hypothesis; but again, this is a mere possibility. To substantiate this interpretation of our passage would require much more robust evidence.

If, by contrast, we were to take the approach advocated by Bhargava, Talageri, Rajaram and Frawley, and Elst, and interpreted the sequencing of regions as indicating migration, the result would be, not a movement Out-of-India, but rather Into India; see Figure 8.2. Such a movement would obviously be difficult to reconcile with the Out-of-India hypothesis. It would of course be compatible with the Iranian In-Migration hypothesis; but as just noted, much more robust evidence would be required to substantiate such an interpretation of our passage.

We must therefore conclude that the *Vidēvdād* passage does not provide cogent evidence for an Out-of-India hypothesis, or for the claim that, in contrast to the Vedic tradition, the Zoroastrian tradition acknowledges an outside origin. Arguments concerning prehistoric movements in the Indo-Iranian linguistic territory, therefore, will have to be based on other evidence or, failing that, must be considered unresolvable.

8.6 Case V: astronomical evidence in the Kauṣītakī-Brāhmaṇa for dating the Vedas?

A passage in the *Kauṣītakī* (or *Śāṅkhāyana*) *Brāhmaṇa* [18] has given rise to numerous attempts to fix the age of the Vedic texts. The basic idea is straightforward: In this passage, the month of *Māgha* occurs at the time of the winter solstice, while later/nowadays it occurs during January/February of the western calendar. Making allowances for the well-known precession of equinoxes, this difference makes it possible in principle to establish the time period at which the passage must have been composed.[30]

[18] *sa vai māghasyāmāvāsyāyām upavasaty udaṅṅ āvartsyann upeme vasanti prāyaṇīyenātirātreṇa yakṣyamāṇās tad enaṁ prathamam āpnuvanti...sa ṣaṇmāsān udaṅṅ eti tam ūrdhve ṣaḷahair anuyanti sa ṣaṇmāsān udaṅṅ itvā tiṣṭhate dakṣiṇāvartsyann upeme vasanti vaiśuvatīyenāhnā yakṣyamāṇās tad enaṁ dvitīyam āpnuvanti sa ṣaṇmāsān dakṣiṇaiti tam āvṛttaiḥ ṣaḷahair anuyanti ṣaṇmāsān dakṣiṇetvā tiṣṭhata udaṅṅ āvārtsyann upeme vasanti mahāvratīyenāhnā yakṣyamāṇās tad enaṁ tṛtīyam āpnuvanti*

(KB 19.3)

He (= the sun) rests at the new moon of *Māgha*, about to turn northward; these (the priests) rest (too), about to sacrifice with the introductory *atirātra*; so they obtain him first... [A clear reference to the winter solstice, after which the sun "turns northward," i.e. begins to rise farther and farther to the north each day]

He goes northward for six months; him they follow with six-day sacrifices in correct order.

Having gone north for six months, he stays, about to turn south; they rest, about to sacrifice with the *viśuvat* (= midsummer) sacrifice; so they obtain him a second time. [A clear reference to the summer solstice, after which the sun "turns south," i.e. begins to rise farther and farther to the south each day]

He goes south for six months; they follow him with six-day sacrifices in reverse order.

Having gone south for six months, he stays, about to return north; they rest, about to sacrifice with the mahāvrata sacrifice; so they obtain him a third time [a clear reference to the winter solstice again].

Unfortunately, the results of early attempts to use this passage for establishing the date of our text, surveyed in Macdonell and Keith 1912: 1: 422–5, are far from straightforward. Estimates range from 2350 BC (Tilak for the related *Taittirīya-Saṁhitā* passage), to 1391 BC (Davis and Colebrook for our text), to as late as 1181 BC (Jones and Pratt), or even 800–600 BC (Macdonell and Keith's conclusion). A recent publication by Rajaram (1995: 41–3) fixes the date even earlier than Tilak, to around 3000 BC.

The question we need to ask ourselves is, "Why this wide range of interpretations?" Clearly, it cannot be a question of the mathematics, which given the precession rate of 1° = roughly 72 years, is simple and straightforward; and scholarly or ideological bias or national origin is not sufficient either to explain, say the difference between Tilak's and Rajaram's conclusions, or between those of, say, Davis and Colebrook versus Macdonell and Keith. The problem, I submit, lies in inherent uncertainties of how to interpret our passage.

To lay the ground for this evaluation, let me introduce the immediately preceding passage in *Kauṣītakī Brāhmaṇa* 19.2, example [19].

[19] *te purastād eva dīkṣāprasavān kalpayante taiṣasyāmāvāsyāyā ekāha upariṣṭād dīkṣeran māghasya vety āhus tad ubhayaṁ vyuditaṁ taiṣasya tv evoditataram iva ta etaṁ trayodaśam adhicaraṁ māsam āpnuvanty etāvān vai saṁvatsaro yad eṣa trayodaśo māsas tad atraiva sarvaḥ saṁvatsara āpto bhavati* /

(KB 19.2)

They establish the consecration soma-pressings before(hand). They should consecrate themselves one day after the new moon of *Taiṣa*, or of *Māgha*, so they say. Now, either (view) is widely proclaimed; but that of *Taiṣa* is more (commonly) proclaimed, as it were. They obtain this thirteenth, additional month. So great indeed is the year as this thirteenth month. So here the entire year is obtained.

Surveying the passages in [18] and [19], a few things can be established with certainty, others with a good degree of likelihood, and yet others remain entirely uncertain.

What is certain from [18] is that at the time of the composition of our text the view was held that the winter solstice occurs at the new moon of *Māgha*. The passage in [19] further makes it fairly likely, although not absolutely certain, that the new moon coinciding with the winter solstice may have been early in the month of *Māgha*; this would explain that the consecration is more commonly set for the first day of the preceding month's new moon – under the assumption that this would make it possible to begin the ritual immediately after the winter solstice. (The less preferred option, the day after the new moon of *Māgha*, would entail a delay of the ritual.) The fact that [19] also mentions an intercalary thirteenth month further makes it likely that the tradition of the *Kauṣītakī Brāhmaṇa* used intercalary months to reconcile the difference between solar and lunar year cycles.

Beyond this, too many crucial elements remain entirely uncertain. These include the following:

1 Was intercalation used on a yearly basis? That is, were the months entirely lunar (consisting of 27 or 28 days), and the thirteenth month was inserted every year? If so, at what point in the cycle was it inserted? If this was not the case – as suggested by the fact that [18] mentions six + six = twelve months for the course of the sun – at what yearly intervals were intercalary months inserted, and what, therefore, was the number of days per month (the Vedic texts range between 27 and 35 days)? Given a rough correlation of 1 day = 1° or 72 years of precession, the difference between 27 and 35 days, that is 8 days, would translate into a variation in time depth of 576 years.

2 If the calendrical cycle was indeed one of twelve solar months, plus intercalary months at certain – unknown – intervals, the new moon of *Māgha* could fall on any day within a 27/28 day window. This introduces a possible variation of about 1,950 years. Moreover, it would suggest that the coincidence of winter solstice and the new moon of *Māgha* was not strictly fixed, but approximate. In that case, we must face the uncertainty of the tolerance of variation that our tradition accepted – one week, more than that, less than that? – and how it resolved cases where the difference between solstice and new moon exceeded that tolerance. Unfortunately, our text does not tell us anything about this; and the overall evidence of the Vedic texts is too heterogeneous to be helpful.

3 Did the month begin with the new moon or with the full moon? As Macdonell and Keith point out, the commentaries are not unanimous on this count, although the majority seem to favor the full moon. The difference of about fourteen days would introduce a possible variation of about 1,000 years.

4 If intercalary months were inserted at certain intervals, rather than on a yearly basis, a further element of uncertainty is introduced, namely the extent to which intercalation managed to maintain synchronization of lunar and solar years, especially as the precession of equinoxes threatened that synchronization. The extent to which a cumulation of slightly incorrect intercalations could have contributed to the difference between the timing of *Māgha* in the *Kauṣītakī Brāhmaṇa* and later (at, say, *Varahamihira's* time, or at present) is truly incalculable. And the problem would become even greater if there had been changes in the method of intercalation.

As noted, none of uncertainties can be resolved on the basis of our text, or of the general Vedic tradition for that matter; and the margin of error is at least of a magnitude of between 576 and 1,950 years. (The latter is what, roughly, separates the extreme proposals – *c*.3000 by Rajaram versus 800–600 BC by Macdonell and Keith.) The philological evidence simply does not permit using our passage(s) as the basis for determining the date of composition of the *Kauṣītakī Brāhmaṇa*, nor does it permit making a rational choice between the wide variety of different estimates that have been proposed. Determining the age of our text and thereby establishing a point of departure for estimating the age of the Vedas, therefore, will have to be based on other evidence or, failing that, will have to be admitted as not being determinable by sound philological means.

8.7 Case VI: Rig-Vedic astronomical evidence for dating the Vedas?

Several publications have taken Rig-Vedic passages containing a form of *brahman* to refer to a solstice or other important point in the solar year, and have taken this interpretation as the foundation for establishing the date of the

Rig-Veda; Elst (1999: 107–8) provides a helpful summary, especially in light of the fact that several of these publications are not available to me.

Tilak (1893) interpreted the *brahman* of the passage in [20] as referring to the "equinox and the fruit of the union between a divine father and daughter, i.e. the two adjoining constellations Mṛgashira/Orion and Rohini/Aldebaran..." (Elst 1999: 107–8) and this is believed to establish that the word *brahman* can indeed refer to a major point in the solar year. Sengupta (1941) took *brahman* in [21] to refer to the summer solstice and, because of the reference to what Elst characterizes as a "non-total eclipse... in the afternoon on the Kurukshetra meridian," used this conjunction to fix the date to 26 July 3298 BC (Sengupta's publication unfortunately is not accessible to me, as a consequence I am not sure which of the two occurrences of *brahman* he takes to refer to the summer solstice.). Rajaram (1995: 106) finds support for the use of *brahman* as referring to "solstice" in the passage in [22]; see his interpretation in [22a]. As Elst (and also Rajaram) notes, Sengupta's "calculation stands or falls with the unusual translation of the word *brahma* [*sic*] as 'solstice'." Elst finds support for this interpretation by "later scriptural references to the same event, *Shankhayana Aranyaka* 1:2, 18 and *Jaiminiya Brahmana* 2.404–410." And he concludes by saying "On the other hand, it is up to the skeptics to come up with a convincing alternative translation which fits the context."

[20] *práthiṣṭa yásya vīrákarmam iṣṇád ánuṣṭhitaṁ nú náryo ápauhat / púnas tád ā́ vṛhati yát kanā́yā duhitúr ā́ ā́nubhṛtam anarvā́ //5//*
madhyā́ yát kártvam ábhavad abhī́ke kā́maṁ kṛṇvāné pitári yuvatyā́m / manānág réto jahatur viyántā sā́nau níṣiktaṁ sukṛtásya yónau //6//
pitā́ yát svā́ṁ duhitáram adhiṣkán kṣmayā́ rétaḥ saṁjagmānó ní ṣiñcat / svādhyò 'janayan ***bráhma*** *devā́ vástoṣ pátiṁ vratapā́ṁ nír atakṣan //7//*
sá īṁ vṛ́ṣā ná phénam asyad ā́jau smád ā́ páraid ápa dabhrácetāḥ / sárat padā́ ná dákṣiṇā parāvṛ́ṇ ná tā́ nú me pṛśanyò jagṛbhre //8//

(RV 10.61)

Whose manly action (*Sāyaṇa*: semen) had spread out, desiring, (that) man put then aside (what he had) set out (to do). He pulls it back again that which was inserted from (= in) the virgin daughter, (he) the undefeatable.

When it was in the middle of (what was) to be done, in the encounter, the father making love with the young woman, the two left behind a little (*Sāyaṇa*: alpam) semen, going apart, poured down on the back (of the earth), on the abode/yoni of the good deed.

When the father mounted his daughter, having intercourse, he poured down semen on the earth. The Gods produced ***bráhman*** 'equinox' (?) or 'blessing' and created Vastoṣpati (*Sāyaṇa*: Rudra), the protector of vows.

Like a bull he (*Sāyaṇa*: Vastoṣpati) threw foam in the battle/encounter; at the same time he went back and forth, of weak = uncertain (?) mind. She ran to the southern locations like someone banished (saying/thinking) "These allures of mine did not take."

[20′] *utā́si maitrāvaruṇó vasiṣṭhorvá́śyā* ***brahman*** *mánasó 'dhi jātáḥ / drapsáṁ skannáṁ* ***bráhmaṇā*** *daívyena víśve devā́ḥ púṣkare tvādadanta //*

(RV 7.33.11)

And you, *Vasiṣṭha* are the son of *Mitra* and *Varuṇa*, O ***brahman*** 'priest', born from *Urvaśī* from (her) mind. The All-Gods took you, the shedded drop (of *Mitra* and *Varuṇa's* semen [see verse 13]), in the lotus blossom with divine ***bráhman*** 'spell/blessing'.

[21] *ā́ yāhy ádribhiḥ sutáṁ sómaṁ somapate piba / vṛ́ṣann indra vṛ́ṣabhir vṛtrahantama //1//...*

... / mā́dhyandine sávane matsad índraḥ //4d//
yát tvā sūrya svàrbhānus támasā́vidhyad āsuráḥ / ákṣetravid yáthā mugdhó bhúvanāny adīdhayuḥ //5//
svàrbhānor ádha yád indra māyā́ avó divó vártamānā avā́han / gūḷháṁ sū́ryaṁ támasā́pavratena (/) turī́yeṇa ***bráhmaṇā́****vindad átriḥ //6//*
mā́ mā́m imáṁ táva sántam atra irasyā́ drugdhó bhiyásā ní gārīt / tvám mitró asi satyárādhās taú mehā́vatam váruṇaś ca rā́jā //7//
grā́vṇo ***brahmā́*** *yuyujānáḥ saparyán kīríṇā devā́n námasopaśíkṣan / átriḥ sū́ryasya diví cákṣur ā́dhāt svàrbhānor ápa māyā́ aghukṣat //8//*
yáṁ vaí sū́ryaṁ svàrbhānus támasāvidhyad āsuráḥ / átrayas tám anv avindan nahy ànyé áśaknuvan //9//

(RV 5.40)

Come, drink the soma pressed with stones, O lord of soma, O bull, Indra, with the bulls, greatest Vṛtra-slayer.

...

... at the midday pressing, may Indra enjoy himself.

When the asuric *Svarbhānu* had hit you with darkness (as with an arrow), O *Sūrya* (= O sun), the creatures appeared like someone confused, not knowing his surroundings.

When at that time you, *Indra*, destroyed *Svarbhānu's* wiles/magic, unfolding under the sky, *Atri* found, by means of the fourth ***bráhman*** 'summer solstice' (?) or 'prayer, spell', the sun hidden with illegal darkness.

Let him, the betrayer, not swallow me here out of envy and fear, (me) being yours. You are *Mitra*/friend of true favor; let these two help me here, (you) and King *Varuṇa*.

Atri, the ***brahmán*** 'summer solstice' (?) or 'priest, spell-caster' who joins the pressing stones and honors the Gods with mere[31] (?) bowing, he has placed the eye of the sun in the sky; he has hidden the wiles/magic of *Svarbhānu*.

The sun indeed whom the asuric *Svarbhānu* hit with darkness, the *Atris* found him again; others were not able.

[22] *ā́śásanaṁ viśásanam átho adhivikártanam / sūryā́yāḥ paśya rūpā́ṇi (/) tā́ni* ***brahmā́*** *tú śundhati*

(RV 10.85.35)

(a) Behold the forms of the Sun Goddess, behold the hues of her garments; the border, the head and the division – which [*sic*] *brahma* [*sic*] relieves her. (Rajaram in Rajaram and Frawley 1997: 201)

(b) A slaughtering, a cutting up, and then a further cutting. Behold the colors of *Sūryā* (the bride); but the ***brahmán*** 'priest, spell-caster' cleans them.

(c) (It is like) the slaughtering, cutting up, and cutting to pieces. – Behold the colors of *Sūryā*! But the enchanter cleans them.[32]

As the translations in [20]–[21] and [22b/c] show, it is indeed possible to come up with alternative translations which, in each case, fit both the narrow context of the verse in which *brahman* occurs, and the broader context of the entire hymn and/or its use in the ritual or its interpretation by traditional Indian commentators. Moreover, unlike Elst's summary argument, based on interpretations by Tilak, Sengupta, and Rajaram, these translations do not confuse *bráhman* (neuter) 'prayer, spell, blessing' with *brahmán* (masculine) 'priest, spell-caster, etc.', and their well-established meanings and difference in meaning, and do not require unusual interpretations which cannot be supported by independent evidence in the Rig-Veda or elsewhere in the Vedic tradition.

The problematic nature of Tilak's, Sengupta's, and Rajaram's interpretations becomes even clearer once we take a closer look at the relevant passages.

Let us begin with [20]. The verses referred to by Tilak/Elst, including verse 7 in which *bráhman* (neuter) occurs, form part of a longer passage (verses 2–11), whose central theme is the shedding of semen and its consequences. Verses 5–8 more specifically relate to the common Vedic myth of a primordial father–daughter incest which, as the general Vedic context shows, needs to be either avenged (by Rudra) or, in this case (verse 7), must be set right by divine intercession – in terms of a *bráhman* (neuter) 'blessing'. As a consequence, the natural interpretation of verse 7 would be 'When the father mounted his daughter, having intercourse he poured down semen on the earth. The Gods produced a blessing and created *Vastoṣpati*, the protector of vows.' This conclusion is supported by [20′], where again the Gods produce a *bráhman* (neuter) 'blessing', this time on the divine birth of *Vasiṣṭha* through *Urvaśī*, the apsaras. Nothing in [20], or in the larger context of the hymn or of the Vedic tradition, or in *Sāyaṇa's* commentary, points to an astronomical interpretation. The burden is on those claiming such an interpretation for [20] to demonstrate either that the same/a similar interpretation is appropriate for [20′], or to explain why such an interpretation is not appropriate for [20′] – or for any of the many other occurrences of *bráhman* (neuter) outside [20] and [21].

One problem with [21] is that there is no overt connection in this hymn between the first four verses and the remainder of the hymn, which is one of several Vedic versions of the *Svarbhānu* myth. As a consequence, the fact that verse 4 talks about the *mādhyandina savana* cannot automatically be taken as situating the rest of the hymn in time. Second, there is nothing in verses 6–9 that identifies the eclipse as a partial one – an interpretation which I take to be crucial for establishing the date of July 26, 3298 BC. Rather, statements such as *gūḷháṁ sūryaṁ támasā́pavratena* 'the sun hidden by illegal darkness' suggest a complete eclipse. Most important, the two occurrences of *brahman*, the first neuter, the second masculine, are perfectly compatible with the usual meanings 'prayer, spell' and 'priest, spell-caster' respectively. In fact, the last verse, not referred to in Elst's summary, secures the interpretation of verse 8 as referring to an action by the *brahmán* (masc.) **'priest'** *Atri*, by claiming that 'the *Atris* found him (the sun) again; others were not able'. The interpretation of the first occurrence of *brahman* (neuter) in the collocation *turī́yeṇa bráhmaṇā* as meaning 'with the fourth prayer or spell' is supported by the parallel passages in TS 2.1.2.2 and ṢB (or *Tāṇḍ.*) 6.6.8, in which the Gods overcome *Svarbhānu* only on the fourth attempt. Nothing in our passages calls for an astronomical interpretation; and those advocating such an interpretation owe it to us to explain why that interpretation is limited just to the passages in [20]–[22], and does not occur elsewhere. As for the two later Vedic passages which are claimed to support Sengupta's interpretation of RV 5.40, I have made a thorough examination of one of these, JB 2.204–10 (the other text was not available to me). While the JB text does indeed talk about solstice (winter and summer), it does *not* localize the solstice in space and time, and it does *not* relate it to a solar eclipse. Put differently, it provides no evidence that would support Sengupta's specific astronomical interpretation.

Finally, as is well known, the passage in [22] comes from the Rig-Vedic wedding hymn. The null hypothesis therefore would be an interpretation which is in keeping with this context; and any other interpretation would require more than casual justification. Now, while there can be some question over the exact interpretation of verse 35 – what is the meaning of *ā́śásanaṁ viśásanam átho adhivikártanam* in this context, and how precisely does this collocation relate to the following *rūpā́ṇi* 'colors' or 'forms'? – the recitation of this verse (together with verses 29, 30, and 34) in the ritual at the giving away of the bride's garment (see Āp.GS 9.11), combined with the extended context of the wedding hymn, makes it likely that an interpretation along the lines of Geldner [22c] is the most appropriate. Under this interpretation the various words for slaughter suggest the blood stains (*rūpā́ṇi*) on the bridal garment which, though natural after consummation of marital union, are inauspicious because of their blood. Before the bridal garment can be given away, then, a priest or spell-caster must somehow purify the garment and remove the inauspicious stains.

As mentioned earlier, Elst has thrown out a challenge to those disagreeing with the astronomical interpretation that he advocates "to come up with a convincing alternative translation which fits the context." The preceding discussion has met that challenge. Moreover, Elst admits (and so does Rajaram) that the interpretation of "*brahma*" on which the astronomical interpretation rests is "unusual." The preceding discussion has, I hope, demonstrated that the interpretation is not only "unusual," but also philologically dubious.

As in all the other cases examined in this chapter, this does of course not mean that therefore Sengupta's fourth millennium BC date for the Rig-Veda is incorrect. It simply means that the evidence in favor of that date is not sufficient, and that attempts to establish a date for the Rig-Veda on the basis of astronomical evidence contained in the text must look for philologically better grounded evidence. Until and unless such evidence is found, however, we will have to argue the date of the Rig-Veda on the basis of other, non-textual evidence or, failing that, we will have to admit our inability to determine the date.

8.8 Conclusions

The fact that closer investigation of each of the six cases examined in this chapter has led to negative results may be disappointing and even depressing for those who look to the Vedic texts for clues to resolve important issues about the prehistory and early history of South Asia/India. But even if we believe that the Vedas are historical documents, rather than simply *apauruṣeya* and thus beyond the reach of any historical investigation, it is important to remind ourselves that whatever their original and/or secondary purposes may have been, they were not intended as data bases for latter-day historians. Whatever historical evidence they may contain, therefore, can only be gleaned by a careful, philologically well-grounded reading of the lines – and between the lines – of the texts. If that reading, then, fails to provide answers to historical and prehistorical questions that concern us, it is better to admit this than to arbitrarily choose one or another of several conflicting and poorly established interpretations. In this manner, at least, we leave the issue open for further discussion, rather than closing the debate, on the incorrect assumption that we have found a satisfactory answer. (Personally, I feel that most of the evidence and arguments that have been offered in favor either of the Aryan In-Migration hypothesis or of the Out-of-India hypothesis are inconclusive at closer examination.[33] But see Hock [2002] on the issue of what I there call the "horse culture complex."[34])

Even more significant, I believe, is the methodology which I have employed. Throughout I have endeavored to live up to the desiderata outlined at the beginning, namely being *transparent* and *vulnerable* – transparent by providing supporting evidence that is easily open to verification, and vulnerable by being open to challenge and potential falsification. As I stated at the outset, this, I believe, is the only way that we can establish a common ground for those working in Vedic studies. Without this common ground there is nothing to evaluate the many conflicting theories without either resorting to questioning each others' motives, or saying "Trust me, trust me." As I tell my students: If people merely say "Trust me, trust me," don't trust them, don't trust them. And as to questioning each others' motives, it is good to note that people as different in their motives as Elst and Zydenbos have stated on the Indology List that what really counts is the evidence and its interpretation – even racists and communalists can come to correct results if their evidence and their methodology are correct (however much we may deplore their ideologies and biases).

Acknowledgments

This is a considerably expanded version of a paper read at the July 2000 meeting of the World Association for Vedic Studies in Hoboken, NJ, and submitted for publication in the Proceedings. I am grateful to the organizers for inviting me to give this presentation.

Notes

1 This section draws on Hock 1993.
2 With the qualification on p. 7 that the Indo-Europeans were of 'unknown racial characteristic (though it is not unlikely that they were Nordic originally [!])...'
3 'Indra half dem...Arier...in den Kämpfen um das Sonnenlicht....machte er...die schwarze Haut untertan.'
4 'die schwarze Haut.'
5 'die schwarzen Ureinwohner.'
6 'Fünfzigtausend Schwarze warfst du nieder. Du zerschlissest die Burgen wie das Alter ein Gewand.'
7 'Neben die Sonne dich stellend, daß deine, des Unsterblichen, Gestalt in die Augen fällt....'
8 'Aus Furcht vor dir zogen die schwarzen Stämme fort, indem sie kampflos ihren Besitz zurückließen....'
9 'Er schloß die Schwarzen aus mit den feuerfarbigen Wesen (...).'
10 'Die Schwarzen sind wohl die schwarze Rasse und im mythologischen Hintergrund die Paṇis oder die Mächte der Dunkelheit, die rötlichen Wesen oder Mächte... die Mächte des Lichtes... aruṣá und kṛṣṇá ist sonst der Gegensatz von Morgen und Nacht....'
11 'Durchkreuze die vielen gottlosen Tücken und laß uns, du Gabenreicher, die Sonne gewinnen.'
12 'die schwarze Haut vertreibend.'
13 'die Unholde oder die unarische Rasse.'
14 'die schwarze Decke, d.h. die Finsterniss.'
15 'Läutere dich, du Ausgezeichneter, erfülle die beiden großen Welten, (wie) Uṣas, wie Sūrya mit den Strahlen.'
16 'Der Vṛtratöter Indra sprengte die dasischen (Burgen), die die Schwarzen in ihrem Schoß bargen, der Burgenbrecher. Er schuf für Manu Land...'.
17 '...der...den mit den Schwarzen Schwangeren (die Leibesfrucht) abtrieb...'.
18 'die (Preßsteine) blasen durch Zaubermacht die dem Indra verhaßte schwarze Haut von Erde und Himmel weg.'
19 'die schwarze Decke, d.h. die Finsterniss.'
20 'Töter der Schwarzen.'
21 'Der Nichtweiße ist der dunkelfarbige Nichtarier...'.
22 'die nicht glänzende, d.h. dunkle (Wolke)... schlagend.'
23 The interval between [7a] and [7b] is a little larger; but [7b] explicitly mentions the *dasyus*, making it legitimate to relate it to [7a].
24 Witzel's reference, 1.12.13 must be a typo.

25 If anything, 6.20.12 = 1.174.9 would refer to a passage across the **sea**; and the *Paṇis*, whom *Saramā* visits in RV 10.108, live beyond the river Rasā in the extreme northwest (see Verse 1) – this passage thus does not provide strong evidence for an Aryan movement into India/South Asia.

26 Without reference to either Talageri or Bhargava.

27 A shorter version is found in *Yašt* 10.

28 It could of course be even further north (in the areas later held by the Massagetae and the Sakas). However, Skjærvø acknowledges that Gnoli (1989: 38–51) may be right in assuming that the *airiianəm vaējah* "was simply the invention by priests who wished 'to place their Prophet at the centre of the world'."

29 Regions 12–14 could mark additional markers of the southern or eastern boundaries. If region 13, *Caxra*, can be confidently identified with modern Carx in Southeast Afghanistan, near Ghazna, it might be considered a transitional boundary marker, between southwestern 10–11 and more northeastern 15.

30 The following discussion supersedes what I had to say on this issue in Hock 1999 which unfortunately was not philologically well grounded.

31 The exact meaning of *kīrí(n)* in this context is not clear; elsewhere a meaning 'praising, praiser' seems appropriate.

32 '(Es ist wie) das Schlachten, Zerlegen und Zerschneiden. – Sieh die Farben der Sūryā! Aber der Beschwörer reinigt sie.'

33 This includes Jha and Rajaram's (2000) claimed decipherment of the Indus script which identifies the language as Sanskrit of the *sūtra* period. As noted by several scholars on the Indology List, including Witzel and Farmer, even if the phonetic values attributed to the Indus signs should be correct, the decipherment leaves far too much latitude for interpretation by proposing a single sign for all vowel-initial *akṣaras* and by assuming that vowels are not indicated. As a consequence, a sequence of V (= any vowel) + p (= *p* followed by any vowel) could designate Skt *upa, apa, api, āpo, apo*, and thanks to the assumption that endings often are not written out, *āpiḥ* and all other inflected forms of the word, all inflected forms of *ắp-* 'water', and even Engl. *up*. What is especially disconcerting (and à propos for this chapter) is the fact that many of the Sanskrit interpretations offered are not well-formed Sanskrit. For instance, Jha and Rajaram offer a reading *isādyattaḥ marah* which they interpret to mean 'Mara (forces of destruction) controlled by Ishvara', referring 'to the cosmic cycle of creation and destruction. *Yattah* is derived from the root 'yam', meaning to control…' (2000: 167–8). Setting aside faulty transcriptions such as *isād* for intended *īśād*, we can observe at least two problems of a rather elementary structural sort. One of these is the implicit assumption that the ablative/*pañcamī* can be used to designate the agent/*kartṛ* of a passive construction (the correct case is the instrumental/*tṛtīyā*). The other is the belief that consonant doubling applies freely in Vedic and thus can also apply to single consonants between vowels (hence *yata-* 'controlled' → *yatta*), whereas the Vedic *prātiśākhyas* agree on permitting such doubling only in consonant groups (as in *atra* 'here' → *attra*).

34 Notice that my argument in Hock (2002) is not affected by whether or not there is incontrovertible skeletal evidence for horses in the Indus Civilization or whether Jha and Rajaram's "artist's reproduction" of a reconstituted "Horse Seal" (2000: 177) can be maintained in the face of extensive criticism on the Indology List and elsewhere; see for instance Steve Farmer (7/24/00, 9:31, 9:37, 9:41 p.m.) and Witzel (7/25/00, 1:40 a.m.), both on the Indology List. The "horse culture complex" involves not just the presence of horses, but of domesticated horses, their use with two-wheeled battle chariots, and their significance in the Vedic ritual. The first uncontroversial evidence for something that can be considered a horse culture complex is found in the late phases of the Indus civilization, in Pirak (near the Bolan Pass), together with other cultural changes, and in Swat (near the Khyber Pass) – that is, in areas that would have been first affected by an in-migration. (See e.g. Kenoyer 1995: 226–7 and Kennedy 1995: 46.)

References

Basham, A. L., 1954. *The Wonder that was India*. New York: Macmillan.

Bhargava, P. L., 1956 (1971). *India in the Vedic Age: A History of Aryan Expansion in India*. Lucknow: Upper India Publishing House. [Non vidi; cited by Talageri 1993a,b.]

Biswas, S. K., 1995. *Autochthon of India and the Aryan Invasion*. (Re-written History Series, 1.) New Delhi: Genuine Publications and Media.

Chatterji, S. K., 1960. *Indo-Aryan and Hindi*, 2nd edition. Calcutta: Mukhopadhyay.

Childe, V. G., 1926 (1987). *The Aryans: A Study of Indo-European Origins*. New York: Dorsett Press.

Deshpande, M. M., 1978. "Genesis of Ṛgvedic Retroflexion: A Historical and Sociolinguistic Investigation." In *Aryan and Non-Aryan in India*, edited by M. M. Deshpande and P. E. Hook. Ann Arbor, MI: The University of Michigan Center for South Asian and Southeast Asian Studies, pp. 235–315.

Elizarenkova, T. J., 1995. *Language and Style of the Vedic ṛṣis*. Albany, NY: State University of New York Press.

Elst, K., 1999. *Update on the Aryan Invasion Debate*. New Delhi: Aditya Prakashan.

Frawley, D., 1994. *The Myth of the Aryan Invasion of India*. New Delhi: Voice of India.

Geldner, K. F., 1951. Der Rig-Veda..., 3 vols, posthumously edited by Charles R. Lanman. Cambridge, MA: Harvard University Press.

Gnoli, G., 1989. *The Idea of Iran: An Essay on its Origin*. Serie Orientale Roma LXII. Rome: Istituto Italiano per il Medio ed Estremo Oriente (cited from Skjærvø 1995).

Gonda, J., 1975. *Vedic Literature* (A history of Indian literature, 1:1.). Wiesbaden: Harrassowitz.

Graßmann, H., 1872 (1964). *Wörterbuch zum Rig-Veda*. Wiesbaden: Harrassowitz.

Hale, W. E., 1986. *Ásura in Early Vedic Religion*. Delhi: Motilal Banarsidass.

Hock, H. H., 1975. "Substratum Influence on (Rig-Vedic) Sanskrit?," *Studies in the Linguistic Sciences*, 5(2): 76–125.

——, 1984. "(Pre-)Rig-Vedic Convergence of Indo-Aryan with Dravidian? Another look at the Evidence," *Studies in the Linguistic Sciences*, 14(1): 89–108.

——, 1993. "A Critical Examination of some Early Sanskrit Passages Alleged to Indicate Dialectal Diversity. Comparative-historical Linguistics: Indo-European and Finno-Ugric," Papers in honor of Oswald Szemerényi III, edited by B. Brogyanyi and R. Lipp. Amsterdam and Philadelphia, PA: Benjamins, pp. 217–32.

——, 1996a. "Pre-Ṛgvedic Convergence Between Indo-Aryan (Sanskrit) and Dravidian? A Survey of the Issues and Controversies." In *Ideology and Status of Sanskrit: Contributions to the History of the Sanskrit Language*, edited by J. E. M. Houben. Leiden: Brill, pp. 17–58.

——, 1996b. "Subversion or Convergence? The Issue of Pre-Vedic Retroflexion Reexamined," *Studies in the Linguistic Sciences*, 23(2): 73–115.

——, 1999. "Through a Glass darkly: Modern 'Racial' Interpretations vs. Textual and General Prehistoric Evidence on *ārya* and *dāsa/dasyu* in Vedic Society." In *Aryan and Non-Aryan in South Asia: Evidence, Interpretation, and Ideology*, edited by J. Bronkhorst and M. Deshpande. Harvard Oriental Series, Opera Minora, Vol. 3, Columbia, MO: South Asia Books, pp. 145–74.

——, 2002. Wem gehört die Vergangenheit? Früh- und Vorgeschichte und indische Selbstwahrnehmung. "Arier" und "Draviden." Konstruktionen der Vergangenheit als

Grundlage für Selbst- und Fremdwahrnehmungen Südasiens, edited by Michael Bergunder and Rahul Peter Das (Neue Hallesche Berichte. Quellen und Studien zur Geschichte und Gegenwart Südindiens, 2), pp. 232–50.

Hock, H. H. and B. D. Joseph, 1996. *Language History, Language Change, and Language Relationship: An Introductioin to Historical and Comparative Linguistics*. Berlin/New York: Mouton de Gruyter.

Jha, N. and N. S. Rajaram, 2000. *The Deciphered Indus Script: Methodology, Readings, Interpretations*. New Delhi: Aditya Prakashan.

Kennedy, K. A. R., 1995. "Have Aryans been Identified in the Prehistoric Skeletal Record from South Asia? Biological Anthropology and Concepts of Ancient Races." In *The Indo-Aryans of Ancient South Asia: Language, Material Culture, and Ethnicity*, edited by G. Erdosy. Berlin and New York: de Gruyter, pp. 32–66.

Kenoyer, J. M., 1995. "Interaction Systems, Specialized Crafts and Culture Change: The Indus Valley Tradition and the Indo-Gangetic Tradition in South Asia." In *The Indo-Aryans of Ancient South Asia: Language, Material Culture, and Ethnicity*, edited by G. Erdosy, Berlin and New York: de Gruyter, pp. 213–57.

Kuiper, F. B. J., 1991. *Aryans in the RigVeda* (Leiden Studies in Indo-European, 1.) Amsterdam/Atlanta, GA: Rodopi.

Kulke, H. and D. Rothermund, 1986 (1990). *A History of India*. New York: Dorsett.

Macdonell, A. A. and A. B. Keith, 1912 (1958). *Vedic Index of Names and Subjects*. Delhi: Motilal Banarsidass.

Mansion, J., 1931. *Esquisse d?une histoire de la langue sanscrite*. Paris: Geuthner.

Parpola, A., 1988. "The Coming of the Aryans to Iran and India and the Cultural and Ethnic Identity of the dāsas," *Studia Orientalia*, 64: 195–302. (An unauthorized reprint is found in the *International Journal of Dravidian Linguistics*, 17(2): 85–229, same year.)

Rajaram, N., 1995. *The Politics of History: Aryan Invasion Theory and the Subversion of Scholarship*. New Delhi: Voice of India.

Rajaram, N. S. and D. Frawley, 1995. *Vedic Aryans and the Origins of Civilization: A Literary and Scientific Perspective*. St. Hyacinthe, Québec: World Heritage Press. (Not accessible to me.)

——, 1997. *Vedic Aryans and the Origins of Civilization: A Literary and Scientific Perspective*, 2nd edition. New Delhi: Voice of India.

Rau, W., 1957. *Staat und Gesellschaft im alten Indien nach den Brāhmaṇa-Texten dargestellt*. Wiesbaden: Harrassowitz.

Renou, L., 1956. *Histoire de la langue sanskrite*. Lyon: AIC.

Risley, H. H., 1891. "The Study of Ethnology in India," *Journal of the Anthropological Institute of Great Britain and Ireland*, 20: 235–63.

Sengupta, P. C., 1941. "The Solar Eclipse in the Rgveda and the Date of Atri," *Journal of the Royal Asiatic Society of Bengal Letters*, 7: 92–113. (Not accessible to me.)

Sjoberg, A. F., 1990. "The Dravidian Contribution to the Development of Indian Civilization: A Call for a Reassessment," *Comparative Civilizations Review*, 23: 40–74. (Offprint circulated through the Center for Asian Studies, University of Texas at Austin.)

Skjærvø, P. O., 1995. "The Avesta as Source for the Early History of the Iranians." In *The Indo-Aryans of Ancient South Asia: Language, Material Culture, and Ethnicity*, edited by G. Erdosy. Berlin and New York: de Gruyter, pp. 155–76.

Talageri, S. G., 1993a. *Aryan Invasion Theory and Indian Nationalism*. New Delhi: Voice of India.

——, 1993b. *The Aryan Invasion Theory: A Reappraisal*. New Delhi: Aditya Prakashan. [≈ 1993a, omitting the first, Hindutva-ideological chapter.]

Thomas, F. W., 1904. "Discussion of Rapson 1904," *Journal of the Royal Asiatic Society*, 1904: 460–71.

Tilak, B. G., 1893 (1955). *Orion: Researches into the Antiquity of the Vedas*. Pune: Tilak Brothers. (Not accessible to me.)

Trautmann, T. R., 1999. "Constructing the Racial Theory of Indian Civilization." In *Aryan and Non-Aryan in South Asia: Evidence, Interpretation, and Ideology*, edited by J. Bronkhorst and M. Deshpande. Harvard Oriental Series, Opera Minora, Vol. 3, Columbia, MO: South Asia Books, pp. 277–93.

Witzel, M., 1995. "Ṛgvedic History: Poets, Chieftains and Politics." In *The Indo-Aryans of Ancient South Asia: Language, Material Culture, and Ethnicity*, edited by G. Erdosy. Berlin and New York: de Gruyter, pp. 307–52.

Zimmer, H., 1879. *Altindisches Leben*. Berlin: Weidmann.

9

VEDIC ASTRONOMY AND EARLY INDIAN CHRONOLOGY

Subhash Kak

9.1 Introduction

The use of Vedic astronomy in fixing early Indian chronology has been contentious, but recent discoveries have strengthened the case of its use. The earlier criticism was based mainly on the argument that no credible evidence supported the belief that the Vedic people knew anything but primitive astronomy. Furthermore, the generally accepted model of the presence of the Vedic people in India simply did not support the dates – some of which go as far back as the fourth millennium BC – that emerged from Vedic astronomy. Inconvenient internal dates of texts, such as *c.*1300 BC (or 1800 BC as argued by Achar 2000b) in the case of *Vedāṅga Jyotiṣa*, were explained away as a result of poor observations in a tradition that lacked a sound practice of observational astronomy. Although there was circularity in this reasoning, it carried weight in some circles.

The idea that observational astronomy was lacking in India was part of the larger view that India was a civilization of imagination and it lacked real science (Inden 1990). This position, which arose out of colonialist attitudes of the nineteenth century, is negated by the discovery of the earliest geometry and mathematics in India (Seidenberg 1962, 1978), the outstanding grammatical and logic traditions (Rao and Kak 2000), and advanced traditions of medicine, chemistry, and technology (Ray 1956; Subbarayappa 1971).

Meanwhile, the question with regard to astronomy itself has changed for a variety of reasons: first, Billard showed that the belief that India did not possess a tradition of observational astronomy was wrong (Billard 1971; van der Waerden 1980); second, archaeological discoveries reveal to us that Sarasvatī – the great river of the Ṛgvedic times – dried up before 1900 BC, suggesting that parts of the Ṛgveda must be at least as old as that epoch (Feuerstein *et al.* 1995); third, discovery of an hitherto unknown astronomy in the Vedic texts that establishes the credibility of the internal astronomical dates from the texts (Kak 1992–2000); fourth, a variety of evidence that indicate that the Indian cultural tradition represents a continuity that goes back at least about 10,000 years (Kenoyer 1998); fifth, computer reconstruction of ancient skies indicate that the Vedic astronomical references unambiguously point to the third millennium BC (Achar 2000a,b,c).

The archaeological record relating to antiquity and continuity of the Indian tradition means that the Vedic dates are not inconsistent with it. The finding about the relative sophistication of Vedic astronomy means that we must consider these dates carefully, especially if there is other independent evidence that supports them.

The focus of this chapter is to summarize recent findings of Vedic astronomy up to the *Vedāṅga Jyotiṣa* period. We review the altar astronomical code, ideas related to the size and the nature of the planetary system and the motions of the sun and the moon, and show how this astronomy constitutes a sophisticated system based on sound observations. We show that the chronological framework revealed by Vedic astronomy is entirely consistent with the literary evidence from the texts as well as the new archaeological findings. We visit several Vedic astronomical dates and show how these dates are in broad agreement with the new chronological markers obtained through a study of altar astronomy.

9.2 Vedic knowledge

The fundamental idea pervading Indian thought from the most ancient times is that of equivalence or connection (*bandhu*) among the *adhidaiva* (*devas* or stars), *adhibhūta* (beings), and *adhyātma* (spirit). These connections, among the astronomical, the terrestrial, the physiological, and the psychological, represent the constant theme in the discourse of Vedic texts. These connections are usually stated in terms of vertical relationships, representing a recursive system; but they are also described horizontally across hierarchies where they represent metaphoric or structural parallels. Most often, the relationship is defined in terms of numbers or other characteristics. An example is the 360 bones of the infant – which later fuse into the 206 bones of the adult – and the 360 days of the year. Likewise, the tripartite division of the cosmos into earth, space, and sky is reflected in the tripartite psychological types.

Although the Vedic books speak often about astronomical phenomena, it is only recently that the astronomical substratum of the Vedas has been examined (Kak 1992–2000). One can see a plausible basis behind the connections between the astronomical outer and the biological inner, stressed in the Vedas. Research has shown that all life comes with its inner clocks. Living organisms have rhythms that are matched to the periods of the sun or the moon. There are quite precise biological clocks of 24 hours (according to the day), 24 hours 50 minutes (according to the lunar day since the moon rises roughly 50 minutes later every day) or its half representing the tides, 29.5 days (the period from one new moon to the next), and the year. Monthly rhythms, averaging 29.5 days, are reflected in the reproductive cycles of many marine plants and those of animals.

The menstrual period is a synodic month and the average duration of pregnancy is nine synodic months. There are other biological periodicities of longer durations. These connections need not be merely numerical; in its most general form is the *Upaniṣadic* equation between the self (*ātman*) and the universe (*brahman*).

It is tempting to view *jyotiṣa*, the science of light and astronomy, as the fundamental paradigm for the Vedic system of knowledge. *Jyotiṣa* is a term that connotes not only the light of the outer world, but also the light of the inner landscape. Astronomy is best described as *nakṣatra-vidyā* as in the *Chāndogya Upaniṣad*, but because of its popularity we will also use *jyotiṣa* in its narrow meaning of astronomy. As defining our place in the cosmos and as a means to understand the nature of time, astronomy is obviously a most basic science.

That astronomy reveals that the periods of the heavenly bodies are incommensurate might have led to the notion that true knowledge lies beyond empirical (*aparā*) knowledge. On the other hand, it is equally likely that it was an analysis of the nature of perception and the paradox of relationship of the perceptor to the whole that was the basis of Vedic thought, and the incommensurability of the motions in the sky was a confirmation of the insight that knowledge is recursive.

This Vedic view of knowledge seems to have informed the earliest hymns so it does not appear to be feasible to answer the question of which came first. Neither can we now answer the question whether *jyotiṣa* as pure astronomy was a precursor to a *jyotiṣa* that included astrology.

Analysis of texts reveals that much of Vedic mythology is a symbolic telling of astronomical knowledge. This has been pretty well established for other mythologies as well (de Santillana and Dechend 1969). Astronomy was the royal science not only because it was the basis for the order in nature, but also because the inner space of man, viewed as a microcosm mirroring the universe, could be fathomed through its insights.

The importance of *jyotiṣa* for agriculture and marking rites and festivals is clear. Different points in the turning year were marked by celebrations. The year, beginning with the full moon in the month *Phālguna* (or *Caitra*), was divided into three four-monthly, *cāturmāsya*, sacrifices. Another way of marking the year is by a year-long *dīkṣā*. The year was closed with rites to celebrate *Indra Śunāśīra* (*Indra* with the plough) to "obtain the thirteenth month"; this thirteenth month was interposed twice in five years to bring the lunar year in harmony with the solar year. This closing rite is to mark the first ploughing, in preparation for the next year. Symbolically, this closing was taken to represent the regeneration of the year. Year-long ceremonies for the king's priest are described in the *Atharvaveda Pariśiṣṭa*; these include those for the health of horses, the safety of vehicles, and so on.

The *Gṛhyasūtras* describe rites that mark the passage of the day such as the daily agnihotra. Three soma pressings, at sunrise, midday, and sunset, were a part of the daily ritual of *agniṣṭoma*. Then there were the full and new moon ceremonies. Longer soma rites were done as *sattras*, sessions of twelve days or more. It is clear that *Jyotiṣa*, as astronomy plus astrology, played an extremely important role in the lives of the Vedic people. The underlying measurement basis was sidereal – with respect to the stars – and this required careful observation. The division of the month into thirty *tithis*, each of which is slightly smaller than a solar day, required abstraction and measurement.

9.2.1 Altars

Altar ritual was an important part of Vedic life and we come across fire altars in the Ṛgvedic hymns. Study of Vedic ritual has shown that the altar, *adhiyajña*, was used to show the connections between the astronomical, the physiological, and the spiritual, symbolically. That the altars represented astronomical knowledge is what interests us in this chapter. But the astronomy of the altars was not systematically spelled out although there are pointed references in many texts including the tenth chapter of the *Śatapatha Brāhmaṇa*, entitled "*Agnirahasya*." The Ṛgveda itself is viewed as an altar of mantras in the *Śulbasūtras*.

Altars were used in relation to two basic types of Vedic ritual: *Śrauta* and *Gṛhya*. This ritual marked specific points in the day or the year as in the soma rituals of *agniṣṭoma* and *agnicayana*. The *Śatapatha Brāhmaṇa* describes the twelve-day *agnicayana* rite that takes place in a large trapezoidal area, called the *mahāvedi*, and in a smaller rectangular area to the west of it, which is called the *prācīnavaṃśa* or *prāgvaṃśa*. The text says clearly that *agnicayana* represents ritual as well as knowledge.

The *mahāvedi* trapezium measures thirty *prakrama* on the west, twenty-four *prakrama* on the east, and thirty-six *prakrama* lengthwise. The choice of these numbers is related to the sum of these three equaling one-fourth the year or ninety days.

The nominal year of 360 days was used to reconcile the discrepancies between the lunar and solar calendars, both of which were used. In *mahāvedi* a brick altar is built to represent time in the form of a falcon about to take wing, and in the *prācīnavaṃśathere* are three fire altars in specified positions, the *gārhapatya*, *āhavanīya*, and *dakṣiṇāgni*.

The *gārhapatya*, which is round, is the householder's fire received from the father and transmitted to the descendents. It is a perpetual fire from which the other fires are lighted. The *dakṣiṇāgni* is half-moon shaped; it is also called the *anvāhāryapacana* where cooking is done. The *āhavanīya* is square. Between the *āhavanīya* and the *gārhapatya* a space of a rough hourglass is dug out and strewn with grass; this is called the *vedi* and it is meant for the gods to sit on.

During the agnicayana ritual the old *āhavanīya* serves the function of the original *gārhapatya*. This is the reason why their areas are to be identical, although one of them is round and the other square. In addition eight *dhiṣṇya* hearths are built on an expanded ritual ground.

Agnicayana altars are supposed to symbolize the universe. *Gārhapatya* represents the earth, the *dhiṣṇya* hearths represent space, and the *āhavanīya* altar represents sky. This last altar is made in five layers. The sky is taken to represent the universe therefore it includes space and earth. The first layer represents the earth, the third the space, and the fifth the sky. The second layer represents the joining of the earth and space, whereas the fourth layer represents the joining of space and sky.

Time is represented by the metaphor of a bird. The months of the year were ordinarily divided into six seasons unless the metaphor of the bird for the year was used when *hemanta* and *śiśira* were lumped together. The year as a bird had the head as *vasanta*, the body as *hemanta* and *śiśira*, the two wings as *śarada* and *grīṣma*, and the tail as *varṣā*.

The Vedic sacrifice is meant to capture the magic of change, of time in motion. Put differently, the altar ritual is meant to symbolize the paradoxes of separation and unity, belonging and renunciation, and permanence and death. The *yajamāna*, the patron at whose expense the ritual is performed, symbolically represents the universe.

The ritual culminates in *yajamāna* ritual rebirth, which signifies the regeneration of his universe. In other words, the ritual is a play dealing with paradoxes of life and death enacted for the *yajamāna*'s family and friends. In this play symbolic deaths of animals and humans, including the *yajamāna* himself, may be enacted.

9.2.2 Evolution of Vedic thought

How did the use of altars for a symbolic representation of knowledge begin? This development is described in the *Purāṇas* where it is claimed that the three altars were first devised by the king *Purūravas*. The genealogical lists of the *Purānas* and the epics provide a framework in which the composition of the different hymns can be seen. The ideas can then be checked against social processes at work as revealed by textual and archaeological data.

As we will see later in this chapter, there existed an astronomical basis to the organization of the Ṛgveda itself; this helps us see Vedic ritual in a new light. That astronomy could be used for fixing the chronology of certain events in the Vedic books was shown more than a hundred years ago by Tilak, Dikshit, and Jacobi. This internal evidence compels the conclusion that the prehistory of the Vedic people in India goes back to the fourth millennium and earlier (Dikshit 1969). On the other hand, new archaeological discoveries show a continuity in the Indian tradition going as far back as 8000 BC (Shaffer and Lichtenstein 1995). These are some of the elements in accord with the view that the Vedic texts and the archaeological finds relate to the same reality. One must also note that the rock art tradition in India has been traced back to an even greater antiquity (Wakankar 1992). Whether this tradition gave birth to the Harappan tradition is not clear at this time.

Recent archaeological discoveries establish that the Sarasvatī river dried up *c.*1900 BC which led to the collapse of the Harappan civilization that was principally located in the Sarasvatī region. Francfort (1992) has even argued that the *Dṛṣadvatī* was already dry before 2600 BC. The region of the Sarasvatī and the *Dṛṣadvatī* rivers, called *Brahmāvarta*, was especially sanctified and Sarasvatī was one of the mightiest rivers of the Ṛgvedic period. On the other hand, *Pañcaviṃśa Brāhmaṇa* describes the disappearance of Sarasvatī in the sands at a distance of forty days on horseback from its source. With the understanding of the drying up of Sarasvatī it follows that the Ṛgvedic hymns are generally anterior to 1900 BC but if one accepts Francfort's interpretation of the data on the *Dṛṣadvatī* then the Ṛgvedic period includes the period before 2600 BC.

It is most significant that the *Purāṇic* king-lists speak of 1924 BC as the epoch of the *Mahābhārhata* war, that marked the end of the Vedic age. This figure of 1924 BC emerges from the count of 1500 years for the reigns prior to the Nandas (424 BC), quoted at several places in the *Purāṇas*, as corrected by Pargiter (1922). Since this epoch is virtually identical to the rough date of 1900 BC for the catastrophic drying up of the Sarasvatī river, it suggests that the two might have been linked if not being the same, and it increases our confidence in the use of the Indian texts as sources of historical record.

9.3 *Nakṣatras*

The Ṛgveda describes the universe to be infinite. Of the five planets, it mentions *Bṛhaspati* (Jupiter) and *Vena* (Venus) by name. The moon's path was divided into 27 equal parts, although the moon takes about $27\frac{1}{3}$ days to complete it. Each of these parts was called a *nakṣatra*. Specific stars or asterisms were also termed *nakṣatras*, and they are mentioned in the *Ṛgveda* and *Taittirīya Saṃhitā*, the latter specifically saying that they are linked to the moon's path. The Ṛgvedic referring to thirty-four lights apparently means the sun, the moon, the five planets, and the twenty-seven *nakṣatras*. In later literature the list of *nakṣatras* was increased to twenty-eight. Constellations other than the *nakṣatras* were also known; these include the *Ṛkṣas* (the Bears), the two divine Dogs (Canis Major and Canis Minor), and the Boat (Argo Navis). The *Aitareya Brāhmaṇa* speaks of *Mṛga* (Orion) and *Mṛgavyādha* (Sirius). The moon is called *sūrya raśmi*, one that shines by sunlight.

The *Śatapatha Brāhmaṇa* provides an overview of the broad aspects of Vedic astronomy. The sixth chapter of the book provides significant clues. Speaking of creation under the aegis of the *Prajāpati* (referring either to a star or to abstract time) mention is made of the emergence of *Aśva*, *Rāsabha*, *Aja*, and *Kūrma* before the emergence of the earth. It has been argued that these refer to stars or constellations. Viśvanātha Vidyālaṇkāra (1985) suggests that these should be identified as the sun (*Aśva*), Gemini (*Rāsabha*), Capricorn (*Aja*), and Cassiopeia (*Kūrma* or *Kāśyapīya*). Vedic ritual was based on the times for the full and the new moons, solstices and the equinoxes. The year was known to be somewhat more than 365 days and a bit less than 366 days. The solar year was marked variously in the many different astronomical traditions that marked the Vedic world. In one tradition, an extra 11 days, marked by *ekādaśarātra* or an eleven-day sacrifice, were added to the lunar year of 354 days. According to the *Taittirīya Saṃhitā* 5 more days are required over the nominal year of 360 days to complete the seasons, the text adding that 4 days are too short and 6 days are too long. In other traditions, *gavām ayana*, "the walk of cows or intercalary periods," varied from 36 days of the lunar sidereal year of 12 months of 27 days, to 9 days for the lunar sidereal year of 13 months of 27 days, to bring the year in line with the ideal year of 360 days; additional days were required to be in accord with the solar year.

The year was divided into two halves: *uttarāyana*, when the sun travels north, and *dakṣiṇāyana*, when the sun travels south. According to the *Kauṣītaki*

Brāhmaṇa, the year-long sacrifices began with the winter solstice, noting the occurrence of the summer solstice, *viṣuvant*, after six months.

The *nākṣatra* names of the months began with *Caitra* in spring, although some lists begin with *Phālguna*. Since the months shift with respect to the 12 *nakṣatra* about 2,000 years per *nakṣatra*, this change in the lists indicates a corresponding long period. The lists that begin with *Caitra* mark the months thus: *Caitra*, *Vaiśākha*, *Jyaiṣṭha*, *Āṣāḍha*, *Śrāvaṇa*, *Bhādrapada*, *Āśvina*, *Kṛttikā*, *Mārgaśira*, *Pauṣya*, *Māgha*, *Phālguna*. That this scheme goes back to the Ṛgvedic period has been argued by Achar (2000c). The earliest lists of *nakṣatras* in the Vedic books begin with *Kṛttikā*, the Pleiades; much later lists dating from sixth century CE begin with *Aśvinī* when the vernal equinox occurred on the border of *Revatī* and *Aśvini*. Assuming that the beginning of the list marked the same astronomical event, as is supported by other evidence, the earliest lists should belong to the third millennium BC. The *Taittirīya Saṃhitā* 4.4.10 and *Śatapatha Brāhmaṇa* 10.5.4.5 each mention twenty-seven *nakṣatras*. But there was also a tradition of the use of twenty-eight *nakṣatras*. The *Atharvaveda* 19.7 lists these twenty-eight together with their presiding deities; the additional *nakṣatra* is *Abhijit*. The lists begins with *Kṛttikā* (Pleiades) where the spring equinox was situated at that time.

9.4 Ritual, geometry, and astronomy

We have mentioned that the altars used in the ritual were based on astronomical numbers related to the reconciliation of the lunar and solar years. The fire altars symbolized the universe and there were three types of altars representing the earth, the space, and the sky. The altar for the earth was drawn as circular whereas the sky (or heaven) altar was drawn as square. The geometric problems of circulature of a square and that of squaring a circle are a result of equating the earth and the sky altars. As we know these problems are among the earliest considered in ancient geometry.

The fire altars were surrounded by 360 enclosing stones, of these 21 were around the earth altar, 78 around the space altar, and 261 around the sky altar. In other words, the earth, the space, and the sky are symbolically assigned the numbers 21, 78, and 261. Considering the earth/cosmos dichotomy, the 2 numbers are 21 and 339 since cosmos includes the space and the sky.

The main altar was built in five layers. The basic square shape was modified to several forms, such as falcon and turtle, built in five layers, of a thousand bricks of specified shapes. The construction of these altars required the solution to several geometric and algebraic problems.

Two different kinds of bricks were used: the special and the ordinary. The total number of the special bricks used was 396, explained as 360 days of the year and the additional 36 days of the intercalary month. By layers, the first has 98, the second has 41, the third has 71, the fourth has 47, and the fifth has 138. The sum of the bricks in the fourth and the fifth layers equals 186 *tithis* of the half-year.

The number of bricks in the third and the fourth layers equals the integer nearest to one-third the number of days in the lunar year, and the number of bricks in the third layer equals the integer nearest to one-fifth of the number of days in the lunar year, and so on.

The number of ordinary bricks equals 10,800 which equals the number of *muhūrtas* in a year (1 day = 30 *muhūrtas*), or equivalently the number of days in 30 years. Of these 21 go into the *gārhapatya*, 78 into the eight *dhiṣṇya* hearths, and the rest go into the *āhavanīya* altar.

9.4.1 Equivalence by area

The main altar was an area of $7\frac{1}{2}$ units. This area was taken to be equivalent to the nominal year of 360 days. Now, each subsequent year, the shape was to be reproduced with the area increased by one unit.

The ancient Indians spoke of two kinds of day counts: the solar day, and *tithi*, whose mean value is the lunar year divided into 360 parts. They also considered three different years: (1) *nakṣatra*, or a year of 324 days (sometimes 324 *tithis*) obtained by considering 12 months of 27 days each, where this 27 is the ideal number of days in a lunar month; (2) lunar, which is a fraction more than 354 days (360 *tithis*); and (3) solar, which is in excess of 365 days (between 371 and 372 *tithis*). A well-known altar ritual says that altars should be constructed in a sequence of 95, with progressively increasing areas. The increase in the area, by one unit yearly, in building progressively larger fire altars is 48 *tithis* which is about equal to the intercalation required to make the *nakṣatra* year in *tithis* equal to the solar year in *tithis*. But there is a residual excess which in 95 years adds up to 89 *tithis*; it appears that after this period such a correction was made. The 95 year cycle corresponds to the tropical year being equal to 365.24675 days. The cycles needed to harmonize various motions led to the concept of increasing periods and world ages.

9.4.2 The Ṛgvedic altar

The number of syllables in the *Ṛgveda* confirms the textual references that the book was to represent a symbolic altar. According to various early texts, the number of syllables in the *Ṛgveda* is 432,000, which is the number of *muhūrtas* in 40 years. In reality the syllable count is somewhat less because certain syllables are supposed to be left unspoken.

The verse count of the *Ṛgveda* can be viewed as the number of sky days in 40 years or 261 × 40 = 10,440, and the verse count of all the Vedas is 261 × 78 = 20,358. The *Ṛgveda* is divided into 10 books with a total of 1,017 hymns which are placed into 216 groups. Are these numbers accidental or is there a deliberate plan behind the choice? One would expect that if the Ṛgveda is considered akin to the five-layered altar described in the *Brāhmaṇas* then the first two books should correspond to the space intermediate to the earth and the sky.

Table 9.1 The altar of books

Book 10	Book 9
Book 7	Book 8
Book 5	Book 6
Book 3	Book 4
Book 2	Book 1

Table 9.2 Hymns in the altar of books

191	114
104	92
87	75
62	58
43	191

Now the number that represents space is 78. When used with the multiplier of 3 for the 3 worlds, this yields a total of 234 hymns which is indeed the number of hymns in these 2 books. One may represent the Ṛgvedic books as a five-layered altar of books as shown in Table 9.1. When the hymn numbers are used in this altar of books we obtain Table 9.2.

The choice of this arrangement is prompted by the considerable regularity in the hymn counts. Thus the hymn count separations diagonally across the 2 columns are 29 each for Book 4 to Book 5 and Book 6 to Book 7 and they are 17 each for the second column for Book 4 to Book 6 and Book 6 to Book 8. Books 5 and 7 in the first column are also separated by 17; Books 5 and 7 also add up to the total for either Book 1 or Book 10. Another regularity is that the middle three layers are indexed by order from left to right whereas the bottom and the top layers are in the opposite sequence.

Furthermore, Books $[4 + 6 + 8 + 9] = 339$, and these books may be taken to represent the spine of the altar. The underside of the altar now consists of the Books $[2 + 3 + 5 + 7] = 296$, and the feet and the head Books $[1 + 10] = 382$ The numbers 296 and 382 are each 43 removed from the fundamental Ṛgvedic number of 339.

The *Brāhmaṇas* and the *Śulbasūtra* tell us about the altar of *chandas* and meters, so we would expect that the total hymn count of 1017 and the group count of 216 have particular significance. Owing to the pervasive tripartite ideology of the Vedic books we choose to view the hymn number as 339×3. The tripartite ideology refers to the consideration of time in three divisions of past, present, and future and the consideration of space in the three divisions of the northern celestial hemisphere, the plane that is at right angle to the earth's axis, and the southern celestial hemisphere.

The number 339 is simply the number of disks of the sun or the moon to measure the path across the sky: $\pi \times 108 \approx 339$ The number 216 represents the distance to the sky, which was twice the distance of 108 to the sun. The Ṛgvedic code then expresses a fundamental connection between the numbers 339 and 108.

The number 108 is actually the average distance that the sun is in terms of its own diameter from the earth; likewise, it is also the average distance that the moon is in terms of its own diameter from the earth. It is owing to this marvelous coincidence that the angular size of the sun and the moon, viewed from the earth, is more or less identical. It is easy to compute this number. The angular measurement of the sun can be obtained quite easily during an eclipse. The angular measurement of the moon can be made on any clear full moon night. An easy check on this measurement would be to make a person hold a pole at a distance that is exactly 108 times its length and confirm that the angular measurement is the same. Nevertheless, the computation of this number would require careful observations. Note that 108 is an average and due to the ellipticity of the orbits of the earth and the moon the distances vary about 2 to 3 percent with the seasons. It is likely, therefore, that observations did not lead to the precise number 108, but it was chosen as the true value of the distance since it is equal to 27×4, because of the mapping of the sky into 27 *nakṣatras*. The diameter of the sun is roughly 108 times the diameter of the earth, but it is unlikely that the Indians knew this fact.

There also exists evidence that the periods of the planets had been obtained by this time.

9.5 The planetary system

The Ṛgveda asserts that the universe is infinite in extent (e.g. RV 1.52.13). It suggests that the sun is at the center of the universe (RV 1.35.7–9) as the rays of the sun are supposed to range from the earth to the heavens. More evidence is to be found in the *Brāhmaṇas*. For example, the *Śatapatha Brāhmaṇa* (*ŚB* 6.1.10–6.2.4) gives us a brief account of the creation of the universe where several elements related to the physical and the psychological worlds are intertwined. Within this account the description of the physical world is quite clear. It begins with the image of a cosmic egg, whose shell is the earth (6.1.11). From another cosmic egg arises the sun and the shell of this second egg is the sky (6.2.3). The point of this story is to suggest that the universe was perceived at this point in the shape of an egg with the earth as the center and the sun going around it below the heavens. The stars are seen to lie at varying distances with the polestar as the furthest.

The *Atharvaveda* 10.7 presents an image of the frame of the universe as a cosmic pillar (*skambha*). In this, the earth is taken to correspond to the base (10.7.32), the space to the middle parts, and the heavens to the head. The sun, in particular, is compared to the eye (10.7.33). But there is no evidence that this analogy is to be taken in a literal fashion. One can be certain that in the Vedic period, the sun was taken to be less distant than the heavens.

The motions of all the heavenly bodies is considered to be uniform as in the system of circular motions of the sun and the moon in the *Vedāṅga Jyotiṣa*. But it is clear from the manner in which the notion of *tithi* worked that these circular motions relate to the mean positions, and there was awareness that the actual motions deviated from the ideal positions of the mean planets.

The idea of the uniform motion implied that the relative distance of a body from the earth was determined by its period. This set up the following arrangement for the luminaries: the moon, Mercury, Venus, the sun, Mars, Jupiter, Saturn (Frawley 1994).

Since the sun is halfway in this arrangement, it is reasonable to assume that the distance to the sun was taken to be half of the distance to the heavens. The notion of the halfway distance must date from a period when the actual periods were not precisely known or when all the implications of the period values for the size of the universe were not understood. It is not clear that a purely geocentric model was visualized. It appears that the planets were taken to go around the sun which, in turn, went around the earth. One evidence is the order of the planets in the days of the week where one sees an interleaving of the planets based on the distance from the sun and the earth, respectively; this suggests that two points of focus, the earth and the sun, were used in the scheme. Further evidence comes from the fact that the planet periods are given with respect to the sun in later texts such as the one by *Āryabhaṭa*. It appears that the purely geocentric model may have been a later innovation.

The *Pañcaviṃśa Brāhmaṇa* (*PB*) deals with various rites of different durations. The rites appear to have an astronomical intent as given by their durations: 1 through 40 days (excepting 12), 49, 61, 100, and 1,000 days; 1, 3, 12, 36, 100, and 1,000 years. The rites provide a plan for marking different portions of the year and also suggest longer periods of unknown meaning. In *PB* 16.8.6 we have a statement about the distance of the sun from the earth:

> *yāvad vai sahasraṃ gāya uttarādharā ity āhus tāvad asmāt lokāt svargo lokaḥ*
>
> The world of heaven is as far removed from this world, they say, as a thousand earths stacked one above the other.

Let R_s represent the distance between the earth and the sun, R_m be the distance between the earth and the moon, d_s be the diameter of the sun, d_m be the diameter of the moon, and d_e be the diameter of the earth. Since the sun is considered halfway to the sky, the *PB* statement implies that $R_s \approx 500d_e$. We have already mentioned that the moon and the sun were taken to be about 108 times their respective diameters from the earth ($R_s \approx 108d_s$ and $R_m \approx 108d_m$).

Considering a uniform speed of the sun and the moon and noting that the sun completes a circuit in 365.24 days and the moon 12 circuits in 354.37 days, we find that $R_m \approx (354.37 \times 500)/(365.24 \times 12)\, d_e$ or $R_m \approx 40d_e$. By using the relationship on relative sizes that $R_s \approx 108d_s \approx 500d_e$ we know that $d_s \approx 4.63d_e$. Assuming that the diameter of the earth was at some time in the pre-Siddhantic period estimated to be about 900 *yojanas*, the distance to the moon was then about 36,000 *yojanas* and that to the sun about 450,000 *yojanas*. In fact, to account for the long periods of Jupiter and Saturn, the sun should be closer to the earth than the midpoint of the heavens. Alternatively, one could assume that the distance of the heavens is beyond $1{,}000d_e$ and perhaps also that the distance of the sun is somewhat less than $500d_e$.

A theory on the actual diameters of the sun, the moon, and the earth indicates a knowledge of eclipses. The RV 5.40 speaks of a prediction of the duration of a solar eclipse, so relative fixing of the diameters of the earth, the moon, and the sun should not come as a surprise.

Also note that the long periods of Jupiter and Saturn require that the sun be much closer to the earth than the midpoint to the heavens, or push the distance of the heavens beyond the $1{,}000d_e$ of *PB* and perhaps also make the distance of the sun somewhat less than $500d_e$. We do see these different modifications in the models from later periods. The idea that the sun is roughly 500 or so earth diameters away from us is much more ancient than Ptolemy from where it had been assumed to have been borrowed by the Indians.

Did the idea that $R_s \approx 500d_e$ originate at about the time of *PB*, that is from the second millennium BC, or is it older? Since this notion is in conflict with the data on the periods of the outer planets, it should predate that knowledge. If it is accepted that the planet periods were known by the end of the third millennium BC, then this knowledge must be assigned an even earlier epoch. Its appearance in a book dealing primarily with ritual, must be explained as a remembrance of an old idea. We do know that *PB* repeats, almost verbatim, the Ṛgvedic account of a total solar eclipse.

It is certain that the synodic periods were first computed because the longest period, the 780 days of Mars, is not too much larger than twice the sun's period. With Mars as the furthest body in a primitive model, the sun's distance will have to be reduced to about 0.47 of the furthest point. In order to accommodate the stars, the sun will have to be brought even nearer. When the sidereal orbits of the planets were understood, sometime in the Vedic period, the space beyond the sun had to be taken to be vast enough to accommodate the orbits of Jupiter and Saturn. The noncircular motions of the planets would require further changes to the sizes of the orbits and these changes represent the continuing development of this phase of Indian astronomy. The theory that $R_s \approx 500d_e$ was so strongly entrenched that it became the basis from which different Greek and later Indian models emerged. Ptolemy considers an R_s equal to $600d_e$ whereas *Āryabhaṭa* assumes it to be about $438d_e$. Thus the Greek and the later Indian modifications to the basic idea proceeded somewhat differently.

9.5.1 The sizes of the planets

The ideas on planet sizes can be seen to evolve from those in the *Purāṇas* to the *Siddhāntas*. The *Purāṇas* confusingly combine two different theories, one related to the departure from the ecliptic by the moon and the other on the sidereal periods. The planets are listed in the correct sequence, supporting the view that the planet periods were known. The order of the angular sizes are correctly shown as Venus, Jupiter, Saturn, Mars, Mercury although the fractions stated are not accurate.

9.6 The two halves of the year

The *Brāhmaṇas* recognize that the speed of the sun varies with the seasons. The year-long rites of the *Brāhmaṇas* were organized with the summer solstice (*viṣuvant*) as the middle point. There were two years: the ritual one started with the winter solstice (*mahāvrata* day), and the civil one started with the spring equinox (*viṣuva*). Vedic rites had a correspondence with the different stages of the year and, therefore, astronomy played a very significant role. These rites counted the days up to the solstice and the latter half of the year, and there is an asymmetry in the two counts. This is an astronomical parameter, which had hitherto escaped notice, that allows us to date the rites to no later than the second millennium BC.

The *Aitareya Brāhmaṇa* (4.18) describes how the sun reaches the highest point on the day called *viṣuvant* and how it stays still for a total of 21 days with the *viṣuvant* being the middle day of this period. In *PB* (chapters 24 and 25), several year-long rites are described where the *viṣuvant* day is preceded and followed by three-day periods. This suggests that the sun was now taken to be more or less still in the heavens for a total period of seven days. So it was clearly understood that the shifting of the rising and the setting directions had an irregular motion. *Śatapatha Brāhmaṇa* (*ŚB* 4.6.2) describes the rite called *gavām ayana*, the "sun's walk" or the "cows' walk." This is a rite which follows the motion of the sun, with its middle in the *viṣuvant* day. *Yajurveda* (38.20) says that the *āhavanīya* or the sky altar is four-cornered since the sun is four-cornered, meaning thereby that the motion of the sun is characterized by four cardinal points: the two solstices and the two equinoxes. The year-long rites list a total of 180 days before the solstice and another 180 days following the solstice. Since this is reckoning by solar days, it is not clear how the remaining four or five days of the year were assigned, but this can be easily inferred. Note that the two basic days in this count are the *viṣuvant* (summer solstice) and the *mahāvrata* day (winter solstice), which precedes it by 181 days in the above counts. Therefore, even though the count of the latter part of the year stops with an additional 180 days, it is clear that one needs another four or five days to reach the *mahāvrata* day in the winter. This establishes that the division of the year was in the two halves of 181 and 184 or 185 days. Corroboration of this is suggested by evidence related to an altar design from the *Śatapatha Brāhmaṇa* (*ŚB* 8.6) (Kak 2000b). This altar represents the path of the sun around the earth. The middle point, which represents the earth and the atmosphere, is at a slight offset to the center. This fact, together, the fact that the number of bricks in the outer ring are not symmetrically placed, shows that the four quarters of the year were not taken to be symmetric.

This inequality would have been easy to discover. The Indians used the reflection of the noon-sun in the water of a deep well to determine the solstice days. If one assumes that the two halves of the year are directly in proportion to the brick counts of 14 and 15 in the two halves of the ring of the sun, this corresponds to day counts of 176 and 189. This division appears to have been for the two halves of the year with respect to the equinoxes if we note that the solstices divide the year into counts of 181 and 184. The apparent motion of the sun is the greatest when the earth is at perihelion and the least when the earth is at aphelion. Currently, this speed is greatest in January. The interval between successive perihelia, the anomalistic year, is 365.25964 days which is 0.01845 days longer than the tropical year on which our calendar is based. In 2,000 calendar years, the date of the perihelion advances almost 35 days; in 1,000 years, it advances almost a half-year (175 days). This means that the perihelion movement has a cycle of about 20,000 years.

In the first millennium BC, the earth was at perihelion within the interval prior to the winter solstice. Thus, during this period, the half of the year from the summer solstice to the winter solstice would have been shorter than the half from the winter solstice to the summer solstice. This is just the opposite of what is described in the rites of the *Brāhmaṇas*. It is interesting that the Greeks discovered the asymmetry in the quarters of the year only *c*.400 BC. The *Śatapatha Brāhmaṇa* reference to unequal halves of the year predates the Greek discovery of it by centuries.

The count of about 181 days from the winter to the summer solstice would be true when the perihelion occurs before the summer solstice. This will require it to move earlier than mid- to late June and no earlier than mid- to late December. In other words, compared to 400 BC, the minimum number of months prior to October is four and the maximum number of months is ten. This defines periods which are from 6,850 years to 17,150 years prior to 400 BC. These periods appear too early to be considered plausible and this may reflect the fact that the measurements in those times were not very accurate. Nevertheless, it means that the first millennium BC for the rites of the *Brāhmaṇas* is absolutely impossible. Since the *Śaptapatha Brāhmaṇa* has lists of teachers that go through more than fifty generations, we know that the period of the *Brāhmaṇas* was a long one, perhaps a thousand years. To be as conservative as possible, one may consider the period 2000–1000 BC as reasonable for these texts. The Vedic *Saṃhitās* are then assigned to the earlier fourth and third millennium BC.

9.7 The motions of the sun and the moon

The *Vedāṅga Jyotiṣa* (VJ), due to Lagadha, describes some of the astronomical knowledge of the times of altar ritual. It has an internal date of *c*.1350 BC, obtained from its assertion that the winter solstice was at the asterism *Śraviṣṭā* (Delphini). Achar (2000b) argues that a proper identification of β Delphini means that this date be corrected to 1800 BC.

VJ describes the mean motions of the sun and the moon. This manual is available in two recensions: the earlier Ṛgvedic VJ (RVJ) and the later Yajurvedic

VJ (YVJ). RVJ has 36 verses and YVJ has 43 verses. As the only extant astronomical text from the Vedic period, we describe its contents in some detail. The measures of time used in VJ are as follows:

1 lunar year	= 360 *tithis*
1 solar year	= 366 solar days
1 day	= 30 *muhūrtas*
1 *muhūrta*	= 2 *nāḍikās*
1 *nāḍikā*	= $10\frac{1}{20}$ *kalās*
1 day	= 124 *aṁśas* (parts)
1 day	= 603 *kalās*

Furthermore, five years were taken to equal a *yuga*. An ordinary *yuga* consisted of 1,830 days. An intercalary month was added at half the *yuga* and another at the end of the *yuga*. What are the reasons for the use of a time division of the day into 603 *kalās?* This is explained by the assertion that the moon travels through 1,809 *nakṣatras* in a *yuga*. Thus the moon travels through one *nakṣatra* in $1\,\frac{7}{603}$ sidereal days because $1{,}809 \times 1\,\frac{7}{603} = 1{,}830$, or the moon travels through one *nakṣatra* in 610 *kalās*. Also note that 603 has 67, the number of sidereal months in a yuga, as a factor. The further division of a *kalā* into 124 *kāṣṭhās* was in symmetry with the division of a yuga into 62 synodic months or 124 fortnights (of 15 *tithis*), or *parvans*. A *parvan* is the angular distance traveled by the sun from a full moon to a new moon or vice versa.

The VJ system is a coordinate system for the sun and the moon in terms of the 27 *nakṣatras*. Several rules are given so that a specific *tithi* and *nakṣatra* can be readily computed. The number of risings of the asterism *Śraviṣṭhā* in the *yuga* is the number of days plus five (1,830 + 5 = 1,835). The number of risings of the moon is the days minus 62 (1,830 − 62 = 1,768). The total of each of the moon's twenty-seven asterisms coming around sixty-seven times in the *yuga* equals the number of days minus twenty-one (1,830 − 21 = 1,809).

The moon is conjoined with each asterism sixty-seven times during a yuga. The sun stays in each asterism $13\frac{5}{9}$ days. The explanations are straightforward. The sidereal risings equals the 1,830 days together with the five solar cycles. The lunar cycles equal the sixty-two synodic months plus the five solar cycles. The moon's risings equal the risings of *Śraviṣṭhā* minus the moon's cycles. This indicates that the moon was taken to rise at a mean rate of 1,830/1,768 = 24 hours and 50.4864 minutes.

Although a mean *tithi* is obtained by considering the lunar year to equal 360 *tithis*, the determination of a *tithi* each day is by a calculation of a shift of the moon by 12° with respect to the sun. In other words, in 30 *tithis* it will cover the full circle of 360°. But the shift of 12° is in an irregular manner and the duration of the *tithi* can vary from day to day. As a practical method a mean *tithi* is defined by a formula. VJ takes it to be 122 parts of the day divided into 124 parts.

Each *yuga* was taken to begin with the asterism *Śraviṣṭhā* and the synodic month of *Māgha*, the solar month *Tapas* and the bright fortnight (*parvan*), and the northward course of the sun and the moon. The intercalary months were used in a *yuga*. But since the civil year was 366 days, or 372 *tithis*, it was necessary to do further corrections. As shown in Section 9.6, a further correction was performed at 95 years, perhaps at multiples of 19 years.

9.8 *Nakṣatras* and chronology

Due to the precession of the earth's polar axis the direction of the north pole with respect to the fixed background stars keeps on changing. The period of this precession is roughly 26,000 years. Polaris (α Ursae Minoris) is the Pole star now but *c*.3000 BC it was α Draconis which was followed later by β Ursae Minoris; in CE 14,000 it will be Vega. The equinoxes and the solstices also shift with respect to the background stars. The equinoxes move along the ecliptic in a direction opposite to the yearly course of the sun (Taurus to Aries to Pisces rather than Pisces to Aries to Taurus and so on).

The vernal equinox marked the beginning of the year. The sun's position among the constellations at the vernal equinox was an indication of the state of the precessional cycle. This constellation was noted by its heliacal rising. The equinoctial sun occupies each zodiacal constellation for *c*.2,200 years. Around 5000 BC it was in Gemini; it has moved since into Taurus, Aries, and is now in Pisces. The sun spends about $13\frac{1}{3}$ days in each *nakṣatra*, and the precession takes the equinoxes across each *nakṣatra* in about a thousand years.

In terms of the nakṣatras, the vernal equinox was in *Puśya* around 7200 BC, Punarvasu around 6100 BC, *Ārdrā* in 5100 BC, *Mṛgaśiras* in 4000 BC, *Rohiṇī* in 3100 BC, *Kṛttikā* in 2200 BC, *Bharaṇī* in 1300 BC, and *Aśvinī* in 300 BC. Since the shift across a *nakṣatra* takes place in approximately thousand years, each of the dates should be considered approximate to within a couple of hundred years, especially because we are not sure how exactly the beginning of a *nakṣatra* was defined.

Since the Vedic texts are an anthology of ancient hymns and legends (redacted according to an astronomical plan at a much later date), we would expect them to reflect many of these early dates, just as *Kalevala*, the Finnish national epic which was written down only in the nineteenth century, contains references to astronomical events that occurred thousands of years ago. There are some references in the Ṛgveda that have been interpreted as a memory of the vernal equinox in the *Puśya* and *Punarvasu nakṣatras*. One of these is a winter solstice in *Aśvinī* (RV 1.117.22 and 1.84.10), which would represent *c*.6000 BC. Bal Gangadhar Tilak (1893) pointed out that the occurrence of the winter solstice with the full moon of *Māgha* at the time of *Taittirīya Saṃhitā* corresponded to 2350 BC; he further suggested that the winter solstice had, in earlier periods, coincided with *Phalgunī* and *Caitrī* corresponding to the periods of 4000–2500 BC and 6000–4000 BC.

K. D. Abhyankar (1992) has sought the earliest Vedic astronomy in an *Aśvinī* calendar dating back to 7000 BC. Noting that the winter solstice occurs now in the *Mūla nakṣatra* with niryana longitude of 247°, he uses precession and a supposed date of the corresponding winter solstice in the Vedic times to arrive at this epoch.

9.8.1 Vernal equinox in Orion

We are on firmer ground about the vernal equinox in Orion, as in the story in the *Aitareya Brāhmaṇa* of *Prajāpati* (the lord of the year) feeling love for his daughter *Rohiṇī*. He takes the form of a stag (*Mṛgaśiras*, Orion) and approaches her, who is in the shape of a doe. The gods disapprove and Rudra (*Mṛgavyādha*, Sirius) pierces Orion. This represents the time when the vernal equinox was moving from *Mṛgaśiras* to *Rohinī* (Aldebaran). This is confirmed by the fact that *Mṛgaṣiras* had another name: *Agrahāyana*, "the beginning of the year." Tilak in his book, *Orion*, argued that the Greek Orion derives from the Vedic *Agrahāyana*. This epoch of the shifting of the vernal equinox is roughly 4000 BC.

The list of *nakṣatras* beginning with *Kṛttikā* indicates that it was drawn up in the third millennium BC. Scholars have also argued that a subsequent list began with *Rohiṇī*. This view is strengthened by the fact that there are two *Rohinīs*, separated by fourteen *nakṣatras*, indicating that the two marked the beginning of the two half-years.

Thirteen-and-a-half *nakṣatras* ending with *Viśākhā* were situated in the northern hemispheres; these were called *devanakṣatras*. The remaining *nakṣatras* ending with *Bharaṇī* that were in the southern hemisphere were called *yamanakṣatras* (*yama*: twin, dual). This classification in the *Taittirīya Brāhmaṇa* (1.5.2.7) corresponds to 2300 BC.

The *Śatapatha Brāhmaṇā* speaks of a marriage between the Seven Sages, the stars of the Ursa Major, and the *Kṛttikās;* this is elaborated in the *Purāṇas* where it is stated that the *ṛṣis* remain for a hundred years in each *nakṣatra*. In other words, during the earliest times in India there existed a centennial calendar with a cycle of 2,700 years. Called the *Saptarṣi* calendar, it is still in use in several parts of India. Its current beginning is taken to be 3076 BC. On the other hand, notices by the Greek historians Pliny and Arrian suggest that, during the Mauryan times, the calendar used in India began in 6676 BC. It is very likely that this calendar was the *Saptarṣi* calendar with a beginning at 6676 BC. Around 500 CE, a major review of the Indian calendar was attempted by astronomers. *Āryabhaṭa*, *Varāhamihira* and others used the *nakṣatra* references that the *Saptarṣi* were in *Maghā* at the time of the *Mahābhārata* war to determine its epoch. *Āryabhaṭa* declared the war to have occurred in 3137 BC (the *Kaliyuga* era begins 35 years after the war), and *Varāhamihira* assigned it 2449 BC. It has been suggested that this discrepancy arose because the change in the number of *nakṣatras* from the earlier counts of twenty-seven to the later twenty-eight was differently computed by the two astronomers. It is quite likely that the fame of the *Kaliyuga* era with its beginning assigned to 3102 BC prompted a change in the beginning of the *Saptarṣi* era to about the same time, namely, to 3076 BC. The shifting of seasons through the year and the shifting of the northern axis allow us to date several other statements in the books.

The *Kauṣītaki Brāhmaṇa* (4.4) speaks of the full moon night in *Phālguna* as the beginning of the year which corresponds to about 4000 BC. The same text (19.3) places the winter solstice in the new moon of *Māgha*; this could refer to a time as early as 1400 BC. The *Śatapatha Brāhmaṇa* (2.1.2.3) has a statement that points to an earlier epoch where it is stated that *Kṛttikā* never swerves from the east. This corresponds to 2950 BC. This date is supported by an examination of the actual sky map of that period (Achar 2000a). The *Maitrayaānīya Brāhmaṇa Upaniṣad* (6.14) refers to the winter solstice being at the mid-point of the *Śraviṣṭhā* segment and the summer solstice at the beginning of *Maghā*. This indicates 1660 BC. The *Vedāṅga Jyotiṣa* (Yajur 6–8) mentions that winter solstice was at the beginning of *Śraviṣṭhā* and the summer solstice at the mid-point of *Āśleṣā*. This corresponds to *c*.1350 BC (Sastry 1985). On the other hand, Achar (2000b) argues that a proper identification of β Delphini pushes this date to 1800 BC. It should be noted that these dates can only be considered to be very approximate. Furthermore, these dates do not imply that the texts come from the corresponding period; the text may recall an old tradition. A chronology of the Vedic period by means of astronomical references was attempted by the historian of science P. C. Sengupta. Among other evidence, Sengupta uses the description of the solar eclipse in RV 5.40.5–9 to fix a date for it. These dates should be considered along with the recent work of Achar (2000a,b,c). The changes in the beginning of the *Nakṣatra* lists bring us down to the Common Era; at the time of *Varāhamihira* (550 CE) the vernal equinox was in *Aśvinī*. To summarize, we can divide up the Vedic period into three main subdivisions:

1 *Early Vedic period (6000?–4000 BC)* This period is remembered in several legends of the Vedic texts.
2 *Ṛgvedic period (4000–2000 BC)* Composition of most of the Ṛgvedic hymns, development of the altar astronomy.
3 *Brāhmaṇic astronomy (2000–1000 BC)* Reflects the phase after the drying up of the Sarasvatī river. The *Brāhmaṇas* speak of the river being lost in the sands of the desert. This is a conservative and rough picture. If the Ṛgveda praises the Sarasvatī as a river that runs to the sea and the river is now known to have dried up by 1900 BC, then the closure of the Ṛgvedic period in about 2000 BC is justified. If the river dried up a thousand years earlier, as some scholars have suggested, then the periods will have to be adjusted correspondingly. Obviously, we don't address the question of the date at which the texts became frozen into their currently known forms. The final version of the texts could very well have come somewhat later, just as new editions of the Bible are still being created.

The *Purāṇic* memory of the *Mahābhārata* war having occurred in 1924 BC may represent the transference of a much earlier event to a cataclysmic event that was geological in nature. The memory of the war in popular imagination may represent the conflation of two different actual events.

9.9 Astronomy and literature

There are several ways to check the dates that emerge from Vedic astronomy. The texts have genealogies of kings and *ṛṣis* that help us establish relative chronologies in many cases. The *Purāṇic* king lists speak of roughly a hundred generations before the *Mahābhārata* war. The Greek historians inform us that the Indians during the time of the Mauryas remembered more than 150 generations of kings spanning over 6,000 years (we assume that these lists remember the prominent kings only). Then there are various remembered lines of teachers that show up at various places in the texts. Specifically, the *Bṛhadāraṇyaka Upaniṣad* remembers a line of sixty teachers. We don't know how many years should be assigned to each teacher but this line could span substantially more than a thousand years. Furthermore, there are traditions regarding the date of the *Mahābhārata* war. Although there is disagreement about the date – ranging from 3137 BC according to the *Kaliyuga* tradition to 1924 BC according to the *Purāṇic* accounts (where we take that the separation of 1,050 years from the war to the Nandas in some *Purāṇas* is actually a misprint for a separation of 1,500 years, as argued by Pargiter and others) – we are speaking of events that reach into the third millennium BC. The geographical focus of the Vedic texts is in the Sarasvatī region of India so we can have no other conclusion excepting that the texts reflect a tradition that existed in this region. There are those who suggest that the Vedic people are latecomers into India and their texts represent a translation into Sanskrit of an earlier Indian culture. But this position confuses history of ideas with racial history. Even if this hypothesis were true we would still be talking of the ancient tradition rooted in India, irrespective of which ethnic or linguistic group has been responsible for its safekeeping and transmission to our times. Furthermore, such a position lies outside scientific discourse, because we have no means of either disproving or proving it. Neither is this the most economic hypothesis that would explain our evidence.

Vedic texts are not to be tied to any specific ethnic or linguistic group. They could very well have been composed by speakers of a multilingual culture. This pattern of the use of one elite language by speakers of many other mother tongues has been repeated in India for millennia and it continues to our day. From the texts, it cannot be said whether the Vedic tradition was the only tradition in northwest India at that time. Indeed, it is very likely that other cultural traditions coexisted with it. Just as Europeans, when they arrived in the Americas, found a great diversity of languages and cultures, Vedic India consisted of many different ethnic and linguistic groups.

9.10 Concluding remarks

The chronological frame provided by Vedic astronomy does not answer the question about the original homeland of the Vedic people. All it says is that the Vedic people have been in the Indian geographical region going back at least seven or eight thousand years. We cannot rule out the presence of other groups during this period in this region. To get an idea of social diversity, we must depend on an analysis of the literary evidence and attempt correlations of this evidence with the archaeological record. From the astronomical data, it is certain that the Vedic people were in India during the *Rohiṇī* period of 4000 BC. But did the Vedic people come to India prior to, say, 6000 BC? This question lies outside the scope of Vedic studies. At that time horizon, we get close to a period when there may have been large migrations of people across continents at the end of the last Ice Age.

In my view, it is wrong to speak of an absolute dichotomy of invasions versus noninvasions into India. Such a dichotomy must be rooted to a definite time window. Writing specifically about the second millennium BC, Mark Kenoyer says: "There is no archaeological or biological evidence for invasions or mass migrations into the Indus Valley between the end of the Harappan phase, about 1900 B.C. and the beginning of the Early Historic period around 600 B.C." (Kenoyer 1998: 174). Other studies have shown that there is no break in the biological record between 4500 BC and 800 BC (Kennedy 1995). To speak of an age much before this time is to enter the realm of speculation.

To conclude, we ask why astronomical evidence has for so long been disregarded. Irrespective of the sophistication of Vedic astronomy, it is clear that references such as that of the shifting of the vernal equinox from Orion are unambiguous. References to astronomical events of 4000 BC shouldn't have been surprising if we are not surprised by a memory of equally ancient astronomical events in the myths of the Finns or the Polynesians. The rejection of the astronomical evidence was due to the acceptance as fact of the theory of Aryan invasions in the second millennium BC. The demands of the Occam's razor rule out scenarios of invasions or mass migrations into India during the period indicated by Vedic astronomy, so why have some people persisted with such scenarios? The distinguished anthropologist, Edmund Leach, thought that a racist view of history was behind the mind-set that caused serious scholars to believe in the myth of Aryan invasions:

> Where the Indo-European philologists are concerned, the invasion argument is tied in with their assumption that if a particular language is identified as having been used in a particular locality at a particular time, no attention need be paid to what was there before; the slate is wiped clean. Obviously, the easiest way to imagine this happening in real life is to have a military conquest that obliterates the previously existing population!
>
> The details of the theory fit in with this racist framework... Because of their commitment to a unilineal segmentary history of language development that needed to be mapped onto the ground, the philologists

> took it for granted that proto-Indo-Iranian was a language that had originated outside either India or Iran. Hence it followed that the text of the Rig Veda was in a language that was spoken by those who introduced this earliest form of Sanskrit into India. From this he derives the myth of the Aryan invasions. QED.
>
> The origin myth of British colonial imperialism helped the elite administrators in the Indian Civil Service to see themselves as bringing "pure" civilization to a country in which civilization of the most sophisticated (but "morally corrupt") kind was already nearly 6,000 years old. Here I will only remark that the hold of this myth on the British middle-class imagination is so strong that even today, 44 years after the death of Hitler and 43 years after the creation of an independent India and independent Pakistan, the Aryan invasions of the second millennium BC are still treated as if they were an established fact of history.
>
> (Leach 1990)

Further understanding of ancient India requires a paradigm shift, away from preoccupation with establishing priority for one race or another or one linguistic group or another. For correct understanding we must accept the reality of mutual interactions among ancient people. The parallels in ancient mythologies (de Santillana and Dechend, 1969) are most likely a result of these interactions. New examples of cultural intercourse between India and the West have become clear through the work of Kazanas (1999), Napier (1986, 2001), and Taylor (1992). This interaction was unquestionably in both directions.

References

Abhyankar, K. D., 1992. "A Search for the Earliest Vedic Calendar." In *Issues in Vedic Astronomy and Astrology*, edited by H. Pandya, S. Dikshit, and M. N. Kansara. New Delhi: Rashtriya Veda Vidya Pratishthan.

Achar, B. N. N., 2000a. "On the Astronomical Basis of the Date of Satapatha Brahmana," *Indian Journal of History of Science*, 35: 1–19.

——, 2000b. "A Case for Revising the Date of Vedanga Jyotisha," *Indian Journal of History of Science*, 35: 173–83.

——, 2000c. "On the *caitradi* Scheme," *Indian Journal of History of Science*, 35: 295–310.

Billard, R., 1971. *L'astronomie Indienne*. Paris: Publications de l'ecole francaise d'extreme-orient.

Dikshit, S. B., 1969. *Bharatiya Jyotish Shastra*. Lucknow: Hindi Samiti (Original edition, 1896).

Feuerstein, G., S. Kak, and D. Frawley, 1995. *In Search of the Cradle of Civilization*. Wheaton: Quest Books.

Francfort, H. P., 1992. "Evidence for Harappan Irrigation System in Haryana and Rajasthan," *Eastern Anthropologist*, 45: 87–103.

Frawley, D., 1994. "Planets in the Vedic literature," *Indian Journal of History of Science*, 29: 495–506.

Inden, R., 1990. *Imagining India*. Cambridge: Blackwell.

Kak, S., 1992. "Astronomy in the Vedic Altars and the Ṛgveda," *Mankind Quarterly*, 33: 45–55.

——, 1993a. "Astronomy in Śatapatha Brāhmaṇa," *Indian Journal of History of Science*, 28: 15–34.

——, 1993b. "Astronomy of Vedic Altars," *Vistas in Astronomy*, 36: 117–40.

——, 1993c. "The Structure of the Rigvedic," *Indian Journal of History of Science*, 28: 71–9.

——, 1993d. "Planetary Periods from the Rigvedic code," *Mankind Quarterly*, 33: 433–42.

——, 1994/95. "The Astronomical Code of the Rigveda," *Puratattva: Bulletin of the Indian Archaeological Society*, 25: 1–30.

——, 1995a. "The Astronomy of the Age of Geometric Altars," *Quarterly Journal of the Royal Astronomical Society*, 36: 385–96.

——, 1995b. "From Vedic Science to Vedānta," *The Adyar Library Bulletin*, 59: 1–36.

——, 1996. "Knowledge of Planets in the Third Millennium B.C.," *Quarterly Journal of the Royal Astronomical Society*, 37: 709–15.

——, 1997. "Archaeology and Literature," *Current Science*, 73: 624–7.

——, 2000a. "Astronomy and its Role in Vedic Culture." Chapter 23 in *Science and Civilization in India, Vol. 1, The Dawn of Indian Civilization, Part 1*, edited by G. C. Pande. Delhi: Center for Study in Civilizations, pp. 507–24.

——, 2000b. *The Astronomical Code of the Ṛgveda*. New Delhi: Munshiram Manoharlal.

——, 2000c. "Birth and Early Development of Indian Astronomy." In *Astronomy Across Cultures: The History of Non-Western Astronomy*, edited by H. Selin. Dordrecht: Kluwer Academic Publishers, pp. 303–40.

Kazanas, N., 1999. "The Ṛgveda and Indo-Europeans," *Annals of the Bhandarkar Oriental Research Institute*, 80: 15–42.

Kennedy, K. A. R., 1995. "Have Aryans been Identified in the Prehistoric Skeletal Record from South Asia? Biological Anthropology and Concepts of Ancient Races." In *The Indo-Aryans of Ancient South Asia*, edited by G. Erdosy. Berlin: Walter de Gruyter, pp. 32–66.

Kenoyer, M., 1998. *Ancient Cities of the Indus Valley Civilization*. Oxford: Oxford University Press.

Leach, E., 1990. "Aryan Invasions over Four Millennia." In *Culture Through Time, Anthropological Approaches*, edited by E. Ohnuki-Tierney. Stanford, CA: Stanford University Press, pp. 242–3.

Napier, A. D., 1986. *Masks, Transformation, and Paradox*. Berkeley, CA: University of California Press.

——, 2001. "Masks and Metaphysics in the Ancient World." In *Mind, Man and Mask*, edited by S. C. Malik. New Delhi: Indira Gandhi National Centre for the Arts/Aryan Books International, pp. 3–15.

Pargiter, F. E. 1992. *Ancient Indian Historical Tradition*. London: Oxford University Press.

Rao, T. R. N. and S. Kak, 2000. *Computing Science in Ancient India*. New Delhi: Munshiram Manoharlal.

Ray, P. C., 1956. *History of Chemistry in Ancient and Medieval India*. Calcutta: Indian Chemical Society.

de Santillana, G. and H. von Dechend, 1969. *Hamlet's Mill: An Essay on Myth and the Frame of Time*. Boston, MA: Gambit.

Sastry, T. S. Kuppanna, 1985. *Vedāṅga Jyotiṣa of Lagadha*. New Delhi: Indian National Science Academy.

Seidenberg, A., 1962. "The Origin of Geometry," *Archive for History of Exact Sciences*, 1: 488–527.

——, 1978. "The Origin of Mathematics," *Archive for History of Exact Sciences*, 18: 301–42.

Sengupta, P. C., 1947. *Ancient Indian Chronology*. Calcutta: University of Calcutta Press.

Shaffer, J. and D. L. Lichtenstein, 1995. "The Concept of Cultural Tradition and Paleoethnicity in South Asian Archaeology." In *The Indo-Aryans of South Asia*, edited by G. Erdosy. Berlin: Walter de Gruyter.

Subbarayappa, B. V., 1971. *A Concise History of Science in India*. New Delhi: Indian National Science Academy.

Taylor, T., 1992. "The Gundestrup Cauldron," *Scientific American*, 266 (3): 84–9.

Tilak, B. G., 1893. *The Orion*. Pune: Tilak Brothers.

Vidyālaṇkāra, V., 1985. *Śatapatha Brāhmaṇastha Agnicayana Samīkṣā*. Bahalgarh: Ram Lal Kapur Trust Press.

van der Waerden, B. L., 1980. "Two Treatises on Indian Astronomy," *Journal for History of Astronomy,* 11: 50–8.

Wakankar, V. S., 1992. "Rock Painting in India." In *Rock Art in the Old World*, edited by M. Lorblanchet. New Delhi: Indira Gandhi National Centre for the Arts, pp. 319–36.

10

THE TEXTUAL EVIDENCE

The Rigveda as a source of Indo-European history

Shrikant G. Talageri

10.1 Introduction

The question of the original homeland or Urheimat of the Indo-European family of languages is not a settled one: although most writers on the subject would support a theory that the family originated in "South Russia," a general term for a large area stretching northwestwards from the Caspian Sea or for any specific part of this area, and spread by expansions and/or migrations to the other areas historically inhabited by speakers of Indo-European languages, this theory is not supported by the main academic disciplines involved in the study of the Indo-European homeland question, *particularly in respect of the presence of these languages at the easternmost end of the Indo-European spectrum, that is, in South Asia.*

While linguists, by and large, continue to support this theory, and to maintain that the Indo-Aryan languages of South Asia were brought into this region by immigrants or invaders in the second millennium BC, archaeologists are increasingly rejecting this theory on the ground that the evidence of archaeology, physical anthropology, and cultural continuity in South Asia from the neolithic period onwards disproves the idea that any such immigration or invasion ever took place, or at least that it could ever have taken place within the time-frame dictated by the exigencies of the chronology suggested by Indo-European dialectological studies (Erdosy 1995: x–xii).

For the purpose of this chapter, I will leave aside the implications and details of the linguistics versus archaeology debate, and only examine, to the extent possible within the scope of the chapter, the third academic discipline, apart from linguistics and archaeology, which has a direct bearing on the subject of the Indo-Aryan languages in India and, by extension, on the subject of the Indo-European migrations and expansions: namely, the study of textual sources, which in this context, means specifically the study of the evidence in the Rigveda.

The evidence in the Rigveda is examined by me in comprehensive detail elsewhere (in my book *The Rigveda – A Historical Analysis*, Aditya Prakashan,

New Delhi), which, at the time of writing, is in print, and I will present a brief summary of this evidence in the present chapter.

The examination covers the following aspects of the Rigveda:

1 A comparative examination of the mythology of the Rigveda and the mythologies of other Indo-European branches.
2 An examination of the internal chronology and geography of the Rigveda.
3 An examination of references in the text which have a bearing on the origins and migrations of other branches of the Indo-Europeans.

10.2 Comparative mythology

The study of comparative Indo-European mythology has shown that it is possible to reconstruct a common or Proto-Indo-European mythology, or at least to identify elements common to different Indo-European mythologies.

The results of this study produce a picture which is very difficult, if not impossible, to reconcile with any of the possible scenarios in which the composers of the Rigveda are treated as immigrants into India who composed the text at the end of a long series of migrations from South Russia to the northwest of India, the greater part of the alleged journey being carried out in the close company of the Iranians.

According to the standard theory of Indo-Aryan immigration into India:

(a) The Indo-Iranians, as a more or less single undifferentiated group, separated from the other Indo-European groups in the Indo-European homeland itself: according to Victor H. Mair, for example, the Indo-Iranians were already separated from the Tocharian and Anatolian branches by 3700 BC; from the Germanic, Baltic, Slavonic, Italic, Celtic, and Albanian branches by 3200 BC; from the Greek branch by 2500 BC; and from the Armenian branch by 2000 BC (Mair 1998: 848–52).

(b) After separating from all the other branches, the original Indo-Iranians, still as a single undifferentiated group, migrated to Central Asia, and settled down there for a considerable period of time. So considerable a period of time, in fact, that the original immigrants were absorbed into the local populations and almost completely lost their original racial features and characteristics: according to Michael Witzel,

> even before their immigration into South Asia, (they) completely 'Aryanised' a local population, for example, in the highly developed Turkmenian-Bactrian area which yielded the BMAC, involving both their language and culture. This is only imaginable as the result of the complete acculturation of both groups.
>
> (Erdosy 1995: 113)

As a result:

> By the time they reached the Subcontinent they were already racially mixed:... they may have had the typical somatic characteristic of the ancient populations of the Turanian/ Iranian/Afghan areas and may not have looked very different from the modern inhabitants of the Indo-Iranian borderlands.
>
> (Ibid.)

(c) The process of immigration into the northwestern parts of India was equally a complex one. As pointed out by George Erdosy, the movement into the northwestern parts of India was not part of a process of "cataclysmic invasions, for which there is little evidence indeed," but of "more gradual and complex phenomena" (Erdosy 1995: XV). Witzel, in the same volume, characterizes it as a "gradual trickling in, and subsequent rise in dominance, of Vedic tribes in the Punjab": the process was so gradual that their "genetic impact would have been negligible and... would have been 'lost' in a few generations in the much larger gene pool of the Indus people" (Erdosy 1995: 113).

(d) The process of development of the Vedic language and culture in the Punjab was also a long and complex one: according to Witzel,

> Such a process may have evolved in the manner of the Mitanni (and, in a different context, much of Hittite) culture: initial domination by Indo-Aryan speaking, somatically and to some extent culturally already 'Turanian' tribes in the Panjab, followed by quick acculturation.
>
> (Erdosy 1995: 114)

Speaking about the language of the Rigveda, Witzel refers to the conclusions of F. B. J. Kuiper who "traces the influence of the substratum in the use of *iti*, in the two forms of the gerund which presupposes a long time of 'subliterary' usage prior to acceptance into the high, poetical language, and in the spread of retroflex sounds such as ṭ, ḍ, ṇ, and ṣ" in the language of the Rigveda, and endorses Kuiper's conclusion that "between the arrival of the Aryans... and the formation of the oldest hymns of the Rigveda, a much larger period must have elapsed than is normally thought." Witzel therefore sums up the situation: "in contrast to its close relatives in Iran (Avestan, Old Persian), Vedic Sanskrit is already an *Indian* language" (emphasis in the original) (Erdosy 1995: 108).

The Rigveda, it must be noted, is, according to this theory, the *end product* of this very long and complex chain of events and circumstances.

The character of Rigvedic mythology, in relation to the mythologies of the other Indo-European branches, however, stands in sharp contrast to the scenario described earlier:

(a) The mythology of the Rigveda represents the most primitive form of Indo-European mythology: according to A. A. Macdonell, for example, the Vedic gods "are nearer to the physical phenomena which they represent, than the gods of any other Indo-European mythology" (Macdonell reprint 1963: 15).

In fact, the original nature-myths, in which the mythological entities and the mythological events in other Indo-European mythologies are rooted, can, in the vast majority of cases, be identified or traced only through the form in which the myths are represented in the Rigveda.

(b) All the other Indo-European mythologies, individually, have numerous mythological elements in common with Vedic mythology, but very few with each other (and even these are ones which are also found in Vedic mythology).

Thus, the only recognizable Indo-European elements in the mythologies of the various Indo-European peoples of ancient West Asia are those which they, separately, share with the mythology of the Vedas: Hittite *Inar* (Indra); Kassite *šūriaš* (Sūrya), *Maruttaš* (Marut), and *Inda-bugaš* (Indra-Bhaga); and Mitanni *Indara* (Indra), *Mi-itra* (Mitra), *Nasha-at-tiya* (Nāsatya), and *Uruwna* (Varuṇa).

Likewise Baltic *Perkunas* (Parjanya) and Slavonic *Pyerun* (Parjanya), *Svarog* (Svarga), *Ogon* (Agni), and *Bog* (Bhaga) have their parallels in Vedic mythology.

As Griffith points out in the preface to his translation of the Rigveda: "the deities, the myths and the religious beliefs and practices of the Veda throw a flood of light upon the religions of all European countries before the introduction of Christianity" (Griffith 1887).

In many cases, it is almost impossible to recognize the connections between related mythological entities and events in two Indo-European mythologies without a comparison of the two with the related Vedic versions. Thus, for example, the Teutonic *Vanir* are connected with the Greek *Hermes* and *Pan*, but it is impossible to connect the two except through the Vedic *Saramā* and *Paṇi*: as we have shown in detail in our book (Talageri 2000), the Teutonic *Vanir* and Greek *Pan* are cognate to the Vedic *Paṇi*.

Even the main Vedic myth which relates to the Saramā–Paṇi theme, found in the Rigveda in X 108, and in later developed forms in the Jaiminīya Brāhmaṇa (II 440–2) and the Bṛhaddevatā (VIII 24–36), is found in both the Teutonic and Greek mythologies in transformed versions which bear absolutely no similarities with each other, but which are both, *individually*, clearly recognizable as developments of the original Vedic myth.

The myth, as it is found in X 108, incidentally, is itself an evolved and anthropomorphized form, located in the *latest* of the ten Books or Maṇḍalas of the Rigveda, of an original nature-myth, found referred to at various places in earlier parts of the Rigveda, according to which "Saramā is the Dawn who recovers the rays of the Sun that have been carried away by night" (Griffith's footnote to I.62.3) or by the Paṇis who are "fiends of darkness" or "demons who carry away and conceal the cows or rays of light" (Griffith's footnote to I.151.9).

(c) Iranian mythology, which should share to some extent at least the same character as Vedic mythology (since it is held that it was the *undivided Indo-Iranians*, and not the Indo-Aryans alone, who separated from the other Indo-European groups in South Russia and migrated to Central Asia where they shared a common culture and religion), on the contrary, *has no elements in common with other Indo-European mythologies* (other than with Vedic mythology itself).

It is difficult to understand how any objective analyst of Vedic mythology could fail to recognize the fact that the uniquely primitive and representative character of Vedic mythology is *totally incompatible* with a theory which treats the Rigveda as the *end-product* of a long and complex chain of events and circumstances involving a long period of separation of the original Indo-Aryans from the other Indo-Europeans, long migrations (over long periods of time) from South Russia to Central Asia and later to India, complete racial transformations *en route* (so that the "Indo-Aryans" who finally entered India bore little, or no, racial resemblance to the original "Indo-Aryans" who left South Russia), and a long stay in the Punjab where the (new or transformed) Indo-Aryans merged into the local population, lost all memories of their original habitats and journeys, and developed a uniquely *Indian* Indo-Aryan language before they commenced the composition of the Rigveda.

10.3 Internal chronology and geography

The geography of the Rigveda is held to be one of the strongest pieces of evidence in the text about the immigration of the Indo-Aryans through the northwest into the interior of India.

However, this conclusion is based, *not* on any analysis of the internal chronology and geography of the text, but on a bare assumption that if, as they *must* have, the Indo-Aryans entered into India from the northwest, then the Rigveda must give evidence of this circumstance, and the references to more western areas in the Rigveda must necessarily be older than references to more eastern areas. The argument that the Rigveda proves the immigration of the Indo-Aryans from the northwest into the east is thus a purely circular argument.

A proper perspective on the implications of the geographical references in the Rigveda cannot be had without first sorting out the internal chronology of the text.

The basis for the internal chronology of the Rigveda is the division of the text into ten Books or Maṇḍalas, which clearly represent more or less distinct epochs of Rigvedic composition and, hence, of Rigvedic history.

I have analyzed this chronology in detail in my book (Talageri 2000), and will merely present a summary of the criteria used, and the results obtained:

1. The first criterion is that of the relationship between the composers of the hymns in different Maṇḍalas: when Maṇḍala A contains hymns by a composer who is an ancestor of a composer in Maṇḍala B, it will be natural to assume that Maṇḍala A is older than Maṇḍala B.
2. The second criterion is that of references within the hymns in one Maṇḍala to the composers of hymns in another Maṇḍala: when a hymn in Maṇḍala D refers to a composer in Maṇḍala C as a figure from the past, it will be natural to assume that Maṇḍala C is older than Maṇḍala D.

3 The third criterion is that of references within the hymns to kings and Ṛṣis (other than composers, who have already been dealt with) who are contemporaries in some Maṇḍalas; and figures from the past in others: when Maṇḍala E refers to a king or Ṛṣi as a contemporary figure, and Maṇḍala F either refers to the same king or Ṛṣi as a figure from the past, or to a descendant of that king or Ṛṣi as a contemporary figure, it will be natural to assume that Maṇḍala E is older than Maṇḍala F.

Three different criteria are used, and the criteria are not used selectively (i.e. taking the names of a few selected composers and kings) but in totality (i.e. all the names of composers and kings, who are common to two or more Maṇḍalas, are taken into consideration), and the unanimous results are as follows:

Maṇḍalas 6, 3, and 7, in that order, stand out as representing the Early Period of the Rigveda.
Maṇḍalas 4 and 2, in that order, represent the Middle Period of the Rigveda.
Maṇḍalas 5, 8, and 9, in that order, represent the Late Period of the Rigveda.
Maṇḍala 10 represents the Very Late, or Final, Period of the Rigveda.
Maṇḍala 1 stands out as a Maṇḍala whose period stretches out from the pre-Middle (but post-Early) period to the Very Late, or Final, period of the Rigveda.

The above chronological order, separately obtained on the basis of each of the three criteria already cited, is further confirmed by the following factors:

(a) The chronological order of the Maṇḍalas (i.e. 6, 3, 7, 4, 2, 5, 8, 9, 10) is confirmed by a consideration of the rigidity of their family structures: that is, Maṇḍala 6 represents the most rigid family structure, where every single hymn and verse is composed by members of one single branch of one single family of composers; Maṇḍala 10, at the other end of the spectrum, has the loosest family structure, where not only are the hymns composed by Ṛṣis belonging to almost every single family in the Rigveda, but where, in a very large number of cases, even the very family identity of the composers is unknown; and all the other Maṇḍalas, exactly in the order obtained by us, represent stages or progressions from the rigid structure of Maṇḍala 6 to the loose structure of Maṇḍala 10.

(b) The general chronological order is also confirmed by a consideration of the method of attribution of hymns: in the older Maṇḍalas, hymns composed by the descendants of an important or eponymous composer are generally attributed to that ancestral composer himself, but in later Maṇḍalas, hymns are generally attributed to the actual composer himself. There is a general consensus that the six family Maṇḍalas (Maṇḍalas 2–7) are older than the nonfamily Maṇḍalas (Maṇḍalas 1, 8–10). It is significant that the family Maṇḍalas, except for Maṇḍala 5 (which, as per our analysis, is the latest of the family Maṇḍalas), follow the older method, while the nonfamily Maṇḍalas, except for Maṇḍala 1 (which, as per our analysis, is the oldest of the nonfamily Maṇḍalas), follow the later method.

The chronological order of the Maṇḍalas (6, 3, 7, 4, 2, 5, 8, 9, 10) becomes crucial for our analysis of the geography of the Rigveda.

An examination of the geographical factors in the Rigveda (rivers, places, animals), gives us the following picture.

1 In the oldest period of the Rigveda (the period of Maṇḍala 6), the Vedic Aryans were settled in the areas to the east of the Sarasvati, that is, in present-day Haryana and Uttar Pradesh.
2 Toward the ending of the Early Period (Maṇḍalas 3 and 7), the Vedic Aryans expanded westwards into the Punjab.
3 By the Middle Period, and in the Late Period of the Rigveda, the geographical horizon of the Vedic Aryans had spread as far westwards as the southeastern parts of Afghanistan.

A chronological and geographical analysis of the Rigveda, thus, not only contradicts the assumption that the Vedic texts depict a movement from the northwest to the east, but, in fact, proves, beyond any shadow of doubt, that the movement was from the east to the northwest.

10.4 Indo-European groups

The theory of Indo-Aryan immigrations into India involves only the Indo-Aryans: it does not involve any other Indo-European group, not even the Iranians, who, according to this theory, parted company with the Indo-Aryans in Central Asia or Afghanistan itself (or, according to some writers, in "eastern Iran," but this is often a euphemism for Afghanistan).

However, the evidence in the Rigveda contradicts this assumption: it is clear, from the evidence in the hymns, that major Iranian groups like the Persians (Iranian *Parsua* = Vedic *Parśava*), the Parthians (Iranian *Parthava* = Vedic *Pārthava*), the Pakhtoons (Vedic *Paktha*), and the Baluchis (Vedic *Bhalāna*), at the very least, all of whom are named in the Rigveda as "Anu" tribes, opponents of the Vedic king Sudās in the Dāśarājña battle (the battle of the ten kings) in Maṇḍala 7, *were settled in the heart of the Punjab in the Early Period of the Rigveda.* (The Purāṇas name another "Anu" tribe settled in the Punjab: the Medes, Iranian *Madai* = Puranic *Madra*.)

The battle represents a major conflict in which the Vedic people, who were settled to the *east* of the Sarasvati river in earlier times, expanded westwards into the Punjab, clashed with a confederation of the "Anu" tribes then inhabiting the region, and defeated them. This resulted in a movement of sections of these tribes from the Punjab to areas further west (starting with Afghanistan).

This battle, it must be noted, took place in the Early Period of the Rigveda, and is dated, by modern western scholars, to *at least* as early as the middle of the second millennium BC: for example, Witzel notes that the Sarasvati is "prominent in Book 7: it flows from the mountains to the sea (7, 95, 2) – which would put the battle of 10 kings prior to 1500 BC or so due to the now well-documented dessication of the Sarasvati (Yash Pal *et al.* 1984)" (Erdosy 1995: 335).

The ancestors of the Persians, Parthians, Pakhtoons, and Baluchis were therefore settled in the Punjab "prior to 1500 BC or so" on the evidence of the Rigveda, and the Vedic Aryans were settled to their east, to the east of the Sarasvati River.

The recorded presence of these Iranian groups in areas further west is much later to the period of the Dāśarājña battle, and even to the very latest date (1000 BC) assumed for the Rigveda as a whole by Western scholars. The Encyclopaedia Britannica records:

> By the mid-ninth century BC two major groups of Iranians appear in cuneiform sources: the Medes and the Persians. Of the two, the Medes were the more widespread, and, from an Assyrian point of view, the more important. What is reasonably clear from the cuneiform sources is that the Medes and Persians (and no doubt other Iranian peoples not identified by name) were moving into western Iran *from the east*.
>
> (emphasis ours) (Encyclopaedia Britannica 1974, Vol. 9, 832)

Likewise the *Larousse Encyclopaedia of Mythology* confirms:

> *We find no evidence of the future 'Iranians' previous to the ninth century BC.* The first allusion to the Parsua or Persians, then localized in the mountains of Kurdistan, and to the Madai or Medes, already established on the plain, occurs in 837 BC in connection with the expedition of the Assyrian king Shalmaneser III. About a hundred years afterwards, the Medes invaded the plateau which we call Persian (or Iran) driving back or assimilating populations of whom there is no written record...
>
> (emphasis ours) (Larousse Encyclopaedia of Mythology 1959: 321)

More recently, P. Oktor Skjærvø reiterates that " 'Persians' are first mentioned in the 9th century BC Assyrian annals: on one campaign, in 835 BC, Shalmaneser (858–824 BC) is said to have received tributes from 27 kings of Paršuwaš; the Medes are mentioned under Tiglath-Pileser III (744–727 BC)" (Erdosy 1995: 156).

To conclude, the textual sources not only flatly contradict any ideas of any immigration of Indo-Aryans into India from the northwest after a separation from the Iranians, but they provide strong and conclusive textual evidence in favor of the idea of an Indian homeland. In this, the textual evidence is in harmony not only with the evidence of archaeology (which rejects the idea of an Indo-Aryan immigration into India), but, with the evidence of more definitive linguistic criteria such as the evidence of place names and river names as noted by Witzel (Erdosy 1995: 105–7).

References

Encyclopaedia Britannica, 1974. *The New Encyclopaedia Britannica*, 15th edition, Vol. 9. Chicago, IL: Encyclopaedia Britannica.

Erdosy, George (ed.), 1995. *Indo-Aryans of Ancient South Asia – Language, Material Culture and Ethnicity*. Berlin: Walter de Gruyter.

Griffith, Ralph T. H., 1987. *Hymns of the Rgveda* (complete translation of the text). New Delhi: Munshiram Manoharlal Publishers Pvt. Ltd.

Larousse Encyclopaedia of Mythology, 1959. *The Larousse Encyclopaedia of Mythology*, translated by Richard Aldington and Delano Ames. London: Batchworth Press Ltd.

Macdonell, A. A., 1963 (reprint). *The Vedic Mythology*. Varanasi: Indological Book House.

Mair, Victor H. (ed.), 1998. *The Bronze Age and Early Iron Age Peoples of Eastern Asia, Volume II*. Washington, DC: The Institute for the Study of Man (in collaboration with) The University of Pennsylvania Museum Publications.

Talageri, S. G., 2000. *The Rigveda – A Historical Analysis*. New Delhi: Aditya Prakashan.

11

INDOCENTRISM

Autochthonous visions of ancient India[1]

Michael Witzel

11.1 Introduction

The "Aryan question" is concerned with the immigration of a population speaking an archaic Indo-European (IE) language, Vedic Sanskrit, who celebrate their gods and chieftains in the poems of the oldest Indian literature, the Ṛgveda, and who subsequently spread their language, religion, ritual, and social organization throughout the subcontinent. Who were the "Aryans"? What was their spiritual and material culture and their outlook on life? Did they ever enter the Indian subcontinent from the outside? Or did these people develop indigenously in the Greater Panjab?

This, the "Aryan" question, has kept minds and politicians busy for the past 200 years; it has been used and misused in many ways. The discussion has become a cottage industry in India during recent years. This chapter attempts to present many[2] of the *pros* and *contras* for the (non-)occurrence of a movement of an "Aryan" population and its consequences. First, a detailed summary of the traditional "western" theory (Sections 11.1–11.11), then the recent Indian counter-theories; this is followed by an evaluation of their merits (Sections 11.12–11.24); the chapter concludes with some deliberations on the special kind of "discourse" that informs and drives the present autochthonous trend.

11.2 Materials: texts, dates, locations

Most of our evidence on the ancient "Aryans" comes from the texts and from the linguistic and cultural data contained in them.[3] The Vedas are a large collection of texts, orally composed and orally transmitted, perfectly, well into this millennium, almost like a tape recording. The oldest is the Ṛgveda (Ṛgveda Saṃhitā (RV), with many hymns of RV 10 as a late addition). The Old Iranian texts are quite similar to those of the Vedas. The five long Gāϑā (Yasna 28–53) are the RV-like poems by Zaraϑuštra himself; the Yasna Haptaŋhāiti is a collection of Mantras used for fire worship. The rest of the Avestan texts is post-Zoroastrian.

The East Iranian texts of the Avesta are as elusive to absolute dating as the Vedic ones (Witzel 1972, 2000).

However, the Ṛgveda, whose geographical horizon is limited to the Panjab and its surroundings, does not yet know of iron but only of the hard metal copper/bronze (Rau 1974, 1983; *ayas* = Avest. *aiiah* "copper/bronze"). Iron is only found in later Vedic (Ved.) texts, where it is called, just as in Dravidian (Drav.) **cir-umpu*, the "black metal" (*śyāma, kṛṣna ayas*). It makes its appearance in South Asia only by *c.*1200 or 1000 BCE.[4] The RV, thus, must be earlier than that.[5] The RV also does not know of large cities such as that of the Indus civilization but only of ruins (*armaka*, Falk 1981) and of small forts (*pur*, Rau 1976). Therefore, it must be *later* than the disintegration of the Indus cities in the Panjab, at *c.*1900 BCE. A good, possible date *ad quem* would be that of the Mitanni (Mit.) documents of Northern Iraq/Syria of *c.*1400 BCE that mention the Ṛgvedic gods and some other Old Indo-Aryan (IA) words (however, in a form slightly preceding that of the RV).[6] Post-RV texts (AV, etc.) whose geographical horizon stretches from Bactria (*Balhika*) to *Aṅga* (Northwest Bengal) mention iron for the first time and therefore should be contemporaneous or slightly rather later than 1200/1000 BCE. The early *Upaniṣads* precede the date of the Buddha, now considered *c.*400 BCE (Bechert 1982, 1991 sqq.) and of the re-emergence of cities *c.*450 BCE (Ersdosy 1988). On the whole the period of the four Vedas seems to fall *roughly* between *c.*1500 BCE[7] and *c.*500 BCE.[8]

Dating the Avestan (Avest.) texts, too, rests only on internal evidence (Skjærvø 1995). The Old Avest. texts reflect a copper/bronze (*aiiah*) culture; the younger texts might to some extent overlap with the expansion eastwards of the Median realm (*c.*700–550 BCE). Zaraϑuštra who spoke Old Avest. should be dated well before this time. Current estimates range from the fourteenth to the seventh century BCE.[9]

11.3 Immigration

Any type of immigration has increasingly been denied in India, especially during the past two decades, and more recently also by some Western archaeologists. How likely is an immigration scenario for people speaking IA, on the basis of comparable cases from Indian and non-Indian history? Beginning with the prehistoric migrations starting with the move of Homo Sapiens "Out of Africa" some 50,000 years ago, we actually *do know* that one group after the other has entered the Indian subcontinent, as immigrants or as invaders, in historical times.[10] In addition, small-scale semi-annual transhumance movements between the Indus plains and the Afghan and Baluchi highlands continue to this day (Witzel 1995: 322, 2000).

Why, then, should all immigration, or even mere transhumance trickling in, be excluded in the single case of the IAs, especially when the linguistic and cultural evidence (Sections 11.8, 11.21–11.23) so clearly speaks for it? Just one "Afghan" IA tribe that did not return to the highlands but stayed in their Panjab winter quarters in spring was needed to set off a wave of acculturation in the plains, by transmitting its 'status kit' (Ehret) to its neighbors.[11] Given the frequency of movements, large and small, into South Asia via the northwestern (and other) corridors persisting until this day, the vehement denial of *any* such possibility (Section 11.8 sqq.) is simply unreasonable (and can only be explained psychologically).

The important, clinching factor (Sections 11.6–11.7) to decide the question is that the IAs, as described in the RV, represent something definitely *new* in the subcontinent. Both their spiritual and much of their material culture are new; these *and* their language link them to the areas west and northwest of the subcontinent, and to some extent beyond, to the Ural area and to Southern Russia/Ukraine. The obvious conclusion should be that these new elements *somehow* came from the outside.

Indeed, the western relatives of the IAs the *Paršumaš* (Persians), and the people who brought IA elements to the Mit. (*c.*1460–1330 BCE) and the Kassites[12] who, as a first wave, preceded them in Mesopotamia, all are *intrusive* (cf. Drews 1989). The same may be assumed for the Greater Panjab, where a new element brought in *new* items such as the domesticated horse and the horse-drawn chariot (Section 11.20), and IE/IA style poetry, religion, and ritual. A massive, if gradual introduction of some, if not all IA traits seems the only viable conclusion (see later, on Ehret's model).

Denial of immigration into the area of an already existing culture has recently been asserted by some archaeologists as well; they posit a purely local, indigenous development of cultures, for example, by the British archaeologist Lord Renfrew (1987)[13] and by some Americans such as Shaffer (1984), Shaffer and Lichtenstein (1999) who think that new languages were introduced by way of trade and by taking over of new models of society.

If there was immigration, who then were the autochthonous inhabitants of the subcontinent? They can in fact *still* be traced in the substrates of the RV and of modern languages: an unknown Indo-Gangetic language has supplied about 40 percent of the agricultural terminology in Hindi (a typical feature already for the RV, Kuiper 1955, 1991).[14] Again, such a scenario is met with in many other areas of the world.[15] (See later in Section 11.5.)

11.4 Acculturation

In spite of vague reminiscences of older homelands,[16] even the earliest RV hymns clearly reflect South Asian realities, in other words, they were already composed in the Greater Panjab. They also include many non-Sanskritic words and names, those of non-Aryan "foreigners" (*Kīkaṭa*, *Pramaganda*, etc.) and demons (*Śambara*, *Cumuri*, etc.) But also those of noblemen and chiefs (*Balbūtha, Bṛbu*) and occasionally of poets (*Kavaṣa*, *Kaṇva*, *Agastya*, *Kaśyapa*). All these non-IA words do not have a Ved. or IE background (see later in Section 11.5, n. 28), something that can be determined by purely linguistic means. Such words are *impossible* either in Ved. or in Indo-Iranian (IIr) or IE in general (Mayrhofer 1986: 95, Szemerényi 1970: 90 sqq.); this is a point almost universally neglected by autochthonists (Section 11.8 sqq.).

In the RV, *arya/ārya* does *not* mean a particular "people" or even a particular "racial" group but all those who had joined the tribes speaking Vedic Sanskrit and adhering to their cultural norms (such as ritual, poetry, etc.) – as had been underlined for decades.[17] The *Others*, such as the *Kīkaṭa* (RV 3.53), who inhabit the Greater Punjab *together* with the *Ārya*, are even declared "not to be fit to deal with cows." They form the amorphous group of the *Dasyu* "the foreigner, the enemy." While the *ārya* frequently fight among themselves, their main enemies are the *dasyu* who are portrayed in typical half-mythical fashion as "foreign devils" and demons.

There must have been a long period of acculturation between the local population and the "original" immigrants speaking IA. Indeed, the bulk of the RV represents only some five generations of chieftains (and some five generations of poets).[18] The famous chieftain of the *Bharata*, *Sudās*, is one of the latest mentioned. On the other hand, a number of tribal federations (*Anu-Druhyu*, *Yadu-Turvaśa*, etc.) preceded that of the *Pūru* and the *Bharata* who were dominant in the middle and late RV period (Witzel 1995, 1997). It is during the long period of *initial* acculturation, for the most part not present in our RV, that some of the linguistic (and cultural) features (Kuiper 1955, 1991) of the early (pre-)Ṛgvedic period must have evolved. They include new grammatical formations such as the absolutives in *-tvā*, *-tvī*[19] and *-ya* for verbs with preverbs (Tikkanen 1987). Absolutive formation corresponds, among others, to Drav. verbal structure, but absolutives are *not* found in Iranian. Significantly, *Vasiṣṭha* the self-proclaimed (Iranian?) immigrant author of much of book 7, avoids them.[20] Only constant contact and bilingualism between speakers of Old Indo-Aryan (OIA) and of the local language(s) of the Greater Panjab could produce such innovations and calques.[21]

Local influence is indeed what the non-IE part of RV vocabulary suggests, by Kuiper's count some 380 words or about 3.8 percent of the vocabulary of the RV (Kuiper 1991, 1995: 261). Such local substrate words can easily be identified because of their isolation within the IE-derived IA vocabulary, that is, they always do not have Iranian, Slavic, etc. counterparts. Frequently, their sounds and syllable structure are non-IE as well. This is a point so far completely neglected or simply derided[22] by the advocates of the autochthonous theory.[23]

11.5 Linguistic substrates

Since the very concept of a linguistic substrate (Anttila 1989: 154 sqq.) is often misunderstood (discussion by Bryant 1999), a brief characterization is in order (Witzel, forthc. a,b). Most words in early Ved. that do not conform to IE/IIr word structure (including sounds, root structure and word formation) and have no clear IE/IIr etymology must belong to a preceding language, a non-IA *substrate*; some of them, however, are loans from a neighboring non-IA language (*adstrate*, the favored position by those autochthonists who recognize that they actually have a problem, see e.g. Lal 1997). It is, however, important to underline that it is the phonetic and grammatical *structure* that does not fit the IE/IIr/IA one of Vedic

Sanskrit. Not just etymology (which may remain unsolvable in some cases[24] and is, in others, not even necessary),[25] but *all* the structural features are of equal importance here.[26]

A word that superficially looks IE/IA, such as *Kosala*, is simply disqualified linguistically by its *-s-*,[27] or, words such as *kīnāśa*, *kīkaṭa*, *pramaganda*, *balbūtha*, *bṛsaya* can by no means be explained in terms of IE: (1) there are no IE/IA roots such as *kīn*, *kīk*,[28] *mag*, *balb*, *bṛs* as only roots of the format {(s)(C) (R) e (R) (C/s)} are allowed;[29] (2) the sound *b* is very rare in IE; (3) suffixes such as *-ā-ś*, *-ṭ*, *an-d/-a-nd-*, *-būth-/bū-th-* are not found in IE/IA; and (4) only *ṣ* (but not *s*) is allowed in Ved. after *i*, *u*, *r*, *k*. In addition, these words do not have any cogent IE/IA etymologies.

The use of such formal, structural categories immediately allows to detect many words as being non-IE, and as originally non-IA. Just as for IE and IA, similar structural rules exist Drav. and for Munda.[30] A comparison of these data frequently allows to *narrow down* the origin of a word,[31] though this has hardly been done in practice (Witzel, forthc. a,b).[32] Instead, etymological discussions deal, by and large, with vague similarities of ancient Ved., (old) Drav. and *modern* Munda words. To quote (*pseudo-*)Voltaire: etymologies, "where consonants count little and vowels nothing."

There are, thus, clear and decisive rules in place that allow to narrow down, and in many instances even to determine the origin of Ved. words. Throwing up one's hands in postmodern despair (Bryant 1999), and certainly, a haughty, nontechnical dismissal (Talageri 2000) are misguided.

The range of the non-Indo-Aryan words of the RV is perhaps even more interesting than their number. They include names for local plants and animals,[33] and a large number of agricultural terms, which are not expected in the vocabulary of the largely pastoralist IAs who left the tedious job of the ploughman (*kināśa*) and farming in general (*tilvila*, *phala*, *pippala*, *khala*, *lāṅgala*, etc.) to the local people. Instead, they preserved only a few general IE terms, such a *yava* "barley, grain," *kṛṣ* "to scratch, plough."[34] Some local river names, always a very resistant part of the vocabulary, are preserved as well.[35]

In sum, an early wave of acculturation of the immigrant speakers of Old IA (Ved.) and the local population has seriously influenced not just popular IA speech but even the highly traditional poetic language and many other aspects of their traditional IIr culture, religion, and ritual. This "Indianization" of the IAs began even *before* our extant RV texts (Kuiper 1967, 1991). A certain amount of codification of this process can be detected with the formulation, in the Puruṣa hymn (RV 10.90), of the system of the *four* classes (*varṇa*) instead of the more common IE three, which system has been called, by P. Mus, "the first constitution of India."

On the Iranian side, however, one has so far observed very little of linguistic and other acculturation (Skjærvø 1995). However, it would be surprising and is erroneous to state, as has generally been done, that O. Pers., Avest., etc. seem to have been affected very little by the preceding (substrate) languages of the great

Bronze Age cultures, such as those the BMAC, Shahri Sokhta, Mundigak, Tepe Yahya, and Elam.[36] There are, indeed, quite a number of words that are foreign even in Indo-Iranian[37] and there is a host of unstudied Iranian words taken from the various local substrates (Witzel 1999a,b, forthc. a,b). This feature is of extreme importance in evaluating the linguistic materials that speak for the immigration of speakers of OIA into the subcontinent.

11.6 Cultural continuity?

While the intrusive traits of IA language, poetics, large parts of IA religion, ritual, and some aspects of IA material culture are transparent, the obvious continuity of local cultures in South Asia, as prominently seen in archaeology, is another matter. Yet, how much of the culture of semi-sedentary tribes on the move (Scythians, Huns, Turks, Mongols) would indeed be visible in the archaeological record?[38] Further, the constantly shifting river courses in the Panjab may have obscured many of the shallow remnants of the IA settlements: temporary, rather rickety resting places (*armaka*, Rau 1983). Third, the IAs are known, from their own texts, to employ the services of the local populations.[39] Continuity of local styles thus is to be expected a priori. However, when traditional style pottery with traditional paintings, such as in the early post-Indus Cemetery H culture, appears *together* with a new burial style, that is cremation or exposition and subsequent deposition of the bones in urns, *and* with a new motif painted on them, that is, a small human, a "soul," drawn inside a traditionally painted peacock, then all of this draws our attention. The bird-soul motif seems to reflect Ved. beliefs about the souls of the ancestors moving about in the form of birds (Vats 1940; Witzel 1984; Falk 1986). While this assemblage seems to indicate early acculturation, more data are necessary to confirm that the still little known Cemetery H culture in Harappa and Cholistan is one reflecting IA presence.

Presence of IA speakers would rather be indicated by the introduction of their specialty, the horse-drawn chariots with spoked wheels, horse furnishings, etc. When such items are found, there is a good chance that this represents IAs, but alternative scenarios cannot be excluded; tribes that were influenced and/or pushed forward in front of them, such as the Mit. and Kassites in Mesopotamia and the Hyksos in Egypt (Drews 1989); or, simply, neighboring local tribes that had adopted some facets of IA material culture early on.

Ideally, an "Aryan" archaeological site would include the remnants of horses and chariots, horse furnishings, a Ved. ritual site with (three) fire places nearby (preferably west of a river), a rather primitive settlement pattern with bamboo huts, implements made of stone and copper (bronze), some gold and silver ornaments, but with *local* pottery, evidence of food that includes barley, milk products, meat of cattle, sheep and goat, and some wild animals. However, this particular archaeological set (or part of it) has not yet been discovered, unless we think of the Swat Valley finds, *c.*1400 BCE (Gandhara Grave Culture, 1700–). Swat is known in the RV (8.19.37) as IA territory, *Suvāstu* "good ground."[40]

In sum, we have to look out for a '*Leitfosssil*', a clear indicator of IA culture such as the chariot and Ved. ritual sites. The obvious continuity of pottery styles, taken alone, tells little.[41] *All aspects* of material and spiritual culture, of linguistics as well as genetics, have to be taken into account.

11.7 Palaeontology and genetics

Autochthonists, however, also maintain that there is no evidence of *demographic* discontinuity in archaeological remains during the period from 4500 to 800 BCE,[42] and that an influx of foreign populations is not visible in the archaeological record.[43]

The revisionists and autochthonists overlook, however, that such refutations of an immigration by "racially" determined IAs still depend on the old, nineteenth-century idea of a massive *invasion* of outsiders who would have left a definite mark on the genetic set-up of the local Panjab population. Presently we do not know how large this particular influx of linguistically attested outsiders was. It can have been relatively small, if we apply Ehret's model (1988, derived from Africa, cf. Diakonoff 1985) which stresses the *osmosis* (or a "billiard ball," or Mallory's *Kulturkugel*) effect of cultural transmission.

Ehret (1988) underlines the relative ease with which ethnicity *and* language shift in small societies, due to the cultural/economic/military *choices* made by the local population in question. The intruding/influencing group bringing new traits may initially be small and the features it contributes can be fewer in number than those of the preexisting local culture. The newly formed, combined ethnic group may then initiate a recurrent, *expansionist* process of ethnic and language shift. The material record of such shifts is visible only insofar as new prestige equipment or animals (the "status kit," with new, intrusive vocabulary!) are concerned. This is especially so if pottery – normally culture-specific – continues to be made by local specialists of a class-based society.[44]

Similar things could be said about Archaic Greece, or post-Jōmon Japan, but that would lead too far here. As will be seen later, the descriptions given just now fit the Indus/Ved. evidence perfectly.

11.8 Intruders or autochthons?

The preceding discussion (Sections 11.1–11.7) presupposes that groups speaking OIA (Ved.) were an intrusive element in the North-West of the subcontinent. This is strenuously denied by advocates of an autochthonous origin of the IAs (always called "Aryans"). Their Indocentric counter-theories range from: (1) a mild version, insisting on the origin of the Ṛgvedic IAs in the Panjab, the "autochthonous" or indigenous school;[45] (2) a more stringent but increasingly popular "Out of India" school[46] which views the Iranians and even *all* IEs emigrating from the Panjab, to the; (3) most intense version, which has all languages of the world derived from Sanskrit: the "Devabhāṣā school," which is mostly – but not solely – restricted to traditional Pandits.[47]

In these views,[48] though often for quite different reasons, any immigration or trickling in – nearly always called "invasion" – of the (Indo-)Aryans into the subcontinent is suspect or simply denied. The *Ārya* of the RV are supposed to be just another tribe or group of tribes that have *always* been resident in India,[49] next to Dravidians, Mundas, etc. The theory of an immigration of IA speaking *Ārya* ("Aryan invasion") is simply seen as a means of British policy to justify their own intrusion into India and their subsequent colonial rule: in both cases, a "white race" was seen as subduing the local darker colored population.

However, present (European, American, Japanese, etc.) Indologists do not maintain anything like this now, even less so after the recent genetic discoveries that link all present humans to a fairly recent common origin, and all non-Africans to an even more recent emigration by some 10,000 people "Out of Africa," some 50,000 years ago: the problem of an "Aryan invasion" into India is as relevant or irrelevant to Indologists as Bantu "invasion" of central, east, and southern Africa, or the polar Na-Dene deep into North America.

While the "invasion model" was still prominent in the work of archaeologists such as Wheeler (1966: "Indra stands accused"), it has been supplanted by much more sophisticated models[50] over the past few decades (see Kuiper 1955 sqq.; Thapar 1968; Witzel 1995). This development has *not* occured because Indologists were *reacting*, as is now frequently alleged, to *current Indian criticism* of the older theory. Rather, philologists first, and archaeologists somewhat later, noticed certain inconsistencies in the older theory and tried to find new explanations, a new version of the immigration theories.

Linguists and philologists such as Kuiper 1955, 1991; Emeneau 1956; Southworth 1979; archaeologists such as Allchin (and Allchin) 1982, 1995; and historians such as Thapar 1968, all have maintained that the IAs and the older local inhabitants ("Dravidians," "Mundas," etc.) have mutually interacted from early on, that many of them were frequently bilingual, and that even the RV already bears witness to that. They also think, whether explicitly following Ehret's model (1988; cf. Diakonoff 1985) or not, of smaller infiltrating groups (Witzel 1989: 249, 1995; Allchin 1995), not of mass migrations or military "invasions." However, they still maintain, and for good reasons, that *some* IA speaking groups *actually entered* from the outside, via some of the (north)western corridors of the subcontinent.

Autochthonists, however, maintain in this *one* case that there has not been *any* influx at all, conveniently forgetting that most humans have emigrated out of Africa as recently as some 50,000 years ago. Instead, some simply *reverse* the "colonial" invasion theory and discover an *emigration* from India (the "Out of India Theory," OIT): a truly Indocentric view of the world, echoed by quite similar ones now found in other parts of Asia. They like to utilize some of the arguments of current archaeology, for example, those of Shaffer (1984) and those of Shaffer and Lichtenstein (1995, 1999), who stress indigenous cultural continuity from *c.*7000 BCE well into the semi-historic times of the first millennium, which he declares to be evident according to the *present* state of archaeology.[51] Consequently, he protests the "linguistic tyranny" of earlier models. This is a much too narrow, purely archaeological view that neglects many other aspects, such as all of spiritual and some of material culture, but it is grist on the mills of the autochthonists.

Since language is of crucial importance for this argument, it needs to be addressed here in great detail. However, the revisionists and autochthonists have almost completely overlooked this type of evidence, or they have outrightly denied it. Recently some have begun to pay attention (see Bryant 1999, 2001; cf. also Elst 1999), however, still in an unprofessional manner (Talageri 1993, 2000).[52] Unfortunately, this was in large measure even true for the apparently lone IE scholar in India, S. S. Misra[53] (1992).[54]

However, opponents of the theory of an IA immigration or trickling in, whether revisionists, autochthonists, or OIT adherents must *also* explain the linguistic, textual, archaeological, geographical, astronomical, and other scientific data (Section 11.13 sqq. see Witzel 2001b) to become credible.

11.9. On scientific procedure

Like all scientific theories the theory of an immigration into South Asia by speakers of IA has to be constantly and thoroughly (re-)investigated. Scholarship is an *ongoing* dialectical process. However, all too frequently old and long given up positions are brought up by revisionists and juxtaposed to recent ones in order to show "contradictions" in what is called "the western approach." This is improper procedure. Natural scientists do not seriously discuss pre-Copernican or pre-Darwinian systems any longer.[55]

New evidence has to fit in with the *general framework* established by the many, completely unrelated observations in the various branches of scholarship; otherwise a particular theory is revised or discarded. But, deducing a complete "paradigm shift" based on *isolated* facts is quite common in the contemporary effort to rewrite Indian (pre-)history, where even hard scientific facts are *explained away* and with the help of new, auxiliary, *ad hoc assumptions*. Rather, Occam's razor applies.

In the ensuing discussion, therefore, we frequently have to reinvent the wheel and have to restate, sometimes even to prove well-known and well-tested principles and facts: this includes those of comparative linguistics (summaries by Hock 1986; Anttila 1989; Szemerényi 1970, 1996; Beekes 1995), comparative epic studies (Parry 1930–32, 1971; Lord 1991), of South Asian archaeology (Allchin 1995; Kenoyer 1998; Possehl and Gullapali 1999), Indus epigraphy (Possehl 1996a), of zoology and botany (Meadow and Patel 1997, Meadow 1998), or the evidence contained in the texts, as established by philology over the past two centuries (Witzel 1997).

In spite of the autochthonists' stress on the "hard sciences," all too frequently "scientific facts" are quoted which, on closer observation, are not hard facts at all. Each single item brought up for discussion must therefore be scrutinized well. For example, an unsuspecting reader may take for granted that LANDSAT photos show the drying up of the Sarasvatī River in 1900 BCE (Kak 1994a; cf. Gupta 1996). But

LANDSAT or aerial photos cannot by themselves indicate historical dates (cf. § 25 Witzel 2001b). Or, some selected linguistic data, such as *supposed* change from an older *aśva-* 'horse' (as in Skt) to Latin *equu-s* (Misra 1992), are used to indicate an Iranian and IE emigration from India. This contradicts standard (IE *and* non-IE) linguistic knowledge (Hock 1999). Such single, often erroneous facts, are simply made part of an *inclusivistic*, Indocentric belief system that *encapsulates*, in facile fashion, older mythical and religious ideas (Witzel 1986, 1992, 1998).

In short, facts from the various sciences must match, before a certain new theory can be accepted. If the linguistic, textual, archaeological, anthropological, geological, and other facts contradict each other, the new theory is in serious difficulty. *All* exceptions have to be explained, and well within plausible range; if they cannot, the theory does not hold. It *never* is proper working procedure that such inconsistencies are explained away by *ad hoc* assumptions and new theories, in other words, by special pleading. Occam's razor applies.

11.10 On linguistic procedure

Besides genetics and archaeology it is language, and the spiritual culture embodied in language and texts, that are crucial for any theory of an influx of speakers of OIA into the subcontinent.

Linguistic evidence is available since the earliest forms of Sanskrit (Ṛgvedic OIA) and Zarathustra's Gāϑās in Iran. The materials transmitted by language obviously point to the culture of its speakers and also to their original and subsequent physical surroundings. In addition, language has its own archaeology: the various subsequent historical "layers" of a particular language can be uncovered when painstakingly using well-developed linguistic procedures (see later).

However, linguistic data and even more so, linguistics, have generally been neglected by the autochthonists.[56] When actually used, the linguistic ideas and "arguments" of the autochthonists are far off the internationally accepted norms and procedures. Therefore, a discussion of their proposals and beliefs does not only take up much space but *must* be convoluted and torturous; in addition, it is often very technical.

Like other sciences, language study is not something that can be carried out by amateurs, even though an "everyone can do" attitude is widespread as far as one's mother tongue and language in general are concerned, especially so in etymology and the (often assumed) origin and the (frequently lacking) history of individual words. Here, total amateurism is the rule. "Oakish" etymologies, such as *England* from *aṅguli* 'finger', or *abād* from *bath* (Gupta 1990b), go back to the tradition of Plato's Kratylos or the equally unscientific explanations of *Yāska's Nirukta*, and beyond.[57] Assyria is derived from *asura*, Syria from *sura*, Phoenicians from *Paṇi*, Hittites (Khet) from *Kaṭha*, Mit. from *Maitrāyaṇīya*, etc. (Surya Kanta 1943; Bhagavad Datta repr. 1974; Gupta 1990a,b, etc.).

In comparative linguistics, however, it is not similarity that counts but the *regularity* of sound correspondences (see later), though they outwardly may appear non-intuitive. To quote one of the most hackneyed, non-intuitive examples: the correct equation, sound by sound, of Skt *dvā(u)*, Latin *duo* = Armenian *erku* < *tku* < *tgī* < *twī* < IE * *dwī* (The sign '<' means "derived from"; * indicates not attested, reconstructed forms).

Worse than comparing look-alikes is the trend, in the South Asian context, of cross-family comparison (Drav. and IA, IA, and Munda, etc.) that is especially widespread and has completely wrong results, as such comparisons are, again, simply based on overt similarities between words. Frequently, such comparisons are justified by positing a unified prehistoric South Asian linguistic area (*Sprachbund*, see Section 11.14).

However, in order to provide some concrete background to all such claims the theory and working methods of comparative linguistics have to be stated in brief form. Language is a communicative device similar to other auditory or visual signs, sign language, or even gestures. The devices used in language are based on sounds and meanings attached to (groups of) sounds. Their combinations are structured grammatically as words and sentences. The sounds of language are easily analyzable physical features as they are produced by the interactions of the vocal tract, tongue, mouth, and nose. The production of sounds, their frequency (in Hz) etc., all can be measured by instruments and can be described in a strict fashion. The same applies to their combinations as words (root, affixes, accent, etc.) and sentences (syntax).

Second, the sounds (or meanings) of a language change over time, sometimes very quickly.[58] Such sound changes are not random, but involve each word of a particular language and, as has been known for the past 130 years, they follow a fixed pattern (*Lautgesetze*) that is only disturbed by some analogies or dialect forms.

Due to such historical developments in sounds, grammar, and meaning, each language has many levels of development, just as the geological or archeological levels in the ground. The various historical levels are attested in writing (modern English; Shakespeare's, King James Bible; Chaucer's; Old Saxon Bible) or in outlying dialects (Scottish Engl. *bright* [brext]). Certain languages, such as English, become largely unintelligible within a span of five hundred to a thousand years.

The changes of the sounds and the grammar of a language and its dialects can be described and analyzed. The result is a series of changes that make up, just as in biology or genetics, a "family tree" of changes and grammatical innovations in dialects and related languages, the cladistic tree. Furthermore, since sound changes in each language concerned occur *across the board*, they are regular and their description results in the famous regularity of sound correspondences (*Lautgesetze*).

Comparison of various (more or less conservative) dialects and of obviously similar and related languages, in the case of English: Dutch, German, Scandinavian, and Gothic, then shows that these regular sound changes in all these languages lead back to a common, reconstructable Germanic ancestor that is different from that of other European (etc.) languages, the ancestors of Celtic,

Italic, Greek, Slavic, or IIr, which in turn lead back to a common, well-reconstructed ancestor language, (Proto-)IE (PIE). Each one of these groups has *innovated* in phonetics and grammar with respect to the others and thus is clearly defined, like the various species in biology by their very innovations which lead, for example, from the various Galapagos finches back to a common source, the finch, and from this to the prehistoric early birds, the reptiles etc.

Just as in biology (taxonomy, the human pedigree, genetics, etc.) or in manuscript study (setting up of a stemma), the occurrence of common innovations *always* indicates that the innovative group has split off from the core group, and obviously is to be dated *later* than the core.

Languages, especially as far as their "skeleton" of sounds and grammatical forms are concerned, can be compared and arranged just as living beings are by paleontology and now, genetics. The resulting tree-like (or cladistic) arrangement will be used in the following discussion.

The matter is much more complex, though, when it comes to the changes in the meaning of words and the meaning of grammatical forms. Here, careful study of the oldest available texts will aid the reconstruction of the meanings of proto-forms.

Once the set of rules has been established, the theory requires that we can make predictions about the form of words in each related language, and at all its historical stages, whether attested in writing (or in a remote dialect) or not. Predictions are of course only possible as the theory is based on a strict set of rules and subrules that are derived from the "hard science" part of language, that is sounds and their groupings as words. Such predictions were possible especially after the more developed form of IE linguistics emerged, *c.*1870 CE, with the establishment of regular sound correspondences (*Lautgesetze*) by the Leipzig *Junggrammatiker* school.

Such predictions forecast the shapes and forms of words in the various related languages and always "get it right" when not disturbed by analogy. In other words, give me a Sanskrit or IE word, and I will predict its Old (or Modern) English form, whether already found in an old manuscript or a rare dialect or not. However, the predictions include also items that had not been observed in any IE language, for example, the proposal by the young F. de Saussure more than a century ago (1879), of a set of unknown sounds, later called laryngeals (h_1, h_2, h_3). They have disappeared, with a few indirect traces, in all then known IE languages. When Hittite finally was deciphered and read in 1916, h_2 was still found written (in words such as *peḫur* = Grk, *pūr* = Engl. *fire*).[59] In other words, just as the existence of the planet Pluto was predicted by astronomy, so were the laryngeals, in both cases decades before the actual discovery.

Finally, just like living beings in nature, languages can be influenced by the surroundings, that is, by other languages, but they cannot "breed" with other species, that is, there is no such thing as a truly "mixed" language. Even if two languages strongly interact, the result still has most of the grammatical features of one of the "ancestors." English still is Germanic though it has a large (Norman) French vocabulary and *some* grammatical forms taken over and expressed, in calque, by Anglo-Saxon means: not **beautifuller*, but "more beautiful" (< *plus beau*). To confuse this kind of interaction with genetic relationship is a common mistake in India, these days, where the unrelated Drav., Munda and IA language families are assumed to be the direct descendants of some sort of hypothetical ancient "Prākṛta" or Bronze Age pan-Indian language (see later in Section 11.14).

After this brief but necessary theoretical excursion we can investigate the details of the autochthonous theories, albeit, due to the lack of linguistic sophistication of autochthonists, in necessarily torturous detail.

11.11 Vedic, Iranian, and Indo-European

Even the most stalwart autochthonists have not denied that Vedic Sanskrit is closely related to Old Iranian (and to the other IE languages).[60] However, this relationship is explained by an *emigration* westwards of the Iranians and the other IEs *from* the Panjab (see later). Vedic Sanskrit is indeed so closely related to Old Iranian that both often look more like two dialects than two separate languages (e.g. *tam mitram yajāmahe : təm miϑrəm yazamaⁱde* 'we worship *Mitra*'). However, that does not necessitate at all that the Old Iranian dialects were introduced to into Iran from the east, from India, just as little as Low German dialects from England.[61]

Rather, the comparison of the many common features found in Ved. IA and Old Iranian have led to the reconstruction of a common parent, IIr, spoken (at least) *c.*2000 BCE, by a group of people that shared a common spiritual and material culture (see Sections 11.3–11.4). Beyond that, the comparison of IIr and other IE languages has allowed similar reconstructions for all IE languages from Iceland and Ireland to Xinjiang (Tocharian). This theory was first developed in the early nineteenth century and has been tested extensively (and confirmed by new discoveries).

As a branch of Eastern IE, IIr shares many peculiarities with other eastern IE languages such as Balto-Slavic: in sounds (**ḱ > š/ś* : Lithuanian *ašvò* (fem.), IIr **ac'ua* > E.Ir. *aspa*, Ved. *aśva*, but note western IE: Lat. *equus* "horse," O. Irish *ech*, and Tocharian *yuk*, *yakwe*); also in vocabulary (Skt *dina* 'day', O. Slav. *dinⁱ*: Lat. *dies*, cf. Schrader 1890: 312), and perhaps even in mythology: Skt *Parjanya*, Lith. *Perkūnas*, O. Slav. *Perunᵘ* (Schrader 1890: 414). The IIr parent language can be reconstructed by comparative linguistics, and large parts of the IIr spiritual and material culture as well, by *carefully* using the method of linguistic paleontology.[62]

Yet, in spite of the various "tests" comparative linguistics, whether IE or Bantu, has undergone for some 200 years, some revisionists and autochthonists even call into question the theories and methods of comparative linguistics as such. Some of them clearly lack an understanding of the principles at work.[63] In addition, they make use of the *expected* scholarly differences of opinion to show that the whole "theory of (IE) linguistics" does not work or is an "unproved theory" (Rajaram 1995: 144, 217) or a "petty conjectural pseudo-science" (2000, *passim*). (If so, linguistics would hardly be taught at universities all over the world; this is not astrology!) Rajaram *et al.* neglect (a) that any science progresses and that certain opinions of the nineteenth century cannot be juxtaposed to those of the twentieth century, and (b) that in any contemporary field of science[64] there is a certain range of generally agreed facts but also a certain range of difference of opinion, such as between traditionalists, radical skeptics,[65] and those proposing new solutions to old or recently noticed problems. In short, there always are conflicting interpretations of the materials at hand that are discussed in dialectical fashion. Some interpretations are merely possible, others probable, and still others have actually been proved and have subsequently been shown to be correct.

Still, the autochthonous school maintains that the very assumptions at the basis of the genealogical, family (cladistic) tree model of the IE language family is wrong and deride it (cf. Elst 1999: 119; see discussion by Bryant 1999), or contest it *just* for the Indian linguistic area (see later). Actually, various models have been proposed and tested for the development from Proto-IE to the individual languages, to begin with, the "family tree" model (A. Schleicher's *Stammbaumtheorie*, 1861–62), or a theory of dialectal waves of innovation emanating from a certain center (Joh. Schmidt's *Wellentheorie*, 1872). Further, sociolinguistic theories include the development of PIE as a sort of camp language (another *Urdu*, so to speak), a new Pidgin or Creole, based on diverse original languages that eventually spread beyond its own rather limited boundaries, for example, with the introduction of horse-based pastoralism (Kuz'mina 1994; Anthony 1995, 2000, etc.).

Some autochthonists (Talageri 1993, 2000; Kak 1994a; Elst 1999: 159) use rather simplistic linguistic models, such as the suggestion that population increase, trade, the emergence of agriculture,[66] and large-scale political integration led to the extinction of certain languages and to a transfer of other languages across ethnic groups. However none of them in isolation, nor a combination of all of them, lead to the surprising spread of IE languages inside and outside the subcontinent.[67]

Autochthonists further neglect that language replacement, visible during the Ved. period, depends on a range of various sociolinguistic factors and not on single (monolateral!) factors such as the presence of nomads, increasing population density, etc. Rather, the situation differs from case to case, and the important factors for any particular replacement must be demonstrated, in the case of early India, the change from the language(s) of the urbanized Indus civilization to that of the pastoralist IAs. It certainly cannot be done, in Indocentric fashion, by positioning the homeland of the ("non-tropical") IE language inside India and make its speakers emigrate, across the Indus area, toward Iran and Europe (see later in Sections 11.22–11.23).

Instead of the, by now, "traditional" comparative linguistics, the revisionist and autochthonists propose (a) the Out of India theory, often based on (b) a prehistoric Indian Sprachbund (of 3000–5000 BCE). Both will be discussed in the following sections.

11.12 "Out of India" theories

The direction of the spread of languages and linguistic innovations cannot *easily* be determined, unless we have written materials (preferably inscriptions). Therefore, *theoretically*, a scenario of an IE emigration from the Panjab is possible. But some linguistic observations such as the distribution of languages, dialect features, substrate languages, linguistic paleontology, words for cultural and natural features in the languages concerned, etc. all argue against the Out of India scenarios.

Out of India theorists such as Elst (1999: 122, 124 etc.), Talageri (1993, 2000), Misra (1992), Aiyar (1975), etc. envision an IE homeland in South Asia, to be more precise, in the Gangetic basin (Talageri 1993, 2000; Elst 1999: 118 sqq.). Talageri simply assumes, without any linguistic, archaeological, or paleontological sources and proof,[68] that in "prehistoric times the distribution of the languages in India may have been roughly the same as it is today"[69] (1993: 407) and that "a major part of the IEs of southeastern [*sic!*] Uttar Pradesh migrated to the west and settled down in the northwestern areas – Punjab, Kashmir, and the further north-west,"[70] subsequently to venture further west.[71] This view is based on data about peoples "clearly mentioned and described in the Puranas."[72] Writing prehistory like this *naively* relies on texts that were composed millennia after the facts, and those are the products of a lively Bardic tradition (Parry 1971; Rocher 1986; Lord 1991; Brockington 1998), influenced by Brahmanical redactors (Horsch 1966; Söhnen 1986). In spite of what Pargiter (1913) and even Smith (1973) have tried to establish, we cannot write the history of archaic and ancient India based on the legendary Epic and *Purāṇic* accounts that were composed during the middle ages (Witzel 1990, 1995, 2001a,b).

Yet, Talageri actually knows, *somehow*, which IE group moved first and which later, and by which route (2000: 263).[73] This truly Indocentric, pseudo-*Purāṇic* fantasy is confidently self-characterized as: "This whole description is based on the most logical and in many respects the *only possible*, interpretation of the facts... Any further research, and any new material discovered on the subject, can only confirm this description... there is no possible way in which the location of the Original Homeland in the interior of northern India, so faithfully recorded in the Puranas and confirmed in the Rigveda, can ever be disproved" (1993: 408).[74] This is discussed later in the chapter.

In order to achieve his southeastern UP homeland, Talageri has not only to *rely* on the *Purāṇas* and the Epics, he also has to *read them into* his RV evidence (Witzel 2001a), though *pretending* to use only the RV itself to interpret the RV (Talageri 2000)[75] as this strengthens his case for a Gangetic homeland.[76] Nothing in the RV points to the knowledge of the lower Gangetic *Doāb*.[77] Nevertheless, the single appearances of *Jahnāvī* in the RV at 1.116.19 and 3.56.6 are made out to refer to the Ganges, which is clearly based on post-Vedic identifications.[78] Both passages clearly refer to a *Jahnāvī* which translators and commentators (including *Sāyaṇa*) have taken as a tribal designation[79] or an ancient clan (deity) which could have "settled" anywhere.[80]

Talageri's view is not conclusive even for the location of the *Yadu-Turvaśa*, *Anu-Druhyu* and *Pūru* tribes of the RV, which is far from clear for most of the Ṛgvedic period.[81] His opinion on the "western" "emigrant" Ṛgvedic tribes (*Anu*, *Druhyu*) is derived from that of the Epic and *Purāṇic* accounts of the Panjab and of the western neighbors of India, found first in *late* Ved. texts (ŚB and BŚS 18.13: 357.6 sqq., 18.44: 397.8 sqq.). It is "the view from the center," *Kurukṣetra*, a view that was not yet present in Ṛgvedic times as the thirty-odd competing tribes did not have a "center" then.[82] In post-RV texts, however, *all* tribes and peoples outside the Center, the *Kuru*(*-Pañcāla*) realm, are regarded as "outsiders" (*bāhīka* ŚB 1.7.3.8, *udantya, mleccha, asurya*), and they are characterized by their "incorrect" speech and obnoxious behavior (ŚB 9.3.1.24, the Panjabis) and lack of proper *śrauta* ritual (ŚB 13.5.4.19, the *Kāśi*!). The Panjabis (*Bāhīka*) as well as the Banarsis (*Kāśi*) and the southern Biharis (*Aṅga*) are denigrated by middle Ved. texts.[83] This attitude[84] continued with respect to the west which was under constant and continuing threat of immigration, incursion, and occasional invasion from the Afghan highlands (cf. Rau 1957: 14). The Epic and *Purāṇic* accounts simply build on such late Ved. precedents: the Panjabis are regarded as "fallen Ārya," or in the words of BŚS, the *Gandhāri* have emigrated (from the center).[85] Again, nothing of this is found in the RV yet, instead we find the (post-Ṛg)Vedic attitude against "outsiders," the Other.

To combine some notices in the RV on the *Anu-Druhyu* with the much later, actually mistranslated *Purāṇic* story[86] about an emigration from India as statement of *fact* is as far-fetched. This Indocentric view is, in fact, just as mythic as the Roman insistence of their descent from the heroes of Troy (Vergil's Aeneid), or as the many tales about the lost tribes of Israel.[87] To use such legends, concocted long after the fact, as indications of actual historical events is completely anachronistic, and in fact unscientific.

11.13 "Innovative" linguistics and autochthonism

While Talageri's case is one of a nationalistic[88] non-linguist grappling with the very rudiments of linguistics, one of the few specialists of historical and comparative linguistics in India, Misra (1992), reportedly was unaffected by such influences. However, in his recent book he has taken[89] a step back beyond what is already well known and demonstrable. His results conform, intended or not, with the autochthonist and Indocentric view. He even overlooks the *hard facts*, that is, in his denial of PIE laryngeals as precursors of the actually *written* Hittite laryngeal sounds (Misra 1974, 1992). In general, he simply *rewrites*, on an *ad hoc* basis, much of IE (and general) linguistics. The technical details cannot be discussed here at length (for which see Hock 1999; Witzel 2001b). In sum, Misra's *ad hoc* rules do not make for a new system, they are a throwback to the early stages of IE comparative linguistics when strict rules of sound correspondences (*Lautgesetze*) had not yet been established by the Leipzig *Junggrammnatiker* School, at *c.*1870. It simply is uncontested among linguists of any persuasion and any country that the remarkable, *grammatically regular* features of PIE are part and parcel of the parent language, the original PIE.

This language was at first confined to a still unknown area in a temperate (not a tropical!) climate, while autochthonists place the homeland of IE inside South Asia, or in certain parts of India (Misra 1992), or even in the southeastern Gangetic basin (Talageri 1993, 2000), – that is, in Indocentric fashion and not unexpectedly, in their own home land, India.[90] Further, Misra's dating of IE and of the RV, based on this "new" reconstruction, rests on the similarity of *his* "early nineteenth century" style PIE (looking altogether like Sanskrit) with reconstructed Proto-Finno-Ugric (Uralic) forms, for which he accepts the *guess* of Uralic linguists, a date of 5000 BCE. That guess is not any better than the various guesses for PIE, at 3000 or 4500 BCE. In sum, Misra's whole "system" rests on guesswork and on demonstrably faulty reconstructions.

To go into some of the details,[91] Misra's small book of 110 pages (1992)[92] is a curious collection of linguistic data spanning the Eurasian continent, from Tamil to Uralic (Finno-Ugric), and from IE, Ved. and Mit. IA to European Gypsy (Romani). It has the curious conclusion, typical of much autochthonous writing:

> ...the most original and orthodox (*sic!*) Indo-European speech, Sanskrit, was spoken in India ... This was a nice place to live. People would not like to go to places like Europe... On the other hand, there is definite evidence of spread of Aryans (or Indo-Europeans) in different parts of Europe...[93] The Finno-Ugrian contact with Indo-Aryans speaks of the movement of Vedic Aryans from India to that area. Therefore it is likely that Pre-Vedic Aryans also might have gone out of India in several waves. ...The Iranian people were the last to leave...based on the linguistic analysis or relative affinity with Sanskrit.
>
> (Misra 1992: 100 sqq.)

Misra's main thesis, emigration *from* India, has already been refuted, on some linguistic grounds, by Hock (1999). However, as Misra is now quoted by autochthonists as *the* major linguistic authority who has provided "proof" for the OIT, some of his other conclusions must be discussed here.

As quoted earlier, Misra maintains (1992: 94) "the borrowed elements in the Uralic languages show borrowed Ṛgvedic forms in 5000 BC." Unfortunately, his discussion is based on two wrong premises: Harmatta's list of IA/Iranian loans in Uralic[94] and Misra's own "unorthodox" but faulty reinterpretation of IIr and IA data.

Misra's date of the RV "beyond 5000 BC" (1992) is based on the *guess* of Finno-Ugric scholars for Uralic (PFU). The exact form of IIr loan words in PFU are much more important. For these early loans, Misra relies on the faulty listings and materials of Harmatta (1992) which are outdated both as far as IIr as well as PFU are concerned. Joki 1973; Rédei 1987; Katz (1985, cf. now 2001b) have recently worked on this problem; all are not mentioned by Misra.

Harmatta has arbitrarily divided his materials into eleven stages, ranging from 4500–1000 BCE, of 300 years each, with various unlikely positions within that scheme.[95] Misra's faulty, nineteenth-century type reconstruction of IE (see Hock 1999) allows him to classify "most of the loan words . . . to be traced to Indo-Aryan. Of special importance is the borrowing traced to the earliest period (5000 BCE), *which is clearly Vedic Sanskrit*" (my italics, 1992: 24). This refers to words that are actually pre-IA,[96] rather PIIr as they retain *c'* > Ved. *ś*, or *š* instead of Ved. *ṣ*, or the PIE vowels *e, o* instead of the later, Common IIr and Ved. *a*. Misra's use of Burrow's (1973: 23–7) and Abayev's (1992: 27–32) materials suffers from the same methodological fault: forms that easily can be derived from IIr, such as Mordwinian *purtsos, purts* (reflecting IIr **parc'as* [part^{s}as]) are declared by Misra as having come from the much later OIA (Ved.), in spite of their obvious retaining the old pronunciation *c'* [t^{s}] and *not* the Ved. *-ś-*.[97] All of this produces a confused and confusing scenario.

The loans into PFU were not Misra's Sanskrit-like ones; rather they took place at the stage of PIIr (perhaps even at that of late common PIE). PFU has taken over a substantial number of loan words ranging from plants and animals to customs, religion, and the economy.[98]

Misra's new dating of the RV at 5000 BCE, thus, is clearly impossible. It would be so, anyhow, due to the many contradictions raised by monolateral reasoning that he simply does not even notice: at 5000 BCE the RV could not contain the domesticated horse, chariot, copper/bronze weapons, etc. Instead, as the PFU loan words point to a pre-Ṛgvedic language (PIIr, even some pre-PIIr), the RV must actually be considerably *later* than the reconstructed PFU (supposedly of 5000 BCE). All of which fits in well with the "traditional" scholarly date for this text, in the second millennium BCE, which is roughly contemporary with the other early IE texts in Hittite, Mit. IA, and early, Mycenean Greek. I leave aside here Misra's faulty interpretation of Mit. IA words (see Section 11.16) and his curious but inappropriate use of Gypsy materials, a language that actually did emigrate from India, but thousands of years later, in medieval times (Witzel 2001b).[99]

11.14 A prehistoric pan-Indian linguistic area?

Next to the Out of India theory, the other new and equally misleading linguistic scenario is that of a very ancient, prehistoric Indian linguistic area (*Sprachbund*). Aiyar (1975), Waradpande (1993) and (nat.) scientists such as Kak (1994b), or mostly on the internet, the banker Kalyanaraman (1999, 2000) contend that two of the major language families of South Asia, IA (i.e. IE) and Drav. are not (very) different from each other. Both would rather represent two forms of an old South Asian Proto-language, which they call, variously, a Prakrit[100] or just the Indian Bronze Age language.

A forerunner of this idea is Aurobindo (cf. Talageri 2000). He and others confused the (ultimately correct) feeling of an all Indian *cultural* unity with that of *linguistic unity*.[101] For example, Swaminatha Aiyar writes:

> ... from a linguistic point of view also, Dravidian is more comparable to Indo-Aryan than to any other language family in the world... But Dravidian may be the first to have been separated and went north. Next the centum people separated and left through the Himalayan passes to Caspian or Pamir and then to Europe etc. The satem speakers left after that, batch by batch. The last batch might have been the Iranians.
>
> (1975, quoted with approval by Misra 1992: 73–8)

The first part of the quote confuses descent (genetic relationship) of languages with secondary mutual influences of neighboring languages (South Asian linguistic region, *Sprachbund*).

The issue at hand is whether there ever was such a thing as a common South Asian or Indian "Prakrit." Kalyanaraman, Kak (1994b), or Misra (1992) simply (or handily) confuse the relatively new concept of a South Asian linguistic area (*Sprachbund*) with the "genetic" relationship, based on cladistics, of the languages involved.

The *Sprachbund* idea was developed early in the twentieth century when linguists noticed that several disparate languages in the Balkans shared many features. These include Rumanian, Macedonian, Bulgarian, Serbian, Greek, and Albanian – all IE languages from various quite diverse subfamilies.[102] However, they have stayed together for a long time, and have had intermingled settlements for some 1500–2000 years. Consequently, bilingual speakers have influenced each other considerably, especially in syntax and by mutual loan words. Yet, there still is no "new Balkan language" or a "Balkan language family" in sight. The basic vocabulary of these six languages and most of their grammatical *formantia* still are very different from each other.

The same applies to South Asia, where the idea of a linguistic area was pioneered by Emeneau (1956) and Kuiper (1967).[103] But, *unlike* the Balkans, South Asia has at least three different large language families:[104] IE, Drav., Munda, which have nothing in common, either in basic vocabulary or in word structure or in grammatical formantia.[105] Over the past few millennia, these three (as well as the other) language families of South Asia have converged to a large degree, including phonetics (retroflexes, see Section 11.17), word formation (Munda changed from a monosyllabic language with prefixes into a polysyllabic one working with suffixes) and syntax (spread of absolutives, see Tikkanen 1987, or sentence structure preferring SOV arrangements, see Hock 1986).

The spread of such convergent items has been taken by some (Kak 1994b) as a sign that the various South Asian languages are underway to form a new Indic language family. This is overstating the matter by not just a little margin. Tamil speakers do not use Hindi words in their *basic* vocabulary, nor do Bengali speakers basic Santali words, nor Kashmiri speakers Burushaski words, nor Nepali speakers Tibetan words, and vice versa. And, the various grammars involved still are far apart from each other, in spite of all the converge features evoked earlier.

In sum, the proponents of a "common" South Asian Proto-language/'Prakrit' and a "new S. Asian language family *in statu nascendi*" confuse the outcome of a long stay together and original "genetic descent." To state things differently, this simply is bad linguistics and special pleading.

11.15 Autochthonous linguistics and homelands

The two positions described earlier, that of a prehistoric Indian linguistic area (*Sprachbund*) and the (often linked) assumption that one of them involved the IE group of languages that then would have moved "out of India," are not tenable for the reasons already mentioned and for those to be discussed in detail in the following sections.

First of all, as regards an IE homeland inside India, we would expect an original clustering of the various IE subgroups inside India, in other words, a clustering of innovations, right from the period of close proximity and of constant linguistic exchanges between the speakers of the PIE language and its incipient dialects. This kind of evidence has been observed in various parts of the world: closely packed areas of related languages indicate original habitat, while a geographically wide spread of one (sub)family points to recent expansion. Bantu covers all of Central, East, and South Africa while its parent group, Niger-Congo, has a very dense arrangement of diverse languages in West Africa.[106] Or, the large array of English dialects in England, and the very few but widely spread variants outside England (North America, Australia, etc.) clearly point to England as the place of origin.

The actual spread of IE across Eurasia points in the same direction. The famous Satem innovations (*k*' > *c*' etc.) are limited to the IE languages in the east of the IE settlement area.[107] Clearly, the older Centum block has been split by the Satem innovations, with Celtic, Greek etc., in the west and Tocharian in the east. This clustering indicates that IIr is a *secondary* southeastern extension of eastern (Satem) IE, and that Ved. is a further, in fact the latest, easternmost one of these Satem branches; for a recent summary, see Hock (1986: 452, 1999). In short, the "dialectal features" in the arrangements of (P)IE languages indicate a general expansion of IE westwards and eastwards from an unknown center, somewhere close to the geographical center before the precolonial expansion of IE languages (over Siberia, the Americas, etc.).

Other items include the temperate, nontropical core vocabulary of IE (Section 11.23) or early IE loans from Semitic somewhere in the Near East such as ***wVjn*-, IE **woin*- 'wine' (Nichols 1997: 143), words that are *not* found in India. Or, on a typological level, there is the intermediate position of PIE between the Uralic and the various (NW/NE and S) Caucasian language families (Nichols 1997, 1998).

This would indicate an original settlement of the ancestor language somewhere in (the steppes of South) Eastern Europe. However, many early IE languages of that region have disappeared since,[108] and the SE steppes were subsequently settled by the North Iranian Scythians, several Turkic and Mongolian (Kalmyk) steppe peoples, and finally by Slavs.[109] This area is also at the fault line between the western Centum and eastern Satem languages and of certain syntactic features of IE (Hock 1999: 15).

All such observations make an Indian homeland of PIE a priori unlikely. Hock (1999) has adduced a further reason why this cannot be the case: all early dialectal differences in PIE, supposedly developed inside India, would have been exported, at various periods, and would have *exactly* reconstituted themselves geographically, all over Europe and the Near East, in the *same* geographical relationship as originally found in the hypothetical Indian homeland. This scenario certainly needs very special pleading, and simply falls prey to Occam's razor.[110]

11.16 Telling absences: lack of Indian characteristics west of India

Further, the case *against* an Indian homeland of PIE, and conversely, *for* a non-Indian homeland of PIE, Proto-IIr, and even of Proto-IA (pre-Vedic), can be made by observing the total absence of typical South Asian features (both local and OIA) in the other IE languages west of India. These include absence of typical Indian features and grammatical innovations in Mit. IA, Old Iranian, and the rest of IE, as well as the lack of typically Indian words for South Asian plants, animals, technology, etc. All of them should have been exported along with the emigration from India of the Iranians and other IEs. Proponents of the Indian homeland and Out of India theories as well as those of an early Indian *Sprachbund* would have to explain cogently why all these typical Indian features did not make it westward, beyond the Khyber and Bolan passes: collective amnesia? This problem, in typical monolateral fashion, is simply overlooked.

To begin with the language most closely related to Vedic Sanskrit, Mit.-IA. This language is attested by a number of OIA loan words (Mayrhofer 1979, EWA III 569 sqq.) in the non-IE Hurrite language of the Mit. realm of northern Iraq/Syria (*c.*1460–1330 BCE). The loans cover the semantic fields of horses, their colors, horse racing, and chariots, some important "Vedic" gods, and a large array of personal names adopted by the ruling class. However, the Mitanni documents do not show any typical *South Asian* influence.[111]

These remnants of IA in Mit. belong to an early, pre-Ṛgvedic stage of IA, seen in the preservation of IIr *-zdh-* > Ved. *-edh-*, IIr *ai* > Ved. *e*, as well as in the absence of retroflexion.[112] How could all of this be possible at *c.*1400 BCE if one supposes an emigration from India, in some cases (Misra 1992) even *after* the supposed hoary date of the RV (5000 BCE)? The RV, after all, is a text that already *has* all these features.

It also is important to note the typical innovations of OIA in Mit. IA which attest to their early existence *outside* South Asia in Mesopotamia, in the earlier Mit.-IA habitat in the Zagros Mountains, and beyond in Greater Iran. Such typical OIA (Ved.) linguistic innovations include *aika-vartana* (*a-i-ka-ua-ar-ta-an-na*) 'one turn'[113] instead of Ir. *aiva-* or general IE **oino* > **aina*. Still, the vocabulary does not yet show signs of typical *South Asian* influence: for example, there is no retroflexation in *mani-nnu*, or the Southwest Iranian, Elam. O.P. **bara-mani* and in the East Iranian dialect, Avest.: *ma^{i}ni* (in spite of the very specific, phonetic alphabet used by the Zoroastrians!) But retroflexation is precisely what is found once OIA enters South Asia: RV *maṇi* 'jewel'.[114] Mit. IA also does not have typical South Asian loan words such as *āṇi* 'lynch pin'.

The Mit. loan words also share some IIr religious innovations, such as the new *Asura* gods *Varuṇa*, *Mitra*, *Indra*, and the *Nāsatya*[115] and the new the concept of *Ṛta* (Iran. *Arta*, in *very late* Avest. pronunciation = *aša*),[116] and perhaps the newly introduced ritual drink, *sauma*, IIr **sauma* (Ved. *soma*, Avest. *haoma*).[117] There is extensive proof for the use of the domesticated horse (*ašuua*, cf. names for horse colors[118]), the chariot (*rattaš*) and chariot racing.[119]

To see in some of these words a post-RV form of OIA, a "Prakrit" (Misra 1992; Elst 1999: 183)[120] is misguided as this form is due to the peculiarities of the cuneiform writing system. Mit. IA *seems* to fit in well (at dates *c.*1400 BCE) with Misra's theory of an early RV at 5000 BCE as he regards some of the Mit. words as representing post-Vedic, Middle Indo-Aryan (MIA) developments. He assumes (repeated by Elst 1999: 183) MIA replacement of *v-* by *b-* as in Mit. *biriya-* < Ved. *vīrya* (rather, *priya-*, see EWA I 139), or MIA assimilation of clusters in Mit. *satta* < Ved. *sapta* 'seven'.

However, it has been asserted for long that *satta* in *satta-vartana* 'seven turns' has been influenced by Hurrite *šinti* 'seven'[121] as *sapta* could easily be written in cuneiform. The words starting with *b-* such as *bi-* did not receive their *b-* from a MIA pronunciation of *vi*,[122] as Misra maintains, but are due to the fact that Mit. does not allow initial *v-* (Diakonoff 1971: 30, 45) which Misra, surprisingly, does not know. Clearly, all such forms are due to the exigencies of cuneiform writing and Hurrite pronunciation found in the Mit. realm. In short, the Mit. IA words are not Prakritic but pre-Ṛgvedic (see earlier).

In sum, Mit.-IA is older than the RV and cannot have come from the Panjab or India in general, but must have been spoken on the north-eastern border areas of Mesopotamia; finally, it influenced the Hurrite language of the Mit. that belongs, just like its later relative in Urartu, to the North (Eastern) Caucasian group of languages (Diakonoff 1971, 1986). Thus, Misra's early "Middle Indo-Aryan" at 1400 BCE simply evaporates, along with his early RV at 5000 BCE.[123] We are back at the "traditional" dates.

Indeed, some of the rather indirect IA influx into the Near East may have been earlier than the one visible in Mit. (Drews 1989). The Kassite conquerors of Mesopotamia (*c.*1677–1152 BCE) have a sun god *Śuriiaš*,[124] perhaps also the *Marut* and maybe even *Bhaga* (*Bugaš*?), as well as the personal name *Abirat(t)aš* (*Abhiratha*); but otherwise, the vocabulary of their largely unknown language hardly shows any IA influence, not even in their many designations for the horse and horse names[125] (Balkan 1954).[126]

If one now thinks through, exemplarily, the implications of the autochthonous theory, the ancestors of the Mit. IAs would have left India very early indeed (well before the favorite autochthonist hoary date of the RV, 2600–5000 BCE). They would have done so with the Ṛgvedic dialect features (*ai* > *e*, *zdh* > *edh*) *not yet* in place, and without any of the alleged MIA forms of Misra (*satta*, etc.), but *with* the typical OIA and IIr terms for horses and chariot racing (*before* their invention and introduction into South Asia *c.*2000–1700 BCE, Meadow 1996, 1998)! They would also have done so *without* any of the local South Asian innovations (no retroflex in *mani-*, etc.) that are already found in the RV ("at 5000 BCE"). Mit.-IA also is *without* any particularly local Indian words (lion, tiger, peacock, lotus, lynch pin *āṇi*), all of which would have been "selectively" forgotten while *only typical* IIr and IE words were remembered. In short, a string of contradictions and improbabilities. Occam's razor applies.[127]

11.17 Absence of retroflexes west of India

Turning back in time, or in the cladistic scheme, to the closest relative of OIA, Old Iranian, we will note a few typical innovations that separate it from IA, further below. However, Old Iranian (Old Persian, Avest., etc.) also contains clear evidence that does not allow for its emigration from India westwards, but rather requires a scenario that posits the introduction of Iranian into the Iranian plateau *before* it ever reached the borders of the Indian subcontinent. One such feature is the complete absence of typical Indian words referring to nature and culture (see below Sections 11.16 and 11.23) that simply could not have been forgotten *en masse* "while crossing the Bolan pass."

Another feature is the absence of retroflex sounds (*ṭ*, *ṭh*, *ḍ*, *ḍh*, *ṣ*, *ṇ*) in Old Iranian. Retroflexion is also found sporadically in some other parts of the world (Hock 1986), such as in Scandinavia or Australia (innovative in both cases). However, it is typical for South Asia when compared to its neighboring regions, that is Iran, West/Central Asia, the Himalayas, and Southeast Asia.[128]

Again, in the autochthonous scenario, the hypothetical emigrants from India would have lost the typical South Asian "bending back of their tongues" as soon as they crossed the Khyber or Bolan Passes: not even Old Iranian (East Iran. Avest.) has these sounds. But, conversely, the Baluchi, who originally were a West Iranian tribe, have *acquired* retroflexion – just in *some* of their dialects – and *after* their arrival on the borders on the subcontinent, early in the second millennium CE (Hoffmann 1941; Hamp 1996; cf. Hock 1996). The same has happened to other late, incoming western Iranian groups such as Parachi and Ormuri that are found in Eastern Afghanistan, and also to some local Iranian Pamir languages such as Wakhi. Clearly, retroflexion affects those *moving into* the Eastern Iranian borderland/Indus plain. Importantly, the most widespread appearance of retroflexes is among the cluster of Hindukush/Pamir languages, that is the languages surrounding these mountains in the east (Nuristani/Kafiri, Burushaski, Dardic, and the rest of these northernmost IA languages) as well as in the north (some of the Iranian Pamir languages: Wakhi, Yigdha, Sanglechi, Ishkashmi, Khotanese Saka), as detailed by Tikkanen (in Parpola 1994: 166). Retroflexes *may* also have belonged to (a *part* of) the Central Asian/Afghanistan substrate of the RV (Witzel 1999a,b). Retroflexion clearly is a northwestern regional feature that still is strongest and most varied in this area. In sum, retroflexion affects all those moving into the East Iranian borderland, the Indus plain and the subcontinent.[129]

Had retroflexion indeed been present in the pre-Iranian or the Proto-Iranian coeval with the (Ṛg)Vedic period, its effects should be visible in Old Iranian, at least in Avest.[130] which was spoken in East Iran, that means in a large part of the territory of modern Pashto (which has retroflexes indeed).

Cases such as IIr **waj'h-tar* > **waj'dhar* 'the one who pulls' > Avest. *vaštar*, but > Ved. *voḍhar-* 'draft ox' present perhaps the best testimony for the several stages of conditioned reflexes in the development from IE to Ved. A change from Ved. *voḍhar-* > Avest. *vaštar-* (à la Misra) is plainly impossible in any version of phonetics, as also *voḍhar-* > IE **wek'h-tor-* (as in Latin *vec-tor*). Missing consonants as in *vo-ḍhar-* do not suddenly (re-)emerge out of the blue in other languages, and *not* as *-š-* in Iranian, as *-k-* in Latin, or as *-k-* in Gaulish *Vectur-ius*, or as *-g-* as in Engl. *wagon*. Rather, with the IE theory, they all stem from IE **weg'h-tor-*. (All of this is neglected, monolaterally, by Misra 1992).[131] In sum, the well-known rules of IE sound changes explain the development of the root *vah* (IE **weg'h*) without problem, while any OIT theory would have great difficulty to get from *voḍhar-* to any Avestan, Latin, English, etc. form.[132]

(Old) Iranian, which has kept the older sound sequences, allows for a relative and even for absolute dating: **aždh* > *oḍh* is parallel to **sazd-* > *sed*, that is, both are post-Indo-Iranian and even post-Mitanni, which keeps the sequence *azd*. In other words, Ṛgvedic is younger than the Mit. words preserved at *c*.1450–1350 BCE. At any rate, RV *-ed-* is definitely younger than the Mit. forms because the IIr form **sazdai* > Ved. *sede* (3 sg. perf., cf. Avestan *hazde* 'he has sat') has already spawned a number of analogical formations in the RV that are *not* conditioned by *-azd-*. These are found even in the older sections of the RV.[133]

In all these cases the retroflex is late and localizable, that is, Ved. *innovation* (in the Hindukush area?) that is not shared by Iranian and the other IE languages. In short, this innovation is rather *low down* on the "family pedigree," in cladistics. Any biologist would classify a similar development in biological materials as a clear indicator of a late development, as an *innovation*, – in this case, one that separates Ved. IA/OIA from the rest of IA, IIr, and IE.[134] In other words, Vedic Sanskrit does *not* represent the oldest form of IE, as autochthonists often claim.

The same conclusion can be reached when studying local Panjab loan words in the RV (Witzel 1999a,b) and their lack in Old Iranian texts.

11.18 Absence of local Indian words and grammatical innovations in Iranian

The *hypothetical* emigrants from the subcontinent would have taken with them a host of "Indian" words – as the Gypsies (Roma, Sinti) indeed have done. But, we do not find any typical Old Indian words beyond South Asia, neither in the closely related in Old Iranian, nor in Eastern or Western IE, except for the few, commonly borrowed words of culture (*Wanderwörter*), such as recent imports into English (*orange*, *tea/chai*, or *curry*, *punch*, *veranda*, *bungalow*), or the older ones of the type *rice*, *beryl*, *hemp*, etc.[135] In an OIT scenario, one would expect "emigrant" Indian words such as those for lion, tiger, elephant, leopard, lotus, bamboo, or some local Indian trees,[136] even if some of them would have been preserved, not for the original item, but for a similar one (e.g. English [red] squirrel > North American [gray] squirrel).

There should be at least *a few* terms of *tropical* plants that would have been exported (north)westwards,[137] perhaps with changed meanings. This is not the case. Designations for typical Indian plants and animals that should be found in IE and especially in Iranian, do not even appear in Iran, not to speak of Central Asia or Europe.[138] Nor do we find *retained* Indian names for plants/animals, although at least some of them are actually *still found* in Iran: the lion,[139] the tiger,[140] the lotus (seen on Behistun sculptures), etc. Other words that have occasionally been used for the autochthonous argument, such as *kapi* 'monkey', *siṃha* 'lion' or *ibha* 'elephant' are rather dubious cases.[141] Instead of Indian words we find, for example, for *siṃha* 'lion', other words such as Iran. *šer*, Grk. *līs*, Lat. *leō(n)* (Witzel 1999a,b, forthc. b), and similarly, Grk/Latin ones for 'tiger', 'lotus', etc. Many of them come from a Mediterranean/Near Eastern substrate, but not, as expected in any OIT scenario, from the South Asian one visible in Ved.

In sum, no typical Indian designation for plants or animals made it beyond the Khyber/Bolan passes. The only clear exception possible *would* be the unlikely case of the birch tree, found in India only high up on the mountain ranges of Kashmir, whose IE name **bhṛg'ho-* is found all the way from India[142] to Europe: Ved. *bhūrja* (Kaṭha Saṃhitā); Ir. Pamir dial. *furz*; Shugni *vāwzn* < **barznī*; Osset. *bœrs(œ)*; Lith. *béržas*; Serbo-Croat. *bréza*; German *Birke*; Engl. *birch*, etc. (cf. Section 11.22, n. 175). The other "European" trees that are found in the northwest of the subcontinent and beyond up to Russia/Urals, are *absent* from Sanskrit vocabulary[143] (Section 11.23).

This situation has always been well explained by the assumption of IE linguists that these European/Caucasus/Ural tree names were remembered (sometimes, in the Central Asian steppes and deserts, only in old sayings or in poetry?) down to the very doorsteps of South Asia in Afghanistan. Or, they were applied to similar items but were utterly forgotten in the tropical South Asia as there were no similar trees for which these IE names could be used.

The autochthonous theory again must introduce the improbable *auxiliary* assumption that *all such temporate climate words* have been forgotten *inside* the subcontinent after, or even as soon as, the Iranians (and other IEs) *supposedly* crossed the Suleiman Range and the Khyber/Bolan passes into Afghanistan and Iran.

On the other hand, many if not most of the typical South Asian plant and animal names have clear, non-IE, local origins. In other words, they are loan words into Ved. from the local South Asian languages[144] (e.g. RV *mayūra* 'peacock', *vrīhi* 'rice', etc.). Others are new formations, built on the basis of IE words, for example, 'elephant': *hastin* (+ *mṛga*) 'the (wild animal) with the hand'[145] or perhaps *vyāghra* 'tiger'.[146] These new formations must have been introduced when the *immigrating* speakers of IA (*not* the Iranians!) were first faced with them in the Greater Panjab. Autochthonists (Elst 1999; Talageri 2000; etc.) denounce such cases as poetic or descriptive formations, or as dialect designations which can happen at any stage in the history of a language (e.g. Vulgar Latin *caballus* > French *cheval*, etc. for older *equus*). However, such monolateral critics once again overlook the wider context, the *complete absence* of *original* IE/IA words for *South Asian* plants/animals built with clear IE *roots* and/or *word structure*.

The absence of IE/IA words for local plants and animals clearly militates against any assumption that pre-IA, Proto-IIr, or PIE was the *local* language of the Panjab or even of Uttar Pradesh during (pre-)Harappan times. This also agrees with the fact that most of the South Asian loan words in the Ṛgveda, excluding some Central Asian imports (Witzel 1999a,b, forthc. b), are *not* found in Iran and beyond.[147] These words include Kuiper's (1991) *c*.380 'foreign words' in the RV. Again, not all of them could have been "lost" as soon as the *hypothetical* IE or Iranian emigrants crossed over into Iran and beyond. One would at least expect a *few* of them in the "emigrant" languages. They could have survived in the west and could have acquired a new meaning, such as British Engl. *corn* 'wheat' > 'maize' in America. The Gypsies, after all, have kept a large IA vocabulary alive, over the past 1000 years or so, during their wanderings all over the Near East, North Africa, and Europe (e.g. *phral* 'brother', *pani* 'water', *karàl* 'he does').

No amount of special pleading will convince an independent (linguistic) observer of a scenario that relies on the total loss of all *typical* South Asian words in Iranian and *all the other* "emigrant" IE languages. Again, Occam's razor requires to scrap the theory of an IE emigration from the Panjab to the West.

11.19 Absence of local Indian influences in Indo-Iranian

As has been indicated earlier, Avest. and Old Persian share many innovations with Ved., when compared to Eastern (Satem) IE or the rest of PIE. This was, of course, the initial reason to set up the IIr group of languages as a separate branch of IE. The occurrence of common innovations *always* indicates a split off from the core group, which obviously is *later* than the core (see earlier).

Some innovations, stemming from the IIr period, are met with in Old Iranian (pronoun *ah-am* 'I', Avest. *azəm*;[148] Nom.Pl. *aśvāsa-as*, Avest. *aspåŋhō* 'horses' etc.). This is attributed to the common source language rather than to OIA influencing the neighboring Old Iranian dialects (as clearly witnessed in the examples given earlier).

On the other hand, while we can observe some changes common to all Iranian languages (*s* > *h*, *p*, *t*, *k* + consonant > *f*, *ϑ*, *x* + cons., etc.), Avest. often is quite archaic, both in grammar and also in vocabulary, while Ved. seems to have progressed much more toward Epic and Classical Sanskrit (loss of injunctive, moods of the perfect, aorist, etc.). The Avest. combination within a sentence of neuter plural nouns with the singular of the verb is hardly retained even in the other older IE languages. The Old Avest. of Zaraϑuštra, thus, is frequently even more archaic than the RV and therefore simply too old to have moved out of India *after* the composition of the RV (*supposedly*, before 2600–5000 BCE).

In other words, Iranian simply lacks the many *innovations* that characterize Ved., innovations that are not found among the other IE languages either, for example the absolutives in *-tvā, -ya*, ntr. pl. in *-āni*,[149] *jabhāra* for *jahāra, Jamadagni* (= Avest. *jimaṯ*) next to the innovative RV *gamad*, or the generalization of the Ṛgvedic *e*-perfects, derived from IIr **sazdai* (Avest. *hazde*) > Ved. *sede*, spawning many analogical formations such as *mene*. Since sound changes and grammatical changes are not random these Ved. innovations must have occurred well after Ved. had separated from late IIr/pre-Iranian, thus: IE → E. IE → IIr → Ved., namely, IIr → Iranian.

It would be against all rules of comparative linguistics in IE or in any other language family (and of general cladistics, as in biology), to assume that such late Ṛgvedic developments would represent old IE ones (Misra 1992) and that cladistic branching should *not apply just in the single case of IA*.[150] Vedic Sanskrit may be regarded as *devabhāṣā* but it is subject to the same developments as any other spoken language. One can only conclude that Proto-Iranian (> Avest., O. Persian) split off from IIr and thus, from pre-Old IA (> Ved., Mit. IA, etc.) at an *early* date. Because of the early split, Old Iranian preserved some archaic features, while also developing innovations on its own.

All of this points to a separation of Proto-Iranian and Proto-OIA at some time *before* the RV and before Mitanni-IA. It cannot have happened *inside* South Asia as the even the close geographical neighbor, Avest. (spoken in most of Afghanistan, Witzel 2000) lacks all those typically South Asian words that are local loans into Vedic (Section 11.5, Witzel 1999a,b).

In sum, Proto-Iranian was never spoken in the Panjab and the many linguistic archaisms in Old Iranian cannot readily be explained by a *supposed* early Iranian emigration from India.

How can the autochthonists then deal with archaisms found in Iranian that are *not* found in Vedic? In an autochthonous scenario, such archaisms ought to have been preserved in the Panjab, side by side with the RV (where there is no trace of them). They must have been forgotten, miraculously, by peoples *all over* the subcontinent (just like names of trees and other examples mentioned earlier, Section 11.15 sqq.)[151] once the Iranians *supposedly* left it (Elst 1999: 122, 124 sqq.), taking with them and retaining these very archaic features. However, when and where should this exodus have happened? Southwestern, Central Southern and Northern Iran was occupied, in the third millennium BCE, by non -IE peoples.[152] Iranian, IIr, or IE influences are nowhere to be seen.[153] Further, Iranian does not show any typical local Indian elements (see earlier).[154] Again, the required collective amnesia, surprisingly one restricted just to *certain archaic* items just *inside* India, does not make for a good case. It is, again, one of very special pleading.

While all such emigration schemes are possible in a purely *theoretical* scenario, there are a number of arguments that render it impossible. Some of them, notably the question of separate innovations, have been listed by Hock (1999). The actual distribution of IE (and IIr) dialect features simply does not allow for all-IE innovations *after* a supposed Iranian/IE exodus from India.[155]

One can add the early close links of IIr (and, later, early Iranian) with Uralic in Southern Russia and in the Ural and Western Siberian regions (see Section 11.13), and the new terminology coined for the horse-drawn chariot (*ratha/raϑa*), first introduced in the Southern Russia/Ural area *c.*2000 BCE (see Section 11.20). This list, which could be extended, clearly points to the areas *north* of the ancient Near East, and strongly militates against the assumption of an original Indian homeland of OIA, IIr, and, worse, of IE (see Sections 11.21–11.23).

Further, if the Iranians (and IEs) emigrated from India, why we do not find "Indian bones" of this *massive* emigration in Iran and beyond? Indian skeletons are, as Kennedy informs (1995, 2000), remarkably different from Near Eastern ones.[156] Again, autochthonists would have to argue that mysteriously only *that* section of the Panjab population left westwards which had (then actually not attested!) "non-Indian" physical characteristics, – very special pleading indeed. Thus, to adopt an Indocentric OIT stance *precisely mirroring* the IA immigration theory based on "trickling in" is not possible as this "trickling out" would comprise *all subfamilies* of IE, from Tocharian to Celtic, and would constitute a much more *massive* emigration, or "invasion" as Misra (1992) calls it, than any type of IA influx *into* India.

The IE theory can explain the materials found in the various languages much more satisfactorily. In one phrase, *the Iranian languages simply miss the Indianization of IIr*, with all its concurrent innovations in grammar and vocabulary.

11.20 Dating Indo-Aryan and Iranian innovations

As could be seen, it is sometimes difficult to argue against some of the autochthonists' assumptions purely on *general* linguistic grounds as language changes cannot easily be tied to certain areas, unless there is evidence from inscriptions and clearly localizable texts.

However, a good indicator of the time frame of IIr and its daughter languages, O. Iran. (Avest.) and OIA (Ved.), is found in the word for the horse-drawn chariot, Sanskrit *ratha*, O. Iran. *raϑa*. This word is attested in the oldest IIr texts, in the RV and in the Avesta, also with the secondary formation Ved. *rath-in-*, O. Avest. *raϑ-ī* 'the one who has a chariot, charioteer'. Even more tellingly, it appears in the inherited archaic compound, with a locative case ending in its first member, RV *rathe-ṣṭha*, Avest. *raϑaē-šta-* 'charioteer' (cf. also *savye-ṣṭha* 'warrior').

The autochthonous theory would have the RV at *c*.5000 BCE or before the start of the Indus civilization at 2600 BCE. Therefore, the Iranians or other IEs *should have exported* the chariot from South Asia at that early time. But, the chariot is first found in a rather archaic form ("proto-chariot"), betraying its origin in a oxen-drawn wagon (Ved. *anas*, PIE **weg'h-o-*, *wagon*, *veh-icle*), at *c*.2000 BCE, in Ural Russia and at Sintashta, West and East of the Urals. As its invention is comparatively late, the western IE languages retain, not surprisingly, the older meaning of the IE word, *$roth_2o$-"wheel" (Lat. *rota*, Germ. *Rad* 'wheel'); they simply have moved away, from the original, central IE region (such as the Ukraine/Ural steppes) westwards into Europe[157] before this particular development took place.

An autochthonist counterargument could maintain that the newly introduced chariot spread quickly from the Near East or Central Asia all over the Iranian and Indian world, along with its IIr name, **ratha*. It would thus belong only to a secondary historical level (after that of the earlier "Panjab Indo-Europeans"). This argument, however, would again run into a number of difficulties. Strangely, the word in its new meaning of 'chariot' never reached the neighboring Proto-Slavic tribes, nor the other European "emigrants" on the western side of Eurasia,[158] while it is known to the close neighbors, the (Northern) Iranians and the Mitanni-IA. Worse, the word and the object are found already in the RV (*supposedly*, pre-Indus, 2600 or *c*.5000 BCE!), well *before* its invention.[159] In short, multiple insurmountable contradictions emerge.

The word *cakra* 'wheel' may be a much older adaptation from Sumerian, *gil-gul* 'wheel' and GIŠ*gígir* 'wagon,' to IE *k^we-k^wl-o-* > IIr *cakra*, taken over from the Near East at the time of invention of the wheel and the wagon (Littauer and Crouwel 1996). However, IE *$roth_2o$, in the newly specialized meaning *ratha* 'chariot', is restricted to IIr and its early archaeological attestation puts PIIr, again, close to the Urals. On the other hand, there are common PIE words in Ved. (and O. Iran.) for the cart or four-wheeled wagon (*anas*) and its constituent parts , such as *akṣa* 'axle', *ara* 'spoke, pin', *nabhya* 'nave', *yuga* 'yoke', *raśmi*, *raśanā* 'reins', etc. (for details see EWA, s.v.) They are much older, PIE, as they refer to the more primitive technology of solid wheel, oxen-drawn wagons and carts that was developed (from sledges) in Mesopotamia during the late fourth millennium.

If according to the autochthonous theory, the Iranians had emigrated westwards out of India well before the RV (2600–5000 BCE), how could both the Indians (in the Panjab) and the Iranians (from the Ukraine to Xinjiang) have a common, inherited word for the – not yet invented – horse-drawn chariot as well as a rather ancient word for the charioteer? Both words must have been present at the time of the IIr parent language: as the linguistic evidence shows, the technical innovation was already IIr (note Proto-IIr **th* that regularly developed to > Ir. *ϑ*, as in O. Iran. *raϑa*), and it must have happened at the place of its invention,[160] in the steppe plains near the IIr River *Rasā* (Volga).

Consequently, the occurrence of **ratha* in IIr at *c*.2000 BCE shows that its *import* was carried out, along with many other IIr items of culture and religion, from the South Russian/Central Asian steppes *into* the subcontinent, and not vice versa. *This is one of the few clear cases where we can align linguistic innovation with innovation in material culture, poetics and myth, and even with archaeological and historical attestation.*[161] Therefore, we have to take it very seriously. The various revisionist or autochthonous dating schemes that circumvent the important innovation in technology and language dealing with the quick horse drawn, spoke-wheeled chariot at *c.*2000 BCE are doomed to failure.[162]

After this review of "systematic absences" in non-IA languages belonging to the IE family of grammatical and some cultural items that must have been present in India in any autochthonous scenario,[163] we can now turn to (predictable) items that further delineate IE, IIr, and IA in time and place.

11.21 Linguistic innovations and migrations

The relative dating of OIA can be further specified if we take into account older, western IE (Centum) versus younger (Satem) innovations. Terms that are *old* in IE include PIE *$*g^wow$-* 'cow', **dyew-* 'heaven' and their archaic accusative forms *$*g^w\bar{o}m$, *dyēm* with PIE dissimilation of *-w-* (i.e. instead of an expected, regular *$**g^w\bar{o}wm$, **dyēwm*). They should have existed already in a hypothetical "IE Panjab." However, the dissimilated PIE forms are reflected in various old IE languages, as Ved. *gām* 'cow', Hom. Grk. *boun/bōn*, Ved. *dyām* 'heaven', Grk *zēn*, etc. (EWA I 479, 752). In any autochthonous theory, this archaic dissimilation would either be due to pre-split PIE dialects *inside* India (already refuted by Hock 1999, earlier) or to the extremely unlikely subsequent, *individual* development of the *same* traits outside India, after the IE languages would have left the subcontinent.[164] Just like the supposed "individual" innovations in *dyām* and *gām*, such eastern IE developments (cf. Hock 1986: 451 sq.) would have to be *re-imports* from their focus in Eastern Europe/Central Asia back into India – all convoluted cases of very special pleading.

To correlate such relative dates (e.g. PIE *$*g^w\bar{o}$-* > IIr *gā-* > Ved. *gā-*, or PIE *k'm̥tom* > IIr *c'ata* > Ved. *śata*), with other early IE languages, we can take a look at their first traces, with Hittite *c.*2000–1600 BCE in Anatolia, Mycenean Greek at *c.*1400–1200 in Crete, Mitanni-IA. in North Syria/Iraq at 1450–1350 BCE. All PIE and IIr terms and forms must precede these dates by a *large* margin as even archaic languages, such as Vedic and Hittite, are separated from each other by *several* levels of subsequent innovative developments. The date of the dispersal of the earliest, western IE languages (including Tocharian, eastwards) can be estimated in the early third millennium BCE.

Further dates can be supplied by a study of important cultural features such as the common IE reconstructed word for copper/bronze, or the vocabulary connected with the heavy oxen-drawn wagon (see later). They point to the end of the fourth or the beginning of the third millennium as a date ad quem, or rather post quem for the last stage of commonly shared PIE.

The autochthonous theory would, again, have to assume that all Indian (Ved.) innovations mentioned earlier would have been carried out *after the speakers of*

Iranian (and/or all other IE languages) had left the subcontinent. In this Indocentric scenario (Talageri 1993, 2000, etc.), the Centum languages (Celtic, Germanic, Latin, Greek, etc.), then the Satem languages (Slavic, etc.), would have followed each other by a time span of at least a few hundred years. Iranian would have been the last to emigrate from India as it is closest to Vedic. It should have left well before *c*.1000 BCE, when West Iranian is first found on the eastern borders of Mesopotamia.[165]

The relative dates discussed earlier allow to put such claims into a distinct relief, especially when such extraordinary early dates as 5000 BCE are claimed for the RV (Misra 1992). Granting this for argument's sake (though impossible on text-internal, cultural grounds), the *hypothetical old* RV would have the comparatively *modern* form of OIA (derived < IIr < PIE); nevertheless, it would *precede* that of the very archaic Hittite (*c*.2000–1600 BCE) by a margin of some 3000 years. We know, of course, that Ved. is not *earlier* than Hittite but clearly *later*, that is, lower in the cladistic scheme, than the 'family tree'. It is also *later* than Eastern IE (Satem innovations, *RUKI*, cf. Hock 1986, 1999), *later* than Proto-Indo-Iranian (*e*, *a* > æ, *k'* > *c'*, *o* > *ā* in open syllables), and even later than pre-Vedic (*c'* > *ś*, or *zd*(*h*) and *j'* > Ved. *h*, which still preserved as š [*ž*] < *j'h* in Mit. IA at 1400 BCE, see later in Section 11.16, n. 111). In short, all of the above indicates that neither time nor space would agree with an OIT scenario.

In other words, all linguistic scenarios that assume such hoary dates for the RV and an IE emigration out of India (such as Misra 1992; Talageri 1993, 2000; Elst 1999) are not just badly deliberated but plainly impossible: PIE, while still in the Panjab, would *not* yet have developed all the traits found in non-OIA languages (Satem, etc.), while their close neighbor, the "old" RV, would *already* have gone through all Satem, IIr, pre-Vedic and RV innovations some 7,000 years ago – an unlikely scenario, to say the least. Still, as such, the "old", Ṛgvedic OIA would miraculously have exercised early influences on the rather distant Uralic languages in South Russia/Urals/West Siberia,[166] while the close non-IA IE neighbors of Uralic (O. Iran., Baltic, etc.) would *not*. All of this is obviously impossible on grounds of space and time. Misra *et al.* have not thought through their idiosyncratic and *ad hoc* scenarios.[167] To do so and to think *for* them is really not *our* job, but that of the proponent(s) of the new theory. They should have done their homework.

11.22 Culture and migrations

The matter can still further be elucidated by observing some cultural and natural features found in PIE. According to the autochthonous theories the various IE peoples (the "*Anu, Druhyu*" of Talageri 1993, 2000) and their languages *hypothetically* left India (*c*.5000–4000 BCE). If put to a test by archaeology and linguistics, these "emigrations" would *rather* have to be set at the following latest possible dates.[168]

- At *c*.3000–2500 BCE, West IE leave westwards, possessing 'copper/bronze' (Ved. *ayas*, Lat. *aes*; etc.); with the wagon, but not yet possessing the chariot: Lat. *rota* 'wheel', Grk *kuklo-* 'wheel', Tocharian *kukõl*, *kokale* 'wagon', etc.

(note the *new* formation Grk *hárma(t)-* 'chariot', Pokorny 1959: 58); all parts of the heavy, solid wheel-wagon drawn by oxen (*ukṣan*, etc.) are IE: *akṣa, ara nābha* 'nave'; Germ. *Rad* Lat. *rota;* domesticated horse, used for riding: *$*h_1ek'wo$ >* Lat. *equus*, O. Irish *ech*, Toch. *yuk, yakwe.*

- At *c*.2500–2000, East IE, with Satem characteristics (*$*h_1ek'wo$*, O. Lith. *ašvà*), but still no chariots: Lith. *ratas* 'wheel, circle', Slav. *kolo* 'wheel'.
- At *c*.2000, IIr unity, with the new *ratha* 'chariot' introduced from Volga/Ural/North Caucasus area; and with *cakra* 'wheel, chariot'; the domesticated horse (and the chariot) enter India after 2000 BCE, probably about 1700 BCE; innovative Asura (*Āditya*) gods, with artificial formations (*Arya-man* = Avest. *Airiia-man*, etc.).
- At *c*.1500–1000, Iranians move southwards into Iran: with chariot, Asuras, but keep archaic traits in grammar.
- At *c*.1000, West Iranians are attested beyond the eastern borders of Mesopotamia, in Media and later in the Persis (Assyrian inscriptions).

According to this list, again, all Ved. linguistic innovations (with the RV set at 5000 BCE by the autochthonists) and some East IE innovations, such as the IIr chariot, would have happened *before* the supposed emigration of the Iranians, etc. from India. This is linguistically and archaeologically impossible, unless one uses the auxiliary, equally unlikely hypothesis that some IIrs left India before 2000 BCE and *reimported* the chariot into India (Elst 1999). All such arguments need very special pleading. Occam's Razor applies.

11.23 Nature, plants, animals, and migrations

The autochthonous scenario of an IE emigration from the Panjab also contradicts all we know about PIE material culture (e.g. horse, wagon, the late chariot) as well as climate-based vocabulary, all of which traditionally have been used to indicate a temperate PIE homeland with cold winters, somewhere in Eastern Europe–Central Asia,[169] in an area that included at least *some* (riverine?) tree cover and partially overlapped with the Russian/Siberian *taiga* woodlands (note PIE **medhu* 'honey', Pre-IIr *mekše* 'bee').

Generally, the PIE plants and animals are those of the temperate climate: animals include the otter, beaver, wolf, bear, lynx, elk, red deer, hare, hedgehog, and mouse, and plants include birch, willow, elm, ash, oak, (by and large, also the beech[170]) juniper, poplar, apple, maple, alder, hazel, nut, linden, hornbeam, and cherry (Mallory 1989: 114–16).

Typical IIr words indicating a temperate climate, all with an IE root and suffix structure, include, among others: 'wolf',[171] 'snow/winter',[172] 'birch tree' (*bhūrja*,[173] Pamir Dial. *furz*, Osset. *bærs(œ)*, etc.) which is found on the northwestern borders of the subcontinent (highlands of Kashmir) while some weaker arguments can be made for the willow (> Ved. *vetasa* 'cane, reed', see earlier n. 142), maybe the fir (*pītu?*) or the aspen (*varaṇa?*). But why are all the other IE trees those of a colder climate that are non-existent in Indian languages, even when the neighboring Iranians have some of them, for example, in the eastern Afghan mountains (fir, oak,[174] willow, and poplar)?

It is *theoretically* possible that these words belonged to the *supposed* original IE/IA vocabulary of the northwestern Himalayas. Even if we take into account that the Panjab has cool winters with some frost and that the adjoining Afghani and Himalayan mountains have a long winter season, neither snow nor birch are typical for the Panjab or the Indian plains.[175] Therefore, words such as those for 'wolf' and 'snow' rather indicate linguistic memories of a colder climate than an export of words, such as that for the high altitude Kashmirian birch tree, to Iran, Central Asia, and Europe.

Assuming, for argument's sake, the autochthonous scenario, one should rather ask: how *did* the IE tree names belonging to a cooler climate ever get exported out of India where these trees do *not* exist? One would have to use the auxiliary assumption that such trees were only found in the colder climate of the Himalayas and Pamirs, thus were part of the local South Asian vocabulary, and that they would then have been taken along, in the westward movement of the emigrants.

But, even this special pleading does not work: some of the typical temperate PIE trees are *not* found in the South Asian mountains. Yet, they have good Iranian and IE names, *all* with proper IE word formation. Interestingly, these words have not always been formed from the same stem, which reflects normal (P)IE linguistic variation and is not due to *completely new*, individual, local formation in one or the other IE language. Rather, the PIE variations in the name of the beech,[176] fir (and resin), and oak (see earlier) use the same roots and several of the available PIE suffixes. In other words, these cool climate, temperate trees and their names are already PIE.

If the indigenous theory of an emigration Out of India would apply, *one* or *two* typical "Indian" PIE (dialect) forms of tree names should have been taken and spread westwards, such as is the case with the two loans from Chinese, *chai* or *tea*. The opposite is the case. The individual IE languages have the *same* PIE word, or they have slightly innovated within the usual PIE parameters of ablaut and suffixes.

In short, whatever way one turns the evidence, all points to some original IE tree names of the temperate zone that were exported southwards. Some of them therefore exhibit a slight change in meaning; a few others possibly are applications of old, temperate zone names to newly encountered plants, such as 'willow' > 'reed, cane'. Again, this change in meaning indicates the path of the migration, from the temperate zone *into* India.

The countercheck, the search for Indian plant names in the west, such as lotus, bamboo, Indian trees (*aśvattha*, *bilva*, *jambu*, etc.), comes up with nothing. Such names are simply not to be found, also not in a new meaning[177] (see earlier Sections 11.16 and 11.23). The lack is significant, as the opposite case, import into South Asia, is indeed found. Again, this evidence points to an *introduction* of the IA language into India, not an export "*Out of India*."

The same kind of a scenario is found with the typical PIE animals; they, too, belong to a temperate climate. While some of them such as the wolf or bear occur in South Asia as well, albeit in slightly different species (such as the South Asian black bear), others are found, just as some of the tree names, only in new, adapted meanings. For example, the beaver is not found inside South Asia nowadays. It occurs, however, even now in Central Asia, its bones have been found in areas as far south as Northern Syria and in mummified form in Egypt, and it is attested in the Avesta (*baβri*),[178] which is related to the descriptive term, IE **bhebhru* 'brown, beaver.' This is widely attested: O. Engl. *bebr*, *beofor*, Lat. *fiber*, Lith. *bēbrus*, Russ. *bobr, bebr-* (Pokorny 1959: 136). The respective word in Vedic, *babhru(-ka)*, however, means 'brown, mongoose' (Nenninger 1993) as there is no Indian beaver. While the mongoose is not a water animal, some Indian types of mongooses vaguely look like a "beaver", and clearly, the IE/IIr term for "beaver" has been used, inside South Asia, to designate the newly encountered brown animal, the mongoose, cf. American Engl. *(mountain) lion* for *puma*. The mongoose occurs in the subcontinent, but in Greater Iran only in its southeastern-most corner, in Baluchistan.[179]

The opposite direction of the spread of the word, "Out of India," is not possible as it is not Ved. *babhru* (or Avest. *baβri*) that spread westwards (following Misra 1992), but its regular derivatives of the original (and traditional) IE source, **bhebhru*. The hypothetical export of Ved. *babhru* would have to suppose subsequent individual sound changes, mysteriously resulting in the various attested IE forms that simply cannot occur if one starts from Ved. *babhru*. The same applies to the meaning. All "emigrating" IEs would mysteriously have agreed to substitute the beaver for the Indian mongoose.[180]

Other South Asian animal names are not "exported" either. Occam's razor applies: all things being equal, it is easier to assume import into South Asia of animal names of the temperate zone.

All of the above is not favorable for an emigration scenario. Rather, PIE has a number of temperate/cold climate plants and animals which never existed in South Asia but which can be reconstructed for all/most of PIE; their names follow IE rules of word formation (root structure, suffixes etc.) and exhibit the typical formational possibilities of IE (ablaut, exchange of various suffixes).

A few of them that designate flora and fauna actually occurring inside South Asia have been retained in Ved. (such as bear *ṛkṣa*, wolf *vṛka*, otter *udra*, birch *bhūrja*, etc.) and their designations have been used for the *local* form of the animal or plant in question. But most of the IE plants and animals are *not* found in India and their designations have either been adapted for the animals or plants of a tropical climate (as is the case with the beaver > mongoose *babhru*, 'willow' > 'reed'), or they have simply *not* been used any longer and died out.

According to the autochthonous theory, these temperate climate, non-Indian plant and animal names would have to be new words that were coined only when the various IE tribes had already emigrated out of India. However, again, all of them are proper IE names, with IE roots and suffixes, and with proper IE word formation. It would require extraordinary special pleading to assume that they all were created *independently* by the various emigrant IE tribes, at different times, on different paths, but always from the *same* IE root in question and (often) with the *same* suffixes. How could these "emigrants" know or remember exactly which roots/suffixes to choose on encountering a new plant or animal? Occam's razor applies again, and the opposite assumption carries: IE words of the flora and fauna of the temperate zone were adapted to a tropical climate wherever possible. We see immigration into, instead of emigration "Out of India."

11.24 Summary of the evidence

On the whole, all of the linguistic data and the multitude of proposed or possible autochthonous scenarios based on them lead to the same kinds of *culs de sac* or *Holzwege*.

There is *no evidence* at all for the development of IE, IIr, and even of pre-OIA/Vedic *inside* the subcontinent. It is contradicted, among other items, by the Iranian and Mit. evidence. An *emigration* of the Iranians and other IEs[181] from the subcontinent, as supposed by autochthonists, is *excluded* by the linguistic evidence at large. To maintain an Indian homeland of IE, IIr, and Pre-OIA requires multiple special pleading of a sort and magnitude that no biologist, astronomer, or physicist would tolerate.

Simply put, *why should we allow special, linguistic pleading just in the case of India*? There is nothing in the development of human language in India that intrinsically differs from the rest of the world. Occam's razor applies.

So far, most of the linguistic evidence presented in the previous sections has been largely neglected by the autochthonists,[182] and if it has been marshaled at all, it has been done so *ad hoc*, in a monolateral fashion, and while disregarding linguistic counter evidence as well as the larger picture supplied by related sciences. This unfortunately is the case even with the lone, autochthonously minded Indian historical linguist, Misra. His *rewriting* of IE linguistics remains incidental and idiosyncratic, and it results in multiple contradictions, just as the rest of the theory. Autochthonists must do a lot of homework in trying to contradict the linguistic data discussed earlier (Sections 11.13–11.23) before they can hope to have any impact on linguistic discussions.

Conversely, the data derived from linguistic study are consistent throughout: they clearly indicate that an Eastern IE language, the Ved. branch of IIr, has been *Indianized* and has phonetically and grammatically *innovated after* its arrival in the Hindukush and the Panjab, while Iranian has escaped this influence as it did not enter the subcontinent then.

Exactly how the IA language *and* the *IA spiritual and material culture* of the archaeologically still little traced IA speaking tribes – as expected for people on the move! – was introduced, that is still an open and very much debated question. It can be traced securely, so far, only in the evidence coming from the texts (horses, chariots, religion, ritual, poetics, etc.), perhaps in the Gandhāra Grave

Culture (starting *c.*1700–1600 BCE, Allchin 1995: 50), and from the features of the language itself that have been discussed here at length. Possibly, genetic evidence, especially that deriving from studies of the male Y chromosome, may add to the picture in the near future. It indicates several major movement of bearers of the Y chromosome types IV, V, VI, and some later intrusions, such as types IX, X (Francalacci 2001).

11.25 The autochthonous theory in context

The autochthonous theory, in its various forms, leaves us with many *monolateral* assertions and, consequently, with multiple internal contradictions as far as time frame, cultural content, archaeological, zoological, astronomical, mathematical, linguistic, and textual data are concerned.[183] If such contradictions are noticed at all by the revisionist and autochthonist writers – Elst (1999); Frawley (1994); Klostermaier *et al.* (1997) do not! – they are explained away by new, auxiliary assumptions and theories, that is, by *special pleading*, and frequently by *extraordinarily* special pleading. In short, all things being equal, the new, disjointed Indocentric theory falls prey to Occam's razor.

If we would in fact assemble all the monolateral autochthonous "evidence" (as has been attempted here and in Witzel 2001b) and think it through, torturous as it may prove to be, we would have to rewrite not only Indian history, but also many sections of archaeology, historical linguistics, Ved. literature, historical geography, zoology, botany, astronomy, and so on. To apply the new Indocentric "theory" consistently would amount to a "paradigm shift" in *all* these fields of study. But biologists, for example, would not be amused. In other words: *why should there be "special rules" in all these sciences only as far as evidence from South Asia is concerned*?

Such features make the autochthonous theory particularly unfavorable as a replacement of earlier explanations.[184] A "paradigm shift" can be maintained, as has been shown time and again in the preceding sections, only by using very special pleading. If the model of a transhumance type immigration or trickling in of speakers of OIA, and subsequent steadily increasing acculturation, is to be replaced, then such a new revisionist/autochthonous model has not yet been found, and it has certainly not yet been shown to be probable. The burden of proof squarely rests on the shoulders of the advocates of the new autochthonous theory.

To conclude, even when neglecting some individual quirks,[185] the various autochthonous proposals simply do not present a coherent and cogent picture. Rather, they consist of monolateral, disjointed fragments, disproved by other evidence that is taken from the contemporaneous local context. They almost completely neglect the linguistic evidence, and they run into serious chronological and geographical difficulties: they have horse-drawn chariots in South Asia before their actual invention, horses in South Asia before their introduction from Central Asia. They have the use of iron tools at 1900 BCE before its first use at *c.*1200–1000 BCE. They have the Ṛgvedic Sarasvatī flowing to the ocean while the

RV indicates that it had already lost its main source of water supply and must have ended in a terminal lake (*samudra*), just like its East Iranian namesake, the *Harax^{v}a^{i}tī* which flows in to the Hamum Lake. They must also distort, against philology, the textual evidence of the RV to make it fit supposed Harappan fire rituals, the use of the script, a developed town civilization and its stratified society of traders and artisans, and international maritime trade. And, they must rewrite the literary history of the Vedas to fit in improbable, hoary dates for the composition of its texts, so that they agree with *supposed contemporary* astronomical *observations* – when everything else in these texts points to much later dates.[186]

Finally, they have the OIA, or even the IE Proto-language, developing in the Panjab or even further east in northern India while all non-IA[187] linguistic and historical evidence, including that of linguistic paleontology, clearly points to areas further northwest and west. They maintain, in Indocentric fashion, an Indian homeland for IE while the expected early South Asian loan words are entirely missing in all non-IA IE languages, including even the neighboring Old Iranian. Conversely, such loans are already copious in (Ṛg)Vedic and are traceable to South Asian substrate sources.

Curiously, even the alleged historical development of the Aryan "invasion theory" is not correct as it is usually narrated.[188] It was *not* developed and formulated in the nineteenth century to show that the Vedas were composed before the "Aryans" mixed with the indigenous "races" and to underline that the British conquest was similar to the "Aryan conquest." In fact, during the early period of IE linguistics the home of the IE language was thought, in the typical Romantic fashion of the day, to be in India or in innermost Asia. The concept of the IE language family, though first formulated, and not yet scientifically, by two late eighteenth-century British citizens (Lord Monboddo and William Jones), was *not* developed by British imperialists but by Danish and German scholars of the romanticism era, such as F. Bopp (1816); it was further developed in the later nineteenth century by German linguists such as the Leipzig *Junggrammatiker* school whose members had no interest at all in British imperial designs (cf. Kennedy 1995; Trautmann 1999). The theory of an immigration into or invasion of South Asia by speakers of IA, based on the familiar concept of the Hunnic and Germanic invasions of the Roman empire, and the idea of an IE "race" emerged only later in the nineteenth century and they were not even generally accepted; for example, the concept of an "Aryan race" was *rejected* by the now-maligned Oxfordian Indologist Max Müller (1888) or, at length, by the German Indo-Europeanist Hermann Hirt (1907).

Present day non-Indian scholars, however, no longer have any colonialist or "Eurocentric" agendas and scholars, anyhow, do not feel the need to defend "traditional" Western conclusions and theories of the nineteenth or twentieth centuries.[189] Present day "western scholarship" (which is not restricted to Occidental countries) is very much aware of its own historical situation and theoretical position; yet, it is firmly rooted, (postmodernism by and large excluded) in the enlightenment tradition.

Notwithstanding the internal social and political reasons for the clash between recent Indian historiography (locally, now often termed "Marxist") and the new wave of revisionist and nationalistic writing that culminates in the Indocentric "Out of India Theory," it is its very emergence and increasing popularity, as late as two generations after Indian independence, that must surprise. The revisionist Indocentric project, with the *exact* (*anti-colonialist*) *opposite*[190] of the "Aryan Invasion Theory," certainly is not guided by the principles of critical theory but takes, time and again, recourse to pre-enlightenment *beliefs* in the authority of traditional religious texts such as the *Purāṇas*. In the end, it belongs, as has been pointed out earlier,[191] to a different "discourse" than that of historical and critical scholarship. In other words, it continues the writing of religious literature, under a contemporary, *outwardly* "scientific" guise.[192]

The revisionist and autochthonous project, then, should not be regarded as *scholarly* in the usual post-enlightenment sense of the word, but as an apologetic, ultimately *religious* undertaking aiming at proving the "truth" of traditional texts and beliefs. Worse, it is, in many cases, not even scholastic scholarship but a *political* undertaking aiming at "rewriting" history out of national pride or for the purpose of "nation building" with "one people, one nation, one culture." *Am ind'schen Wesen soll die Welt genesen*?

If such writings are presented under a superficial veneer of objective scholarship they must be exposed as such,[193] at least in the context of critical post-enlightenment scholarship. Alternatively, they could simply not be taken seriously as historiography and could be neglected (which seems to be the favorite attitude of most scholars in Indology/Indian Studies). In both cases, however, they must be clearly *understood* and described as traditional, (semi-)religious writings. Therefore, they should be regarded and used, not as scholarly contributions, but as *objects for the study* of the traditional mind – uncomfortable as this might be for some of their proponents, many of whom combine, in facile fashion, an education in science with a traditional mindset.[194]

Now, more than fifty years after Indian independence, one would expect scholars to have gained some distance from colonial times and it should not be regarded as a *scholarly*, but simply as a political undertaking to "rewrite" history for the purpose of national pride or "nation building." We know to what such exercises have lead during the past century.

If the present wave of apologetic, revisionist, and nationalistic writing should continue unabated, and if it should remain unchecked by post-enlightenment scholarship, future historians will look back at these excesses of the end of the twentieth century and the beginning of the twenty-first century in the same way as some now like to do with regard to the nineteenth century. And they will criticize the present generation of scholars for having looked the other way – for whatever reason.

It remains for us to hope[195] that the recent spate of revisionist, autochthonous, Indocentric, and chauvinistic writings will not lead to similar, real life consequences as those that we have witnessed during the twentieth century.

Abbreviations

AV	Atharvaveda Saṃhitā
Avest.	Avestan
BŚS	Baudhāyana Śrautasūtra
DEDR	Burrow and Emeneau 1984
Drav.	Dravidian
EJVS	Electronic Journal of Vedic Studies (Boston, 1995–)
EWA	Mayrhofer 1956–76
Germ.	German
Grk	Greek
IA	Indo-Aryan
IE	Indo-European
IIr	Indo-Iranian
Iran.	Iranian
KEWA	Mayrhofer 1986–96
Lat.	Latin
Lith.	Lithuanian
MIA	Middle Indo-Aryan
Mit.	Mitanni
MT	Mother Tongue (Boston: ASLIP 1995–)
NIA	New Indo-Aryan
O. Engl.	Old English
OIA	Old Indo-Aryan
O. Iran.	Old Iranian
OP	Old Persian
O. Pers.	Old Persian
Osset.	Ossetic
PIE	Proto-IE
Pkt	Prakrit
RV	Ṛgveda Saṃhitā
Skt.	Sanskrit
Toch.	Tocharian
Ved.	Vedic
Ved. Index	Macdonell–Keith 1912

Notes

1 A first, 120 pp. version of this chapter has appeared in 2001 (*EJVS* 7–3) which may be consulted for many of the more technical details. Some very recent publications are necessarily not yet included for discussion in this update, such as the summary and discussion of the problem by E. Bryant 2001 or J. V. Day 2001. However, many of Bryant's points are already included here as we both have discussed them intensively at Harvard while he was preparing his book for publication. See also the recent, quite critical update by a *non*-occidental scholar, Toshiki Osada 2000 (in Japanese).

2 Due to consideration of space, this chapter is by and large restricted to linguistic features. For deliberations on texts, philology, archaeology, history, and the various natural sciences see Witzel *EJVS* 7–3, 2001b.

3 For details on texts, their localization and linguistic levels see Witzel 1987a, 1989, 1997.

4 Archaeological dates for iron had been creeping up over the last few decades; however, according to Possehl and Gullapalli 1999, and Agrawal and Kharakwal (in press) the introduction of iron in Northwest India is close to 1000 BCE. Occasional use of meteoric iron predates that of smelted iron.

5 For autochthonous dates, placing the RV thousands of years earlier, see later Section 11.13 sqq., n. 73. Talageri (2000, see later, n. 74) introduces traditional legendary data to achieve such hoary dates; for a critique, see Witzel 2001a.

6 See later Section 11.16, n. 111, on *vašana [važana]*, and *-az- > e.*

7 Maximally, but unlikely, 1900 BCE, the time of the disintegration of the Indus civilization. The IA influx must be pre-iron age (1200, or even 1000/900 BCE).

8 Max Müller had come to a similar chronology. Nowadays this is misrepresented by the autochthonists, especially Rajaram (1995), who accuses Müller to have invented this chronology to fit in with Bishop Usher's biblical calculations!

9 Y. Avest. *Bāxδī* 'Bactria', which corresponds to AV *bahlika*, indicates a lower limit for Zarathustra of *c.*1200–1000 BCE (Witzel 1980).

10 Tribal groups: Saka, Yue Ji (Tukhara, Kushana, Abhīra, Gurjara; large armies: Darius' Persians, Alexander's, and the Bactrian Greeks; Chinese via Tibet, Ladakh, and Nepal; Arabs to Sindh; Ahom Tai to Assam; Huns, Turks, Moghuls, Iranians, Afghans via the northwestern passes, and so on.

11 See Section 11.7. Constant interaction of "Afghan" pastoral highlanders and Indus plain agriculturists could have set off the process (see Witzel 2000). After the collapse of the Indus civilization, many of its people moved eastwards (Shaffer 1999), leaving much of the Indus plains free for IA style cattle breeding.

12 See Balkan 1954. However, many wrong data are found with the following authors: Elst (1999: 183), Rajaram and Frawley (1997: 123). (Kikkuli's) manual is not at all "written in virtually pure Sanskrit" (Rajaram and Frawley 1997: 123). Elst (1999: 184) has the [Aryan] Kassites immigrate "from Sindh to Southern Mesopotamia" as a "conquering aristocracy" in a "planned invasion." Actually, the Kassite language belongs to an altogether unknown language group (Balkan 1954). From what sources did these writers derive their innovative insights?

13 Speaking of other areas of Eurasia; in the case of South Asia, however, he thinks of elite dominance achieved through IA immigration/invasion.

14 *Nahalī*, a small IA language spoken on the Tapti river in Madhya Pradesh, has at successively "lower" levels of vocabulary, 9 percent Drav., 36 percent Korku (Munda), and some 24 percent without any cognates (Kuiper 1962: 50, 1966: 96–192; *Mother Tongue II-III*, 1996–97); these low-level words belong to the oldest language so far traceable in India (Witzel 1999a,b).

15 For example, England with numerous IE immigrations and invasions (Celts, Romans, Anglo-Saxons, Vikings, Danes, and Normans – and now Caribbeans and South Asians). There is a strong non-Indo-European substratum in English, with common words as *sheep*. All of Europe has been subject to the same kind of Indo-European "invasions," read: 'immigration and/or acculturation'.

16 That is, of the Bactria-Margiana area and even from further afield: river names (Witzel 1987a, 1999a,b; Hintze 1998), mountains and mountain passes, and tribal names. Such names retain pre-Old Iranian forms and all are aligned along the *expected* route of immigration *into* the subcontinent, from the northern steppes via Margiana/Bactria to Herat/Arachosia and Eastern Afghanistan. Individuals such as the great *Ṛṣi Vasiṣṭha* and his clan (RV 7.33.1–3), and whole tribes such as the *Bharata* and *Ikṣvāku* (*Jamin īya Brāhmaṇa* 3.327–8: Caland §204), are described as crossing the Sindhu or the

Satlej/Beas (RV 3.33). Later Vedic texts continue to report such movements; for details see Witzel 2001b. (Incidentally, nowhere in the Vedas do we hear of an out of India, *westward* movement (see n. 72; Section 11.12), as some "Out of India" proponents would have it nowadays). The Iranian textual materials on immigration are even more meager but they provide similar indirect reminiscences. However, *A^iriianąm Vaējah* (Vīdēvdād 1), usually understood as the "original" (northern, e.g. Choresmian) home of all *A^iriia* of the Avesta is "the best of all places and settlements" in the highlands of central Afghanistan (Witzel 2000), right in the center of all the "Iranian" lands of the Avesta, a region typical for transhumance pastoralism. *A^iriianąm Vaējah* is certainly *not* located inside India (Misra 1992: 39; Elst 1999: 197 sq.; Talageri 2000), nor does it have any bearing on the original home of all Iranians, or even of the speakers of Indo-Iranian (Witzel 2000).

17 Kuiper 1955, 1991; Thapar 1968; Southworth 1979, 1995; Witzel 1995.

18 Witzel 1987a, 1995. Talageri's claims (2000) of a hoary RV with some two thousand years of composition are impossible in any version of textual and linguistic history, see below, n. 74 and Witzel 2001a.

19 Based on the archaic suffix – *tu*, as in *gatvā*, a calque formed from the old IE stem – *tu* which then became fossile (*-tvī tum*, *tave*, etc.), see Kuiper 1967.

20 The speakers of IA and the local population must have interacted on a bilingual basis for a long period, *before* the composition of the present RV hymns with their highly hieratic, poetical speech (Kuiper 1991, 2000). A relative date can be inferred from Mitanni-IA (at *c.*1400 BCE), predating the extant RV (see Section 11.16).

21 Such as the absolutives, or the use of *iti* (Kuiper 1967); perhaps also some Prakrit-like forms (*jyotiṣ*, *muhur*, etc.) which have been disputed as such, see Kuiper 1991: 2, 27 sqq., 79; 2000, aan de Wiel 2000.

22 Rajaram, a scientist, engineer, and mathematician by training, speaks of "unproved conjectures" (1995: 219), etc., and regards comparative linguistics as "unscientific," – strange, for a science that can make correct *predictions*! See later, Section 11.10.

23 With the – only very partial – exception of Elst 1999 and Talageri 1993, 2000. Surprisingly, Talageri (1993: 205) finds that "the overwhelming majority of Sanskrit names for Indian plants and animals are derived from Sanskrit and Indo-European" (Bryant 1999: 74). A brief look into KEWA, EWA (Mayrhofer's "unclear" etc.), never used by him, would have convinced him of the opposite. But, linguistic arguments are "hairsplitting" (2000: 248, 299) or just "a linguistic ploy."

24 Especially when the underlying language is not one of the known ones (IA, Proto-Drav., Proto-Munda, Proto-Burushaski, etc.) but one of the unknown Gangetic languages (such as "Language X," Masica 1979) or from the Panjab-based prefixing Para-Munda language (Witzel 1999a,b); cf. Bryant 1999: 73.

25 In the heavily Anglicized *Massachusetts*, for example, place names such as *Massatoit*, *Massachusetts*, *Wachusetts*, *Montachusetts*, *Cohasset*, *Neponset*, *Mattapoisett*, *Mattapan*, *Mashpee*, *Chicopee*, *Nantucket*, *Pawtucket* are without English etymology and immediately recognizable.

26 Entirely misunderstood by those autochthonists (quoted by Bryant 1999: 72) who merely delight in pointing out the differences in etymological proposals by IE, Drav., or Munda proponents. Further, Drav. and Munda linguistics are not yet as developed as IE/IA. There always will be cases that *allow* multiple interpretation, even after application of the structural rules of IA/IE, Drav., Munda, described below; for details see Witzel forthc. a.

27 *Pace* the non-specialist, out of hand dismissal by Talageri 2000: 248, 299; see, rather, Anttila 1989: 156 for a detailed discussion.

28 With the exception of the onomatopoetic **kik* in 'magpie', Skt *kiki-* in *kikidīvi* (EWA 1349); **mag/meg* does not exist in IE.

29 C = consonant, M = voiced/mediae, T = unvoiced/tenues, R = resonants = *y/w/r/l/n/m*; not allowed are the types Rce- or Rse- (Skt **ṛka*, **usa*, etc.), and the types: **bed*, **bhet*,

tebh*, **pep*, **teurk/tekt* (Skt **bad*, *bhat*, *tabh*, *tork*). See Mayrhofer 1986: 95, Szemerényi 1970: 90 sqq. In short: (S) (T) (R) e (R) (T/S) where T = all occlusives, R = resonant; forbidden are M – M (bed*), M – T (**bhet*), T – M (**tebh*), same occl. in one root, such as: no **pep* (except **ses* 'to sleep'), final 2 occl. or final 2 sonants, no: **tewrk*, **tekt*; but *s-Teigh*, etc. are allowed.

30 The basic Drav. word structure (*ə* = long or short vowel) is (C)*ə*(C), and suffixes have the structure: -C, -C*ə*, -CC*ə*, -CCC*ə*; after a root -C the vowels *-a-*, *-i-*, or *-u* are inserted.

31 This contradicts those autochthonists (cf. Bryant 1999: 80) who simply reject the notion of an unknown (lost) language as a source. But it does not deter linguistic amateurs such as Talageri (1993: 200) who speaks of "a twilight zone of *purely hypothetical* non-existent languages."

32 IA etymologies are now discussed with a complete explanation of all of their constituent parts, of related roots and of suffixes employed. For the complexities of establishing a proper etymology see the thirty-six items in Hoffmann 1992: 761–66. However, the Drav. *DEDR* is only a list of related words without further explanation; a Munda etymological dictionary is only in collection stage, not to speak of other languages of the subcontinent.

33 Cf. the discussion by Bryant 1999: 75. If the IAs would have been autochthonous to the Greater Panjab, these "local" words should be IA, while in fact they are "foreign," non-IE/IA (see Witzel 1999a,b). It is quite a different problem (Bryant 1999: 76) that many plant names in IE do not have a clear etymon. Still, they are IE, IA in phonetics and *word structure* and as such, *inherited* from PIE into IA. PIE is of course not the "first language," and many such names (their "root") must have been inherited into PIE, from Nostratic, for example; still, they can be reconstructed for PIE and conform to its structure. Talageri (1993: 206) simply does not understand how the language developed over time, from pre-PIE to Iir, to IA, when declaring such words simply as Aryan colloquial or slang. *All remain within the fold!*

34 For the problems of the root *sā* 'to sow', *sītā* 'to furrow', *sīra* 'plough' see EWA II 733.

35 Details in Witzel 1999a, cf. Bryant 1999: 78. Significantly, there is a cluster of non-IA names in eastern Panjab and Haryana (including the local name of the Sarasvatī, (**Vi<šam>bal/ž!*), where the successor cultures of the Indus Civilization continued for a longer period of time.

36 Due to the surprising neglect by Iranists of etymological studies of Old Iranian (not to speak of Middle Iranian where we even do not have comprehensive dictionaries).

37 Witzel 1995, 1999a,b, in detail: forthc. b; Lubotsky, forthc; Bryant's proposal (1999: 77) that the non-IE loanwords in Iranian must come from the Proto-IIr that was spoken in Eastern Iran before the Iranians moved in cannot be substantiated. The individual P-Iran. and P-IA forms of such loans often differ from each other (Witzel 1999a,b, forthc. b, Lubotsky, forthc.) which is typical for repeated loans from a *third* source.

38 The remnants of the Huns, for example, have been found only recently in some Hungarian graves; otherwise we would only know about them from the extensive literary and historical record (and the name of "Hungary"). Similarly, the Huns in India are only known from historical records and from the survival of their name as *(Hara-)Hūṇa* in the Mahābhārata or *Hūṇ* in some Rajasthan clans and *Hūṇdeś*, just north of the Indian border, in Western Tibet.

39 For agriculture, Kuiper 1955, 1991; for washing, Witzel 1986, and especially for pottery, Rau 1983.

40 However, with sponsors of sacrifice that bear strange names: *Vayiyu*, *Prayiyu*. One may also think of part of the assemblage of the Cemetery H culture of the Panjab.

41 Some archaeologists simply restrict themselves to report the findings of archaeology and *intentionally* neglect all the linguistic and spiritual data of the texts; in fact, some denounce them as "linguistic tyranny" (Shaffer 1984). This is not helpful in approaching a *complete* picture of the early history of the subcontinent.

42 J. Lukacs asserts unequivocally that no significant population changes took place in the centuries prior to 800 BC; see now Kennedy 1995, 2000.

43 The remnants of the Harappan Cemetery H people etc., all are physically very close to each other, while the people of Mohenjo Daro stand somewhat apart. "Aryan bones" have not been found. (Kennedy 1995, 2000; cf. Meadow 1991, 1998; Meadow and Patel 1997).

44 Similarly, Anthony and Vinogradov (1995);

> Language shift can be understood best as a social strategy through which individuals and groups compete for positions of prestige, power, and domestic security...a linkage between language and access to positions of prestige and power... A relatively small immigrant elite population can encourage widespread language shift among numerically dominant indigenes in a non-state or pre-state context if the elite employs a specific combination of encouragements and punishments. Ethnohistorical cases...demonstrate that small immigration and concurrent language takeover is absent, the texts often allow such deductions, e.g. for Mesopotamia.
>
> (W. von Soden 1985: 12)

45 Aurobindo, Waradpande 1993; Kak 1994b, etc., see Elst 1999: 119; Talageri 2000: 406 sqq.; Lal 1997: 281 sqq.

46 S. S. Misra 1974, 1992, 1999; Talageri 1993, 2000; Frawley 1994; Elst 1999; Klostermaier 1989, 1997, 1998, 2000 etc.

47 For summaries see Hock 1999; Talageri 2000. The exact opposite is seen in deriving Skt. from Arabic in a book published in Pakistan: Mazhar 1982.

48 The list of such internet and printed publications waxes by the month. There now exists a closely knit, self-adulatory group, churning out long identical passages, copied in cottage industry fashion. A "canonical" list would include, among others: Choudhury 1993; Elst 1999; Danino 1996; Feuerstein *et al.* 1995; Frawley 1994; Kak 1994a,b; Klostermaier (in Rajaram and Frawley 1997) 1998, 2000; Misra 1992; Rajaram 1993, 1995; Rajaram and Frawley 1995, 1997; Rajaram and Jha 2000; Sethna 1981, 1989, 1992; and Talageri 1993, 2000, where Choudhury stands somewhat apart by his *extreme* chauvinism. They and others frequent the internet with letters and statements ranging from scholarly opinions and prepublications to inane accusations, blatant politics, and hate speech; such ephemeral "sources" are not listed and discussed here.

49 Nobody explains *when* that should have been, after the exodus from Africa now put at 50000 BCE.

50 Elst disingeneously insists on calling any migration or even a "trickling in" an "invasion." However, immigration/trickling in and acculturation obviously are entirely different from a (military) invasion, or from overpowering and/or eradicating the local population. Incidentally, the idea of *Indra* destroying the "fortification walls" of the Indus towns was not created by Wheeler but his collaborator at the time, V. S. Agrawal (Witzel 2001b).

51 The underlying but unexpressed assumption is that late Neolithic Baluchistan is somehow typical or instrumental for all of subcontinental civilization of the following millennia. While the origin of wheat agriculture in the Indus Valley is to be sought in the eastern hills of the Baluchistan/Afghanistan ranges, the South (millet, see Science Magazine, Volume 294, 2 November 2001: 989) and the East (rice) stand apart in this and in many other aspects of early culture. The famed "continuity" thus is only a very partial one. Then, as now, the subcontinent was a mosaic of cultures.

52 Talageri, though mentioning the value of linguistics (2000: 415), merely compares some words in look-alike, Nirukta fashion, without any apparent linguistic background. Elst is better prepared philologically and linguistically, yet still lacks linguistic sophistication and his linguistic evaluation (1999: 118 sqq. 137) is lacuneous; instead, we find numerous speculations of when and how the *hypothetical Indian* IEs emigrated from India.

53 His (only?) trip to an international meeting in Dushanbe in 1977, duly noted in the introduction to his 1992 book, provided him with some contacts, unfortunately not always the right ones, see his rather uncritical use of Harmatta's materials (Section 11.13, n. 95). At this time, however, he still advocated a (more or less) conventional time scheme (Drobyshev 1978: 89–90) with PIE at 5000–3500 BCE, "Satem stage" 3500–2000, IA 2500–2000, ancient IA languages 2000–1000, middle IA languages 1000–200 BCE. His "conversion" to an Indocentric view came only in 1992 (see Section 11.13 sqq.).

54 Bryant (1999) reports that he found, already in 1994–95, that a majority of Indian scholars "had rejected the Aryan invasion/migration completely, or were open to reconsider it."

55 However, one should also not confound the autochthonous theories of the past two centuries (Dayanand Sarasvati, B. B. Tilak, etc.) with the present wave of Indigenism.

56 The only exception so far is a thin book by the Indian linguist S. S. Misra (1992) which bristles with inaccuracies and mistakes (see later), and some, though incomplete discussion by Elst (1999). Elst (PhD Leuven, Belgium) typically delights, in his "Update" (1999), in speculating about an Indian *Urheimat* of IE and a subsequent emigration, with "Indian" invasions of Europe, neglecting that linguistic (and other) data speak against it, see Hock 1999 and Section 11.15 sqq. (and cf. n. 81!). Others such as Rajaram (1995: 144, 217, 2000 *passim*) or Waradpande (1993), though completely lacking linguistic expertise, simply reject linguistics as "a petty conjectural pseudo-science" with "none of the checks and balances of a real science." They overlook the fact that a good theory *predicts*, for example, in predicting pre-Greek *k^w or the IE laryngeals (see Section 11.10); both of which have been shown to be correct upon discovery of new languages (Mycenean Greek, Hittite).

57 This has been tradition ever since the *Brāhmaṇa* texts (*Rudra* from *rud* 'to cry', *putra* from the nonexistent word **put* 'hell', *bhairava* from *bhī+rav+vam*, etc.).

58 Even within ten years, according to a recent East Coast study; or note that speakers of (educated) London English early in the twentieth century pronounced 'but' as [bət], now as [bʌt], or more recently, 'has' [hæz] as [hāz], etc.

59 Or the unattested, early Greek/pre-Greek *k^w, which was discovered in writing when Mycenean Greek was deciphered in 1952, see earlier.

60 Though Talageri (2000) even refuses the link of Vedic with Iranian.

61 As will be seen later (Section 11.18), there are a number of features of Old Iranian (such as lack of typical South Asian substrate words, Section 11.16 sqq.) which actually *exclude* an Indian origin. Such data have not been discussed yet, in scholarly fashion, by the autochthonists.

62 Generally, against its use, Zimmer (1990) and cf. Cowgill (1986: 66–8); but note its usefulness, when not used in single or isolated cases but in larger context, such as in the discussion of plants and animals (Section 11.23).

63 Waradpande 1989; Kak 1994b; Talageri 2000, etc.; discussion in Bryant 1999, cf. Elst 1999.

64 Note, for example, the discussion among scientists about the *various* paleo-channels of the Sarasvatī (Sarsuti-Ghaggar-Hakra), in Radhakrishnan and Merh (1999), or the first appearance of the horse in South Asia (Meadow 1998), both discussed in Witzel 2001b.

65 Such absolute skepticism is always welcome as a hermeneutic tool; but, it has to be relativized: one may maintain that linguistic paleontology does not work (Zimmer 1990), but how then is it that IE words for plants and animals *consistently* point to a temperate, not a tropical climate and to a time frame *before* the use of iron, chariots, etc.? The few apparent inconsistencies can be explained easily (e.g. "elephant," etc., see later n. 127, 149).

66 Elst 1999: 159 sq. stresses, like many other autochthonists, that "India was the best place on earth for food production" and that "a generous country like India must have

had a large population," both unsubstantiated articles of faith. The Indus Valley has only gradually been settled from the Baluchi/Afghani hills, and the Gangetic plain remained very sparsely settled for much longer. (Cf. also the negative description of the Panjab by Eastern Iranians, in Vīdēvdād, see n. 52). For Elst, however, "the ancient Hindus colonized the world" while India in reality, by and large, has been a *cul de sac*. Autochthonists also wonder why a "large population" could take over IA language(s) brought in by a few tribes. They should note, for example, that a trade language, the coastal Swahili, by now covers most of Eastern Africa (largely, without Islamization!).

67 In fact, most of the factors just mentioned were *not* present during the early Ved. period which saw the introduction and spread of IA all over the Greater Panjab.

68 For details see later; for example, note that even the typical Panjab features of climate and geography would not agree with a supposed "tropical" PIE language in the Gangetic Basin (see Section 11.22). For the distribution of prehistoric languages in India see rather Witzel 1999a,b, 2001b.

69 That is "the Dravidian languages being spoken in the south, Austric in the east, the Andamanese languages in the Andaman Islands, the Burushaski language in Northern Kashmir, Sino-Tibetan languages in the Himalayan and far eastern border areas, and the IE languages certainly in more or less their present habitat in most of northern India."

70 He continues: "where they differentiated into three groups: the Pūrus (in the Punjab), the Anus (in Kashmir) and the Druhyus (in the northwest and Afghanistan)"; cf. Talageri 1993: 196, 212, 334, 344–5; 2000: 328, 263.

71 Talageri 1993: 407 "... major sections of Anus... developed into the various Iranian cultures. The Druhyus spread out into Europe in two installments."

72 Actually, based on one misrepresented passage given by Talageri 1993: 368 and 2000: 260 sq., typical for several autochthonists, twice in *untranslated* form, which makes it easy to impute any meaning desired, in case: a "first historical emigration... of the Druhyu into the areas to the north of Afghanistan (i.e. into Central Asia and beyond)." See, with variants, *Brahmāṇḍa* 2.74.11, *Brahma* 13.152, *Harivaṃśa* 1841, *Matsya* 48.9, *Vāyu* 99.11, cf. also *Viṣṇu* 4.17.5, *Bhāgavata* 9.23.15, (see Kirfel 1927: 522): *Pracetasaḥ putraśataṃ rājānaḥ sarva eva te // Mlecchарāṣṭrādhipāḥ sarve udīcīm diśam āśritāḥ*, which means *not* that these '100'(!) kings conquered the "northern countries" way beyond the Hindukush or Himalayas, but that all these '100' sons of Pracetās (a descendant of a 'Druhyu'), kings of Mleccha kingdoms, are 'adjacent' (*āśrita*, or 'inhabiting') to the mountainous "northern direction," – which since the Vedas and *Pāṇini* has signified Greater *Gandhāra* and its many local "Rājas" of one valley or the other (Dir, Swat, Bannu, etc.); *contra* Witzel 2001a.

73 "The first series of migrations, of the Druhyus, took place... with major sections of Druhyus migrating northwards from Afghanistan into Central Asia in different waves. From Central Asia many Druhyu tribes, in the course of time, migrated westwards, reaching as far as western Europe. These migrations must have included the ancestors of the following branches... a. Hittite. b. Tocharian. c. Italic. d. Celtic. e. Germanic. f. Baltic. g. Slavonic. ... The second series of migrations of Anus and Druhyus,... took place much later, in the Early Period of the Rigveda [*sic!*], with various tribes migrating westwards from the Punjab into Afghanistan, many later on migrating further westwards as far as West Asia and southwestern Europe. These migrations must have included the ancestors of the following branches (which are mentioned in the Dāśarājña battle hymns [Nothing of this is actually found in the battle hymn, RV 7.18, and is pure fantasy based on 'P.N. Oak type' etymologies such as *Alina* = *Hellenes*, – MW]: a. Iranian. b. Thraco-Phrygian (Armenian). c. Illyrian (Albanian). d. Hellenic. Talageri, thankfully, even has the solution of the enigma of the Indus language (Parpola 1994; Witzel 1999a,b): "The Indus Valley culture was a mixed culture of Pūrus and Anus" (1993: 408), in his view, Ved. and Iranian speaking people.

74 Luckily for us, the author names his two main sources: the *Purāṇas* and the Ṛgveda. The reliability of *Purāṇic* and Epic sources is discussed above (Witzel 2001a,b, 1995, 1990), and the RV does not support his theory either: it simply does not know of, or refer to central and eastern Northern India. Talageri achieves such evidence by twisting the facts his way, see the discussion of Jahnāvī, n. 90, Witzel 2001a.

75 Of course, one of the basic requirements of philology (Witzel 1995, 1997). But Talageri's analysis of the RV (2000) is based on two extraneous facts: the post-Ṛgvedic list (of late Vedic times) of authors (*Ṛṣi*) of the RV hymns and the contemporaneous (Late *Brāhmaṇa*) arrangement of the RV hymns by *Śākalya*. His results, consequently, do not reflect the Ṛgvedic but the Late Vedic situation of, say, 500 BCE (Witzel 2001a), though he refuses to concede the point. Typically, he does not know of the seminal work of the young Oldenberg 1888.

76 The Ganges is only mentioned twice in the RV, once directly in a late hymn (10.75.5), and once by a derived word, *gāṅgya* in a late addition (6.45.31).This occurs in a *tṛca* that could be an even later addition to this *additional* hymn, which is too long to fit the order of the arrangement of the RV, see Oldenberg 1888.

77 The context of the RV rivers Sarayu and Gomatī sometimes – based on medieval and modern sources – mentioned in secondary literature as of the Ganges Doāb, is one of the western hills and mountains, in Afghanistan (Witzel 1987a:193, 1999, 2001a,b).

78 Note Mbh 1.3722 etc., son of *Ajamīḍha*, his daughter = *Gaṅgā*. – *Jāhnāvī* at Mbh 3.8211; *Jāhnava* at *Pañcaviṃśa Brāhmaṇa* 22.12; cf. *Jahnu*'s descendants at *Aitareya Brāhmaṇa* 7.18, *Āśvalāyana Śrautasūtra* 12.14, = '*Gaṅgā*' at *BhGītā* 10.31, *Viṣṇu* Pur. 398; cf. Keith and Macdonell, *Vedic Index*.

79 Such an "ancestral goddess", next to *Hotrā*, *Bhāratī*, *Iḍā* and *Sarasvatī*, is seen at RV 2.1.11, etc. That Jahnāvī refers to a river, the Ganges (Witzel 2001a), is an Epic/*Purāṇic* conceit. The word can simply be derived from that of the *Jahnu* clan.

80 Note that the center of settlement in RV 3 is the eastern Panjab and the Sarasvatī area of Haryana, see Witzel 1995: 320.

81 See Keith and Macdonell 1912. Settlement in Kashmir by any Ṛgvedic tribe is very doubtful, see Witzel 1994; in the later *Brāhmaṇa* period, Uttara-Madra (however, *not* as often asserted, Uttara-Kuru) *may* refer to Kashmir. As a curiosity, it might be added, that we would expect tribal names such as Druhyu (or Anu) in Europe, but we only find correspondences meaning "ghost" and "apparition" (Pokorny 1959: 276).

82 However, the Sarasvatī is the political center in the later RV, in Sudās' time. This common attitude is reflected in Manu's concept of *madhyadeśa* (> mod. Nepali *mades* 'Gangetic lowlands'), in ancient and modern China (*zhong guo*, 'the middle land'), etc. In ritual, too, one often regards one's own location as the center of the universe.

83 Witzel 1987a, 1989, 1997. However, the "north," *Gandhāra* and *Uttara-Madra*, (Uttara-Kuru?) are always excluded from such denigration, see Witzel 1989: 101. The Panjabis, however, have been regarded as outsiders since the AV and *Śatapatha Brāhmaṇa*; *Patañjali's Mahābhāṣya* has preserved the oldest "Sikh joke," *gaur bāhīkaḥ* "the Panjabi is an ox."

84 Mellowed somewhat with regard to eastern North India (*Aitareya Brāhmaṇa* 7.18), where the *Andhra*, *Puṇḍra*, *Śabara*, *Pulinda*, etc. are – ahistorically – included as *Viśvāmitra's* sons (Witzel 1997).

85 If this BŚS passage is understood as indicating a Panjab center; for details see Witzel 2001b (EJVS 7–3 and 7–4).

86 See earlier, n. 71 (*contra* Witzel 2001a, cf. n. 42, 86).

87 Note that the Pashtos, in spite of the East Iranian language and some still clearly visible aspects of pre-Muslim IIr culture, claimed to be one of them – The Gypsies (Roma), who actually *have* emigrated from India, rather claim origins in Southern Iraq (Ur!) or Egypt.

88 See his 1993 book "*Aryan Invasion Theory and Indian Nationalism.*"

89 He has written another small book in 1999 (_The Date of the Rigveda and the Aryan Migration: Fresh Linguistic Evidence_) as an answer to Hock (1999); this is not yet available to me. From the excerpts that I have seen it seems that he continues with incidental, _ad hoc_ rewriting of the IE linguistic picture, as discussed below.

90 This familiar "principle" used in deciding the _Urheimat_, (Witzel 2000, and later, Section 11.21 sqq.) is: "the homeland is _at_, or _close to_ the homeland of the author of the book in question." Talageri introduces late Vedic and _Purāṇic_ concepts (see n. 73, 78; cf. Witzel 2001a); not surprisingly, then, the outcome is a Gangetic homeland.

91 Written before I heard of the author's demise. I am sorry that he can no longer reply to the following points. However, as his book has been quoted in virtually every autochthonously minded publication it is important to point out the facts.

92 Note that Talageri's new book (2000) largely restates Misra (who in part restates Aiyar), with the addition of Epic-_Purāṇic_ legends, and thus is a cottage industry exploitation of a now popular trend.

93 Adding, for example, "...The Greeks were invaders and came to Greece from outside...there was a vast substratum of pre-Greek languages...before the Hittite invasion to the area [Turkey] it was peopled by another tribe called Hattic...the Hittite speakers might have gone there in very early days from an original home (which was perhaps India)...The Slavonic people...were invaders...at the expense of Finno-Ugrian and Baltic languages...."

94 Presented at the Dushanbe conference (Asimov 1978) and reprinted in Harmatta 1992: 360–7. Surprisingly, the _historian_ Harmatta is called by Misra "one of the leading Indo-Europeanists." His paper has been used uncritically by many autochthonists who cannot judge such linguistic materials.

95 For example, the development _is_ > _iš_, which is already E. IE (Slavic, IIr, etc.) has been placed at 2000 BCE (as _iś_!), that is 600 years later than the closely related changes _rs_ > _rš_, _ks_ > _kš_, and the same development _appears again_ as PIIr _iś_ > _iš_ at 1700 BCE.

96 Such as Harmatta's FU *_aja_ 'to drive, to hunt', *_porc'as_, _porśas_ 'piglet', *_oc'tara_ 'whip', *_c'aka_ 'goat', *_erśe_ 'male', *_reśme_ 'strap', *_mekše_ 'honey bee', *_mete_ 'honey' (from Harmatta's stages 1–7). Most of the acceptable evidence of Harmatta falls right into the P-IIr period, with the development of PIE labiovelars to velars: *k^w, k^wh, g^w, g^wh > _k_, _kh_, _g_, _gh_, clearly seen in PFU *_werkas_ 'wolf' < PIIr *_vṛka-s_ < PIE *_wḷ_k^w_o-s_ (which Misra takes as RV Sanskrit!) About the same time, the PIE *_k'_, _k'h_, _g'_, _g'h_ developed to _c'_, _c'h_, _j'_, _j'h_. This stage is clearly seen in the _majority_ of the loans into PFU, for example, in *_porc'as_ 'piglet'. The various representations of PIIr *_a_ by PFU _e_, _ä_, _o_, _a_ will be treated elsewhere (Witzel, forthc. a, see Rédei 1987).

97 The older [t^s] is still found in modern Nuristani, e.g. _du.c._ [dut^s] < PIIr _dac'a_ < PIE _dek'ś_, but not in the _linguistically already younger_, but actually around 3,000 years old, forms Ved. _daśa_, O. Iran. _dasa!_

98 Conversely, there is comparatively little FU in IE, not uncommon in a situation of predominant cultural flow from one side. The reason for the early occurrence of word for bee (FU *_mekše_) and honey (PIE *_medhu_) may lie elsewhere, in the usefulness of bee's wax to produce _cire perdue_ metal products, which seem to be earlier in the Taiga woodlands than in the steppes and even further south (Sherratt, forthc.) However, these contacts were not as unilateral as usually depicted. The Northern Iranian, Ossetic, for example, has a number of Permian (Wotyak) words, for example, those meaning 'silver, payment/tax, pawn/rent, pay-off/bribery, fir tree, eyebrow, forehead' (Rédei 1987: 38).

99 A detailed study of Misra's data from the Gypsy (Romani) language is beyond the scope of the present discussion. It is not correct to simply say that MIA _a_ has changed to _e_ in an originally open syllable (in MIA, OIA) and in a non-open syllable remaining _a_: the archaic Balkan Romanes has _kar-_, _karáv_ etc. "to do" (from _karomi_). Romani cannot be used as a parallel to show that PIE _a_, _e_, _o_ derives from an older _a_ (Misra 1992: 81), see Hock 1999; Witzel 2001b.

100 The very idea of a "pan-Indian Prakrit" is, of course, a *contradictio in se*. As any beginner in Sanskrit or linguistics knows, *Prākṛta* always refers to Middle Indo-Aryan that followed the Old India Aryan (Vedic) stage.

101 With the then usual conflation of outward appearance or "race," ethnicity, and language (contra: Hirt 1907), he found that his native people, the Bengalis, and the inhabitants of his new home, Pondicherry, were not so different after all, and that Sanskrit and Tamil tongues may have been two divergent families derived from one "lost primitive tongue."

102 Rumanian from the Western IE Vulgar Latin; Bulgarian, Macedonian, and Serbian from the Eastern IE Southern Slavic; Greek from the Western IE Old Greek; Albanian from the vague Illyrian/Dalmatian (etc.) subfamily; one should probably add Romani (Romanes, the language of the Balkan Gypsies derived from the MIA form of the IIr subfamily), all are much more different from each other than even modern Iranian and IA.

103 For (further) details on the South Asian *Sprachbund* or linguistic area or convergence area, it is useful to consult Hock (1986: 491–512) though it is largely devoted to syntax; cf. also Hock 1996.

104 Nostratic, or Greenberg's *Eur-Asiatic*, are another matter, but even these new theories still do not turn Drav. and IE into Meso-/Neolithic neighbors *inside* India.

105 The situation, thus, is not unlike that of modern Europe: with Uralic (Finnish, Estonian, Hungarian, etc.), Basque, Altaic (Turkish, and the Mongolian Kalmyk), Arabic (Malta), and various Caucasus languages, while the rest, the majority, is IE speaking.

106 The same applies to Austronesian, with a very dense grouping in Taiwan (and then in South East Asia), but with the wider spread of just one subfamily, Polynesian, all across the Pacific. Elst 1999: 126 sq. points, as "proof" for his Indian *Urheimat* of IE, to some other, asymmetric expansions.

107 With the exception of the early "emigrant," the western-type Centum language Tocharian, which actually is the easternmost IE language, in China (Xinjiang); its speakers might have moved even further east after the Centum/Satem split. We can now add the western IE Bangani substrate in the high H.P. Himalayas which is sometimes close to but by no means identical with Tocharian; its ancient speakers may have crossed the Himalayas from the *north* (Xinjiang) and may originally have occupied just the northernmost, alpine pastures part of the H.P. valleys, a situation often found in other high mountain areas.

108 Thracian, Dacian in the Balkans; Hittite, Luwian, etc. in Anatolia; and probably several lost languages in Southern Russia/Ukraine as well (Cimmerian?).

109 The center *may* therefore have been situated somewhere between Greek, Hittite, Armenian in the South and Slavic, (North) Iranian (Scythian, Saka, etc.) in the north, in other words, in the Greater Ukraine; cf. discussion by Nichols (1997, 1998).

110 Elst (1999) includes a long chapter on links of IE with other language families, with a curious mixture of correct and incorrect data (Witzel 2001b), for example, p. 141: Ved. *paraśu* "axe" is not from Mesop. *pilakku* "spindle" (see EWA II: 87, which he surprisingly does not use!), or (p. 145) the logically/linguistically even more surprising statement that, because Drav. and Munda happen to be *attested later* than Vedic, there is no reason to assume early borrowing from these languages into Ved. (as if these languages did not have their own long prehistory, just as Ved.)! He may not regard himself as an OIT theorist but he constantly reflects and advocates this attitude in his writings (see n. 11, 65, 105, 140, 154, 179); for example, he has a curious speculation of a Manu who would have led his "Indo-Europeans" upstream on the Ganges toward the Panjab, ending with (p. 157): "India as a major demographic growth centre from which IE (*sic*!) spread to the north and west and Austronesian to the southeast as far as Polynesia." If this is not autochthonist and Indocentric, what is?

111 Brentjes' pointing to the peacock motif in Mitanni times art (Drobyshev 1978: 95) is a very weak argument (Schmidt 1980: 45 sq.) The Sumerians imported many items from India (Possehl 1996b) and the peacock motif is attested in Mesopotamia well before the Mitannis.

112 Note *-zd-* in *Priyamazdha* (*Bi-ir-ia-ma-aš-da*, Mayrhofer 1979: 47; in Palestine, cf. *Priya-aśva: bi-ir-ia-aš-šu-va*): Ved. *priyamedha*: Avest. *-mazdā*. Or, note retention of IIr *ai* > Ved. *e* (*aika: eka* in *aikavartana*), and retention of *j'h* > Ved. *h* in *vašana(š)šaya* of 'the race track' = [*važhanasya*] cf. Ved. *vāhana-* (EWA II 536, Diakonoff 1971: 80; Hock 1999: 2). Mit. IA also shares the Ṛgvedic and Avest. preference for *r* (*pinkara* for *piṅgala, parita* for *palita*).

113 Thus also Cowgill 1986: 23. Note that Ved. has *eva* "only" < *aiva* = O.Iran. *aiva* "one", and that only MIr. (not O. Iran.) has *ēvak* 'one', with the commonplace MIr. suffix *-ka*.

114 Mayrhofer 1979: 53; cf. RV *maṇi*, Avest. *maⁱni*, Elam. O.P. **bara-mani*, Latin *monīle*, etc.; cf. also Varuṇa as *Uruna*, and Ved. *sthūṇā*, Avest. *stūnā/stunā*, O.P. *stūnā*, Saka *stunā*.

115 Varuṇa (EWA II 515 *a-ru-na, ú-ru-wa-na*, not found in Iran); Mitra (Avest. Miϑra, Mit. *mi-it-ra*); Indra (Mit. *in-da-ra/in-tar*, Avest. *Iṇdra*, see Mayrhofer 1979: 53; *in-tar-ú-da, en-dar-ú-ta* in Palestine, fifteenth century BC; cf. Cowgill 1986: 23); *Indra* is marginalized in Iran; the *Nāsatya* (*na-ša-ti-ya-an-na* = *Aśvin*, Avest. *Nåŋhaiϑiia*. Note also the Hittite *Agniš* (cf. Avest. *dāštāγni*, Ved. *Agni*) another Mit.(-type) import (Mayrhofer 1979: 36, 51: *a-ak-ni-iš*).

116 Contained in names such as *Artasmara* (*ar-ta-aš-šu-ma-ra*), *Artadhāman* (*ar-ta-ta-a-ma*); Mayrhofer 1979: 54 sqq., Cowgill 1986: 23.

117 See now Witzel forthc. b, Staal 2001, Thompson, forthc. (3rd ESCA Harvard Round Table).

118 Kikkuli's book: *bapru-nnu:* Ved. *babhru, binkara-nnu*: Ved. *piṅgala, baritta-nnu*: Ved. *palita*, with Ṛgvedic *-r-* instead of later *-l-*, Mayrhofer 1979: 32, 52–3, cf. Cowgill 1986: 23.

119 One to nine "turns": *a-i-ka-, ti-e-ra-, pa-an-za-, ša-at-ta-, na-a-[w]a-wa-ar-ta-an-na = [aika-, tri-, panca-, satta-* (see later, n. 120), *nava-vartana]*; cf. *tušratta/tuišer-atta* = RV *tveṣaratha.*

120 Elst sees a confirmation of his belief that the RV is of hoary pre-Indus vintage, with subsequent post-Ṛgvedic Prakrit forms in 1400 BCE. MIA forms in the RV, however, are constantly questioned and further reduced, note *jyotiṣ* < **dyaut-is* (C. aan de Wiel 2000).

121 Friedrich 1940; Cowgill 1986: 23; Diakonoff 1971: 81; this is under discussion again, but clearly a Hurrite development: "E. Laroche, *Glossaire de la langue hourrite*:... *šittanna*... comments: "... 'sept', d'après l'indo-arien *šatta-wartanna*. – Forme de *šinti/a*??" S.v. *šinti*$_2$ he says: "Mais *šinti* 'sept' doit encore être séparé... de *šitta*." He also lists a word *šittaa* (long a) from two (Hittite?) Kizzuwadna texts." (pers. comm. by Bjarte Kaldhol, Nov. 5, 2000).

122 Incidentally, this would be *eastern* MIA(!), such as *Māgadhī* (which, however, does not agree with the extreme Rhotacism of Mit.-IA but has *l* everywhere!); western North India has retained *v-*, see Masica 1991: 99 sq. – Other "MIA" features are due to the writing system (*in-da-ra*, etc.); Misra, instead, sees MIA and even NIA. Norman, too, erroneously points to *pt* > *tt (satta)* and a labialization of *a* > *u* after *v* (**ašvasani* > *aššuššanni*), see however, Mayrhofer 1979: 52.

123 The following passage without comment:

> In ancient times in India such *ṛṣis* were very powerful. They were great teachers, researchers, philosophers and scientists. If Agastya had some power he might have helped in bringing down the abnormal height of the Vindhya mountains which created a lack of contact of North and South. Thus, at least this much is likely that due to some factor the height of the Vindhya mountains became

> abnormally high, so that the path for contact of North and South was blocked and due to the growth of population the people in the North had to spread, naturally farther North. They used the routes like the Khyber pass and left it and lost all contact and were finally lost to their people... as a result the Aryans had to go outside to North-West through the Himalayan passes and this consequently was responsible for the spread of Indo-European language family to the outside world.
>
> (Misra 1992: 70)

Is this linguistics, prehistory, a 'scientific' *Mahā-Bhārata*? Or rather just a reverse, Indocentric version of O. Rosenberg's *Myth of the Twentieth Century*?

124 Explained as 'sun god', "*Šamaš*," Mayrhofer 1979: 32; cf. also the war god *Maruttaš* = *Marut-*, and king *Abirattaš* = *Abhiratha;* for details see Balkan 1954: 8.

125 Note, however, *timiraš* = Skt. *timira-* 'dark', cf. Balkan 1954: 29, also 1954: 27 *laggatakkaš* = *lakta* red?

126 The names of some early IA immigrants, according to Harmatta (1992: 374) at *c*.2300–2100 BCE, A-ri-si(< sa')-en = *Arisaina* and *Sa-um-si*(< sa')-en = *Saumasena*, are based on *wrong* interpretations of common Hurrian words (Bjarte Kaldhol, Nov. 6, 2000, see Witzel 2001b).

127 Similarly, the Northern Iran *Parna* (Grk. *Parnoi*, Ved. *Paṇi*) and *Dasa/Dāsa* ~ Avest. (*Aži*) *Dahāka*, ~ Ved. *dāsa Ahīśu*, Lat. *Dahi*, Grk. *Daai*, Avest. *Dåŋha* (:: *Airiia*, cf. Dahae:: Arii), would have escaped their supposed *Panjab* IA enemies (RV *Dasa*, *Dasyu*, *Paṇi*:: *ari*, *Arya*, *Ārya*) northwards well *before* the time of the RV, for example, as *Parna*, still *without* retroflexion and accompanying loss of *-r-*. But, the *Paṇi* occur already in the RV, significantly *not* as real life but already as *mythical* enemies and already *with* retroflexion, while the RV authors are supposed by autochthonists not to know *anything* beyond the Panjab and Uttar Pradesh: multiple contradictions emerge.

128 The map in Parpola 1994 includes Tibetan, but this development is late, and typical for the Lhasa dialect. However, Khotanese Saka, just north of the Pamirs, has retroflexes.

129 But, this does not work vice versa: some of those who move out of India, sooner or later, loose it. However, if this would be taken as proof of OIT, this particular development *cannot* explain words such as Ved. *voḍhar-* which *cannot* turn into Iran. *vaštar-*, Latin *vector*, etc. (see n. 130). The Gypsies (in Turkey, North Africa, Europe) *eventually* lost the retroflexes (when exactly?).

130 Interestingly, the *c*.1000-year-old *Indian* Parsi pronunciation and recitation in Zoroastrian ritual of Avest., while clearly Indianizing as in *xšaϑra* > [*kşatra*], still has not developed retroflexes.

131 In fact, the case of *voḍhar-* is pre-conditioned by the development of IE *k'*, *g'*> IIr *c'*, *j'*, which changed to Proto-Iran. and Pre-Vedic *š*, *ž*, then (in the Hindukush?) to late Pre-Vedic retroflex *š*, *ž*, which *only then* could influence the following consonant (of the *-tar* suffix) to deliver the retroflex "suffix" *-ḍhar-* due to the same (IIr) retrograde Sandhi as seen in *budh+ta* > *buddha* (*ẓh-da* > *ẓḍha*); *then*, the voiced sibilant *ž*. disappeared, normally (as in *lih*: *liẓḍha* > *līḍha*) with compensatory lengthening of the preceding vowel; but, in the particular environment of *voḍhar* (*až* > *o*, just as *az* > *e*) represented by *o* + retroflex consonant (*-tar* suffix), in short: IE **weg*$^{\prime h}$ + *ter* > IIr **vaj*$^{\prime h}$*-tar-* > *vaj'd*^{h}*ar* > pre-Ved. **važdhar-* (note that this stage, minus the *Indian* retroflexion, is still preserved in Mit. IA *vash-ana-* [*vāžh-ana*]) > Ved. *voḍhar-*; as well as IIr **vaj*$^{\prime h}$*tar-* > Proto-Iran. **važdar-* > Avest. *vaštar-*.

132 The special pleading that all Ved. innovations happened only *after* the emigration of the Iranians out of India is made impossible by observing innovations such as *rāṭ/rāj-*, *ṣoḍaśa*, *voḍhar-*, *sede* and others such as the absolutive.

133 For example, *yam* > *yem*: *yemuḥ* 4.2.14, *pac* > *pec*: *pece* 4.18.13 etc.; similarly, examples for the *conditioned* OIA development of retroflexes include: *k'* > *c'* > *ś*,

and *g'* > *j'* > *j* as seen in: IE **wik'-s* > IIr **wic'-š* > Avest. *vīš* / > Ved. *viṭ* 'people, settlement'; IE **rēg'-s* > IIr **rāj'š* > *r*; > Lat. *rēx*, etc.; cf. also Avest. *xšuuaš*: Ved. *ṣaṣ*; Lat. *sex* etc.

134 Autochthonists would again have to take recourse to special pleading, but local loan words from the Panjab substrate (Witzel 1999a,b) already have *unconditioned* retroflexes (such as in *vāṇā*, etc.), and these substrate words are, again, missing in Iranian.

135 See Witzel 1999a,b for details: *karpāsa* cotton, etc.

136 Lion (*siṃha*); tiger (*vyāghra* AV+, *śārdūla* MS+, *puṇḍarīka* lex.), note N. Pers. *bebr*; elephant (*gaja* Manu+, *ibha* RV?, *kuñjara* Epic+), leopard (*pṛdāku* AV, *dvīpin* AV+, Ep., *citra-ka*, etc. lex.), lotus (*padma*, *kamala*, *puṇḍarīka*), bamboo (*veṇu*), or some local Indian trees (*aśvattha*, *śamī*, *bilva*, *jambu*). For the Central Asian substrate names of lion and tiger and their respective (non-)role in BMAC religion, see now Witzel, forthc. b.

137 Elst (1999: 129 sqq.) simply denies the possibility of IE linguistic paleontology and quotes the always skeptic Zimmer (1990) as his crown witness. However, it is precipitous to dismiss carefully applied linguistic paleontology completely, (cf. n. 61).

138 Excluded are, of course, the real exports (*Wanderwörter*) from India such as rice, cotton, beryl, etc., see Witzel 1999a,b.

139 See the Old Pers. sculptures at Behistun, Iran. *šer* (Horn 1893: 178).

140 Iran. *bebr* (Horn 1893: 42), is still found in the Elburz and Kopet Dagh, and as late as the 1970s around the Aral Lake and on Oxus islands in Afghanistan; probably derived from a Central Asian loan word, along with the protoform of *vyāghra* (Witzel forthc. b).

141 Employed by Ivanov-Gramkrelidze (1984, I 443) as proof for the IE homeland in Anatolia/Armenia. However, the *irregular* sound correspondences (otherwise unattested, such as *ele* –:: *i*-, etc.) seen in *i-bha*: *ele-phant-*, or in *kapi*: Engl. *ape*, or *līs*: *leon*, etc. are typical for *loan* words, not for original, inherited PIE vocabulary. Further, Ved. *ibha* (RV) does not even seem to mean "elephant" but "household of a chief" (see later n. 144). For this, and details on *kapi* see Witzel 2001b. Elst (1999: 131), however, incorrectly concludes from the *same* materials that IE came from a *tropical* area, adding (1999: 131–2) a few very unlikely comparisons on his own such as Latin *le-o(n)* from Skt *rav* 'to howl'(!) – which is in fact IE **h₃reu(H)*, Grk *ōromai*, Lat. *rūmor* (EWA II 439), demonstrating his lack of linguistic sophistication (see Witzel 2001b).

142 But only higher than 7000 feet in Kashmir. The reason for the survival of the word in South Asia (Panjabi *bhoj*, etc.) may have been export and common ritual use of birch bark, for example for amulets.

143 Perhaps with the exception of the willow (Avest. *vaēti*, Grk *itéa*, Lat. *vitex*, OHG *wīda*, Lith. *žil-vitis*; see earlier, n. 118, Schrader 1890: 440, 275), growing and attested in Eastern Iran: Pashto *vala* < **vait-iya*, but not found in Vedic/Skt, unless it is retained in (**vaita-sa* >) *veta-sa* "reed, ratan, Calamus," with the expected change in meaning 'willow > reed'. The oak, though found in various forms in Afghanistan, is *not* attested in Skt, except in myth as the inherited name of the IE weather god, Ved. *Parjanya* (see EWA s.v.), who likes oaks, as still heard even today in the German verse telling to avoid oak trees in thunderstorms, '*von Eichen sollst du weichen, Buchen sollst du suchen*!'

144 Autochthonists commonly decry the very *concept* of substrate, see Elst 1999 (much as they now begin to decry the various historical levels based on the genetic analysis of the male Y chromosome) as this would necessarily indicate that Vedic had not been present in Northwest India since times immemorial.

145 RV 1.64.7, 4.16.13 etc., used for words such as Late Ved. *gaja*, *Śatapatha Brāhmaṇa* 14.4.1.24 *mataṅga*, Epic *nāga*, RV(?) *ibha*. Ved. *ibha* is of dubious meaning and

etymology (Oldenberg 1909–12). At least two of the four cases in the RV do not refer to "elephant" but rather to the "retinue train" or the "court" of a chieftain. The meaning "elephant" is attested only in Class. Skt (Manu), Pāli, see EWA I 194; cf. also O. Egypt.', *abw*, EWA III 28.

146 Only, if with Mayrhofer the one "who tears apart?" (KEWA III 274), or "who smells scents by opening [his jaws]"(?) EWA II 593; otherwise, *Vājasaneyi Samhitā śārdūla*, *puṇḍarīka* (lex.), etc.; rather, N. Pers. *bebr* must be compared, see now Witzel forthc. b.

147 For these words of Central Asian origin, see Witzel 1999, forthc. b, Lubotsky forthc.

148 For example, Vedic *ah-am* "I" ' = Avestan *az-əm*, *az-ə̄m*, O. Pers. *ad-am* have added the additional morpheme IIr *-am* (as in *ay-am*, *iy-am*); it was transferred to the rest of the pronouns: *tvam*, *vayam*, *yūyam* as well. This feature is not found in other IE languages: Lat., Greek *egō*, Gothic *ik* (Engl. *I*), O. Slavic *az*^{u}, *jaz*^{u}; it clearly separates IIr from the other Eastern and Western IE languages.

149 Or, the Ṛgvedic normalization in *g-* of the present stems beginning in *j/g-*: IE *g*^{w}*m̥-sk'e-ti* > IIr **ja-šca-ti* > Avest. *jasaiti*:: Vedic *gacchati*. Note that *j* is retained only in traditional names such as *Jamad-agni* and in the perfect, *ja-gām-a*, etc.

150 Autochthonists assume, instead, *early innovation inside* India that would have been exported to Iran. How would that "selection" have been made? Iranian as well as the rest of the IE languages lack all the *typical Indian* innovations found in the RV. Again, too many auxiliary assumptions!

151 The lack of South Asian substrate words in Iranian (cf. Bryant 1999) underlines why (hypothetically) the archaic Iranian traits cannot have been preserved in the Panjab, side by side with the RV, before the *supposed* Iranian move westwards. Any other scenario would amount to very special pleading, again: One can hardly maintain that the Vedic "Panjabis" received these local loans only *after* the Iranians had left. Talageri (2000), against all linguistic evidence, even denies close relationship of both groups.

152 By the Elamians and Western Iranians (Mede, Persians) only after *c.*1000 BCE (cf. Hintze 1998), and by other non-IE peoples before. In Eastern Iran/Afghanistan, according to stray Mesopotamian, archaeological and a few isolated Ved. sources: non-IE settlements, in Southern Iran: Elamian up to Bampur, Meluhhan east of it in Baluchistan/Sindh, and Arattan north of it in Sistan; on the northern fringe – the Bactria-Margiana substratum, visible in IIr (Witzel 1999a,b, 2000, forthc. b).

153 For example, if the Iranians had indeed moved out from the Panjab at an "early date," they would have missed, the *supposed* "Panjab innovation" of the use of the (domesticated) horse (which is already IE: Latin *equus*, etc., but found in the subcontinent only at 1700 BCE), and they would especially have missed the later innovation of the horse-drawn chariot (IIr **ratha*, developed only at *c.*2000 BCE., see Section 11.20). Or, if they had moved out a little later, say, after the Mit. IAs, all of this would have come too late to account for the non-appearance of Iranian tribes in the RV, which has only some (*pre-*)Iranian looking names (Witzel 1999) in book 8, camels (RV 8) and some Afghani rivers (Gomatī in the Suleiman Range, Sarayu in Herat, and Sarasvatī in Arachosia). One cannot make the Iranians move from India to Iran, say, at 5000 or 2600 BCE, then introduce the innovation of horse pastoralism (not present in the subcontinent then!), and then let them take part, at *c.*2000 BCE, in the innovation of the *already IIr* horse-drawn chariot (**ratha*, Section 11.20). As always with such monolateral autochthonous theories, multiple contradictions develop.

154 Another auxiliary theory, for example, of a strong local (Drav., etc.) influence on the RV *only*, as opposed to Iranian – while still in India – is implausible. The autochthonists would have the Vedic innovations occur in the Panjab only *after* the Iranian speakers had left the subcontinent.

155 The old Satem innovations of course include Vedic. Elst supplies a lot of speculation of how the IEs could have left the subcontinent to settle in Central Asia and Europe (1999: 126 sq.).

156 Small, transient and migrating bands and groups such as the IAs or even the larger ones such as the Huns are not easily traced; and, will we ever find archaeological traces of the well attested emigration of a small group such as that of the Gypsies? – Linguistics (see earlier, n. 23) and genetics, however, clinch the case: the Bulgarian Gypsies, for example, have typical Indian mtDNA genes (M type) and Y chromosomes, but these are only to some 30 percent Indian; for the rest they have acquired European genes. This is the exact reversal of the general Indian situation, with some 25 percent of W./C. Asian genes (Section 11.7). How then did the Autochthonists' Indian emigrants "select" their genes on emigration from India, and "export" only 30 percent "proper Indian" ones? Again, this is just as impossible a scenario as the *assumed* earlier (selective) "export" of Indian linguistic features westwards by Talageri's IE = "Druhyu" emigrants (see earlier Section 11.12).

157 Change of meaning "wheel(s)" > "chariot" (*pars pro toto*) is a common linguistic occurrence.

158 Grk. has *hárma/harmatos*, Lat. *currus, curriculum*, also *rota*, as *pars pro toto* word; O. Slav. *kolo*.

159 There have been efforts, of course always on the internet, to push back the dates of chariots and spoked wheels (also implied by Talageri's 2000 years composition period for the RV, see Witzel 2001a,b), to dilute the difference between chariots and carts/four-wheeled wagons, to find horses all over India well before the accepted date of *c*.1700 BCE, to derive the Indian horse from the early Siwalik horse (2.3 million years ago!); there even has been the truly asinine proposition to change the meaning of Skt *aśva* "horse" (*Equus caballus*) and to include under this word the ass/donkey (*gardabha, rāsabha, khara*, etc., *Equus asinus*) and the half-ass/onager (*Equus hemionus khur*). Here, as elsewhere, it is useless to enter into a discussion.

160 Or after its take-over from Mesopotamia, as per Littauer and Crouwel 1996; for the trail of connections see Nichols 1997, 1998 and cf. Drews 1989 for early Near Eastern and Armenian and other trans-Caucasus attestations.

161 For the poetics and myth see EWA, KEWA s.v. *sūrya/svar*, with its phrases and *kennings* for chariot, note 'sun wheel' in Ved., Grk., Old Norse in EWA s.v. *cakra*, etc. See now however, Littauer and Crouwel 1996 for a Near Eastern origin.

162 Other (theoretically) possible scenarios such as a long-distance import, along with that of the horse, from some (North) Iranians near the Urals into the area of the IAs who had remained stationary in the Panjab, run counter to the archaic formation of the words concerned (*ratheṣṭha, savyeṣṭha*) and the clearly secondary, *inherited* form in Iranian (*raϑa*); all would amount, again, to very special pleading.

163 This is *not* the overused argumentum ex nihilo as this absence covers not just one case but *wide ranges* of vocabulary, phonetic, and grammatical innovations found outside India, and as it includes all the relatively recent Indian innovations (see RV *mene* § 19, n. 132).

164 Other such unique Satem and IIr cases involve **kw* > *k*, **k'* > *c'*, then, **ke* > **cæ* > *ca*; the change **e* > **æ* is early in IIr as it is seen in the *cakāra, jagāma* type palatalization, as well as that of **o* > *ā* in *Brugmann* cases (cf. Hock 1999); finally **æ* > Ved./Avest. *a*. Clearly, several long-term developments are involved.

165 However, Iranian has some *pre*-RV features, while it misses all Indian innovations, all of which makes a late emigration impossible, see Section 11.19.

166 Which, *pace* Misra, point to loans made during the IIr and Iranian periods, not in the Ved. period, see earlier.

167 In fact, most of the Autochthonists have not even started to learn the linguistic "trade," and simply reject linguistics out of hand, as mentioned earlier. Misra's new book (1999) is not yet available to me.
168 Note that the following list can be read both in the new, autochthonous/indigenous way, that is of leaving India, or in the "traditional" IE way, of leaving a Southeast European/Central Asian homeland.
169 Geiger 1871: 133 sqq.; Schrader 1890: 271; Hirt 1907: 622; Friedrich 1970; Mallory 1989: 114 sqq.
170 See summary by Cowgill 1986: 86 sq., Blažek 2000/1.
171 Ved. *vṛka*: Avest. *vəhrka*; cf. Lith. *vilkas*, O. Slav. *vl'kᵘ*, Alban. *ulk*, Grk *lūkos*, Lat. *lupus*, Gothic *wulfs* < **wḷkʷos*.
172 Ved. *hima:* Avest. *zim/ziiam*, Grk *khiō'n* 'snow', *-khimos*, Lat. *hiems*, Gaul. *Giamon* Armenian *jiun* 'snow', etc.
173 Only the birch tree is found all the way from India to Europe: *bhūrja* 'betula utilis' (differs slightly from the European one), Iran. Pamir dial. *furz*; Shugni *vāwzn* < **barznī*; Osset. *bœrs(œ)*; Lith. *béržas*; Serbo-Croat. *brèza*; Germ. *Birke*; Engl. *birch*, etc.
174 Cf. the oak/thunder god, Skt. *Parjanya*, Lith. *Perkúnas*, O. Slav. *Perunᵘ*, etc., cf. earlier n. 142. However, the Iranian and NIA Himalayan languages have invented *new* formations for local trees such as the oak (from *vana*, **vañja* 'tree'), willow, etc. (cf. Blažek 2000/1: 84 sq.)
175 This scenario is also contradicted by the evidence of all the other IE "cold climate" words that have *not* been preserved in India, not even in the Northwest or in the Himalayas, and by other, purely linguistic observations, made earlier, Section 11.16 sqq.
176 For the distribution of the word, see Henning 1963; Lane 1967; summary by Cowgill 1986: 86 sq. However, Blažek (2000/1) shows new evidence for an ultimate Nostratic origin ("tree with edible fruits") from Semitic, Egyptian, Berber, Chadic, Dravidian, and Altaic. IE **bhāg-(o)* 'beech' was adapted into various IE languages, for example, with the famous Mediterranean substitution in Greek (due the well-known changing climate in Europe in PIE/post-PIE times) as 'oak', but kept as the temperate climate 'beech' tree in Lat. *fagus*, Germ. *Buche*, Anatolian (Phrygian) *Bákros* 'Dionysos', etc. The word for 'beech' etc. is not found, also not by local adaptation for other trees, in Iranian (Blažek 2001: 84 sq.) or in South Asian languages. Elst (1999: 130), while not mentioning historical climate, simply disposes of the beech argument wholesale.
177 For example, in a hypothetical case: *'fig tree' > *'large tree with hanging twigs', *'willow'. The only exception are certain later cultural loans, plants such as "cotton" or "mustard".
178 The beaver was once actually found south of around 35 degrees North; note a beaver mummy from Egypt (in Paris, Louvre, Witzel 2001b), earlier in Syria, reportedly even in South Asian excavations; however, note Meadow 1996: 404, for the so far generally untrustworthy identifications of mammals in such excavations. Even the supposed early attestation of the beaver in NW South Asia would not matter. First, as this would be a rather isolated example of temperate fauna (or flora) in South Asia, second, as words change their meanings along with changes in environment (see earlier note 176, beech tree): the beaver has in fact died out in all such southern areas (Syria, etc.), after which the word-if *indeed* used in early southern IE languages! – was free for reassignment to other, similar animals (mongoose, etc.), just as the word 'brown' has been used in Europe for the bear. In Avest., beaver skins(*baβri)* occur (because of trade?) as dress of the river goddess *Anāhitā* ('made up of thirty beaver skins') *Yašt* 5.129: "the female beaver is most beautiful, as it is most furry: the beaver is a water animal." However, see the following note.
179 Interestingly, N. Pers. *bebr* < Phl. *bawrak*, Avest. *baβri* 'beaver', is a cat-like, tail-less animal whose skins are used (Horn 1893: 42); the beaver is no longer found in Iran; note also N. Pers. *bibar* 'mouse'.

180 For Elst (1999: 130,132) this is not a problem as he lets the IE *first* live in India and name the mongoose a 'brown one'. Then, when emigrating westward, *each* IE language would mysteriously have transferred this designation *individually* to the beaver, and always in the *later, correct* post-PIE form, as per individual subfamily or language in question. Occam applies: derivation of the various 'beaver' words from Skt *babhru* or an 'Indian' PIE **bhebhru* 'mongoose' is linguistically impossible.

181 The much later emigration of the Gypsies and some others into Central Asia are of course excluded here.

182 With the (partial) exception of Elst (1999), and Talageri (2000), for which see earlier.

183 For more details and some questions not discussed here, see Witzel 2001b, *EJVS* 7–3 and 7–4.

184 Except, of course, if the aim is some 'superior', religious or political motive.

185 Such as Kak's "astronomical code" (1994a) that is precariously piled on a combination of Ṛgvedic brick layers of the still *non-existent Agnicayana* and combined with the structure of the still *non-existent* complete RV collection. Note, that this is not questioned but *favored* by Klostermaier (1997, 1998, 2000), Elst (1999) and other revisionists and autochthonists.

186 For details on all these points see Witzel 2001b.

187 Including even that of Mitanni-IA, see earlier; but excluding, obviously, that of the comparatively quite late IA emigrants, the Gypsies.

188 The most blatant rewriting of nineteenth-century (European) intellectual history (and much else) has been carried out by the mathematician (PhD 1976) and electrical engineer (B.A. 1965) Rajaram (1993, 1995, etc.) who sees missionary and colonialist designs all over Indology. Even a cursory reading of his many repetitive books and press articles will indicate a *new mythology* of the nineteenth century, written for and now increasingly accepted, by some (expatriate) Indians of the twenty-first century to shore up their claims to a largely imagined, glorious but lost distant past.

189 I have clearly pointed to this (1995), when I discussed the various forms of argumentation that have to be avoided in writing ancient Indian history; however, this point has been blatantly disregarded by the autochthonists or believers in the 'Out of India' theories: in many web sites (and in Talageri 2000), these writers excoriate me for my critique of present revisionist/autochthonous writing, but they never mention my criticism of past Western or of certain present archaeological and historical writings (often produced by "Westerners").

190 Forerunners of such sentiments are books such as *Ancient Indian colonization in South-East Asia*, and note the contemporary one by Choudhury, *Indian Origin of the Chinese Nation*: (1990). The simple motto seems to be: 'if you can colonize us, we could do so to others, even long ago!' In sum, Indocentric one-up-manship.

191 Witzel 1995, 1999c.

192 Though the ones pursuing this project use dialectic methods quite effectively, they frequently also turn some traditional Indian discussion methods and scholastic tricks to their advantage, see *Caraka* 3.83, *Nyāyasūtra* 4.2.50; the method is used in *Mahābhāṣya*, and still earlier in some *Upaniṣadic Brahmodyas* (Witzel 1987b, 2003).

193 Such as Rajaram's (2000) case of fraud and fantasy in "deciphering" the Indus seals, see Witzel and Farmer 2000a,b.

194 In view of this, it might not even seem necessary to "decolonialize" the Indian mind (cf. Witzel 1999c).

195 A sign of hope is that recent interviews with Indian College students from all over the country seem to indicate that they have no interest at all in this kind of debate. They are much more practically minded. ("The New Republic," *Times of India*, January 26, 2001.)

References

Abayev, V. I. Pre-history of Indo-Iranians in the Light of Aryo-Uralic Contacts. (Quoted in Misra 1992: xii, 15, 34; cf. Asimov 1977: 73.)

Agrawal, D. P. and J. S. Kharakwal, in press. "Outstanding Problems of Early Iron Age in India: Need of a New Approach." *Proceedings of the Seminar on Early Iron Age, Kumaon University at Nainital, Uttaranchal.*

Aiyar, S. R., 1975. *Dravidian Theories*, Madras: Madras Law Journal Office.

Allchin, B. and Raymond, A., 1982. *The Rise of Civilization in India and Pakistan.* Cambridge: Cambridge University Press.

Allchin, F. R., 1995. *The Archaeology of Early Historic South Asia. The Emergence of Cities and States.* With contributions from George Erdosy, R. A. E. Coningham, D. K. Chakrabarti, and Bridget Allchin. Cambridge: Cambridge University Press.

Anthony, D. and D. R. Brown, 2000. "Eneolithic horse exploitation in the Eurasian Steppes: Diet, Ritual and Riding," *Antiquity*, 74: 75–86.

Anthony, D. and N. B. Vinogradov, 1995. "The Birth of the Chariot," *Archaeology*, 48: 36–41.

Anttila, R., 1989. *Historical and Comparative Linguistics.* Amsterdam/Philadelphia, PA: John Benjamins.

Asimov, M. S. *et al.* (eds), 1978. *Ethnic Problems of the Early History of Central Asia: International Symposium* [= International Symposium on Ethnic Problems of the Ancient History of Central Asia (Second Millennium BC). Dushanbe].

Balkan, K., 1954. *Kassitenstudien I: Die Sprache der Kassiten.* New Haven, CT: American Oriental Society.

Bechert, H. 1991. "The Date of the Buddha reconsidered." In *Indologica Taurinensia*, edited by H. Bechert, 10, 1982, 29–36. *The dating of the historical Buddha/Die Datierung des historischen Buddha, part 1* (Symposien zur Buddhismusforschung IV, 1–2). Göttingen: Vandenhoek und Ruprecht.

Beekes, R. S. P., 1995. *Comparative Indo-European Linguistics: An Introduction.* Amsterdam/Philadelphia, PA: John Benjamins.

Bhagavad Datta, 1974 (reprint). *Vaidika vāṅmaya kā iṭihās.* New Delhi: Mehar Chand Lacchmandas.

Blažek, V., 2000/2001. "The Ever-Green 'Beech' -argument in Nostratic Perspective," *MT* VI: 83–94.

Bopp, F., 1816. *Ueber das Conjugationssystem der Sanskritsprache: in Vergleichung mit jenem der griechischen, lateinischen, persischen und germanischen Sprache. Hrsg. und mit Vorerinnerungen begleitet von Karl Joseph Windischmann.Frankfurt am Main: Andreäischen.*

Brockington, J., 1998. *The Sanskrit Epics.* Leiden/Boston: Brill.

Bryant, E. F., 1999. "Linguistic Substrata and the Indigenous Aryan Debate" In *Aryan and Non-Aryan in South Asia. Evidence, Interpretation and Ideology*, edited by J. Bronkhorst and M. Deshpande. Harvard Oriental Series, Opera Minora, Vol. 3. Cambridge, MA: Harvard University Press, pp. 59–83.

——, 2001. *The Quest for the Origins of Vedic Culture. The Indo-Aryan Migration Debate.* Oxford: Oxford University Press.

Burrow, T., 1973. *The Sanskrit Language.* London: Faber & Faber.

——, 1984. *A Dravidian Etymological Dictionary*, 2nd edition. Oxford: Clarendon Press.

Choudhury, P., 1990. *Indian Origin of the Chinese Nation: A Challenging, Unconventional Theory of the Origin of the Chinese.* Calcutta: Dasgupta & Co.

——, 1993. *The Aryans: A Modern Myth. Part-I. (A Story of a Treacherous Theory that Concerns Every Indian) A Book that Offers Many Things to Think Anew*. New Delhi: Eastern Publishers' Distributor.

Cowgill, W., 1986. In *Indogermanische Grammatik. Band I. 1. Halbband: Einleitung*, edited by J. Kurylowicz and M. Mayrhofer. Heidelberg: Winter.

Dani, A. H. and V. M. Masson (eds), 1992. *History of Civilisations of Central Asia*, Vol. I. *The dawn of Civilisation: Earliest Times to 700 BCE*. Paris: Unesco Publishing.

Danino, M., 1996. *The Invasion that never was/Song of Humanity by Sujata Nahar*. Delhi: Mother's Institute of Research & Mysore: Mira Aditi.

Day, J. V., 2001. *Indo-European Origins: The Anthropological Evidence*. Washington, DC: Institute for the Study of Man.

Diakonoff, I. M., 1971. *Hurrisch und Urartäisch*. München: Kitzinger.

——, 1985. "On the Original Home of the Speakers of Indo-European," *JIES*, 1: 92–174.

Diakonoff, I. M. and S. A. Starostin, 1986. *Hurro-Urartian as an Eastern Caucasian Language*. München: Kitzinger.

Drews, R., 1989. *The Coming of the Greeks*. Princeton, NJ: Princeton University Press.

Drobyshev, M. A. (ed.), 1978. "Ethnic Problems of the Early History of Central Asia," International Symposium, Dushanbe, October 17–22, 1977. Moscow: Central Department of Oriental Literature.

Ehret, Ch., 1988. "Language Change and the Material Correlates of Language and Ethnic Shift," *Antiquity*, 62: 564–74.

Elst, K., 1999. *Update on the Aryan Invasion Debate*. Delhi: Aditya Prakashan.

Emeneau, M. B., 1956. "India as a Linguistic Area," *Language*, 32: 3–16.

Erdosy, G., 1988. *Urbanisation in Early Historic India*. Oxford: British Archaeological Reports.

—— (ed.), 1995. "The Indo-Aryans of Ancient South Asia." In *Indian Philology and South Asian Studies*, edited by A. Wezler and M. Witzel, Vol. 1. Berlin/New York: de Gruyter.

Falk, H. V., 1981. *Árma. Zeitschrift der deutschen morgenländischen Gesellschaft*, 131: 160–71.

——, 1986. *Bruderschaft und Würfelspiel*, Freiburg: Hedwig Falk.

Feuerstein, G., S. Kak and D. Frawley, 1995. *In Search of the Cradle of Civilization*, Wheaton: Quest Books.

Francalacci, P., 2001. The Peopling of Eurasia: The Contribution of Y-chromosome Analysis, 3rd ESCA Harvard Roundtable. At: http://www.fas.harvard.edu/~sanskrit/RoundTable Schedule.html

Frawley, D., 1994. *The Myth of the Aryan Invasion of India*. New Delhi: Voice of India.

Friedrich, J., 1940. "Aus verschiedenen Keilschriftsprachen," 3–4. *Orientalia* (NS), 9: 348–61.

Friedrich, P., 1970. *Indo-European Trees*. Chicago, IL: University of Chicago Press.

Gamkrelidze, T. and V. Ivanov., 1995 [1984]. *Indo-European and the Indo-Europeans*. Berlin: de Gruyter.

Geiger, L., 1871. *Zur Entwicklungsgeschichte der Menschheit*. Stuttgart: J. G. Cotta'sche Buchhandlung.

Gupta, S., 1990a. *A Comparative Etymologic Lexicon of Common Indo-Germanisches [sic] (Indo-European) Words*. Milton, MA: Sverge Haus.

——, 1990b. *Etymologically Common Hydronyms, Toponyms, Personal and Proper Names Throughout the Indo-European Geographic Area*. Milton, MA: Sverge Haus.

——, 1996. *The Indus-Sarasvati Civilization. Origins, Problems and Issues*. Delhi: Pratibha Prakashan.

Hamp, E. P., 1996. "On the Indo-European Origins of the Retroflexes in Sanskrit," *Journal of the American Oriental Society*, 116: 719–23.
Harmatta, J., 1992. "The emergence of the Indo-Iranians: The Indo-Iranian Languages," In *History of civilisations of Central Asia*, Vol. I. *The Dawn of Civilisation: Earliest Times to 700 BCE*, edited by A. H. Dani, and V. M. Masson, Paris: Unesco Publishing, pp. 357–78.
Henning, W. B., 1963. "The Kurdish Elm," *Asia Major* (NS), 10: 68–72.
Hintze, A., 1998. "The Migrations of the Indo-Aryans and the Iranian Sound-Change *s > h*," edited by W. Meid, *Akten der Fachtagung der Indogermanischen Gesellschaft in Innsbruck*, Institut für Sprachwissenschaft der Universität Innsbruck.
Hirt, H., 1907 [1905]. *Die Indogermanen, ihre Verbreitung, ihre Urheimat, und ihre Kultur*, 2 Vols. Strassburg: K.J. Trübner.
Hock, H. H., 1986. *Principles of Historical Linguistics*. Berlin/New York: Mouton de Gruyter.
——, 1996. "Pre-Ṛgvedic Convergence Between Indo-Aryan (Sanskrit) and Dravidian? A Survey of the Issues and Controversies." In *Ideology and Status of Sanskrit: Contributions to the History of the Sanskrit Language*, edited by J. E. M. Houben, Leiden: Brill, pp. 17–58.
——, 1999. "Out of India? The linguistic evidence." In *Aryan and Non-Aryan in South Asia. Evidence, Interpretation and Ideology*, edited by J. Bronkhorst and M. Deshpande. Harvard Oriental Series, Opera Minora, Vol. 3. Cambridge, MA: Harvard University Press, pp. 1–18.
Hoffmann, K., 1941. *Die alt-indoarischen Wörter mit -ṇḍ-, besonders im Ṛgveda*, Diss: München.
——, 1992. *Aufsätze zur Indoiranistik*, edited by S. Glauch, R. Plath, and S. Ziegler, Vol. 3. Wiesbaden: L. Reichert.
Horn, P., 1893. *Grundriss der neupersischen Etymologie*, Strassburg: Trübner.
Horsch, P., 1966. *Die vedische Gāthā- und Ślokalitteratur*, Bern: Francke.
Joki, A. J., 1973. *Uralier und Indogermanen. Die älteren Berhrungen zwischen den uralischen und indogermanischen Sprachen*, Helsinki: Suomalais-ugrilainen seura.
Kak, S., 1994a. *The Astronomical Code of the Ṛgveda*, New Delhi: Aditya Prakashan.
——, 1994b. "On the Classification of Indic languages," *Annals of the Bhandarkar Oriental Research Institute*, 75: 185–95.
Kalyanaraman, S., 1999. *Rigveda and Sarasvati-Sindhu Civilization*. August 1999, At: http://sarasvati.simplenet.com/html/rvssc.htm
——, 2000. *Sarasvati*. Bangalore: Babasaheb (Umakant Keshav) Apte Samarak Samiti.
Katz, H., 1985. *Studien zu den älteren indoiranischen Lehnwörtern in den uralischen Sprachen*, D Litt thesis. Habilschrift München.
——, 2001. *Fremd und Eigen: Untersuchungen zu Grammatik und Wortschatz des Uralischen und des Indogermanischen: in memoriam Hartmut Katz*. Wien: Praesens.
Keith, A. B. and Macdonell, A. A., [1912] 1967. *Vedic Index*. London, reprint Delhi: Motilal Banarsidass.
Kennedy, K. A. R., 1995. "Have Aryans been Identified in the Prehistoric Skeletal Record from South Asia? Biological Anthropology and Concepts of Ancient Races." In *The Indo-Aryans of Ancient South Asia*, edited by G. Erdosy, Berlin/New York: de Gruyter, pp. 32–66.
——, 2000. *God-apes and Fossil Men: Paleoanthropology of South Asia*. Ann Arbor, MI: University of Michigan Press.
Kenoyer, J. M., 1998. *Ancient Cities of the Indus Valley Civilization*. Oxford: Oxford University Press/American Institute of Pakistan Studies.
Kirfel, W., 1927. *Das Purāṇa Pañcalakṣaṇa*, Bonn: K. Schroeder.

Klostermaier, K., 1989. *A Survey of Hinduism*. Albany, NY: SUNY.
——, 1997. *Preface*. In *Vedic Aryans and the Origins of Civilization: A Literary and Scientific Perspective*, 2nd edition, edited by, Rajaram and Frawley, New Delhi: Voice of India.
——, 1998. "Questioning the Aryan Invasion Theory and Revising Ancient Indian History," *ISCON Communications Journal*, 6(1): 1–7.
——, 2000. *Hinduism: A Short History*. Oxford: Oneworld.
Krishnamurti, Bh. K., 2001. *Comparative Dravidian Linguistics. Current Perspectives*. Oxford: Oxford University Press.
Kuiper, F. B. J., 1955. "Rigvedic loan-words." In *Studia Indologica. Festschrift für Willibald Kirfel zur Vollendung seines 70. Lebensjahres*, edited by O. Spies. Bonn: Orientalisches Seminar.
——, 1962. *Nahali, A Comparative Study*. Amsterdam: Noord-Hollandse Uitgevers Maatschappij.
——, 1966. "The sources of Nahali vocabulary." In *Studies in Comparative Austroasiatic. Linguistics*, edited by H. Zide. The Hague: Mouton, pp. 57–81.
——, 1967. "The Genesis of a Linguistic Area," *Indo-Iranian Journal*, 10: 81–102.
——, 1983. *Ancient Indian Cosmogony*, edited by J. Irwin. Delhi: Vikas.
——, 1991. *Aryans in the Ṛgveda*. Amsterdam-Atlanta: Rodopi.
——, 1995. "Foreign Words in the Rgveda," *IIJ*, 38: 261.
——, 2000. "A bilingual Ṛṣi." In *Anusantatyai. Fs. für Johanna Narten zum 70. Geburtstag*, edited by A. Hintze and E. Tichy (Münchener Studien zur Sprachwissenschaft, Beihefte NF 19). Dettelbach: J.H. R'll.
Kuz'mina E. E., 1994. "Horses, Chariots and the Indo-Iranians: An Archaeological Spark in the Historical Dark," *South Asian Archaeology* I: 403–12.
Lal, B. B., 1997. *The Earliest Civilization of South Asia (Rise, Maturity and Decline)*. New Delhi: Aryan Books International.
Lane, G. S., 1967. "The Beech Argument: A Re-Evaluation of the Linguistic Evidence," *Zeitschrift für vergleichende Sprachforschung*, 81: 1970-212.
Littauer, M. A. and Crouwel, J. H., 1996. "The Origin of the True Chariot," *Antiquity*, 70: 934–9.
Lord, A. B., 1991. *Epic Singers and Oral Tradition*, Ithaca, NY: Cornell University Press.
Lubotsky, A., 1998 (in press). "Indo-Iranian Substratrum" (paper read at a conference in Tvarminne, Finland).
Majumdar, R. C., 1953. *Ancient Indian Colonization in South-East Asia*. Baroda: M.S. Gaekwad University.
Mallory, J. P., 1989. *In Search of the Indo-Europeans: Language, Archaeology and Myth*. London: Thames and Hudson.
Masica, C. P., 1979. "Aryan and Non-Aryan Elements in North Indian Agriculture." In *Aryan and Non-Aryan in India*, edited by Madhav M. Deshpande and Peter Edwin Hook. Ann Arbor, MI: Center for South and Southeast Asian Studies, pp. 55–151.
——, 1991. *The Indo-Aryan Languages*, Cambridge, New York: Cambridge University Press.
Mayrhofer, M., 1956–1976. *Kurzgefasstes etymologisches Wörterbuch des Altindischen*. Heidelberg: KEWA.
——, 1979. *Ausgewählte kleine Schriften* (Sigrid Deger-Jalkotzy u. Rüdiger Schmitt, eds): Wiesbaden: Reichert.
——, 1986. *Lautlehre. Indogermanische Grammatik*, Band I, 2. Halbband: Heidelberg: Car Winter.
——, 1986–1996. *Etymologisches Wörterbuch des Altindoarischen*. Heidelberg: Carl Winter.
Mazhar, M. A., 1982. *Sanskrit Traced to Arabic*. Faisalabad: Sheikh Aziz Ahmad.

Meadow, R. H., 1996. "The Origins and Spread of Agriculture and Pastoralism in Northwestern South Asia." In *The Origins and Spread of Agriculture and Pastoralism in Eurasia*, edited by D. R. Harris. London: UCL Press, pp. 390–412.

——, 1998. "Pre-and Proto-Historic Agricultural and Pastoral Transformations in Northwestern South Asia." In *The Transition to Agriculture in the Old World, The Review of Archaeology* (Special Issue edited by Ofer Bar-Yosef), 19: 12–21.

Meadow, R. H. and A. Patel, 1997. "A Comment on: Horse Remains from Surkodata by Sándor B'k'nyi," *South Asian Studies*, 13: 308–15.

Misra, S. S., 1974. *New Lights on Indo-European Comparative Grammar*. Varanasi: Manisha Prakashan.

——, 1992. *The Aryan Problem, a Linguistic Approach*. New Delhi: Munshiram Manoharlal.

——, 1999. *The Date of the Rigveda and the Aryan Migration: Fresh Linguistic Evidence*. Pune: University of Pune.

Mother Tongue. *Journal of the Associtation for the Study of Language in Prehistory*. Boston [in Vol. II–III, 1996–97, several authors deal with Nihali].

Müller, F., 1888. *Biographies of Words and the Home of the Aryans*. London: Longmans Green.

Nenninger, C., 1993. "Wie kommt die Pharaonsratte zu den vedischen Göttern?" *Studien zur Indologie und Iranistik*, 18: 161–8.

Nichols, J., 1997. "The Epicentre of the Indo-European Linguistic Spread." In *Archaeology and Language I*, edited by R. Blench and M. Spriggs. London/New York: Routledge, pp. 122–48.

——, 1998. "The Eurasian Spread Zone and the Indo-European Dispersal." In *Archaeology and Language II. Correlating archaeological and linguistic hypotheses*, edited by R. Blench, and M. Spriggs. London/New York: Routledge, pp. 220–66.

Oldenberg, H., 1888. *Die Hymnen des Rigveda, Band I. Metrische und textgeschichtliche Prolegomena*. Berlin. Wilhelm Hertz.

——, 1912 [1909]. *Ṛgveda. Textkritische und exegetische Noten* (Abhandlungen der königlichen Gesellschaft der Wissenschaften zu Göttingen 11, 13.) Berlin [Repr. Göttingen 1970].

Osada, T., 2000. "Hatashite āriya-jin.no shinnyū.wa atta no ka? Hindū nashonarizumuṇo taitō nakaḍe." *Kokusai Nihon Bunka Kenkyu Sentā Kiyo*. (Nihon Kenkyu) 23, March, Heisei 13. Was there an Aryan Invasion at all? In the Context of the Rise of Hindu Nationalism.

Pargiter, F. E., 1913. *The Purāṇa text of the Dynasties of the Kali Age*. London: Oxford University Press.

Parpola, A., 1994. *Deciphering the Indus Script*. Cambridge: Cambridge University Press.

Parry, M. (n.p. 1930–32). *Studies in the Epic Technique of Oral Verse-making*.

——, 1971. *The Making of Homeric Verse: The Collected Papers of Milman Parry*. Oxford: Clarendon Press.

Pinnow, H. J., 1959. *Versuch einer historischen Lautlehre der Kharia-Sprache*. Wiesbaden: O. Harrassowitz.

Pokorny, J., 1959. *Indogermanisches Wörterbuch*. Bern: Francke.

Possehl, G. L., 1996a. *Indus Age. The Writing System*. Philadelphia, PA: University of Pennsylvania Press.

——, 1996b. "Meluhha." In *The Indian Ocean in Antiquity*, edited by J. Reade, London: Kegan Paul Intl., pp. 133–208.

Possehl, G. L. and P. Gullapalli, 1999. "The Early Iron Age in South Asia." In *The Archaeometallurgy of the Asian Old World*, edited by V. Pigott, Philadelphia, PA: The University Museum, pp. 153–75.

Radhakrishna, B. P. and S. S. Merh (eds), 1999. *Vedic Sarasvati–Evolutionary History of a Lost River of Northwestern India*. Bangalore: Memoir 42 of the Geological Society of India.

Rajaram, N. S., 1993. *The Aryan Invasion of India: The Myth and the Truth*. New Delhi: Voice of India.

——, 1995. *The Politics of History*, New Delhi: Voice of India.

Rajaram, N. S. and D. Frawley, 1997 [1995]. *Vedic Aryans and the Origins of Civilization: A Literary and Scientific Perspective*, 2nd edition. *Foreword* by Klaus K. Klostermaier. New Delhi: Voice of India.

Rajaram, N. S. and N. Jha, 2000. *Deciphering the Indus Script. Methodology, Readings, Interpretations*. Delhi: Aditya Prakashan.

Rau, W., 1957. *Staat und Gesellschaft im alten Indien nach den Brāhmaṇa-Texten dargestellt*. Wiesbaden: O. Harrassowitz.

——, 1974. *Metalle und Metallgeräte im vedischen Indien*. Akademie der Wissenschaften zu Mainz, Abhandlungen der Geistes-u. sozialwissenschaftlichen Klasse 1973, No. 8, Wiesbaden: F. Steiner, 649–82.

——, 1976. *The Meaning of pur in Vedic Literature* (Abhandlungen der Marburger Gelehrten Gesellschaft III/1). München: W. Finck.

——, 1983. *Zur vedischen Altertumskunde*, Akademie der Wissenschaften zu Mainz, Abhandlungen der Geistes-u. sozialwissenschaftlichen Klasse, No. 1. Wiesbaden: F. Steiner.

Rédei, K., 1987. “Zu den indogermanisch-uralischen Sprachkontakten.” *Sitzungsberichte der Österreichischen Akademie der Wissenschaften, Philosophisch-Historische Klasse*, 468 Band. Wien.

Renfrew, C., 1987. *Archaeology and Language*. London: Jonathan Cape.

Rocher, L., 1986. *The Puranas*. Wiesbaden: O. Harrassowitz.

Schleicher, A., 1861–62. *Compendium der vergleichenden grammatik der indogermanischen sprachen*. Weimar, H. Böhlau.

Schmidt, H.-P., 1980. “On Birds and Dogs and Bats,” *Persica* IX, 1–85 and plates I–XI.

Schmidt, J., 1872. *Die verwantschaftsverhältnisse der indogermanischen sprachen*. Weimar, H. Böhlau.

Schrader, O., 1890. *Prehistoric Antiquities of the Aryan Peoples: a Manual of Comparative Philology and the Earliest Culture. Being “Sprachvergleichung und Urgeschichte” of Dr. O. Schrader*. Transl. by Frank Byron Jevons... from the 2d rev. & enl. German ed. with the sanction and co-operation of the author. London: C. Griffin and Company.

Sethna, K. D., 1981. *Karpāsa in Prehistoric India: A Chronological and Cultural Clue*. New Delhi: Biblia Impex.

——, 1989. *Ancient India in a New Light*. New Delhi: Aditya Prakashan.

——, 1992. *The Problem of Aryan Origins From an Indian Point of View. Second extensively enlarged edition with five supplements*. New Delhi: Aditya Prakashan (first edition, Calcutta: S. & S. Publications, 1980).

Shaffer, J. G., 1984. “The Indo-Aryan Invasions: Cultural Myth and Archaeological Reality.” In *The People of South Asia: The Biological Anthropology of India, Pakistan and Nepal*, edited by J. R. Lukas. New York: Plenum, pp. 77–90.

Shaffer, J. G. and D. A. Lichtenstein, 1995. “The concepts of ‘cultural tradition’ and ‘paleoethnicity’ in South Asian archaeology.” In *The Indo-Aryans of Ancient South Asia*, edited by G. Erdosy. Berlin/New York: de Gruyter, pp. 126–54.

Shaffer, J. G. and D. A. Lichtenstein, 1999. "Migration, Philology and South Asian Archaeology." In *Aryan and Non-Aryan in South Asia. Evidence, Interpretation and Ideology*, edited by J. Bronkhorst and M. Deshpande. Harvard Oriental Series, Opera Minora, Vol. 3. Cambridge, MA: Harvard University Press, pp. 239–60.

Sherratt, A. (forthc.) "Patterns of Growth: Nodes and Networks in the Ancient World."

Skjærvø, P. O., 1995. "The Avesta as Source for the Early History of the Iranians." In *The Indo-Aryans of Ancient South Asia*, edited by G. Erdosy, Berlin/New York: de Gruyter, pp. 155–76.

Smith, R. M., 1966. "On the White Yajurveda Vaṃśa," *East and West* (NS) 16: 112–25.

——, 1973. *Dates and Dynasties in Earliest India; Translation and Justification of a Critical Text of the Purāṇa Dynasties*. Delhi: Motilal Banarsidass.

Soden, W. von., 1985. *Einführung in die Altorientalistik*. Darmstadt: Wissenschaftliche Buchgesellschaft.

Söhnen, R., 1986. "Das Gautamīmahātmya und seine vedischen Quellen." In *o-o-pe-ro-si, Festschrift für Ernst Risch zum 75. Geburtstag*, edited by A. Etter. Berlin/New York: de Gruyter, pp. 176–95.

Southworth, F. C., 1979. "Lexical Evidence for Early Contacts Between Indo-Aryan and Dravidian." In *Aryan and Non-Aryan in India*, edited by M. M. Deshpande and P. E. Hook. Ann Arbor, MI: Center for South and Southeast Asian Studies, pp. 191–233.

——, 1995. "Reconstructing Social Context from Language: Indo-Aryan and Dravidian prehistory." In *The Indo-Aryans of Ancient South Asia*, edited by G. Erdosy. Berlin/New York: de Gruyter, pp. 258–77.

Staal, J. F., 2001. "How a Psychoactive Substance Becomes a Ritual: The Case of Soma," *Social Research*, 68: 745–78.

Surya K., 1943. *Kāṭhakasaṃkalana*. Lahore.

Szemerényi, O., 1970. *Einführung in die vergleichende Sprachwissenschaft*. Darmstadt: Wissenschaftliche Buchgesellschaft (= Introduction to Indo-European linguistics) [4th rev. edn]. Oxford: Clarendon Press/New York: Oxford University Press, 1996.

Talageri, St, 1993. *Aryan Invasion Theory and Indian Nationalism*. New Delhi: Voice of India (also = New Delhi: Aditya Prakashan 1993).

——, 2000. *Rigveda. A Historical Analysis*. New Delhi: Aditya Prakashan.

Thapar, R., 1968. *Proceedings of the Indian Historical Congress*.

Thompson, G., 2001. "The relationship Between Vedic and Avestan: The Provenance of Soma, Amshu, and its relation to the BMAC?" Paper presented at *Third Harvard Round Table on the Ethnogenesis of South and Central Asia*, May 12–14; cf. http://www.fas.harvard.edu/~sanskrit/RoundTableSchedule.html

Tikkanen, B., 1987. *The Sanskrit Gerund. A Synchronic, Diachronic and Typological Analysis*. Helsinki: Finnish Oriental Society.

Trautmann, Th., 1999. "Constructing the Racial Theory of Indian Civilization." In *Aryan and Non-Aryan in South Asia. Evidence, Interpretation and Ideology*, edited by J. Bronkhorst and M. Deshpande. Harvard Oriental Series, Opera Minora, Vol. 3. Cambridge, MA: Harvard University Press, pp. 277–93.

Vats, M. S., 1940. *Excavations at Harappa*, Delhi: Manager of Publications, Govt. of India.

Waradpande, N. R., 1989. *The Aryan Invasion, a Myth*. Nagpur: Baba Saheb Apte Smarak Samiti.

——, 1993. "Fact and Fictions about the Aryans." In *The Aryan Invasion, a Myth*, edited by S. B. Deo and S. Kamath. Nagpur: Baba Saheb Apte Smarak Samiti (1989), pp. 14–19.

Wheeler, R. E. M., 1966. *Civilizations of the Indus Valley and Beyond*. London: Thames and Hudson.
Wiel, C. aan de, 2000. "*dy* > *jy*, oder Prākṛtismus im Rigveda?" In *Indoarisch, Iranisch und die Indogermanistik. Arbeitstagung der Indogermanischen Gesellschaft vom 2. bis 5. Oktober 1997 in Erlangen*, edited by B. Forssman and R. Plath. Wiesbaden: Reichert, pp. 535–42.
Witzel, M. Jav, 1972. *apāxəδra. Münchener Studien zur Sprachwissenschaft*, 30: 163–91.
——, 1980. "Early Eastern Iran and the Atharvaveda," *Persica*, 9: 86–128.
——, 1984. "Sur le chemin du ciel," *Bulletin des études indiennes*, 2: 213–79.
——, 1986. "JB palpūlanī. The structure of a Brāhmaṇa tale." *Felicitation Volume B. R. Sharma*, edited by M. D. Balasubrahmaniam. Tirupati: Kendriya Sanskrit Vidyapeetha, pp. 189–216.
——, 1987a. "On the Localisation of Vedic Texts and Schools (Materials on Vedic Śākhās, 7)." *India and the Ancient World. History, Trade and Culture before A.D. 650. P.H.L. Eggermont Jubilee Volume*, edited by G. Pollet. Leuven, pp. 173–213.
——, 1987b. "The Case of the Shattered Head." *Festschrift für W. Rau, StII* 13/14: 363–415.
——, 1989. "Tracing the Vedic dialects." In *Dialects dans les littératures indo-aryennes*, edited by Colette Caillat. Paris: Institut de Civilisation Indienne, pp. 97–264.
——, 1990. "On Indian Historical Writing: The Case of the Vaṃśāvalīs," *Journal of the Japanese Association for South Asian Studies*, 2: 1–57.
——, 1992. "Meaningful Ritual. Structure, Development and Interpretation of the Tantric Agnihotra Ritual of Nepal." In *Ritual, State and History in South Asia. Essays in Honour of J.C. Heesterman*, edited by A. W. van den Hoek, D. H. A. Kolff, and M. S. Oort. Leiden: Brill, pp. 774–827.
——, 1994. "The Brahmins of Kashmir." In *A Study of the Nīlamata – Aspects of Hinduism in Ancient Kashmir*, edited by Y. Ikari. Kyoto: Institute for Research in Humanities, Kyoto University, pp. 237–94. At: http://www.people.fas.harvard.edu/~witzel/KashmiriBrahmins.pdf
——, 1995. "Early Indian History: Linguistic and Textual Parameters." In *The Indo-Aryans of Ancient South Asia*, edited by G. Erdosy, *Indian Philology and South Asian Studies*, edited by A. Wezler and M. Witzel, Vol. 1. Berlin/New York: de Gruyter, pp. 85–125.
——, 1995. "Ṛgvedic History: Poets, Chieftains and Polities." In *The Indo-Aryans of Ancient South Asia*, edited by G. Erdosy, pp. 307–52.
——, 1997. "The Development of the Vedic Canon and its Schools: The Social and Political Milieu." (Materials on Vedic Śākhās 8). In *Inside the Texts, Beyond the Texts. New Approaches to the Study of the Vedas*. Harvard Oriental Series, Opera Minora, Vol. 2. Cambridge, MA: Harvard University Press, pp. 257–345.
——, 1998. "Macrocosm, Mesocosm, and Microcosm. The Persistent Nature of 'Hindu' Beliefs and Symbolical Forms." In *IJHS Symposium on Robert Levy's MESOCOSM*, edited by S. Mittal. *International Journal of Hindu Studies* 1: 501–53.
——, 1999a. "Aryan and non-Aryan Names in Vedic India. Data for the linguistic situation, *c.*1900–500 BC." In *Aryans and Non-Non-Aryans, Evidence, Interpretation and Ideology*, edited by J. Bronkhorst and M. Deshpande. Harvard Oriental Series, Opera Minora, Vol. 3. Cambridge, MA: Harvard University Press, pp. 337–404.
——, 1999b. Early Sources for South Asian Substrate Languages. *Mother Tongue* (extra number), October 1999. At: http://www.people.fas.harvard.edu/~witzel/MT-Substrates.pdf

Witzel, M. Jav., 1999c. "Classical Studies and Indology." In *Reconstitution of Classical Studies. Special Issue: A Report on the First Symposium Towards a Reconstitution of Classical Studies*, edited by H. Nakatani, No. 3. 3/11/Heisei 11, 16–36.

——, 2000. "The Home of the Aryans." In *Anusantatyai. Fs. für Johanna Narten zum 70. Geburtstag*, edited by A. Hintze and E. Tichy (Münchener Studien zur Sprachwissenschaft, Beihefte NF 19), Dettelbach: J. H. R'll, pp. 283–338.

——, 2001a. "Westward ho! The Incredible Wanderlust of the Ṛgvedic Tribes Exposed by S. Talageri." A Review of: Shrikant G. Talageri, *The Rigveda. A Historical Analysis*. (Sāvadhānapattra no. 2) *EJVS* 7–2.

——, 2001b. "Autochthonous Aryans? The Evidence from Old Indian and Iranian Texts," *EJVS* 7–3, 2001. At: http://users.primushost.com/~india/ejvs/issues.html

——, 2003. "Yājñavalkya as Ritualist and Philosopher, and His Personal Language." In *Paitimùna. Essays in Iranian, Indo-European, and Indian Studies in Honor of Hanns-Peter Schmidt*, Volumes I & II, edited by S. Adhami. Casta Mesa, CA: Mazda Publishers, pp. 103–43.

——, forthc. a (n.p.). "The Languages of Harappa." In *Proceedings of the Harappan Congress at Madison 1998*, edited by M. Kenoyer.

——, forthc. b. *Linguistic Evidence for Cultural Exchange in Prehistoric Western Central Asia*. Philadelphia: Sino-Platonic Papers 129, 2003 (in press).

Witzel, M. and S. Farmer, 2000a. "Horseplay in Harappa. The Indus Valley Decipherment Hoax." *Frontline* Vol. 17(Chennai), Oct. 13, 2000, 4–14. At: http://www.frontlineonline.com/fl1720/fl172000.htm, http://www.frontlineonline.com/fl1720/17200040.htm

——, 2000b. "New Evidence on the 'Piltdown Horse' Hoax." *Frontline*, Vol. 17, November 11–24, pp. 126–9. At: http://www.frontlineonline.com/fl1723/fl172300.htm, http://www.frontlineonline.com/fl1723/17231220.pdf;cf. http://www.safarmer.com/frontline/

Zimmer, S., 1990. "On Indo-Europeanization," *JIES*, 18: 141–55.

Part IV

HISTORIOGRAPHY

12

ARYAN ORIGINS

Arguments from the nineteenth-century Maharashtra

Madhav M. Deshpande

The debates on Aryan origins in Maharashtra in the nineteenth century occurred on the background of the emerging Western education in the region under the auspices of the British colonial authorities and the traditional self-definitions by the Brahmanical and non-Brahmanical communities. The Brahmins of the region traditionally viewed themselves as one of the five Drāviḍa Brahmin groups residing to the south of the Vindhyas, with the exception of the Gauḍa Sārasvata Brahmin community from the region of Goa. This community considered itself to be one of the migrant groups from the region to the north of the Vindhyas, a region occupied by the five Gauḍa Brahmin groups. While the Gauḍa-Drāviḍa distinction was traditionally held to be very ancient, brought about by migrations etc. prompted by the epic sage Paraśurāma, both the divisions among Brahmins looked upon themselves to be authentic Āryas in the Dharmaśāstric sense. While the Dharmaśāstras generally considered the three upper Varṇas as belonging to the Ārya group, the Śūdras and others being the non-Ārya groups, the Brahmins in the region of Maharashtra, in the pre-colonial period, came to argue that there were only two Varṇas left on earth in the post-Paraśurāma period. Paraśurāma, according to the epic narratives, is believed to have killed off all the Kṣatriyas on the earth twenty-one times, and hence the Brahmins came to believe that there were no true Kṣatriyas left on earth. The Vaiśya identity was also summarily dismissed in this region, and the Brahmins came to believe that there were only two Varṇas left, the Brahmins and the Śūdras. This belief of the Brahmins played an important role in the emergence of the new theories of Aryan origins in the nineteenth-century Maharashtra. The ruling families of the region, though rejected by the Brahmins as being Śūdras, strenuously attempted to assert their Kṣatriyahood, and in the process a great tension between the Kṣatriyas and the Brahmins developed in the pre-colonial period, and continued into the colonial and post-colonial period. The classes who were below the ruling Kṣatriya families developed their own conceptions, and there emerged competing conceptions and interpretations of Aryan origins in the nineteenth century.

As the British took over the rule of the Maharashtra region from the Brahmin Peshwas in 1818, the colonial authorities initially began sponsoring educational efforts both for traditional Sanskritic learning and vernacular languages. The support for exclusively traditional Sanskrit learning first emerged in the form of setting up a Sanskrit Pāṭhaśālā in Pune providing for the study of traditional Sanskritic subjects. Here, the British authorities attempted to de-emphasize the Vedic studies and encouraged the Śāstric studies, particularly the fields of Astronomy, Mathematics, and Law, hoping that this would gradually push the traditional community of Brahmins in more rational and useful directions. Increasingly, over a few decades, the British were dissatisfied with the management of this Sanskrit College in Pune. This Sanskrit College was eventually closed, and the British authorities opened a modern college, the Deccan College, in Pune in 1860. It was in this college, where modernity and western knowledge first made a major entrance into the consciousness of the Brahmin and non-Brahmin communities of the region. While the first half of the nineteenth century saw the emergence of modernizing Brahmins like Bal Shastri Jambhekar, a more serious turn in the direction of modern education and dissemination of western ideas began with the establishment of the Deccan College. The establishment of the Deccan College and the reduction of the official governmental support for the traditional Sanskrit education was perceived by the Brahmin community of Pune as a threat to the survival of the Sanskritic traditions, and this led to the emergence of purely native Brahmin institutions like the Vedaśāstrottejaka Sabhā and the new Sanskrit Pāṭhaśālā. The emergence of vernacular education with governmental and missionary support also saw another development. In addition to the traditionally educated Brahmin class, this period also saw, even though on a small scale, the emergence of a class of educated non-Brahmins. While the availability of modern western ideas was shared by the newly educated Brahmin as well as the non-Brahmin, given the traditional rivalries between these groups, the Brahmins and the non-Brahmins developed different conceptions of history, and sought support for different political and social movements. Emergence of Indian nationalism in the late nineteenth century also contributed to these conceptual developments. Different interpretations of the Aryan origins owe themselves to these different historical factors.

After Bal Shastri Jambhekar, who is generally considered to be the first Brahmin promoter of modern education in the vernacular languages, there appeared several Brahmins who carried forward the torch of modern education. Among these, we must count the figures of Bhau Daji Lad, Kashinath Telang, Ramkrishna G. Bhandarkar, and Mahadeo Govind Ranade. They constitute a generation of modern Brahmins which dominated the field of modern historical and Indological studies in the second half of the nineteenth century, and trained later generations of native scholars like Bal Gangadhar Tilak, Vishnushastri Chiplunkar, and M. M. Kunte. Bhau Daji, Telang, Bhandarkar, and Ranade were nationalists in their own right and yet were political moderates who saw the benefits of British education and governance toward the emergence of modern India. Among these, Bhandarkar was the only scholar who paid a great deal of attention to the question of Aryan origins, and the linguistic and social history of ancient India.

Bhandarkar's contribution toward an understanding of the Aryan origins may be seen most profoundly in his *Wilson Philological Lectures on Sanskrit and the Derived Languages* delivered in 1877 in Bombay, and published in the form of a book in 1914. In his introductory remarks, Bhandarkar refers to his departure from the traditional Sanskritic modes of thought and the precarious position he had reached among his contemporaries:

> A Shastri or Pandit is esteemed and treated with respect and consideration by his countrymen; the English-knowing Indian may be feared if he holds some Government appointment, but if none, he enjoys no consideration. . . . In one branch of learning, however, *viz.* Sanskrit, an English-knowing Indian may meet with appreciation and esteem at the hands of the learned in Europe. . . . Among his own countrymen he will find sympathy only if he has studied Sanskrit exactly in the old way, but even in this case his heterodoxy, which is the result of his English education, would stand in the way. But there are indications that a more sympathizing and appreciating body of men is growing about us, and the circle will go on widening as education advances. In this, as in other matters, there are hopes that our countrymen will, in the course of time, chiefly through the agency of Government education, adapt themselves to their altered circumstances; and the Hindu's inherent love of learning will gradually extend and engraft itself on the branches of knowledge to which he has been newly introduced by the European.
>
> (1914: 2)

This is the best description of the predicament of the emergence of modernity in Indian education. This modernity and its predicament is here to stay with us in the reception of the new theories of Aryan origins in this region in the nineteenth and the twentieth centuries.

Referring to the developments in historical and comparative linguistics since the days of William Jones, Bhandarkar says:

> The discovery of Sanskrit and the Indian grammatical system at the close of the last century led to a total revolution in the philological ideas of Europeans. . . . But several circumstances had about this time prepared Europe for independent thought in philology. . . . The languages of Europe, ancient and modern, were compared with Sanskrit and with each other. This led to comparative philology and the classification of languages, and a comparison of the words and forms in the different languages led scholars into the secrets of the growth of human speech, and the science of language was added to the list of existing branches of knowledge. The progress made within about fifty years is marvelous, and affords a striking instance of the intellectual activity of the Europeans. In the

> cultivation of Philology and the elaboration of this new science the Germans, of all other nations, have been most prominent, and have done by far the greater portion of the work.
>
> (Ibid.: 5)

Bhandarkar openly acknowledges his debt to this new European philology and is consequently advocating views on Indian history which come as a serious departure from the traditional Indian views.

While his *Wilson Philological Lectures* were specifically focused upon Sanskrit and the derived languages, and not on the Indo-European pre-history of Sanskrit, Bhandarkar acknowledges the essential validity of the construction of the Indo-European language family and the place of Sanskrit within this family: "The languages of the civilized nations of the world have been divided into three families, the Aryan or Indo-European, the Semitic and the Turanian" (Bhandarkar 1914: 15). Bhandarkar then gives a detailed description of languages belonging to the various branches of Indo-European including the Indian branch "consisting of Sanskrit, Pali and the Prakrits, and the modern vernaculars of Northern India and of Ceylon" (Bhandarkar 1914: 15). Referring to the Turanian family of languages, Bhandarkar says that it consists of "the Turkish and the languages of the Mongolian tribes. To this last family the dialects spoken in Southern India are also to be referred" (Bhandarkar 1914: 15). Making general observations, Bhandarkar says: "The Zend approaches Sanskrit the most, but the affinities of this latter with Greek and Latin are also very striking, and such as to convince even a determined skeptic" (Bhandarkar 1914: 15–16). The very historical approach to the study of Sanskrit, not just its pre-history, is a new development in the days of Bhandarkar. With a new historical approach to the study of Sanskrit grammarians, Bhandarkar asserts:

> It therefore appears clear to me that the language in Pāṇini's time was in a different condition from that in which it was in Kātyāyana's. . . . In Pāṇini's time a good many words and expressions were current which afterwards became obsolete; verbal forms were commonly used which ceased to be used in Kātyāyana's time, and some grammatical forms were developed in the time of the latter which did not exist in Pāṇini's.
>
> (Ibid.: 29)

For Indian intellectuals of the nineteenth-century Maharashtra, the notion that the pre-history of Sanskrit was connected with languages like Persian, Greek, and Latin, and that Sanskrit itself had a changing history of its own, were revolutionary ideas. These ideas remained revolutionary for quite some time and did not attain universal acceptance.

Bhandarkar, in examining the relationship between Sanskrit and Pali, begins to develop historically oriented explanations:

> Though [the speakers of Pali] heard conjunct consonants and the diphthongs *ai* and *au* pronounced by the speakers of Sanskrit, as correctly

> as the other letters which they did not corrupt, their organs were not fitted to utter them. These peculiarities may have been natural or acquired. If natural, the people who first corrupted Sanskrit into Pali must have belonged to an alien race which came into close contact with the Āryas and learnt their language. . . . And there is another instance in History of an alien race having treated the sounds of the language of a civilized community in just the same way. The Barbarians who overran Italy and developed the Italian from the Latin, showed the same inability to pronounce the Latin conjuncts, and assimilated them as our Pali ancestors did.
>
> (Ibid.: 47)

The process of the emergence of the Prakrits is accounted for by Bhandarkar by referring to the migration of the Āryas from "the land of the five rivers" to "the country known afterwards as Brahmāvarta and Kurukshetra." This is the country about Thaneśvar, where "they formed a consolidated community in which an aboriginal or alien race was incorporated and the language represented by the Pali was the language of that race" (Bhandarkar 1914: 88). The idea of the Āryas, the speakers of Sanskrit, coming into contact with non-Āryas, and such a contact leading to a degenerative transformation of Sanskrit into Prakrits is an idea not inherently alien to the Sanskritic tradition. But the same tradition does not admit any notion of history for this divine and eternal language, and here Bhandarkar's efforts to find historical origins of and developments in Sanskrit did not go well with his contemporaries. These were departures from the Sanskritic tradition. If the speakers of Sanskrit were Āryas, and if Sanskrit itself resulted from a process of transformation from its Indo-European precursors and underwent later transformations of its own, were the Āryas themselves subject to transformative processes? If the transformations of Sanskrit into Pali were caused by the alien speakers trying to learn the Aryan language, what was it that caused the transformations which resulted into the very existence of Sanskrit itself, and what caused transformations within the very history of Sanskrit? Such questions indeed raise unpalatable issues, and Bhandarkar's own wording suggests that he, as a Brahmin, was himself caught in the middle. Bhandarkar's wording would suggest a belief that the Āryas were not in contact with non-Aryans in "the land of the five rivers." Even admitting that the Indus civilization was not excavated by this time, one still finds this belief difficult to accept, particularly in view of the fact that there are north western Prakrits in Aśokan inscriptions, a fact which was known to Bhandarkar by this time. Bhandarkar finds that the northwestern Prakrits like Paiśācī,

> appear to be truly Aryan. Perhaps then this was the language of an Aryan tribe that had remained longer in the original seat of the race, and was connected with the ancestors of the Teutons, so as to develop a phonetic peculiarity resembling theirs, and emigrated to India at a very late period and settled on the borders. Or it might be that the tribe came to India along with the others, but living in the mountainous countries on the

> border in a sort of rude independence, it developed this peculiarity of pronunciation. . . . Since under this supposition they could not have come in very close contact with their more civilized brethren of the plains, their language did not undergo some of those phonetic modifications which Sanskrit underwent in the mouth of the aboriginal races.
>
> (Ibid.: 94)

So the speakers of northwestern Prakrits were truly Aryan, uncontaminated by contact with the non-Aryans, but not as civilized as the speakers of Sanskrit who did come in contact with the "aboriginal races." Bhandarkar almost seems to believe that the Aryans were not in contact with aboriginal races until they moved from "the land of five rivers" into the interior of India. Thus the linguistic deviations from Sanskrit in the direction of Pali and other Prakrits are caused by the contact of the Āryas with the non-Āryas, while the linguistic deviations from Sanskrit in the direction of the northwestern Prakrits and other IE languages are to be explained by "isolation" at best. This creates an interesting tripartite division: the ethnically pure but less civilized Āryas of the northwest, the pure civilized Āryas of the "land of the five rivers," and the uncivilized non-Āryas of the rest of the Indian subcontinent.

The notion that the ancestors of the Vedic Aryans came to India from outside was acceptable to Bhandarkar. Referring to the Mitanni inscriptions dated to 1400 BC, Bhandarkar (1933: Vol. I, 96) points out the proximity of the Mitannis to the Assyrians. He connects the Assyrians with the Asuras of the Vedas. He says that Atharvaveda (10.3.11: *sa me śatrūn vi bādhatām indro dasyūn ivāsurān*) puts the Dasyus and Asuras together, and comments:

> Is it not unlikely that just as in India the progress of the Aryans was contested by the Dasyus, so was it contested by the Asuras of Assyria and they were thus compared with the Dasyus in some of the passages quoted above. . . . In later times especially when Aryans settled in the regions of the five rivers, . . . the reminiscences of the human Asuras and the fights of the Aryans with them and their civilisation led to the whole subject having transformed itself into a myth of the determined enmity between the Devas and the Asuras.
>
> (1933: Vol. I, 97)

Citing Brunnhofer in support, Bhandarkar argues that "all hymns (of the Ṛgveda) were composed not in the Punjab; but Vedic poetry began when the Indian Aryans lived in a more northerly region. It is the work of poets of North Iran from Caspian Sea to the Punjab" (Bhandarkar 1933: Vol. I, 99). In his lecture in 1888 delivered at the Free Church College in Bombay, Bhandarkar expresses his complete support for the "critical, comparative, and historical method":

> The critical, comparative, and historical methods began to be well understood and employed about the end of the eighteenth century, and

> within a hundred years since that time, an equally amazing progress has been made. ... Before the application of the comparative and historical method the beliefs that the world was created in six days and that the Hebrew was the primitive language of which all the rest were offshoots were equally prevalent.
>
> (Ibid.: 363–4)

He wholeheartedly subscribes to the construction of the IE language family:

> Besides, from all the observation that the great founders of comparative philology have made, they have come to the conclusion that the affinity between the Sanskrit and the European languages dates from prehistoric times, i.e., is due to the fact that the ancestors of us all spoke one and the same language before they separated and formed distinct nationalities. This was long before the time when the Vedas were composed.
>
> (Ibid.: 377–8)

Bhandarkar was a political moderate and, though a nationalist, saw the benefits brought to India by the British rule, and especially by modern education. Even while appreciating the contribution of the Europeans in the development of modern knowledge, Bhandarkar wanted Indians not to lag behind:

> Why should discoveries be made in France, Germany and England, and not in India? ... Surely no costly laboratories are required to enable us to study the ancient literature of our country ... This is a field in which we may successfully compete with Europeans, and in which we enjoy certain peculiar advantages. But these advantages can be turned to account only if we follow their critical, comparative, and historical method. ... And here I feel myself in duty bound, even at the risk of displeasing some of you, to make a passing allusion to the most uncritical spirit that has come over us of praising ourselves and our ancestors indiscriminately, seeing nothing but good in our institutions and in our ancient literature, asserting that the ancient Hindus had made very great progress in all the sciences, physical, moral, and social, and the arts, ... and denying even the most obvious deficiencies in our literature. ... As long as this spirit exists in us, we can never hope to be able to throw light on our ancient history.
>
> (Ibid.: 391–2)

Bhandarkar was fond of referring to the leading western Indologists as Ṛṣis: "Let us ... sitting at the feet of the English, French, and German Ṛṣis,[1] imbibe the knowledge that they have to give, and at least keep pace with them, if not go beyond them" (Bhandarkar 1933: Vol. I, 393). Bhandarkar's liberal political views, his active participation in the movement for social reform, and his open-ended academic approach were not easily palatable to his contemporaries, including many of his students. Vishnushastri Chiplunkar and Bal Gangadhar Tilak were students of Bhandarkar at the Deccan College, and yet their more militant Hindu nationalism and their support of the conservative social agenda led them to frequently differ from Bhandarkar. However, in spite of the tensions between them and Bhandarkar, it is evident that the roots of modern education were planted in the soil of Pune. Of these two, B. G. Tilak went on to develop excitingly new ideas about the original home of the Aryans. But before looking at Tilak's ideas, we need to consider another pioneering figure in the nineteenth-century Maharashtra, Mahadeo Moreshwar Kunte.

Mahadeo Moreshwar Kunte (1835–88) was a remarkable person. In 1859, Kunte finished his high school matriculation and in 1864 received a BA degree from the University of Bombay. In 1867, he was appointed as the head master at a high school in Kolhapur. Until that point, he had not studied Sanskrit. In Kolhapur, he studied Sanskrit in the traditional way, and moved as a head master to Pune in 1871. He started a Marathi publication, *Ṣaḍdarśanacintanikā*, to introduce the philosophical systems in Sanskrit to Marathi readers, and most remarkably, in 1880 he wrote a book, *The Vicissitudes of Āryan Civilization in India*, which was submitted for a competition in Italy where it won a prize. Kunte, though a graduate of the University of Bombay, was not as well trained in Sanskrit philology as R. G. Bhandarkar, and yet his book encompasses many subjects demonstrating his wide reading. Kunte was a political moderate, but opposed the cause of social reform. His 1880 book is dedicated to "James Braithwaite Peile, Esq., C.S., M.A., Acting chief secretary to the Government of Bombay . . . as a token of appreciation of his sympathies with the natives of this country."[2] The book opens with a remarkable motto:

> There is a glorious future before the Āryas in India, now that their activities, dormant for centuries and threatening to become petrified, are likely to be revived and quickened by the ennobling and elevating many-sided civilization which the western Āryas have developed, and which is brought to bear upon them.
>
> (Kunte 1880)

This remarkable statement calling the British "Western Āryas," brothers of the "Indian Āryas" is reminiscent of the statement inscribed on the foundation stone of the Old Indian Institute Building, Oxford, dated to May 2, 1883:

> *śāleyam prācyaśāstrāṇāṃ jñānottejanatatparaiḥ /*
> *paropakāribhiḥ sadbhiḥ sthāpitāryopayoginī //1//*
> *ālbarṭeḍvarḍitikhyāto yuvarājo mahāmanāḥ /*
> *rājarājeśvarīputras tatpratiṣṭhāṃ vyadhāt svayam //2//*
> *aṅkarāmāṅkacandre'bde vaiśākhasyāsite dale /*
> *daśamyāṃ budhavāsare ca vāstuvidhir abhūd iha //3//*
> *īśānukampayā nityam āryavidyā mahīyatām /*
> *āryāvartāṅglabhūmyoś ca mitho maitrī vivardhatām //4//*

> This Building, dedicated to Eastern sciences, was founded for the use of Āryas (Indians and Englishmen) by excellent and benevolent men desirous of encouraging knowledge. The High-minded Heir-Apparent, named Albert Edward, Son of the Empress of India, himself performed the act of inauguration. The ceremony of laying the Memorial Stone took place on Wednesday, the tenth lunar day of the dark half of the month of Vaiśākha, in the Saṃvat year 1939 (= Wednesday, May 2, 1883). By the favor of God may the learning and literature of India be ever held in honour; and may the mutual friendship of India and England constantly increase![3]

While Bhandarkar had deep respect for Western Indologists and was generally a political moderate, I have not detected a reference to "Western Āryas" in his writings. In this respect, Kunte has gone a step ahead. However, Bhandarkar, though not using the expression "Western Āryas," had already gone in the direction of what Thomas Trautmann (1997: 190ff.) calls "The Racial Theory of Indian Civilization." Kunte, however, extends this racial affinity argument beyond Bhandarkar, either out of conviction or to earn favor with his British bosses, or both. In general, Kunte was treated with biting sarcasm by his contemporaries, especially by Vishnushastri Chiplunkar (Chiplunkar 1926: 1039; Rajwade 1980: 12–13).

Besides the notion of racial affinity of the Indians with the British, Kunte repeatedly speaks of "Āryan invasion," "Āryans before invasion," and "India before the Āryan invasion." His 1880 book opens with this introductory comment: "Before the Āryas invaded India, the country was inhabited by races philologically and religiously allied with one another to a considerable extent" (Kunte 1880: xxi). The Āryas, who subjugated the non-Āryas, had a history consisting of important epochs:

> their establishment in India after a long and continued struggle for centuries, the development of their activities by struggle, their prosperity and the consolidation of their power, . . . their expeditions into the different parts of India, their expansion and their attempts at the Āryanization of the enterprising aboriginal races.
>
> (Ibid.: xxi)

The first chapter of Kunte's book is titled "Antecedents of the Ancient Indian Āryas" and it discusses

> the questions of their origin, their mythology, their philology, and their sacrificial system, and shows how they spread out toward the countries of Europe – entering into the history of the Mazdayasnians, and pointing out the causes of the dissensions between them and the Indian Āryas.
>
> (Ibid.: xxv)

The general stages in the development of the history of the Āryas according to Kunte (1880: 2) are:

1 The early history of the Āryan tribes, constituting the Āryan race as a whole.
2 The separation of the tribes and their migration into the western regions.
3 The great schism among the Āryans in Āriana itself and its features.
4 The consequent invasion of India.

In order to reconstruct these stages, Kunte promises to use "materials which can be obtained from the Rik-Sanhitā, Comparative Philology, Comparative Mythology, the Zendavesta and the very extensive sacrificial literature of the Brahmavādins" (Kunte 1880: 3–4). Through his theory of gradual growth, Kunte hopes to demonstrate the rise of the Āryas "from barbarism, to pursue, for some time, pastoral and agricultural life, and when prepared, to form a feudal confederacy, though spontaneous and tacit, and in the fullness of time to develop grand schemes of the invasion and occupation of India" (Kunte 1880: 6–7). His last phrase "grand schemes of the invasion and occupation of India" almost parallels his description of the British rule.

How barbarous were the "original" Āryas as compared to the Āryas in the Ṛgveda? Kunte indeed wants to make a clear distinction between their states of civilization.

> The ancient Āryas were at first, that is, long before they invaded India, savages who hunted wild beasts and lived upon their flesh, the whole animal being cooked. Some of them formed a gang, and intoxicated with the Soma-juice, went a-shooting, yelling as frantically as possible, brandishing their rude javelin-like poles, and overcame their wild adversary in the recesses of a jungle more by dint of a furious onslaught, than by a sustained effort. They had not constructed even rude huts to live in.
>
> (Ibid.: 7)

However, Kunte wants to assure us that references in the Ṛgveda (1.164.43) to cooking a spotted ox are "old or ancient" practices belonging to "times that had long past away" (Kunte 1880: 7, fn. 1). But, while the Ṛgveda retains memories of an ancient past, very different from the civilized Ṛgvedic present, this civilized Ṛgvedic present was evidently a continuity of the civilized state attained by the no-longer-barbarous Āryas already in their "mother country" before they launched their invasion of India. In India, when the now-civilized Āryas reached its borders, they had to fight the uncivilized Dasyus:

> When the long war with the Dasyus ended, when kingdoms on the model of those in their mother country were formed, when the tribes settled, maintaining the same social, religious and political relations with one

> another as before, when the Āryans were duly respected by the aborigines who had learnt submission, when the prestige of Āryan gods was completely established and when Āryan society in India was thoroughly consolidated, it was significantly observed by a poet who naturally expressed a national feeling, that Dhātā – the god of stability – arranged society as it once existed. ... The Āryans attempted at least to reproduce on the banks of the five rivers of the Punjab all that they once possessed and cherished in the plateau of Ariana.
>
> (Ibid.: 21–2)

For Kunte, the Āryas of the Ṛgveda were fully civilized already before they entered India, where they transplanted their already developed social, religious and political institutions, "as the colonists in America transplanted institutions, the growth of the English soil to the banks of the Mississippi and the Hudson" (ibid.). However, there were those pre-Āryan uncivilized Dasyus to deal with in India. Thus a division between the civilized Ārya of the Ṛgveda and the uncivilized Dasyu was at the core of ancient Indian history, and with it the mission to subjugate and civilize the uncivilized. That burden obviously fell on the shoulders of the civilized Āryas, as it did on the shoulders of the civilized British, "the Western Āryas."

Now, let us view "the character of the invading ancient Āryas" through Kunte's narrative. The second chapter of Kunte's book has the title: "The Invasion of India and the Period of Occupation." From their original home, Ariana,

> the Āryas who had resisted all temptations of emigrating from their homes and who had made progress in some arts of peaceful life were compelled to abandon their native country and all that they cherished most, their lands, and pastures, and depart, never to return, toward the East. ... They marched *en masse* with their families, with their servants, with their military bands, with their hordes of husbandmen, with their shop-keepers, and their artisans, clinging to their social institutions, and their sacrificial customs. ... The Āryan community soon came in contact with the aborigines of the Punjab – the Dāsas and the Dasyus.
>
> (Ibid.: 111–12)

However, there was no match between the civilized Āryas and the uncivilized Dāsas and Dasyus. While the Āryas could organize an expedition and use weapons of warfare and "invent new machines," the Dāsas had no weapons "worthy of notice" and they merely congregated "in villages without any social organization." The Āryas had plans and justifications for their actions, while the Dāsas "impulsively declared their intentions, made attacks, or surrendered at discretion." The Āryas were "well-built, strong, fair, attractive in their features," while the Dāsas "were dark, ill-proportioned and repulsive" (Kunte 1880: 113–14). There was every reason for the Āryas to be boastful, their "boastfulness was encouraged and confirmed by the inferiority of the aboriginal races," and Kunte perceives a similar situation in modern India: "The ancient Āryas spoke of their heroes as being the special care of their gods, and magnified their enterprises. The Englishman speaks with pride, glory and self-complacency of his Indian heroes." But there is one major difference: "The ancient Āryas settled in India. The modern Englishman is only a sojourner till [he] makes his fortune" (Kunte 1880: 147–8). This discussion of the significant difference between the ancient Āryas who invaded India and became Indians and the modern Western Āryas who are there just to make a fortune shows that Kunte is not averse to making a political point. With all the appreciation of the help offered by the Western Āryas, Kunte, the politically moderate author, is still a nationalist at heart.

Finally, Kunte is a Brahmin scholar and his Brahmanical approaches to historical reconstruction become gradually clear toward the end of his book. While dealing with the ancient periods, his term "Indian Ārya" is inclusive of the three higher Varṇas, the Śūdra being relegated to the non-Ārya. However, coming closer to modern times, Kunte expresses a pervasive Brahmin belief. Note how the history moves from ancient to modern times in his narrative:

> The Āryas are essentially superior to the non-Āryas. The social history of India is the history of the relative bearing of the two races on one another. ... The division of the Āryas into Brāhmaṇas, Kṣatriyas, and Vaishyas has become obsolete. It is distinctly asserted that there are now only two castes – the Brāhmaṇas and the Shūdras.
>
> (Ibid.: 509)

Thus, looking at the broad picture painted by Kunte, it would seem that there are the Western Āryas, that is, the British, the Indian Āryas, that is, the Brāhmaṇas, and the non-Āryas, that is, all non-Brāhmaṇa communities, all lumped in the Śūdra category. There is clear affirmation in Kunte's work that the "civilizing influences" (p. 516) and the "civilizing power" (p. 517) of the Western Āryas with respect to Indians are similar to the civilizing role of the Ārya Brāhmaṇas with respect to non-Ārya non-Brāhmaṇas. Such roles necessarily involve what Kunte himself calls the "principle of graded subordination" (Kunte 1880: 509). However, Kunte says that there are large

> aboriginal races like the Jats in the Punjab, the Santhals in Bengal, the Gonds and Khonds between the valleys of the Godavari, and the Mahanadi, the Mahars and Dheds of Maharashtra, the Kolis generally on the banks of the rivers, and the Bhills in Central India and the Todors in the Nilgiris – all these are without the pale, both of the Moslems and the Brāhmaṇas. ... Their elevation depends on the civilizing power of the Europeans.
>
> (Ibid.: 517)

While much of Bhandarkar's methodologically sound historical work is still respected by scholars, Kunte's magnum opus, because of its ideological orientation and lack of sound historical methodology, has fallen by the way side. However, in its own days, it had its detractors like Vishnushastri Chiplunkar (1926: 1039) and admirers like Rajwade (1980: 12–13). Vaman Balkrishna Ranade (1925: 53), a contemporary of Kunte who has written a brief account of Kunte's life, praises Kunte's *Vicissitudes* very highly: "Anyone who has had a chance to read this book can attest to the high scholarship and searching intelligence of Mr. Kunte." In its own times, Kunte's book was very influential.

A contemporary of Bhandarkar and a participant in the social and religious reform movements and liberal politics was Justice Mahadeo Govind Ranade. Ranade's historical work focuses more on the period of the Maratha kingdoms, though one sees his treatment of ancient history in some of his writings. In his "Introduction to Mr. Vaidya's Book" one finds the most elaborate references to the period of the ancient Āryas. Here, Ranade is mainly concerned with issues related to social reform, and yet he is making his statements about the need for social reform in the context of reviewing the ancient history of social institutions: "There is abundant reason for hope that an historical study of these institutions will dispel many a false conception of the antiquity and sanctity of the existing arrangements" (M. G. Ranade 1915: 71). In his presentation of the need for reform of the Hindu social practices like child-marriage and ban on widow re-marriage, Ranade points out the similarities of practices among the Hindu Āryas and the Roman Āryas:

> The rise and fall of female rights and status in Hindu Āryan society has a history of its own, at once interesting and suggestive in its analogies to the corresponding developments in the institutions of another kindred stock, the Roman Aryans, who have so largely influenced European ideas. Both began by a complete subordination of the women in the family to the men, and of the men themselves to the head of the family.
>
> (1915: 72–3)

Here, it is clear that Ranade accepts the bond of common ancestry between the Hindu Āryas and the Roman Āryas, something that was common knowledge for his western-educated generation. Ranade likes to argue that the ideals of social reform were already practiced by the ancient Āryas during some early period. However, a decay sets in due to the conflicts of the Āryas with the non-Āryas:

> The Aryan ideals lost their charm, and a lower type of character and morality asserted its predominance as the down-trodden races, which had been driven to the hills, issued from their haunts, and fell upon the demoralized and disunited Aryan kingdoms on all sides.
>
> (Ibid.: 74)

Thus, Ranade would like to believe in a sort of ideal golden period of the ancient Āryas when they were practicing a sort of modern morality and were politically united. All this came to an end through internal demoralization as well as through the external attacks by the non-Āryas. These non-Āryas were a degrading influence upon the Āryas. This was compounded by the degradation which occurred during the rule of the Muslims. Ranade looks upon the British rule as a golden opportunity to return to the ancient ideals of the pure Āryas:

> Fortunately, the causes which brought on this degradation have been counteracted by Providential guidance, and we have now, with a living example before us of how pure Aryan customs, unaffected by barbarous laws and patriarchal notions, resemble our own ancient usages, to take up the thread where we dropped it under foreign and barbarous pressure, and restore the old healthy practices.
>
> (Ibid.: 76)

It is clear that Ranade looks upon the social customs of the British as continuities from the common ancestral Aryan period "unaffected by barbarous laws and patriarchal notions," and the newly found association of the British Aryans with the currently degraded Indian Aryans as an opportunity for the degraded Indian Aryans to go back to their ancient glory.

At the same time, Ranade, the nationalist, is proud of his Āryavarta-India:

> I profess implicit faith in two articles of my creed. This country of ours is the true land of promise. This race of ours is the chosen race. It was not for nothing that God has showered his choicest blessings on this ancient land of Aryavarta. We can see His hand in history.
>
> (Ibid.: 125)

This is what Ranade said in 1893 during his speech at Lahore on the occasion of the Seventh Social Conference. Making such a pro-Ārya and pro-Āryāvarta statement seemed appropriate in a place like Lahore in the very Aryan land of the five rivers. However, Ranade changed his rhetoric in just one year. Speaking in 1894 in Madras at the Eighth Social Conference, Ranade realized that he was speaking to the representatives of the non-Aryan Dravidian south: "Your Dravidian civilization has been always very strong enough to retain the stamp of its individuality in the midst of Aryan inundations, which submerged it for a time" (M. G. Ranade 1915: 133). The benevolent character of the Aryan migration and the superiority of the Aryans of the Āryāvarta became a political liability in the land of Dravidian pride, and Ranade, the emerging politician, quickly changed his rhetoric to fit the changed circumstances. A few years later, in 1899, now speaking to the Thirteenth Social Conference in Lucknow, Ranade said:

> Far in the South, which is now the stronghold of Brahmanical ideas uninfluenced by outside contact, the Aryan civilisation no doubt made its way, but it continued to be an exotic civilisation confined to a small minority of Aryan settlers, so few in numbers that they were overwhelmed by the influences of the earlier Dravidian domination.
>
> (Ibid.: 215)

The political use of history gets more and more confused. If the British Aryans are supposed to help the Indian Aryans to go back to a purer form of Aryan social institutions, what is supposed to happen to the non-Aryan Dravidians of the south? The division of the Brahmin-Ārya from the non-Brahmin non-Ārya, and the division of the Aryan north from the Dravidian south posed complicated problems for the British Aryans, who had to face different demands from these groups. Were they supposed to Aryanize the Indian non-Aryan and re-Aryanize the Indian Aryan, or were they supposed to save the non-Aryan Indian from the domination of the Indian Brahmin-Aryan?

The above dilemmas become more evident when considered from the point of view expressed by a rare non-Brahmin author, Jotirao Phule (1827–90). Phule was born in the Mali "gardener" caste which is traditionally held to be above the untouchables, but below the Maratha castes. In the Brahmin ideology of the period, all non-Brahmins were Śūdras, because it was believed by the Brahmins that the true ancient Kṣatriyas and Vaiśyas had not survived. Thus, the Brahmins were the only representatives of the ancient Āryas, and all other castes, including the ruling Maratha houses were considered as belonging to the Śūdra groups. It is evident from my presentation of the views of Bhandarkar, Kunte, and Ranade that such views had percolated even into the writings of the modern Brahmins of Maharashtra, who perceived their dominant role as analogous to the role of the new colonial rulers, the British Āryas. Phule's writings provide a unique glimpse into the way these relations were viewed by individuals from the non-Brahmin communities. There indeed was no unanimity among the various non-Brahmin groups on such issues. There is enough evidence to show that the ruling Maratha houses of Maharashtra considered themselves to be Kṣatriyas and claimed to belong to the three upper Varṇas, eligible for Vedic ceremonies. Traditionally, the Brahmins of the region did not easily accept this claim. Such issues were raised in 1676 when Shivaji, after establishing a successful kingdom of his own, wanted to be coronated as a Kṣatriya king according to Vedic rites of coronation. The local Brahmins refused to perform this ceremony, claiming that there were no true Kṣatriyas in the world any longer. Finally, a Brahmin from Banaras, Gāgābhaṭṭa, was brought to perform this ceremony for Shivaji. This tension continued into the nineteenth century, when the Maratha king of Kolhapur insisted on having Vedic rites performed for him. These Kṣatriya ruling houses would certainly have claimed to represent the Aryan warrior class. However, there are clear indications that the same ruling Kṣatriya houses would not accord the same Kṣatriya status to other caste groups who were accorded a lower Śūdra status by both the Brahmins and the Kṣatriya houses. Phule's position in this complicated social structure is important. He would like to have the Kṣatriya houses on his side against the domination of the Ārya-Brahmin.

In his numerous publications, Phule presents a picture of history, which is not different in substance from the one seen in the works of the Brahmin authors like Bhandarkar, Kunte, and Ranade. However, his interpretation is very different. Agreeing with the idea that Āryas came into India from outside and subjugated the indigenous groups, Phule identifies these invading Āryas exclusively with

Brahmins. In doing so, he is using the very ideas propagated by Brahmins that the old Kṣatriyas and Vaiśyas have no longer survived, and that there are only Brahmins and Śūdras. However, in the context of the theory of Āryan invasion, the Brahmins become the outsiders, foreigners, and the subjugated Śūdras become the true sons of the soil, the aggrieved people who lost their independence. In Phule's interpretation, those Śūdras who tilled the land (*kṣetra*), became Kṣetriyas "land-owners/land-tillers," and these were the true Kṣatriyas. The invading foreign Ārya-Brahmins came in hordes from Iran and subjugated the pre-Āryan people of the land. In describing the process of subjugation, Phule cleverly uses Brahmanical myths, but turns them upside down. The myth of the axe-wielding Brahmin Paraśurāma killing all Kṣatriyas in the world twenty-one times shows the cruelty of the invading Brahmins. Phule says that the indigenous Kṣatriyas fought Paraśurāma so bravely that they came to be named Mahā-ari "great enemies," but after their subjugation, these brave Mahā-aris were reduced to the status of untouchables (Mahār, cf. Phule 1991: 41). The Vāmana incarnation of Viṣṇu, in the form of a Brahmin boy subjugating the demon Bali through deceit, shows how the Brahmins subjugated the non-Brahmins through deceit. Most of these ideas are frequently repeated in Phule's writings, but are seen in a concentrated form in his *Gulāmgiri* "Slavery" (Phule 1991: 111ff.).

While Bhandarkar, Kunte, and Ranade looked forward to the "civilizing" mission of the British Āryas, at the same time noticing its similarity with the civilizing mission of the ancient Indian Āryas, Phule was urging the British authorities to save the non-Ārya Śūdras from the domination of the Ārya-Brahmin. The clearest expression of this is seen in his "Memorial addressed to the Education Commission" in 1882 (Phule 1991: 233). Phule says:

> I sincerely hope that Government will ere long ... take the glory into their own hands of emancipating my Shudra brethren from the trammels of bondage which the Brahmins have woven around them like the coils of a serpent. ... Away with all Brahmin school-masters.
>
> (1991: 236)

Phule never refers to the British by the term, Ārya, which is reserved only for the despised Brahmins. Phule's construction of the ancient history is thus a mirror image of the history constructed by the Brahmin authors, similar in substance, but opposite in its orientation. Brahmin authors reacted vigorously to Phule, and this reaction is seen particularly in the writings of Vishnushastri Chiplunkar (1926: 441ff., 1020ff.).

Vishnushastri Chiplunkar (1850–82) had the shortest span of life among his contemporaries, and yet his prolific and fiery writings have left a significant legacy of a brilliant mind. Vishnushastri represents a segment of Pune Brahmins very different from the one represented by the moderate Bhandarkar and Ranade. Vishnushastri and B. G. Tilak were students of Bhandarkar, and yet temperamentally differed from him. They despised the moderateness of Bhandarkar and

Ranade and accused them of being British sympathizers. The hoped camaraderie between the Western Āryas and the Indian Āryas seen in the works of Bhandarkar and Ranade was infuriating to Chiplunkar and Tilak, whose political views were more conservative and militant. Their works laid the foundation of the conservative militant Hindu nationalist movement. Vishnushastri does not seem to be opposed to the theoretical construction of the Indo-European language family and the place of Sanskrit within such a family: "It is clear from a good deal of evidence that these (Parsee/Iranian) people belong to the Aryan family. From the similarity of languages and ritual practices, it is established that the ancient Hindus were related to the ancient people of Persia" (Chiplunkar 1926: 606–7). Turning to the origin of the Hindus, Chiplunkar says:

> The origin of this (Hindu) nation is from the Aryan branch, which is considered to be the principal branch of the human race. . . . The original home of these Aryans was probably somewhere in-between Europe and Asia. Such is the conjecture of modern philologists. From that region, different groups of these people went very far in both directions. This is what everyone believes these days. One of these groups came to the east and settled in Iran and another group came and inhabited the land of Punjab. This is the original home of the ancient Hindus. From there, they spread throughout the country.
>
> (1926: 615)

Thus there is not much difference between the historical notions expressed by Bhandarkar, Ranade, and Chiplunkar.

However, here the similarity ends. While from a purely historical point of view, Chiplunkar may not be opposed to expressions like "Western Āryas" or "British Āryas," however, for Chiplunkar, there was no love lost between these two Āryas. In fact, Chiplunkar discusses in great detail how the British hated the Brahmin. He discusses a letter signed by a British person as Elifas in the Bombay Gazette (September 29, 1876) which had the heading "The Native Press and Brahmin Intriguers." The letter says: "When will the Government be awake to the fact that a Brahman is a born-intriguer." Referring to Vishnushastri Chiplunkar, the letter says:

> It is unnecessary to say that he is one of the herd of demi-semi-educated Brahmans, annually let loose on the country from the Government schools and colleges. It is as needless to say that he is a Government servant, a master in an English High School. . . . (He has) a special talent as a caterer to the intellectual and moral wants of the native public.
>
> (Ibid.: 643)

The author of the letter says that it is the Brahmin who stays aloof from the European, and not the European from the Brahmin. The Brahmins believe that "the lowest Brahmin would be defiled by eating with the highest European." Vishnushastri takes the author of this letter to task. So much for the love between the Indian and the British Aryans.

What one notices in the writings of Vishnushastri Chiplunkar is the segment of Brahmins which is caught between the British on one hand and the Śūdras on the other; these Brahmins are waging a fight on both the fronts. In criticizing Jotirao Phule's charges that the Chitpavan Brahmins were born from a funeral fire or that they were invaders from Iran, Vishnushastri angrily asserts that, whatever the origin of the Chitpavan Brahmins, their natural qualities have always manifested themselves before and no mean attacks like the writings of Jotirao are going to diminish those qualities (1926: 1023). Referring to the high intelligence of the Hindu Āryas, Chiplunkar says:

> Another quality (of the Indian Āryas) is their intelligence. Our country is famous for this quality from the very beginning. When the most ancient nations of Europe had not even been born, the people of this land of Āryas had developed high intelligence, and one cannot say that that intelligence has diminished even under the current conditions of [political] down-turn. The power of intelligence, which the Āryas had when they first settled in the land of five rivers, is still the same after the passage of thousands of years.
>
> (Ibid.: 1069)

The notion that the Indian Āryas may themselves be of foreign origin needed to be dealt with more specifically, because it has uneasy implications in that the Indian Āryas become foreigners like the Muslims, the French, and the English. Chiplunkar elaborates an interesting argument in favor of the Indian Āryas:

> Recently, western scholars have determined a theory, based on linguistic and other theories, that this land of India was not originally ours. Of the many Aryan nations which lived near the Caucasus mountains, many went to the east and others to the west. Among them, we and the Iranians are the eastern Aryan nations. The Iranians went to Iran, while we entered this Hindusthan through the region of Punjab. If this explanation is accepted, then like the Muslims, the French, and the English, we are ourselves foreigners. The only thing we can consider is how we behaved among ourselves as well as with the people we subjugated. Recently, it has been determined that there was no caste system in the Vedic times. So, clearly there could not have been the (alleged) domination of the Brahmins. Therefore, we do not need to worry about this period. Eventually, in the evil age of the Purāṇas, the fourfold system of Brahmins, Kṣatriyas, Vaiśyas, and Śūdras entered the land of the Āryas. Even in this period, it is difficult to figure out how these four

> Varṇas came to be determined. It is obvious that each person was assigned to a Varṇa fitting his qualities and abilities. ... How did the Āryas treat the people they subjugated? There is no evidence that the Āryas eliminated the subjugated Śūdras and tribals or fed them to hunting dogs. There is no evidence that any Āryas committed atrocities alleged by Mr. Jotirao Phule.
>
> (Ibid.: 1178–9)

Thus, Vishnushastri counters Phule's charges strongly, and in doing so establishes the superiority of Indian Āryas over the Western Āryas. It was they who tried to eliminate the Red Indians in the American colonies. In fact, Vishnushastri uses the expression "our Western Aryan brothers" (*āmace pāścātya āryabandhu*) sarcastically (1926: 1239). If "our Western Aryan brothers" care for us so much, why don't they just offer us sage advice and retire to their own country, rather than stay here and exploit us (Chiplunkar 1926: 1223). Referring to the mutiny of 1857, Chiplunkar laments? "In this century, there was a chance of getting rid of all foreigners and establishing sovereignty of our Aryan land. However, our Western Aryan brothers found our weakness and set us fighting among ourselves, and that chance was lost" (1926: 1225). Vishnushastri marks a turning point in the use of the expression "our Western Āryan brothers."

Among the personalities considered so far, Bhandarkar was the only trained philologist of modern Maharashtra to deal with the question of Aryan origins. Others based their opinions on derived information and built their arguments to fit the social and political needs as they saw them. B. G. Tilak (1856–1920), on the other hand, had an original approach, an approach based not so much on philology, but on astronomy and geology, and on an ingenious interpretation of Vedic textual materials. Three of his publications bear witness to his scholarly treatment of the subject of Aryan origins. Importantly, unlike many of the other authors, his treatment of the subject rests on purely scholarly grounds, and does not make any reference to the contemporary social or political conditions. This is particularly remarkable considering how deeply he was involved in the nationalist politics of the day. His first publication on the subject was the book *Orion or Researches into the Antiquity of the Vedas*, published in 1893. His second publication was *The Arctic Home in the Vedas*, published in 1903. His third and the last publication on the subject was the book *Vedic Chronology and Vedāṅga Jyotisha* [*Containing also Chaldean and Indian Vedas and other miscellaneous essays*], written in 1913 in the Mandaly jail in Burma and published posthumously in 1925.

Tilak's contribution to this subject is so voluminous and the astronomical, geological, and textual arguments so complex, that it would not be possible to do justice to them in a few paragraphs. What distinguishes Tilak from all others is that he is not just arguing for the Arctic home of the Aryans, in the sense of Indo-Europeans; he is specifically arguing that the descriptions in the Vedic texts themselves are of such high antiquity, and hence the Vedas themselves may be located in the Arctic home. Here is a summary of Tilak's conclusions in his own words:

> 10000 or 8000 B.C. – The destruction of the original Arctic home by the last Ice Age and the commencement of the post-Glacial period.
>
> 8000–5000 B.C. – The age of migration from the original home. The survivors of the Aryan race roamed over the northern parts of Europe and Asia in search of lands suitable for new settlements. The vernal equinox was then in the constellation of Punarvasu, and as Aditi is the presiding deity of Punarvasu, ... this may, therefore, be called the Aditi or the Pre-Orion Period.
>
> 5000–3000 B.C. – The Orion Period, when the vernal equinox was in Orion. Many Vedic hymns can be traced to the early part of this period and the bards of the race seem to have not yet forgotten the real import or significance of the traditions of the Arctic home inherited by them. ...
>
> 3000–1400 B.C. – The Kṛttikā Period, when the vernal equinox was in the Pleiades. The Taittirīya Saṃhitā and the Brāhmaṇas, which begin the series of nakṣatras with the Kṛttikās, are evidently the productions of this period. ... The traditions about the original Arctic home had grown dim by this time and very often misunderstood, making the Vedic hymns more and more unintelligible.
>
> (1903: 453–4)

Summing up his "historical view" of the Vedas, as opposed to the "theological view" of the tradition, Tilak makes three significant points:

> 1 The Vedic or the Aryan religion can be proved to be inter-glacial; but its ultimate origin is still lost in geological antiquity.
> 2 Aryan religion and culture were destroyed during the last Glacial period that invaded the Arctic Aryan home.
> 3 The Vedic hymns were sung in post-Glacial times by poets, who had inherited the knowledge or contents thereof in an unbroken tradition from their ante-diluvian fore-fathers.
>
> (Ibid.: 457)

A succinct critique of Tilak's ideas is offered by Dandekar:

> It is, for instance, difficult to imagine that the Vedic seers had preserved in their oral traditions, for over five thousand years which could have by no means been a period of peace and stability, the memories of the experiences of their ancestors in the arctic region. And why, it may be asked, should these memories have been preserved specifically by the Vedic and the Iranian Aryans? ... The fourth and last Ice-age is now believed

> to have occurred about 50,000 B.C. ... The primarily naturalistic and astronomical interpretation of the Vedic *mantras*, which Tilak adopts, is also not much favoured by the modern Vedists. But the major defect of Tilak's theory is that it has completely ignored the linguistic and archaeological aspects of the question.
>
> (1981: 8–9)

While it is true that Tilak does not bring up any of the contemporary social or political issues while discussing his theory, and argues purely on the basis of evidence as he sees it, his theory can be seen to have some interesting implications. The earlier theories of Aryan migrations as seen in the works of Bhandarkar, Kunte, and Chiplunkar accept the notion of the Aryans coming to India from outside, and yet they seem to connect the composition of the Vedas with the region of Punjab. That makes the Vedas a product of a branch of Indo-European. However, Tilak's theory of the Arctic home in the Vedas takes the descriptions given in the Vedas, if not the Vedas themselves, to a period of 8000–10000 BC. That would almost certainly place the Vedas earlier than the Greeks, the Romans, and the Mitannis. Such a hoary ancestry to the Vedas makes their inheritors, the Indian Aryans, senior brothers to the Western Aryans, in spite of their current condition of subservience to them. At best, it suggests the possibility that the linguistic and the cultural traditions of the Western Aryans may be derived from the more ancient Vedic tradition, and at minimum, their traditions turn out to be younger than the Vedic traditions. Such implications would certainly have an energizing impact on the nationalist movement rooted in the Brahmanical tradition. The possibility that the traditions of the Greeks and Romans could be derived from the Vedic tradition has not been seriously entertained in Tilak's own writings, and yet it is clear that this is the direction that would appear in the works of nationalist Indian authors during Tilak's lifetime. Stanley Wolpert has discussed the significance of Tilak's theories for his nationalistic goals. He shows that Tilak spoke differently on different occasions, more cautious on some than on others. In his *Arctic Home in the Vedas* and similar publications, Wolpert claims, Tilak was "anxious to maintain the guise of scientific impartiality" (Wolpert 1961: 125). The cautious Tilak says:

> It is impossible to demonstrate historically or scientifically that Vedic religion and worship is *absolutely* without a beginning. All that we can say is that its beginning is lost in geological antiquity. ... If theologians are not satisfied with the support which this scientific view accords to their theory about the eternity of the Vedas, the scientific and the theological views must stand, as they are, distinct from each other, for the two methods of investigation are essentially different.
>
> (1894: 37–8)

However, on another occasion, the less cautious Tilak says: "We may, however, still assert that for all practical purposes the Vedic religion can be shown to be beginningless even on strict scientific grounds" (reported in Wolpert 1961: 126). The political significance of Tilak's theories was not lost on his followers. In his Sanskrit biography of Tilak, Chitale (1956: 203) claims that, in the conflict between the Eastern and the Western civilizations, Tilak accomplished the victory of the Eastern civilization over the Western civilization in his publications (*paurvātya-pāścātya-saṃskṛtyoḥ saṅgharṣe paurvātya-saṃskṛter vijayo 'nena grantha-dvaya-nirmāṇena lokamānyaiḥ sampāditaḥ*).

As a representative of this direction in constructing a nationalist version of ancient history, we may consider the prolific writings of Narayan Bhavanrao Pavgee who is the author of a multivolume work *The Bhāratīya Sāmrājya or Hindu Empire*. This was projected to be completed in twenty-two volumes, and eleven volumes had already appeared by 1912. Besides these volumes, he also published in 1912 another work: *The Vedic Fathers of Geology*. Pavgee's work is distinctly inspired, though not constrained by the work of B. G. Tilak, who disagreed with Pavgee's notion of the Āryāvartic home of the Aryans. However, Pavgee's nationalist Hindu ideology is visible throughout his writings, something that cannot be said for the careful work of Tilak. Pavgee's multivolume work is dedicated with love and respect to all Ārya brothers (*ārya-bāndhava*) and sisters (*ārya-bhaginī*) and is intended to express his very strong affection for his dear Ārya mother-land (*dayita-ārya-bhūmi*).

The second volume of his *Bhāratīya Sāmrājya* (1893) is titled: *Āryalok va tyāñce Buddhi-vaibhav* "The Āryan People and the Wealth of their Intelligence." The book begins with a section dealing with the original home of the Āryas (*āryāñce mūla-nivāsa-sthāna*). Pavgee asserts at the very beginning that the Vedas are the oldest literature of mankind, and that the Vedas support the notion that northern India is the original home of not just the Aryans, but of the entire mankind (Pavgee 1893: 2). In his support, he cites Elphinstone's *History of India*:

> It is opposed to their foreign origin, that neither in the code, nor, I believe, in the Vedas nor in any book that is certainly older than the code is there any allusion to a prior residence or to a knowledge of more than the name of any country out of India. Even mythology goes no further than the Himalaya chain in which is fixed the habitation of the gods.
>
> (Pavgee 1893: 3–4)

The Aryan family of languages originated in India, Pavgee (1893: 5) asserts, and it expanded westward from India through the regions of Iran, Greece, Italy, Spain, England, Germany, and Russia. Pavgee mentions the view of western philologists that the Aryans came into India from outside, but he does not support this view. In the ninth volume of his *Bhāratīya Sāmrājya* (1900), titled *Bharatakhaṇḍātīl Nānāvidha Bhāṣā* "Various Languages in India," Pavgee has a section on the original land of the Ārya language, that is, Sanskrit. Pavgee asserts unequivocally that Sanskrit originated in the region of Āryāvarta within India and is the mother of all Aryan languages. All languages such as Marāṭhī, Hindī, Bengalī, Gujaratī,

Iranian, Greek, Latin, German, English, and Polish were born from Sanskrit. They are daughters of Sanskrit (Pavgee 1900: 14). Various originally Ārya groups left their religion and castes and left the original Ārya homeland, and these eventually became the various branches of the Aryan language family. In support of this conclusion, Pavgee offers a large number of passages from Smṛtis and Purāṇas (Pavgee 1900: 16ff.).

In his 1912 book in English, *The Vedic Fathers of Geology*, Pavgee refers to another of his publications that I have not been able to get hold of. However, in this publication, Pavgee tries to outdo the theories of B. G. Tilak. Here are Pavgee's theories in his own words:

> In my work entitled "The Āryāvartic Home and the Aryan cradle in the Sapta Sindhus," or "From Āryāvarta to the Arctic and from the Cradle to the Colony," and in my larger work in Marathi with still greater details, I have endeavoured to prove, by all sorts of evidences, Vedic and non-Vedic, scriptural and profane, scientific and demonstrative, historical and traditional, that we are autochthonous in India; that we were born in Āryāvarta on the banks or in the region of the reputed and the most sacred river the Sarasvatī, which was deemed by our very ancient Vedic ancestors of the Tertiary Period to be the scene where life had first commenced; that our Colony of young adventurers, having emigrated from and left Āryāvarta, had colonised distant lands of Asia, Africa, Europe, and America, and settled in the Arctic and Circum-Polar regions, during the Tertiary Epoch, at a time when the climate of the Arctic regions having been genial, these were fit for human habitation; that at the sight of the new phenomenon of everlasting Dawns, as also of the unusual long days and nights of the Arctic Regions, – to which our colonists from India were not accustomed while living in their Mother-Country-Āryāvarta, – their astonishment and fear knew no bounds; and that at the advent of the great Ice-Age; the once genial climate of the Arctic Regions having been replaced by extreme, not to say unbearable cold, and the higher latitudes having been covered with Ice-caps of enormous thickness, such our colonists as had made settlements there, were compelled to retrace their steps back to their Mother-land Āryāvarta, by the direction of the Snow-clad Himalaya, which was ever in their minds, and which they always remembered and cherished with fondness, as the northern boundary of their Beloved Bhārata-varsha.
>
> (1912: 34–5)

Pavgee attempted to solve all the riddles which Tilak was not able to solve. His theory combined Tilak's Arctic home with an even more ancient Āryāvartic home.[4] While Tilak did not explicitly say that the languages and the cultures of the Greeks and the Romans were derived from the Vedas of the Arctic home, Pavgee went ahead and made these assertions. In arguing against the theories proposed by Western philologists, Pavgee found "convincing" evidence in the

Smṛtis and Purāṇas for the "Out of India" model. In some sense, Pavgee may be credited to be one of the first exponents of this theory, which has gradually become popular among the Hindu nationalists of the twentieth century. In his work, the nationalist ideology and historical reconstruction occupy the same space and they reinforce each other. Beginning with the work of Tilak, and in the work of Pavgee, Bhandarkar's philology takes a back seat, and sciences like astronomy and geology appear as the primary tools for historical reconstruction. Rejecting the primacy of Comparative Philology, Tilak asserts:

> Dr. Schrader, in his *Pre-historic Antiquities of the Aryan Peoples*, gives us an exhaustive summary of facts and arguments regarding primitive Aryan culture and civilisation which can be deduced from Linguistic Palæology, or Comparative Philology, and as a repertory of such facts the book stands unrivalled. But we must remember that the results of Comparative Philology, howsoever interesting and instructive they may be from the linguistic or the historical point of view, are apt to mislead us if we know not the site of the original home, or the time when it was inhabited or abandoned by the ancestors of our race.
>
> (1903: 431–2)

This insistence on the use of physical and mathematical sciences is an important development and is again reminiscent of the induction of these sciences in the search for the "Sindhu-Sarasvat" civilization in modern times. In this new "scientific" adventure into historical reconstruction, Tilak's ideas wielded great influence, particularly in the region of Maharashtra. In the *Vedavidyā* volume of the Marathi Encyclopedia published by S. V. Ketkar (1921: 186ff.), Western views are presented as prima facie views, while Tilak's theory is presented as the *siddhānta* "final conclusion."

Before I conclude this discussion of the nineteenth-century theories about Aryans and their migrations as they developed in Maharashtra, I would like to point out a major factor, besides the emerging nationalism. The participants in this discussion are not neutral personalities. Their own identities are directly involved in the production of their theories. Referring to Prakrit languages used in Aśokan inscriptions, Bhandarkar (1914: 296) says: "They are, however, not recognized as independent languages by our grammarians who treated them *as we treat the Marathi of the lower classes*." Who is this "we?" This is not just a distant observer/scholar "we." This refers to "we, as Brahmins." Thus, the academic scholarship of Bhandarkar and others was inevitably tied to their self-definition as Brahmins. Referring to Bhandarkar, Rosane Rocher (1974: 269) says that his work shows his "upper-class bias," but we may not be able to extricate any scholar from his or her self-definition, and recognizing these self-definitions allows us to see the forces of history at work. The identity of Bhandarkar, Ranade, Kunte, Chiplunkar, and Tilak as Brahmins has as much to contribute to the shape of their theories, as the non-Brahmin Śūdra identity of Phule has to contribute to the shape of his theories. While a careful scholarly writer like Bhandarkar rarely uses expressions like "we, the Brahmins" or "we, the Āryas," expressions like "we, the Āryas," "our Aryan history," "our Aryan land," "our Aryan brothers and sisters," and "what we did in ancient times" abound in the works of Chiplunkar and Pavgee. This collapse of the distance between the object of study and the scholar, especially in the heat of the rising nationalist sentiment, has had serious consequences in the shape of historical scholarship in succeeding decades. This is seen in the works of Vishvanath K. Rajwade, the famous Marathi historian, and, more significantly, in the historical writings of the Hindu Mahāsabhā leader, V. D. Savarkar. The collapse of the gap between the object of historical study and the historian often turns the historian away from his role as a neutral observer and analyst to that of an advocate. This advocacy of a certain point of view, in the cause of self-identity and self-interest, is manifest in the writings of many of the personalities discussed earlier. The stronger this self-advocacy appears in the historical writings of the nineteenth century, a greater shift in the direction of what one may call "Out of India" theory is discerned. As we have noticed, this shift occurred rather slowly, but it was speeded up with the explicit formulations of Pavgee. It is easy to underestimate the impact of Pavgee's publications. However, among the authors discussed here, Chiplunkar and Pavgee were read most widely. Divekar, in his 1981 survey of materials in Marathi on the economic and social history of India (p. 35) says that Pavgee's "multi-volumed *Bhāratīya Sāmrājya* (Pune, 1893) covers such varied subjects as history, geography, education, science, and crafts in ancient India." Though less objective than other works, Pavgee's work in Marathi was easily accessible to wider audiences and that this was one of the few such extensive works in Marathi at this time. The Marathi publications of Chiplunkar, Tilak, and Pavgee, stoking the fire of a resurgent nationalistic Brahmanical spirit, were instrumental in the emergence of the later developments in Hindu nationalism under the leadership of Savarkar and others. The India-centered projection of Ārya-Hindu history was an essential part of this nationalistic Hindu project. Its beginning was already made in the nineteenth century.

Notes

1 During his visit to Vienna to attend the Congress of Orientalists in 1886, Bhandarkar read out his own Sanskrit verses describing the gathering of scholars. In his own words:

> The idea I endeavoured to bring out in these verses... was that this body of holy and learned Ṛṣis, adored by gods and men, that had assembled at Mithilā,... had risen up again at Vienna. ... Aśvala, the priest of Janaka, had assumed the form of Bühler, Yājñavalkya appeared as Weber and Roth, and Śākala as Kielhorn. Kahoḍa manifested himself as Jolly; and the remaining Ṛṣis as Ludwig, Rost, Jacobi, and the rest.
>
> (Bhandarkar 1933: Vol. I, 347)

2 Vishnushastri Chiplunkar (1926: 1039) criticizes Kunte for this dedication, suggesting that this dedication allowed Kunte to escape stringent rules of the Department of Education which prohibited a school teacher from engaging in any other work.

3 For details, see: Trautmann 1997: 4–5.

4 In his recollections of his meetings with Tilak, Pavgee says that beginning in 1894 he had many opportunities to discuss his theories with Tilak. Pavgee says that Tilak never agreed with him on his theory of the Āryāvartic home of the Aryans, and insisted on his idea of the Arctic home of the Aryans (see: S. V. Bapat 1925: 523ff.). It is perhaps this interaction between the two that inspired Pavgee in his later work to incorporate the notion of the Arctic home as a colony of the Aryans from their Āryāvartic home.

References

Bapat, S. B. (ed.), 1925. (In Marathi). *Lokmānya ṭiḷak yāṃcyā āṭhvaṇī va ākhyāyikā* ("Reminiscences about Lokmānya Ṭiḷak"), Vol. II. Pune: Sadashiv Vinayak Bapat.

Bhandarkar, R. G., 1914. *Wilson Philological Lectures on Sanskrit and the Derived Languages* (delivered in 1877). Mumbai: Radhabai Atmaram Sagoon.

——, 1933. *Collected Works*, In three volumes, edited by N. B. Utgikar. *Government Oriental Series*. Pune: Bhandarkar Oriental Research Institute.

Chiplunkar, V., 1926. (In Marathi). *Nibandhamālā* ("Collected Essays by Vishnushastri Chiplunkar"), 3rd edition, edited by V. V. Sathe. Pune: Chitrashala Press.

Chitale, K. W., 1956. *Lokamānya-Ṭiḷaka-Caritam*. Bombay: Published by the author.

Dandekar, R. N., 1981. *Exercises in Indology*, Select Writings 3. Delhi: Ajanta Publications.

Deshpande, M. M., 1979. *Sociolinguistic Attitudes in India: An Historical Reconstruction*. Ann Arbor, MI: Karoma Publishers, Inc.

——, 1993. *Sanskrit and Prakrit: Sociolinguistic Issues*. Delhi: Motilal Banarsidass.

——, 1999. "What to do with the Anāryas? Dharmic Discources of Inclusion and Exclusion." In *Aryan and Non-Aryan in South Asia: Evidence, Interpretation and Ideology*, edited by J. Bronkhorst and M. Deshpande. Harvard Oriental Series, Opera Minora, Vol. 3. Cambridge, MA: Department of Sanskrit and Indian Studies, Harvard University, pp. 107–27.

Divekar, V. D., 1981. *Survey of Material in Marathi on the Economic and Social History of India*. Pune: Bharata Itihasa Samshodhana Mandala.

Ketkar, S. V., 1921. *Mahārāṣṭrīya Jñānakośa. Prastāvanā Khaṇḍa. Part 2. Vedavidyā*. Pune: Mahārāṣṭrīya Jñānakośa Maṇḍaḷa.

Kunte, M. M., 1880. *The Vicissitudes of Aryan Civilization in India*. Bombay: Oriental Printing Press.

Pavgee, N. B., 1893. (In Marathi). *Bhāratīya Sāmrājya, Pūrvārdha, Book 2, Ārya Loka va Tyāñce Buddhivaibhava*. Pune: Published by the author.

——, 1900. (In Marathi). *Bhāratīya Sāmrājya, Uttarārdha, Book 9, Bharata Khaṇḍātīl Nānāvidha Bhāṣā*. Pune: Published by the author.

——, 1912. *The Vedic Fathers of Geology*. Pune: Published by author.

Phule, J., 1991. (In Marathi). *Mahātmā Phule Samagra Vaṅmaya* ("Collected works of Mahātmā Phule"), 5th edition, edited by Y. D. Phadke. Mumbai: Mahārāṣṭra Rājya Sāhitya āṇi Saṃskṛtī, Maṇḍaḷa.

Rajwade, S. R., 1980. (In Marathi). *Āhitāgni Rājvāḍe: Ātmavṛtta* ("Autobiography of Āhitāgni Rajwade"). Pune: Shrividya Prakashan.

Ranade, M. G., 1915. *Miscellaneous Writings of the late Hon'ble Mr. Justice M.G. Ranade*. Pune: Mrs Ramabai Ranade.

Ranade, V. B., 1925. (In Marathi). *Thor puruṣāñcī lahān caritre* ("Brief Biographies of Great Men"), edited by D. V. Potdar. Pune: Sarasvat Prakashak Mandali.

Rocher, R., 1974. "Studies in the Indian Grammarians." *Semiotica*, 12: 263–80.

Tilak, B. G., 1893. *The Orion or Researches into the Antiquity of the Vedas*. Pune: The Manager, Kesari.
——, 1894. *Journal of the Poona Sarvajanik Sabha*, XVII(3): 37–8.
——, 1903. *The Arctic Home in the Vedas*. Pune: The Manager, Kesari.
——, 1925. *Vedic Chronology and Vedanga Jyotisha* (containing also Chaldean and Indian Vedas and other miscellaneous essays). Pune: Messrs Tilak Bros, Gaikwar Wada.
——, 1915. (In Marathi). *Gītārahasya athavā karmayogaśāstra* ("The Secret of the Bhagavadgītā, or the Science of Karmayoga"). First Reprint. Pune: Kesari Office.
Trautmann, T. R., 1997. *Aryans and British India*. Berkeley and Los Angeles, CA: University of California Press.
Wolpert, S., 1961. *Tilak and Gokhale: Revolution and Reform in the Making of Modern India*. Berkeley, CA: University of California Press.

13

ARYAN PAST AND POST-COLONIAL PRESENT

The polemics and politics of indigenous Aryanism

Lars Martin Fosse

> It is legitimate to search for the Indo-Europeans on protohistoric ground, but this is a prolongation of the hypothesis, not a verification of it. The truth of the idea of "Indo-European" lies in the language and the religion, not in archaeology.
>
> (Bernard Sergent)[1]

On October 16, 1996, the Indian newspaper *The Economic Times* published an article, quoted on the Internet, about a conference entitled "Indologists discount Aryan influx theory." The first paragraph reads:

> A conference of over 300 Indologists here has rejected the Aryan Invasion Theory.
>
> The conference on "Revisiting Indus-Saraswati Age and Ancient India," attended by scholars all over the world, was aimed at correcting the "distorted Hindu history," according to Ms Reeta Singh, one of the organisers.
>
> "Recent archaeological discoveries have fully established that there was a continuous evolution of civilization on the Indian subcontinent from about 5000 BC, which remained uninterrupted through 1000 BC. This leaves no scope whatsoever to support an Aryan invasion theory," a resolution at the conference said.
>
> It explained that the term Arya in Indian literature has no racial or linguistic connotations. It was used in the noble sense.
>
> (*The Economic Times*, October 16, 1996)

This remarkable plebiscite shows to what degree the question of Indo-Aryan origins has become politicized. Normally scholarly questions are not made the subject of popular vote. But then the conference was sponsored by various American Hindu organizations, among which we find the Vishwa Hindu Parishad Atlanta Chapter and the Arya Samaj Chicago, both branches of important Indian

Hindu revivalist organizations. According to Ms Singh, "the main challenge in front of us is to get the leadership in the hands of next generation of American Hindus." Apparently, the intention is to influence their views on India's ancient history. Indigenous Aryanism would indeed seem to be part of the identity building deemed necessary for expatriate Indians.

I shall therefore take a closer look at Indigenist Aryanism as an expression of Indian nationalism, and with a particularly close reference to the Hindutva movement while paying a short visit to some of the proponents of the theory. This is relevant because Hindutva has adopted Indigenous Aryanism as a part of its ideology, thereby making it an explicitly political matter as well as a scholarly problem. Although indigenism is supported by Indians who are otherwise not connected to the Hindutva movement, and also by some Western scholars with no connection to the same movement – along with some personalities who would seem to be part and parcel of it[2] – it is important to see what it means to the nationalists and how they proceed to express their views. I shall mainly concentrate upon books produced by amateur scholars whose polemics may not carry much scholarly weight, but who play an important part in India's public debate on the Aryan question. For practical reasons, I shall distinguish between amateur scholars referred to as *polemicists* and professional academics. The latter may of course also act in a polemical capacity, but their training sets them apart from the laymen.

13.1 The indictment of Western Indology

In 1997 the Cambridge archaeologist Dilip K. Chakrabarti published a book called *Colonial Indology. Sociopolitics of the Ancient Indian Past.* It contains an acrimonious attack on Western Indology,[3] accusing it of racism at its worst and paternalism at its best. The vituperative rhetoric and wholesale rejection of Western Indology seem astounding at first sight. But both fit seamlessly into a kind of discourse often associated with Hindu nationalism, where pugnacious and derisive rhetoric frequently is used as a rallying technique while concealing a lack of intellectual substance. Chakrabarti's book differs from the other literature considered in this chapter insofar as the author is a professional academic, able to avoid the intellectual awkwardness that often characterizes the writing of the polemicists discussed later, who have little or no professional training in any of the subjects they argue about so passionately. But Chakrabarti's fundamental message is not much different from the message of the amateurs.

Chakrabarti's book purports to explore the underlying theoretical premises of the Western study of ancient India, premises which the author claims developed in response to the colonial need to manipulate the Indian's perception of the past. In this context gradually an elaborate racist framework emerged, in which the interrelationship between race, language, and culture was a key element. There is more than a grain of truth in this, although it doesn't work as a complete explanation for nineteenth-century Western interest in India. What is more surprising, however, is the claim that "this framework is still in place, and implicitly accepted not merely by Western Indologists but also by their Indian counterparts."[4] This is often the working assumption of indigenist polemicists, but few express it so clearly as Chakrabarti. In fact, he suggests that "one of the underlying assumptions of Western Indology is a feeling of superiority in relation to India, especially modern India and Indians." Western Indologists are portrayed as patronizing and arrogant.[5]

Chakrabarti sees Western Indology as essentially a by-product of the establishment of Western dominance in India. It would seem that this view is based primarily on the history of British dominance in the subcontinent. While the connection between German nationalism and Indology is discussed, French and Italian Indology appear to be almost entirely beyond Chakrabarti's horizon. He is equally critical of mainstream Indian scholars, making short shrift of people who have "toed the Western line." These scholars apparently have no noble motives for maintaining the views they hold but are motivated by a self-serving endeavor to obtain scholarships and other material advantages.[6] "Mainstream" scholars are in polemical indigenist literature almost invariably identified with the political left and usually designated as "Marxists," and Chakrabarti conforms, in this respect too, with traditional Hindutva discourse on the subject. Thus, Chakrabarti, like many populist indigenist polemicists active in the debate, targets the "Westernized" intellectual elites at Indian universities. The alleged "leftist" character of these elites gives Chakrabarti's critique unequivocal political connotations.

The same applies to his critique of nineteenth-century Indology. No one would deny that most Western scholars in this period had opinions and attitudes that were both racist and prejudiced. What is at stake is not Chakrabarti's description and documentation of racism and discrimination, but how he uses this repugnant material as a ploy to delegitimize views of Indian history that are not in line with the politics of modern Indian nationalism. Thus, having given a scathing – and perfectly appropriate – critique of James Mill's[7] view of Indian civilizations, Chakrabarti proceeds in the following manner:

> ...Mill's contempt for ancient India extends to the other Asian civilizations as well and...much of Mill's framework has survived in the colonial and post-colonial Indology. For instance, his idea that the history of ancient India, like the history of other barbarous nations, has been the history of mutually warring small states, only occasionally relieved by some larger political entities established by the will of some particularly ambitious and competent individuals has remained with us in various forms till today.
> (1997: 94)

This critique is thematically related to Chakrabarti's criticism of Rothermund and Kulke's[8] description of the Mauryan empire. Based on the outer distribution of Ashokan edicts, these scholars dispute that Ashoka's empire included the whole of the subcontinent except its southernmost part.[9] Chakrabarti, however, argues that the Mauryan empire had its sway over the whole of South Asia from the southern flank of the Hindukush to the Chittagong coast on the one hand and the southernmost tip of the peninsula on the other. He concludes:

> ...Indians would certainly try to understand the fact that for more than a hundred years in the late fourth, third and early second centuries BC, there was a state which controlled the entire natural geographical domain of south Asia. Not even the British controlled such a large area for such a long period. This fact should in any case be one of the answers to the notion that there have only been divisive tendencies in the political history of India.
>
> (Ibid.: 206)

What is crucial here, is that the description of India as a conglomerate of small, unstable states militates against the romantic notion of Indian civilization that is propagated by the Hindu nationalists. In this political discourse, India's golden past is projected upon the present as a technical device used to prevent the crumbling and disintegration of the Indian state. It is a case of using the past to build the future, and there is no room for a past that does not serve this purpose. The views expressed by Rothermund and Kulke may be disputed for scholarly reasons, but that is not the point here.[10] Right or wrong, their description of India's past has to be discarded by Chakrabarti because it is *functionally pernicious*. And from a rhetorical point of view, sowing doubts about the motives and attitudes of an opponent is more efficient in the context of mass communication than a difficult and often inconclusive professional discussion. Therefore, in the scheme of things, the moral disqualification of Western Indology is crucial, and the attempt to bring about this disqualification runs like a red thread through much of the indigenist literature I am about to consider. Let me state quite clearly that there is nothing innocent about this rhetoric. It is not due to a lack of insight into how "proper" academic discussions are to be conducted. The same kind of rhetoric reverberates in the political discourse of the *Organiser* and other Hindutva publications. Hindu nationalist rhetoric is simply a practical expedient. But it is also, to some extent, a reaction to and the mirror image of the anti-Indian rhetoric of the colonial era.

13.2 The pitfalls of inferred history

The description of India's earliest history is pieced together on the basis of scraps of information culled from ancient literatures, languages, and archaeology. In the Western academic tradition, the spread of Indo-Aryan languages to South Asia is one of the several cases where the presumed migration of Indo-Europeans lead to the dissemination of Indo-European languages in the Eurasian area. At the beginning of the nineteenth century, the origin of these peoples was thought to be in India or somewhere in Asia, but later the cradle land was moved to somewhere in Eurasia and has since then led a rather vagrant existence. Since there are no historical documents giving exact information about the geographical focal point of the Indo-Europeans, this focal point has to be inferred on the basis of incomplete and sometimes highly inadequate data sets which often permit more than one interpretation.

The epistemological complications caused by the nature of the evidence opens up a vast argumentative space which is able to accommodate a large number of hypotheses based on probabilistic and analogical thinking of various kinds. While not all hypotheses are permitted within the perimeter of this space, several contradictory hypotheses are often admissible. Thus, the argumentative space easily lends itself to the creation of a rhetorical discourse where emotional arguments and contentious assertions compensate for the lack of certainty produced by the data. It is a test of professional scholarship that this rhetorical discourse is avoided and that uncertainties are not hidden behind assertive and pugnacious language.

The impressions of the first part of this chapter are based on a close reading of books by four indigenist polemicists: K. D. Sethna, Bhagwan Singh, Navaratna S. Rajaram, and Shrikant Talageri.[11] These writers are not only concerned with the homeland of the Aryans, but also with the divisions of Indian society caused by the "little" nationalisms of the subcontinent and India's import in the context of global culture. None of them seem to be familiar with other ancient Indo-European languages than Sanskrit, and are therefore often forced to quote Western authorities in support of their views rather than developing their own scholarly and technical arguments based on first-hand knowledge of the sources. Central to their project is a critical analysis of the inferential logic used by the Western scholars in their configuration of the available data. Here, they sometimes score points, as the logic they criticize is not always beyond reproach. The literature quoted by the polemicists is largely in English. German Indology seems to be mostly unknown, and French Indology is hardly mentioned at all, in spite of the important contributions from such people as Louis Renou, Georges Dumézil, and J. Filliozat. Consequently, all the works considered here are in various degrees underinformed, all the more so because the English sources have not been fully exploited either. The result is a critique that is largely neglected by Western scholars because it is regarded as incompetent, but which due to its rhetorical force and potential impact in an Indian polemical context cannot be entirely ignored.

13.3 The problem of Aryan origins: K. D. Sethna's response to the theories of Asko Parpola

In 1988 the Finnish Indologist Asko Parpola published a paper called "The coming of the Aryans to Iran and India and the cultural and ethnic identity of the Dāsas." The paper is a brilliant example of inferred history. The author brings together a large number of textual, linguistic, and archaeological data and configures them in such a manner as to present a rational and complex narrative of the Indo-Aryan penetration of India. Parpola's presentation differs considerably from the older and more simplistic theories of an Aryan invasion. Instead of a massive onslaught, he presents a complicated set of migrations that over several centuries lead to an Aryanization of the northwestern part of the continent. He proposes that the Dāsas, Dasyus, and Paṇis[12] mentioned by the Rigveda were the dominant élite of the recently discovered Bronze Age culture of Margiana and Bactria, and that they were the first to introduce the Aryan languages into India around 2000 BC. Around 1800 BC the first wave of Aryan speakers in Greater Iran and in India would seem to have been overlaid by a second wave of Aryans coming from the northern steppes, which eventually leads to the emergence of the syncretistic religions and cultures of the Veda and the Avesta, and of the Mitanni dynasty in the Near East.[13]

K. D. Sethna[14] in an appendix to his book *The Problem of Aryan Origins From an Indian Point of View* presents a critique of Parpola's views.[15] Sethna's rebuttal comprises almost 200 pages of meticulous argumentation, covering a large number of problems. Unlike the other polemicists considered here, he writes without rancour in a polished and courteous style which does not divert attention from his arguments. It is impossible to do justice to Sethna's work here, and I shall have to confine myself to a few points.

The first has to do with the horse question. Parpola states that "a major reason against assuming that the Harappans spoke an Indo-European language is that the horse is not represented among the many realistically depicted animals of the Harappan seals and figurines."[16] He points to the fact that comprehensive bone analyses "by one of the best experts" have yielded the conclusion that there is no clear osteological evidence of the horse in the Indian subcontinent prior to *c.*2000 BC. Sethna counters by attacking Parpola's expert witness. Based on Indian archaeological excavations he introduces the counterclaim that the horse was indeed present prior to the assumed arrival of the Aryans.[17] This is certainly admissible from a methodological point of view, but at the same time, it highlights some of the more fundamental problems of the debate. In his book *Decipherment of the Indus Script* from 1994, Parpola refers to such counterclaims by maintaining that they are not sufficiently documented.[18] Thus we have an intellectual stalemate: if the contenders swear by different authorities in a matter that is crucial to the debate, there can be no progress toward a consensus.

As expected, Sethna disputes Parpola's evidence for an entry into India. He claims that the evidence which according to Parpola indicates colonization at Pirak may be explained by cultural contacts, since there are no "intrusive necropoles."[19] Sethna thereby touches upon a general problem in Indo-European archaeology, where diffusion of artifacts and cultural features without the movement of people have been suggested as an alternative to models based on migrations or invasions not only in the East but also in Western Europe. Sethna furthermore rejects Parpola's suggestion that Rigvedic Aryans entered the Swat valley in 1600–1400 BC. He points out that the presence of the horse may indicate Aryanism in the Swat region, but cannot make the Aryanism Rigvedic on the sole strength of that presence. Instead, he claims that a number of archaeological items rule out a Rigvedic entry in this period.[20] Such items are brickfaced altars dug into the earth and containing a round fireplace with a central cavity. These structures definitely indicate Aryanism, according to Sethna, yet they cannot be related to the Rigveda.

Parpola mentions certain silver objects or objects ornamented with silver in connection with the traits of the Namazga V culture assumed to be Aryan.[21] Here Sethna objects on the basis of the fact that silver is not mentioned in the Rigveda. Thus, on this score the Rigveda according to Sethna goes out of the chronological framework within which Parpola speaks of Aryanism in India or in Greater Iran. Sethna also tries to build a more elaborate argument for assuming that the Rigveda did not in fact know silver.[22] His conclusion is clear: "There cannot be the slightest suspicion of silver in the Rgveda's period." Consequently, the Rigveda must be dated as pre-Harappan.[23] The weakness of this argument is that we have no reason to believe that the Rigveda gives us a complete breakdown of Indo-Aryan material culture. Gold, silver, and copper have in fact been known since 4000 BCE, and to assume that the Rigvedic Aryans knew gold but not silver is counterintuitive. Arguments *ex silentio* are inherently weak, and Sethna would need much stronger indications than the rather feeble ones he presents to convince. He quotes the *Encyclopaedia Britannica* (EB) on the subject,[24] but with less precision than could be wished for. In its chapter on the history of silver, the *EB* states that "silver was discovered after gold and copper about 4000 BC,"[25] but in its chapter on gold, it says that "the history of gold extends back at least 6,000 years, the earliest identifiable, realistically dated finds having been made in Egypt and Mesopotamia *c.*4000 BC."[26] Thus, the chronological difference between the discovery of the two metals may not necessarily be great.

In a similar manner, Sethna argues that the use of cotton was widespread in the Indus Valley civilization, whereas the use of cotton is unknown in the Rigveda. Cotton only turns up in the sūtras, which again would seem to indicate an extremely old age for the Rigveda.[27] However, this does not necessarily follow either. First of all, this is another argument *ex silentio* and does not prove that the Aryans were indeed ignorant of cotton. Second, if the Aryans *actually* were ignorant of cotton, this may be explained by other reasons than hoary age. In fact, much of Sethna's argument in the final analysis hinges on the presumed date of the Veda, which is crucial to the argument presented by many indigenists. I shall have occasion to discuss this problem later in the chapter.

As would be expected, Sethna wants to identify the language of the Harappan culture with Sanskrit, at least in the sense that "it is akin to, if not quite identical with, Rigvedic Sanskrit."[28] If this identification is correct, then there would be no problem dating the Rigveda as pre-Harappan. Here he draws on the views of the archaeologist J. G. Shaffer, who emphasizes the strong continuities linking the Harappan civilization to its antecedents. The problem with this line of argument is of course that material culture and language are not necessarily strongly correlated, so that any arguments for linguistic continuity based on archaeological remains are open to doubt.

An interesting controversy emerges in the analysis of the nature of the Dāsas or Dasyus. Here, Sethna attempts to reject Parpola's view that these are partly mythological, partly human. This concept may seem strange to modern man, but in the Vedic period the border between humans and supernatural beings was fluid. Gods such as Indra or Vishnu had the power of metamorphosis and could change their shape at will, whereas the shape of humans could be changed by supernatural beings. No one denies that some Dāsas are supernatural beings, but most Indologists readily accept that some of them are also human and see no difficult hurdle in this double nature. As enemies, they would naturally qualify as demons. Sethna, however, claims that all Dāsas are nonphysical, nonhuman beings.[29] This is of course a simpler solution than assuming a mixed identity, because as Sethna points out, "if after granting the obviously demoniac character of a good number of named Dāsa–Dasyus, one still opts for the human character of many of them, one is rather at a loss how to demarcate the latter."[30] This is undoubtedly correct, but then many of the problems connected with the interpretation of the Vedas are caused precisely by the ambiguity of the material, which to confound things even more, was often intentional. Nevertheless, Sethna finds arbitrary the whole picture of the Rigvedics conquering human Dāsas.[31] His own interpretation, which sees the Dāsas and Dasyus as representatives of evil, is instead influenced by his guru Sri Aurobindo, whose views on Vedic hermeneutics are at loggerheads with western philological method.[32] The consequence of the spiritual interpretation, however, is clear: if the Dāsas are metaphors of evil, then identifying them with historical peoples is a futile exercise, and they cannot serve as players in a migration scenario. Thus the rejection of Parpola's interpretation of the Dāsas strengthens the Indigenist position by removing the possibility of a Vedic connection with historical migrations.

Sethna's work is both methodical and thoughtful, and where he departs from the traditional academic interpretations this is usually due to a fundamentally different vision of how the arguments are to be weighted rather than due to the ignorance of the arguments used by his opponents. However, his symbolic interpretation of the Vedas in line with Sri Aurobindo's reading creates an unbridgeable gap between the Western interpretations that he criticizes and his own interpretation. Everybody would agree that the Rigveda contains symbolic and allegorical material, but most academic scholars would also see a substantial amount of concrete references in the texts, although the exact nature and meaning of these may be difficult to penetrate more than 3,000 years after they were created. And what Sethna regards as strong evidence would by many academic scholars be regarded as weak or inconsequential, consequently there is little scope for reaching a consensus. These factors imply that his critique, generally speaking, lacks the necessary force to make an impact on the traditional Western academic hermeneutics even if some of his arguments may have a certain relevance within a limited context.

13.4 Bhagwan Singh's theory about Aryan society

Of the writers considered here, Bhagwan Singh[33] would at the outset seem to be the best informed. His bibliography comprises an impressive number of about

600 items, covering a vast field of scholarship. However, Singh's obvious lack of scholarly training robs him of the ability to use his reading to his advantage, and the views presented on the 500 pages of his book fail dismally to convince. I shall take a closer look at his construction of Aryan society and his use of etymologies. According to Singh,

> traditional commentators, working in an age when the social position of merchants had been seriously undermined, could hardly visualize a past when merchants had played a hegemonistic role. Western translators could not get reconciled to the fact that a civilization we meet in the descriptions of the *Ṛgveda* could have prospered at such an early period. They thereafter started with reductive interpretations – a mistake which was not rectified even after the discovery of the Harappan Civilization.
> (1995: xvii)

Singh sees the Aryan culture as a merchant culture, claiming that the first Aryans to turn up in Turkey were traders. He also – somewhat surprisingly – claims it to be generally admitted that the chief divinities – Indra, Agni, Parjanya, the Maruts, and Viṣṇu – are agricultural gods. However, by the time of the Rigveda they had acquired an additional role of guarding the cargo and the members of the caravan from robbers and pirates in addition to "conducting them through safe routes undisturbed by wild beasts and natural calamities."[34] Singh proceeds to claim that the maritime activities depicted in the Rigveda contradict the idea that the Aryans were pastoralists. Instead, they were economically far advanced in comparison to their backward neighbors "who were still in pastoral or gathering stage."[35]

It is obvious that Singh's construction of the Aryans as merchants and agriculturalists with maritime activities is fitted to the Harappan civilization as we know it from the archaeological remains. It can hardly be justified on the basis of the Vedic texts as traditionally interpreted. It is therefore not suprising that he rejects Marshall's arguments against identifying the Harappans with the Aryans.[36] Marshall musters cultural data from the Veda only to conclude that they differ significantly from what we know about the Harappans. Singh's book is a protest against precisely such conclusions. It deals predominantly with material culture and tries to relate data from the Vedas to archaeological material from the Harappans' civilization.

Singh rejects not only the idea that the Aryans migrated into India, he also denies any migrations out of India. Instead, Aryan culture allegedly dissipated through the spread of traders and religious missionaries who had "culturally and linguistically transformed vast areas within an incredibly short period of time."[37] This is a staggering vision, which would seem to need very solid documentation. However, Singh brings no material that credibly demonstrates the activities of his traders and missionaries. At the same time, he rejects the idea that the Vedic people were "semi-barbarous nomads,"[38] since it would be absurd to assume that such people could be found "meditating on philosophical problems."

Singh assumes that abstract thinking and philosophizing need certain material conditions that could not be met within a more or less nomadic society. This is hardly a cogent idea, since even nomadic peoples have religion and consequently also at least a rudimentary philosophy.

Like so many indigenists, Singh offers a discussion of the horse problem. As already mentioned, the horse has not been identified among the cultural artifacts of the Indus Valley culture, and this has been used as an argument for claiming that the Indus Valley culture was not Indo-Aryan.[39] Trying to establish the presence of the horse in India at an early date has therefore become a preoccupation with many indigenists who overlook the fact that it is not really the presence of the horse as such that is of interest, but rather the religious role – or lack of such a role – that it has in the Indus Valley religion. In principle, horses could have been imported to India before the Aryans made their entrance in the arena, but proving this to be the case would not really have much impact on the horse argument.

Singh claims that the Aryans domesticated the ass before the horse, and that this animal was called "horse" or *aśva* (Prakrit *assa*). He goes on to elaborate this hypothesis with a surprising display of warped linguistics and historical ignorance that for most informed readers immediately condemns his book to obscurity, since the rest of his arguments concerning other problems must be assumed to be tainted with the same lack of critical insight and elementary knowledge of method.

Singh makes the mistake of comparing Old English *assa/assen*, Gothic *asilus*, Latin *asinus* etc. with *aśva*, which is assumed to be their origin.[40] This is, of course, impossible, since Sanskrit *aśva* itself is a later derivative of proto-Indo-European **ekwos*. It is remarkable, however, that Singh is aware of the cognates for *horse* and quotes them correctly on page 67. According to Singh, "[w]e find Indo-Aryan (IA) 'ś' preserved as 's' in the East European languages while it is replaced by 'h'/'k'/'q'/'g' in the dialects of Central and Western Europe which received the linguistic impulse from the Anatolian region." Singh has in other words invented a new set of sound laws where Indo-Aryan "ś" is treated as the proto-consonant which somehow produces the results quoted earlier, and he has introduced these sound laws without giving any linguistic arguments to demonstrate that this rewriting of standard historical phonology has a logical basis. It does not disturb Singh that Vedic also has a separate word for ass, *rāsabha*. To the contrary, the "*Ṛgveda* suggests that at an early stage either the distinction between an ass and a horse was so thin that the word *aśva* was applied to both horse and ass, or they knew only the ass as attested by Aśvins, deified 'horsemen', whose vehicle was ass-driven (I.116.2; AB iv.9; KB xviii.1)." The last remark is revealing for Singh's treatment of the Vedic texts. It is in fact true that the Aśvins sometimes use an ass to drive their chariot. So does Indra on occasion (e.g. RV 3.53.5). However, the Aśvins also use horses and birds. The case of AB iv.9 is particularly interesting: here we have an etiological myth the purpose of which is to explain why the ass is the slowest of the traction animals. According to the Brāhmaṇa, this is because the Aśvins won a race against Agni, Uṣas, and Indra with it, thus expending most of its speed and energy for ever. This story hardly tallies with the idea that *aśva* and *rāsabha* are the same animals.

Singh's explanation of the English word *horse* is no better: "Old English *hors*, Old High German *hros*, German *ross*, Icelandic *hross*, Latin *Equus* [!], Greek *hippo*, probably an onomatopoeic [!] term derived from *hreṣā* – neighing of a horse expressing its satisfaction."[41] The fact that these words superficially look alike – although the presence of *equus* and *hippos* in this company defies phonological justification even according to Singh's standards – does not mean that they are related in any way. It is, for one thing, impossible that Sanskrit "h" in *hreṣā* should correspond to a Germanic "h".[42] As for *equus* and *hippos*, they belong etymologically with *aśva*, not with *horse*. Nevertheless, Singh insists that "the earliest domesticated animal known to the so-called Proto-Indo-Europeans as *aśva* was not horse but 'ass', which is exactly the Prakritic form of *aśva* and appears to have gone from the land of Prakrits to the Indo-European field."[43] This argument is based on the idea that the Prakrits are older than Sanskrit which Singh presents more or less as an artificial language. Only later the term is allegedly transferred to the horse exclusively leaving words such as *khura*, *rāsabha*, and *gardabha* for the ass. This is, of course, nonsense, and a perusal of other parts of the book does little to redeem the author.

However, Singh's creation of folk etymologies is not untypical for indigenist literature. The practice sometimes serves political or ideological purposes. A quote from M. S. Golwalkar shows this in a revealing manner: "Our epics and our 'puranas' also present us with the same expansive image of our motherland. *Afghanistan was our ancient Upaganasthan* [my emphasis]; Shalya of the Mahabharata came from there."[44] The invention of false etymologies is therefore not an entirely innocent matter. It can be used to support irredentist policies, particularly when it is accompanied by an uncritical and "historical" reading of ancient epics and scripture. At the same time, such folk etymologies have a long history on the subcontinent, going back to the period of the Brāhmaṇas and beyond. The approach to language they represent is therefore deeply embedded in the Hindu intellectual tradition.

13.5 The polemics of Navaratna S. Rajaram

In the *Organiser* of April 18, 1999, N. S. Rajaram,[45] a mathematician and a computer scientist, expressed the following view on Indological method:

> Western Indology treated Vedic India as a dead civilization such as Egypt and Babylon, and tried to reconstruct the whole thing from scratch. This ignored a large body of existing literary and cultural traditions continuing to the present. The result of this fallacious approach was fantasies like the Aryan Invasion Theory and the idea that the Harappan language and script were "proto-Dravidian," an imaginary language. *The correct approach is to relate archaeological discoveries to Indian literature and tradition. This gives an alternative approach, combining Indian tradition and modern science* [my emphasis], which several of us including

> Dr. Jha, David Frawley, K. D. Sethna and others have been pursuing. The "establishment" scholars, however, seem stuck in the old groove following Western Indology, which is a colonial-missionary construct with no scientific or historical basis.
>
> (*Organiser*, April 18, 1999)

Rajaram's description contains factual errors, as Western Indologists became acquainted quite early with India's traditional theories of knowledge and interpretation. To suggest that archaeological data were not related to Indian literature and tradition is not correct, either. However, the most important part of Rajaram's statement comes at the end of the paragraph: *Western Indology is a colonial-missionary construct with no scientific basis*. To Rajaram, the linguistics that has so dominated Indology is a pseudo-science, "the crown jewel of which is the Aryan Invasion Theory."[46] This parochial view overlooks the fact that linguistics is based on the study of a vast number of languages on a global basis and has a number of far more important concerns than the Aryan invasion theory. Instead, Rajaram describes philology and the linguistic approach to history as the hodgepodge mix of amateur biology, discredited race theories, and defensive reaction to the emergence of archaeology as an empirical science.[47] Applied to the Aryan invasion theory, linguistic analysis was according to Rajaram a new and unproved methodology "used to determine one of the most important issues of human history – how peoples of the largest language family in the world came to be related. Its methodology was assumed to be valid though it had never proved itself in any historical interpretation."[48] This level of insight into the world of philology and linguistics is highlighted by a factual blunder a few sentences later, where the author apparently ascribes knowledge of glottochronology to Max Müller who died half a century before the method was invented.[49]

Rajaram's attack centers upon the inadequacy of philology and linguistics as tools for discussing India's most ancient past. But his critique is in a curious manner directed against these branches of scholarship such as they were in the nineteenth century. The Indological scholarship of that century was allegedly unscientific to a degree that is scarcely comprehensible today. It was riddled with superstitions like belief in the Biblical Creation and the story of Noah and the Flood. The other creation of the period, the "Race Science," is presented as a further testimony to the profound scientific ignorance of nineteenth-century Indologists.[50] This is in spite of the fact that the race science of the last century was the creation of Darwinian biology and a fledgling physical anthropology rather than by philology and linguistics. Although Rajaram is aware of modern work in the Indological field, he uses an extraordinary amount of space discussing the views and personality of Max Müller, who, as far as Western Indology is concerned, has been dead in every possible sense of the word for a century. This is of course due to the position that Max Müller enjoys in India where he still is able to arouse passionate anger and controversy. Many of the other Indologists of the period are rejected as mere dilettantes, mainly missionaries and bureaucrats, who succeeded in making a mark simply because they had the support of the ruling authorities.[51] No trust can be placed in their methods, which are claimed to be totally haphazard and display almost complete ignorance of science and scientific method. According to Rajaram,

> Western Indology today suffers from a weak scholarly base, and is in the main little more than a continuation of nineteenth century trends. The standard of Sanskrit scholarship in Europe and America is not high, and Indologists for the most part are repackaging nineteenth century translations using academic fashions of the moment like Marxism and Freudian analysis.
>
> (Rajaram and Frawley 1995: 41)

The role of race and prejudice in the debate of the last century is well-known,[52] and there is good reason to take exception to it, but the biased rejection of scientific methods that proved highly successful in other studies than Indology, such as in the decipherment of Akkadian, Sumerian, and Egyptian, drains Rajaram's own competence and sincerity of credibility at the very outset. However, his rejection of philology and linguistics has an inherent bearing on Vedic interpretation. The liberation of the Vedas from philology and comparative linguistics means that they can be interpreted ahistorically and therefore in harmony with the needs of the moment. Instead of philology's contextualization of the Vedas as part of a distant civilization, they are returned to their original place of honor in the infinite continuum beyond space-time, from whence they can be recalled and invoked at need to invest new socio-religious phenomena with divine legitimacy. Knowing what the Vedas actually say is not important. Being able to invest them with an appropriate and functional meaning is the heart of the matter. Here the specific methodological requirements of philology and linguistics are the major stumbling blocks.

Rajaram's own arguments center upon four mainstays: archaeology, the river ecology of the ancient North-West, astronomy, and Vedic mathematics. Like most nationalists, Rajaram rejects the idea that the word "Aryan" has an ethnic or racial meaning. It is entirely an honorific.[53] Having dismissed the invasion theory, he sums up: "*the real problems are the chronology of Vedic India and the origin and spread of Indo-European languages*."[54]

Rajaram's focus on chronology, which is highly significant in a Hindutva context, leads to an attack upon Max Müller's tentative approach to the same problem. Müller by common sense reckoning regarded the year 1000 BCE as the lower limit for the composition of the Rigvedic hymns, although he made it clear that this was a conjecture. This, however, does not deter Rajaram from using a fair amount of ink trying to discredit Müller's dating. This dating is claimed to be determined by Biblical chronology and therefore a product of superstition. Since modern Indologists tend to date the composition of the Vedic hymns to roughly the same period as Müller, we must assume that they are guilty of the same primitive motives.

Like Chakrabarti, Rajaram also attacks "the current Indian intellectual scene," which "with its continued attachment to the Aryan invasion theory is little more than a prolongation of the old colonial policies."[55] Their achievement consists of recasting Indian history along Marxist lines. As for many indigenists, important counterarguments are the facts that the "invasion" is unmentioned in the Vedas, and that there are no archaeological traces of the invading Aryans.

Like so many conclusions drawn by both Western scholars and indigenists alike, these views rest upon assumptions that have not been verified. The fact that the invasion is not mentioned in the Vedas is of no consequence to academic scholarship, since a number of peoples do not remember their original homelands, or do not mention them in extant sources. The Hittites have left no memory of their origins, and like other Indo-European peoples of western Asia, their material cultures are purely Asiatic.[56] The Romans had no remembrance of how they entered Italy, they had to invent a Trojan connection. As for archaeology, as important a political event as the Roman conquest of Sicily is impossible to detect in the contemporary habitation sites and tombs.[57] In many cases, the invaders may share the same material culture as the invaded, or look exactly like them. Anthropologically, we need not assume that the migrating Aryans were substantially different from the peoples of the Indus civilization.[58] Thus, both the silence of the early textual sources and the archaeological remains carry less weight in the discussion than assumed by some debaters. They are essentially arguments *ex silentio* and may be explained in a number of ways.

The last part of Rajaram's book deals with India as the source of civilization. He proposes that the presence of Indo-European speakers from India to Ireland going back to prehistoric times may be ascribed to a combination of political and ecological disturbances in the Rigvedic heartland that seem to have taken place at the beginning in the fifth millennium BCE.[59] His evidence presumably suggests that the Rigveda belongs to an earlier layer of civilization that preceded the rise of Egypt, Sumeria, and the Indus Valley.[60] Rajaram emphasizes that the Vedic civilization was predominantly an indigenous evolution, an important point also to Chakrabarti and to nationalists in general. But bolder than Chakrabarti, Rajaram pushes the age of the Rigveda back to the remotest antiquity, almost to the end of the last Ice Age.[61] Going through various kinds of evidence he concludes:

> ...on the basis of archaeology, satellite photography, metallurgy and ancient mathematics, it is now clear that there existed a great civilization – a mainly spiritual civilization perhaps – before the rise of Egypt, Sumeria and the Indus Valley. The heartland of this ancient world was the region from the Indus to the Ganga – the land of the Vedic Aryans.
> (Ibid.: 247)

Here as not infrequently elsewhere, Rajaram rallies the alleged support of modern *scientific* methods to show that the ancient Indians were part of a great civilization that flourished at the beginning of history. The picture presented by natural science is thus far removed from the one found in history books that place the "Cradle of Civilizations" in the river valleys of Mesopotamia. And the mystery of the Indo-European speakers has finally found a solution: *They were part of a civilization that flourished before the dawn of civilizations*.[62] This is India's golden past, this is India as a mother of civilizations, this is the Hindu version of India's history which says that Hindu civilization was the dominant civilization of the world for several millennia before the birth of Christ, the same way as Western civilization has been dominant since the nineteenth century.[63] In a sense, the legitimacy of India's Aryan culture rests upon this historical vision because it pushes the Vedas far back into proto-history, back to the *origo* of human culture, thereby making them the point of departure for other religions as well. Here the Indian perception that the legitimacy and authority of ideas increase with their antiquity clashes with the modern western rejection of yesterday's ideas and the constant search for new and better truths.

13.6 Shrikant Talageri's reinvention of linguistics and philology

One of the consequences of the rejection of Western linguistics and philology is that these branches of scholarship have to be reinvented, and perhaps the most ambitious attempt of such a reinvention in polemicist literature is the work of Shrikant Talageri,[64] a Bombay *literateur* with a wide range of scholarly and cultural interests. In 1993, Talageri published two books[65] where he takes on the whole complex of problems related to the Aryan Invasion Theory with great vigor. In the preface to one of his books he receives both recognition and support from S. R. Rao,[66] one of India's most outstanding archaeologists. The fact that Talageri is thus embraced by a leading Indian scholar implies that his work deserves more attention than would otherwise be the case for a dilettante.

Talageri starts his exposition with the geographical distribution of modern languages, continues with a systematic critique of the evidence pointing to South Russia as the original homeland and then proceeds to a discussion of arguments based on the study of Sanskrit, such as the cerebrals in Vedic Sanskrit, and assumed Austric and Dravidian loanwords in Sanskrit and Vedic Sanskrit versus later Indo-Aryan. His program ends with the racial evidence and a consideration of the evidence in Sanskrit texts. It is a complete and ambitious philologico-linguistic project with physical anthropology thrown in for good measure. At the same time, he develops his own theory of Indo-European history, which of course differs fundamentally from the traditional Western version.

A curious aspect of Talageri's work is the limited number of sources upon which it is based. His bibliography contains some 40 items, the *Larousse Encyclopaedia of Mythology* being his most important source on matters of Indo-European religion. His description of the traditional "invasion theory" is fair, although incomplete and partly obsolete. But in spite of the paucity of material at his disposal, he has no qualms about presenting a new, or at least repackaged, version of Indo-European prehistory. Unfortunately, this new version is not supported by fresh material, and the old material is treated in a highly selective manner. Within the limited space of a medium-sized book, problems of immense complexity are dismissed in a few paragraphs, whereas sweeping statements replace the detailed and painstaking analysis that would be expected from a professional scholar.

Talageri's reinvention of comparative philology is among other things flawed by the fact that he has not understood the principle of sound laws, which makes comparative phonology something of a hard science.[67] This is a shortcoming he shares with other writers such as Rajaram and Bhagwan Singh, both of whom have extremely fanciful views on comparative philology and etymology. The consequence of this lack of technical competence is that Talageri's arguments, devised to reject the traditional academic positions, usually collapse because they are methodologically unsound. However, occasionally he reaches the same conclusions as some Western scholars. This is the case with his discussion of the Brahui language. Talageri rejects the theory that the Brahuis were invading Aryans who adopted the language of the natives as well as the theory that the Brahuis were local Dravidians. Instead, following Grierson, he claims that the Brahuis were Dravidian immigrants from the South. Here he gets support from modern scholars as well.[68] What is remarkable, however, is Talageri's formulation of the chain of events:

> The most likely and logical explanation [...] is that the Brahuis are the survivors of a group of Dravidian immigrants from the south who retained their linguistic identity although their racial identity got completely submerged into that of the native Aryan-speaking population.
>
> (1993b: 122)

This is important to him, since he does not want to accept the presence of Dravidians in the North-West in the Harappan period. There is, however, more than a touch of irony in the fact that he solves his problem by accepting a migration solution that is almost the mirror image of the assumed Aryan migration into India.

If we turn to Talageri's own view of the homeland problem, we find the following presentation:

> The original Indo-European language, which we will here call "proto-proto-Indo-European" to distinguish it from the hypothetical language (proto-Indo-European) reconstructed by European linguists, was spoken in interior North India; but in very ancient times it had spread out and covered a large area extending to Afghanistan, and had developed a number of dialects, which may be classified as follows:
>
> Outer Indo-European dialects: Spoken in Afghanistan and northern Kashmir and the adjoining north Himalayan region.
> Central Indo-European dialects: Spoken in what we may call the "Punjab region" and in southern Kashmir.
> Inner Indo-European dialects: Spoken in the expanse of northern India from the Gangetic region to Maharashtra and from Punjab to Orissa and Bengal.
>
> (1993a: 145)

Here Talageri may have been inspired by Grierson's theory about two sets of Indo-Aryan dialects – one the language of the Midland, and the other the group of dialects forming what Grierson called the Outer sub-branch.[69] Unfortunately, Talageri's model is not closely argued in terms of linguistic data and cultural elements, it is rather stated *tout court*, as if the rejection of the invasion theory is sufficient support for it. He then proceeds to discuss a number of arguments that have been used to support the invasion theory, such as the development of retroflexes or cerebrals in Sanskrit.[70] Talageri rejects the traditional theory which sees these sounds as due to the influence of Dravidian speakers, who in one view of the Indus culture were the original people inhabiting the North-West of India. In this matter, however, he receives a modicum of support from some Western scholars who are not convinced that Dravidian is the cause of the retroflexes.[71] But if it may be doubted that Dravidian languages were responsible for the development of retroflexes in Sanskrit, it is generally accepted that there was a mutual influence between Indo-Aryan languages and Dravidian languages at a later stage, a phenomenon studied within the context of area linguistics. As Dixon points out, if two languages are in contact, and some of the speakers of each have a degree of competence in the other, then they are likely to borrow lexemes, grammatical categories and techniques, and some grammatical forms (in at least one direction, often in both directions). Thus, they gradually become more similar.[72] Every geographical area in which more than one language is spoken, becomes a linguistic area to a greater or lesser extent, and India has been defined as such an area.[73]

However, the similarities between Indo-Aryan and Dravidian languages cannot be due to Dravidian influence, according to Talageri, "since such a circumstance would be linguistically unnatural."[74] This view is based on a statement by Bhadriraju Krishnamurti, who points to the fact that borrowing into Dravidian languages is mostly lexical, whereas Indo-Aryan languages mostly borrow structural features. Krishnamurti suggests that transfer of morphological features "is expected to follow at a more advanced state of language contact, *necessarily presupposing extensive lexical borrowing*." From this statement Talageri extracts an ironclad linguistic law: "Linguistic borrowing always starts out with vocabulary, and it is only at an 'advanced stage' of 'extensive lexical borrowing' that phonological structural features are borrowed; and only later that morphological and syntactic features are borrowed. This is the case everywhere."[75] Unfortunately, it is not. As Dixon shows, "in some contact situations, we find – for a variety of reasons – that lexemes are scarcely borrowed, whereas in other situations they are freely borrowed."[76] Talageri, who is unaware of this, concludes that unless "the normal linguistic laws are to be treated as invalid just in order to accommodate the invasion theorists' insistence that the linguistic structure of Indo-Aryan is borrowed from Dravidian, it will *have* to be accepted that the linguistic structure of Indo-Aryan *cannot possibly be 'borrowed' from Dravidian*."[77] Thus, he avoids the conclusion that Middle Indo-Aryan and New Indo-Aryan have been built on a Dravidian substratum. Instead,

> The correct explanation for the structural similarity between Indo-Aryan and Dravidian languages is that the similar structure is not "borrowed" by any one of the two from the other. It cannot have been borrowed by the Dravidian languages, since there is no evidence to show that this was the original pan-Indo-European linguistic structure; and it cannot have been borrowed by the Indo-Aryan languages since there is no evidence of the "extensive lexical borrowing" which should precede any structural borrowing.
>
> "Indian Aryandom and Dravidiandom are one" simply because the Indo-Aryan languages and the Dravidian languages developed this common linguistic structure conjointly. It is an "Indian" linguistic structure, and not an "Indo-Aryan" or a "Dravidian" one.
>
> (Ibid.: 189)

Strange as it may seem, this is also a political statement. In the final analysis, it may be regarded as a strategy to bridge the chasm that opened up between Tamil Brahmins and non-Brahmins at the turn of the century. This issue also concerned Sri Aurobindo, who wrote: "The distinction between Aryan and non-Aryan, on which so much has been built, seems on the mass of the evidence to indicate a cultural rather than a racial difference."[78] As we have seen already, Sri Aurobindo did not regard the Rigveda's non-Aryan Dāsas or Dasyus as human foes of a different race but as supernatural beings of a demoniac darkness who oppose the inner spiritual adventure of the Rishis. This kind of hermeneutics is one of the several possible strategies undertaken by Hindu nationalists to defuse potentially problematic material in the Vedas.

13.7 The Aryan–Dravidian divide

> In India the problem of Aryan origins has not only a bearing on the remote past. It also has a relevance to the immediate present. Ever since Western historians pronounced, and the historians of our country concurred, that a Dravidian India had been invaded by the Aryans of the Rigveda in the second millenium B.C. there has been a ferment of antagonism, time and again, between the North and the South.
>
> The Northerners, figuring in their own eyes as Aryan conquerors, have occasionally felt a general superiority to the Southerners who have come to be designated Dravidians. The people of the South have often resented those of the North as being, historically, intruders upon their indigenous rights. An unhealthy movement has arisen in Tamil lands, sometimes erupting in violent strength and otherwise flowing as a subtle pervasive undercurrent which tends to make for a touchy and suspicious relationship between the two parts of our subcontinent, in spite of a broad unifying sense of nationhood.
>
> (Sethna 1992: 1)

This subdued description by K. D. Sethna graphically depicts what is a pivotal concern in the debates on Aryanism. It is also a concern to Shrikant Talageri, whose language is more hardhitting: "A certain section of die-hard Leftists in the extreme south had decided, well before 1947, to make political and ideological capital out of the very first premise of the Aryan invasion theory, namely, that Aryans invaded India and drove the Dravidians south. Starting under the name 'Justice Party', this section floated the 'Dravida Kalagam' (DK), claiming to represent a movement of, by, and for the 'Dravidians', to liberate them from 'Aryan dominance'. " This philosophy today constitutes the dominant political current in Tamil Nadu, with the DMK and the AIADMK, linear descendants of the DK, dominating the political scene. Hatred for Brahmins, Sanskrit, Hindi, and Hinduism, forms the main plank of this "Dravidian Movement."[79] To understand the background, we shall have to go back to the end of the nineteenth century and the formation of the non-Brahmin or Dravidian movement.

In the nineteenth century, Brahmins all across India had gained tangible advantages under colonial rule. Tamil-speaking Brahmins had especially reaped rich rewards. Barely 3 percent of the population, they disproportionately dominated the bureaucracy and various professions such as education, journalism, law, and medicine, as well as associational politics, into the 1920s, primarily by getting a head start in English and university education.[80] Because Brahmin domination was ensured by a colonial legal culture which institutionalized Brahmanical social theory as the very foundations of the Raj, all caste Hindus in the south who were not Brahmin were unilaterally considered "Shudra." That amounted to almost three-fourths of the populace of the Madras Presidency and had a very provocative impact on non-Brahmins. The Vellalas in particular were eager to shed the Shudra designation.[81] In addition, Brahmins often combined economic power derived from land ownership with religious authority and further separated themselves from the lower castes while increasing their control over them. Thus, the position of the Brahmins engendered suspicion, if not hatred, in the mind of the non-Brahmin.[82]

Eugene F. Irschick has shown how the colonial authorities in conjunction with local interests tried to influence the settlement pattern of parts of the Tamil population using among other things the reconstruction of a glorious Dravidian past as a means to put an end to the geographical mobility of these population segments.[83] Perhaps even more important in the construction of a Tamil identity was the linguistic work produced by missionaries such as Roberto Di Nobili (1577–1656) and Constantius Beschi (1680–1743), but, above all, of the Rev. Robert Caldwell (1819–91), who in addition to his pioneering work on Tamil and Dravidian linguistics also had ideas about Tamil culture and history that were conducive to the development of a strong national identity among Tamil-speakers.[84] This ethnonationalism was strongly anti-Brahmin. Brahmins were regarded as representatives of an Aryan invasion and held responsible for corrupting the original Dravidian religion,[85] while the Shaiva scriptures were presented as superior to the Vedas. Brahmins were also accused of introducing the caste system into

South India. At the same time, Tamil culture was described as unconnected with the north and northern settlers, and the Tamils allegedly never derived their letters or arts or civilization from the Aryans.[86] Thus, the Dravidian nationalists and particularly the Tamils proceeded to reconstruct a history from scanty sources and conjecture which recalled an antiquity dating from the Indus civilization to the powerful Tamil kingdoms of the South. The political and social consequences for the Brahmins were considerable. Anti-Brahminism was riding high on a tide of reforms directed toward the betterment of the non-Brahmin majority of Madras. These reforms included the establishment of quotas based on caste and religion for civil service posts, ensuring the rights of non-Brahmins in seeking government office.[87] By 1921, the opportunities for Brahmins in the civil service had been considerably reduced, and Brahmins had to take to other professions. The hatred for Brahmins that had been whipped up in the population also led to acts of violence; it is therefore hardly surprising that Brahmins felt the need to respond to the historical picture presented by the Dravidianists.

It is an interesting aspect of the ensuing debate that both Dravidianists and neo-Hindus were able to extract separate narratives of their respective pasts from colonial Indology, and to rewrite these narratives in such a manner that they suited the practical purposes of the two contending groups. If Caldwell had glorified the Dravidian past, other writers saw the religion of the Dravidians as "gross demonolatry" contrasting with the "subtle philosophies" of the Aryan Brahmins. Thus, the neo-Hindus had a basis in colonial Indology upon which to build, and just like the colonial historians, they tended to regard India and Indian culture as coextensive with Hinduism. In many a neo-Hindu narrative, the progressive admixture of aboriginal Dravidians had caused the "fall" of Hinduism from its glorious Aryan beginnings, a decline that was only further exacerbated by the invasions of the Muslims.[88]

In one of the early Brahmin counterattacks on the Dravidianists, Srinivas Aiyangar tried to reconquer Tamil as part of the Brahmin heritage claiming that "... the earliest grammarians of Tamil were Brahmans, their first spiritual instructors were Brahmans, and their first teachers of philosophy were also Brahmans."[89] A Brahmin scholar, R. Swaminatha Iyer, took up the argument from the philological point of view. Evidence showed, he claimed, that "what are known as Dravidian languages are in all their present essential features a creation of Aryan and Aryanised immigrants from the North."[90] It therefore followed that the tradition about Agastya's immigration to the south was not merely a myth, and that the Dravidian civilization of the South was merely the civilization of these Aryan and Aryanised immigrants.[91] Many Brahmins joined the Varnashrama Dharma movement, which tried to promote Brahmin ideals. According to a resolution passed by a conference of this organization, the "Vedas and the Smritis had for their sole object the preservation of the Brahmana race without any admixture of other blood, so that the Vedas may be preserved by a set of qualified people and bred up in a purely Vaidic atmosphere."[92] The movement tried to cajole the non-Brahmins into joining the Brahmins. They too, the reasoning went, were "noble Aryans," and they must "firmly believe that the truly orthodox Brahmin is your real friend and Saviour, both for the life here and for the life beyond."[93] This statement was made in 1918 and in the spirit of Aurobindo and Dayānanda represents an early attempt to co-opt non-Brahmins back into the traditional caste system by presenting them as noble Aryans. This idea of co-Aryanness is still very much alive and forms an important part of Hindutva ideology. So is the rejection of the theory that Sanskrit and the Dravidian languages are unrelated.

From a nationalist point of view, it is clear that the concept of an Aryan–Dravidian divide is pernicious to the unity of the Hindu state, and an important aim for Hindutva and neo-Hindu scholarship is therefore to introduce a counter-narrative to the one presented by Western academic scholarship. Navaratna Rajaram strongly objects to the idea that Dravidian languages are a family unrelated to Sanskrit. According to him, "empirical data provides no support for the existence of Dravidian languages independent of Sanskrit."[94] Quite to the contrary, no trace of any Dravidian language free from the influence of Sanskrit has ever been found. The proto-languages inferred by Western scholars are rejected as imaginary languages created by modern linguists to fill gaps in their theory. Rajaram presents his own views on the subject in the *Organiser*:

> The term Dravida refers simply to a geographical region whereas Arya is a cultural term. Just as the nineteenth century scholars confused race and language in their misuse of the word Arya the same people confused geography, language and culture in the case of the word Dravida. The Aryan–Dravidian divide is essentially a political fraud, the result of colonial-missionary mischief.
>
> (Rajaram 1997)

According to Rajaram, no well-informed scholar today takes either the Aryan invasion or the notion of the foreign origin of the Vedas and the Vedic civilization seriously. Furthermore, he claims that the Aryan–Dravidian divide was created by the colonial rulers, just as they created the Hindu–Muslim divide.[95] Even today the field of Dravidian studies is allegedly dominated by "missionary scholars" like Kamil Zvelebil. Although Zvelebil's scholarship is dubious according to Rajaram, "through a combination of inflated pretensions and the unwillingness of other scholars to expose him, Zvelebil has successfully interposed himself as an arbiter of Dravidian scholarship, and even the Indus script and language!" It is interesting to note that while Rajaram rejects proto-Dravidian as a scholarly phantasy, Talageri elsewhere invokes the same theory to prove a point![96] Indigenist polemicists, like the Western scholars they decry, are equally unable to come up with a unified theory of the Indo-European or Aryan past.

A slightly more sophisticated attempt at getting around the linguistic differences between Dravidian and Indo-Aryan languages has been made by Subhash Kak. In his paper "On the Classification of Indic Languages" he deals with Indo-European and Dravidian. Here he argues that "based on genetic classification, both the Indo-Aryan and Dravidian languages have had common parents and these languages share many typological categories."[97] This he tries to justify by referring to the Nostratic theory, which assumes a linkage of language families – Indo-European, Uralic, Turkic, Mongolian, Tungusic, Dravidian, South Caucasian (Kartvelian), and perhaps Afroasiatic.[98] Kak claims that speakers of these languages interacted strongly resulting in many shared characteristics among the languages. The relationship among the Nostratic languages is ascribed to proximity about eight thousand years ago. Kak suggests the following scenario:

> Around 7000 B.C. the Indo-Europeans were located in the Indus-Sarasvati valleys, northern Iran, and southern Russia; the Afro-Asiatics were in West Asia; and the Dravidians were located just south of the Indo-Europeans in a belt stretching from South India to southern Iran. There existed many trading links between the groups. The Vedic period is to be seen as following a long interactive era between the Indo-Aryans and the Dravidians. The proof of this comes in many Dravidian features of the Vedic language.
> (1994: 192)

Kak's paper is strangely poor on details.[99] At the end, he claims that "attested migrations of the Indo-Iranians into Europe explains the presence of several Dravidian features in the European languages."[100] It is typical that he does not mention *which* features he regards as Dravidian. Nor is his general model well argued with reference to specific archaeological or linguistic material. Yet for all its shortcomings, his paper is probably the best attempt to save a modicum of Indo-European and Dravidian commonality in the incipient phase of these languages. The main problem is that the idea of a Nostratic superfamily, contrary to Kak's contention on page 188, has *not* been increasingly accepted in recent years. According to Dixon, there is no reputable historical linguist anywhere in the world who accepts the claims of the Nostraticists.[101] The reasons are lack of rigor in the methods applied, as well as the fact that several of the language families that are supposed to be related are still in dire need of research. The presumed Altaic family may not exist at all. Thus Kak is really clutching at straws.

It is clear that the opposition to the Aryan invasion theory has a predominantly Brahmin background. But it is interesting that a political leader from the lower part of the social ladder also opposed the theory. B. R. Ambedkar in his book *Who were the Shudras?* took strong exception to it. His reasons for doing so are enlightening:

> The Aryan race theory is so absurd that it ought to have been dead long ago. But far from being dead, the theory has a considerable hold upon people. There are two explanations which account for this phenomenon. The first explanation is to be found in the support which the theory receives from the Brahmin scholars. This is a very strange phenomenon. As Hindus, they should ordinarily show a dislike for the Aryan theory with its express avowal of the superiority of the European races over the Asiatic races. But the

> Brahmin scholar has not only no such aversion but he most willingly hails [*sic*]. The reasons are obvious. The Brahmin believes in the two-nation theory. He claims to be the representative of the Aryan race and he regards the rest of the Hindus as descendants of the non-Aryans. The theory helps him to establish his kinship with the European races and share their arrogance and superiority. He likes particularly that part of the theory which makes the Aryan an invader and a conqueror of the non-Aryan native races. For it helps him to maintain and justify his overlordship over the non-Brahmins.
>
> (Chakrabarti 1997: 228)

Ambedkar's statement shows to what extent the interpretation of history depends upon present needs.The southern Brahmins rejected the invasion theory because it was used to their disadvantage, and Ambedkar rejects it for precisely the same reason, but from a low-caste perspective. In both cases, history is a potent weapon that has to be defused.

13.8 Indigenist rhetoric and the anguish of India

In her book on ethnicity, security, and separatism in India, Maya Chadda comments upon the heavy hand of history on the collective consciousness of the Sikhs. In this connection she quotes Robin Jeffrey who shows how Sikh politicians found it necessary to invoke the past – and to portray past events in a way that did not correspond to any documentary evidence Jeffrey had seen. Jeffrey distinguishes between what he calls the academic history and the rhetorical history of Punjab.[102] It was clear that Sikh politicians were using the imagined past to justify the present and to reconstruct their identities in the context of new developments. In a similar manner, competing versions of the past are found in Kashmir and on Sri Lanka.[103] The phenomenon is not restricted to ethnic nationalism, we also find it in connection with caste history.

The heated polemics against Western Indology may carry an emotional impact that quickly blunts the response of a Western scholar, but there is a strain of sadness in these noisy assertions that is brought out well by Bhagwan Singh, also deploring the moral decrepitude of Western Indology:

> All these aberrations create doubts about the probity of those who disinherited the Vedic Aryans from the legacy of the Harappan civilization even though their's is the only tradition which bemoans its lost glories and has fondly preserved whatever could be preserved as part of its own traditional history. *Deprive them of the Harappan inheritance and there shall be nothing left to make the Aryans feel proud of, whether in India or abroad.* [my emphasis] Indian Aryans are known to be the moving super-computers of history when it comes to loading the bulk of the text in their mind, but they are rejected as halfwits when it comes to recognition of their tradition about which they were so crazy.
>
> (1995: 11)

The cultural anguish so eloquently expressed by Singh reverberates through the Internet. It echoes the sentiments of a complaint made by Golwalkar:

> Our history is for the most part occupied by the Muslim period and, later, the British period. If this is how we teach our children – that they had nothing great in the past, that they have been a beaten people always, that it was only after the advent of Moghuls and, later the English, that this nation began to look forward – in short, that they had no past worthy of pride and no ancestors worthy of emulation, can we expect anything worthwhile from them?
>
> (1992: 55)

India, at the end of the twentieth century, with an immense population of nearly one billion people squeezed in on a territory smaller than the United States and staggering on the brink of a social, environmental, and economic disaster, has reason to agonize. Yet I believe that the psychological roots of this cultural *Angst* are to be found in the late eighteenth and nineteenth century, when India first found itself elevated to cultural stardom by such men as Voltaire, William Jones, and Friedrich Schlegel, only to find itself mocked, rejected, and degraded at the beginning of the twentieth century.[104] Indians not only had to deal with a colonial power which had effective control over their territory, but they also had to face the immensely powerful and terrifying onslaught of modernization and the arrogant will of the British to *redefine* them through British education and Christian mission, thus threatening to supersede the traditional ways of self-imaging and self-definition. Such organizations as the Arya Samaj and Brahmo Samaj were reactions to this colonial mind-game, and the subsequent counter-narratives of primeval grandeur, being reflections of an indophobic Indology now obsolete in the West, became part of India's political discourse and strategies for self-definition. Nineteenth-century Indology survives in Indian debates because its narratives became ingrained in India's visceral intellectual life, the school system, and in the creation of political categories. Although much indigenist rhetoric can be related explicitly to high-caste interests, there is a more general background which cannot simply be explained as right-wing politics. At the end of the colonial era, India was not merely a colony emerging from the political oppression and material exploitation of the past. It was also a wounded civilization looking for a new and regenerated self-assurance. To begin with, other ideological and political preferences prevailed. Now, with the loss of intellectual credibility experienced by the Left after the collapse of Communism and Congress in moral disintegration, this self-assurance has to be sought elsewhere.

13.9 The Hindutva dilemma: Indigenous Aryanism as a political tool

If we turn to the Hindu nationalists at the beginning of this century, we find that Indigenous Aryanism had not yet become integrated into the ideology of the religious Right, at least not in its modern form. Dayānanda Saraswati described the

Aryans of the Vedic era as a chosen people that some time after Creation came down from Tibet into Āryāvarta and then became the "sovereign lords of the earth."[105] However, he also states: "This country is called Āryāvarta because it has been the abode of the Aryas from the very dawn of Creation."[106] The Aryans were in fact the first to settle Āryāvarta, and Dayānanda rejected the Western Orientalist idea that the Aryans came from the Middle East into a country already settled by savages.[107] Bāl Gangādhar Tilak, however, thought that the Aryans had their original homeland in the Arctic region. The German scholar Hans-Joachim Klimkeit suggests that this view may be due to the fact that Tilak was a Chitpavan Brahmin, and that the Chitpavan Brahmins had a myth of origin to the effect that their ancestors had come from the North somewhere outside India.[108] Vināyak Damodar Sāvarkar also accepted the possibility of a non-Indian Aryan extraction. It was Mahādev Sadaśivrao Golwalkar, founder of the Rashtriya Swayamsevak Sangh (RSS), who in political terms settled the matter by claiming that "Hindus came into this land from nowhere, but are indigenous children of the soil always, from times immemorial."[109] It has been pointed out several times that Golwalkar's view is the natural consequence of an ideology that regards the Muslims and Christians as intruders. By the same token, the Aryans would be intruders too, and we have seen that they were indeed decried as such in Tamil Nadu. But it is also proper to see indigenism as a constructive tool within the context of Hindutva organicism.

In Golwalkar's thinking, the Hindus – and thereby the Aryans – were autochthonous to the land of India:

> The origin of our people, the date from which we have been living here as a civilised entity, is unknown to the scholars of history. In a way we are **anadi**, without a beginning. To define such a people is impossible.
>
> We existed when there was no necessity for any name. We were the good, the enlightened people. We were the people who knew about the laws of Nature and the laws of the Spirit. We built a great civilisation, a great culture and a unique social order. We had brought into actual life almost everything that was beneficial to mankind. The rest of humanity were just bipeds and so no distinctive name was given to us. Sometimes, in trying to distinguish our people from others, we were called "the enlightened" – the **Aryas** – and the rest **Mlecchas**.
>
> (1992: 16f)

In Golwalkar's narrative[110] these sons of the sacred mother Bharat have an almost Messianic mission in the world. The term *anadi* has distinct religious overtones and would seem to link the Aryans with the Vedic *puruṣa* or cosmic giant that is also the origin of the *varṇa* system which makes the Indian social order so unique. H. V. Seshadri, present General Secretary of the RSS, contrasts two types of national cohesion, mechanical or organic. The mechanical version has unity at the structural and functional level. The other kind is the cohesion of a living organism. No part of it is joined to it from outside.[111] Whereas mechanical cohesion causes inherent friction, the organic pattern produces harmony. Here, social norms and conventions evolve in tune with the basic motivation of mutual love and co-operation. This harmonious society is comparable to a living organism, and the various limbs and organs co-operate spontaneously with one another and with the entire body. In Seshadri's words, "the founding fathers of our society had, in fact, conceived of it as *Virata Purusha* with thousands of heads, eyes, hands, feet and so on, but with one heart, throbbing all through. That was the kind of living, organic unity sought to be established in the society."[112]

Seshadri's reference to the Rigveda is significant because through the Vedic *varṇa* system it gives the organicist view of society as divine sanction. If Indian nationalism is founded on European nationalism, as social scientists are wont to claim, the modalities of this nationalism are at least in part arch-Indian. It is obvious that Aryans cannot have been extraneous to this societal body at the sacred beginning of Cosmic time. Indian society, modeled on the cosmic giant who is also identical with the sacrifice and in the post-vedic period with the god Viṣṇu, is a model for social harmony, which is one of the fundamental ideological purposes of the caste system: a hierarchical harmony where duties or *dharmas* are distributed among the several castes which are burdened with unequal shares of purity and impurity. The *sanctity* of this vision breaks down if the Aryans are treated as barbaric intruders.

Arvind Rajagopal has suggested that there is a muted but persistent upper caste, brahmin-dominated identity emerging as the dominant, if not the hegemonic, national identity of India.[113] There is much material to document such a claim, and the social vision delineated above is certainly Brahmin in spirit.[114] But this is not the only attempt in India's modern history to create an ideological basis for a unified nation. From the beginning, modern India had to face and absorb a number of ethnonationalisms. Therefore, the Indian nationalists had to create an inclusive interpretation of history – the opposite of what the ethnonationalists were trying to prove.[115] In his construction of Indian history, Jawaharlal Nehru also tried to extract unifying principles that would give India inner cohesion.[116] And for all his democratic principles, he made no bones about using the armed forces in order to integrate the more recalcitrant elements of colonial India. The Hindutva approach differs in method rather than in purpose.

According to Sita Ram Goel, the Nehruvian version of history which has been "sold as secularist in post-independence India" is "no more than a mix of the imperialist versions [of history]."[117] Nehru's vision was of a multi-cultured India, and it was tolerant of the different creeds that were established on India's territory. This vision of multiple separate entities joined in one nation is in the background when Talageri presents the "first principle of Leftist propaganda" as the idea that India is not a nation, but a conglomerate of nations. And the main motive for projecting this "multinational India" theory is to sow the seeds for the eventual breakup of India into its "constituent nations," the alleged rationale behind this being that if India breaks up into small "nations," these would be easier for the Leftists to gobble up one by one. But in Talageri's view a deeper reason for this Leftist attitude is "hatred and contempt for one's own nation, culture, historical ethos and identity" which is "manifested in a psychopathic hatred and contempt for Hinduism, Hindu Nationalism and Hindu culture."[118] It would therefore seem that the general antipathy toward the Left is strongly influenced by the social critique of the Left, which not only threatens traditional views but also high-caste interests. Since academic scholars often share this critical attitude toward India's social system, their scholarly methods are equally branded as Marxist. It is overlooked that the methods applied by India's mainstream academics, by and large, are the same methods that are applied all over the democratic, industrialized world, not only in Indology but also in other disciplines of the humanities and the social sciences. This identification of modern methods with "Leftism" thus serves to alienate Hindutva scholarship from the rest of the academic world. At the same time, ironically the Hindu nationalist stance betrays them as true inheritors of the British Raj, perhaps even more so than the Congress nationalists that preceded them.

Around the beginning of the nineteenth century, both J. G. Herder and Friedrich Schlegel had presented India as the cradle of humanity. In Schlegel's view, Sanskrit was the mother of languages.[119] This Romantic notion of India as the *Urheimat* would seem to have become the destination of the Hindu nationalists' intellectual trajectory toward a more gratifying view on India's past. The rejection of almost 200 years of linguistic and philological scholarship has the result that polemicist arguments often acquire a curiously creaky and distant quality, as if being carried across the expanse of a vast time gap. Even if they occasionally make good points when discussing the logical coherence of some arguments concerning aspects of the migration theory, they are unable to create a convincing counter-model that in a satisfactory manner accounts for the data we *do* happen to know. What they provide, however, is a highly efficient rhetoric with a mobilization potential which serves to promote a new Hindu identity as well as Hindu nationalist policies.

Acknowledgments

This chapter was made possible by substantial grants from The Institute for Comparative Research in Human Culture and the Benneche Foundation. I also owe a great deal of gratitude to Wolfson College, Oxford, which accepted me as Visiting Scholar for the Trinity term of 1999, thus giving me the working conditions and stimuli that I needed to see the work through. Special thanks to Raoul Martens, who supplied me with useful material, although we disagree on most accounts, and to Edwin Bryant who read a draft of this chapter and supplied me with a valuable critique. I have also received valuable comments from Luis Gonzalez-Reimann and Kathinka Frøystad. In addition, thanks to a large number of Internet friends who have given me far more input than I could possibly use, and to Ruth Schmidt who improved my English.

This chapter was finished before the arrival of India's present government, and it would be too complicated to rewrite the relevant paragraphs of the article to harmonize them with the current political situation.

Notes

1 "Il est légitime de chercher les Indo-Européens sur le terrain protohistorique, mais *il s'agit là d'un prolongement de l'hypothèse, non de sa vérification*. La vérité de la notion d' 'Indo-Européen' est dans la langue et dans la religion, elle n'est pas dans l'archéologie" (Sergent 1995: 394).

2 Important persons here would be the astrologer and amateur Indologist David Frawley, the Yoga specialist Georg Feuerstein, and the linguist Koenrad Elst.

3 Chakrabarti does not define "Indology" directly, but in the first sentence of his preface, he refers to the "Western study of ancient India" (p. ix). This would seem to be a fairly adequate definition of Indology as understood in its narrow sense, and particularly related to Sanskrit studies, but at the same time even early Indologists studied contemporary Indian vernaculars, religion and culture. In a modern context, the term Indology would refer to the study of ancient and modern Indic languages as well as the culture, history and religions of India in general. In a number of places, Indology has been replaced by the term "South Asian studies."

4 Chakrabarti 1997: ix.

5 Ibid.: 1.

6 Ibid.: 7.

7 Mill, James (1773–1836). Scottish philosopher, historian, and economist and a prominent representative of Utilitarianism. Mill wrote a History of British India, 3 vol. (1817). The History's severe Utilitarian analysis of Indian civilization also popularized among European readers an image of the subcontinent as perpetually backward and undeveloped.

"Mill, James" Encyclopædia Britannica Online. <http://members.eb.com/bol/topic?eu=54009&sctn=1> (accessed August 18, 1999).

8 The German historians H. Kulke and D. Rothermund published their *A History of India* in 1986. They discuss the Mauryan empire on pp. 61–70.

9 Chakrabarti 1997: 201.

10 The question of the extent of the Mauryan empire is a classical case of historical inference based on insufficient data. Neither the view of Chakrabarti nor the view of Rothermund and Kulke can be proved, and Chakrabarti may therefore opt for an interpretation that is more satisfactory seen from a nationalist point of view without having to twist the data. However, his own interpretation is equally open to criticism, and the *non liquet* remains.

11 Talageri 1993a,b; Rajaram 1993, 1995; Singh 1995; and Sethna 1992.

12 Parpola compares these names with the Iranian ethnic names *daha*, *dahyu*, and *parnoi*.

13 Parpola 1988: 265.

14 K. D. Sethna has since 1949 been the editor of *Mother India*, a Review of Culture. He was educated at St Xavier's School and College in Bombay and at Bombay University with degrees in philosophy and English. During his MA studies he joined the Sri Aurobindo Ashram of Integral Yoga at Pondicherry. His interests are in literature, philosophy, mystical and spiritual as well as scientific thought and ancient Indian history. He has published extensively on a number of subjects.

15 Sethna 1992: 204ff.

16 Parpola 1988: 215.

17 Sethna 1992: 216ff.

18 Parpola 1994: 157.

19 Sethna 1992: 228.

20 Ibid.: 233.

21 Parpola 1988: 205.

22 Sethna 1992: 242ff.
23 Ibid.: 244.
24 Ibid.: 264.
25 "silver processing" Encyclopædia Britannica Online. <http://members.eb.com/bol/topic?eu=119895&sctn=2> (accessed June 22, 1999).
26 "gold processing" Encyclopædia Britannica Online. <http://members.eb.com/bol/topic?eu=119894&sctn=2> (accessed June 22, 1999).
27 Sethna 1992: 246.
28 Ibid.: 263.
29 Ibid.: 330.
30 Ibid.: 333.
31 Ibid.: 335.
32 See for instance Sethna 1992: 107ff.
33 Bhagwan Singh has published a number of works in Hindi, partly of a literary, partly of a philological character.
34 Singh 1995: 18.
35 Ibid.: 29.
36 Ibid.: 8.
37 Ibid.: 12.
38 Ibid.: 50.
39 See for instance Parpola 1988: 196.
40 Singh 1995: 57.
41 Ibid.
42 It is demonstrable that Germanic *h* is derived from I-E **k*, whereas this *k becomes *ś* in Skt. Skt *h* is usually derived from I-E * *gh*.
43 Singh 1995: 58.
44 Golwalkar 1992: 22.
45 N. S. Rajaram has a bachelor's degree in electrical engineering from the B. M. S. College in Bangalore and a PhD in mathematics from Indiana University in Bloomington, USA. He has more than twenty years' experience in teaching and research at several universities in the United States. His areas of research have included probability theory and statistics, artificial intelligence and robotics, and industrial automation.
46 Rajaram 1995: xiii.
47 Ibid.: 186.
48 Rajaram and Frawley 1995: 50. Models for the application of linguistic analysis to demic diffusion were in fact readily available in the shape of historical data on language and cultural diffusion. The nineteenth-century scholars who devised the invasion theories had the most impressive models right in front of them: Since the time of Columbus, Western Europeans had invaded and colonized North America, Meso-America, South America, and Australia. Huge population movements had taken place, and indigenous populations were heavily decimated, partly because of European brutality, partly because of the spread of new diseases. The conquest of Costa Rica almost entirely replaced the indigenous population with Spanish speakers. In Mexico a substantial Spanish element was injected into the population without the indigenous population being annihilated, and with an ongoing genetic and cultural amalgamation as a result (King 1981: 151). The same process applies to the Andean region of South America. In North America the native Americans were chased away from their traditional areas under constant pressure from European settlers. In Russia, there was a substantial annexation of areas in Asia, both to the south and to the east with a concomitant spread of the Russian language and Russian culture. A literary reflex of this expansion was Jules Verne's book *Michael Strogoff: The Courier of the Czar*. One can also mention a large number of colonies with small, but powerful European populations ruling over the natives. But not only that: European scholars

had been raised in a school system where Greek and Roman history was an integral part of the curriculum. This history offered an assorted selection of barbaric migrations, particularly at the end of the Roman empire, which could serve as models for the expansion of the Indo-Europeans. It is therefore hardly surprising that the migration model has come under revision only recently. This has come about by the analysis of language and culture diffusion, where we now are able to see that there are several models available. Invasion – or migration – is only one such model. Japan, for instance, offers a model for cultural diffusion without a concomitant genetic diffusion. The history of the English language in Ireland shows us how a language can spread without a large-scale invasion. During the seventeenth century, a new English-speaking ruling class was settled in Ireland, and the mercantile and professional classes in towns became predominantly English-speaking. By the eighteenth century, the Irish language was confined to the poorer rural people. After 1745 this effect was also evident in Gaelic Scotland. These populous and impoverished communities were ravaged by economic failure in the nineteenth century, and survivors began a rapid shift to English. In 1700, four/fifths of the Irish population spoke Irish, and the English spoken in Ireland was not different from the English spoken in Britain. Three hundred years later, only one/seventh of the Irish population speak Irish, and the English spoken in Ireland is substantially different from the English of Britain (Pokorny 1968 [1936]: 180).

49 The method was proposed by Morris Swadesh in 1951 and is based on studies of the lexicon, which undergoes gradual changes so that an assumed specific percentage of the core vocabulary is lost with time. The method is controversial for several reasons and does not play a major role in modern linguistics. When used, it is usually because other methods are unavailable. For a short description, see Lehmann 1993: 35ff.

50 Rajaram 1995: xiv.

51 Ibid.: 52.

52 See for instance Trautmann (1997), who gives a better and more balanced picture of the situation than Chakrabarti.

53 Rajaram and Frawley 1995: 19.

54 Ibid.: 21.

55 Ibid.: 42.

56 Hencken 1955: 2.

57 Ibid.: 32.

58 See for instance chapter VI of Sergent 1997.

59 Rajaram and Frawley 1995: 205.

60 Ibid.: 206.

61 Ibid.: 209.

62 Ibid.: 248. The emphasis is mine. Rajaram ascribes the end of the Indus culture to an ecological disaster. His chronology looks like this: 8000 – ending of the last Ice Age; 3750 – ending of the Rigvedic Age; 3100 – ending of the Vedic Age; the Mahābhārata war; 3000 – beginning of the Harappa-Sūtra period; 2700–2200 – high Harappan–Sumerian civilization; *c.*2350 – founding of the Akkadian empire by Sargon of Akkad; 2200 – Drought begins: the beginning of the end of the Harappan and Akkadian civilizations; 2200–1900 – end of the ancient world. All dates BCE.

63 Sita Ram Goel in the preface to Talageri 1993: v.

64 Shrikant G. Talageri was educated in Bombay where he lives and works. He has been interested in wildlife, comparative music, religion and philosophy, history and culture, and linguistics. He has made a special study of the Konkani language, his mother tongue.

65 Talageri 1993a,b. The two books are partly identical, as they have much text in common, and the reappraisal of the Aryan invasian theory would seem to be a remake of the *Aryan Invasion Theory and Indian nationalism.*

66 Talageri 1993a: v–ix: "The author of the present book, Shrikant G. Talageri, has taken great pains to examine the archaeological, literary, linguistic and anthropological evidence both for and against the Aryan invasion and non-Indian home of the Aryans and come to the reasonable conclusion that the Indo-Aryans lived in the Indus Valley and neighbouring countries long before the European Aryan speakers in Central Asia. I am sure his findings based on comprehensive study research will put an end to much publicized Aryan invasion theory."

67 Thus, he for instance tries to derive the word gaja, "elephant" from the Sanskrit root garj- "to roar," which is phonetically impossible (Talageri 1993a: 170). A derivation from garj- would have given garjaka- or garjiki. Nor could gaja- have gone through a Prakrit language, which would have given gajja- with a heavy first syllable. Bhagwan Singh simply rejects the relevance of sound laws: "... to talk of the laws governing an entire linguistic area is absurd. There is no language in the world which has perfect grammatical rules. Not even Sanskrit. How can we talk of phonetic laws governing such a large number of dialects and what sense is there in taking the assumed PIE roots seriously when we can not reconstruct old English by comparison of English spoken in the commonwealth countries?" (Singh 1995: 330).

68 See for instance Sergent 1997: 81ff.

69 See Chakrabarti 1997: 130. Chakrabarti refers to this as the "Outer Band." Grierson uses the terms "Inner sub-branch" and "Outer sub-branch" of Indo-Aryan languages, see *Linguistic Survey of India*, vol. 1, Part 1 (1927), p. 117.

70 Retroflexes do not occur in any other ancient Indo-European languages, but are for instance well known in modern East Norwegian and Swedish.

71 See for instance (Hock 1996) and (Sergent 1997: 137). Based on physical anthropological material, Sergent rejects the idea that the Harappans were Dravidians, and instead classifies them as Indo-Afghan. In Sergent's opinion, only the southernmost part of the Indus Valley culture was populated by Dravidians. This fits nicely with Hock's view that retroflexes may be explained as an internal development in Indo-Aryan languages.

72 Dixon 1997: 15.

73 Ibid.: 16.

74 Talageri 1993a: 186.

75 Ibid.: 186f.

76 Dixon 1997: 27.

77 Talageri 1993a: 187.

78 Quoted in Sethna 1992: 175. According to Sethna, Aurobindo argues that "there is nothing in the present ethnological features of the country" to prove the common theory that there was, from outside India, a penetration of "a small body of fair-skinned barbarians into a civilized Dravidian peninsula." The quotation from Aurobindo is from *The Secret of the Veda*, published by the Sri Aurobindo Ashram, Pondicherry, 1971. According to Patricia M. Greer (pers. comm.), Sri Aurobindo's various writings on the Veda and his translations of some of the hymns, originally published in the "Arya" (a periodical in which Sri Aurobindo serialized many of his major works) between August 1914 and 1920, were brought together and published in book-form in 1956 under the general title "On the Veda." The title of the volume, however, was later changed to the more significant "The Secret of the Veda." That re-titling took place for the 1972 "Centenary Edition" of Sri Aurobindo's works. Sri Aurobindo died in 1950. In recent years, the Sri Aurobindo Ashram Archives have published many unpublished translations and chapters on the Vedas found among Sri Aurobindo's papers.

79 Talageri 1993b: 38. DMK and AIADMK are the acronyms for the Dravida Munnetra Kazhagam and the All India Anna Dravida Munnetra Kazhagam respectively.

80 Ramaswamy 1997: 27.

81 Irschick 1969: 295.
82 Hardgrave 1965: 11.
83 Irschick 1994.
84 Irschick 1969: 279.
85 Ibid.: 294.
86 Ibid.: 291f.
87 Hardgrave 1965: 19–21.
88 Ramaswamy 1997: 26.
89 Irschick 1969: 298.
90 Ibid.
91 Ibid.: 298f.
92 Ibid.: 299f.
93 Ibid.: 300.
94 Rajaram 1995: 177.
95 Rajaram 1997.
96 Talageri 1993a: 163.
97 Kak 1994: 187.
98 Dixon 1997: 38.
99 Kak here clashes with Talageri who argues strongly to prove that there was no Dravidian influence on Vedic. As far as academic lingustics is concerned, Kak seems very superficially informed.
100 Kak 1994: 193.
101 Dixon 1997: 44.
102 Chadda 1997: 54.
103 Ibid.: 49ff.
104 Thomas Trautmann has coined the phrases *indomania* and *indophobia* for these two extremes. For the French and German reactions to India, see Figueira (1994).
105 "The Aryans of the Vedic era are described as a chosen people to whom 'the formless God revealed perfect knowledge of the Veda'. Some time after Creation, they came down from Tibet into Aryavarta – a virgin territory between the Himalayas and Vindhya mountains, the Indus and the Brahmaputra – and then became the 'sovereign lords of the Earth', whose inhabitants they instructed in Sanskrit, the 'mother of all languages'" (Jaffrelot 1996: 16). Jaffrelot refers to Dayānanda's book *The Light of Truth*, pp. 248, 277–9, and 341–5. In fact, the word that Dayānanda uses for Tibet, Triviṣ-apa, may also mean Heaven, and it is unclear which meaning he had in mind. A difference in meaning may not have existed for him (Ashok Aklujkar, pers. comm.).
106 Saraswati 1975 [1849: 729]. I am grateful to Luis Gonzalez-Reimann for this reference.
107 Jordens 1997: 254.
108 Klimkeit 1981: 233.
109 The quotation is from "We, or our nationhood defined," p. 37, quoted in Jaffrelot 1996: 55.
110 The publication mentioned here is a selection of writings from Golwalkar's 700 page *magnum opus* with the same name.
111 Seshadri 1991: 17.
112 Ibid.: 19.
113 Rajagopal 1996: 112.
114 The high-caste background and bias of the Sangh parivar is discussed in Jaffrelot 1998.
115 Chadda 1997: 27.
116 Ibid.: 28f.
117 Talageri 1993b: v.
118 Ibid.: 9.
119 Figueira 1994: 207ff.

References

Chadda, M., 1997. *Ethnicity, Security, and Separatism in India*. New York: Columbia University Press.

Chakrabarti, D. K., 1997. *Colonial Indology: Sociopolitics of the Ancient Indian Past*. New Delhi: Munshiram Manoharlal Publishers Pvt. Ltd.

Dixon, R. M. W., 1997. *The Rise and Fall of Languages*. Cambridge: Cambridge University Press.

Figueira, D., 1994. *The Authority of an Absent Text. Authority, Anxiety, and Canon. Essays in Vedic Interpretation*. Albany, NY: State University of New York Press.

Golwalkar, M. S., 1992. *Bunch of Thoughts*. Bombay: Society of Hindu Missionaries.

Hardgrave, R. L., 1965. *The Dravidian Movement*. Bombay: Popular Prakashan.

Hencken, H., 1955. "Indo-European Languages and Archaeology," *American Anthropologist*, 57(6): 1–68.

Hock, H. H., 1996. *Pre-Rgvedic Convergence between Indo-Aryan (Sanskrit) and Dravidian? A Survey of the Issues and Controversies*. In *Ideology and Status of Sanskrit. Contributions to the History of the Sanskrit Language*, edited by J. E. M. Houben. Leiden–New York–Köln: E. J. Brill: 17–58.

Irschick, E. F., 1969. *Politics and Conflict in South India. The Non-Brahman Movement and Tamil Separatism, 1916–1929*. Berkeley and Los Angeles, CA: University of California Press.

——, 1994. *Dialogue and History. Constructing South India, 1795–1895*. Berkeley, CA: University of California Press.

Jaffrelot, C., 1996. *The Hindu Nationalist Movement and Indian Politics 1925 to the 1990s*. New Delhi: Penguin Books India Ltd.

——, 1998. *The Sangh Parivar Between Sanskritization and Social Engineering*. In *The BJP and the Compulsions of Politics in India*, edited by T. B. Hansen and C. Jaffrelot. Delhi: Oxford University Press: 332.

Jordens, J. T. F., 1997. *Dayananda Sarasvati. His Life and Ideas*. Delhi: Oxford University Press.

Kak, S., 1994. "On the classification of Indic languages." *Annals of the Bhandarkar Oriental Research Institute*, 75: 185–95.

King, J. C., 1981. *The Biology of Race*. Berkeley, CA: University of California Press.

Klimkeit, H.-J., 1981. *Der politische Hinduismus. Indische Denker zwischen religiöser Reform und politischem Erwachen*. Wiesbaden: Otto Harrassowitz.

Lehmann, W. P., 1993. *Theoretical Bases of Indo-European Linguistics*. London and New York: Routledge.

Parpola, A., 1988. "The Coming of the Aryans to Iran and India and the Cultural and Ethnic Identity of the Dasas." *Studia Orientalia*, 64: 195–302.

——, 1994. *Deciphering the Indus Script*, Cambridge: Cambridge University Press.

Pokorny, J., 1968 [1936]. *Substrattheorie und Urheimat der Indogermanen. Die Urheimat der Indogermanen. Darmstadt, Wissenschaftliche Buchgesellschaft*. CLXVI: 176–213.

Rajagopal, A., 1996. *Expatriate Nationalism: Disjunctive Discourses*. In *Quest of a Secular Symbol*, edited by R. Ghose. Indian Ocean Centre & South Asian Research Unit. Perth: Curtin University of Technology: 109–139.

Rajaram, N. and D. Frawley, 1995. *The Vedic Aryans and the Origins of Civilization. A Literary and Scientific Perspective*. New Delhi: Voice of India.

Rajaram, N. S., 1993. *Aryan Invasion of India : The Myth and the Truth*. New Delhi: Voice of India.
——, 1995. *The Politics of History: Aryan Invasion Theory and the Subversion of Scholarship*. New Delhi: Voice of India.
——, 1997. *Colonial-missionary Mischief, not Scholarship. Origins of Aryan-Dravidian Divide*. New Delhi: Organiser (December 14, 21).
Ramaswamy, S., 1997. *Passions of the tongue: Language Devotion in Tamil India, 1891–1970*. Berkeley, CA: University of California Press.
Saraswati, D., 1975 [1849]. *The Light of Truth (Satyarth Prakash)*. New Delhi: Sarvadeshik Arya Pratinidhi Sabha.
Sergent, B., 1995. *Les Indo-Européens*. Paris: Payot.
——, 1997. *Genèse de l'Inde*. Paris: Payot.
Seshadri, H. V., 1991. *The Way*. New Delhi: Suruchi Prakashan.
Sethna, K. D., 1992. *The Problem of Aryan Origins. From an Indian Point of View. Second Extensively Enlarged Edition with Five Supplements*. New Delhi: Aditya Prakashan.
Singh, B., 1995. *The Vedic Harappans*. New Delhi: Aditya Prakashan.
Talageri, S. G., 1993a. *The Aryan Invasion Theory: A Reappraisal*. New Delhi: Aditya Prakashan.
——, 1993b. *Aryan Invasion Theory and Indian Nationalism*. New Delhi: Voice of India.
Trautmann, T. R., 1997. *Aryans and British India*. Berkeley, CA: University of California.

14

CONCLUDING REMARKS

Edwin F. Bryant

The solution to the Indo-European problem has been one of the most captivating intellectual projects of the last two centuries, and the problem has resulted in a massive amount of scholarship – the vast majority of which has been produced by European and American scholars – attempting to reconstruct the proto-language of the Indo-European speakers, locate the original homeland where it was spoken, and conjecture on the social and cultural life of the proto-speakers. Naturally, the pursuit of the origins of Western civilization has caused scholars to attempt to reconstruct the proto-histories of non-European countries that happen to partake of the Indo-European language family, such as India – indeed, the discovery of the Indo-Aryan side of the family was especially relevant, or, more precisely, foundational, to the whole endeavor. Not surprisingly, and as has become unavoidably evident of late to anyone in the field of South Asian studies, the reconstruction of the history of the Vedic and pre-Vedic Indo-Aryan speakers is not just of relevance to the field of Indo-European studies, but also of intense interest to many scholars in the modern day, postcolonial context of ancient Indian historical reconstruction. In India, in particular, many scholars understandably are committed to exerting a major role on the construction and representation of the history of South Asia, and this to a great extent involves revisiting and scrutinizing the versions of history inherited from the colonial period.

The purpose of this volume has been to bring together different voices and attempt to portray differing views on the origins of the Vedic speakers, that is, on whether the Indo-Aryan side of the family were immigrants into the Indian subcontinent, or indigenous to it. The data involved in this issue are vast and, in the specialized academic culture of the present day, beyond the command of any individual scholar. The chapters here run the spectrum of positions on this issue. On one side, there are the "Out-of-India" proposals of Elst, Misra, and Talageri. Elst, perhaps more in a mood of devil's advocacy, toys with the evidence to show how it can be reconfigured, and to claim that no linguistic evidence has yet been produced to exclude India as a homeland that cannot be reconfigured to promote it as such. Talageri and Misra are among the very few Indigenists who have ever attempted to bring any innovative *positive* evidence to bear on the greater Indo-European problem (most typically deconstruct the endeavors of others). Talageri prioritizes the Ṛgvedic testimony, and Misra brings some new perspectives on the Finno-Ugric loans.

Adjacent to this is the Indigenous position of Lal. Although the corollary of an indigenous Indo-Aryan population must be that all the Indo-Europeans came from India, Lal, like almost all of his colleagues in Departments of History and Archaeology in South Asia who have taken an interest in the problem of Indo-Aryan origins, shows no concern with the greater Indo-European problem, or the location of the proto-homeland, but only with the evidence connected with the Indo-Aryans. As far as he is concerned, the evidence so far produced to suggest their intrusive origins does not stand to close scrutiny. Shaffer, too, calls on scholars to cease perpetuating outdated interpretations of South Asian proto-history without regard for archaeological data, which he argues do not support Western intrusive cultural influence as responsible for supposed major discontinuities in the South Asian archaeological record. His chapter stresses the continuity of cultural development stretching back to the seventh millennium BCE, with nothing in the archaeological record firmly locating the Indo-Aryans outside of South Asia. Kak's concerns, in turn, are neither with the Indo-European homeland nor even the indigenousness of the Indo-Aryans. His conviction, like Tilak's before him (who did accept an external origin of the Aryans, albeit in the North Pole) is that the Vedic texts are far older than the date commonly assigned to them. These chapters give a good sense of the range of what has been termed "revisionist" scholarship (I do not use this term with the derogatory sense that it has accrued, but in its literal sense of scholarship that is prepared to revise, that is, revisit and reconsider theories and versions of history formulated over the last two centuries).

On the other side of the spectrum is Witzel, whose focus in his chapter is in laying out in considerable detail the reasons he feels an Indian homeland is an unambiguously untenable position. His chapter covers the gamut of evidence – philological, linguistic, archaeological, and astronomical. Kenoyer, focusing on the archaeological evidence, also opposes the Indigenist position, particularly the attempt at attributing a Vedic presence to the Indus Valley civilization (IVC). He cautiously proposes that the social, economic, and ideological restructuring of previously marginal groups in the post-Harappan period may correspond to some of the various communities described in the Vedic texts. Finally Parpola, examines the archaeological and linguistic data from Central Asia, and offers a hypothesis of the trans-Asiatic trajectory of the Indo-Aryans that he feels best accounts for both types of evidence.

Somewhere in the middle are the chapters of Hock and Lamberg-Karlovsky, who are neither promoting a position on this issue, nor critiquing an opposing point of view. Hock discusses five different cases of Vedic interpretation where the passages in question and their interpretation do not provide cogent support for the hypotheses they are supposed to support. He feels that most of the evidence and arguments that have been offered in favor either of the Aryan In-Migration hypothesis or of the Out-of-India hypothesis are inconclusive at closer examination, and offers several examples of how insufficient evidence is produced in support of a point of view. Lamberg-Karlovsky outlines in some detail the many possibly insurmountable problems and hasty conclusions that have resulted from attempting to convincingly correlate the Indo-Aryans, and their predecessors the Indo-Iranians, with archaeological cultures. Finally, Fosse and Deshpande's chapters provide important glimpses at how Aryanism cannot be separated from issues of identity and the politics of representation.

I should probably declare my own opinion at this point, in accordance with the imperatives of postmodernism: as I made clear in Bryant (2001) I still remain agnostic – I have not found the available evidence sufficient to fully resolve the issue to my full satisfaction. On the one hand, I find most of the evidence that has been marshaled to support the theory of Indo-Aryan migrations into the subcontinent to be inconclusive upon careful scrutiny, but on the other, I have not been convinced by an Out-of-India position, since there has been very little of significance offered so far in support of it. At the same time, I find all the IE homeland proposals offered so far to be highly problematic and unconvincing. Therefore, the entire homeland-locating enterprise, with its corollary of Indo-Aryan origins, despite the increase in the body of data available on the issue, has not advanced much further in my mind than the opinion expressed by Max Müller two centuries ago that the original point of origin is probably "somewhere in Asia, and no more."

Indo-European historical reconstruction does not take place in a vacuum; there are ideological issues at stake in contested history. While it remains a fascinating problem, the discussion over Indo-Aryan origins has unfortunately recently become increasingly political, emotional, polemical, and strident, and it is now increasingly difficult for scholars of South Asia to have a cordial exchange on the matter without being branded a "Hindu nationalist," "western neo-colonialist," "Marxist secularist" or some other such simplistic and derogatory stereotype. One does not have to lurk for long on any one of a number of South Asian list sites to soon encounter the issue and the diametrically opposed views that it generates, views that are often invariably articulated in condescending, hostile, and emotional tones. As a result, the moderator of the principal Indology list serve has completely banned discussion of the topic at the time of writing. Clearly, there is a lot more at stake, here, than the existence or absence of innocuous horse bones in the Indus Valley, or the different possible ways of accounting for the curious non-Indo-European linguistic features in the Ṛgveda.

Having just completed a book discussing the range of data involved in this issue, as well as some of the socio-politico-religious contexts of their interpretations over the last two centuries (Bryant 2001), I have little new to add here, and since it is unlikely that the debate will be resolved to the satisfaction of even a majority of scholars any time in the foreseeable future, I take the opportunity of these concluding statements to sieve through my own work on this issue, and reiterate and summarize some of the main reasons as to why there might be such impassioned controversy over the Indo-Aryans in the first place. In my analysis of the problem, there are three main reasons why many (but, let us be clear, by no means all) Indian scholars (and some Western ones) have seen fit to revisit or question the theory of external origins of the Indo-Aryans. The first is suspicion of the motives of the scholars who pieced together the theory in the nineteenth century in the first place, the second is the extreme malleability of much of the evidence itself, and the third is the imperatives of Hindu nationalism (although this latter element, while certainly underpinning much of the scholarship of the Indigenous school, cannot be indiscriminately applied to anyone reconsidering the early history of the subcontinent as I have stressed elsewhere, Bryant 2001).

Consequently, since it seems to be inappropriate for the co-editor of a volume that has invited contributions from scholars representing views on both sides of the issue to use the platform of a conclusory chapter to judicate over some of the migratory or anti-migratory viewpoints expressed in the pages of this volume, a task that I leave to the judgment of the reader, I will consider here a few of the most often quoted examples of both Indo-Aryan discourse and Indo-Aryan data in an attempt to show that, while the polemics the issue invokes is lamentable, the fact that there is a growing controversy is understandable and, indeed, in my view, inevitable. Since Fosse's chapter gives some important insights into some of the nationalistic dynamics underpinning the concern over Aryan origins for Hindu nationalism, I will limit my comments on Indo-Aryan discourse to aspects of its appropriation in nineteenth-century Europe. I will prune my comments on Indo-Aryan data from excessive supporting detail, technicalities, and references – for which the reader can refer to Bryant 2001 – and cut to the chase, focusing on some of the most important issues that, in my view, need further scholarly attention in the matter of Indo-Aryan origins.

14.1 The discourses

The first shadow cast over the reception of the "discovery" of the Sanskrit language and literatures in the late eighteenth century, and the implications these bore for the chronology and history of European civilization, was the pro- (or anti-) Christian bias it provoked among certain scholars. If accepted at face value, the Sanskrit material, as scholars such as William Jones well knew, threatened to subvert the absolute authority of Mosaic history, a prospect he and many of his contemporaries found unacceptable, since they felt obliged to believe in the sanctity of the venerable books of Genesis (1788: 225). Accordingly, there were efforts made either to make the Hindu chronology conform to that of Genesis, which Jones and others attempted to do, or, to herald the newly discovered material as evidence that discredited the Bible, as other segments of the intelligentsia such as Voltaire set out to do. Either way, the Sanskrit material was filtered through the position European scholars took on the bible in the late eighteenth and early nineteenth century.

But even well after Adam was no longer in the picture, biblical sensitivities were replaced by colonial ones, and there was a very cool reception in some circles to Max Müller's disclosure to a rather ungrateful world that the British and the rickshaw pullers of Calcutta were of the same racial family (Legge 1902: 710).

Müller noted the mood of the day:

> They would not have it, they would not believe that there could be any community of origin between the people of Athens and Rome, and the so-called Niggers of India. The classical scholars scouted the idea, and I still remember the time, when I was a student at Leipzig and begun to study Sanskrit, with what contempt any remarks on Sanskrit or comparative grammar were treated by my teachers . . . No one ever was for a time so completely laughed down as Professor Bopp, when he first published his Comparative Grammar of Sanskrit, Zend, Greek, Latin and Gothic. All hands were against him.
>
> (1883: 28)

Elsewhere, Müller, who was effusive in his admiration for things Indian compared to some of his contemporaries, noted that some of his colleagues would be horror-struck at the idea that the humanity they meet with in India should be able to teach Europeans any lesson (ibid.: 7). The most absurd arguments found favor for a time, if they could only furnish a loophole by which to escape the unpleasant conclusion that Greek and Latin were of the same kith and kin as the language of the black inhabitants of India (Müller 1875: 164). The extremes of Indophobic discomfort with the connection of Sanskrit with Greek and Latin was exemplified by the ludicrous conviction of the Scottish philosopher Dugald Stewart who, without knowing a word of the language, proposed that Sanskrit wasn't a cognate of Greek, it *was* Greek. It had been borrowed by the brahmanas during Alexander's conquest, and adopted to keep their conversations inaccessible to the masses. The developing pressure to justify the colonial and missionary presence in India prompted, in certain circles, the denigration of Indian civilization, and the shunning of embarrassing cultural and linguistic ties with the Indians. At the beginning of the nineteenth century, India was considered the cradle of civilization as the homeland of the Aryans, but, by the century's end, it was viewed by some as its grave.

Nonetheless, linguistic reality soon proved to be unavoidable, and colonial sensitivities had to find other means of negotiating with the corollaries of the Indo-European language connection. This was soon manipulated in all manner of ways. Some voices in the colonial power did not hesitate to point out that the government of India by the English had been rendered appreciably easier by the discoveries which have brought home to the educated of both races their common Aryan parentage (Maine 1875: 18–19). From this perspective, what had taken place since the commencement of the British Government in India was only a reunion of the members of the same great family. Müller himself had earlier expressed that the same race to which the first conquerors and masters of India belonged had now returned to accomplish the glorious work of civilization, which had been left unfinished by their Aryan brethren (1847: 349). Havell took it upon himself to speak on behalf of the Indians who, in his perception, accepted British rule because "they recognize that the present rulers of India . . . are generally animated by that same love of justice and fair play, the same high principles of conduct and respect for humanitarian laws which guided the ancient Aryan statesmen and law givers in their relations with the Indian masses" (1918: vi). Clearly, the Aryan connection could turn out to be a politically shrewd card to play because "in thus honouring our Aryan forerunners in India we shall both honour ourselves and make the most direct and effective appeal to Indian loyalty" (ibid.: ix).

There were a variety of other occasions when the Aryan connection could prove to be useful. Devendraswarup argues that after the British were shaken by the Great Revolt of 1857, they soon found a reason to stress their common Aryan bond with the Brahmans, preponderant in the rebellious Bengal Native Infantry, where they had once minimized it. The same Risley who had once voiced relief that the new science of racial anthropology exempted the need for Europeans to affiliate themselves with the Hindu side of the family, did not hesitate in his 1881 Bengal Survey on the Races, Religions and Languages of India, to allot common Aryan descent liberally to the Indian groups who were predominant in the British army such as the Rajputs, Jats, and Brahmans (Chakrabarti 1997: 127). The Aryan connection was manipulated at will, although such scholars refused to follow the notion to its logical conclusion: that consanguinity entitled contemporary India to a moral parity with Great Britain, and ultimately, to national independence (Maw 1990: 36). Certain Christian evangelists also found advantages in discourses of Aryan kinship, exhorting the Indians to shake off their enslavement to the Indo-European gods and embrace Christ, as the Europeans had done many centuries earlier (e.g. Hastie 1882).

I will do no more than make a cursory reference to the appropriation of Aryanism in Germany, since this has been adequately covered elsewhere (Poliakov 1971; Day 1994). Suffice it to say that statements from Tacitus led some Germans to believe that they were a people indigenous to the area they inhabited. Since they were members of what was known, at the time, as the Aryan language family, and since there was no indication that the Aryans had entered this area from anywhere else, the residents there must have been the pure descendants of the original Aryans. Their physical traits, by extension, since they had not been mixed with elements from any other people, must be those of the original Aryans – blond, fair, and blue eyed. This conclusion was fortified with dubious readings of certain passages in the Vedic texts of fair invading Aryans clashing with snub-nosed indigenous *Dasas*, and German Aryanism proceeded inexorably to its well-known teleology.

I will add this Dasa case to Hock's examples, as a further philological example of the selective interpretation of evidence, because it especially aroused the indignation of a number of Indian scholars. It involves the adjective *anāsa*, a term which describes the much maligned *dasyu* enemies of the *ārya*s in one instance. The term can be legitimately construed as *a-nāsa* 'without nose', or *an-āsa*, 'without mouth', or 'uncouth', as Sāyana, the earliest commentator on the *Ṛgveda* had construed it. But, in the context of nineteenth-century philology, the fact that many European scholars were combing through the Vedic texts in search of evidence of the Aryan invasion certainly influenced the choice of possible interpretations, and the former option became standardized, to the indignation of certain Indian scholars: "[T]o hang such a weight of inference as the invasion and conquest of India by the straight nosed Aryans on the solitary word *anāsa* does certainly seem not a very reasonable procedure" (Iyengar: 6). From Iyengar's perspective, beneath all the excitement exhibited by Western scholars about the battles between the invading Aryas and native Dasyas in the *Ṛgveda* was but the echo of a war of cult with cult and not one of race with race.[1]

Interest in the Indo-European homeland problem seemed to wane during the decades after the war perhaps because many prehistorians avoided this issue in reaction to the political abuses of archaeology under the Nazis and the explicit racism which was the ultimate outcome of the Romantic search for ethnic origins in Germany (Sherratt 1988: 459). The last two decades or so, on the other hand, have seen an explosion of renewed interest. However, even after 200 years of intense speculation, there is still no significant consensus as to either the location of the Indo-European homeland or the nature of its language speakers. Scholars hardly agree on even the most basic details of the IEs – their culture, their origins, or even their very existence – any more in the present, than they did in the past.

Typically, a convincing and detailed proposal offered in one field, that is, archaeology, is completely contradicted by evidence from another, that is, linguistics (and vice versa) and even within disciplines scholars radically disagree with each other. Any attempt to isolate or highlight one aspect of the data as paramount is inevitably countered by contradictory conclusions produced by other factors. One need only consider a few of the current theories in the field to realize how little consensus there is, even on basic issues: the archaeological data has been used by the Gimbutas (1997) school to reconstruct an aggressive, mounted, nomad IE warrior from the harsh, cold, and austere northern environment of the Steppe Kurgan culture in the fourth millennium BCE, and by Renfrew (1987) to reconstruct a gentle, sedentary agriculturist proto-Indo-European in Anatolia in the seventh millennium BCE; the linguistic evidence has been used by Gamkrelidze and Ivanov (1995) to reconstruct a warm and exotic Near Eastern Indo-European homeland with tropical elephants and monkeys, and by Nichols (1997) to reconstruct a Bactrian homeland.

Given the religious, colonial, and imperial corollaries that were brought to bear on the data associated with the Indo-European speakers and their Eastern offshoots the Indo-Aryans, and given the resulting complete lack of consensus regarding their point of origin despite over two hundred years of intense research, it is hardly surprising that in the sensitive postcolonial climate of recent years, many Indian scholars are going to wonder why on earth they should feel obliged to retain theories pertaining to the origins of their Vedic forefathers that emerged from such contexts during the nineteenth century:

> Instead of letting us know definitely and precisely where the so-called original home of the Aryans lay, they drag us into a maze of conjectures clouded by the haze of presumptions. The whole subject of the Aryan problem is a farrago of linguistic speculations or archaeological

> imaginations complicated by racial prejudices and chauvinistic xenophobia. It is high time we extricate ourselves from this chaos of bias and belief.
> (B. Prakash: xliv)

To conclude, then, I suggest that the discussion on Indo-Aryan origins could be conducted in a more sensitive fashion if European and American scholars keep in mind the dubious legacy of scholarship in the history of the Indo-European quest in the West. In addition, the vast range of speculations regarding the location of the elusive homeland has not helped inspire confidence in those observing this confusion from outside of Western academic circles. From the other side, while pointing out colonial biases is fair game, tremendous advances were nonetheless made in the collection of data and the methods of interpreting them in the nineteenth century, and all nineteenth-century Western scholars cannot be tarred and feathered with the same brush. Suspicion of colonial motives does not justify a priori jettisoning the theories emanating from this period, nor make the data disappear. Moreover, to indiscriminately assume in a blanket fashion that present day Indologists of the twenty-first century subscribe to the ideological orientations of the nineteenth century, and to imply that there have been little or no advances in data accumulation and interpretation over the last century and more exhibits a methodological predisposition that would be viewed incredulously in any other academic field of study. There were, and still are, very good reasons to believe in Aryan migrations and there remains solid empirical data that need to be confronted and addressed if one chooses to tackle a problem like that of the Indo-Aryans. It is to this that we turn to next.

14.2 The data

In addition to suspicion of European biases and motives in the initial construction of Indo-European history, and to the complete lack of consensus among scholars as to the location of the homeland of the original Indo-European speakers, much of the evidence associated with the Indo-Aryans, whether philological, linguistic, or archaeological, can prove to be extremely malleable if one is prepared to consider it from different perspectives. It can thus be construed in sometimes diametrically opposed ways by scholars approaching the issue with differing presuppositions and expectations.

14.2.1 The substratum evidence

The "substratum" evidence in Vedic texts is one example of data relevant to the early history of the Indo-Aryans being continually presented through one interpretatory model to the almost complete exclusion of others. I use the term substratum in the sense of an indigenous language being subsumed and displaced by an alien incoming language. In this process, the indigenous language affects the dominant language by depositing into it some of its own linguistic features, such as vocabulary or morphology. These linguistic features form a substratum in the dominant language which can be discerned by diligent linguists. American English displaced the native languages of North America, for example, but borrowed many words from them including place names. A principal reason why South Asia had been excluded relatively early as a potential Indo-European homeland was that it showed evidence of a pre-Indo-European linguistic substratum – considered to have been of Dravidian, Munda, or other unknown languages (South Europe had also been eliminated for the same reasons – north Spain and southwestern France had a pre-Indo-European substratum in the form of Basque, and Italy had Etruscan). I do not find this explanation necessarily wrong. Nor, with a certain amount of finetuning here and there, do I find it particularly inadequate. But I do believe that it is not the only way of accounting for the evidence, and therefore it cannot be heralded in its own right as *proof* that the Indo-Aryans must have invaded India.

There are several points that have not been adequately taken into consideration in the discussion of this evidence. First of all and most importantly, in the verifiable modern and historical period, the Dravidian languages in the South and the Indo-Aryan ones in the North, are continuing to greatly influence each other linguistically (and undergoing a process of linguistic convergence by the developing and sharing of areal features, such that some even go so far as to suggest that a new language family might eventually develop which will be neither strictly Dravidian nor Indo-European [Andronov 1964; Dasgupta 1982]), but this has nothing to do with substratum; adstrata or various expressions of bilingualism are the principal factors involved. I use the term *ad*stratum to refer to a situation is which languages influence each other due to being geographically adjacent to each other, as opposed to one being superimposed on another (such as the present-day languages of Europe which are adjacent to each other, but borrow lexical terms from each other as a result of cultural exchanges or other types of interaction). Since adstratum accounts for the ongoing influences between Dravidian, Munda, and the Indo-Aryan languages in the present day, how do we exclude the possibility that a similar situation might not also account for the shared influences between these languages in the less-verifiable pre- and proto-historic period?

Since the Dravidians speakers are also generally considered immigrants into the subcontinent, the suggestion, first made by Bloch (1924, 1928–30) that perhaps these relevant linguistic features could have been borrowed by Indo-Aryans from invading Dravidians, as opposed to by Dravidians from invading Indo-Aryans, is another possibility that has yet to receive serious scholarly attention. Of substantial importance is Witzel's conviction that there was no Dravidian influence in the early Ṛgveda. He divides the Ṛgveda corpus into three distinct chronological layers on linguistic grounds, and finds that Dravidian loans only surface in layer II and III, and not in the earliest level at all. On the basis of certain linguistic evidences, such as Munda type prefixes, he prefers to consider the pre-Aryan language an early form of Munda. Dravidian, in Witzel's scenario, was a later intruder which, interestingly, he is prepared to consider as having arrived at about the same time as the pre-Indo-Aryan languages (1998, 2000), consequently, the subsequent influences of Dravidian on later Indo-Aryan were the result of an adstratum relationship between these two languages. (There is no consensus as to the origin of Dravidian, and any attempt to establish a date for proto-Dravidian is ultimately in the nature of guesswork.)

If the Dravidian influences in the Vedic texts could have been caused by adstratum (or superstratum), then how do we exclude the possibility that all the various innovations visible in Indo-Aryan, whether Dravidian, Munda, Masica's (1979) unknown "language x," or anything else, could not have been the result of these other languages intruding on an Indo-Aryan one (as opposed to vice versa) and acting as adstratum or superstratum rather then substratum? I use the term superstratum to refer to a situation where an alien intruding language, rather than displacing an indigenous language, becomes subsumed by it, but not before affecting the dominant language in some fashion (English, for example, intruded into India, but did not displace the languages on the subcontinent, although it did pass many loan words into them). If Dravidian could have influenced Indo-Aryan through adstratum or superstratum interactions, and *not* through a substratum relationship, then why could Munda (or other languages) not likewise have done so? In short, convergence, or any type of borrowing or similarities between languages, whether lexical or structural, does not *necessitate* a situation of a linguistic substratum.[2]

The second point relevant to any discussion on substratum, is that there still remains a difference of opinion among linguists as to whether a number of the non-Indo-European features visible in the Vedas might not be spontaneous developments, rather than borrowings from a substratum. H. H. Hock (1975, 1984, 1996), for one, has consistently challenged the notion that the linguistic convergences on these and other linguistic features in the Indian languages could only have been due to a Dravidian substratum. For the most part, he argues that many of the innovative features Indo-Aryan shares with Dravidian actually have parallels in other Indo-European languages and are therefore more likely to have been internal developments and not borrowings from any other language at all. There are three linguistic features innovative to the *Ṛgveda* that have been the subject of the most discussion; there is, phonologically, the introduction of retroflexes which alternate with dentals in Indo-Aryan; morphologically, the gerunds (absolutives, or verbal participles that is, *hatvā* instead of *jaghanvān*); and syntactically the use of *iti*, a postposed quotative marker. Hock cites examples of retroflexion occurring in other Indo-European languages, and proposes that this trait could have been an indigenous development (the possibility of the cerebrals in Sanskrit being a spontaneous phenomenon has been current since Bühler in 1864 and no agreement has yet been reached after a discussion extending over more than a century). Likewise, Hock lists occurrences of gerunds and participles (absolutives) in other Indo-European languages as well as usages of the quotative marker *iti* (see also, e.g. Tikkanen, 1987, who finds that adstratum influences could just as easily account for the commonalty of gerunds between Indo-Aryan and Dravidian as substratum). Moreover, there seems to be an unquestioned assumption that it was invariably Indo-Aryan that borrowed these features from Munda, Dravidian, or whatever, despite the fact that the possibility of Indo-Aryan spontaneously evolving some of the syntactical innovations and then influencing Dravidian or Munda, as opposed to being influenced by them, has yet to be excluded. As for Brahui, it could have been separated from the other languages by the Indo-Aryan invasion or it could represent a migration [from the South] – the two inferences are equally probable.

The character of the non-Indo-Aryan loan words in the Vedic texts is another area that has received considerable attention as evidence of a pre-Indo-Aryan population. The borrowing and coining of words for flora and fauna peculiar to any area such as India, as opposed to possessing "primitive" terms for them (i.e. terms possessing an IE root) generally indicates to linguists that the thing in question is new and unfamiliar to the speakers of a language. In the Indic case at least, this is seen as evidence that the Indo-Aryans were immigrants into an area that possessed unfamiliar fauna and so consequently borrowed the local terms for these items from the preexisting indigenous natives (or coined new terms for them). These latter were eventually subsumed by the immigrants, but their existence can be inferred from such lexical items in the Vedic texts in the form of a substratum. For the present discussion, the problems and controversies involved in the identification of loanwords will be avoided (although there is not a single case in which a *communis opinio* has been found confirming the foreign origin of a Ṛgvedic word).

Kuiper finds that several words from his list were agrarian in nature, and hence testified to an (originally) non-Indo-Aryan agrarian population that was more or less integrated into a society of a predominantly nomadic pastoralists (1991). Masica found 80 percent of the agricultural terms in Hindi to be non-Aryan – 55 percent of which were of unknown origin (what is especially important to note, here, is that out of the total number of items in the survey, only 4.5 percent have Austro-Asiatic, and only 7.6 percent Dravidian etymologies, and even in these categories many of the etymologies are uncertain) (pp. 129–39). The poor showing of all these South Asian languages cause him to postulate the existence of another unknown language (or languages) existing as linguistic substrata in Indo-Aryan times. He labels this tongue "language x."

However, even in this regard, the existence of a pre-Aryan linguistic substratum, while providing a perfectly acceptable explanatory model, does not have to be the only means of accounting for the many botanical terms in Sanskrit that do not have Indo-European etymologies. Foreign botanical items have been continually imported into the subcontinent since time immemorial (millet, sorghum, etc.), and it is more than probable that some of them have maintained their original foreign names. In many cases, these non-Indo-Aryan designations could be traceable to other language families – the linguistic history of such words could tell us much about the origin of their referents. In this category of words, then, it is the plant, not the Aryans, who would be the intruders to the subcontinent. In addition, the same basic possibilities outlined earlier for Dravidian and Munda linguistic relationships need to be considered: to what extent can these unknown items ascribed to "language x" be the result of loans, or adstratum relationship between Indo-Aryan tribes and other unknown ones, rather than the result of substratum?

Indo-Aryan speakers in India are still importing and cultivating new crops and retaining their foreign names to this very day. They have been doing so throughout history. One need only go to one's local supermarket to experience this principle: exotic fruit from other countries are imported into our societies (and sometimes even transplanted and grown locally) while nonetheless retaining their original foreign names which soon become part of our own vocabularies. Therefore, although the foreign names for flora may very well be indicative of a pre-Indo-Aryan substratum, this need not be the only explanation; these terms could simply be loans denoting items imported into a preexisting Indo-Aryan speaking area by trade over the millennia. Only the etymologies of terms for plants indigenous to the Northwest of the subcontinent have the potential to be conclusive. If the Indo-Aryans were native to the Northwest, one would expect Indo-Aryan terms for plants native to the Northwest. If such plants could be demonstrated as having non-Indo-Aryan etymologies, then the case for substratum becomes more compelling.

There is ample evidence of foreign personages and tribes in the Vedic period. Kuiper lists some 26 names of Vedic individuals who have non-Indo-Aryan names with which Mayrhofer concurs (Kuiper 1991: 6–7). Witzel (2000) points out that twenty-two out of fifty Ṛgvedic tribal names are not Indo-Aryan, with a majority of them occurring in later books. He sees these as direct takeovers of local names of tribes or individuals inhabiting the subcontinent before the arrival of the Indo-Aryans. While this may well be an economical explanation, there nonetheless remains the possibility that such tribes and individuals may have been itinerant individuals or groups intruding upon a preexisting Indo-Aryan community, as opposed to migrating Indo-Aryan speaking groups intruding upon non-Indo-Aryan ones.

The non-Indo-Aryan nature of the terms and names noted earlier also has to be juxtaposed with the fact that the place and river names in northern India are almost all Indo-Aryan. Place and river names are, to my mind, the singlemost important element in considering the existence of a substratum. Unlike people, tribes, material items, flora and fauna, they cannot relocate or be introduced by trade, etc. (although their names can be transferred by immigrants). Place names tend to be among the most conservative elements in a language. Moreover, it is a widely attested fact that intruders into a geographical region often adopt many of the names of rivers and places that are current among the peoples that preexisted them, even if they change the names of others (i.e. the Mississippi river compared to the Hudson, Missouri state compared to New England).

With this in mind, it is significant that there are very few non-Indo-Aryan names (and almost none whose etymologies are completely uncontested) for rivers and places in the North of the Indian subcontinent, which is very unusual for migrants intruding into an alien language-speaking area. All the place names in the *Ṛgveda*, which are few in number, are Indo-Aryan, or at least sanskritized (Witzel 1998). Of course, it could be legitimately argued that this is due to the Aryans sanskritizing the names of places and rivers in the Northwest as seems to have been the case in Nepal (Witzel 1993), but the lack of non-Indo-Aryan terms for toponomy and hydronomy in this area nonetheless does deprive us of essential data that have been fundamental in establishing the existence of substrata in other languages, and is remarkable when compared with the durability of place designations elsewhere. The same applies to rivers. River and place names cannot be loanwords, or be the result of adstratum unlike the rest of the material outlined earlier. Only if it can be convincingly demonstrated that the majority (and not just two or three exceptions which could have been named by itinerant tribes) of Indo-Aryan hydronomic and topographic terms could not have evolved from PIE roots, does the case for substratum become much more compelling.

There is also another very significant reason why Migrationists need to eliminate this possibility of a post-Indo-Aryan arrival of Dravidian and Munda. As Witzel has stressed, from the perspective of those who have ventured to argue for a hypothetical South Asian homeland, the Iranians could not have left the subcontinent much before the composition of the *Ṛgveda* due to the proximity of the languages. Why, then, did even Iranian (what to speak of earlier stages of Indo-European) not share the innovations Indo-Aryan shared with Dravidian and/or Munda and/or other unknown languages, such as the retroflexes, etc.? Why do most of these South Asian areal features seem to stop at the Khyber Pass, so to speak (although Hock 1993, does notes that some of the innovations, especially retroflection, are shared by eastern Iranian and so did ripple out from South Asia). An indigenist position would presumably argue that the Dravidians (and any other language group influencing Indo-Aryan such as Munda) intruded into an Indo-Aryan speaking area after the Iranians had left.

Let us pursue this possibility, not for the purpose of promoting it as factual, but with a view of finetuning our thoughts on this issue. It is important to reiterate, here, that if Witzel is correct in determining that Dravidian did not, in fact, affect the oldest layers of the Ṛgveda, then he has provided evidence that the Dravidian speakers interacted with the Indo-Aryan speakers *after* the earliest Vedic period, as adstratum, and therefore even further after the split with the Iranians (and other Indo-Europeans), irrespective of *where* that split took place. If this is the case with the Dravidian speakers, it is not unreasonable to consider the possibility that the Munda speakers could have been a slightly earlier interaction that was pre-early Ṛgveda, but post-Indo-Iranian, but, again, one that affected Indo-Aryan as adstratum. The first issue to be dealt with in this case by any Out-of-India position, of course, is chronological, and Witzel has rightly pointed out the relevance of the philo-archaeological evidence of the horse and chariot, here. But, aside from these important points, it is not clear to me that there is anything in the non-Indo-European *linguistic* evidence preserved in the Ṛgveda that has so far been introduced into the discussion that can militate against a Dravidian and Munda, etc., ad- or superstratum (irrespective of whether the Indo-Aryans were migrants or indigenes).

14.2.2 Linguistic paleontology

Linguistic paleontology is another aspect of the linguistic evidence that has received a tremendous amount of attention in the history of the homeland quest.

But it seems fair to note that very few linguists today put much stock in this method. While the premise of the method is actually quite brilliant – linguistic paleontology involves hypothesizing about the social, religious, political, economic, ecological, cultural, and geographical environment of pre- and proto-historic cultures from linguistic fossils, or cognate terms, preserved in the various members of a language family – there are simply far too many problems that have been identified with the present state of the method to rely on it for determining the geology, environment, habitat, or nature of the homeland. From well before the time of Keith (1933), who cautioned that linguistically we may assert that the Indo-Europeans knew butter but were unacquainted with milk, knew of snow but were ignorant of rain, and had feet, but preserved no terms for hands, the method has been subject to a litany of complaints by linguists (Fraser 1926; Dhar 1930; Pulgram 1958; Colemann 1988; McNairn in Anthony 1995; Krell 1998). Most recently, and of relevance to the present discussion, Krell (1998), who feels the old, pliable crutch of linguistic paleontology should certainly be abandoned (p. 280), points out that the reconstructed lexicon may well represent a linguistic continuum of several millennia into which different lexical items were introduced at different stages in different places. Most importantly, she reiterates the common objection that it is virtually impossible to identify the exact or even approximate referent of a reconstructed lexical item since historical linguistics has shown numerous examples of how dramatically the meaning of a given word can shift in the course of a few centuries, let alone several millennia (as a side note, her analysis of the evidence of linguistic paleontology produces a proto-economic culture that was agricultural with knowledge of navigation, rather than the often assumed pastoral one of the Kurgan Steppe).

The main data from this method utilized in favor of an Indo-Aryan migration is the fact that exotica unique to the Indian subcontinent does not have cognates in other Indo-European languages, and thus is not constructable to proto-Indo-European (PIE). Also, conversely, items that are reconstructable to PIE do not have Indo-Aryan cognates. With regard to the former argument, Friedrich (1970), for example, in his taxonomy of Indo-European trees, proposes that linguistic paleontology reveals eighteen different categories of trees which were known to the ancient Indo-Europeans, all of which were known to the Slavs. He suggested that this might mean that the Slavic speakers resided in an ecological area approximately corresponding to that of the PIEs. In sharp contradistinction, the paucity of these eighteen stocks attested in Tocharian, Anatolian, and Indic suggested to him movement into a radically different environment (p. 169).[3]

But as has been pointed out since the time of Max Müller (1887), who favored a Bactrian homeland, if the Indo-European tribes had, hypothetically, journeyed forth from an Eastern homeland, they would obviously have encountered strange trees, animals, and fauna that did not exist in the East and for which they would have coined new terms or borrowed names from the indigenous people resident in those areas. Such new lexical terms would obviously not surface in Indo-Aryan,

Tocharian, and Anatolian, since the objects they denoted did not exist in those places. The result would be a large number of common terms in the western IE languages (since they are numerically greater), and a smaller number in Indo-Iranian, but it may be erroneous to reconstruct a proto-form from such terms simply because there are a large number of cognates, or make conclusions from this as to the location or nature of the homeland. It has long been established since the nineteenth century that cognates of a term must be evidenced in both the eastern and western branches of Indo-European in order to be even considered as a possible proto-form – precisely to eliminate the possibility of assigning items to PIE that are only evidenced on one side of the language family as a result of belonging to a later post-dispersal period – but it is not always clear that this methodological precaution is followed by those promoting the temperate climate of east Europe or the steppes. Also, it seems relevant to note, here, that Buck finds that for most of the Indo-European trees that have been reconstructed, the root connections are mostly obscure and the same applies to the inherited names of animals. Friedrich found only three roots for his reconstructed trees that could be cogently connected with an IE verbal root; the great majority of PIE tree names are unanalyzable nominal roots, and for their reconstruction the most relevant branches of linguistics are phonology and semantics (p. 155). Anyone of a mind to postulate a South Asian homeland would anticipate precisely the findings of Friedrich and others – terms with numerous cognates in the languages west of India beginning in Iran (but with obscure root connections due, perhaps, to being borrowings from local substratum), that do not exist in Vedic (e.g. Dhar 1930). Along the same lines, linguists favoring an Anatolian homeland, account for the parallel lack of Hittite cognates in the same way (Gamkrelidze and Ivanov 1995: 573; Dolgopolsky 1989: 18).

The same objections have been raised with regard to the exotic items unique to India but unattested elsewhere. The argument basically holds that since the terms for exotica typical of India have no cognates elsewhere, then these terms could not have been in PIE, and therefore PIE could not have been spoken in the areas, such as India, where such exotica are to be found. The argument goes back at least to Lassen in 1851, but was immediately dismissed by his colleagues: "the want of animals specifically Asiatic . . . can be explained simply by the fact of these animals not existing in Europe, which occasioned their names to be forgotten" (Weber: 10). Max Müller also rejected this line of argument on the grounds that if the elephant and the camel had really been known by the united Aryans, when living in Asia, it would have been natural that, when transplanted to the northern regions, their children who had never seen a camel or elephant would have lost the name for them (1887: 101). Some Indian scholars (e.g. Dhar: 30) found it revealing that some linguists propose that Western tree, etc, names have been utterly forgotten in South Asia, but hold the reverse possibility, of Eastern exotica being forgotten in western climes, to be special pleading.

Here, too, modern day linguists utilize arguments similar to Dhar's to support an Anatolian homeland.

> The importance of [terms in the proto-language designating plants, animals and other geographically bound concepts] should not be overestimated. If a given proto-language was spoken in an area outside that of its daughter languages, specific words designating features of the ancient habitat are not usually preserved in the attested languages. Therefore, if a language ancestral to a group of European languages originated in Africa, we would not be able to find in the extant lexical stock ancient words for 'giraffe' and 'elephant' which could suggest its African origin.
>
> (Dolgopolsky 1987: 8)

In actual fact, Gamkrelidze and Ivanov have even assigned PIE status to animals unique to India such as the monkey[4] and elephant in support of their Anatolian homeland (and Dolgopolsky 1987, considers the term **singh*, lion, as one of the few PIE animal terms that appear to be fairly reliable on the basis of Indic *si»ha* and Armenian *inj* 'panther'). Since the former's reconstructions are not without controversy, we will not let them detain us here, but they do show that there are always etymological surprises in store when scholars approach the data with different presuppositions and inclinations, and they do further problematize the value of linguistic paleontology in the homeland quest – there are a number of perfectly qualified linguists who find that linguistic paleontology supports not the cold temperate landscape of the steppes, but a warmer and more exotic southern one.

14.2.3 Other linguistic data

To my mind, the main pressing item from Gamkrelidze and Ivanov's reconstructions likely to be raised as an objection against an Indian homeland is the much later appearance of the horse in the South Asian archaeological record as opposed to its much earlier use in the steppes, where it was domesticated 6,000 years ago (Anthony *et al.* 1991: 94). I will return to this later. As far as the usefulness of linguistic paleontology is concerned, the point of the earlier comments is not in any way to suggest that the evidence supports an Indian homeland, a proposal which I feel has provided scanty positive data with which to recommend itself, the point is to suggest that this is not the type of data that is likely to convince those already suspicious of the ambiguous nature of the linguist evidence that has typically been marshaled so far to insist on the migration of the Indo-Aryans into the subcontinent from an external homeland. We can see how evidence can be radically reconstrued by scholars with differing presuppositions in the case of the loanwords that have been transmitted from the Indo-Iranian languages into the Finno-Ugric language family. This language family was probably spread throughout North Europe and Northwest Asia in the pre-historic period. Finno-Ugric contains numerous loan words that, depending on the linguist, have been identified as either Indo-Iranian, Iranian, or Indo-Aryan, indicating that these languages must have been adjacent to Finno-Ugric in pre-historic times. Since there is absolutely no evidence suggesting the presence of Finno-Ugric speakers near the Indian subcontinent, it is reasonable to conclude that Indo-Iranian speakers must have been present in northwest Central Asia. How, then, could they have been indigenous to India or, even, the far Northwest of the subcontinent and Afghanistan?

But here, too, we have seen how Misra has reconstrued the evidence in a manner completely opposed to that which has been prevalent up to now. Misra argues that all the loans are from Indo-Iranian[5] into Finno-Ugric – there are no loans from Finno-Ugric in Indo-Iranian – and that therefore the Indo-Iranians never went from the area neighboring the Finno-Ugrics down to Iran and India; they went from India to the Caspian Sea area where they encountered Finno-Ugrics. The argument is that had the Indo-Iranians been neighbors with the Finno-Ugrics in the regions to the North of the Caspian Sea for so many centuries, then both languages would have borrowed from each other. If the Indo-Iranians, as per the standard view of things, had then journeyed on toward their historic destinations in the East, they should have brought some Finno-Ugric loans with them in their lexicons, at least a few of which should be expected to have surfaced in the earliest textual sources of India and Iran. Of course, as with everything else, counter arguments can be brought forth such as the power dynamics of sociolinguistics whereby a lower status group may borrow terms from a higher one without the latter, in turn, borrowing from them. But in and of itself, the argument is no more unreasonable than the (perfectly acceptable) Migrationist explanation, and it shows how easily much of the linguistic evidence can simply be flipped around by those inclined to do so.

Other linguistic traces are equally as amenable to renegotiation. The names of rivers common to both Iran and India, such as the Iranian Haravaiti and Harāyu, which correspond to the Indian Sarasvatī and Sarayu could either have been transferred from Iranian rivers to Indian ones, or vice versa, as Lal, Talageri, and Elst have argued herein. Scholars have conventionally interpreted these transferals as evidence of the movement of the Indo-Aryans toward India from the Caspian Sea area via Iran. This remains a straightforward and reasonable way of accounting for this evidence, but as has been noted (and as was pointed out as far back as Müller), it would be just as plausible to assume that Sarasvatī was a Sanskrit term indigenous to India and was later imported by the speakers of Avestan into Iran (Erdosy: 42). The same applies to other Indo-Aryan traces in river terms spread across Russia and adjacent areas. It also applies to the Mitanni Indo-Aryans: there is nothing in the Near Eastern documents themselves that favors any direction of movement, and archaeologists have pointed out that there is not a single cultural element of Central Asian, Eastern European, or Caucasian origin in the archaeological culture of the Mitannian area (Brentjes: 146), which is the area from where they are typically considered to have originated.

As for the arguments concerning the homogeneity of Indo-Aryan in the subcontinent, Elst, following Dhar (1930), has provided one alternative way of accounting for this, but one has only to consider Nichols' model of language spread to find another example of how theoretical models can be reversed when viewed by different perspectives. The argument holds that if PIE had developed dialectical isoglosses in India in the manner outlined earlier, why would all of the different dialects have emigrated to eventually become distinct languages, leaving only one solitary language behind? Why did some of the dialectical variants germinating in any hypothetical PIE in South Asian not remain to develop into other non-Indo-Aryan, IE languages on the subcontinent itself? After all, Sanskrit developed into a variety of mutually incomprehensible, distinct languages in the historic period, such as Braj, Bengali, Punjabi, Gujarati and Marathi, etc. So why would PIE not likewise have developed into other distinct IE languages in addition to Sanskrit in the subcontinent itself in the proto-historic period? Why did they all emigrate? Viewed in this light, this evidence speaks against a South Asian homeland, since the homeland of the Indo-Europeans should presumably be found wherever the greater variety of language forms are evidenced. The Indo-Iranian languages being homogeneous are more peripheral to the area of greatest variety and must have therefore been peripheral to the homeland. In other words, it is more probable that one or two groups moved out from a geographical matrix which had become linguistically heterogeneous, than that many linguistically distinct groups moved out from a linguistically homogeneous area (see Hock 1999b, for further dialectical problems incurred by any Indian homeland hypothesis, and Elst's comments in this volume). Again, this is a rational, satisfying explanation.

But, Johanna Nichols (1997, 1998) presents an alternative model for the epicenter of the Indo-European linguistic spread which addresses this eastern homogeneity in a strikingly different manner. Nichols' Indo-European homeland thesis, which is the most recent homeland theory at the time of writing, places the origin of the Indo-Europeans well to the east of the Caspian Sea, in the area of ancient Bactria-Sogdiana. Since this is adjacent and partly overlapping the area where the Out-of-India/Indigenist school would place the homeland, her theory merits some attention. Nichols' theory is partly predicated on the geographical relationship between loan words emanating from Mesopotamia into Indo-European via other language families (see Nichols 1997 for details), and partly on her assertion that the principle that the area of greatest heterogeneity of a language family is indicative of its locus of origin is demonstrably false for the languages of Central Asia. She cites Iranian, which spread over enormous stretches of Asia in ancient times, and Turkic, which likewise spread over major portions of Asia, as examples of languages whose greatest diversity occurred in refuge areas on the western periphery of their point of origin.

In Nichols' Bactrian homeland, PIE *expands* out of its locus eventually forming two basic trajectories. The language range initially radiates westward engulfing the whole area around the Aral sea from the northern Steppe to the Iranian plateau. Upon reaching the Caspian, one trajectory expands around the sea to the North and over the steppes of Central Asia to the Black Sea, while the other flows around the Southern perimeter and into Anatolia. Here we have a model of a continuous distribution of PIE without postulating any migrations whatsoever.

By the third or second millennium BCE we have the proto-forms of Italic, Celtic, and perhaps Germanic in the environs of Central Europe and the proto-forms of Greek, Illyrian, Anatolia, and Armenian stretching from northwest Mesopotamia to the southern Balkans (1997: 134). Proto-Indo-Aryan was spreading into the subcontinent proper, while proto-Tocharian remained close to the original homeland in the Northeast.

As this expansion was progressing into Europe, a new later wave of IE language, Iranian, is spreading behind the first language spread. Sweeping across the steppes of Central Asia, the Caucuses and the deserts of north Iran, the Iranian dialects separated the two preceding trajectories – which up till that time had formed a continuum – into two non-contiguous areas (one in Central Europe to the North of the Caspian Sea, the other in Anatolia to its south). Along the same lines, Iranian separates Tocharian from the other languages. In time, the two original trajectories coincided in the Balkans. The southern trajectory had meanwhile formed a continuous chain of Dacian, Thracian, Illyrian, Greek, and Phrygian spreading from west Anatolia to the Danube plain (ibid.: 136). From the northern trajectory, Italic spread to Italy from Central Europe, and Celtic to its historic destination, followed, in time, by Germanic which was followed, in turn, by Balto-Slavic. All of these languages spread by expansion – there are no migrations throughout this whole immense chronological and geographical sequence.

The corollary of Nichols model is that the assumed variegatedness of the western languages is only due to the fact that the later Iranian language had spread and severed the contiguity of the northern and southern IE trajectories (which had previously formed an unbroken continuity around the east coast of the Caspian) thereby making them appear noncontinuous while leaving behind Indo-Iranian and a stranded Tocharian to the east. The variegatedness of western languages is actually due to their situation on the western periphery of the original locus, or homeland. This model might also address the issue of why PIE did not evolve into more dialects in the putative homeland: the later westward spread of Iranian obliterated all of the eastern parts of the proto-continuum except for Indo-Aryan to its east, and the isolated Tocharian to the Northeast.

14.2.4 Archaeology: the Indus Valley civilization

While some of the earlier examples have hopefully given some sense as to how some of the linguistic evidence can either be brought into question, or reconfigured when viewed by those disposed to challenge established paradigms, most of the arguments raised by the detractors of the Indo-Aryan Migration theory deal with the archaeological evidence. In fact, since there is so little opportunity available for the study of historical linguistics in India, and as a result of the failure of finding any tangible archaeological evidence of the Indo-Aryans whatsoever (see Lal and Shaffer in this volume), it is a number of archaeologists from the subcontinent who have been the most vociferous in their opposition to the theory. The main debate focuses on the cultural and linguistic identity of the

Indus Valley civilization (IVC) for obvious reasons, with a growing number of Indian archaeologists questioning the divide between the vast urban civilization, and the Vedic Aryans.

Rao and Thapar's identifications (Lal 1984) of fire pits in the Indus site of Kalibangan as "sacrificial altars" created a stir and a string of similar identifications elsewhere (e.g. Rao 1993). However, their usefulness proved limited since, as Dhavalikar (1995) pointed out, these could have simply been ovens used for cooking or baking. The correlation of the Sarasvatī with the Hakra/Ghaggar seemed the most promising piece of evidence that might have vindicated the Indigenist School. The argument is that the *Ṛgvedic* hymns describe a mighty river, the Sarasvatī, flowing down to the ocean, situated exactly where the Hakra/Ghaggar river bed has been found. Even though all the other Vedic rivers correspond to present-day rivers, the Sarasvatī corresponding to the description of the texts is nowhere to be found, and she has always been considered mythological until the discovery of a river bed, called the Hakra on the Pakistan side of the border, and the Ghaggar on the Indian side. Determining the date when this dry river bed was once a mighty river flowing down to the ocean is seen as powerful archaeological evidence that must be taken into consideration when dating the composition of the *Ṛgveda*, and that also has a direct bearing on the relationship between the Indo-Aryan composers of the hymns and the IVC.

However, apart from the problems involved in dating the bed, and the variety of opinions offered in this regard, one is still left with the problem of determining whether the Sarasvatī known to the composers of the hymns was the full-flowing river of the fourth millennium BCE, the more diminished version of the third millennium, or a dwindling body of water sometime in the first half of the second millennium BCE. Advocates of the Aryan Migration theory can still claim that the Indo-Aryans could have arrived during or toward the end of the Indus civilization and then settled down on the banks of the river. For these and other reasons, the Sarasvatī evidence, although exciting, failed to convince its detractors. Positive evidence, then, associating the Indo-Aryans with the ruins of the IVC, has yet to be produced.

14.2.5 The horse evidence

If the Indo-Aryan speakers cannot be identified positively, can they at least be excluded as a presence in the IVC by the use of negative evidence? Since the time of Sir John Marshall, the absence of the horse has been the mainstay of the belief that the speakers of the Vedic language must have succeeded the Harappan civilization. The horse is clearly an animal highly valued in the Vedic world. It is perfectly reasonable to expect that if the Aryans were native to the Indus Valley their presence would be evidenced by remains of the horse there. Such evidence, or lack thereof, has become crucial to – and almost symbolic of – the whole Aryan controversy. The horse, as a result, is presently "the most sought after animal in Indian archaeology" (A. K. Sharma: 75).

The earliest undisputed evidence of horses in the Indian subcontinent is generally dated to around the early second millennium BCE. In the opinion of many scholars, this paucity of horse bones in India indicates that the Indo-Aryans entered this region well after dispersing from their original homeland. The domesticated horse has been the primary animal for which scholars have tried to account in the homeland quest, since it is culturally central to the various IE traditions, and was possibly known to the undivided Indo-Europeans. This lacuna in the Indian archaeological record tends to haunt any attempt to argue for an Indian *urheimat*, and even any efforts to correlate the IVC with the Vedic culture, which is a horse-using one. Since this animal has become almost synonymous with the Vedic Aryans and, by extension, the whole Indo-Aryan migration debate, the horse evidence is of great relevance to this discussion.

Some caveats seem to be in order, here: the first point that needs to be established is that, in terms of its proto-Indo-European pedigree, there seems to be a widespread opinion among linguists, going back at least to Fraser (1926), that considering **ekwos* to have been a domesticated horse involves accepting some major assumptions which can easily be called into question. We don't know if the term referred to *equus caballus* Linn or some other type of equid in the proto-period, we don't know if it referred to a domesticated horse or a wild horse, and, allowing that it did refer to a domesticated *equus caballus* Linn, we cannot rule out the possibility that it was a late loanword that circulated around the IE-speaking area (D'iakonov 1985; Coleman 1988; Diebold 1987; Zimmer 1990; Dolgopolsky 1993; Lehmann 1993). Clearly, if the word for horse could have circulated *after* the dispersal of the IEs, and then been restructured according to individual dialects, then stating that the IEs knew the horse *before* their dispersal and must therefore have inhabited an area wherein the horse is native (and eliminating other areas where the evidence for the horse is a later phenomenon) is barking up the wrong tree.

Furthermore even if **ekwos* does refer to a PIE domesticated *caballus* Linn, horse domestication may well have occurred in the steppes, since this is the natural habitat of the animal, but it is an unwarranted assumption to then conclude that the IE homeland must have also been in the same area. The horse could have been very well known to the proto-Indo-Europeans in their original homeland without the horse necessarily being a native of that homeland, or they themselves its domesticators. Of course, in the Indian context, irrespective of the referent of PIE **ekwos*, there is little dispute that the *Ṛgveda* does refer abundantly to *equus caballus* Linn, and one cannot fault scholars using the first appearance of these specific horse bones in the archaeological record as an approximate *terminus post quem* for this text. However, although the horse has always been highly valued in India – from the Vedic, through the Epic, and up to the Sultanate period, it has always been an elite item – it has always been an import from the Northwest and never indigenous (although foreign breeds have been imported and bred on the subcontinent with varying degrees of success, especially up in the Northwest – later Vedic texts speak about the fine horses of Kandahar and other places). One must accordingly be wary of making the Indo-Aryans themselves overly synonymous with the horse, since the horse could have been imported in the proto-historic period, just as it has been throughout the historic period, but this in itself need not indicate a priori that the Indo-Aryans were imports as well, especially if the domestic horse was a post-Indo-European development that circulated throughout the various dialects as Lehmann (1993) has argued, or an item known only in some areas where the proto-Indo-European dialects were spoken as Colemann (1988) has suggested.

The exact species of the equid is the crucial issue here. A number of identifications of horse bones in the Indus Valley civilization have been made over the years, some of which have been accepted by scholars such as Lal, earlier, and at least one of which, the findings at Surkotada (*c*.2100–1700 BCE) was accepted by a horse specialist, Bökönyi (see Sharma 1974). But other experts, such as Meadows (1997), remain unconvinced, since the remains could have appertained to either *Equus caballus* Linn, or to some other member of the horse family. As an aside, to pronounce unambiguously that there is *no* evidence of the horse in the IVC, on one side, or to insist that there is conclusive evidence, on the other, are both somewhat sleights of hands. A more precise statement is that there is some evidence of the horse, but it has been contested. There is no *uncontested* evidence because there are only minor differentiating features between the various species of *Equus*. *Equus hemionus khur*, for example, is indigenous to the Northwest of the subcontinent, but it is *Equus caballus* that is the sought-after Aryan steed.[6] The differences between the species are either difficult for experts to identify or, unless the specific distinguishing parts of the skeleton are found (certain teeth and the phalanges – toe bones – are particularly important for differentiating equid subtypes), impossible to determine with certainty.

Obviously, the horse would never have been an issue had it not been linked with the Aryans – were it not for the politicization of the issue, the reports of horse evidence in the Indus Valley, albeit sparse, would hardly have raised any eyebrows. In any event, scholars have every right to use the first appearance of horse bones in the archaeological record as an approximate dating marker for this text. Moreover, even allowing the Surkotada finds, unless horse bones are undeniably found in the early, pre- and mature Harappan strata, the Indo-Aryan speakers may be allowed a degree of synthesis with the later Harappan civilization, but their status as intruders, albeit somewhat earlier than previously held, will still not be considered convincingly undermined to the satisfaction of all.

But, irrespective of the differences between Meadows and Bökönyi, one caveat should be kept in mind here – the horse lacuna in the archaeological record could possibly be due to the elite and rare nature of this beast which may have been the preserve of martial and sacrificial contexts and thus unlikely to turn up in normal archaeological contexts – if it was not eaten on a significant scale for food, or buried with the deceased, it is unlikely to show up in large quantities in the archaeological record. The chariot is a good example of the limitations of relying on the archaeological record for the purposes of dating a cultural group. The earliest archaeological evidence of the chariot is sometime between the fourth and first century BCE (Gaur 1983). If we accept the dates assigned by most scholars to the *Ṛgveda*, namely, 1500–1200 BCE, the chariot as known to this text must have unquestionably been in existence on the subcontinent for a millennium or so before becoming evidenced in iconographic form just before the common era. The archaeological *argumentum ex silentio* clearly shows its limitations in this period during which we know the chariot was extant from the literary evidence but it has not been verified archaeologically. Obviously, the further back in time we go, the more the likelihood of finding such iconographic evidence decreases.

The chariot evidence compels us to acknowledge that the paucity or absence of an Indo-Aryan diagnostic item in the archaeological record might not mean the absence of that item and nor, therefore, of the Indo-Aryans, otherwise the chariot evidence would compel us to date the appearance of the Indo-Aryans on the subcontinent to just before the common era. The excavations at Mehrgarh are another example: they threw the date for evidence of agriculture back *two entire millennia*, and subverted the view that agriculture and urbanization were both diffused from West Asia. This clearly underscores the danger of establishing theories predicated on *argumentum ex silentio* in the archaeological record. Having said this, however, it seems fair to add that the burden of proof lies with anyone arguing for the existence of the horse or chariot in the IVC – which an Indigenous case must argue.

14.3 Urbanity and the Vedas

The other argument that usually surfaces in denying the Indo-Aryans a presence in the IVC, again since the time of Marshall, is the fact that the early Vedic texts seem to make no explicit mention of towns. How, then, could the Indo-Aryans have been the progenitors of such a sophisticated civilization (while Lal, in this volume, holds that the Vedic *pur* refers to a fort, Rau 1976, depicts it as a wattle hut)? This seems a fairly reasonable argument, but, here too, there are a few further points that should be considered.

First, archaeology is revealing large settlements in the Punjab even in the post-Harappan period, in the very time and place when few question that the Aryans were very much present

> Sites such as Harappa continued to be inhabited and are still important cities today... Late and post-Harappan settlements are known from surveys in the region of Cholistan... the upper Ganga-Yamuna Doab... and Gujarat. In the Indus Valley itself, post-Harappan settlement patterns are obscure, except for the important site of Pirak... This may be because the sites were along the newly-stabilized river systems and lie beneath modern villages and towns that flourish along the same rivers.
>
> (Kenoyer 1991: 30)

Pirak, a site in the Punjab in first half of the second millennium BCE – right when and where most Migrationists would place the intruding Indo-Aryans – is a town of some size. Data from Bahawalpur, the region in Pakistan most thoroughly surveyed, suggests an *increase* in size in the settlements of the Late Harappan period in comparison to the Harappan period, and a shift to the East (Shaffer 1993: 57). So the hymns may not be sparse in urban references due to ignorance or unfamiliarity with large settlements and urban towns, this lacuna may rather be a peculiarity of the texts.

Second, even if the composers of the Vedic hymns did not primarily live in the cities of the Indus Valley, this fact in and of itself does not mean that the Harappans could not have been Indo-Aryan speakers: a language family can obviously encompass urban dwellers as well as village dwellers as is obvious all over the world today. It is important to stress in this regard that anyone promoting Dravidian or Munda, as the language of the Indus Valley will anyway have to accept an identical situation: urban Dravidian or Munda speakers coexisting with nonurban tribal Dravidian or Munda speakers (some of which have remained tribal to this day). The southern Dravidian culture and eastern Munda culture were radically different from that of the Indus Valley in the third millennium BCE, so if hypothetical urbanized Harappan Dravidians or Mundas could have coexisted on the subcontinent with their nonurbanized linguistic brethren to the South or East, then Indo-Aryan speakers could have done likewise. Therefore, even if the *Ṛgveda* does not elaborately describe the flourishing cities of the Indus, there is no way to discount the possibility that it could still have been the product of an Indo-Aryan pastoral society that coexisted with an Indo-Aryan urban one. As Witzel points out, the possibility of urban centers being known to the Indo-Aryans cannot simply be dismissed, since, although there is no mention of towns in the Vedic texts, this may be due to the cultural tendency of the Brahmins who could preserve their ritual purity better in a village than in a busy town (1989: 245).

Finally, there are two obvious routes to the Indian subcontinent from the Caspian Sea area: a northern route from the northeast of the Caspian Sea through the steppes of Central Asia and down through Afghanistan and into India, to which Parpola is partial, and a southern route from the southeast of the Caspian Sea through the deserts and plains of North Iran and into Afghanistan. Whether one favors the northern route or the southern, one will nonetheless have to accept that the Indo-Aryans passed through the Bactria Margiana Archaeological Complex (BMAC) or, as some have argued (e.g. Sarianidi 1993a,b), were the founders of this civilization. Given this, attention must be drawn to the fact that the BMAC was a sophisticated civilization consisting of fortified towns. Structures that have been identified as temples, were "monumental" (Sarianidi 1993a: 8); the Gonur "temple" occupies an area of 2 hectares (from a total area of 22 hectares) and was surrounded by walls up to 4 meters thick. Indeed, according to later excavators of BMAC sites, the extensive distribution of the BMAC, together with the considerable size of their cities and the monumental nature of single architectural units, combine to suggest that the BMAC was a sociopolitical phenomenon of considerable magnitude that appears to mirror a state structured polity of power (Hiebert and Lamberg-Karlovsky 1992).

Anyone accepting the Indo-Aryan identity of the BMAC (or of any of the sites of the southern route, which will be touched upon later), cannot then use the argument that the Indo-Aryans could not have resided in towns on the grounds of an apparent lack of urban references in the *Ṛgveda*. Even if it is argued that the Indo-Aryans were not the founders of the BMAC, but arrived toward the end of this civilization (they were initially held to have destroyed it until, as with the IVC, it was realized that no traces of destruction have been found), they nonetheless must surely have passed through this whole area on their way to India and would therefore have been aware of, and interacted with, such towns. Accordingly, it becomes very hard to deny the possible residence of the Indo-Aryans in, or coexistence with, urban centers. All this further underscores the point that lack of urban references in the *Ṛgveda* is not an acceptable indicator of the Indo-Aryan's ignorance of urban centers.

Also of relevance to the previous discussion on the Indus Valley is the fact that although the horse was certainly utilized in the BMAC as attested by its representation on grave goods, no horse bones have been discovered there (despite the fact that an unusually high number of animal bones have been found). Absence of horse bones, then, does not equal absence of horses, nor necessarily of Indo-Aryans. A final related point is that the Vedas make no mention of temples, or temple structures. What are we to make of "ceremonial centers" at the sites of Togolok 21 and Gonur 1 that have been identified in the same BMAC where we have fire worship and the ritual usage of hallucinogens in a temple-like setting? (Sarianidi 1977, 1990, 1993b)[7] Any acceptance that these identifications, if correct, are the handiwork of Indo-Aryans, or that the Indo-Aryans passed through this area (which they must have done from a point of origin outside the subcontinent) will entail reconsidering certain stereotypes such as the Indo-Aryans knew no urban centers or temples and that the failure of archaeologists to uncover horse bones equals the real-life absence of horses in a society.

Ultimately, the answer to the linguistic identity of the Indus Valley lies in our hands, but it has yet to yield its secret, despite a plethora of attempts (see Possehl 1996). If the Indus script turns out to represent an Indo-Aryan language during this period there would be massive implications and corollaries for the entire IE homeland problem, especially since shards found in Ravi suggest that the script may go back as far as 3500 BCE (Meadows 1997). In other words, an Indo-Aryan script on the subcontinent at a time frame when the Indo-Europeans were still more or less undivided (most IEists hold that the IEs were still undivided till sometime between 4500 and 3500 BCE) would constitute a formidable argument for any one choosing to locate the IE homeland in India. And all the ink spilt on attempting to date the Veda *c.*1200 or 1500 BCE will merit the skepticism that Indigenous Aryanists have generally directed to such efforts. All in all, two centuries worth of IE speculation will be subverted overnight.

On the other hand, if the script turns out to be any language other than Indo-Aryan, then the Indigenous case no longer merits much further serious scholarly consideration (although there could still have been Indo-Aryan pastoralists interacting with these Indus Valley urban centers from very ancient times, even if the dominant language of the latter turns out to be non-Indo-Aryan). But their case, at least to my mind, will be closed. No doubt, die-hards on both sides will attempt to reconfigure things to salvage their respective points of view, but either attempt to do so at that point become even more interesting subjects for historiographical and sociological analysis in my estimation. Kenoyer, earlier, has pointed out that it is a priori unlikely that the script be Vedic, since the early texts do not mention writing. On the other hand, one might also question why, if the script were Dravidian or Munda, it did not surface at some point in the Dravidian and Munda speaking areas to the East and South. Again, as with everything else, explanations on both sides can be found if one is committed to finding them – on one side, one could either argue that the Vedas may not mention writing because the priestly caste emphasized oral learning, and the script was a creation of the merchant community, while, on the other side, one could argue that the Dravidian or Munda residents of the Indus Valley were literate while their fellow language speakers elsewhere were not, a disjunction that can still be seen between rural and urban communities in many parts of the world today. Whatever language is contained in the script, it would be unwise for decipherers, in my opinion, to eliminate either Sanskrit, Vedic, or Munda as possible candidates.

As for the overland trail of the Indo-Aryans, Lamborg-Karlovsky has given a good sense of some of the problems involved in correlating linguistics and archaeology. At least on a theoretical level (if not in practice), it is by now universally acknowledged that the spread of a material culture need not at all correspond to the spread of a language group, any more than a material innovation or development within a material culture need be reflective of the intrusion of a new language group. There is no more consensus regarding the identification of the Indo-Iranians in the archaeological record, than that of the Indo-Europeans. Both the northern and southern routes have diametrically differing archaeological cultures. Both have been identified with the Indo-Aryans in a variety of ways by a variety of different scholars.

We have included in this volume two quite distinct views on the trans-Asiatic saga of the Indo-Aryans and their predecessors, the Indo-Iranians. Parpola presents us with a quite specific alignment of archaeological cultures with chronological linguistic levels from Indo-European to Indo-Iranian, and Lamberg-Karlovsky has dwelt at length on the problems involved with attempting to identify language groups such as the Indo-Iranians and their descendents with any Central Asian culture such as the Andronovo, the most commonly identified in this regard. Bypassing the major liberties scholars sometimes take in interpreting pottery or other innocuous items of material culture in terms of Vedic or Avestan religious narrative (see Bryant 2001), the most obvious problem in identifying the Indo-Aryans in Central Asia can be stated quite succinctly: no traces of steppe cultures have been detected south of the Hindukush. As Francfort notes, nothing allows us to question the proposal that the Andronovians of Tazabagjab are the Indo-Iranians as much as the fact that they vanish on the fringes of sedentary Central Asia and do not appear as the ephemeral invaders of India at the feet of the Hindukush (1989: 453). The main obstacle facing scholars arguing for an Indo-Aryan element in southern sites can also be stated equally as succinctly: the southern route, across the Gorgan Plain in southern Turkmenistan and northeastern Iran is littered by the sites of sophisticated urban centers. How does this fit with the assumed pastoral non-urban nature of the Indo-Aryans?

14.4 The dating of the Veda

If much of the linguistic and archaeological evidence is ambiguous or malleable, there is still a massive chronological obstacle to an Indigenous Aryan position. How far back could Indo-Aryan have existed on the subcontinent? Since all eternity? Everything hinges on the date of the Vedas. As Witzel has discussed at length, unless a much greater antiquity for the Vedic corpus could be convincingly demonstrated the Indigenous case completely looses all plausibility.

In addition to the horse and chariot evidence, another philological item that can be correlated with archaeology, first mentioned in the *Atharvaveda* (11.3.7; 9.5.4) and again in the *Śatapatha Brāhmaṇa*, is *kṛṣṇa ayas*, 'black metal/bronze' namely, iron. This first appears in the archaeological record, including the Deccan, in a variety of places by the thirteenth to tenth century BCE. One would have difficulty on philological grounds, accordingly, in placing the *Ṛgveda*, too much earlier than the *Atharvaveda* since the language of this text, although later, is not sufficiently different enough to warrant an interval of too many centuries. The iron evidence strongly supports the *communis opinio* which will place the date of the *Ṛgveda* somewhere within a 1900–1200 BCE bracket.

But even this contention is not without problems since, in actual fact, although there is no evidence for awareness of smelted iron technology, iron ore and iron items have been uncovered in eight bronze age Harappan sites, some going back to 2600 BCE and earlier. In Mundigak, for example, five iron items dated between 2600–2100 BCE were found including a copper/bronze bell with an iron clapper, two iron "buttons" on a copper/bronze rod, an iron button on a copper/bronze mirror, and two indistinct lumps of "carbonates of iron" (see Possehl 1999, for further details). Some of these seem to be items of everyday use. So there was an awareness of iron, which may have been encountered accidentally during the smelting of copper, and a willingness to exploit it.

Therefore the 1900–1200 BCE bracket seems to be justified provided we can be assured that the *kṛṣṇa ayas* of the texts refers to smelted iron objects and not to iron ore. After all, *kṛṣṇa ayas* simply means 'black metal', and items made of black metal go back to the Bronze Age in Harappa, whether they were 'smelted or not.'[8] This does somewhat minimize the persuasiveness of the 1100 BCE date for the *Atharvaveda* on the grounds that it refers to *kṛṣṇa ayas*. The black metal could have been accidentally encountered as a by-product of the smelting of copper, manipulated in some of the ways noted earlier, and referred to as the 'black' *ayas*. We simply don't know.

From the Indigenous side, one is most likely to encounter the astronomical evidence when dealing with issues of Vedic antiquity. Hoch has touched on this, as have the opposing views of Kak and Witzel. I will select here only one of the numerous claims pertaining to the astronomical evidence, the references to *Kṛttikā* (Pleiades), because this evidence is another excellent example of how differing presuppositions lead one side of the debate to minimize the plausibility of certain aspects of this data and prioritize others, and the other side to minimize and prioritize very different interpretative possibilities.

Bal Gangadhar Tilak was the first to produce a variety of passages from the *Brāhmaṇa*s that described the year beginning with the sun in *Kṛttikā* at the vernal equinox which would have occurred around 2500 BCE. For example, he noted that the earlier texts often refer to the *Kṛttikā* as the beginning, or mouth '*mukham*', of the year. Moreover, *Kṛttikā* always heads up the lists of *nakṣatra*s in the earliest texts, thereby paralleling *Aśvinī*, which headed up the later lists of *nakṣatra*s, and definitely corresponded to the vernal equinox, in historical times. As further evidence that this beginning must have once occurred at the vernal equinox, Tilak pointed out that the *Vedāṅgajyotiṣa* explicitly places the vernal equinox with the sun very close to *Kṛttikā* (due, in his opinion, to being composed a little later, when the equinox had shifted a little due to precession).

Immediately after Tilak and Jacobi (1909, who reached similar conclusions at the same time, but independently of Tilak) had published their astronomical arguments, another scholar, S. B. Dikshit, drew attention to another passage from a *Brāhmaṇa* text that he felt supported their contentions. He translates the passage as follows: "[one] should, therefore, consecrate [the sacred fires] on *Kṛttikā*. These, certainly, do not deviate from the Eastern direction. All other *nakṣatras* deviate from the Eastern direction" (p. 245).[9] Dikshit interpreted the passage as indicating that *Kṛttikā* was situated due east, as opposed to the other stars which were either to the left, or to the right of this point. This suggested to him that they were situated on the celestial equator during the vernal equinox, or that their declination was nil when the passage was composed. Nowadays, *Kṛttikā* is to the North of the celestial equator, due to the precession of the equinoxes. Dikshit calculates that the brightest star of this *nakṣatra* would have been on the equator around 2990 BCE.

A number of other Indian astronomers have produced other passages supporting these, or related contentions, such as, more recently, Jean Filliozat, who points out that in spite of the systematic doubt from Thibaut and Whitney to such proposals, the ancient dates attributed to these Vedic texts find some support in the Buddhists lists (p. 125). She points out that a variety of later Buddhist texts, which have borrowed the order of the *nakṣatras* in the Vedic lists more or less exactly, have divided the *nakṣatras* into four parts, with *Kṛttikā* heading up the list as protectors of the East. She notes that the references to this *nakṣatra* suggesting its placement at the vernal equinox are too frequent and dissimilar to have been a later interpolation.

The first explicit statement of a year beginning at the vernal equinox is in the *Vedāṅgajyotiṣa* which places the vernal equinox in 10° of the constellation *Bharaṇī*, the winter solstice in the beginning of *Śravanā*, the summer solstice in the middle of *Āśleṣā* and the autumnal equinox in 3° of *Viśakhā*. Astronomers have assigned this conjunction dates ranging from 1391 BCE to 1181 BCE (Keith and Macdonell 1912: 423). This evidence is important since it bolsters the value of the astronomical data pointing to a 2500 BCE date for the passages noted earlier from the *Brāhmaṇa*s which are earlier texts, and would require the *Ṛgveda* to be dated earlier still. Even the *Vedāṅgajyotiṣa*, since the time of Max Müller (1892), and despite containing such specific information regarding the position of all four equinoctial and solsticial points, has not been unanimously accepted as a reliable record of the second millennium BCE.

Thibaut (1895) and Whitney (1895) were the main critics of the proposals of Tilak and Jacobi (and their objections are echoed by later scholars such as, most recently, Pingree, 1973). Thibaut felt that the vernal equinox is not explicitly referred to in the *Brāhmaṇas* and that "we must... disabuse our minds of the notion of the equinoxes... having been of any importance for the Hindus previous to the... influence of Greek astronomy" (1895: 90). He also pointed out that there is no proof that the boundaries between the *nakṣatras* as known in the *Brāhmaṇas* and the *Vedāṅgajyotiṣa* were the same as those known in the later period: a few degrees inexactitude can translate into centuries or a millennium or more of chronological difference. In other words, even if the sun did rise in *Kṛttikā* at the vernal equinox, how can one be sure that this *nakṣatra* corresponded to the same portion of the celestial sphere in the ancient period as it did in later times? Whitney's main objection to the whole method of Jacobi and Tilak is that "nothing in the *Ṛg-Veda* nor in the *Brāhmaṇas*, and nothing in the later Sanskrit literature, tends in any degree to give us the impression that the ancient Hindus were observers, recorders, and interpreters of astronomical phenomena" (1895: 365).

Thibaut and Whitney, in such remarks, vividly highlight the major difference dividing the two opposing camps on this whole issue: were the ancient Indo-Aryans able to chart and coordinate the precise motions of the sun and the moon in the celestial sphere in an organized and accurate fashion, or did their needs simply require a basic and approximate observation of the heavens sufficient to synchronize certain human activities? Tilak's first assumption, which he shares with Jacobi, is that although certain basic astronomical observations, such as solstices and equinoxes, are not specifically mentioned in the early texts, this does not mean that they were unknown to the Indo-Aryans. These scholars attempt to demonstrate that the ancient Indo-Aryans, who were definitely aware of the *uttarāyaṇa* and *dakṣiṇāyaṇa*, northern and southern movements of the sun, and hence the solstices, were also more specifically aware of the equinoxes. Moreover, they were capable of determining these with some degree of accuracy, even if such knowledge is not explicitly detailed in the oldest texts. Tilak found it difficult to understand why scholars were reluctant to allow the Indo-Aryans the simple ability of dividing the sky into twenty-seven equal segments so that the moon would appear to rise in a different part of the heavens, or *nakṣatra*, each night. All that a simple observatory would require, he noted, is twenty-seven poles planted equidistant in a circle around a house or open space with the observer occupying the same central space every day. Likewise, the estimation of the equinoxes could be accomplished by the simple act of tracing and counting the different daily length of the shadow of a stick, that is, by the simple act of inferring that midway between a day that is shorter than the night, and a night that is shorter than the day, must be a time with equal day and night, feats that he felt could surely not have been beyond the *nakṣatra darṣa* 'observer of the lunar mansions' about whom there are references in the *Brāhmaṇas*.[10] One could, of course, counter this by arguing that it might not, actually, be so easy to determine the longest or shortest shadow measurements to the exact day since the daily change of size would be very small. Moreover, we known that Babylonian observers, whose activities were recorded, were watching the night sky for a millennium or more before coming up with the idea of an equally divided zodiac, so this idea does not appear to have been immediately obvious to them.

The attempts to defend, or refute, the validity of this type of astronomical evidence are predicated on a series of assumptions. Depending on how one evaluates which set of assumptions are more or less reasonable, one will be inclined to approve, or disapprove, of the conclusions proposed. Those advocating the astronomical method believe that the ancient Indo-Aryans must have had certain specific astronomical skills. Although these are not specifically delineated in the earliest texts that have come down to us, they can be inferred from statements made in these texts. These skills would include the ability to divide the celestial sphere into twenty-seven *nakṣatras* corresponding to the twenty-seven-day lunar sidereal month. The *nakṣatra* system corresponds to the same stars as it does in the historical period. Two principal days for beginning the year were the winter solstice and the vernal equinox. The Indo-Aryans were well aware of both these year beginnings and could calculate them with some degree of accuracy. The information contained in the *Vedāṅgajyotiṣa* is to be understood in its own terms (i.e. as per the assumptions outlined earlier).

The basic presupposition of those opposed to such conclusions, in their turn, is that non-mention of these specific astronomical abilities in the earliest texts indicates non-acquaintance with such skills and anything more than this is simply speculation. If the Indo-Aryans did have precise observational and computational astronomical abilities, why did they not record them or why did any hypothetical record of these disappear? Even explicit astronomical specifications such as those found in the *Vedāṅgajyotiṣa* have to be regarded as unreliable for chronological purposes on the grounds that there is no guarantee that the earliest Indo-Aryan astronomers had exactly the same *nakṣatra* map, or the same degree of accuracy, in their earlier calculations as they developed in the later period (nor perhaps were these so important or relevant earlier in time). Also, if one is to impartially consider all possibilities, even if we allow that these references are valid astronomical observations, proponents of Indo-Aryan migrations can still argue that they refer to primordial memories that were retained by the Aryans during their overland trek to India, which they then inserted in later texts. Of course, proponents of the Indigenist school understandably feel that they are as valid a chronological indicator as anything else that has been brought forward to date the Vedic texts. In any event, it seems rather precarious to rest the whole dating of the *Ṛgveda* and other Vedic texts primarily on references to single items, whether this be the references to *Kṛttikā*, for an earlier date, or to the adjective *kṛṣṇa* supplementing the word *ayas*, for a later date.

To conclude the discussion of the data, then, while the horse and chariot evidence cannot be simply brushed aside, it will only be the decipherment of the script that will prove decisive in this whole issue to the satisfaction of most scholars, since the recent discovery suggests that the script could go back to 3500 BCE (providing, of course, that it encapsulates the same language throughout). If it turns out to be a language other than Indo-Aryan, then obviously the Indigenist position need no longer detain the consideration of Indologists or serious scholars of ancient history. In my opinion, this eventuality will be the only development that will convince a large number of scholars that the Aryans were, indeed, immigrants into India. On the other hand, an Indo-Aryan decipherment will radically alter the entire Indo-European homeland-locating landscape, not just the protohistory of the subcontinent. If it is Indo-Aryan, *everything* will need to be reconsidered – Indo-Aryans, Indo-Iranians, and Indo-Europeans. We can note that Ventris, the decipherer of Linear B script from Crete, was amazed to see Greek emerge from Linear B – he was expecting to see a pre-Indo-European language, the *consensus gentium* of his day. The answer, after all is said and done, is written on the seals. If it is not Indo-Aryan, then the standard Migrationist scenario will likely remain an excellent rendition of events which can always be updated and improved as new evidence surfaces.

In the meantime, the idea of an Aryan immigration into India has by no means been disproved, and remains a perfectly plausible way of accounting for at least some of the presently available evidence. Even so, Indigenists have raised some significant criticisms against the theory that cannot just be brushed aside, and this, in my opinion, requires that the more sober voices from the Indigenous Aryan school cannot be denied representation in discussions concerning Indian proto-history. Moreover, the opinions of significant numbers of Indian intellectuals about the history of their own country cannot simply be relegated to areas outside the boundaries of what is considered worthy of serious academic attention. Neglected viewpoints do not disappear, they simply reappear with more aggression due to frustration at being ignored.

Indo-Europeanists will likely consider the Indigenist position a rather myopic view since (with the exception of some of the views expressed in this volume) it tends to restrict itself primarily to the history of only one member of this huge language family with much less concern as to how the other members got to be where they are. Indeed, the most serious obstacle the Indigenous position faces is that, like it or not, it must inherit the corollary of arguing for an indigenous Indo-Aryan language group, namely, that the other IEs left the subcontinent for their destinations to the West. Granted there are significant problems with all the IE homeland proposals but, clearly, an Indian homeland theory is even more subject to the type of criticism that can be vented on other homeland theories because very little serious positive evidence has so far been offered to support it – the Indigenist school tends to limit its concerns primarily to deconstructing the opinions of others rather than offering anything very positive that can account for the entirety of the IE problem. But this myopia itself, while unlikely to convince most scholars that the homeland might really have been in northwest South Asia and adjacent regions to its west, can nonetheless be seen as a contribution to the field if it forces or inspires us to reevaluate some of our inherited assumptions, and take a fresh look at the entirety of the evidence. And attention must always be paid to the *context* of interpretation – from all sides – as well as the actual range of interpretations. I have noted something of the influences that impinged on European scholarship in the nineteenth century. India is certainly not immune from similar forces – the present volatile situation in India has made Western, and many Indian, scholars particularly concerned about the repercussions of communal interpretations of history in that country as Fosse's chapter demonstrates.

However, although the promotion of Indigenous Aryanism is undoubtedly extremely important to notions of identity and to the politics of legitimacy among certain Hindu nationalists, such concerns are not representative of all the scholars who have supported this point of view. There are other important concerns also motivating such reconsideration of history: the desire of many Indian scholars to reexamine the reconstruction of the religious and cultural history of their country that was put in place during the heyday of European imperialism and colonialism. Although there are doubtlessly nationalistic and, in some quarters, communal agendas lurking behind some of this scholarship, its principal feature is anti-colonial/imperial – I have expressed concern at what I have termed a type of Indological McCarthyism creeping into areas of Western, as well as certain Indian, academic circles, whereby *anyone* reconsidering the status quo of Indo-Aryan origins is instantly and a priori dubbed a nationalist, communal or, even worse, a Nazi (Bryant 2001).

One must also note that the interpretation of evidence being presented by the Indigenous Aryan group cannot be opposed *because* of the nationalist element since this would equally be allowing ideological beliefs to manipulate historical interpretation. It is a fact, albeit one difficult to acknowledge, that nationalistic influences have produced great advances in knowledge, not just in science and technology, but also as a result of resources channeled into humanistic disciplines such as archaeology. Indeed, one might well wonder how much research would have been invested in the Indo-European problem in the first place, had it not been for its relevance to European imperialism and nationalism.

On the other side, this is no longer the colonial period; it is still a postmodern one where suppressed and subaltern views are, if anything, much in vogue. Whatever may have been the motives of nineteenth-century Indologists, it is hard to imagine why present-day Western Indologists might still feel impelled to preserve an "Aryan Migration" theory for no good reason. The fact is that most scholars have been generally unconvinced by the limited exposure they have had with Indigenist viewpoints because of the poor and selective quality of the arguments they encounter, not because they somehow have some strange compulsion to insist on an external origin for this language group. Unless attitudes to this issue change from all sides, the divide between individuals in Western academic circles, Indo-Europeanists as well as Indologists, and the growing number of scholars, primarily in India, sympathetic to the Indigenous position (or, at least, suspicious of the Migrationist one), as well as between so-called "leftists" and "rightists" in the subcontinent itself (see Bryant 2001) will simply become more pronounced and acrimonious. And this will simply impede exchange between differing opinions and points of view, which is essential to any progressive field of study.

In conclusion, any objective and honest attempt at presenting a comprehensive account of the pre-historic period in South Asia should give a fair and adequate representation of the differences of opinion on this matter, as well as of the criticisms that can be levied against any point of view. With regards to the charge of "throwing up one's hands in post-modern dispair" (vide Witzel earlier), I suggest that rather than simply dwelling only on the defects of Migrationist theories on one side, and exclusively pointing out the obstacles of an Out-of-India position on the other, it seems incumbent on those of us at least attempting to approach the ideals of objective scholarship to discuss the *valid* problems that have been pointed out on both sides, even if we feel one version of events better accounts for the entirety of the evidence. This means acknowledging valuable criticisms even if we find them embedded in a greater context of proposals that we might feel has little value, as well as acknowledging the weaknesses in our own views. There is all-too-often a mocking and condescending tone adopted by disputants of this issue, and a tendency of simply highlighting and ridiculing the most outlandish aspects of an opponents arguments while ignoring any coherent points that might counter one's own position. There is also a tendency to immediately resort to tactics of casting *ad hominem* aspersions – lumping those who hold an opposing view point, whether Migrationist or Indigenist, into simplistic categories and branding them "nationalist," "neo-colonialist," "traditionalist," "Marxist," or some other such disparaging label – even when there is nothing in the writing of the author so charged to merit such whitewashing. The Indo-Aryan problem is likely to remain unresolved for the foreseeable future, so we might as well attempt to address it in a cordial fashion.

Notes

1 For further examples of questionable translations of Vedic passages and the influence of nineteenth-century physical anthropology, see Hock in this volume and 1999, and Trautmann 1997.

2 Nor does adstratum and superstratum interaction require that there were large groups of people on the move. Bloch (1928–30) was the first to point out that individual literary men from the Deccan could have imported Dravidian terms into classical Sanskrit (in which case, many of the terms would be provincialisms rather than real borrowings). The massive amount of Sanskrit vocabulary borrowed by the Dravidian languages, after

all, would have been imported by individual *brāhmaṇas* from the North rather than as the result of any major movement of population. These individual Sanskrit-speaking *brāhmaṇas* who went south were the cause of very extensive lexical adoptions by the Dravidians, but this has nothing to do with linguistic substrata. The reverse possibility, of individual southerners going north and importing Dravidian lexica into Sanskrit, seem to be substantiated for Bloch by the fact that many of the Dravidian loans did not survive to be inherited by the later Indo-Aryan vernaculars (although this explanation does not work so well for structural influences, which require more extensive interaction).

3 See also the salmon argument (e.g. Thieme 1964) which still has its adherents (e.g. Diebold 1991).

4 Moreover, the monkey, *kapi*, is actually an example of what could be a Dravidian loan in the proto-Indo-European period.

5 As a side note, Misra, in addition to reversing the direction of language flow, is of the opinion that most of the words can be accounted for as Old Indo-Aryan forms and not Iranian. Shevoroshkin (1987) also considers them to be Indo-Aryan (and even MIA). D'iakonov (1985) and Dolgopolsky (1993) consider them Indo-Iranian. Gamkrelidze and Ivanov, in contrast, are quite specific that they should be interpreted as early Iranian, and not as Indo-Iranian, or even less as Old Indic (1983: 67). Joki also considers them to be mostly Iranian or Middle Iranian (1973: 364–5).

6 Rajaram argues that the RV 1.162.18 speaks of a horse with thirty-four ribs. He states that this corresponds to the equids native to India, and not to the European and Central Asian varieties which have thirty-six ribs (Bharatiya Pragna 2.10, October 2000).

7 Although, see Nyberg (1995) for a dissenting view on these hallucinogens, and Sarianidi (1999) for a response.

8 In actual fact, it has yet to be discounted that some of these Harappan items might even have been smelted: "none has been analyzed to determine their technical properties and we do not known which of them is meteoric and which (if any) were smelted" (Possehl 1999b).

9 *Śatapatha Brāhmaṇa* (II. 1.2. 2–3).

10 *Vājasaneyi Saṃhitā, xxx. 10; Taittirīya Brāhmaṇa*, iii. 4. 4. 1.

References

Andronov, M., 1964. "On the Typological Similarity of New Indo-Aryan and Dravidian," *Indian Linguistics: Journal of the Linguistic Society of India*, 25: 119–26.

Anthony, D. W., 1986. "The 'Kurgan Culture', Indo-European Origins, and the Domestication of the Horse: A Reconsideration," *Current Anthropology*, 27(4): 291–313.

Anthony, D., D. Y. Telegin, and D. Brown, 1991. "The Origin of Horseback Riding," *Scientific American*, December: 94–100.

Bloch, J., 1924. "Sanskrit et Dravidien," *Bulletin de la Societe de Linguistique de Paris*, 76: 1–21.

——, 1928–30. "Some Problems of Indo-Aryan Philology," *Bulletin of the School of Oriental Studies*, 5: 719–56.

Brentjes, B., 1981. "The Mitannians and the Peacock." In *Ethnic Problems of the History of Central Asia in the Early Period*. Moscow: Soviet Committee on the Study of Civilizations of Central Asia, pp. 145–8.

Bryant, E. F., 1991. "Linguistic Substrata and the Indo-Aryan Migration Debate," *Aryan and Non-Aryan in South Asia. Harvard Oriental Series*, 3: 59–83.

——, 1998. "The Indo-Aryan Invasion Debate: The Logic of the Response." Proceedings from the 10th Annual Indo-European Conference at UCLA. Monograph Series 32: 205–28.

Bryant, E. F., 2001. *In Quest of the Origins of Vedic Culture: The Indo-Aryan Invasion Debate*. New York: Oxford University Press.
——, 2002. "The Indo-Aryan Invasion Debate and the Politics of Identity," *Neue Hallesche Berichte. Quellen und Studien zur Geschichte und Gegenwart Suedindiens*, edited by Bergunder, Michael and Das, Rahul Peter. Halle: Verlag der Franckeschen Stiftungen, pp. 206–31.
Chakrabarti, D. K., 1997. *Colonial Indology: the Sociopolitics of the Ancient Indian Past*. New Delhi: Munshiram Manoharlal.
Coleman, R., 1998. "Book Review of *Archaeology and Language* by Colin Renfrew," *Current Anthropology*, 29(3): 449–53.
Dales, G. F., 1964. "The Mythical Massacre at Mohenjo-Dara," *Expedition*, 6(3): 36–43.
Dasgupta, P., 1982. "On Conceiving of South Asia as a Linguistic Area," *Indian Linguistics: Journal of the Linguistic Society of India*, 43(3–4): 37–48.
Day, J. V., 1994. "The Concept of the Aryan Race in Nineteenth-Century Scholarship," *Orpheus*, 4: 15–48.
Devendraswarup, 1993. "Genesis of the Aryan Race Theory and its Application to Indian History." In *The Aryan Problem*, edited by S. B. Deo and Kamath Suryanath. Pune: Bharatiya Itihasa Sankalana Samiti, pp. 30–9.
Dhar, L., 1930. *The Home of the Aryas*. Delhi: Delhi University Publications.
Dhavalikar, M. K., 1995. "Fire Altars or Fire Pits?" In *Śrī Nāgābhinandanam*, edited by V. Shivananda and M. V. Visweswara. Bangalore: Nagaraja Rao.
D'iakonov, I. M., 1985. "On the Original Home of the Speakers of Indo-European," *Journal of Indo-European Studies*, 13(1 and 2): 92–174.
Diebold, R. A. Jr., 1987. "Linguistic Ways to Prehistory." In *Proto-Indo-European: The Archaeology of a Linguistic Problem*, edited by Susan Skomal and Edgar Polomé. Washington, DC: Institute for the Study of Man, pp. 19–71.
——, 1992. "The Traditional View of the Indo-European Palaeoeconomy: Contradictory evidence from Anthropology and Linguistics." In *Reconstructing Languages and Cultures*, edited by Edgar C. Polomé and Werner Winters. Berlin: Mouton de Gruyter, pp. 317–67.
Dikshit, S. B., 1985. "The Age of the Satapatha Brahmana," *Indian Antiquary*, 24: 245–6.
Dolgopolsky, A., 1987. "The Indo-European Homeland and Lexical Contacts of Proto-Indo-European with other Languages," *Mediterranean Language Review*: 7–31.
——, 1989. "Cultural Contacts of Proto-Indo-European and Proto-Indo-Iranian with Neighbouring Languages," *Folia Linguistica Historica*, VIII(1–2): 3–36.
——, 1990–93. "More About the Indo-European Homeland Problem," *Mediterranean Language Review*, 6–7: 230–48.
Erdosy, G., 1989. "Ethnicity in the Ṛgveda and its Bearing on the Question of Indo-European Origins," *South Asian Studies*, 5: 35–47.
Filliozat, J., 1969. "Notes on Ancient Iranian and Indian Astronomy," *Journal of the K. R. Cama Oriental Research Institute*, 42: 100–35.
Francfort, H.-P., 1989. *Fouilles de Shortughaï. Recherches sur l'asie Centrale Protohistorique*. Paris: Diffusion.
Fraser, J., 1926. "Linguistic Evidence and Archaeological and Ethnological Facts," *Proceedings of the British Academy*, 12: 257–72.
Friedrich, P., 1970. *Proto-Indo-European Trees*. Chicago, IL: University of Chicago Press.
Gamkrelidze, T. V. and V. V. Ivanov, 1983. "The Migration of Tribes Speaking the Indo-European Dialects from their Original Homeland in the Near East to their Habitations in Eurasia," *Soviet Studies in History*, XXII (1–2): 53–95.

——, 1995. "The Indo-European and the Indo-Europeans." In *Trends in Linguistics Studies and Monographs*, 80. Berlin: Mouton and Gruyter.

Gaur, R. C., 1983. *Excavations at Atranjīkherā*. Delhi: Motilal.

Gimbutas, M., 1997. *The Kurgan Culture and the Indo-Europeanization of Europe*, edited by Miriam Dexter and Karlene Jones-Bley. Washington, DC: Institute for the Study of Man.

Hastie, W., 1882. *Hindu Idolatry and English Enlightenment*. Calcutta: Thacker.

Havell, E. B., 1918. *The History of Aryan Rule in India*. London: John Murray.

Hiebert, F. T. and C. C. Lamberg-Karlovsky, 1992. "Central Asia and the Indo-Iranian Borderlands," *Iran*, XXX: 1–15.

Hock, H. H., 1975. "Substratum Influence on (Rig-Vedic) Sanskrit?" *Studies in the Linguistic Sciences*, 5(2): 76–125.

——, 1979. "Retroflexion Rules in Sanskrit," *South Asian Languages Analysis*, 1: 47–62.

——, 1984. "(Pre-)Rigvedic convergence of Indo-Aryan with Dravidian? Another look at the evidence," *Studies in the Linguistic Sciences*, 14(1): 89–107.

——, 1993. "Subversion or Convergence? The Issue of Pre-Vedic Retroflexion Reexamined," *Studies in the Linguistic Sciences*, 23(2): 73–115.

——, 1996. "Pre-Ṛgvedic Convergence between Indo-Aryan and Dravidian? A Survey of the Issues and Controversies." In *Ideology and Status of Sanskrit*, edited by Jan E. M. Houben. Leiden: Brill.

——, 1999a. "Through a Glass Darkly: Modern 'racial' interpretations vs. textual and general prehistoric evidence on Arya and dasa/dasyu in Vedic Indo-Aryan society," *Aryan and Non-Aryan in South Asia. Harvard Oriental Series Opera Minora*, 3: 145–174.

——, 1999b. "Out of India? The Linguistic Evidence." *Aryan and Non-Aryan in South Asia. Harvard Oriental Series Opera Minora*, 3: 1–18.

Iyengar, S., 1914. "Did the Dravidians of India Obtain their Culture from Aryan Immigrant [*sic*]." *Anthropos*: 1–15.

Jacobi, H., 1909. "On the Antiquity of Vedic Culture." *Journal of the Royal Asiatic Society*: 721–6.

Joki, A. J., 1973. *Uralier und Indogermanen*. Helsinki: Suomalis.

Jones, W., 1788. "On the Gods of Greece, Italy, and India," *Asiatic Researches*, 1: 221–75.

Keith, A. B., 1909. "On the Antiquity of Vedic Culture," *Journal of the Royal Asiatic Society*: 1100–6.

——, 1933. "The Home of the Indo-Europeans." In *Oriental Studies in Honour of Cursetji Erachi Pavry*, edited by J. D. Cursetji Pavry. London: Oxford University Press, pp. 189–99.

Keith, A. B. and A. A. Macdonell, 1912 (1967). *Vedic Index of Names and Subjects*. Delhi: Motilal Banarsidass.

Kenoyer, J. M., 1991, "Urban Process in the Indus Tradition: A Preliminary Model from Harappa." In *Harappa Excavations 1986–1990*, edited by Richard H. Meadows. Madison, MD: Prehistory, pp. 29–60.

Krell, K. S., 1998. "Gimbutas' Kurgan-PIE Homeland hypothesis: a Linguistic Critique," *Archaeology and Language II*, edited by Roger Blench and Matthew Spriggs. London: Routledge, pp. 267–89.

Kuiper, F. B. J., 1991. *Aryans in the Rigveda*. Leiden Studies in Indo-European 1. Atlanta: Rodopi.

Lal, B. B., 1984 "Some Reflections on the Structural Remains at Kalibangan." In *Frontiers of the Indus Civilization*, edited by B. B. Lal and S. P. Gupta. New Delhi: Books and Books, pp. 55–62.

Lassen, C., 1867 (1851). *Indische Alterthumskunde*. London: Williams & Norton.
Legge, F., 1992. "The Home of the Aryans," *Academy*, LXIII: 710–11.
Lehmann, W. P., 1993. *Theoretical Bases of Indo-European Linguistics*. London: Routledge.
Maine, Sir H. S., 1875. *Lectures on the Early History of Institutions*. New York: Henry Holt.
Marshall, Sir J., 1931. *Mohenjo-Daro and the Indus Civilization*. London: Arthur Probsthain.
Masica, C., 1979. "Aryan and Non-Aryan Elements in North Indian Agriculture." In *Aryan and Non-Aryan in India*, edited by M. Deshpande and P. Hook. Ann Arbor, MI: University of Michigan, pp. 55–151.
Maw, M., 1990. *Visions of India*. Frankfurt: Verlag Peter Lang.
Meadows, R., 1997. "A Comment on 'Horse Remains from Surkotada' by Sandor Bokonyi," *South Asian Archaeology*, 13: 308–15.
Misra, S. S., 1992. *The Aryan Problem: A Linguistic Approach*. New Delhi: Munshiram Manoharlal.
Müller, F. M., 1847. "On the Relation of the Bengali to the Arian and Aboriginal languages of India." Report of the British Association for the Advancement of Science, pp. 319–50.
——, 1875. *The Science of Language*. New York: Scribner.
——, 1883. *India: What Can it Teach us?* London: Longmans.
——, 1985 (1887). *Biographies of Words and the Home of the Aryas*. New Delhi: Gayatri.
Nichols, J., 1997. "The Epicentre of the Indo-European Linguistic Spread." In *Archaeology and Language I*, edited by Roger Blench and Matthew Spriggs. London: Routledge, 1997.
——, 1998. "The Eurasian Spread Zone and the Indo-European Dispersal." In *Archaeology and Language II*, edited by Roger Blench and Matthew Spriggs. London: Routledge, pp. 220–66.
Nyberg, H., 1995. "The Problem of the Aryans and the Soma: The Botanical Evidence." In *The Indo-Aryans of Ancient South Asia*, edited by G. Erdosy. Berlin: Walter de Gruyter.
Oldenberg, H., 1894. "Der Vedische Kalender und das Alter des Veda," *Zeitschrift der Deutschen Morgenlšndischen Gesellschaft*, pp. 629–48.
Pingree, D., 1973. "The Mesopotamian Origin of Early Indian Mathematical Astronomy," *Journal for the History of Astronomy*, 4: 1–12.
Poliakov, L., 1971. *The Aryan Myth*. London: Sussex University Press.
——, 1996. *Indus Age: The Writing System*. Philadelphia, PA: University Press.
Possehl, G. L., 1999. "The Early Iron Age in South Asia." In *The Archaeometallurgy of the Asian World*, edited by V. Pigott. University Museum Monograph 89, MASCA. Research Papers on Science and Archaeology Volume 16. Philadelphia, PA: University of Pennsylvania, 153–75.
Prakash, B., 1966. *Rgveda and the Indus Valley Civilization*. Hoshiapur: Vishveshvarananda Institute.
Pulgram, E., 1958. *The Tongues of Italy*. Cambridge, MA: Harvard University Press.
Rao, S. R., 1993. *Lothal*. "The Aryans in Indus Civilization." In *The Aryan Problem*, edited by S. B. Deo and Suryanath Kamath. Pune: Bharatiya Itihasa, pp. 173–80.
Rau, W., 1976. *The Meaning of Pur in Vedic Literature*. München: Wilhelm Fink Verlag.
Renfrew, C., 1987. *Archaeology and Language*. New York: Cambridge University Press.
Sarianidi, V., 1977. "New Finds in Bactria and the Indo-Iranian Connections." In *South Asian Archaeology*, edited by Maurizio Taddei. Naples: Istituto Universitario Orientale, pp. 643–59.

——, 1987. "South-West Asia: Migrations, the Aryans and Zoroastrians," *International Association for the Study of the Cultures of Central Asia Information Bulletin*, 13: 44–56.
——, 1990. "Togolok 21, An Indo-Iranian Temple in the Karakum," *Bulletin of the Asia Institute*, 4: 150–6.
——, 1993a. "Margiana in the Ancient Orient," *International Association for the Study of the Cultures of Central Asia Information Bulletin*, 19: 5–28.
——, 1993b. "Recent Archaeological Discoveries and the Aryan Problem." In *South Asian Archaeology*, edited by Adalbert Gail and Gerd Mevissen, pp. 251–64.
——, 1993c. "Margiana and the Indo-Iranian World." In *South Asian Archaeology*, edited by A. Parpola and P. Koskikallio, pp. 667–80.
——, 1999. "Near Eastern Aryans in Central Asia," *Journal of Indo-European Studies*, 27(3–4): 295–326.
Shaffer, J. G., 1993. "Urban Form and Meaning in South Asia: the Shaping of Cities from Prehistoric to Precolonial Times," *Studies in the History of Art*, 31: 53–67.
Sharma, A. K., 1974. "Evidence of Horse from the Harappan Settlement at Surkotada," *Purātattva*, 7: 75–6.
Sherratt, A., 1988. "Review of Archaeology and Language by Colin Renfrew," *Current Anthropology*, 29: 458–63.
Sheveroskin, V. "Indo-European Homeland and Migrations," *Folio Linguistica Historica*, 7: 227–50.
Smith, G. (n.d.) *The Conversion of India*. New York: Young People's, *n.d.*
Thibaut, G., 1895. "On Some Recent Attempts to Determine the Antiquity of Vedic Civilization," *Indian Antiquary*, 24: 85–100.
Thomason, S. G. and T. Kaufman, 1988. *Language Contact, Creolization, and Genetic Linguistics*. Berkeley, CA: University of California.
Tikkanen, B., 1987. *The Sanskrit Gerund: A Synchronic, Diachronic and Typological Analysis*. Helsinki: Studia Orientalia.
Tilak, L, n.d (a) *The Orion*. Poona: Messrs Tilak Bros.
——, n.d (b) *The Arctic Home in the Vedas*. Poona: Messrs Tilak Bros.
Trautmann, T. R., 1997. *Aryans and British India*. Berkeley, CA: University of California Press.
Tripathi, R. S., 1967. *History of Ancient India*. Delhi: Motilal Banarsidass.
Weber, A., 1857. *Modern Investigations on Ancient India*. trans. Fanny Metcalfe. London: Leipzig.
Whitney, W. D., 1895. "On a Recent Attempt by Jacobi and Tilak to Determine on Astronomical Evidence the Date of the Earliest Vedic Period as 4000 BC," *Indian Antiquary*, 24: 361–9.
Witzel, M., 1989. "Tracing the Vedic Dialects." In *Dialectes dans les Littérateurs Indo-Aryennes*, edited by C. Caillat. Paris: Institut de Civilisation Indienne, pp. 97–265.
——, 1993. "Nepalese Hydronomy: Towards a History of Settlement in the Himalayas," *Nepal Past and Present*. New Delhi: Sterling.
——, 1998. "The Languages of Harappa." Proceedings of the Conference on the Indus Civilization, Madison.
——, 2000. "The Home of the Aryan." Anustantatyai Fs für Johanna Narten zum 70. Geburtstag, *Beihefte Münchener Studien zur Sprachwissenschaft*, edited by A. Hintze and E. Tichy. Dettelbach: J. H. Roell, pp. 283–338.

Zimmer, S., 1988. "On Dating Indo-European: A Call for Honesty," *Journal of Indo-European Studies*, 16(3–4): 371–5.
——, 1990a. "On Indo-Europeanization," *Journal of Indo-European Studies*, 18(1–2): 140–55.
——, 1990b. "The Investigation of Proto-Indo-European History: Methods, Problems, Limitations," In *When Worlds Collide*. Karoma, pp. 311–44.

INDEX